29th EDITION

WRECKS & RELICS

KEN ELLIS

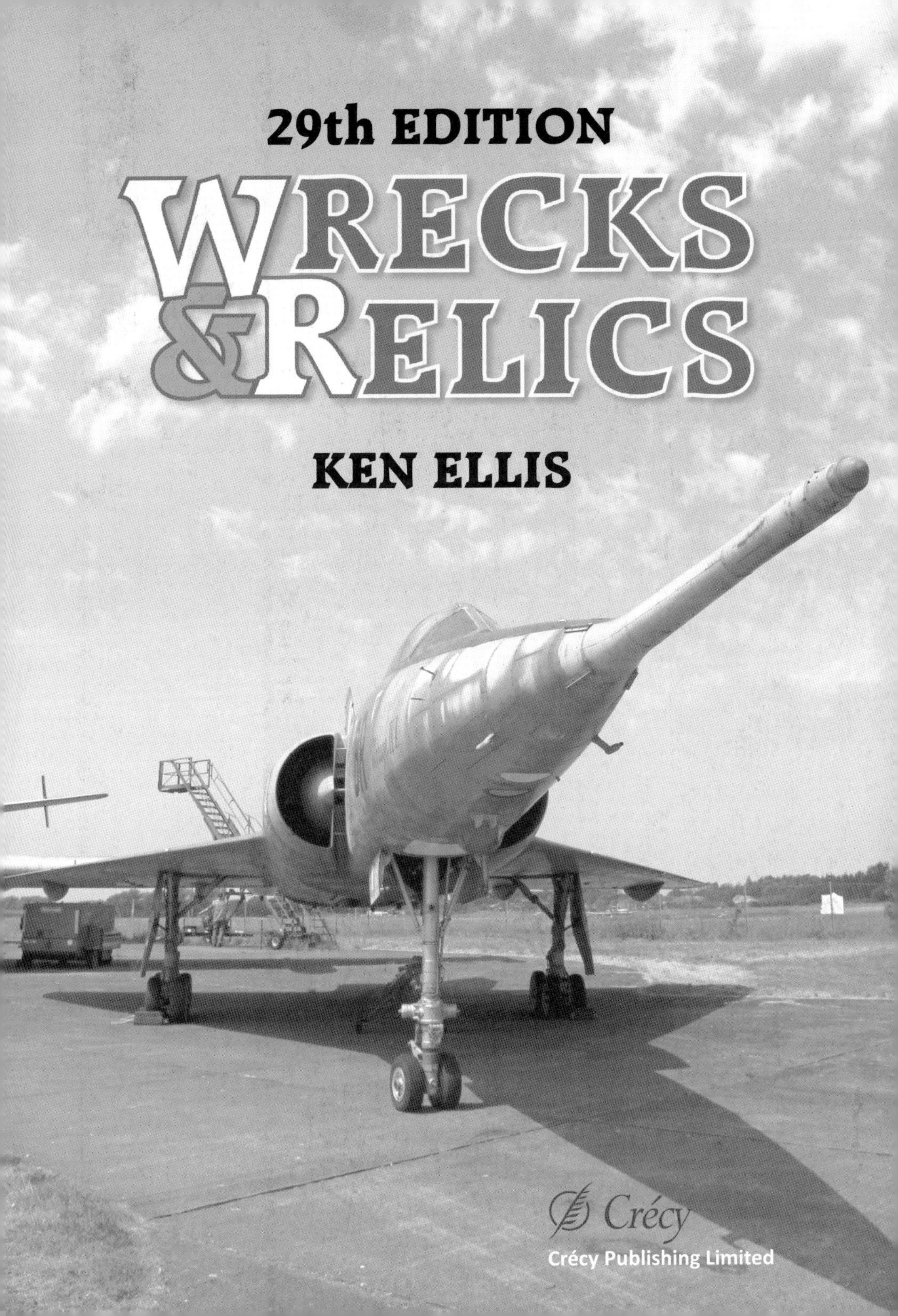

Crécy

Crécy Publishing Limited

CONTENTS

Front Cover: Newquay Cornwall Airport – St Mawgan to most readers – hopefully will continue to commemorate the airfield's maritime heritage with Shackleton AEW.2 WL795: Sep 2022. ***Col Pope***
Rear Cover:
Main: Jaguar GR.1A XX741 in full steam, Bentwaters, May 2023. ***Jake Wallace***
Middle left: Fantastic repatriation, Lockheed 12A G-AFTL, Northampton Airport – aka Sywell – Mar 2023. ***Nigel Bailey-Underwood***
Middle centre: ATP 'G-MAUD', Isle of Man Airport, Ronaldsway, Sep 2022. ***Tony McCarthy***
Middle right: Buccaneer S.2B XX894 flexing its wings, Cotswold Airport – pronounced Kemble – Nov 2023. ***Jake Wallace***
Lower left: Positioning Hawk T.1A XX306, Leeming Bar, Jul 2023. ***Dave Thomas***

Title Page: Yorkshire Air Museum's Mirage IVA No.45, June 2023. ***Col Pope***

This twenty-ninth edition published by
Crécy Publishing
1a Ringway Trading Estate, Shadowmoss Road
Manchester M22 5LH
www.crecy.co.uk

ISBN 9781800353046

Printed in Turkey by Pelikan

PREFACE

A long time ago, in a land far, far away – well, it was 1974 and Liverpool – I took on compiling the fourth edition of *Wrecks & Relics*, which weighed in at 86 pages. That was followed every other year by 25 more editions, piling in another 7,322 pages. Excuse me while I stretch my maths: 2024 take away 1974 comes to *50 years*. That's five decades, half a century, or in old money a *shedload* of time.

It is the moment to hand over the controls... I am very pleased that my colleague and good friend David Willis has slipped into the P1 seat. Over the years the *W&R* 'family' of dedicated enthusiasts and preservationists has supported and encouraged me to chronicle the ups and downs of Britain's aviation heritage. I know that all will give David the same welcome and inspiration.

By way of marking the 50-up milestone a photo-spread of the *W&R4* era occupies the Appendix A slot. Having received a lot of – mostly favourable – comments from my extended diatribe in *W&R28*: a second helping appears overleaf.

A good friend who helps run a regional museum once remarked that it was a good thing that I *wrote* about aircraft preservation rather than *physically* taking part. He knows my total lack of practical skills only too well. He meant his comment as praise, that through my writing endeavours many more deserving aircraft were extant and cherished than would have been had I worked on them instead. I hope that is the case. Many thanks and best wishes to you all.

Be seeing you... ***Ken Ellis***
People's Republic of Rutland

CockpitFest, Newark Air Museum, June 2022, around dinner time... "Would you be interested in taking on *Wrecks & Relics*?" Struggling not to spray a mouthful of cheesecake over Ken, several questions ran through my mind; Could I, Would I, Can I get another slice? At that point, Ken had invested 48 years in the series – it was his baby. I had just a quarter of a century in aviation publishing, initially on *World Air Power Journal* and *Wings of Fame*. A chance meeting hanging out of an Army Lynx ('Ride of the Valkyries' playing in my head) resulted in three years with *AirForces Monthly*, before working on *International Air Power Review* and *Flightpath*. Over the years sub-editors progressed from rolling their eyes at the mere mention of my name to the high praise of "that wasn't too bad"; time to go freelance! Gigs compiling the news for *AIR International* and *Today's Pilot* meant I didn't starve, while nearly a decade as part of the team updating *Jane's All the World's Aircraft* introduced me to flying machines other publications didn't know existed. So, I believed I could and decided I would; the answer to Ken's question had to be "yes". Afterall, there would be cake – obviously I'd have to continue *W&R's'* fine tradition of gastronomic recommendations...

David Willis
Wittering
February 2024

30th Edition deadlines

Images by **1st December 2025**. If you are new to contributing images to *W&R*, please get in touch beforehand for details of resolution required and how best to send. **Comments and notes** by **10th January 2026**. Thanks for your support!

email: **wrecksandrelics@gmx.co.uk**
'Snail mail' via Crécy Publishing – address on page 2

Got them all? *W&R4* (1974) all the way through to *W&R28* (2022) and you're holding *W&R29* – fifty years' worth. Also included are some of the one-offs, including the all-colour *Album* (2003) and the 'collections' trilogy: *Lost* (2012), *Great* (2013) and *Local* (2017). *W&R1* and *W&R2* (1961 and 1963) were compiled by the late D J Stephens, *W&R3* (1968) by S G Jones. Up to *W&R9* (1984) published by Merseyside Group of Aviation Enthusiasts/Merseyside Aviation Society; *W&R10* to *W&20* (2006) by Midland Counties Publications/Midland Publishing. And since by the ever-patient Crécy Publishing.

AND ANOTHER THING...

Weighty issues

Dougie Kerr and his capable team at the Solway Aviation Museum were 'pipped at the post' when Beverley C.1 XB259 was auctioned at Fort Paull in February 2021. Since then, it has languished as the practicalities of such a beast dawned on the successful bidder. The Carlisle crew has stepped into the breach with a plan to rescue the venerable airlifter. To quote a now retired museum curator: "...but acquisition is the simplest bit." Formally opened in May 1996, Solway's roots go back to the early 1960s. This longevity reflects the museum's thorough understanding of the long term nature of the commitment and I'm sure many readers will join in wishing them well in the gargantuan task and make a donation.

The Preface of *W&R*28 dwelt on the importance of the Boeing 747 to Britain's aviation heritage, bemoaning the lack of a national museum adopting one of the British Airways retirees. In October 2023 G-BYGC succumbed to the recycler's skills at St Athan, Wales, and was followed by G-CIVN at Kemble – sorry, Cotswold, Glos – by year's end. The pair flown into Dunsfold, Surrey, in late 2020 face an uncertain future as the former airfield is destined to become a massive housing estate. At Cotswold, G-CIVB was officially opened on 11th February 2022 after extensive work to make it a viable visitor centre. *Victor-Bravo*'s custodian is a *commercial* operation with no responsibility to uphold the nation's aeronautical legacy, but it shows just what *can* be done with a mixture of passion and determination.

Inevitable and unenviable

Newark Air Museum features in two 'episodes' in these pages – turn to page 23 for the bewildering saga of Typhoon DA4 ZH590 and page 169 for a shrewd judgement on the prospects for Canberra PR.7 WH791. The ramifications of the MoD's 'decision' regarding the Typhoon is a troubling, inconsistent, precedent. While WH791 was the last intact PR.7 in the UK, the Canberra as a breed is well served. In many ways, its fate was sealed before it arrived at Newark. Towards the end of its *26 years* on the gate at Cottesmore, I remember marvelling that someone had stuck a cut-out picture of a goldfish on the outside of the nose glazing just below the *water line* clearly visible *inside*! Upon arrival at Newark, with the benefit of inspection of the dismantled airframe, a well-planned and immediate restoration by the then owners *may* have arrested the decay. Year upon year of inertia left Newark with an inevitable and unenviable decision.

Increasingly, British museums are going to have to reach similar conclusions with exhibits that are beyond realistic help. It is unavoidable that more will face reduction to usable parts as curators assess priorities. To re-quote a *W&R* adage that is fast becoming a catch phrase: "Is your Dassault Mystère really necessary?"

Nothing lasts forever

We record two more museums that have had to close as plans for the site they occupied changed. After 35 years of opening to the public, the Fenland and West Norfolk Aviation Museum closed its doors for the last time on 28th October 2022. The airframes held were not the collection's real treasure, that lay in the incredible array of artefacts displayed so lovingly within. In a shining example of co-operation, the City of Norwich Aviation Museum offered to absorb much of this exceptional material. Amid the sadness of closure, the planned and careful wind-down of this museum was laudable.

Three days after Fenland and West Norfolk shut, the Cornwall Aviation Heritage Centre bade farewell to its final visitors. The circumstances of this termination are examined in greater depth on pages 39 and 40. Several scrappings resulted from the demise but the changing nature of airframe dismemberment adds a new dimension to the 'future proofing' of collections. The Cornwall museum claims that the two jetliners would cost £60,000 to dismantle and process – cash that was beyond its resources. (VC10 ZA148 was axed in November 2023, its cockpit travelling to St Athan; the forward fuselage of BAC 111 ZH763 was saved by Southampton-based Solent Sky.) Health and safety rulings and procedures, proper disposal, site insurance and many other costs and 'legals' need to be charged – gone are the days when a 'scrappie' would remove a redundant airframe 'for free' with a knowing wink.

Now, we turn to Finningley – sorry, Doncaster Sheffield Airport – which announced its closure on 13th July 2022 and the last flights took place on Bonfire Night that year. The Vulcan to the Sky Trust was informed that its tenancy would not be renewed beyond July 2023. The organisation and Vulcan XH558 are still in place, hoping upon hope that things may change – see page 275 for more details. If no fairy tale solution is found, the Vulcan will need to be moved by road, a scheme for a one-off ferry flight having already been quashed. This brings about a dilemma. It is a likely assumption that the trust will make an application to the Lottery, or other funding bodies, to cover what will be exceptional dismantling, transportation and re-assembly costs plus infrastructure to house the delta at its destination. (Hendon's XL318 was moved by road from Scampton but it was done in the days when the RAF put its manpower and machinery to the task as a training exercise for its 'smash and crash' specialists – that is surely no longer an option.) Would such a grant represent best use of capital? It *could* be argued that in those circumstances the optimal place for such an endowment would be Rochford – sorry, London Southend Airport – where the Vulcan Restoration Trust *already* has XL426 inside a burgeoning visitor centre and stages regular taxi days and special events. Just saying...

Top: Cornwall Aviation Heritage Centre line-up, October 2022. Left to right: Hawk T.1 XX240; Hunter GA.11 WV256; Hunter T.8C WT722; Lightning F.53 'XS935'; Tornado F.3 ZH553; Canberra T.4 'VN799'; Tornado GR.4 ZA398. (The Hawk and Tornados 'guesting' from the Joint Aircraft Recovery and Transport Squadron enclave.) *David Willis*

Bottom: Boeing 747 G-BYGC's last days, St Athan, October 2023. *Chris England*

ACKNOWLEDGEMENTS

Overseeing the draft, adding to it and refining it were: **Dave Allport**, **David Bennett, Andy Marden**, compiler of *Military Aviation Review's* excellent *Out of Service* feature, **Alistair Ness**, monitored Scotland and via his column in the Central Scotland Aviation Group's superb *Scottish Air News*; **Nigel Price**, **David E Thompson**, for the north of England and other travels; **Ian Thompson**, tackled all things the island of Ireland; **David Willis** cast a diligent eye over the shape of things to come; **Andy Wood** looked after Lincs, Notts and Yorks, directly and via his column in the ever-brilliant *Humberside Air Review*. Despite their combined prowess, all mistooks our awl mein.

Cover and layouts by **Rob Taylor**. With many thanks to **Jeremy Pratt** and the team at **Crécy Publishing**. The map was created by the much-missed **Pete West**.

Many thanks also go to: **Neil** and **Heather Airey**, Lakes Lightnings; **Alan Allen** Vampire and Wasp collector; **Stuart Allen**, ARV G-BOGK; **Andrew Appleton**; **Steve Austin**, Stoneykirk Aviation Museum; **Nigel Bailey-Underwood**; **Philip Bedford**, South East Aviation Enthusiasts Group; **Steve Bell**, Norfolk and Suffolk Aviation Museum; **Rowland Benbrook**; **John Berkeley**; **M S 'Dicky' Bird**; **Rowley Birkin QC**; **David Blades**; **Kevin Bowen**, Heathrow Trident Collection; the late **Alec Brew**, Tettenhall Transport Heritage Centre; **Geremy Britton**, Aircraft Preservation Foundation; **Ben Brown**, Sywell Aviation Museum; **Peter Budden**, Hurn; **Matt Buddle**, Lightning XR754; **Harry Bunn**; **David J Burke**; **Ian Burningham**; **Ray Burrows**, Ulster Aviation Society; **Mike Cain**; **John Camp**, Boxted Airfield Historical Group; **Richard Capper**; **Ian Chadwick**; **Ray Challis**, Venom J-1573; **Gavin Carr**, 'Flea' restorer; **Russell Carter**; **Nick Challoner**; **David Charles**, North East Land Sea and Air Museums; **Richard Clarkson**, Vulcan Restoration Trust; **Ricky Clarkson**; **Ken Cloke**; **Pete Coe**; **John Coghill**, **Philip Cole**, Medway Aircraft Preservation Society; **John Coleman**, Essex notes; **Dave Collier**; **David Collins**, DH Hornet Project; **Peter Colwill**; **Glyn Coney**; **Marcus** and **Carolyn Cordran**, Buccaneer 'XN979'; **Nigel Coward**; **Roger Creed**, Auster restorer; the late **Paul Crellin**; **Alan Curry**; **Brian Curtis**, Wight Aviation Museum; **Terry Dann,** Stow Maries and others; **Mike Davey**, Phantom and cockpit guru; **Clive Davies**, Gloster Aviation Club and Canberra WT333; **David Davis**; **Tom Davis**; **Gary Dean**, P-51 perfectionist; **Brian Downs**; **Ian Doyle**; **Alan Drewett**, Jet Age Museum; **Colin Durrant**, Suffolk Aviation Heritage Museum; **Tony Dyer**, Air Defence Collection; **Mike Eastman**, Aircraft Restoration Group; **Peter Elliott**; **Don Ellis**; **Chris England**, south Wales and others; **Derek Ferguson; Bill Fern**, South Yorkshire Aircraft Museum; **First Dog on the Moon**; **Murray Flint**, refinishing maestro; **Nick Foden**, Pup G-AXDW; **Pete Friar**; **Ron Fulton**, Boscombe Down Aviation Collection; **Mal Function**, health and safety specialist; **Graham Gaff**, East London Aviation Society and UK military master; **Bruce Gordon**, Vampire star-maker; **David Grainger**; **Gilmar Green**; **Daniel Glover**; **Ian Greenhalgh**; **Mark Griffiths**, Blackbushe Heritage Trust; **Richard Hall**, Lightning XS420; **Mark Harris**; **Ian Haskell**; **Andrew Hawkins**, Firefly restorer; **Graham Haynes**, Bentwaters Cold War Museum; **Mark Hazell**; **Howard Heeley**, Newark Air Museum; **Phil** and **Lynn Hewitt**; **Roderick Ho**; **Norman Hobbs**, Britten-Norman Aircraft Preservation Society; **Steve Hobden**; **David Hodgkinson**; **Andy Hone**; **Jon Horswell**; **Jonathan Howard**, The Aeroplane Collection and Vampire owner; **Ian Humphreys**; **Mike Hutchinson**; **Lars-Erik Ingerlo**; **Mike Ingham**; **David S Johnstone**; **John Kenyon**; **Dougie Kerr**, Solway Aviation Museum; **Tim Kershaw**, Jet Age Museum; **Howard King**, Martlesham Heath Control Tower Museum; **Simon King**; **Max** and **Ritch La Rue-Blood**, Leicester Aircraft Restoration Workshop; **Garry Lakin**; **Jackson Lamb; Martin Law**; **Andrew Lee**, Trident G-AWZI; **Chris Mabbott**; **Baz Manning**; **Roger Marley**, Hawker Demon project; **Paul Marsh**; **Brian Matthews**; **Tony** and **Brenda McCarthy**; **Ross McNeill**, Hurricane and PR.9; **Alan Measles**; **Megan's Dad**; **Ian Metson**; **Paul Merriman**; **Paul Middleton**; **Frank Millar**, Canberra restorer; **Alf Milliken**; **Steve Milnthorpe**, Boston craftsman; **Michael Miskin**; **Robert Mitchell**; **Naylan Moore**, Doncaster People's Front / South Yorkshire Aircraft Museum; **Dave Murray**; **Leo Murray**, Irish notes and his own collection; **John Newton**; **John Nixon**, Millom Heritage and Art Centre; **Peter A Norris**; **John Parish**; **Alan Partington**, Catford Independent Air Force; **Dr I Pertbottom**; **John 'Skeeterless' Phillips**, rotorcraft 'sleuthing'; **Mike Phipp**, Bournemouth and more; **Darren J Pitcher**; **Nigel** and **Anne Ponsford**, Ponsford Collection; **Geoffrey Pool**, Bruntingthorpe, Hunter owner; **Col Pope**, East Anglia and Essex; **Adam Poultney; Alan Preece**; **Mark Presswood**; **Les Rawlins**, Heathrow Trident Collection; **Steve Richards**; **Mark Roberts,** Aerobilia; **Neil Rodgers**; **Andy Shemans**, Sywell Aviation Museum; **John Sharpe**, Boscombe Down Aviation Collection; **Andy Simpson**; **Jim Simpson**, Morayvia, Scotland and more; **Peter Sinclair**; **Tom Singfield**; **Bill Skinner**, Thorpe Camp; **Keith Skinner**; **Graham Sparkes**, Hooton Park Trust; **Peter Spooner**; **James Stables**, South Yorkshire Aircraft Museum and cockpiteer; Trevor Stone; **Gareth Symington**; **Pete Tasker**; **Steve Taylor**, Wight Military and Heritage Museum; **Dave 'Mr Shifter' Thomas**, Classic British Jet Collection and Bruntingthorpe stalwart; **Hugh Trevor**, Lightning historian and cockpit owner; **Martin** and **Lynn Tydeman**, Gazelle XZ337; **Sam Tyler**; **David Underwood**, glider restorer; **Priti Vacant**; **Graham Vale**, East Midlands Airport Volunteers Association; **Jake Wallace**, TBAG, Buccaneers and more; **David Wells**; **Michael Westwood**; **Mark Whitnall**; **John Wickenden**; **John Wiseman**; **Wodewick the Wobber**; **Les Woodward**...

Massive shout-out to **Steve Wright** for essential morale boosting from 1980 to the Sunday *W&R29* went to press.

...and Pam and Rascal

BEFORE YOU START...

Many readers will be familiar with the 'rules of engagement': **major recent changes are highlighted in bold**.

Scope: *Wrecks & Relics* serves to outline, in as much detail as possible, the status of all known PRESERVED (ie in museum or other formalised collections, under restoration etc); INSTRUCTIONAL (ie static airframes in use for training); and STORED or DERELICT (ie out of use for a long period of time, as a rescue trainer, scrapped or damaged etc) aircraft in the UK and Ireland and HM Forces airframes based on Crown Territory.

The following exceptions apply: airworthy aircraft not part of a specific collection and/or readily accessible to the public; including the happily greatly expanding number of 'warbird airlines'; aircraft that fall into any of the above categories for only a short period – generally less than a year.

Airframes will only be considered if they are ***at least* a cockpit or a flightdeck**. The former is the full depth of the fuselage, the latter is cut at the floor, with the lower fuselage removed. A **'tidying up'** of 'less interesting' light aircraft – most *W&R* readers will innately know what they are – with **lapsed certification** has been carried out in this edition. Several owners have pointed out that expired 'paperwork' does not necessarily make an aircraft a 'wreck' or a 'relic' and the compiler agrees: while flightless they may well be inspected and cherished. **De-registration** is a far more practical 'measure', more easily definable and the civvie equivalent of Struck off Charge. With similar logic, unfinished homebuilds and/or microlights are also largely ignored unless within a museum or collection: one person's long incomplete project may well be someone's well-active pride and joy. **Balloon baskets/gondolas** (envelopes on their own are *not* considered) and **civilian gliders** are included *only* if they are part of a public-accessible museum. Some discretion has been allowed to cover 'vintage' British-built and military gliders. Coverage of **drones**, UAVs, what-have-you is limited to British or US military types or the the occasional 'important' type (eg Airbus Zephyr) and V-1 'doodlebugs' (real or ersatz). Airframes at dive sites are listed separately - see Appendix D.

Locations: Are listed by county/province and then alphabetically. County boundaries are as given by the Ordnance Survey and as defined by the Local Government Act. Entries for Scotland, Wales, Northern Ireland and Ireland are purely alphabetical. From 1st April 1996 Scotland and Wales were wholly divided into 'Single Tier' Unitary Authorities, with their 'Counties' now having little administrative meaning.

Directions are given after each place name. Readers should note that these are *to the town or village mentioned* and ***not*** necessarily to the actual site in question. Directions are *not* given in the following instances: where the location is a large city or town; where specific directions to the site are not fully known; or at the request of several aircraft owners – who have every right to preserve their peace and quiet – some locations have been 'generalised'.

If you find yourself frustrated locating the now *former* Robin Hood Airport, turn to the Locations Index which includes alternative names. (For Robin Hood, *W&R* adopts the CAA-accepted Doncaster Sheffield Airport, while hankering for when it was Finningley.) A form of notation relating to the status of an 'aerodrome' is given: 'Aerodrome' signifies a civilian flying ground used by aircraft up to King Air, 'biz-jet' etc size. 'Airfield' is used to signify a flying ground used by the armed forces, test establishments or manufacturers. 'Airport' is used to denote a flying ground that takes 'serious' sized airliners on a regular basis. International Civil Aviation Organisation four-letter location indicators are also included. For privacy and security purposes, private strips etc are frequently *not* denoted as such.

Unless otherwise stated, *all* locations in this work are PRIVATE and entry to them *is strictly by prior permission, if at all.* A mention in this book does not imply *any* right of access.

◆ Signifies visitor and location details. This is often used to draw attention to locations that particularly *do not* allow access or where prior permission is required. No attempt is made to give GPS or Google mapping references. With a two-year publication 'span' **opening times are no longer given** and readers are urged to use the 'Contact' segment to satisfy themselves that the venue will be open when they visit. Telephone number(s), email and websites are given, where known. Note: websites, Facebook references etc are given for information only; no recommendation of content is to be implied.

Entries and Aircraft Listings: As *W&R* covers a two-year period, in this case 2022-2024, beyond the location header there is a narrative explaining the status of the entry and outlining any airframes that have moved since the last edition. Those departing are given underlined forwarding references, including the county, or province, where further reference can be found within the book. This allows the reader to follow the more energetic examples around. Any aircraft that fall out of any of the categories above, or are exported, will not have forwarding references. 'Ownership' or 'custodianship' of airframes within this work is not to be inferred as definitive.

Column 1: Aircraft are listed alpha-numerically, using the following rubric. British civil first (except in Ireland where EI- comes first), followed by British Gliding Association and 'B Condition' (or 'trade plate') markings. Then overseas civil registrations in alpha-numeric order.

British military serials follow (with reversal again in Ireland) followed by overseas military listed by country – ie France before Netherlands before USA. Anonymous airframes are inserted where it is thought most logical. Incorrect or fictitious registrations and serials are marked in quotes, eg 'VZ999' or 'G-BKEN'. A dash (–) is used to denote an airframe that has no confirmed primary identity. Entries new to a heading in this edition are marked *. **No attempt has been made to note if an identity is worn or not on the airframe.**

Column 2: Is devoted to individual codes, eg 'Z' or '109', *believed* worn on the airframe. Deck (eg 'O') and shore base (eg 'VL') codes for Fleet Air Arm aircraft are *not* noted.

Column 3: Type/designation; sometimes abbreviated. Design *origin* has been chosen, eg Blackburn Buccaneer, not Hawker Siddeley. (Although Column 6 contains manufacturer details, where location may differ, or for a sub-contractor, for major types, homebuilds do not get this treatment.) Reference to the *Index I Types* will provide a cross-reference. (Major rethinks of types, eg Short's extensive morphing of the Tucano, Slingsby's restructuring of the Fournier RF-6B, and Westland's re-engineering of the Whirlwind, Wessex and Sea King is, however, acknowledged, although not the latter company's 'badge engineering' on the Gazelle and Puma.)

To acquaint readers with the nature of the types listed, some abbreviations and a symbol are used: Believed airworthy, at time of going to press. CIM: Purpose-built instructional/training airframe, not intended for flight: Classroom Instruction Model, or even Module. EMU: Purpose-built test and evaluation airframe, not intended for flight, in most cases using prototype or production jigs and tooling: Engineering Mock-up. FSM: Full-scale model, often a faithful external reproduction of an aircraft, but using construction techniques completely unrelated to the original, frequently in fibreglass. Replica or rep: Reproduction, ie a faithful, or near-faithful copy or a facsimile of a type, using construction techniques and proportions in keeping with the original. The UK MoD has dropped the full stop from its designations: the Hawk these days is a T1 not T.1. *W&R* ignores this *pointless* (geddit?) 'innovation' and remains consistent.

Column 4: Devoted to civil registrations allocated, but not worn. Also here are *correct* identities when an incorrect or fictitious identity is presented in Column 1. Lapsed British civil registrations are also placed here.

Column 5: Year manufactured; in most cases when first flown. Dates from 1925 *onwards* are given as two digits, eg 67 = 1967, or 07 = 2007. Airframes pre-1924 have the year in full, eg 1914. In some cases, it has been possible only to give a 'stab' at the build date in which case they are given as follows: c36. With some aircraft that have never flown, if no other data is given, then the date first registered is used, eg r76. Where it is impossible to give a date a wavy dash – ~ – is given. (An impeccable source tells me this character is a 'tilde' – who knew?)

Column 6: Brief historical details are given, in a necessarily abbreviated form. In each case, units, operators, previous identities etc are listed in *reverse* order, ie the *last* location, user or identity is given *first*. Seasoned readers should have little trouble with these potted histories and the *Abbreviations* section lists the most-used alphanumeric soup. Also given here are other applicable identities, maintenance serials, heritage registers etc.

Much work has gone into showing, wherever possible, when an airframe stopped flying. This is relatively easy with UK civil registered aircraft – see the next paragraph. With British military the abbreviation SOC (struck off charge) has been used as a wide *generic* term, to avoid endless abbreviations and definitions. The date given may well be when the airframe in question *was* struck off, but it may also apply to its being sold (either intact or as scrap), transferred to display purposes, or to a museum, or similar. Occasionally, last flown dates are given.

Where a date is given prefixed 'CoA' (Certificate of Airworthiness), this is the date at which it lapsed and is given as an *indication* of how long the airframe has been flightless. The term 'CoA' is a catch-all and used for all levels of certification, eg including Permit to Fly, Ferry Permit etc. Where an airframe has suffered an accident, this is given as 'Crashed' or 'Cr', no attempt has been made to try to delineate or infer the severity, or nature, or blame of the incident. 'De-reg' refers to the date when a registration was formally cancelled from the civil register. It should be borne in mind that in some cases the 'paperwork' can lag behind the reality, sometimes by decades. Particularly for museum aircraft an attempt has been made to show how long a collection has had an airframe. Mostly, this is noted as 'arrived', but in some cases 'acquired' is used to signify that the airframe was taken on while the collection was based elsewhere, or similar.

Column 7: Used for footnotes – eg [7] and explained at the base of the listing.

Column 8: 'Last noted' dates are given primarily to help historians to trace the status (or demise) of an airframe and perhaps to alert readers intending a visit as to the 'currency' of the information given. The CAA seeks 'No Flight' Declarations (NFD) from registered (but *not* de-registered) aircraft. There's nothing better than a physical sighting, but where many years have gone by, to give an *indication* of continued existence dates prefixed N quote the NFD. Please note: this date does *not necessarily* relate to the location under which the aircraft is listed.

ENGLAND

Scotland
Northumberland &
Tyneside
Isle of Man
Cumbria
Durham &
Cleveland
North Yorkshire
Lancs
East
Yorkshire
West Yorkshire
Merseyside
Greater
Manchester
South
Yorks
Cheshire
Derbys
Notts
Lincs
Staffs
Wales
Shropshire
Leics
Norfolk
W Mids
Cambs
Hereford &
Worcester
Warks
Northants
Suffolk
Beds
Gloucestershire
Bucks
Herts
Essex
Oxon
Greater
London
Wiltshire
Berkshire
Somerset
Surrey
Hants
Kent
Devon
Dorset
W Sussex
E Sussex
Cornwall
Isle of Wight

BEDFORDSHIRE

Includes the unitary authority of Luton

BEDFORD

A Skeeter is at a *private* venue in the *general* area. Although dated, the Nord is *believed* to be current at a *different* site.

	Reg	Type	Yr	History	Note	Date
❑	G-BPMU	Nord 3202	59	ex Little Staughton, G-BIZJ, N22546, ALAT F-MAIX. De-reg 15-6-20		N4-16
❑	XL809	Saro Skeeter AOP.12 G-BLIX	58	ex PH-HOF, Moordrecht, XL809, 26 Rgt, 652, 22 Flt, 654, 652. SOC 12-12-68		12-21

BOZEAT on minor road east of the town, south of Wellingborough

Skirmish Outdoor Activity Centre: ◆ *Prior permission* **only** | **https://skirmishcentral.com**

	Reg	Type	Yr	History	Note	Date
❑	–*	Cessna 150 / 152	~	cockpit, first noted 11-22		11-22
❑	N340SC*	Cessna 340	83	ex Cranfield, VH-SPS. First noted 11-22		11-22

CARDINGTON east of the A600 south of Bedford

Any reader who has not viewed the two awesome 700ft-long airship sheds is missing out. The northern-most example, No.1, was completed in 1916. The other was dismantled at Pulham, Norfolk, in 1928 and re-erected alongside its cousin. The giant structures are used occasionally by modern-day airships. ◆ *No access, but plenty of public vantage points.*

CRANFIELD AERODROME east of Newport Pagnell EGTC

Cranfield University / Cranfield Aerospace: The Farnborough-based **Air Accident Investigation Branch** (AAIB) has an enclave alongside the airfield with a couple of airframes for instruction. Jetstream 31 G-NFLA was ferried to St Athan, Wales, 15th April 2023. ◆*On an active airfield; access* **only** *by prior permission* | **www.cranfield.ac.uk**

	Reg	Type	Yr	History	Note	Date
❑	G-BWWW	BAe Jetstream 3102	83	CoA 26-6-17, de-reg 25-10-22. First noted 4-20	[1]	2-23
❑	G-COAI	Cranfield A1 Eagle	76	ex G-BCIT. De-reg 6-2-20		1-20
❑	'G-DHEA'	HSA HS.125-3B G-OHEA	67	ex Hatfield, G-AVRG, G-5-12. CoA 7-8-92; de-reg 23-6-94. Trailer-mounted, rescue training		2-23
❑	G-DOCB	Boeing 737-436	91	ex BA. Flew in 23-10-14. CoA 15-2-15, de-reg 2-7-15. 'Cranfield University' titles, kept under an 'awning'		1-24
❑	G-REDU*	Aérospatiale Super Puma	98	ex Bond, CoA 22-5-09, de-reg 26-2-09. Ditched 18-2-09	[2]	2-24
❑	G-VUEM	Cessna Citation 501	81	ex G-FLVU, N83ND, N4246A, LV-PML, N67749. Crashed 19-11-10, de-reg 14-7-11. Fuselage, AAIB		2-24
❑	SP-KWN	BAe Jetstream 3212	89	ex LN-FAC, N856TE, N422AM, G-31-856. Flew in 2011. Rescue training		2-23
❑	XX387	Sud Gazelle AH.1	75	ex Arborfield TAD.014, Fleetlands, 651, 661, 657, 16/5 Lancers. Westland-built. Crashed 15-12-92		4-19
❑	XZ668	Westland Lynx AH.7	81	ex M Wallop, 63, 3 Rgt, 653. Ditched 18-8-95		4-19

■ **[1]** The registration derives from its first operator, the Distillers Company - *Triple-Whisky*! Modified by BAE Systems as the ASTREA – Autonomous Systems Technology Related Airborne Evaluation and Assessment – test-bed. Used to pioneer integration of UAVs within airspace used by 'inhabited' aircraft. It flew a 500-mile sortie in April 2013 totally under the command of a ground-based team, with the on-board crew only monitoring proceedings. **[2]** Written out of *W&R27* (p8) as moving to Selby, N Yorks: this was not the case.

Lightning T5 Group: (Note name change.) Russell Carpenter and friends keep this wonderful machine 'in steam'.
◆ *Occasional open days, or* **only** *by prior arrangement* | **www.facebook.com/groups/**

	Reg	Type	Yr	History	Note	Date
❑	XS458 'T'	EE Lightning T.5	65	ex Binbrook, LTF, 11, LTF, 5-11 pool, LTF, 5, 226 OCU. SOC 24-6-88		1-24

Also: Maintaining and storing HS.146s is a local speciality - only long-termers are covered. Seneca G-BMUT has been deleted.

	Reg	Type	Yr	History	Note	Date
❑	G-BADJ	Piper Aztec 250	72	ex N14279. CoA 2-8-08, de-reg 24-11-21. Fuselage. F/n 11-20		10-22
❑	G-BFSR	Cessna F.150J	69	ex OH-CBN. Reims-built. CoA 17-7-09, de-reg 30-10-18		4-21
❑	G-DLAL	Beech King Air 90	75	ex N816RL, N66BP, N816EP, N900MH, N2187L. CoA 17-3-14, de-reg 10-6-21		2-23
❑	G-JOTR*	HSA HS.146-RJ85	96	ex G-CHFE, OO-DTJ, G6-294. Woodford-built. CoA 2-4-22. Arrived 17-3-22		2-23
❑	G-JOTS*	HSA HS.146-RJ100	99	ex OO-DWJ, G-6-355. Woodford-built. CoA 30-11-24. Arrived 11-4-22		2-23

❑ G-OFOA	HSA HS.146-100	83	ex Biggin Hill, G-BKMN, EI-COF, SE-DRH, G-BKMN, G-ODAN. Hatfield-built. CoA 13-7-17, de-reg 6-12-17. Arrived 27-6-17		1-23
❑ G-OFOM*	HSA HS.146-100	90	ex N3206T, PK-DTA, G-BSLP, G-6-144. Woodford-built. CoA 4-10-22. Arrived 17-3-22		2-23
❑ G-SMLA	HSA HS.146-200	85	ex JOTA Aviation, N880PS, G-OZRH, EI-DDF, G-OZRH, N188US, N364PS. Hatfield-built. Arrived 22-10-20. Inst		1-23
❑ G-TZII	Thorp T.211	03	CoA 29-8-08. AD Aerospace-built		2-23
❑ G-WEFX	HSA HS.146 RJ100	00	ex G-ILLR, HB-IYU, G-CGAC, G-6-379. Woodford-built. CoA 16-6-20	[1]	2-23

■ **[1]** *Fox-Xray* acquired to act as an 'electrification' test-bed for Airbus/Rolls-Royce/Siemens as the E-Fan X. The programme was axed in March 2020 with little or no work carried out on the airframe.

Locally: A *private* location in the *general* area.

❑ XD547* 'Z'	DH Vampire T.11	54	ex Cantley, Elgin, Felixkirk, Dumfries, Aberfoyle, Strathallan, Milngavie, Glasgow, CATCS, 8 FTS, 1 RS, 263. SOC 22-3-71. Hawarden-built		7-23
❑ XH328	DH Vampire T.11	56	ex Cantley, London Colney, Duxford, Hurn, Cranfield, Hemel Hempstead, Croxley Green, Bushey, Keevil, Exeter, 3 CAACU, 60. Hawarden-built. SOC 22-6-71. Cockpit		7-23

DUNSTABLE west of Luton

Peter Underwood: The Martin project is at a workshop in the locality. See also Kite ADJ BGA.310 at Shuttleworth, Beds.
◆ ***Private*** location in the *general* area, ***no*** public access

❑ G-AEYY*	Martin Monoplane	37	ex Eaton Bray, Hitchin, Bishop's Stortford, Stoke-on-Trent, Meir. De-reg 3-6-98. Fuselage. Arrived 7-1-18	[1]	9-23

■ **[1]** Incorporated DH.53 Humming Bird components, including the wings - see J7326 at Shuttleworth, Beds. Following a crash in late 1937 it was rebuilt with a new fuselage.

EATON BRAY Peter Underwood relocated Martin Monoplane G-AEYY to Dunstable, Beds, by the summer of 2023.

FLITWICK northwest of Luton, north of J12 of the M1

Roger Creed: Continues to progress on *Charlie-November* ◆ *Prior permission* **only** | **roger.creed52@gmail.com**

❑ G-AHCN	Auster J1N Alpha	46	CoA 6-12-11, de-reg 29-9-14. Fuselage, arrived 6-12	[1]	1-24

■ **[1]** Wings destined for G-AHCN are from J1 G-AJDW.

HATCH off the B658, southwest of Sandy

Skysport Engineering: ◆ **Strictly** ***prior permission*** **only** | **www.skysportengineering.co.uk**

❑ AXB	Slingsby Skylark 2	56	BGA.733, ex Lyveden. CoA 30-6-02	[1]	9-21
❑ F-ANHO	Comper Swift	33	ex France, HB-OXE, CH-352. Fuselage		1-19
❑ N5595T	Douglas C-47A-85-DL Skytrain	43	ex Thruxton, Blackbushe, G-BGCG, Spanish AF T.3-27, N49V, N50322, USAAF 43-15536. Long Beach-built		12-23

■ **[1]** Prototype Skylark 2, flown by Flt Lt Douglas Bridson up to 30,000ft.

HENLOW on the A6007 southwest of Biggleswade

RAF Signals Museum: As part of the wind-down of the RAF station, the museum must vacate its premises by the end of June 2024. This will bring to an end 24 years in residence. Always a pioneering collection, it owed its origins to the artefacts amassed by 1 Radio School when it was at Locking, Somerset. The final open day is scheduled for 4th May 2024 after which an 'everything must go' operation will swing into gear. Loan items will be returned to benefactors: Interested parties in other items for disposal should register – see the website for details: **www.rafsignalsmuseum.org.uk**

RAF Henlow: Full closure is now set at 2026. The Gazelle/Lynx/Typhoon are/were with the **RAF Centre of Aviation Medicine**.

❑ WT612	Hawker Hunter F.1	54	ex Halton, Credenhill, Yatesbury 7496M (29-11-57), A&AEE, Rolls-Royce. Displayed, since 1984	1-24
❑ XZ312	Sud Gazelle AH.1	76	ex Shawbury, Wattisham, 3 Regt. Westland-built. Cockpit	12-14
❑ ZD250 '636'	Westland Lynx HAS.3S	82	ex 702, 815, 702, 815, 702, 815, 829, 702. First noted 4-12	10-19
❑ –	Eurofighter Typhoon EMU	~	cockpit. First noted 7-18	7-18

LEIGHTON BUZZARD

Fly A Flight: Within Leighton Buzzard Garden Centre. Dogfights in a wholly synthetic Spitfire and Messerschmitt Bf 109 are offered in addition to a fixed-base sim using one of the many cockpits generated from the strip-downs at Cotswold, Glos.

◆ *Prior permission* **only** | **www.flyaflightsimulatorexperience.com**

❑ EI-DYG*	Boeing 737-800	08	ex Cotswold, Ryanair. Crashed 10-11-08. Cockpit	7-22

LONDON LUTON AIRPORT

EGGW

❑ G-AOVS	Bristol Britannia 312	58	ex Redcoat, 'G-BRAC', Lloyd, BOAC. CoA 31-7-79, de-reg 7-5-81. Fuselage. Rescue training	12-23
❑ VP-BJW	Boeing 737-301	87	ex Cotswold, KD Avia, N563AU, N348US, N328P. Last flight 29-4-10. Forward fuselage. Rescue training	7-22

LUTON Last noted in January 2020, the cockpit of HS.125 G-AXDM had appeared at Billericay, Essex, by June 2022.

MEPPERSHALL Last noted in July 2019, S.205 G-BBRX has been deleted.

SHUTTLEWORTH AERODROME or Old Warden

EGTH

Shuttleworth Collection: The scope and variety of the collection, on wings and on wheels, need not be re-iterated here. Two exhibits carry notices that convey their importance: the Blériot is 'the world's oldest flying aeroplane and engine' and the Blackburn is 'the world's oldest airworthy British aeroplane'. There is a tremendous cafe, and a truly barmpot decision to charge visitors to use it, even if all they were after was a cuppa and a look at activity on the aerodrome, was thankfully overturned early in 2023.

In March 2022 Moth G-EBLV, Blackburn B.2 G-AEBJ and Avro XIX G-AHKX, previously on loan from BAE Systems, were handed over to the Richard Shuttleworth Trustees. Backing up the transfer was a tidy £75,000 towards their upkeep. Blériot BAPC.9 is on loan at Coventry, Warks.

Supporting in many ways is the **Shuttleworth Veteran Aeroplane Society** (SVAS - hence Super Cub G-SVAS - **www.svasweb.org**) which publishes the excellent *Prop-Swing*. Don't overlook the Swiss Garden, an enchanting 'diversion'.

Departures: Privately owned Hawker Cygnet G-EBJI and Aeronca C.3 G-ADRR flew off to Breighton, E Yorks, on 30th May and 14th June 2022, respectively. Wallis WA-116 G-ARZB left by March 2023 to a location in 'Cambridgeshire' for the proposed 'museum' - see also 'Off-site' below. Chilton DW.1 replica G-CDXU had moved on by July 2022.

◆ *Signed from the A1 | Biggleswade, SG18 9EP* | **01767 627927** | **enquiries@shuttleworth.org** | **www.shuttleworth.org**
Please note*: The hangar complex in the southeast corner is* **not** *available for inspection. Some aircraft listed below may occasionally move to 'the other side' but are regarded as 'front-of-house' exhibits. A hopefully obvious 'one-off' abbreviation is used below - OW for Old Warden (aka Shuttleworth) 'returnees'.*

❑ G-EAGA		Sopwith Dove replica ✈	90	ex 'Essex', OW, Hatch. Skysport-built. Arrived 5-15	[1]	1-24
❑ G-EBHX		DH Humming Bird	1923	ex Lympne No.8. Acquired 1-9-60. *L'Oiseau Mouche* Crashed 1-7-12. CoA 4-4-13	[2]	3-23
❑ G-EBIR		DH DH.51 ✈	1924	ex VP-KAA, G-KAA, G-EBIR. Acquired 7-65. Aircraft Transport & Travel Ltd colours		1-24
❑ G-EBJO		ANEC II ✈	1924	ex Radcliffe on Trent, OW, West Malling, Lympne 1924 No.7. Acquired 1-37		1-24
❑ G-EBLV		DH.60 Moth ✈	1925	ex Hatfield. Arrived 1993. See note above		1-24
❑ G-EBNV	'4'	English Electric Wren II ✈	1923	BAPC.11, ex Warton, Ashton, Samlesbury, Preston, Science Museum, Lympne No.4. Acquired 15-9-57	[3]	1-24
❑ G-EBWD		DH.60X Moth ✈	28	acquired 21-1-32	[4]	1-24
❑ G-AAIN		Parnall Elf II ✈	32	ex Southend, Fairoaks, Badminton. Acquired 7-51		1-24
❑ G-AANG	No.13	Blériot XI ✈	1910	BAPC.3, ex Ampthill, Blackfriars, Hendon. Acquired 1935. See above		1-24
❑ G-AANH	No.43	Deperdussin ✈	1910	BAPC.4, ex *Those Magnificent Men...*, Ampthill. Acquired 1935		1-24
❑ G-AANI	No.9	Blackburn Monoplane ✈	1912	BAPC.5, ex Wittering. Acquired 1937		1-24
❑ G-AAPZ		Desoutter I ✈	30	ex Higher Blagdon, OW. Acquired 5-1-35		1-24
❑ G-AAYX		Southern Martlet ✈	30	ex Shoreham, Redhill, Staverton, Woodley. Acquired 1955		1-24
❑ G-ABAG		DH Gipsy Moth ✈	30	'arrived' 1-04	[1]	10-21
❑ G-ABVE*		Arrow Active 2 ✈	32	ex Breighton, OW. Arrived 7-22	[5]	1-24

❑ G-ACSS	'34'	DH Comet ✈	34	ex Hatfield, Farnborough, OW, Leavesden, Hatfield, London Colney, Gravesend, G-ACSS, K5084 A&AEE, RAE, AA&EE, RAE, G-ACSS. *Grosvenor House*. Acquired 30-10-65		1-24
❑ G-ACTF		Comper Swift ✈	32	ex Rhos, VT-ADO. Acquired 16-8-96. *The Scarlet Angel*		1-24
❑ G-ADGP	'8'	Miles Hawk Speed Six ✈	35	ex White Waltham, OW, Southampton, USA, OW. Phillips & Powis-built. Arrived 10-5-18		1-24
❑ G-AEBB		Mignet HM.14 'Flea'	36	ex Southampton. CoA 31-5-39, de-reg 1-12-46 Acquired 1968	[6]	1-24
❑ G-AEBJ		Blackburn B.2 ✈	36	ex Brough, Warton, Blackburn, 4 EFTS, Brough, Hanworth. Arrived 3-08. See notes above	[7} [8]	1-24
❑ G-AEOA*		DH Puss Moth	31	ex Great Dunmow, ES921, 5 GCF, 1660 CU, 5 GCF, ATA. CoA 27-6-95. Arrived 12-22	[1]	1-24
❑ G-AEXF		Percival Mew Gull *replica* ✈	36	ex Breighton, OW, Sudbury, OW, Squires Gate, Booker, Yeadon, Blackbushe, France, ZS-AHM. Arrived 6-10-13	[9]	1-24
❑ G-AGSH		DH Dragon Rapide 6 ✈	45	ex Hurn, Lower Upham, EI-AJO, G-AGSH, Dominie NR808 n/s. Brush-built. Arr 27-2-09. BEA c/s, *Jemma Meeson*	[10]	1-24
❑ G-ARSG	'12'	Avro Triplane IV replica ✈	64	BAPC.1, ex *Those Magnificent Men...* Hampshire Aero Club-built. Acquired 1966		1-24
❑ G-ASPP	'12A'	Bristol Boxkite replica ✈	64	BAPC.2, ex *Those Magnificent Men...* F G Miles-built. Acquired 1966		1-24
❑ G-BFIP		Wallbro Mono replica	78	ex Reymerston, Flixton, Shipdham, Swanton Morley. CoA 22-4-82, de-reg 28-3-01. Arrived 20-3-15	[11] [12]	2-22
❑ G-CAMM	'6'	Hawker Cygnet replica ✈	92	ex Hucknall, G-ERDB. Arrived 1995	[13]	2-22
❑ G-IBRO		Cessna 152 II	85	ex Leicester, EI-BRO. Crashed 3-3-05, de-reg 29-6-05. Fuselage, rescue training. Arrived mid-2009, on 'far side'	[14]	8-22
❑ G-SVAS		Piper Super Cub 150 ✈	61	ex G-BGWH, ST-ABR, G-ARSR, N10F. Acquired 13-10-08. See note above		1-24
❑ G-TATR*	'29'	Travel Air R replica ✈	12	ex Turweston. Aero Antiques-built. Arrived 24-6-22	[15]	3-23
❑ ADJ		Slingsby Kirby Kite	37	BGA.310, ex Tibenham. Acquired 2011. Restoration, off-site	[16]	1-24
❑ AQQ		EoN Primary ✈	c47 G-ALPS	BGA.580, ex Hatch, Duxford, Henlow, Twinwood Farm, Cranfield, G-ALPS (de-reg 7-2-63). Acquired late 1960s		1-24
❑ –		Fauvel AV.36CR Monobloc ✈	55	BGA.1999, ex Booker, RAFGSA, F-CBSH. Wassmer-built Arrived by aero-tow from G-SVAS 16-7-14		1-24
❑ –		Dixon Ornithopter	c1912	BAPC.8, ex Dunstable. Acquired 1960s		1-22
❑ –		Lilienthal replica	06	BAPC.439, ex St Albans. Arrived 4-07	[17]	1-22
❑ –		Lilienthal biplane replica	06	BAPC.437. Donated 11-12	[18]	1-22
❑ –		Pilcher Bat Mk.3 replica	08	BAPC.337, ex St Albans. Arrived 11-08	[17]	1-22
❑ –		Pilcher Triplane replica	03	BAPC.441, arrived 2006	[19]	3-18
❑ NC8115		Travel Air D-4000	29	Arrived 8-9-20	[20]	9-22
❑ '1264'		Bristol Scout C replica ✈	15 G-FDHB	ex '1611', '1264'. Bristol Scout Group, Ludlow-built. First noted 10-15. Returned to '1264' by 7-22	[21]	1-24
❑ '9917'		Sopwith Pup ✈	1920 G-EBKY	ex 'N6181', 'N5180', 'N5184', West Malling, Kingston. Acquired 1937	[22]	1-24
❑ 'B1162'	'F'	Bristol F.2B ✈	1918 G-AEPH	ex Filton, Watford, D8096, 208. Acquired 2-52 22 Sqn colours, France 3-18, by 11-20		1-24
❑ 'C1096'	'3'	Royal Aircraft Factory SE.5a replica ✈	03 G-ERFC	ex F-AZBF, Le Bourget, Selby. Arrived 8-18. Tested 19-10-18. 56 Sqn colours	[23]	3-23
❑ 'C4918'		Bristol M.1C replica ✈	81 G-BWJM	ex Dewsbury. 'C' Flight, NAW-built. Acquired 28-10-97. 72 Sqn colours	[24]	1-24
❑ 'D1851'	'X'	Sopwith Camel F1 replica	01 G-BZSC	ex Batley. NAW-built. Arrived 28-8-13, first flown 18-5-17. *Ikanopit*, 70 Sqn colours	[24]	1-24
❑ 'E3273'		Avro 504K ✈	1918 G-ADEV	ex G-ACNB, H5199, 'E3404', *Reach for the Sky* (1955), Woodford, Portsmouth, Windermere, 504N BK892, CLE, G-ADEV, London and Provincial-built 504K H5199. Acquired 1958. 77 Sqn colours, red-blue roundels	[25]	1-24
❑ F904		Royal Aircraft Factory SE.5a ✈	1918 G-EBIA	ex 'D7000', Farnborough, Whitley, G-EBIA, F904 84 Sqn. Wolseley-built. Acquired 8-59. 92 Sqn colours	[26]	1-24

	Serial	Code	Type	Year	Reg	History	Note	Date
❑	'N6290'		Sopwith Triplane *replica* ✈	80	G-BOCK	ex Dewsbury. NAW-built. Arrived 6-90. 8 Sqn RNAS colours, *Dixie II*	[24] [27]	1-24
❑	K1786		Hawker Tomtit ✈	31	G-AFTA	ex Dunsfold, Langley, Hawker, Castle Bromwich, Braunstone, RAF 5 GCF, 23 GCF, 3 FTS. Acquired 5-60		1-24
❑	'K2585'		DH Tiger Moth ✈	42	G-ANKT	ex Mk.II T6818, Aston Down, 21 EFTS. Morris-built. Acquired 9-72. CFS 'sunburst' colours	[28]	1-24
❑	'K3241'		Avro Tutor ✈	33	G-AHSA	ex HSA, K3215, 61 OTU, 41 OTU, Hawarden SF, CFS. Acquired 1959. CFS 'sunburst' colours		1-24
❑	'K5414'		Hawker Hind (Afghan) ✈	37	G-AENP	BAPC.78. ex 'K5457', Kabul, Afghan AF. Acquired 1970. 'XV' - 15 Sqn colours		1-24
❑	'K7985'		Gloster Gladiator I ✈	37	G-AMRK	ex '423' *and* '427', L8032, 'N2308', L8032, 'K8032', Gloster, Ansty, Hamble, 8 MU, 61 OTU, 1624F, 2 AACU. Acquired 7-11-60. 73 Sqn colours	[29]	1-24
❑	K8203		Hawker Demon I	37	G-BTVE	ex Hatch, Cardington, 2292M, 9 BGS, 9 AOS, 64. Boulton Paul-built. Arr 23-7-09. CoA 4-9-18, 64 Sqn c/s	[30]	1-24
❑	'N3788'		Miles Magister I ✈	41	G-AKPF	ex 'V1075', Shoreham, Sandown, Shoreham, V1075, 16 EFTS. Phillips & Powis-built. Arrived 9-01	[31]	3-23
❑	P6382		Miles Magister I ✈ ✈	39	G-AJRS	ex 'G-AJDR', P6382, 3 EFTS, 16 EFTS. Phillips & Powis-built. Acquired 3-4-70		1-24
❑	'V9367'	'MA-B'	Westland Lysander III ✈	42	G-AZWT	ex 'V9441', Duxford, Strathallan, RCAF 2355. Acquired 1997. 161 Sqn colours		1-24
❑	Z7015	'7-L'	Hawker Sea Hurricane I ✈	39	G-BKTH	ex Duxford, Staverton, OW, Loughborough, Yeovilton, 759, 880. CCF-built. Acquired 21-2-61. 880 Sqn colours		1-24
❑	AR501	'DU-E'	V-S Spitfire V ✈	42	G-AWII	ex Duxford, Thurleigh, Henlow, Loughborough, CGS, 61 OTU, 1 TEU, 58 OTU, 422, 312, Culmhead Stn Flt, 504, 310. Westland-built. SOC 21-3-46. Arr 6-61. 312 Sqn colours		1-24
❑	'TX176'		Avro XIX Srs 2 ✈	46	G-AHKX	ex Woodford, Strathallan, Kemps, Treffield, Smiths. Arrived 29-6-02. Coningsby SF colours. See notes above		1-24
❑	XA241	JJS	Slingsby G'hopper TX.1	53		BGA.4556, ex Cambridge, Croydon. Arrived 12-95. Stored		1-14
❑	XF603		Percival Provost T.1 ✈	55	G-KAPW	ex Cranfield, Filton, Bristol, 27 MU, CAW, RAFC. SOC 12-9-67. Acquired 2-11-01. RAF grey / green camo	[32]	1-24
❑	'18671'		DHC Chipmunk T.10 ✈	52	G-BNZC	ex G-ROYS, 7438M, WP905 CFS, 664, RAFC. Hawarden-built. Acquired 3-00. RCAF colours		1-24
❑	'S-11'		Ryan ST-A ✈	40	N7779	ex USA, N288Y, VH-AGZ, RAAF A50-31. Arrived 8-20 First flight on site 8-3-21. Dutch Naval Air Service c/s	[33]	3-23
❑	U-88*	'RV'	Bücker Bü 133C Jungmeister ✈	40	G-CMCX	ex N35BU, HB-MKL, N35133, D-EIIV, Swiss AF U-88. Dornier Werke-built. Arrived 17-5-22	[34]	3-23
❑	'BB+EJ'*		Focke-Wulf FW 44J Stieglitz	36	G-EJBB	ex Fishburn, York, Finnish AF SZ-35. Arrived 31-7-23	[35]	8-23
❑	–	'28'	Polikarpov Po-2 *Mule* ✈	44	G-BSSY	ex N588NB, ZK-POZ, N588NB, G-BSSY, YU-CLB, Yugoslav AF 0094, Sov AF. Acquired 31-7-03. Soviet c/s	[36]	1-24

■ **[1]** Dove, Moth G-ABAG and Puss Moth on loan from Andrew and Paul Wood. (See also Great Dunmow, Essex.) **[2]** Prototype Humming Bird, first flown 1-10-23. **[3]** G-EBNV is substantially the unregistered Lympne trials No.4, which had been with the Science Museum until 1945, with engine parts from the original G-EBNV (Lympne No.3). **[4]** G-EBWD was bought by Richard Ormonde Shuttleworth for £300 from Brooklands School of Flying on 21-1-32. **[5]** G-ABVE owned by Coventry-based Ben Cox. **[6]** 'Flea' built by Kenneth Owen at Southampton; Authorisation No.31 issued 2-3-36. **[7]** B.2 used parts from G-ACLD - crashed 16-6-51 - during restoration in the late 1950s. **[8]** See Brough, E Yorks, for *another* 'G-AEBJ'. **[9]** Most famed for the Cape Town out-and-back dash by Alex Henshaw in 2-39. This machine suffered an accident 7-8-65 and was donated to the Historic Aircraft Preservation Society - later Reflectaire - and allowed to rot at Squires Gate. Much reconfigured/rebuilt G-AEXF was restored 1972-1978 and to stress how little of the original survived, it was given a PFA project number - hence the 'replica' suffix. See under Tattershall Thorpe, Lincs, and Hendon, Gtr Lon, for *more* 'G-AEXFs'. **[10]** Rapide on loan from Philip Meeson. **[11]** Wallbro on loan from the Wallis family estate. **[12]** Replica of the original built by brothers Horace Samuel Wallis and Percival Valentine Wallis (hence Wallbro), respectively the father and uncle of the late Wg Cdr Ken Wallis, and flown at Cambridge, 4-7-1910. *India-Papa* built by Ken and his cousin Geoffrey – ie son of Percival – first flown 10-8-78. **[13]** G-CAMM, built by Don Cashmore. Don also built the Bristol M.1 replica at Cosford, Shrop. **[14]** Rescue training airframe G-IBRO was written out of *W&R27* (p10) but serves on. **[15]** G-TATR owned by Richard Seeley. **[16]** Rebuilt in 1982 using the fuselage, port wing and elevator of BGA.327 plus parts from BGA.310. Under restoration by Peter Underwood, see Dunstable, Beds. **[17]** Lilienthal No.11 'Standard Flying Apparatus' circa 1894 and the Pilcher ('Standard' also referred to as 'Normal'.) Bat Mk.3 built by Eric Littledike of St Albans, Herts. **[18]** Built for Shuttleworth by Carsten Brinkmeier in Germany, a replica of the 'Kleiner Doppeldecker' (Little Biplane) of 1895. *Another* Brinkmeier replica, a 'Normalapparat' ('Normal' or 'Standard' is stored against a wall in Hangar 5. Labels describe it as "centre section, 'fuselage' and tailfin". The Normalapparat is essentially the lower component of the Doppeldecker. **[19]** At the time Percy Pilcher was killed at Stanford Hall, Leics, on 18-9-1899 (see Stanford, Leics and Edinburgh, Scotland) he was working on a weight-shift powered triplane. A team from Cranfield University and Bill Brooks of Mainair Sports built a modern-day version for a TV film in 2003. It was flown for the first time on 29-8-03 by Bill Brooks. On 5-9-03 it managed a ¼ mile flight. It was presented to Shuttleworth by the TV company. **[20]** D-4000 owned by Mike South and Richard Seeley. **[21]** Scout on loan from Bristol Scout Group. **[22]** G-EBKY first 'surfaces' as a two-seat version of the Pup, the Sopwith Dove, registered to D L Hollis Williams 3-25. This one was part of a cache of unfinished examples stored at Kingston and acquired by DHW for £5. Stored at West Malling from 1933, it went to Richard Shuttleworth in 1937 and given Pup status. **[23]** SE.5 On loan from Tom Harris – see also Duxford, Cambs. Construction began by John Tetley of Selby in the late 1980s - see also G-BKDT at Elvington, N Yorks - completed by the French Memorial Flight at Le Bourget and first flown in France. In the colours of Canadian Henry 'Hank' Burden DSO DFC 56 Sqn. **[24]** NAW - the former Northern Aeroplane Workshops, Dewsbury. **[25]** The 504's history prior to being discovered at Portsmouth where it had been kept by Airspeed is problematical. It was converted to 504K status from what is believed to have been a glider or banner-towing 504N. The 'accepted' identity is G-ADEV, but as this ended up with an ATC unit in Windermere (as 3118M) in 1942, this is doubted. It was registered as G-ACNB in 12-82 but took up G-ADEV in 4-84. Its latest guise is as a night-fighter with 77 Home Defence Sqn, based at Turnhouse, Scotland, 1918. **[26]** As revealed in *Above the Trenches* (Shores/Franks/Guest, Grub Street, 1990) Major Charles E M Pickthorne, CO of 84 Sqn, shot down a Fokker D.VII while flying F904 on 8-11-18. **[27]** Production of Triplanes came to 152 and as the late Sir Thomas Sopwith decreed that *Charlie-Kilo* should be considered as a late production example, it is known at Old Warden as No.153. **[28]** Tiger Moth is a composite of three acquired by the collection in 1966, making its first flight in 10-77. **[29]** Gladiator in the colours of Plt Off 'Cobber' Kain. **[30]** Demon restored at Hatch, Beds and on loan from Demon Displays Ltd. **[31]** David Bramwell's N3788 is a composite, using the centre section of G-AIUA (see Balcombe, W Sussex), rear fuselage of G-ANLT, wings of G-AHYL plus others. N3788 was 'demobbed' on 27-8-47 becoming G-ANLT; its RAF pedigree was ex 169 Sqn, 2 FIS, 2 FTS, 5 EFTS, 8 EFTS, 27 E&RFTS. **[32]** XF603 painted as one delivered to the Sultan of Oman's Air Force. **[33]** Ryan owned by Arnaldo Leon. **[34]** Jungmeister registered to Bucks-based D E Starkey. **[35]** Stieglitz registered to Oldstead Aero. **[36]** The Po-2's US registration pays homage to the Soviet all-woman 588th Night Bombing Regiment which flew nuisance raids against the Germans, earning the pilots the nickname 'Night Witches'.

Flying Restorations Ltd: Moved into to a workshop on the 'far side' - ie *strictly* non-public - in January 2020, having previously been located at Hatch, Beds. Work on a replica Farman Longhorn and an Airco DH.2 is under way.
◆ **Strictly** *prior appointment* **only**

❑ G-ADKK*	DH Hornet Moth	35	ex W5749, 529, 79, 1 PRU, 6 CPF, G-ADKK. CoA 5-12-20		9-22
❑ J7326*	DH Humming Bird	24 G-EBQP	ex London Colney, Hatch, Audley End, Bishop's Stortford, Hamble, Henlow, Farnborough, J7326, RAE, A&AEE. Crashed *and* de-reg 21-7-34. Arrived 7-21	[1]	9-23

■ **[1]** Humming Bird has the wings of Martin Monoplane G-AEYY - see Dunstable, Beds - which itself used a set of DH.53 wings, probably from J7325. It is on loan from Terry Pankhurst and Peter Kirk. J7326, served on trials with the Airship R-33 in 1925.

Kennet Aviation and **Kennet Engineering:** On the 'far side' - ie *strictly* non-public. Two airframes, registered to Kennet's Tim Manna, are still at the former base, North Weald, Essex: 'JP' 'XD693' (G-AOBU) and Skyraider 126922 (G-RADR). Airworthy Texan '8084' (G-KAMY) shares its time between here, North Weald and Yeovilton.

Provost T.1 XF690 (G-MOOS) arrived from Yeovilton, Somerset, by late 2022: it decamped to St Athan, Wales, 21st December 2023. ◆ **Strictly** *prior appointment* **only**

Flying Restorations gives Hummingbird J7326 a public airing at Old Warden, September 2023. *Terry Dann*

❑ G-ABYA*	DH Gipsy Moth	32	CoA 25-5-17. Stored		7-22
❑ AA810	V-S Spitfire PR.IV	G-PRID 41	ex Norway, 1 PRU. Lost near Trondheim 5-3-42	[1]	1-20
❑ LA564	V-S Seafire F.46	46 G-FRSX	ex N Weald, Newport Pagnell, Redbourn, Newark, Southend, Charnock Richard, Carlisle, Anthorn, 738, 767, A&AEE. SOC 29-6-51. First noted 4-17	[2]	10-20
❑ SR462	V-S Seafire F.XV	45 G-TGVP	ex Sandown, N Weald, USA, N462XV, N9413Z, Burma, 'UB415', UB414, G-15-225, SR462 n/s. SOC 5-6-52. Westland-built. Arrived by mid-2020	[3]	10-20
❑ SX300	V-S Seafire F.17	46 G-RIPH	ex N Weald, G-CDTM, Twyford, Warwick, Leamington Spa, Warrington, Bramcote A2054/ A646 (9-6-53), 728. Westland-built. First noted 6-18	[2]	10-20

■ **[1]** Kennet manages this project for Spitfire AA810 Restoration Ltd - **www.spitfireaa810.co.uk** **[2]** LA564 and SX300 are registered to Seafire Displays Ltd. **[3]** SR462 registered to Dubai-based Tim Percy. His father, the late Lt Cdr Terence Gerard Vaughan 'Pablo' Percy flew this machine; its civil registration reflects his initials.

Also, off-site: **Wallis Heritage Ltd** has been created as custodian to the fleet of Ken Wallis autogyros. Reportedly a 'visitor centre' is envisaged and the entire store was cleared and moved to an undisclosed location in 'Cambridgeshire' by late 2022: G-ARRT, 'G-ARZB' (G-AVDH), G-ASDY, G-ATHM, G-AVDG, G-AVJV, G-AVJW, G-AXAS, G-AYVO, G-BAHH, G-BGGU, G-BGGW, G-BLIK, G-BMJX, G-BNDG, G-SCAN, G-VIEW, G-VTEN.

THURLEIGH, north of Bedford, east of the A6

306th Bomb Group Museum: Sited in the wartime small arms and ammunition store, while the central theme is the Flying Fortress-equipped 306th, the 'home front' and Thurleigh's Royal Aircraft Establishment days are also covered.

◆ *Follow signs for Bedford Technology Park and Bedford Autodrome, MK44 1QT* | **www.facebook.com/306thmuseum/** | **www.306bg.co.uk**

TWINWOOD FARM near Clapham, off the A6 north of Bedford

Twinwood Museums: The tower has been turned into a Glenn Miller era 'shrine'. It was from Twinwood that the legendary band leader departed for France in a Noorduyn UC-64 Norseman on 15th December 1944, never to be seen again. As well as the Glenn Miller Museum, the site also boasts the Twinwood Aviation Museum, the 'Under Fire' exhibition covering the wartime fire service, the Summer of '44 Museum and other displays, all within former RAF accommodation buildings.

◆ *Twinwood Road, Clapham, MK41 6AB* | **info@twinwoodfestival.com** | **www.twinwoodevents.com**

BERKSHIRE

Includes the unitary authorities of Bracknell Forest, Reading, Slough, Windsor and Maidenhead, Wokingham

BINFIELD north of the B3034, northwest of Bracknell

Delta Force Paintball: Cannon Lane. ◆ *Prior arrangement* **only** | **www.paintballgames.co.uk**

❑ XZ606*	'O'	Westland Lynx AH.7	79	ex Billericay, Upminster, Ipswich, Middle Wallop. First noted -21	10-23

Although the references are somewhat dated, the contents of a *private* store in the *general* area are *thought* unchanged.

❑ G-ASXF	Brantly 305	r64	ex Thruxton, Biggin Hill, CoA 16-2-79, de-reg 24-5-82	4-11
❑ G-AYNS	Airmaster H2-B1	r70	ex Redhill. CoA 13-2-73, de-reg 30-5-84. In container	5-17
❑ G-BPCJ	Cessna 150J	69	ex Solihull, Tattershall Thorpe, N61096. *Charlie*. Damaged 25-1-90; de-reg 4-7-90	5-17

BRACKNELL

A *private* owner locally is *believed* to still have a 'JP' cockpit.

❑ XM417	'D'	Hunting Jet Provost T.3	60	ex Hednesford, Fownhope, Halton 8054BM (23-10-69), Shawbury, 6 FTS, 7 FTS, 2 FTS. Cockpit	5-17

COLNBROOK Boeing 737 cockpit G-CEAF moved to Penn, Bucks, on 28th February 2022.

GREENHAM COMMON east of the A339 south of Newbury

Greenham Common Tower: A combination of village centre, café, space-for-hire, and museum with impressive views of the area. The tower opened to the public on 8th September 2018.

◆ *Burys Bank Road, RG19 8BZ.* | **01635 44145** | **info@greenhamtower.org.uk** | **www.greenhamtower.org.uk**

HUNGERFORD on the A4 east of Marlborough

A *private* workshop in the *general* area is at work on a Chilton and a Tiger. ◆ **Strictly** *prior permission* **only**

❑ G-AFGH	Chilton DW.1	38	ex Billingshurst. CoA 7-7-83		N11-23
❑ G-AMCM	DH Tiger Moth	42	ex DE249, A&AEE, 29 EFTS, 7 EFTS, 18 EFTS, Glider Pilot Exercise Unit, 296. 297. SOC 8-6-50	[1]	4-20

■ **[1]** Registered to Australian-based owners.

LAMBOURN on the B4000 north of Hungerford

A Hurricane is *believed* to be at a *private* workshop in the area. ◆ *Prior arrangement* **only**

❑ KZ191	Hawker Hurricane IV	43	ex N Weald, Fowlmere, Israel, 351, 1695 Flt, AFDU. SOC 26-9-46	1-15

LANGLEY on the B470 north of the junction of the M4 and A4, east of Slough

Langley Academy: Langley Road. On the site of the former Hawker flight test airfield, the connection is marked by a 'Flea' on loan from the Brooklands Museum. ◆ *Prior arrangement* ***only*** | **www.langleyacademy.org**

❑ 'G-ADRY'	Mignet HM.14 'Flea'	c67	BAPC.29, ex Brooklands, Aberdare, Swansea. Suspended in foyer, on loan. Arrived 8-10	[1]	1-24

■ **[1]** Built using some original 1930s parts by P D Roberts of Swansea, circa 1967, completed by 1978.

MAIDENHEAD

Maidenhead Heritage Centre: Includes 'Grandma Flew Spitfires', a tribute to the gallantry of the men and women of the Air Transport Auxiliary. Headquartered at nearby White Waltham, ATA was nicknamed 'Anything to Anywhere' from its initials. A pre-bookable Spitfire simulator is also available. The website is a mine of information and imagery.

◆ *18 Park Street, Maidenhead, SL6 1SL* | **01628 780555** | **www.maidenheadheritage.org.uk** | **www.atamuseum.org**

Also: A Harvard and a Hunter are at a *private* location in the area. At *another* venue a Bristol 170 flightdeck is kept.

❑ C-FDFC		Bristol 170 Mk.31	54	ex Fleet, Enstone, G-BISU Instone, ZK-EPH, NZ5912, ZK-BVI, G-18-194. Crashed 18-7-96. Flightdeck	6-20
❑ KF435	'5666'	NAA Harvard T.2B	44	ex Swindon, Guildford, Duxford, Ottershaw, Booker, Camberley, Sandhurst, 1 FTS, 2 FTS, 22 SFTS, 20 FTS, 11 (P)AFU. Noorduyn-built. SOC 24-9-57. Arrived 25-9-14	10-23
❑ XL592	'Y'	Hawker Hunter T.7	58	ex Booker, Kemble, Exeter, Scampton 8836M (31-8-84), 1 TWU, TWU, 229 OCU. Arrived 7-14	10-23

WELFORD or Welford Park, north of the M4, west of junction 13 (A34)

RAF Welford Historical Society: During 2023 the Ridgeway Military and Aviation Research Group merged with the Families, Friends and Veterans of RAF Welford group to create the historical society. Located within the former World War Two airfield, now known as Welford Park, this a *private* museum.

The cockpit of C-47A 42-93510 'CM' moved to Old Sarum, Wilts, on 16th March 2022, on long term loan.

◆ *Prior appointment* **only** | **contact@rafwelfordhistoricalsociety.org** | **www.rafwelfordhistoricalsociety.org**

❑ –	Airspeed Horsa replica	c76	BAPC.609. Ex *Bridge Too Far*, fuselage	1-24

WHITE WALTHAM AERODROME south of the A4 southwest of Maidenhead EGLM

Shoot Aviation: Billed as "Europe's largest provider of aviation sets and content for film and TV" the company has extensive facilities, including 'The Bond Hangar' and 'Ops Room' on the southern perimeter. Turnaround is swift on a lot of airframes: many are brought in for a particular job and leave again and others don't meet *W&R's* coverage criteria. Recent examples include an Agusta 109 in mid-2022; an anonymous SCAN 30 (French-built Grumman Widgeon) and a Heinkel He 111 cockpit (provenance unknown) both noted in June 2023. Such items are not listed - only long-ish termers are given here. Lynx HAS.3 XZ238 migrated to Bournemouth, Dorset, 8th August 2023.

◆ **Strictly** *prior appointment* **only** | **www.shootaviation.com**

Shark-mouthed Tornado ZA355, September 2023. *Terry Dann*

	Identity		Type	Year	History / fate	Note	Last noted
❑	F-BAOZ		Nord Pingouin	82	ex Montelimar, French mil No.92		8-21
❑	N247CK		Canadair Challenger 600S	82	ex *Kingsman* (2014), G-NREG, N247CK. De-reg 15-2-16		9-23
❑	'N247CK'		Piper Navajo 310 G-BLFZ	79	ex PH-RWS, N3538W. De-reg 27-1-17		6-22
❑	N623NP		Grumman Gulfstream III	82	ex St Athan, Hurn, N723MM, N891MG, N802GA, N303GA. Last flight 2-12. Arrived 23-9-21		11-21
❑	N2700		Fairchild C-119G-FA Flying Boxcar	51	ex Ingatestone, Balcombe, Redhill, N Weald, Manston, 3C-ABA, Belgian AF CP-9, C-119F 51-2700. Cockpit		5-21
❑	RP-C7935*		Airbus A320-200	01	ex OE-IHM, LY-SPK, SP-HAB, G-TCAC, N411MP, C-FRAA, G-TCAC, C-FRAA, G-ERAA, C-FRAA. Last flight 26-12-21. Fuselage, first noted 4-23		6-23
❑	–		Boeing 737-400	~	cockpit, first noted 9-21		9-21
❑	'R3119'*	'UP-A'	Hawker Hurricane FSM	~	first noted mid-2020		10-23
❑	XZ220*		Westland Lynx AH.7	80	ex Higher Purtington, South Clifton, Weeton, Hixon, M Wallop, 671, 667, 657, 3 Rgt/662, 653,1 Rgt, 651, 661, 651, 654, 669, 657,659, 669, 654. Cabin and tail. F/n 12-23		12-23
❑	ZA355	'EA'	Panavia Tornado GR.1	80	ex Swansea, Selby, Lossiemouth 9310M, 15, TTTE. SOC 31-5-01. Arr 9-18. Desert 'pink', *MiG Eater* colours	[1]	12-22
❑	ZB506		Westland Sea King Mk.4X	82	ex Charlwood, Horsham, Boscombe Down, QinetiQ, DERA, DTEO, DRA, RAE. Sectioned. First noted 2-21		12-22
❑	ZF116	'WP'	Westland Sea King HC.4	86	ex Charlwood, Colsterworth (?), Gosport, 845, 848, 772. Sectioned. Arrived 21-1-20		5-21
❑	ZG889		Westland Lynx AH.9A	91	ex Ipswich, M Wallop, Staverton. SOC 23-9-16. Arr 10-8-21		8-21

■ **[1]** Painted in the colours of 40+ 'ops' Gulf War veteran ZA447, which is still extant at Cosford, Shropshire.

Aerodrome:

	Identity	Type	Year	History / fate	Note	Last noted
❑	G-AFLW	Miles Monarch	38	Phillips & Powis-built. CoA 30-7-98, de-reg 3-5-01		3-22
❑	G-BZMT	Piper Warrior III	00	ex N4147D. De-reg 28-7-15. Rescue training, f/n 2-20		2-20
❑	SE-GVH	Piper Tomahawk 112	~	ex Little Staughton, Chessington. Cockpit	[1]	10-22
❑	HS554	Fairey Swordfish II G-RNMZ	43	ex Canada, C-GEVS, RCAF (SOC 2-8-46), 745 Sqn FAA, RCAF. Blackburn-built. Arrived 23-7-19	[2]	4-21

■ **[1]** Tomahawk cockpit tours around local events with the Joystick Club. **[2]** Registered to White Waltham Airfield Ltd. The wings and tail are under restoration at Elmsett, Suffolk. See also Hurricane I P3966 (G-LNWZ) at Elmsett.

WINDSOR

Sydney Camm Memorial: In Alexandra Gardens, Barry Avenue, a Hurricane honours its Windsor-born designer.

	Identity		Type	Year	History / fate	Note	Last noted
❑	'R4229'	'GN-J'	Hawker Hurricane FSM	12	BAPC.334, pole-mounted, unveiled 20-7-12. 249 Sqn c/s	[1]	12-22

■ **[1]** Commissioned and financed by the Sir Sydney Camm Commemorative Society.

WOKINGHAM south of the M4 and A329(M) southeast of Reading

A1 Motor Spares: Highland Avenue

	Identity	Type	Year	History / fate	Last noted
❑	G-BSGV	Rotorway Executive	90	Hythe-built. De-reg 7-4-95	10-21

WOODLEY east of Reading

Museum of Berkshire Aviation: A delight in the scope and detail of its contents, the visitor needs to be constantly reminded that all of this took place within the boundaries of the county. Add to this delicious names such as Handley Page and Miles and you are set for an engaging visit.

◆ *Mohawk Way, RG5 4UE.* | **0118 944 8089** | **email** via website | **www.museumofberkshireaviation.co.uk**

❑ G-ALMN		EoN Primary	c48	BGA.589 / AQZ, ex Farnborough, G-ALMN, BGA.589. Last flown 7-5-50, CoA 4-51. Arrived 2004	[1]	1-24
❑ G-APWA		HP Herald 100	59	ex Southend, BAF, PP-SDM, PP-ASV, G-APWA. CoA 6-4-82, de-reg 29-1-87. Arrived 29-8-92. BEA colours	[2]	1-24
❑ G-MIOO		Miles Student 2	57	ex N Weald, Bruntingthorpe, G-APLK, Cranfield, G-MIOO, Duxford, G-APLK, Glasgow, Shoreham, XS941, G-35-4. Crashed 24-8-85, de-reg 1-11-96. Arrived 1997	[3]	1-24
❑ –		Goodwin-Kent GK3	~	BAPC.573, ex Turweston. Arrived 7-6-21	[4]	1-24
❑ –	'465'	EoN 460-1	65	BGA.1288 / BWG, CoA 27-4-97. Arrived 27-5-09		1-24
❑ –		Broburn Wanderlust	46	BAPC.233, ex Farnborough. Arrived 28-11-92		1-24
❑ TF-SHC		Miles Martinet TT.1	43	ex Iceland, MS902, Reykjavik SF, 251. Cr 18-7-51. Arr 3-96		1-24
❑ 'L6906'		Miles Magister I G-AKKY	40	BAPC.44, ex Brooklands, Woodley, Wroughton, Frenchay, G-AKKY (de-reg 12-4-73), T9841, 11 EFTS, 16 EFTS. Phillips & Powis-built. Arrived 26-4-91		1-24
❑ XG883	'773'	Fairey Gannet T.5	57	ex Cardiff, Yeovilton, 849, Culdrose SF. SOC 8-6-70. Arrived 24-3-96	[5]	1-24
❑ XJ389		Fairey Jet Gyrodyne G-AJJP	49	ex Cosford, Southampton, G-AJJP (de-reg 9-11-50), XD759. Arrived 6-94	[6]	1-24
❑ 'XP849'		Westland Scout AH.1	63	ex B' Down, M Wallop. Arrived 13-10-10. ETPS colours	[7]	1-24

■ **[1]** EoN Primary donated by Pat Pottinger. **[2]** First production Dart-powered Herald, born at Woodley, built there by HP (Reading) Ltd and first flown 30-10-59. **[3]** Student on loan from Aces High's Mike Woodley. **[4]** Unfinished homebuild, by D Kent, based upon a racer designed by C J Goodwin in the early 1960s. **[5]** On loan from the Fleet Air Arm Museum. **[6]** RAF Museum elected to gift the Gyrodyne to the museum in early 2022. **[7]** Scout is *largely* XP895, last at Middle Wallop and crashed 10-11-66. It has the boom of XP854 - for the latter see Abridge, Essex.

BUCKINGHAMSHIRE

Includes the unitary authority of Milton Keynes

DENHAM AERODROME Last noted in November 2018, Squirrel II G-TOPS has been deleted.

HALTON AIRFIELD on the A4011 (camp) and east of the B4544 (airfield), north of Wendover EGWN

Trenchard Museum and **James McCudden Flight Heritage Centre**: The skeletal replica of the Halton Aero Club Mayfly biplane of 1927 is one of many highlights – including *three* functioning Link Trainers – within this impressive collection.

◆ *Halton Camp, HP22 5PG* | **email** via website | **www.trenchardmuseum.org.uk**

Halton Aero Club Mayfly replica, February 2023. *David Blades*

❑ 'G-EBOO'		HAC Mayfly replica	22	BGA.338. Fuselage frame on show by 2-23	[1]	1-24
❑ RA905		Slingsby Cadet TX.1	c45	BGA.1143. ex RAFGSA.273, RA905. CoA 14-3-00		1-24
❑ WB626		DHC Chipmunk T.10	50	ex Aylesbury, South Molton, Fownhope, Firbeck, Houghton--on-the-Hill, Southampton, Swanton Morley, Bicester, Kemble, Hendon SF, 5 FTS, 18 RFS. SOC 12-9-73. Hatfield-built. Cockpit		1-24
❑ WZ772		Slingsby Grasshopper TX.1	52	ex Middle Wallop, Halton, 1 MGSP, Brentwood		6-22
❑ XF522		Hawker Hunter F.6	56	ex Bletchley, Milton Keynes, Aylesbury, Halton, 92, 66, 92. SOC 8-1-63. AWA-built. Cockpit, on trailer. 92 Sqn colours		6-22
❑ XR574	'72'	Folland Gnat T.1	63	ex Cosford, Halton, Cosford 8631M (8-10-79), Kemble, 4 FTS, CFS, 4 FTS, CFS, 4 FTS, CFS, 4 FTS		1-24

■ **[1]** Replica of the two-seat Halton Aero Club biplane of 1927, designed by Hugh Latimer-Needham.

RAF Halton: The station is set to close in 2025. The Hunter is with **2409 Squadron ATC** (Herts and Bucks Wing).

❑ VZ568	'C'	Gloster Meteor F.8	50	ex Sennybridge, 4 SoTT, St Athan 7261M (12-10-55), 63. Cockpit. Arrived by 3-19	[1]	7-23
❑ XF527		Hawker Hunter F.6	56	ex 1 SoTT 8680M (2-4-81), Laarbruch SF, 4 FTS, CFE, 19, Church Fenton SF, Linton SF. Displayed, since 5-86		7-23
❑ XW303	'127'	BAC Jet Provost T.5A	70	ex Cosford, Halton 9119M (16-9-91), 7 FTS, 1 FTS	[2]	7-23
❑ XW364	'MN'	BAC Jet Provost T.5A	71	ex Cosford 9188M (5-5-93), Shawbury, 3 FTS, RAFC, CFS, 1 FTS. Arrived 22-10-12, rescue training		7-23
❑ XZ630		Panavia Tornado GR.1	77	ex St Athan, Brüggen 8976M (24-8-88), BAe, A&AEE. Parade ground, since 1-04		7-23

■ **[1]** The rest of VZ568 was still to be found on the Sennybridge ranges in July 2021. **[2]** The fuselage of 'JP' XW303 serves/served as a jump on the equestrian course.

HIGH WYCOMBE or Walter's Ash, northwest of Naphill, north of the town

RAF High Wycombe: Headquarters, Air Command has a pair of full-scale models on display within the grounds.

❑ 'P7666'	'EB-Z'	V-S Spitfire FSM	c09	BAPC.335. Gateguards UK-built. *Observer Corps*, 41 Sqn colours. Displayed since 2009		10-23
❑ 'V7467'	'LE-D'	Hawker Hurricane FSM	c14	BAPC.378. Gateguards UK-built. 242 Sqn colours. Displayed since 2014	[1]	10-23

■ **[1]** For what it's worth, there is *another* 'V7467' - see Duxford, Cambs.

LAVENDON on the A428 west of Bedford

Tony Collins: Award-winning cockpit restorer Tony also owns and operates the **Lavendon Narrow Gauge Railway**. Canberra B(I).6 WT319 which had been 'on detachment' at Doncaster, S Yorks, since mid-2021, has been transferred to Wingless Wonders there. ◆ *Prior arrangement or on railway open days*

❑ WT684		Hawker Hunter F.1	54	ex Doncaster, Firbeck, Long Marston, Brize Norton, Reading, 71 MU 'fleet' Bicester 7422M (8-4-57), 229 OCU, DFLS. Cockpit		1-24
❑ XD235	'148'	V-S Scimitar F.1	58	ex Ingatestone, Welshpool, Southampton, Ottershaw (?), Foulness, FRU, 803. SOC 20-3-70. 803 Sqn colours. Cockpit		1-24
❑ XN651	'705'	DH Sea Vixen FAW.2	61	ex Bletchley, Bristol, Culdrose A2616 (29-7-71), SAH, 766, FAW.1, 893. Hatfield-built. 890 Sqn colours. Cockpit		1-24
❑ XS898	'BD'	EE Lightning F.6	66	ex Bruntingthorpe, Cranfield, Binbrook, 11, 5. SOC 24-6-88. Cockpit		1-24
❑ XW541		Blackburn Buccaneer S.2B	71	ex Welshpool, Ingatestone, Stock, Foulness, Honington 8858M (21-5-85), St Athan, 12, 16, 15. Cockpit		1-24
❑ J-1632	'V'	DH Venom FB.50 G-VNOM	56	ex Cantley, London Colney, Cranfield, Bridgend, Bruntingthorpe, Cranfield, G-VNOM (de-reg 27-6-11), Swiss AF. Swiss-built. Cockpit, 145 Sqn colours. Off-site	[1]	1-24

■ **[1]** Representing WK418 which served 145 Sqn at Celle, W Germany, as 'V' (and later 'G'), 1954-1957.

LONG CRENDON on the B4011, northwest of Thame

A 'JP' is kept at a *private* location in this area.

❑ XW432	'MX'	BAC Jet Provost T.5A	72	ex Ipswich, Cosford 9127M (14-10-91), Halton, 1 FTS, Leeming SF, 3 FTS. First noted 8-14	9-22

MILTON KEYNES

Milton Keynes College: Innovation and Technology Centre. ◆ *Prior arrangement* **only** | **www.mkcollege.ac.uk**

❑ G-TINA	SOCATA Tobago	80	ex Little Snoring. CoA 29-10-14, de-reg 29-10-14		8-16

British Balloon Museum and Library (BBML): The *nominal* base for the huge collection, stored across a wide range of sites. BBML is beyond the scope of *W&R* but if such things float your boat, its extensive website is **www.bbml.org.uk**

PENN on the B474 northwest of Beaconsfield

A Boeing 737 cockpit is with a *private* owner in the *general* area.

❑ G-CEAF*	Boeing 737-229	74	ex Colnbrook, Hurn, European, G-BYRI, OO-SDD, EC-EEG, OO-SDD. Last flight 1-12-08, CoA 3-4-09, de-reg 24-1-11. Cockpit. DHL colours. Arrived 28-2-22		2-22

PITSTONE between the B489 and B488 north of Tring

The Heritage Park - Pitstone Green Museum: Norman Groom's impressive Lancaster cockpit replica was offered for auction on 24th November 2022, with a guide value of £100,000. It moved to Manston, Kent, by February 2023.

TURWESTON AERODROME north of the A422, east of Brackley EGBT

Bianchi Aviation Film Services: Travel Air N6268 was exported to Miami, USA, in 2023.◆ **Strictly** *prior arrangement* **only**

❑ G-AWXZ	Stampe SV-4C	49	ex Booker, F-BHMZ, Fr mil, F-BCOI. SNCAN-built. CoA 8-8-14		4-23
❑ G-BAAF	Manning-Flanders MF.1 replica	75	ex Stow Maries, Booker, Compton Abbas, Booker, Old Warden, Booker. PPS-built. CoA 6-8-96. Off-site	[1]	3-22
❑ 'No.10'	Blériot XI replica G-BPVE	99	ex Stow Maries, Booker, Compton Abbas, Booker, N1197. CoA 29-6-01. Arrived 16-11-21		5-23
❑ N6161	Sopwith Pup G-ELRT	1917	ex Duxford, St Leonards. CoA 25-4-2018	[2]	4-23
❑ 'N6377' 'R'	Sopwith Camel replica G-BPOB	73	ex Stow Maries, 'B2458', Booker, Compton Abbas, Booker, N8997. Tallmantz Aviation-built. CoA 2-7-19. RNAS colours		4-23
❑ 'MS824'	MS 'N' replica G-AWBU	70	ex Stow Maries, Booker, Compton Abbas, Booker. CoA 28-4-04. PPS-built. Arrived 16-11-21	[1]	5-23
❑ '107/15'	Fokker E.III replica G-AVJO	67	ex Stow Maries, '422/15', Booker, Compton Abbas, Booker. PPS-built. CoA 5-4-04. Arrived 16-11-21	[1]	5-23
❑ –	Fokker Dr.I replica	~	ex Stow Maries, Booker, USA. Unfinished airframe. Off-site		3-22
❑ U-95	Bücker Jungmeister G-BVGP	40	ex Booker, F-AZMN, G-BVGP, F-AZFQ, N215696, HB-MIE, D-EIII, HB-MIE, Swiss AF U-95. Dornier-built. CoA 22-8-18		5-23

■ **[1]** PPS – Personal Plane Services, predecessor company to Bianchi Aviation Film Service. **[2]** Registered as a 'Sopwith Scout'.

Also: Reference page 7, Jodel G-AXXW and Seneca G-BBLU have been deleted.

❑ G-AXPG*	Mignet HM.293	71	ex Bicester, Sedlescombe. CoA 20-1-77. Arrived 30-3-22	[1]	4-23
❑ G-CLKX	DHC Chipmunk T.10	50	ex Wickenby, York, Canada (?), WB555, 7924M, Lpl UAS, Birm UAS, 2 SoTT Flt, Debden SF, 4 SoTT Flt, Glas UAS, 43 GCF, MCCF, Ox UAS. Hatfield-built. Crashed 26-4-66		5-20
❑ F-PFUG	Adam RA-14	~	ex Breighton, Boston. Cockpit. First noted 12-19		5-23
❑ 854	Ryan PT-22 Recruit G-BTBH	42	ex Audley End, Chichester, N854, N50993, 41-20854. CoA 31-6-13. Arrived 12-20		9-22

■ **[1]** HM.293 used as a travelling display by the LAA.

TWYFORD on minor roads northeast of Bicester

A Spitfire is *believed* to under restoration at a ***private*** workshop in the *general* area.

❑ AD540	V-S Spitfire V	41	ex Trelonk, Twyford, Dumfries, Carsphairn, 242, 122. *Blue Peter*. CBAF-built. Crashed 23-5-42, excavated 5-93		6-20

WYCOMBE AIR PARK or Booker, on the B482 southwest of High Wycombe EGTB

Stampe G-GMAX made its first flight after rebuild on 12th May 2023.

❑ G-AWMF	Piper Super Cub 150	68	ex N4356Z. CoA 3-3-14. First noted 6-18		11-18
❑ –	Pilatus P.2 FSM	88	BAPC.395, ex Parkhouse, PPS, *Indiana Jones and the Last Crusade* (1989). Fuselage, Luftwaffe colours		7-21

CAMBRIDGESHIRE

Includes the unitary authority of Peterborough

ABBOTS RIPTON on the B1090 north of Huntingdon

Commando Elite Paintball and Airsoft Centre: ◆ *Prior arrangement* **only** | **www.commandoelitepaintball.co.uk**

❑ XN554 Hunting Jet Provost T.3 61 ex Layer Marney, Hadleigh, Ipswich, North Luffenham, Halton 8436M (16-1-75), St Athan, Shawbury, CFS. Camouflaged. First noted 4-18 3-22

ALCONBURY northwest of Huntingdon at the A1/A14 junction

Much of the former airfield is used for civilian purposes and known as Alconbury Weald.

USAF Alconbury, 423rd Air Base Group: The USAF enclave is 'parented' by Molesworth.

❑ '01532' Northrop F-5E Tiger II FSM 80 BAPC.336. Displayed, unveiled 27-4-81. 527th TFTAS colours 10-23

The Stirling Aircraft Project: The workshop moved to a location near Stilton, Cambs, in December 2020.

BOTTISHAM north of the A14 east of Cambridge

Bottisham Airfield Museum: The museum is centred on the remaining wartime buildings, including the 375th Fighter Squadron's ready room and a new-build Nissen hut. The former Duxford P-51 FSM has been extensively refurbished and painted in the colours of Bottisham's 361st FG CO, Colonel Thomas J Christian.

◆ *CB25 9BU* | **01223 813952** | **info@bottishamairfieldmuseum.org.uk** | **www.bottishamairfieldmuseum.org.uk**

❑ '413410'* 'E2-C' NAA P-51D Mustang FSM 91 BAPC.255, ex Duxford '463209', London. 361st FG colours, *Lou IV / Athelene*. Unveiled 18-6-22 1-24

❑ –* NAA P-51D Mustang FSM ~ 'climb-in' cockpit 1-24

BRAMPTON east of the A1/A14 junction

High Harthay Outdoor Pursuits: *May* still have the Navajo. ◆ *Prior arrangement* **only** | **www.highharthay.co.uk**

❑ E.18-2 '42-71' Piper Navajo 70 ex Bentwaters, Fownhope, Spanish AF, N7314L. Fuselage 9-20

BURWELL on the B1102 northeast of Cambridge

A Lynx is kept at a *private* location in the *general* area.

❑ XZ196 Westland Lynx AH.7 79 ex Ipswich, M Wallop, Fleetlands. First noted 10-17 7-23

CAMBRIDGE AIRPORT or Teversham EGSC

Marshall Aerospace: As speculated in *W&R28*, the company's aeronautical side is bound for Cranfield, while the specialist vehicle element is heading for Alconbury. The current site is destined to be a mix of retail park and housing no doubt: 2030 remains the timeline.

Hercules C.4 ZH868 Julia flew in on 20th June 2023: taken September 2023. *David Willis*

Swedish Air Force C-130Hs 84001 and 84003 were roaded out in early July 2022, routing through Immingham Docks on the 5th. As foretold in *W&R28*, the former is bound for the museum at Linkoping; the latter for display at Satenas. From late 2020 Cambridge began to host the RAF Hercules C.4 fleet and the residue of the C.5s. MoD put fourteen of them up for disposal prior to the official bow-out: the last RAF 'Herk' flight was performed by C.4 ZH870 *Jemma* when it/her touched down here on 28th June 2023. This was a full *seven years* premature and, to the author and doubtless loads of readers, crazy. With respect to the Airbus Atlas – aka the A400 or Tottenham Court Road (check your road map!) – it ain't no 'Herk'.

The C-130 market is buoyant, so these wonderful machines may not grace Teversham for long, but in case that is not so, here goes, with arrival dates: **C.4s** ZH865 16-5-23; ZH866 20-3-23; ZH867 28-6-23; ZH868 20-6-23; ZH869 24-5-23; ZH870 28-6-23; ZH871 21-6-23; ZH872 9-2-23; ZH874 12-9-22; ZH875 7-4-22; ZH877 30-1-23; ZH878 19-12-22; ZH879 28-2-23; **C.5s** ZH888 8-12-20 (and SOC 17-8-21);ZH889 16-6-23.

❑	XV201	Lockheed Hercules C.1K	67	ex 1312F, LTW, USAF 66-8551. Flightdeck	[1]	3-20
❑	XV208	Lockheed Hercules W.2(mod)	67	ex TP400 test-bed, Met Res Flt, A&AEE, 48, USAF 66-8558. Arrived 27-4-05. Last flown 30-9-09. Cockpit	[2]	1-22

■ **[1]** XV201 was intended for Sri Lanka as CR-882 but was not delivered. Sections were delivered to Winterbourne Gunner/Porton Down, Wilts. **[2]** Unofficially named 'Snoopy', the famous weather-recon Herk's cockpit is stripped of its 'met' gear and much else.

CHIPPENHAM north of Newmarket

This is *another* Chippenham, far from Wiltshire. A 'SHAR' and a Tornado are kept at a ***private*** location in the *general* area.

❑	ZD899* 'AT-1'	Panavia Tornado F.2	84	ex Selby, Bury, Selby, Boscombe Down, Warton. Last flown 2004. Black, 43 Sqn 1916-2006 c/s. F/n 6-23	[1]	7-23
❑	ZH811* '002'	HS Sea Harrier F/A.2	98	ex Selby, Culdrose, Shawbury, Yeovilton, 801, 899. Last flight 28-3-06. Arrived by 6-22		7-23

■ **[1]** Carries the serial 'ZG757' to port: this was the jet that 43 Squadron used for its 90th anniversary celebrations.

DUXFORD AERODROME south of Cambridge, Junction 10 M11 EGSU

Imperial War Museum (IWM): It didn't start well... I quote from the Preface of *W&R27* regarding Typhoon DA4 ZH590: "After eleven years of pondering, IWM arrived at this conclusion: 'As a prototype, this airframe is an experimental model and not representative of a production or operational aircraft.' To quote one of my 'regulars': 'Terrific, can I have their TSR.2?'" Curatorial aerobatic rationales aside, the transfer to Newark was a superb accolade to the Nottinghamshire museum. So, DA4 was slid from Duxford to Newark in *W&R27* in eager anticipation, but with the caveat 'Due'. After that, ZH590 remained steadfastly in Cambridgeshire.

Under the incredibly diplomatic heading 'Disappointing News', the Newark Air Museum (NAM) issued a press release on 2nd November 2023 announcing that the hand over of DA4 was not going to happen. Awaiting a joint statement from IWM and the RAF Newark magnanimously noted: "Apart from thanking the staff at IWM Duxford for their support throughout the project... at this time the NAM trustees do not wish to make any further statement about the complex and at times baffling situation." But this was not just a case of non-appearance, the statement continued: "[NAM] trustees are mindful that a number of people have made financial contributions towards the costs associated with planned move of DA4... ...all of the funds raised were used towards the cost of laying an additional hardstanding area behind the museum café that would have allowed for the safe reconstruction of DA4." Disillusioned, out-of-pocket and the time and effort could well have been employed in another project...

The NAM missive was closely followed by the joint IWM/RAF explanation: "It is a condition of all MoD donations that they be given first refusal should IWM choose to deaccession and dispose of an aircraft. In the case of the Typhoon DA4 the MoD have [sic] been consulted and have found a new home for the aircraft as a Ground Training Aid at RAF Cosford. Whilst we understand there may be disappointment that the aircraft is not being transferred to Newark Air Museum, the new home for the Typhoon offers continued public benefit through its training of RAF engineers of the future."

It's important to note that IWM is a frustrated bystander in all of this. It took the MoD an incredibly long time for those wheels to go around... This conclusion could have been drawn in 2019 as it clearly does not relate to an all-of-a-sudden 'policy' change. Having only just woken up to the situation – or having dragged its feet since 2020 – the MoD sprang into dynamic action, removing ZH590 to Cosford, Shropshire, on 29th November 2023.

It was to be expected that *W&R* readers would have a lot to say about this, and bless them, they did. The following is a digest of their responses. As regards the author's views, I'll adopt the Francis Urquhart *House of Cards* stance: "You *may* think that. I couldn't possibly comment." **[1]** "Will Cosford 'ring fence' DA4 for Newark when they've finished with it as a teaching aid?" [Assuming NAM still has the stomach to take it on.] **[2]** "Will [NAM] be compensated for its pre-preparation and [the hardstanding] and diversion from other projects?" **[3]** "When does MoD's 'statute of limitations' expire on museums that have received a donation and wish to pass same on to another organisation?" **[4]** "Does this 'decision' affect potential transfers to Typhoons to the wider British museum community?" **[5]** "Has this 'decision', anything to do with a five-sided structure in a land far, far away?"

The first listing is essentially devoted to Hangar 4, which contains the 'Air Defence Collection' of fighter types, Hangar 5 the main restoration hangar and miscellaneous IWM airframes. Nos.2 and 3 continue their role of housing the 'flyers' – see below. Several airframes are stored, away from public gaze, and are listed separately.

See also the 'HQ', IWM South Lambeth, London, IWM North at Manchester, Gtr Man, and two other London-based (but non-*W&R*) venues: HMS *Belfast* and the Churchill War Rooms - details via the website.

Mustang FSM '463209' had been transferred to Bottisham, Cambs, by late 2021.

◆ *CB22 4QR* | **01223 835000** | **duxford@iwm.org.uk** | **www.iwm.org.uk**

Serial	Code	Type	Year	History	Note	Date
❑ 2699		Royal Aircraft Factory BE.2c	1916	ex South Lambeth, Duxford, South Lambeth, 192, 51, 50. Ruston, Proctor-built. Acquired 1920, arrived 10-12		1-24
❑ E2581	'13'	Bristol F.2B	1918	ex South Lambeth, Cardington, South Kensington, Crystal Palace, 2 GCF, 30 TDS, SE Area HQ Flt, 1 Comm Sqn, 39. SOC 22-4-20, acquired 16-12-1922		1-24
❑ 'R7059'	'LY'	V-S Spitfire I FSM	06	BAPC.394, ex 'X4474', 'R6915', 'X4178'. PR.VII PRU 'pink' colours by 12-23		12-23
❑ 'V7467'	'LE-D'	Hawker Hurricane FSM	00	BAPC.267, ex 'P2954', 'R4115', S' Lambeth. 242 Sqn c/s	[1]	1-22
❑ 'Z2315'	'JU-E'	Hawker Hurricane IIb	41	BAPC.643, ex TFC, Russia. Arrived 9-97, unveiled 13-6-00	[2]	1-24
❑ Z2033*	'275'	Fairey Firefly TT.1 G-ASTL	44	ex Yeovilton, Duxford, Staverton, G-ASTL de-reg 2-3-82, TT.1 SE-BRD, White Waltham, Ringway, Hamble, G-6-3, F.I Z2033, 731. 1771 Sqn colours, *Evelyn Tentions*. Arrived 17-8-23	[3]	1-24
❑ HM580	'KX-K'	Cierva C.30A G-ACUU	34	ex Staverton, Elmdon, G-AIXE, HM580, 529, 1448 Flt, G-ACUU, AST Hamble. CoA 30-4-60. Acq 1978. 529 Sqn c/s		1-24
❑ LZ766		Percival Proctor III G-ALCK	44	ex Staverton, Tamworth, G-ALCK, CoA 19-6-63, de-reg 19-8-65, HQBC, 21 EFTS. Arrived 1978		1-24
❑ PN323		HP Halifax A.VII	45	ex South Lambeth, Duxford, S' Lambeth, Duxford, Staverton, Radlett. Fairey-built. SOC 28-5-48. Acquired 1979, arrived 9-12. Cockpit		1-24
❑ WK991		Gloster Meteor F.8	53	ex South Lambeth, Kemble, 7825M, 56, 46, 13 Gp Comm Flt, Northern Sector Flt. Arrived 10-12-63		1-24
❑ WM969	'10'	Hawker Sea Hawk FB.5	54	ex Culdrose A2530 (14-5-64), FRU, 806, FB.3, 811, 898. Arrived 20-1-77		1-24
❑ WZ590	'49'	DH Vampire T.11	53	ex Woodford, Chester, St Athan, 8 FTS, 5 FTS, 228 OCU. Hawarden-built. SOC 9-12-68, arrived 4-5-73. 5 FTS c/s		1-24
❑ XD826*		Vickers Valiant BK.1	57	ex Rayleigh area, Cardiff-Wales 'WZ826', Abingdon, Stratford, Cosford, Feltwell 7872M (5-3-65), 543, 232 OCU, 138, 90, 7. Cockpit. Arrived 9-12-22		1-24
❑ XE627	'T'	Hawker Hunter F.6A	56	ex Brawdy, 1 TWU, TWU, 229 OCU, 1, 229 OCU, 54, 1, 54, Horsham St Faith SF, 54, 229 OCU, 92, 65. Arrived 14-11-86. 65 Sqn colours		1-24
❑ XF708	'C'	Avro Shackleton MR.3/3	59	ex Kemble, 203, 120, 201. Arr 22-8-72. 203 Sqn colours		1-24
❑ XG797	'277'	Fairey Gannet ECM.6	57	ex Arbroath, 831, AS.4, 700, 810. SOC 7-8-68, arrived 21-5-72. 831 Sqn colours, 'Flook' logo		1-24
❑ XH648		HP Victor B.1A (K2P)	59	ex 57, 55, Honington Wing, 15, 57. Arrived 2-6-76		1-24
❑ XH669*		HP Victor K.2	59	ex Rayleigh area, Waddington 9092M, *Black Buck* -82, 55, 57, Witt Wing, A&AEE. Accident 21-6-90. Cockpit. Arr 9-12-22		1-24
❑ XH897		Gloster Javelin FAW.9	58	ex A&AEE, BSE, 5, 33, FAW.7, 25. Flew in 24-1-75		1-24
❑ XS567	'434'	Westland Wasp HAS.1	64	ex Lee-on-Solent, A2719[2] (5-6-86), 829, 703, 829. Arrived 8-92. *Endurance* Flt colours		1-24
❑ XS576	'125'	DH Sea Vixen FAW.2	64	ex Sydenham, 899, 893, 899. Hawarden-built. Arrived 17-3-72. 899 Sqn colours		1-24
❑ XV474	'T'	McD Phantom FGR.2	69	ex Wattisham, 74, 56, 23, 29, 56, 23, 19, 2, 31, 17, 14, 17. Flew in 13-10-92. 74 Sqn colours		1-24
❑ XV712	'66'	Westland Sea King HAS.6	72	ex Gosport, 814, 820, 814, 820, 810, 820, 706, 826, 706, 814. Arrived 27-5-10. 'Tiger' colours		1-24
❑ XV865		Blackburn Buccaneer S.2B	68	ex Coningsby 9226M, Lossiemouth, 208, 12, 237 OCU, 208, 12, 208, 237 OCU, FAA, 809, 736. Arr 21-1-99. 208 Sqn c/s		1-24
❑ XZ194	'V'	Westland Lynx AH.7	78	ex M Wallop, 671 Sqn, 7 Regt, AH.1. Arrived 15-4-13		1-24

❑ ZA469	'029'	Panavia Tornado GR.4	83	ex Marham, GR.1, 617. Arrived 27-3-18		1-24
❑ A-549		FMA Pucará	c81	ex ZD487, ex Boscombe Down, Yeovilton, Stanley, Argentine AF. Arrived 10-83		1-24
❑ 1190	'4'	Messerschmitt Bf 109E-3	40	ex Hurn, Buckfastleigh, Canada, USA, Canada, 'White 4' 4/JG 26, II/JG 26. Force-landed 30-9-40. Arrived 17-3-98		1-24
❑ 100143		Focke Achgelis Fa 330A-1	44	ex Farnborough. Weser Flug-built. Arrived 16-1-77		1-24
❑ 120235	'6'	Heinkel He 162A-1	45	ex South Lambeth, Duxford, S' Lambeth, Cranwell, Brize Norton, Farnborough AM.68, JG 1, Leck. Acquired 1960, arrived 1-13		1-24
❑ –		Fieseler Fi 103 (V-1)	45	BAPC.93, ex Cosford	[4]	1-24
❑ –		Fieseler Fi 103 (V-1) rep	~	on original launch ramp, near American Air Museum		1-24
❑ 501		Mikoyan-Gurevich MiG-21PF *Fishbed*	c70	ex St Athan, Farnborough, Hungarian AF. Arrived 11-97		1-24
❑ –		Mitsubishi A6M5 *Zeke*	c44	ex South Lambeth, Duxford, South Lambeth, ATIAU-SEA. Cockpit. Acquired 1955, arrived 10-12		1-24
❑ 1133		BAC Strikemaster Mk.80A G-BESY	76	ex Warton, Saudi AF, G-BESY (de-reg 18-4-83), G-27-299. Arrived 22-3-00		1-24

■ **[1]** For what it's worth, there is *another* 'V7467' at High Wycombe, Bucks. **[2]** Hurricane 'Z2315' *could* be BE146 if its upper cowling is anything to go by. BE146 was sent to Russia 2-10-41. **[3]** Firefly served as the aerodynamic prototype for the T.1 trainer from 5-46, eventually adopting a 'B Condition' identity. **[4]** Fi 103 on loan from RAF Museum.

'AirSpace': Within is 'Airborne Assault', based on the contents of the Parachute Regiment and Airborne Forces Museum, previously at Aldershot, Hampshire. The cockpit of Hermes *Delta-Golf* is accessible, and the fuselage contains displays. Concorde's 'snoop' droops on occasions. Referring to the introduction narrative to the Duxford section, in an attempt at consistency, IWM announced in October 2022 that Jaguar GR.1B XX108's test and trials pedigree was not optimal and offered it for disposal. As yet, it has not moved...

❑ G-AFBS		Miles Magister I	39	ex Staverton, Bristol, G-AKKU, BB661, 10 FIS, 8 EFTS, G-AFBS. CoA 25-2-63, de-reg 22-12-95. Phillips & Powis-built. Arrived 1978		1-24
❑ G-ALDG		HP Hermes 4	50	ex Gatwick, Silver City, Britavia, Airwork, BOAC. CoA 9-1-63,de-reg 12-10-68. BOAC c/s, *Horsa*. Fuselage	[1]	1-24
❑ G-ALFU		DH Dove 6	49	ex CAFU Stansted. CoA 4-6-71, de-reg 14-11-72	[1]	1-24
❑ G-ANTK		Avro York	45	ex Lasham, Dan-Air, MW232, Fairey, 511, 242. Last flight 30-4-64, de-reg 27-10-64. Dan-Air colours	[1]	1-24
❑ G-APDB		DH Comet 4	58	ex Dan-Air, MSA 9M-AOB, BOAC G-APDB. Hatfield-built. Flew in 12-2-74, de-reg 18-2-74. BOAC colours	[1] [2]	1-24
❑ G-AXDN		BAC/Sud Concorde 101	68	ex Fairford. Flew in 20-8-77, CoA 30-9-77, de-reg 10-11-86	[1] [3]	1-24
❑ G-USUK		Colt 2500A hot-air balloon	87	CoA 19-8-87, de-reg 21-8-90. Gondola. *Virgin Atlantic Flyer*		1-24
❑ –		Airspeed Horsa II	~	BAPC.396, ex Aldershot. Cockpit, Airborne Assault		1-24
❑ –		Hawker Hunter F.6	57	ex Wroughton, S' Kensington, Kingston G-9-185 (9-2-64), Dutch AF N-250. Fokker-Aviolanda-built. Cockpit	[4]	1-24
❑ –		Pilcher Hawk replica	30	BAPC.57, ex St Albans, Wroughton, Hayes, South Lambeth. Arrived 11-04. In foyer	[5]	1-24
❑ D5649		Airco DH.9	1917	ex St Leonards-on-Sea, Hatch, Bikaner, India, RAF/RFC. Waring & Gillow-built. Arrived 19-4-07		1-24
❑ F3556		Royal Aircraft Factory RE.8	1918	ex South Lambeth, Cardington, Crystal Palace, Tadcaster, Radford, no service. Daimler-built. *A Paddy Bird from Ceylon*. Acquired 20-2-1920	[6]	1-24
❑ N4877	'MK-V'	Avro Anson I G-AMDA	38	ex Staverton, Elstree, Derby AW, G-AMDA (CoA 14-12-62, accident 7-11-72, de-reg 9-9-81), Watchfield SF, 3 FP, ATA, 3 FPP. Acquired 1978. 500 Sqn colours		1-24
❑ 'N6635'	'25'	DH Tiger Moth	c42	ex 'DE998', ARC, Stamford, Hooton, Warmingham, 'K2572', Hereford, Lutterworth, Holme-on-Spalding Moor. Arrived 5-3-02. 22 EFTS colours		1-24
❑ V3388		Airspeed Oxford I G-AHTW	40	ex Staverton, Elstree, Boulton Paul G-AHTW (CoA 15-12-60, de-reg 3-4-89), V3388 n/s. DH-built. Arrived 1978		1-24
❑ 'V9673'	'MA-J'	Westland Lysander III G-LIZY	40	G-LIZY (de-reg 18-4-89), RCAF 1558, V9300. Acquired 1991. 161 Sqn colours		1-24

	Serial	Code	Type		Built	History	Note	Date
❑	KB889	'NA-I'	Avro Lancaster X	G-LANC	44	ex Bitteswell, Blackbushe, G-LANC (de-reg 2-9-91), RCAF 107 MRU, 428. Victory Aircraft, Canada-built. Arrived 14-5-86. 428 Sqn colours		1-24
❑	ML796	'NS-F'	Short Sunderland MR.5		44	ex La Baule, Moisdon-le-Rivière, Aéronavale, 27F, 7FE, RAF 230, 4 OTU, 228. Rochester-built. Arr 9-7-76. 201 Sqn c/s		1-24
❑	NF370	'NH-L'	Fairey Swordfish III		44	ex South Lambeth, Gosport, Stretton, RAF n/s. Blackburn-built. Acquired 30-6-52. 119 Sqn colours		1-24
❑	TA719	'56'	DH Mosquito TT.35	G-ASKC	45	ex Staverton, *Mosquito Squadron* (1968), Staverton, G-ASKC (crashed 27-7-64, de-reg 3-9-64), *633 Squadron* (1963) 'HJ898', Shawbury, 3/4 CAACU, 4 CAACU, Shawbury, B.35. Acquired 1978. CAACU TT colours		1-24
❑	–		Hawker Typhoon		~	ex South Lambeth. Cockpit, in education area		10-20
❑	TG528		HP Hastings C.1A		48	ex Staverton, 24, 24-36, 242 OCU, 53-99 pool, 47. Last flight 24-1-68, arrived 1-4-79. 24 Sqn colours		1-24
❑	VN485		V-S Spitfire F.24		47	ex Kai Tak 7326M, Hong Kong Aux AF, 80. South Marston-built. Last flown 21-4-55, arrived 18-7-89		1-24
❑	WH725		EE Canberra B.2		53	ex Wroughton, 50, 44. Arrived 8-3-72. 50 Sqn colours	[7]	1-24
❑	XJ824		Avro Vulcan B.2		61	ex 101, 9-35, 9, 230 OCU, 27. Arrived 13-3-82		1-24
❑	XK936	'62'	W'land Whirlwind HAS.7		57	ex Wroughton, 705, 847, 848, 701, 820, 845. Arr 28-10-75		1-24
❑	XM135	'B'	EE Lightning F.1		59	ex Leconfield, Leuchars TFF, 226 OCU, 74, AFDS. Flew in 20-11-74. 74 Sqn colours	[8]	1-24
❑	XR222		BAC TSR.2 XO-4		64	ex Cranfield, Weybridge. Unflown, arrived 21-3-78		1-24
❑	XS863	'304'	Westland Wessex HAS.1		65	ex A&AEE, ETPS, 826, 706, 815. Arrived 8-10-81		1-24
❑	XT581		Northrop Shelduck D.1		65	ex Old Darby, Army. Acquired 8-78	[9]	10-18
❑	XX108		SEPECAT Jaguar GR.1B		72	ex St Athan, BAe Warton, G-27-313, DERA, A&AEE. Last flown 28-5-02, arrived 29-10-03. See notes above		9-23
❑	XZ133	'10'	HS Harrier GR.3		76	ex S' Lambeth, St Athan, 4, 1, 1417 Flt, 233 OCU. Arr 2-9-93		1-24
❑	ZA465	'FF'	Panavia Tornado GR.1B		83	ex Lossiemouth, 12, 617, 17, 16. Flew in 25-10-01		1-24
❑	18393		Avro Canada CF-100 Canuck Mk.4B	G-BCYK	55	ex Cranfield, G-BCYK, RCAF, 440, 419, 409. Flew in 29-3-75, de-reg 15-9-81		1-24
❑	03-33120		General Atomics MQ-1B		03	arrived 13-4-18	[10]	1-24

■ **[1]** Duxford Aviation Society airframes - see below. **[2]** *Delta-Bravo* operated the first ever scheduled service New York to London 4-10-58. Total time 36,269 hours, 15,733 landings. **[3]** *Delta-November* factoids: total hours 632, landings 273. **[4]** Repurchased by HSA and the rest of N-250 was re-worked as Indian T.66D S-581 in 1967. **[5]** Pilcher Hawk is on loan from Eric Littledike - see also Old Warden, Beds. **[6]** RE.8 was issued to the RAF on 25-10-18 and sent to France on Armistice Day, 11-11-18. It probably flew for no more than 2 hours in total. **[7]** Canberra B.2 on loan from the RAF Museum. **[8]** XM135 made famous 'unpiloted' circuits of Lyneham 22-7-66 with engineer Wg Cdr Walter Holden at the controls. It has a total time of 1,343 hours. **[9]** See Weybourne, Norfolk, for 'another' 'XT581'. **[10]** Predator held on behalf of the National Museum of the USAF, USA.

American Air Museum (AAM): Declared as "no longer meets purpose" in September 2021, TBM-3E '46214' (69327) was moved to Hangar 3 in November 2022 and made the trek to Birkenhead, Merseyside, 5th April 2023, having been gifted to the as yet unproven Battle of the Atlantic Experience. Around the north end of the Grade II listed building is a series of plate glass monoliths entitled 'Counting the Cost' – each of which poignantly depicts the losses of 'Mighty Eighth' aircraft – and of course crews.

	Serial	Code	Type		Built	History	Note	Date
❑	'S4513'	'1'	SPAD XIII replica	G-BFYO	78	ex 'S3398', Yeovilton, Land's End, Chertsey, G-BFYO (CoA 21-6-82, de-reg 14-10-86), D-EOWM. Arrived 17-6-96		1-24
❑	'34064'	'8U'	NAA TB-25J-30-NC Mitchell		45	ex Shoreham, Dublin, Prestwick, Luton, N7614C, USAF, TB-25J / ETB-25J / EB-25J, USAAF B-25J 44-31171. Arrived 29-11-76. *Little Critter from the Moon*		1-24
❑	155529	'114'	McD F-4J(UK) Phantom	ZE359	67	ex Wattisham, 74, ZE359, US Navy 155529, VF-171, VF-31, VF-74, VF-33. Flew in 10-7-91. USN VF-74, *America* colours		1-24
❑	'217786'	'25'	Boeing PT-17 Kaydet		42	ex Swanton Morley, Duxford, CF-EQS, Evergreen, New Brunswick, Canada, 41-8169. Arrived 11-77	[1]	1-24
❑	'226413'	'UN-Z'	Republic P-47D-30-RA Thunderbolt		45	ex USA, Chino, N47DD, Harlingen, Peru AF FAP 119 and 545, USAAF 45-49192. Crashed 9-2-80. Acquired 11-85. 56th FG c/s as 'Hub' Zemke's a/c, *Oregon's Britannia*	[2]	1-24
❑	'238133'		Boeing B-17G-95-DL Flying Fortress		44	ex '231983', *Mary Alice*, Creil, IGN F-BDRS, N68269, 44-83735. Douglas-built. Last flown 1971, arrived 1975		1-24

	Serial	Code	Type	Yr	History	Note	Date
❑	315509	'W7-S'	Douglas C-47A-85-DL Skytrain G-BHUB	44	ex Aces High G-BHUB (de-reg 19-10-81), *Airline*: 'G-AGIV', 'FD988' and 'KG418', Spanish AF T.3-29, N51V, N9985F, SAS SE-BBH, 315 TCG, 316 TCG, USAAF 43-15509. Long Beach-built. Acquired 7-80. 37th TCS / 316th TCG c/s		1-24
❑	'411631'	'MX-V'	NAA P-51D-25-NA Mustang	44	ex '472218', South Lambeth, Duxford, RCAF 9246, USAAF 44-73979. Inglewood-built. Acquired 12-71. *Etta Jeanne II*, 82nd FS, 78th FG colours. Unveiled 10-14	[3]	1-24
❑	44-51228	'493'	Consolidated B-24M-25-FO Liberator	44	ex Lackland, EZB-24M 44-51228. Ford-built. Arrived 29-6-99. *Dugan*		1-24
❑	461748	'Y'	Boeing TB-29A-45-BN Superfortress G-BHDK	45	ex G-BHDK (de-reg 29-3-84), China Lake, 307th BG, Okinawa. *It's Hawg Wild* (stb). Flew in 2-3-80. 307th BG colours		1-24
❑	–		NAA Harvard II	42	ex N Weald, Dutch AF B-168, FE984, RCAF, 2 FIS, USAAF 42-12471. Acquired 1988		1-24
❑	56-0689		Boeing B-52D-40-BW Stratofortress	57	ex 7th BW Carswell, 96th BW, 7th BW, 99th BW, 7th BW, 96th BW, 99th BW, U-Tapao, 509th BW, 454th BW, 306th BW, 99th BW, 91st BW, 509th BW, 494th BW, 95th BW, 28th BW. Wichita-built. Flew in 8-10-83		1-24
❑	56-6692		Lockheed U-2CT-LO	56	ex Alconbury, 9th SRW, 100th SRW, U-2C, 6515th TS, U-2F, 6515th TS, CIA, U-2C, 4080th SRW, CIA. Last flown 28-12-87, arrived 26-6-92. Modified to single-seat configuration		1-24
❑	61-17962		Lockheed SR-71A Blackbird	66	ex Palmdale, 9th SRW, 9th SRW Det 4 Mildenhall, 9th SRW. Arrived 5-4-01	[4]	1-24
❑	67-0120		GD F-111E-CF Aardvark	69	ex Upper Heyford, 20th TFW, 57th TTW, 442nd TFTS, 27th TFW. Arr 19-10-93. *The Chief*, 78th TFS, 20th TFW c/s	[5]	1-24
❑	72-21605		Bell UH-1H Iroquois	72	ex Coleman Barracks, ATCOM, 158th Av Regt. Arr 15-7-97		1-24
❑	76-0020		McDD F-15A-15-MC Eagle	76	ex AMARC Davis-Monthan, 102nd FIW, 5th FIS, 33rd TFW, 36th TFW. Last flown 25-10-93, arrived 4-01. 5th FIS c/s		1-24
❑	77-0259	'AR'	Fairchild A-10A-FA Thunderbolt II	79	ex Alconbury, 10th TFW, 128th TFW, 111th TASG, 128th TFW, 81st TFW. Flew in 6-2-92		1-24
❑	–		GD F-111F-CF Aardvark	~	escape module	[6]	1-24
❑	–		McDD F-15 Eagle	~	ex 48th TFW, Lakenheath. Cockpit simulator, *Eagle Drivers*		1-24

■ **[1]** PT-17 is a composite, having used elements of 42-17786 during its restoration (which was carried out by Eastern Stearman). **[2]** P-47 *Oregon's Britannia* was a major reconstruction based upon large elements of P-47D 45-49192 not used in the composite that created The Fighter Collection's machine *No Guts, No Glory* (now exported). **[3]** Previously well-known as *Big Beautiful Doll*, the P-51 wears the colours of Lt Col H H Lamb's P-51K; Lamb is credited with 5½ 'kills', two of them in 'this' Mustang. **[4]** SR-71 achieved world altitude record 28-7-76 of 85,068ft. **[5]** *The Chief* carried out 19 operational missions during DESERT STORM, 1991. **[6]** Previously quoted as coming from 72-1447 but this is in private hands in The Netherlands.

Store: Some airframes are held out of public gaze at various locations on the site. Schweizer TG-3A 252983 moved to Lasham, Hampshire, on 4th May 2022. Cadet TX.3 XN239 travelled to Long Kesh, N Ireland, by September 2022.

	Serial	Code	Type	Yr	History	Note	Date
❑	'AD937'	'AF-O'	V-S Spitfire V FSM	c18	ex ARC. Acquired c2019. GB Replicas-built. AFDU colours		8-20
❑	XP281		Auster AOP.9	61	ex St Athan, AFWF, M Wallop. NEA 8-11-68	[1]	6-19
❑	9893		Bristol Bolingbroke IVT	42	ex ARC, BAM, OHB, Canada, RCAF. Fairchild Canada-built	[2]	6-19

■ **[1]** XP281 on loan from Army Flying Museum, Middle Wallop, Hampshire. **[2]** Bolingbroke 9893 nose along with the fuselage/centre section of G-MKIV (RCAF 10038, crashed 21-6-87) and the outer wings of 9893.

Duxford Aviation Society (DAS) - **The British Airliner Collection**: The following DAS airframes are within 'AirSpace' (see earlier). Hermes G-ALDG, Dove G-ALFU, York G-ANTK, Comet 4 G-APDB, Concorde G-AXDN. The cockpit of Viscount G-OPAS is on loan to the Bournemouth Aviation Museum, see Bournemouth Dorset. | **www.das.org.uk**

	Serial	Type	Yr	History	Note	Date
❑	G-ALWF	Vickers Viscount 701	52	ex Speke, Cambrian, British Eagle, Channel, BEA. Last flown 12-4-72, de-reg 18-4-72, arrived 21-2-76. BEA colours, *Sir John Franklin*	[1]	1-24
❑	G-ALZO	Airspeed Ambassador 2	52	ex Lasham, Dan-Air, Handley Page, Jordan AF 108, BEA. CoA 14-5-72, de-reg 10-9-81. Dan-Air colours	[2]	1-24
❑	G-AOVT	Bristol Britannia 312	58	ex Luton, Monarch, British Eagle, BOAC. Flew in 29-6-75, de-reg 21-9-81. Monarch c/s; repaint completed 1-17	[3]	1-24
❑	G-ASGC	Vickers Super VC10	65	ex BA, BOAC, BOAC-Cunard, BOAC. Flew in 15-4-80, de-reg 22-4-80. BOAC-Cunard colours	[4]	1-24
❑	G-AVFB	HS Trident 2E	67	ex BA, Nicosia, Cyprus 5B-DAC, BEA. Flew in 13-6-82, de-reg 9-7-82. BEA colours	[5]	1-24

	Reg	Code	Type	Civil reg	Year	History	Note	Date
❑	G-AVMU		BAC 111-510ED		68	ex Hurn, BA, BEA. Last flight 4-3-93, de-reg 12-7-93. BA colours. *County of Dorset*	[6]	1-24
❑	G-BEVT		BN Trislander		77	ex Aurigny. CoA 13-7-17. Flew in 21-6-17	[7]	1-24
❑	ZE701		HSA HS.146 CC.2	G-CMEU	85	ex Northolt, 32, QF, G-6-029, ZE701, G-6-029, ZE701, G-5-03. Hatfield-built. Arrived 24-1-22	[8]	1-24

■ **[1]** *Whisky-Fox* completed 28,299 flight hours and 25,398 landings. **[2]** *Zulu-Oscar* made the last-ever flight by the type in 10-71. **[3]** *Victor-Tango* factoids: completed 35,739 flight hours and 10,760 landings. **[4]** *Golf-Charlie* totted up 54,623 flight hours and 16,415 landings. **[5]** *Fox-Bravo* was damaged by ground fire at Nicosia during the Turkish invasion of Cyprus, 7-74 and remained grounded until 5-77. It completed 21,642 flying hours and 11,726 landings in 1982. **[6]** *Mike-Uniform*'s stats: 45,541 landings, 40,280 hours. **[7]** *Victor-Tango* served with Aurigny throughout its career: around 86,000 flights, total time just shy of 28,000 hours. **[8]** Three days after ZE701 made its last ever flight it was registered to Lingfield-based Aircraft Maintenance Services; the paperwork needed to smooth engine and ancilliaries sales from a *civilian*, instead of a military airframe.

Note: Duxford hosts a wide range of individual airworthy aircraft. The situation with some of these can be fluid and therefore difficult to cover in a book with a two-year 'life'. An increasing number of warbirds are offering flight experiences, or the opportunity to fly alongside a classic. Some are long-term residents, others frequent bases elsewhere - eg Goodwood, Lashenden, Sywell. Several of the resident 'fixed base operators' also house and maintain private owner warbirds and historic types. The status of such machines is in constant flux, and they are not given a formal listing here.

Aircraft Restoration Company (ARC): While specialising in Spitfires, ARC tackles a wide variety of projects. The company also operates and/or maintains aircraft on behalf of other organisations. Only the ARC 'core' fleet and long-term restoration projects are given here: unless noted all are registered to ARC, Aircraft Spares and Materials or Propshop.

The **Hawker Typhoon Preservation Group** delivered a kit-of-parts to ARC in June 2021 as fund-raising momentum for this ambitious venture reached the point where restoration/reconstruction could ramp up. The project includes the former Booker, Bucks, Typhoon cockpit and the rear fuselage of former 174 Squadron RB396 from the Netherlands (shot down 1st April 1945), a Napier Sabre and a large cache of plans. ARC is initially centring on the cockpit section while at Sandown, Isle of Wight, Airframe Assemblies is tackling the rear fuselage. See also Northampton, Northants, for Tempest G-TMPV. More details on: **www.hawkertyphoon.com** Restoration complete, Spitfire PR.19 PS890 (F-AZJS) returned to France on 12th August 2020. ◆ *ARC buildings* **not** *open to public inspection* | **www.aircraftrestorationcompany.com**

	Reg	Code	Type	Civil reg	Year	History	Note	Date
❑	G-DHCZ		DHC Beaver AL.1 ✈		60	ex G-BUCJ, XP772, M Wallop, Beverley, Leconfield, M Wallop, 15 Flt, 667, 132 Flt, AFWF	[1]	1-24
❑	G-EDMK		Boeing A75N1		42	ex EC-AST. Stored awaiting restoration	[2]	3-20
❑	SE-BRG		Fairey Firefly TT.1	G-CGYD	44	ex Sweden, Svensk Flygtjanst, FAA Mk.I DT989, 767, 766, Arr 10-2-04. Under restoration in Buildings 66 and 425		1-24
❑	'L6739'	'YP-Q'	Bristol Bolingbroke IVT ✈	G-BPIV	43	ex 'R3821', 'L8841', 'Z5722', G-BPIV, Strathallan, Canada, RCAF 10201. Fairchild Canada-built. 23 Sqn colours	[3]	1-24
❑	N3200	'QV'	V-S Spitfire Ia ✈	G-CFGJ	39	ex Sandown, Duxford, Braintree, Mimoyecques, Calais, 19. Shot down 26-5-40. Acquired 9-7-15. 19 Sqn colours, *Duxford*	[4]	1-24
❑	P9373		V-S Spitfire I	G-CFGN	39	ex 92, shot down 23-5-40, near Boulogne. CBAF-built Arrived 19-1-11. Stored	[5]	3-20
❑	V9312	'LX-E'	Westland Lysander TT.IIIA ✈	G-CCOM	39	ex N9309K, Canada, RCAF, RAF, 4, 613, 225. SOC 1-10-46. Arrived 4-6-03. 225 Sqn colours		1-24
❑	'X9556'	'S'	Supermarine Walrus I	G-WLRS	34	ex G-RNLI, Audley End, 'Sussex', Southampton, Gt Yarmouth, Winchester, Southampton, W2718, 276, 751, 764. Saro-built. Arrived 22-3-18	[2] [6]	7-23
❑	'AX733'	'K'	Grumman FM-2 Wildcat	G-KINL	43	ex Old Warden, G-CHPN, N49JC, Seattle, Pensacola, N49JC, N70637, N20HA, N68760, USN 86690. General Motors-built. Arrived 27-4-16; first flown 11-10-22. 805 Sqn colours. Crashed 6-7-23	[2] [7]	12-23
❑	BL688*		V-S Spitfire V	G-LFVE	41	ex Trelonk, G-CJWO (de-reg 18-7-22), Twyford, 58 OTU, 41 OTU, 58 OTU, 63, 316, 335th FS USAAF, 610, 132. CBAF-built. Crashed 29-5-45, excavated 1982		7-22
❑	BS548*		V-S Spitfire Tr.IX	G-CMOD	42	ex Sandown, France, 341, 402, 340. Shot down 17-4-43. Salvaged 2012	[8]	2-23
❑	MB293		V-S Seafire IIc	G-CFGI	42	ex Braintree, Malta, 879, 887, A&AEE. Crashed 31-10-44. Salvaged off Malta 4-94. Stored	[5]	3-20
❑	MJ444*		V-S Spitfire IX	G-LEGD	43	ex Sandown, 443, 403, 411. Shot down Belgium 13-1-45. Salvaged 2020. First noted 12-23	[9]	12-23

	Serial	Marks	Type	Year	Reg	History	Note	Date
❑	PL258		V-S Spitfire IX	44	G-NSFS	ex Netherlands, 331 Sqn, PL258. Shot down 29-12-44. CBAF-built. Stored	[10]	3-20
❑	PL983		V-S Spitfire PR.XI ✈	44	G-PRXI	ex Sandown, Duxford, Goudhurst, N Weald, Biggin Hill, Duxford, E Midlands, Stonebroom, Duxford, Old Warden, Vickers G-15-109, N74138, PL983, 2, 4, 1 PP		1-24
❑	PT462	'SW-A'	V-S Spitfire Tr.IX ✈	44	G-CTIX	ex Bryngwyn Bach, N462JC, G-CTIX, Winchester, Mk.IX, Duxford, Israel, IDFAF 4X-FOM, 20-67, Italian AF MM4100, PT462, 4 SAAF, 253. CBAF-built. Arr 9-17. 253 Sqn c/s	[11]	1-24
❑	PV202	'JW'	V-S Spitfire Tr.IX ✈	44	G-CCCA	ex 'W3632', 'QV-I', 'AI-E', 'H-98', '161', G-TRIX, G-BHGH, IAC 161, G-15-174, PV202, 412, 33. CBAF-built. 33 Sqn c/s		1-24
❑	'RB396'		Hawker Typhoon IB	44	G-TIFY	project arrived 24-6-21. See notes above		1-24
❑	RK858		V-S Spitfire IX	43	G-CGJE	ex TFC, CIS, USSR, Sov AF, RK858 n/s. CBAF-built. Missing, Archangel region, 1947, salvaged 1992. Stored		3-20
❑	RK912		V-S Spitfire IX	44	G-CLCS	ex Italy, 93. Crashed 19-4-45. Arrived 5-10-10. Stored		3-20
❑	RN203		V-S Spitfire XIV	45	G-CLCT	ex Germany, 130. Crashed 19-4-45. Salvaged 2002. Stored		3-20
❑	RX168		V-S Seafire III	45	G-BWEM	ex Trelonk, Duxford, Swindon, Exeter, Andover, Norwich, Battle, Dublin, IAC 157 (SOC 27-10-53), RX168, Australia, India. Westland-built. Stored		3-20
❑	XX658		SAL Bulldog	74	G-SMAT	ex local store, G-BZPS, East Low UAS, Cam UAS, Oxford UAS, Cam UAS, 2 FTS. Arrived 20-12-19	[12]	1-24
❑	'2'		Hispano HA-1112-M1L Buchón ✈	49	G-AWHK	ex G-BWUE, Breighton, Sandown, Breighton, Duxford, N9938, *Battle of Britain* (1968), G-AWHK, Spanish AF C.4K-154. JG27 colours by 4-21	[13]	1-24
❑	2100	'V7+1H'	Focke-Wulf Fw 189A-1	c42	G-BZKY	ex G-BZKY (de-reg 9-1-08), Sandown, Sandtoft, Lancing, USSR, Luftwaffe. Shot down 4-5-43. Recovered 1991		1-24
❑	–*	'FI+S'	MS Criquet	47	G-BIRW	ex East Fortune, Duxford, G-BIRW, OO-FIS, F-BDQS. CoA 3-6-83. Arrived by 11-23		12-23
❑	1747		NAA Harvard IV ✈	53	G-BGPB	ex '20385' N Weald, Port AF 1747, WGAF BF+050, AA+050, 53-4619. CCF-built. Port AF colours. *Taz*		1-24

■ **[1]** G-DHCZ, is as close to DHC-2 as the alphabet will allow. **[2]** Registered to Tom Harris - see also Shuttleworth, Beds. **[3]** Registered to Blenheim (Duxford) Ltd. Nose from Battle of Britain veteran Mk.If L6739 (former 23 Sqn night-fighter SOC 31-12-40) to make a *representative* Mk.I. This nose was previously an electric-driven car conversion. The original nose of Mk.IVT 10201 is on show. The **Blenheim Society** works tirelessly to support the restoration of *India-Victor*: **www.blenheimsociety.com** **[4]** Gifted to the IWM and registered to it 1-12-15. When N3200 was shot down, 19 Sqn had applied the unit code 'QV-' but no individual letter. **[5]** UK registered to Mark One Partners LLC. *Golf-November and Golf-India* both cancelled as sold in the USA 11-1-16. **[6]** W2718 retired to 15 MU Wroughton 14-2-46 and acquired by Somerton Airways of Cowes, Isle of Wight. Beyond that it went to Norman Grogan who widened the fuselage and turned it into a caravan. Bless, him, he did not throw *any* of it away, leaving it as a time capsule. It was presented to the then Hall of Aviation at Southampton, Hampshire, in the mid-1980s. In 10-89 was acquired by Dick Melton who returned it to a biplane amphibian at Winchester, Hampshire, and then Great Yarmouth, Norfolk. **[7]** FM-2 served in California in the 1950s as a Hardwick Special HG.1 'bug-bomber'. **[8]** Two-seater conversion, fuselage with Airframe Assemblies 2022; registered to Pays Air Service, Australia, as a Mk.IXT. **[9]** MJ444 another two-seater conversion, registered to Aero Legends – see also Hythe and Lashenden, Kent. **[10]** Registered to the Norwegian Spitfire Foundation. **[11]** There is *another* 'PT462' at Moffatt, Scotland. **[12]** XX658 registered to Skysmart MRO. **[13]** Bf 109 with RR Merlin 500 built by Hispano. G-AWHK has the fuselage of C.4K-154 - a *Battle of Britain* non-flyer, the rest from C.4K-102.

B-17 Preservation Ltd: *Sally B* is Britain's largest privately-operated warbird. Determination keeps this magic machine going: no lottery grants, government hand-outs or other funding. Its lifeblood is the ***Sally B* Supporters Club**, donations from the public, the grit of its engineering team and the expertise of its operator, Elly Sallingboe.

◆ *PO Box 92, Bury St Edmunds, IP28 8RR* | **b-17preservation@sallyb.org.uk** | **www.sallyb.org.uk**

	Serial	Marks	Type	Year	Reg	History	Note	Date
❑	'124485'	'DF-A'	Boeing B-17G-105-VE ✈ Flying Fortress	44	G-BEDF	ex N17TE, IGN F-BGSR, 44-85784. *Sally B* (port), *Memphis Belle* (starboard)		1-24

Classic Wings / Spectrum Leisure: Maintenance base is at Clacton, Essex – which see. The fleet includes: Rapides G-AKIF, HG691 (G-AIYR) and TX310 (G-AIDL); Tiger Moths DE974 (G-ANZZ) and PG657 (G-AGPK). Please note not all will be present at any one time. ◆ *Viewable during normal museum hours and at airshows* | **www.classic-wings.co.uk**

The Fighter Collection (TFC) and the **Friends of the Fighter Collection** support group. Beech D.17S G-BRVE flew off to a new home at Breighton, E Yorks, on 6th August 2022. Sea Fury T.20S WG655 (G-INVN) force-landed close to Duxford on 4th August 2020. Thankfully there was no serious injuries to the pilots, but the aircraft was badly damaged: it was de-registered on 14th April 2021. Offered for sale during 2022, it was trucked out in late 2023, likely bound for the USA.

◆ *Open to the public during museum hours.* | **www.fighter-collection.com**

	Serial	Code	Type	Year / Reg	History	Note	Date
❑	N5903		Gloster Gladiator II	39 G-GLAD	ex Yeovilton, 'N2276', 'N5226', Old Warden, Eastleigh, Ansty, 61 OTU. Arrived 30-11-94. CoA 30-6-18. 72 Sqn colours		1-24
❑	S1581	'573'	Hawker Nimrod I ✈	32 G-BWWK	ex St Leonards-on-Sea, St Just, Henlow, 802. Acquired 2004. 802 Sqn colours		1-24
❑	EP120	'AE-A'	V-S Spitfire V ✈	42 G-LFVB	ex Audley End, Duxford, St Athan 8070M, Wattisham, Boulmer, Wilmslow, St Athan, 5377M (13-7-45), 53 OTU, 402, 19, 501. CBAF-built. Arrived 1-93. *City of Winnipeg*, 402 Sqn colours	[1]	1-24
❑	'JV579'	'F'	Grumman FM-2 Wildcat ✈	44 G-RUMW	ex Monroe, USA N4845V, 86711. Arrived 25-4-93. 846 Sqn colours		1-24
❑	'KD345'	'A-130'	Vought FG-1D ✈ Corsair ✈	45 G-FGID	ex N8297, N9154Z, USN 88297. Goodyear-built. Arrived 4-86. 1850 Sqn, SEAC colours		1-24
❑	PK624		V-S Spitfire F.22	45	ex St Athan, Abingdon 8072M, Northolt, Uxbridge 'WP916', N Weald, 9 MU, 614. CBAF-built. SOC 4-2-54. Arrived 11-10-94		12-21
❑	VX281	'120'	Hawker Sea Fury T.20S	49 G-BCOW	ex Yeovilton G-RNHF, N Weald, Yeovilton, N Weald, USA N281L, N8476W, G-BCOW, DLB D-CACO, G-9-64, VX281, 738, 736. 799 Sqn colours. Crashed 28-4-21		11-21
❑	VX653		Hawker Sea Fury FB.11	49 G-BUCM	ex Hendon, Yeovilton, Lee-on-Solent, Lossiemouth 'XV653', FRU, 811, 738, 736. SOC 10-3-59. Arr 24-11-91		1-24
❑	'A19-144'		Bristol Beaufighter XI	45	ex Melbourne, Sydney, Drysdale, RAAF A8-324. DAP-built. SOC 8-8-49. Arrived 1991	[2]	1-24
❑	No.82		Curtiss Hawk 75A-1 ✈	39 G-CCVH	ex NX80FR, Chino, France, Cazaux, GC II/5. Acquired 1990. French AF colours	[3]	1-24
❑	'MM6976'	'85-16'	Fiat CR-42 Falco	41 G-CBLS	ex Audley End, Italy, Sweden, RSweAF (as a J11) Fv2524. Acquired 1995, arrived 23-2-06. On site from 6-7-18	[4]	1-24
❑	–		Nakajima Ki-43 Hayabusa	c44	ex Australia. Stored		3-18
❑	'20'		Lavochkin La-11	c45	ex Monino, USSR. Arrived 5-93. Stored		3-18
❑	-		Curtiss P-36C Hawk ✈	38 G-CIXJ	ex N80FR, Chino, USAAC 38-210. Arrived 25-6-15		1-24
❑	'160'	'10AB'	Curtiss P-40C Warhawk ✈	41 G-CIIO	ex N80FR, Chino, Russia, Sov AF, USAAF 41-13357. Arrived 9-6-14		1-24
❑	–	'X-17'	Curtiss P-40F-15-CU Warhawk ✈	41 G-CGZP	ex VH-PIV, Wangaratta, Espiritu Santo, 44th FG, 347th FG, 41-19841. Arr 7-11. 85th FS, 79th FG c/s, *Lee's Hope*		1-24
❑	21714	'201'	Grumman F8F-2P Bearcat ✈	48 G-RUMM	ex NX700HL, N1YY, N4995V, 121714. Acquired 3-6-81. VF-20 colours, Lt Cdr 'Whiff' Caldwell's aircraft		1-24

■ All registered to Patina Ltd, unless noted. **[1]** EP120 in the colours of 402 'City of Winnipeg' Sqn RCAF as flown mostly by its CO, Sqn Ldr Geoffrey W Northcott; he chalked up the bulk of his 8 'kills' in EP120: 3 x Bf 109 and 3 x Fw 190. **[2]** 'Beau' has large elements reputed to be from Mk.XIs A19-144 (ex RAF JM135) and A-19-148 (JL946) with the cockpit from an Australian-built Department of Aircraft Production example. **[3]** G-CCVH wears GC II/5 colours to port and Lafayette Esc 'chief's head' to starboard; the latter also being TFC's logo. **[4]** Fiat in the colours of an example that force landed in Norfolk 11-11-40.

Historic Aircraft Collection of Jersey (HAC): The Hurricane and Spitfire have been operated under the **Polish Heritage Flight** banner since November 2019. See under St Leonards-on-Sea, East Sussex, for HAC's closely related Retrotec. Criquet G-BPHZ was trucked to Audley End, Essex, 19th January 2023. Hind L7181 (G-CBLK) moved to St Leonards-on-Sea, on 4th October 2023. ◆ *Viewable during normal museum opening hours* | **www.facebook.com/historicaircraftcollection/**

	Serial	Code	Type	Year / Reg	History	Note	Date
❑	E8894		Airco DH.9 ✈	1918 G-CDLI	ex St Leonards-on-Sea, India, 47, 30. Vulcan Motor-built.	[1]	1-24
❑	K3661	'562'	Hawker Nimrod II ✈	34 G-BURZ	ex St Leonards-on-Sea, Henlow, Ashford, 802. 802 Sqn colours		1-24
❑	K5674		Hawker Fury I ✈	35 G-CBZP	ex St Leonards-on-Sea, Duxford, St Leonards-on-Sea, SAAF 215, 13, RAF 43. *Queen of North and South*, 43 Sqn c/s		1-24
❑	'P2954' 'P3935'	'WX-E' 'WX-D'	Hawker Hurricane XII ✈	42 G-HURI	ex 'R4175', 'P3700', 'Z5140', 'Z7381', TFC, Coningsby, Coventry, Canada, 71. CCF-built. 302 Sqn colours by 5-23 - 'P2954' to stb, 'P3935' to pt		1-24
❑	BM597	'RF-M'	V-S Spitfire Vb ✈	42 G-MKVB	ex Audley End, Fulbourne, Church Fenton, Linton-on-Ouse, Church Fenton, St Athan, 5718M, 58 OTU, 317. CBAF-built. 303 Sqn colours	[2]	1-24

■ **[1]** DH.9 and Hind registered to Aero Vintage, all others to HAC. **[2]** Registered to Aerial Spitfire Icons Mark 5 Pty 11-5-23.

Old Flying Machine Company (OFMC): ◆ *Viewable during normal museum hours and at airshows* | **www.mh434.com**

❑ MH434 'ZD-B' V-S Spitfire IX ✈ 43 ex Booker, COGEA Nouvelle OO-ARA, Belgian AF SM-41,
G-ASJV Fokker B-13, Netherlands H-68, H-105 322, MH434, 349, 222, 350, 222. CBAF-built. 222 Sqn colours, *Mylcraine* 1-24

Plane Sailing Ltd / Catalina Aircraft Ltd: Acting in support of the Canso (PBY-5A equivalent) and uniting those interested in Catalinas is the **Catalina Society**, which publishes the excellent *Catalina News*.

◆ *Viewable frequently during normal museum opening hours and at airshows*

❑ '433915' Consolidated Canso A ✈ 44 ex C-FNJF, CF-NJF, F-ZBBD, CF-NJF, F-ZBAY, CF-NJF, RCAF
G-PBYA 11005. Canadian-Vickers built. 5th ERS colours, *Miss Pick Up* 1-24

EVERSDEN on the A603 west of Cambridge

A Tiger is *believed* to be stored at a *private* location in the area.

❑ G-AZDY DH Tiger Moth 44 ex F-BGDJ, French AF, PG650 n/s. Morris-built. CoA 18-8-97 N1-23

FOWLMERE AERODROME north of the A505, west of Duxford, on the B1368 EGMA

By April 2022 Cessna 303 G-IKAP had moved on – no 'forwarding address'.

GRANSDEN LODGE AERODROME north of the B1046 west of Longstowe

Cambridge Gliding Centre: ◆ *Prior arrangement* **only** | **www.camgliding.uk**

❑ ZE500 Grob Viking T.1 85 BGA.3005, ex Sealand. Crashed 26-8-87. Forward fuselage 8-21

GREAT ABINGTON at the junction of the A11 and A505 southeast of Cambridge

TWI Group: In Granta Park, part of the 'Cambridge Science Cluster' high-tech zone, an Eclipse is on show. The biz-jet was the first to employ the TWI-pioneered friction stir-welding technique. **www.twi-global.com**

❑ N504EA Eclipse 500 05 ex USA. First noted 4-17. See notes above [1] 1-22

■ **[1]** Fourth Eclipse prototype; donated by Eclipse Aerospace and prepared for display by Marshall Aviation Services.

HOUGHTON on the A1123 east of Huntingdon

Jon Wilson: Keeps his Canberra cockpit at a *private* location in the area.

❑ WJ567 EE Canberra B.2 53 ex Wyton, 100, 85, MinTech, 45, RNZAF, 45, 59, 149. HP-built. Cockpit 10-21

LINTON on the A3107 east of Duxford

No.2523 (Linton) Sqn Air Cadets: Chipmunk WG362 was auctioned by Agility in May 2023 and moved to Grimsby, Lincs.

LITTLE GRANSDEN AERODROME south of the B1046, south of Great Gransden EGMJ

Cambridge Bomber and Fighter Society: ◆ *Prior arrangement* **only**: *annual open day* | **www.cbfs.org.uk**

❑ 'K1928' Hawker Fury I 31 BAPC.362, fuselage, off-site [1] 1-24

❑ L1639 Hawker Hurricane I 38 BAPC.402, ex 504, 85. Shot down 14-5-40. Composite [2] 1-24

■ **[1]** Being built up from a variety of sections. K1928 served mostly with 43 Sqn, suffering an accident at Tangmere 19-5-37. It later became instructional airframe 2196M. **[2]** Restoration takes identity from the cockpit area and other elements salvaged from the crash site of L1639. No.504's CO, Sqn Ldr J B Parnall was killed when L1639 was shot down operating from Marcq in France.

Also: Cessna 152s G-BOFL and G-BOFM had moved to Sedlescombe, E Sussex by August 2022.

LITTLE STAUGHTON AERODROME south of the A45, west of Eaton Socon

Continuing the clear out: Cessna 172 G-BHUJ, Tomahawks G-BKAS and OO-RAB, all last noted in August 2019, have been deleted. That leaves just one long-termer... ◆ *Prior arrangement* **only**

❑ G-BTZP SOCATA Tampico 92 de-reg 18-6-08 7-21

MADINGLEY at the junction of the A1303 and A14 west of Cambridge

Cambridge American Forces Cemetery: Perhaps when visiting Duxford, take a trip to Madingley and a walk through the beautifully kept grounds, amid row after row of graves and impressive memorials. | **www.abmc.gov**

MARCH on the A141 south of Wisbech

Ian and **Gary Morton**: Are hard at work returning a former CAFU Dove to 'flight checker' status.

❑ G-ANAP DH Dove 6 53 ex Pershore, Bristol, CAFU Stansted. CoA 6-9-73, de-reg 31-8-73. Cockpit 6-23

No.**1220 (March) Squadron Air Cadets**: The unit's 'JP' procedure trainer, previously on loan at West Walton Highway, Norfolk, has been 'parked' here for want of a confirmed 'home'.

❑ –* Hunting Jet Provost CIM ~ ex West Walton Highway. See notes above 2-22

PETERBOROUGH

Aerospace Experience: On the Woodston Industrial Estate, declaring itself the "UK's leading flight experience company", has a major location at Gatwick with full-motion, wholly 'synthetic' simulators. The Peterborough base boasts a full motion Phantom; one of two modified from former US Navy airframes (F-4Ns?) to train RAF pilots on the well-potent F-4J(UK).

◆ *Prior arrangement* **only** | **www.aerospace.experience.uk/f4-phantom**

❑ –* McD F-4 Phantom ~ ex Wattisham. Ferranti-modified. See note above 12-23

The Blue Bell: Werrington. A notice near the Lynx's 'cab' door reads: "By all means look, but don't enter! Dangerous pipes and children-eating sharks live inside!" The wall side of an outbuilding boasts an impressive mural of a Spitfire.

❑ XZ655* 'A' *and* '3' Westland Lynx AH.7 80 ex Weeton, Hixon, M Wallop, 671, 655, 664, 655, 664, 671, 657, 651, 652, 655, 652. Cabin. First noted 8-20 2-24

PETERBOROUGH (CONINGTON) AERODROME east of the A1, south of Wansford EGSF

Last noted in October 2019, Cessna 150 G-BFKF has been deleted.

❑ XW410 'MR' BAC Jet Provost T.5A ex 'Norfolk', Selby, Cosford 9125M, Shawbury, 1 FTS, RAFC, 3 FTS. Cockpit, first noted 3-18 3-22

RAMSEY on the B1096 west of Chatteris

No.**511 (Ramsey) Squadron Air Cadets**: *Should* still have the Chipmunk cockpit.

❑ WK584 DHC Chipmunk T.10 52 ex Bawtry, Church Fenton, Linton-on-Ouse, 7556M, Edzell SF, Oxf UAS, Glas UAS, 11 RFS. Hawarden-built. Cockpit 3-19

SAWSTON east of the A1301 north of Duxford

An Auster is under restoration at a *private* location in the *general* area.

❑ WZ679* Auster AOP.9 56 ex Coventry, Peterborough, Cranfield, Wroughton, Marlborough, Aborfield 7863M (17-9-64), 656 1-23

STILTON off the A1(M) south of Peterborough

The Stirling Aircraft Project: The workshop moved to the general area during December 2020. Using as many original items as possible, the creation of the forward fuselage and crew stations of a Mk.III makes good progress. The finished item will carry the markings of EE944 'HA-H' which crashed at Tempsford at the end of an SOE sortie on 5th March 1944.

◆ *Prior arrangement* **only**. | **info@stirlingproject.com** | **www.stirlingproject.co.uk**

❑ –* Short Stirling III re-creation 95 BAPC.388, forward fuselage - see above 1-24

UPWOOD southeast of Peterborough, west of Ramsey

Matt Buddle: Keeps his Lightning cockpit in the locality. The cockpit of Harrier GR.3 XZ993 moved to Welshpool, Wales, as far back as 28th April 2017. ◆ *Prior arrangement* **only**

❑ XR754 EE Lightning F.6 65 ex Doncaster, Firbeck, Walpole, King's Lynn, Stock, Honington 8972M, Binbrook, 11, 5-11, 23, 5, A&AEE. Last flown 22-6-88. Cockpit 4-22

WATERBEACH on the A10 north of Cambridge

Waterbeach Military Heritage Museum: Housed in a building near the entrance to the former barracks, the museum – dedicated to the memory of Oliver Errington – covers the legacy of the airfield and its final days as an Army base.

◆ *Denny End Road, CB25 9PA* | **01223 861846** | **waterbeachmilitarymuseum@waterbeach.org** | **www.waterbeachmilitarymuseum.org.uk**

WHITTLESEY on the A605 east of Peterborough

Locally, an Auster is being worked on at a *private* location.

	Reg		Type	Yr	Details	Note	Date
❑	G-AOGV		Auster J5R Alpine	56	CoA 17-7-72		N11-23

WITTERING AIRFIELD on the A1 south of Stamford — EGXT

RAF Wittering: Within the base is the **Harrier Heritage Centre** which is available to *pre-booked* groups (max 12 people) presently on Wednesdays. | **wittering.heritage.centre@gmail.com**

	Reg		Type	Yr	Details	Note	Date
❑	XV279		HS Harrier GR.1	67	ex 8566M (8-2-78), WLT *The Plastic Pig*, Farnborough, Culdrose, A&AEE, BSE, Ferranti, HSA		7-23
❑	XV779		HS Harrier GR.3	70	ex 8931M (23-1-87) 'gate' 1988-2011, 233 OCU, 3, Wittering SF, 3, 20, GR.1, 20, 4, 1, 4. 4 Sqn colours	[1]	7-23
❑	XW923		HS Harrier GR.3	71	ex 8724M, 1417 Flt, 233 OCU, 1, GR.1. Crashed 26-5-81, Belize. 20 Sqn colours. Cockpit		7-23
❑	XZ146	'S'	HS Harrier T.4	76	ex North Luffenham 9281M (17-12-97), Shawbury, 20, 233 OCU, Gütersloh SF, 233 OCU, 4, 3, T.2. 20 Sqn colours		7-23
❑	ZD318		BAe/McDD Harrier GR.7A	85	ex Cottesmore, GR.7, Warton, Boscombe Down, Ferranti, Warton, GR.5. Last flown 11-7-07	[2]	7-23
❑	162068		BAe/McDD AV-8B Harrier II	84	ex Cottesmore, 9250M, VMAT-203. Fuselage	[3]	7-15
❑	162964		BAe/McDD AV-8B Harrier II	87	ex Boscombe Down, St Athan, Warton, USMC, VMA-542, -223, -231, -542. Cockpit in 4 Sqn colours		7-23

■ **[1]** XV779 belly-landed at Wildenrath 16-12-74; cockpit replaced by a spare. *Original* nose can be found at Selby, N Yorks. **[2]** Circa 1998 ZD318 suffered a landing accident and was fitted with the wing of ZD348. **[3]** The original fuselage of BuNo 162068 which was rebuilt as AV-8B+ 165310. Modified by the heritage centre to resemble a GR.7.

Among the resident units is **71 (Inspection and Repair) Squadron** engaged on maintenance trials.

	Reg		Type	Yr	Details	Note	Date
❑	XX351		HS Hawk T.1A	81	ex Shawbury, 4 FTS, 100, 19, 208, 234, 1 TWU. Bitteswell-built. SOC 25-1-16. Arrived 12-1-16. Sectioned, 71 Sqn		5-18
❑	ZD469	'59A'	BAe/McDD Harrier GR.7A	90	ex Cottesmore, Kandahar, 3, GR.5A. Damaged 14-10-05. *Christine*. On display from 28-4-11, 1 Sqn colours	[1]	1-24
❑	ZE651*		Grob Viking T.1	85	ex BGA.3081. Arrived 20-8-21. 71 Sqn		8-21
❑	ZJ810		Eurofighter Typhoon T.3	04	ex Coningsby. SOC 21-2-19. Arrived by 8-20. Fuselage, 71 Sqn		1-23

■ **[1]** ZD469 was damaged in a mortar attack at Kandahar 14-10-05 and declared Cat 5 2-5-08 - total time 1,500.05 hours.

WYTON on the B1090 northwest of St Ives

RAF Pathfinders Archive: Within the RAF enclave is an incredible volunteer-run archive, dedicated to the Pathfinder Force; including material from crash sites. In association with the Pathfinder Collection, there is an exhibition within the base heritage centre. The revised website is a mine of information.

◆ *Prior arrangement* **only** – *visit request form on website* | **email** via website | **www.raf-pathfinders.com**

RAF Wyton: An enclave within the former airfield includes **Joint Force Command** and the **Joint Forces Intelligence Group**.

	Reg		Type	Yr	Details	Note	Date
❑	XH170		EE Canberra PR.9	60	ex 8739M (27-1-82), 39, RAE, 58. Displayed, since 27-1-82		1-24

Also: A Chipmunk cockpit is held in the area.

	Reg		Type	Yr	Details	Note	Date
❑	WP927		DHC Chipmunk T.10 G-ATJK	52	ex South Molton, Ingatestone, London Colney, Ashton-under-Lyne, Crosby, 8216M (4-8-72), Hamble G-ATJK (1965-1968), MCS, Oxf UAS, Lon UAS, Detling SF, London UAS. Hawarden-built. Cockpit		10-23

CHESHIRE

ALDFORD on the B5130 south of Chester

Eaton Hall: Investigations in the spring of 2022 revealed that the anonymous plinth-mounted Gazelle had moved on.

BURTONWOOD south of the M62, west of Warrington

RAF Burtonwood Heritage Centre: Little of the once huge USAF Burtonwood air base remains; cars that hurtle down the M62 are following the course of the main runway. The centre, to the south of the motorway and on the former domestic Site 4, has amassed an incredible collection of artefacts and images to tell the tale of this great airfield.

◆ *From M62 J8 or 9, Shackleton Close, WA5 9YZ* | **email** via website | **www.rafburtonwoodheritagecentre.co.uk**

❑ N31356	Douglas DC-4-1009	46	ex '44-42914', N Weald, C-FTAW, EL-ADR, N6404. Last flown 9-02. Forward fuselage. Arrived 8-12-15	1-24

CHESTER

Airframes listed here are in the *general* area, at *separate* venues and all ***only*** available by prior arrangement.

Air Pulford - Panavia Tornado Restorations: Simon Pulford owns Tornado F.2 cockpit ZD938 at Doncaster, S Yorks. Sioux AH.1s XT148 and XT236 arrived here by November 2022, before trekking to Dumfries, Scotland, 2nd April 2023.
simonpulford@btinternet.com

Andy Blair: Andy's 'JP' will wear CFS silver and Dayglo when completed.

❑ XN549	Hunting Jet Provost T.3	61	ex Warrington, South Molton, Book, Shawbury, Halton, '8235M'/8335M (21-3-73), Shawbury, 1 FTS, CFS. Cockpit	1-18

Nick Foden: Work on the Pup continues. AA-5A OO-GCO has been scrapped. | **grummanaa5a@googlemail.com**

❑ G-AXDW	Beagle Pup 100	69	ex Caterham, Cranfield. Crashed 26-2-09, CoA 31-3-09, de-reg 5-8-09	1-24

Ian Starnes:

❑ XR654	Hunting Jet Provost T.4	63	ex Barton, Chelford, Macclesfield, Hurn, Coventry, Puckeridge, Hatfield, Shawbury, CAW, 3 FTS, 6 FTS. SOC 25-11-71. Cockpit	3-19
❑ –	Fieseler Fi 103 (V-1) FSM	15	BAPC.327, ex Parbold. Built by Mike Davey. Arrived 8-15	8-15

CREWE on the A51 southeast of Nantwich

Obsolete Aviation: Matt Gilbey is undertaking this challenging restoration on an 'as and when' basis. The project was given a Spirit of *CockpitFest* award at Newark, June 2022. ◆ *Prior arrangement* **only** | **obsoleteaviation@gmail.com**

❑ ZG875	Westland Sea King HAS.6	90	ex Market Drayton, Gosport, 819, 820, 814. Accident 12-6-99, SOC 30-10-00. Cockpit, acquired 2015	6-23

HOOTON PARK north of Junction 6 of the M53, near Eastham Locks

Hooton Park Hangars (HPH): (Note, new name.) A milestone in the development of the site came on 14th May 2022 with the opening of Hangar 16 as the main display hall. Working hand-in-hand with **The Aeroplane Collection** (TAC), the Griffin Trust and the CH21 Home Guard Living History Group, HPH is creating a unique visitor centre among the Grade II* 'Belfast Truss' (General Service) hangars at this famous former airfield. TAC proudly has the masthead rider 'Preserving Aviation Heritage since 1962' having been founded as the trail-blazing Northern Aircraft Preservation Society (NAPS).

The restored Messenger is a joy to behold and testament to TAC's capabilities. *Uniform-India* was based at Hooton in the mid-1950s. It is displayed without its outer wings; they will be completed and attached in due course. There are plans afoot to take on a more complete Gemini, with the TAC composite acting as a source of spares.

Please note: Not all airframes will be on show to visitors, either in workshops, or storage.

Disposals: Tutor CHQ (XN247) to Dumfries, Scotland, 15-10-22; Cadet TX.1 RA848 to Doncaster, S Yorks, 15-10-22; Chipmunk T.10 cockpit WG303 to Carlisle, Cumbria, 8-2-23; Cadet TX.1 XA293 to Doncaster, S Yorks, by 12-22; Sioux AH.1 XT148 and XT236 to Chester, Cheshire, by 11-22. Additionally, McBroom BAPC.204 and MW 100 BAPC.310 were transferred to the Weston-super-Mare based British Hang-Gliding Museum on 6th June 2023. Auster G-AJEB and Chipmunk WB584 are both due for disposal from inventory and moving on during 2024.

◆ *Airfield Way, CH65 1BQ* | HPT: **0151 327 3565** | **info@hootonparktrust.co.uk** | **www.hootonparkhangars.co.uk** | TAC: **tac.secretary.web@gmail.com** | **www.theaeroplanecollection.org**

Reg	Type	Year	Details	Notes	Date
❑ G-EBZM	Avro Avian IIIA	28	ex Manchester, Higher Blagdon, Peel Green, Stretford, Lymm, Speke, Huyton, Ringway, Hesketh Park. CoA 20-1-38, de-reg 1-12-46. Acquired 3-11-62. Arrived 12-21	[1] [2]	1-24
❑ G-ADAH	DH Dragon Rapide	35	ex Manchester, East Fortune, Peel Green, Booker, Dyce, Allied AW, Northern & Scottish, British Airways, Hillman's. CoA 9-6-47, de-reg 18-2-59. Acquired 11-10-70, arrived 12-21. Allied Airways colours, *Pioneer*	[1]	1-24
❑ 'G-ADYO' 'BHP.1'	Mignet HM.14 'Flea'	36	BAPC.12, ex Manchester, East Fortune, Chester-le-Street, Newcastle, Wigan, Stockport, Rishworth. Acquired 13-6-64. Arrived 11-21	[1] [3]	1-24
❑ G-AFIU	Luton Minor	c38	ex Barton, Wigan, Stoke, Breighton, Wigan, Peel Green, Pembroke. De-reg 31-3-99. Acquired 1971	[1] [4]	1-24
❑ G-AHUI	Miles Messenger	46	ex Pulborough, Henley, Woodley, Cranfield, Bushey, Caistor, Handforth, Wolverhampton, U-9. De-reg 21-11-73. Acquired 8-02. See notes above	[1] [5]	1-24
❑ G-AIGP	Auster J1 Autocrat	46	ex Spilsby .CoA 30-10-73, de-reg 31-10-73. Arrived 10-12-21	[6] [7]	1-24
❑ G-AJEB	Auster J1N Alpha	46	ex Manchester, Hooton, Warmingham, Brize Norton, Wigan, Cosford. CoA 27-3-69, de-reg 9-6-81. Acquired 28-6-75. See note above.	[1]	1-24
❑ 'G-AKHZ'	Miles Gemini	47	ex Pulborough. Composite, stored. See notes above	[1] [8]	1-24
❑ G-AOUO	DHC Chipmunk T.10 WB730	50	ex Halton, RAFGSA, WB730, 11 RFS. Hawarden-built. CoA 3-4-14, de-reg 10-5-19. Arrived 3-17	[1] [9]	1-24
❑ G-APUD	Wallis-Bensen B-7MC	59	ex Manchester, Firbeck, Nostell Priory, Wigan, Biggin Hill. CoA 27-9-60, de-reg 27-2-70. Acquired 4-72, arrived 11-21	[1] [10]	1-24
❑ G-ARGB*	Auster 6A Tugmaster	46	ex Newark-on-Trent, Waddington, AOP.6 VF635, 662, 1901 Flt. CoA 21-6-74, de-reg 30-5-84. Arrived 25-10-22	[1]	1-24
❑ G-ARTM*	Beagle Terrier 1	50	ex Newark-on-Trent, Chirk, Auster T.7 WE536, 651, 657, Schwechat SF. Cr 28-5-70, de-reg 12-9-73. Arr 25-10-22	[1]	1-24
❑ AKQ	Slingsby T.8 Tutor	46	BGA.466, ex Stamford, Tibenham. Martin Hearn-built. Arrived 31-8-14	[6] [11]	1-24
❑ AKW	Slingsby T.8 Tutor G-ALKP	46	G-ALKP, BGA.469, ex Stamford. Martin Hearn-built. Arrived 26-7-19	[6] [11]	1-24
❑ –	Slingsby Tutor G-ALPU	47	BGA.473, ex Melton Mowbray, G-ALPU, Cranfield, BGA.473. CoA 12-87. Martin Hearn-built. Arrived 10-6-12. Stored	[6] [11]	1-24
❑ '14'	Roe Triplane replica	c53	BAPC.6, ex Manchester, London, Southend, Irlam, Peel Green, Old Warden, Woodford. Avro, Woodford-built. 'Bullseye Avroplane'. Acquired 24-10-69, arrived 11-21	[1] [12]	1-24

Auster Autocrat G-AIGP, a Merseyside denizen in the late 1940s and 1950s. *Ian Humphreys*

	Serial	Code	Type	Year	History	Notes	Last noted
❑	–		Sopwith Baby replica	78	BAPC.137, ex North Stainley, Land's End, Chertsey. Arrived 12-5-18. Restoration project	[6]	1-24
❑	–		Mignet HM.14 'Flea'	36	BAPC.201, ex Millom, Llandwrog, Talysarn. Fuselage	[13]	1-22
❑	–		DH Dragon Rapide FSM	01	BAPC.280, ex Crowne Plaza - Liverpool, 'G-AJCL', 'G-ANZP', 'G-AEAJ'. Cockpit, first noted 8-21	[6] [14]	1-24
❑	–		UFM Easy-Riser	~	BAPC.652, ex Manchester	[1]	1-22
❑	'D8118'*	'T'	Sopwith Camel scale rep	c21	BAPC.567, ex Chalford. Built by Graham Holmes. Arr 2-23	[1]	1-24
❑	P9451		V-S Spitfire I	40	ex 610. Crashed 11-12-40. Cockpit, restored 'space frame'. Arrived by 6-15. Stored	[15]	6-23
❑	EM840* G-ANBY		DH Tiger Moth	43	ex Middle Wallop, Shawbury, -?-, G-ANBY (de-reg 30-4-59) Rochester, 21 EFTS. Morris Motors-built. SOC 25-9-53. Arrived 28-1-23	[16]	1-24
❑	'PV144'*	'4D-A'	V-S Spitfire FSM	20	BAPC.581, ex Carlisle. David Price-built. 74 Sqn colours. Arrived 4-23	[6]	1-24
❑	RM169* G-ANVY	'4-47'	Percival Proctor IV	44	ex Colchester, Great Oakley, SE-CEA, RM169, 4 RS. Hills-built. Arrived 27-10-23		1-24
❑	WB584*		DHC Chipmunk T.10	50	ex Carlisle, Newcastle, Morpeth, East Fortune, Manston, Kilmarnock, Edinburgh 7706M (16-1-61), Shawbury, Debden CF, 11 GCF, Tangmere SF, Glasgow UAS, 8 FTS, Bristol UAS, 12 RFS, 22 RFS. Hatfield-built. Cockpit, trailer-mounted. Arrived by 7-23. See note above.		1-24
❑	WG477* G-ATDP		DHC Chipmunk T.10	51	ex Scampton, Birkdale 8362M (22-8-73), G-ATDP (de-reg 15-1-68), G-ATDI ntu, Marham SF, MECS,114, Bristol UAS, Aberdeen UAS, 11 RFS, 2 BFTS, 25 RFS, Liv UAS, 25 RFS. Hawarden-built. Cockpit, arrived 28-1-23		1-24
❑	WH132	'J'	Gloster Meteor T.7	51	ex Leconfield, Chelmsford 7906M (17-7-66), Kemble, CAW, CFS, CAW, 8 FTS, 207 AFS. Arrived 5-10-17	[6]	1-24
❑	WP978*		DHC Chipmunk T.10	53	ex Stamford, Chivenor, Exeter, Little Rissington 7467M (19-8-59), 4 SoTT CF, 663. Hawarden-built. Cockpit. Arrived 10-4-22	[6] [17]	1-24
❑	WT520		EE Canberra PR.7	55	ex Biddulph, Warton, Lytham St Anne's, Eaglescott, Burntwood, Swinderby, Manby 8184M (8-10-71), 8094M, 31, 17, 1, 17, 31, 80. Short-built. Cockpit. Arrived 7-19	[6]	1-24
❑	XD624	'O'	DH Vampire T.11	55	ex Haverigg, Swinton, Ringway, Macclesfield, CATCS, CNCS, Church Fenton SF, 19. SOC 15-12-70. Fairey-built. Acquired 20-3-11. Wings from XD425	[1] [18]	1-24
❑	–		Fairey Gannet T.2	c56	BAPC.309, ex Caernarfon, Buxton ATC, Sealand, Hooton Park, Tangmere, Fleetlands. Cockpit. Arrived 20-7-12	[1]	1-24

■ **[1]** TAC airframe. **[2]** G-EBZM was registered to Merseyside Aero and Sports Ltd, trading as the Liverpool and District Aero Club, based at Hooton Park, in February 1929, plying the skies on that side of the Mersey for three years. Restoration included the wings tail and undercarriage of Mk.IVM G-ABEE, itself a composite with Mk.IVM G-ACKE. **[3]** 'Flea' built by S O Whiteley at Rishworth, Yorks: did not fly. It is painted as the example built by Brian Henry Park in Wigan; the link being that the Scott A.2S from the original G-ADYO is fitted to BAPC.12. **[4]** G-AFIU designated Parker CA.4 from its builder, C F Parker of Pembroke. It differed little from the LA-4 except for the rear fuselage decking. Started in 1938, it was never finished. Includes wings and tail of G-ATWS, built 1966 in Derby - de-reg 8-2-82. **[5]** Messenger is largely based on Mk.2A G-AHUI, centre section of Mk.2 G-AILL (see also Stratford-upon-Avon, Warks), fins and rudders from Mk.2A G-AJFF - 'biography' relates to G-AHUI. *Uniform-India*, owned by E C Francis of Chester, was based at Hooton Park 1954 to 1957. G-AHUI presented to TAC by the Miles Aircraft Collection 8-02. Also held is the extreme forward cockpit 'slice' of Mk.2A G-AKIO, salvaged from Barton. **[6]** HPH airframe. **[7]** G-AIGP which was bought new by Wright Aviation in November 1946: one of Wright's ventures being the Liverpool Aero Club. As such G-AIGP was based at Hooton Park and just across the Mersey at Speke until January 1956. **[8]** Gemini is centred upon: Mk.1A G-AKHZ with the rear fuselage of Mk.1A G-ALUG, bits of Mk.1 G-AKGD, among others. **[9]** 'Supermunk' with Lycoming O-360. **[10]** Built from a Bensen kit by Wg Cdr Kenneth Horatio Wallis at his then home of Southwick, Sussex, and first flown by him 23-5-59. **[11]** Martin Hearn Ltd of Hooton Park, no less. **[12]** Triplane was originally on loan from the Shuttleworth Trust; title transferred to TAC on 20-11-19. **[13]** 'Flea' BAPC.201 transferred to a private owner, expected to remain on site. Built by Idwal ap Ieuan Jones at Talysarn, Wales, in 1936. Elements from this - undercarriage and other metal parts - are in 'Flea' 'G-EGCK' at Caernarfon, Wales. **[14]** Built by Mike Davey as 'gate guardian' for the Crowne Plaza at the *original* Liverpool Airport. Reduced to a cockpit 2019. To be hands-on exhibit. **[15]** Spitfire cockpit, owned by Mike Davey - see also under Liverpool, Merseyside - and Graham Sparkes, is a 'space-frame' reconstruction from recovered items with no attempt to restore, merely to conserve it in a similar manner to accident investigation piece-togethers. 610 (County of Chester) Sqn was Hooton-based 1936-1939, 1946-1957. **[16]** G-ANBY, this machine was last heard of, unconverted, at Rochester in April 1960 when it was said to have been scrapped. **[17]** 663 Sqn was Hooton-based 1949-1957. **[18]** Wings of XD624 are fitted to WL505 – see West Raynham, Norfolk.

KNUTSFORD on the A537 west of the M6

Oliver Valves: Parkgate Industrial Estate, as well as the family business, it is the home of the incredible ***private*** collection established by Mark and Michael Oliver. 'JP' T.5A XW330 had departed by late 2022 – no 'forwarding address'.
◆ *Available for inspection by prior arrangement* **only**

	Reg	Code	Type	Yr	History	Note	Date
❑	G-BRZG		Enstrom F-28A	73	ex Ipswich, Tattershall Thorpe, N9053. CoA 20-10-13, de-reg 18-5-18. First noted 8-19		1-24
❑	–		Slingsby Tutor	47	BGA.791, ex Hooton Park, VM684, 26 GS, 49 GS. Arr by 8-14		1-24
❑	5X-UUX		Westland Scout Srs 1 G-BKLJ	69	ex Ipswich, E Dereham, Tattershall T', Heysham, Panshanger, G-BKLJ, Uganda Police. Arrived by 5-15		1-24
❑	'B6447'		Sopwith Camel rep	11	BAPC.385, *Susan*	[1]	1-24
❑	P8088	'NK-K'	V-S Spitfire IIa G-CGRM	41	ex Brooklands, Oxford, Sleap, Ibsley, 61 OTU, CGS, 61 OTU, 19, 152, 118, 66. CBAF-built. Crashed 16-9-44. *Bette* and *Borough of Lambeth*. Arrived 18-2-13		1-24
❑	'W3850'	'PR-A'	V-S Spitfire V FSM	08	BAPC.304, ex Leeming. Built by Royal British Legion, Ripon branch. 609 Sqn colours. *Irene*		1-24
❑	ZA399	'AJ-C'	Panavia Tornado GR.1	82	ex Selby, Cosford 9316M, St Athan, 617, 15, 20, TWCU. *Plt Off Warner Ottley DFC*		1-24
❑	ZD992	'724'	HS Harrier T.8	87	ex Ipswich, Cranfield, Yeovilton, 899. Crashed 16-11-00		1-24
❑	13605		Messerschmitt Bf 109G-2 G-JIMP	42	ex Lancing, North Russia, 6/JG5 *Yellow 14*. Shot down 21-6-43.		1-24
❑	–*		Fieseler Fi 103 (V-1) FSM	~	BAPC.640		1-24

■ [1] Camel built by Peter Grieve's Flight Engineering of Carlisle, and to quote its website is an "aluminium-framed flying replica designed by Robert Baslee in the USA. It uses original instrumentation and fittings."

LOWER KINNERTON on minor road south of the A55 Broughton

Outpost Paintball: This extensive site also includes the *cockpitless* but otherwise – relatively – intact Vampire T.11 XH312.
◆ *Prior arrangement* **only | www.outpostpaintball.co.uk**

	Reg	Code	Type	Yr	History	Date
❑	G-ATFF	'53'	Piper Aztec 250C	65	ex Halfpenny Green, N5769Y. CoA 15-5-05	9-21

NANTWICH west of Crewe

Hack Green Secret Nuclear Bunker: A 'JP' is on show in the grounds.
◆ *French Lane, Baddington, CW5 8BL* | **01270 262610 | coldwar@hackgreen.co.uk | www.hackgreen.co.uk**

	Reg	Code	Type	Yr	History	Date
❑	XS179	'20'	Hunting Jet Provost T.4	63	ex Manchester, Salford, Halton '8237M' (8337M - 9-83), Kemble, Shawbury, CAW, RAFC. Arrived 15-1-13	1-24

RIXTON on the A57 east of Warrington

Moat Cafe: Contrary to *W&R28* (p37) the Rallye is *not* within Ramswood Nurseries, although that is close by.

	Reg	Code	Type	Yr	History	Date
❑	G-WCEI		MS Rallye Minerva	73	ex Squires Gate, G-BAOC. De-reg 11-12-14. First noted 4-15	12-23

SANDBACH on the A534 northeast of Crewe

The Andover was a regular at the Glastonbury Festival and is stored at a yard in the town.

	Reg	Code	Type	Yr	History	Date
❑	XS641	'Z'	HS Andover C.1(PR)	67	ex Cosford 9198M (10-1-94), Shawbury, 60, 115, 46, 84, SAR Flt, 84. Forward fuselage	2-20

WARRINGTON

Jonathan Howard: keeps his Vampire in the area. ◆ *Prior arrangement* **only | email@jhoward.org.uk**

	Reg	Code	Type	Yr	History	Date
❑	VZ193		DH Vampire FB.5	49	ex Chelmsford, Doncaster, Firbeck, Malmesbury, Hullavington, 229 OCU, 247. EE-built. SOC 29-5-59. Cockpit	1-24

WIDNES

Vintage Barn: Birchfield Road. Displays the cockpit of a 'Super Shed'.

	Reg	Code	Type	Yr	History	Date
❑	G-SSWM		Short 360-100	84	ex Liverpool, Coventry, Streamline Av, SE-KCI, G-OAAS, OY-MMB, G-14-3648. CoA 14-10-06, de-reg 6-6-07. Cockpit	10-21

WINSFORD on the A54 south of Northwich

Classic Autos: In the Woodford Park Industrial Estate has a 'gate guardian'.

❑	ZE691	'710'	HS Sea Harrier F/A.2	87	ex Queensbury, Ipswich, St Athan, Yeovilton, 899, 801, 899, 800, 899, 801, 800. Crashed 4-2-98. Arrived 7-08	1-24

Also: At a *private* workshop in the *general* area AOP.6 G-BKXP departed for Belgium on 23rd September 2022. Jodel G-BITO has been deleted under the 'clear-up' instigated on page 7.

❑	G-AGLK		Taylorcraft Auster 5D	44	ex RT475 n/s. CoA 15-7-14	6-18

CORNWALL

BODMIN AERODROME east of the A30, north of Bodmin EGLA

❑	G-BMFZ		Cessna F.152 II	85	Reims-built. CoA 27-5-10, de-reg 13-12-10. Fuselage		7-19
❑	–*		Eastbourne Mono rep	c20	ex St Mawgan, Brooklands. Fuselage frame, first noted 8-23		8-23

■ **[1]** Unfinished replica of Eastbourne Aviation Company's first original type, 1911.

CALLINGTON on the A390 southwest of Tavistock

A Lightning is kept at a ***private*** location in the area.

❑	XR755	'BN'	EE Lightning F.6	65	ex Binbrook, 5, 5-11 pool. SOC 21-6-88	7-21

CULDROSE AIRFIELD on the A3083 south of Helston EGDR

HMS *Sea Hawk*: The station's guardian is on its way to its *seventh* decay on duty.

❑	WF225		Hawker Sea Hawk F.1	53	ex 'XE225', A2623, A2645 (4-6-58), FRU, 738, 802. AWA-built. Displayed, since 1958	10-23
❑	XV673	'27'	Westland Sea King HU.5	70	ex Fleetlands, 771, 706, HAS.1, 706. 819, 824, 826, 706 Arrived mid-2015, placed on display 23-3-16	10-23
❑	XV786	'123'	HS Harrier GR.3	70	ex A2611[3], A2615 (5-6-91), St Athan, 3, 4, 1, 4. Cockpit	9-21
❑	XX280*	'280'	HS Hawk T.1A	79	ex 736, FRADU, 19, 6 FTS, 234, 92, 1 TWU, TWU. First noted 7-23, displayed	10-23

The **School of Flight Deck Operations** (SFDO) is the main 'user' of *W&R* airframes. 'DD' codes relate to the 'dummy deck' the trainees work on. Anachronistic since the advent of the F-35, the entire SFDO 'SHAR' fleet had been disposed of by the end of 2023. Removals to date, all to St Athan, Wales: XZ440 14-11-23; ZD579 5-1-24; ZE690 7-11-23; ZE692 21-11-23; ZH797 27-10-23; ZH802 27-10-23; ZH813 19-12-23 and Harrier T.8 ZB603, 5-1-24.

❑	XX510	'DD69'	Westland Lynx HAS.2	73	ex A2683[2], Gosport, Lee-on-S' A2772, A2601[2] (10-10-89), Foulness, Boscombe Down, A&AEE, RAE, A&AEE		9-19
❑	XZ248	'DD02'	Westland Lynx HAS.3S	78	ex A2854 (18-8-10), Yeovilton, 702, 815, 702, 815, 702, 815, 702, 815, 829, 815		9-18
❑	ZD634*	'503'	W'land Sea King HAS.6	85	ex Gosport, A2845 (12-3-09), 771, 810, 819, A&AEE, 819. First noted 7-19		10-23
❑	ZF641		EHI EH 101 PP1	87	ex Fleetlands, Westland. Arrived 18-6-98	[1]	10-23
❑	'AV511'	'DD511'	EHI Merlin EMU	~	ex Yeovil. Arrived 16-11-99		9-19
❑	–	'GTA-02'	Lockheed Martin F-35B	16	Gateguards UK-built. First noted 5-17	[2]	5-17
❑	–	'GTA-03'	Lockheed Martin F-35B	16	Gateguards UK-built. Delivered 10-8-16	[2]	9-19
❑	–	'GTA-04'	Lockheed Martin F-35B	16	Gateguards UK-built. First noted 9-16	[2]	6-18
❑	–		Lockheed Martin F-35B	16	Gateguards UK-built. First noted 5-17	[2]	5-17

■ **[1]** Prototype Merlin, first flown 9-10-87. **[2]** A quartet of F-35B full-scale, towable mock-ups are in use. They are reported to have adapted Tornado undercarriage units and water tanks so that different weights can be set during towing training. At least one of these has an opening canopy to enable rescue procedure tuition. *Three* noted in use 10-23.

DAVIDSTOW MOOR on minor road west of the A39 and Camelford

Davidstow Airfield and **Cornwall at War Museum**: Occupying several former RAF buildings; is dedicated to the armed services and to wartime life in the county. The display hall was erected during 2016.

◆ *Nottles Park, PL32 9YF* | **07799194918** | **hq@cornwallatwarmuseum.co.uk** | **www.cornwallatwarmuseum.co.uk**

❑ XG164		Hawker Hunter F.6	56	ex Poole, Shawbury, Halton 8681M (2-4-81), Kemble, West Raynham SF, 74, 111. 111 Sqn c/s. Arrived 15-7-14	[1]	1-24
❑ XG831	'396'	Fairey Gannet ECM.6	57	ex Helston, Culdrose SAH-8, A2539 (20-5-66), 831, AS.4. Arrived 16-2-08		1-24
❑ XK627		DH Vampire T.11	56	ex Hurn, Felmersham, Lavendon, Barton, Bacup, Hazel Grove, Woodford, Chester, St Athan, 8 FTS, CFS. Hawarden-built. SOC 3-12-68. Cockpit		1-24
❑ XW999		Northrop Chukar D.1	71	ex Culdrose, 792. Arrived 26-9-09		1-24
❑ XZ791		Northrop Shelduck D.1	c84	ex Culdrose, Portland. Arrived 26-9-09		1-24
❑ ZG347		Northrop Chukar D.2	00	ex Culdrose, 792. Arrived 26-9-09	[2]	1-24
❑ –		Fieseler Fi 103 (V-1) FSM	~	BAPC.345		1-24

■ **[1]** Hunter XG164 has the starboard wing of T.7 XL623. The port wing is at Beck Row, Suffolk. The fuselage of XL623 – with *altogether* different wings – is at Dunsfold, Surrey. **[2]** Mike Draper's exceptional *Sitting Ducks and Peeping Toms* records ZG347's first and only flight on 22-2-01 from a ship in the South West Approaches. Salvaged, it 'clocked' 16 minutes total time.

Davidstow Moor RAF Memorial Museum: Occupying what was the sergeants' shower block and within room after room of carefully presented artefacts tell the story of the personnel, units and locals that came together on the moor to do long-ranging battle. ◆ *Camelford, PL32 9YF* | **01840 213266** | **www.davidstowmemorialmuseum.co.uk**

HELSTON on the A3083 north of Culdrose

The Flambards Experience: There are many attractions within, including 'Britain in the Blitz' and a Falklands display.
◆ *Clodgey Lane, TR13 0QA* | **01326 573404** | **info@flambards.co.uk** | **www.flambards.co.uk**

❑ –	BAC/Sud Concorde EMU	c68	ex Filton, cockpit, instrument layout trials	1-24
❑ WG511	Avro Shackleton T.4	52	ex Colerne, St Mawgan, MOTU, Kinloss Wing, MOTU, 120, 42. Cockpit	6-22

LAND'S END on the A30 southwest of Penzance

Land's End: The Bölkow portrays the example that was flown by the Cornwall Air Ambulance from St Mawgan.
◆ *Sennen, TR19 7AA* | **01736 871501** | **visitorscentre@ landsend-landmark.co.uk** | **www.landsend-landmark.co.uk**

❑ 'G-CDBS'	Bölkow Bö 105D	G-BCXO	73	ex 'G-BOND', D-HDCE. CoA 23-5-94, de-reg 4-3-92	1-24

LISKEARD on the A38 northwest of Plymouth

Castle Motors / **Castle Air**: The dramatically-posed Lightning graces the heliport on the A38 to the southeast of the town.

❑ XS936	EE Lightning F.6	67	ex Binbrook, 5, 11, LTF, 5/11, LTF, 5, 11, 23. SOC 21-6-88	9-23

LIZARD on the A3083 south of Helston

Haelarcher Farmhouse B&B and Helicopter Glamping: The Lynx sleeps two, offers great views and sausages!
◆ *Lizard Head Lane, TR12 7NN* | **info@haelarcher.co.uk** | **https://haelarcher.co.uk**

❑ ZD566*	Westland Lynx HMA.8	85	ex Ipswich, Fleetlands, 702, HAS.3, 702. Arrived 16-12-22	1-24

MABE BURNTHOUSE on the A39 northwest of Falmouth

A plant hire yard in the locality has a Lynx.

❑ XZ648	'7'	Westland Lynx AH.7	80	ex Weeton, Hixon, M Wallop, 847, 653, 656, 664, 661, 662, 671, LCF. First noted 8-21	5-23

■ **[1]** Fitted with the boom of XZ680 – see East Grinstead, W Sussex.

NEWQUAY CORNWALL AIRPORT or St Mawgan, off the A3059, northeast of Newquay EGDG

Former **Cornwall Aviation Heritage Centre** (CAHC): In August 2022 CAHC announced it would be shutting down due to the termination of its lease by Cornwall Airport Ltd. The collection closed its doors on 31st October 2022. Strident calls for an eight-month deferral of notice to enable relocation to a nearby – non-airfield – venue came to nought and 11th April 2023 was declared as the deadline to vacate. From then the sale of airframes and dispersal of loaned aircraft began. Cornwall Airport Ltd is owned by Cornwall Council and its business plan includes the vigorous development of St Mawgan as 'Spaceport Cornwall'. A Canadian company, Space Engine Systems, was announced as taking over the lease of the site. (On 9th January 2023 Virgin Orbit's *Launcher One* rocket failed to put its multiple payload into orbit after launch from the St Mawgan-based Boeing 747 *Cosmic Girl* and that the venture filed for bankruptcy protection on 4th April 2023.)

Arising from the ashes of the Classic Air Force, which foundered in 2014, CAHC opened to the public in September 2015. That Classic Air Force, an organisation with greater financial and commercial 'clout', had failed to make a go of an aviation visitor centre at the airport, did not bode well but there were high hopes that CAHC's lower 'bottom line' would prevail. In the end, the prospect of considerable investment, including government support, and much-needed employment, far outweighed CAHC prospects. A naive belief that aviation heritage is more deserving than other businesses is not a guarantee of longevity. CAHC is not the first aviation museum to have its tenure ended and it won't be the last... Appeals to have the decision overthrown became increasingly acrimonious so much so that Cornwall Council is hardly likely to look favourably upon a proposal for an aviation museum anywhere else in the county.

Salvaging the One-Eleven and the VC10 would be a ludicrously expensive exercise, but in a classic *Catch-22* situation, CAHC claim that the two jetliners would cost £60,000 to scrap on site. As this edition closed for press the fate of several airframes remains unresolved and it will be *W&R30* before the full extent of this sorry tale can be concluded. Major airframes believed to remain on site in late 2023 but destined to be removed/scrapped are marked # below.

Disposals: Everett Gyroplane G-ULPS was returned to its Falmouth-based owner by 10-22; Eastbourne Monoplane replica to Bodmin, Cornwall, by 8-23; Balliol WN149, Sea Hawk FGA.6 WV798 and Vampire T.11 WZ450 to North Weald, Essex, 5-7-23; Canberra T.22 cockpit WT525 to Doncaster, S Yorks, 9-6-23 via brief stop-over at Bruntingthorpe, Leics; Hunter T.8C WT722 to Bournemouth, Dorset, 2-8-23; Hunter GA.11 WV256 to Bury St Edmunds, Suffolk, 1-8-23; 'JP' T.4 cockpit XP642, Nimrod SIM and Tornado SIM to Exeter Airport, Devon, by 10-23; Pembroke C.1 XK885 reported to departed to 'Yorkshire' by mid-2023; Nimrod cockpit XV148 relocated to Old Sarum, Wilts, 27-4-23; Harrier GR.3 XV753 to St Athan, Wales, 29-6-23; VC10 K.3 ZA148 succumbed 11-23; its cockpit travelling to St Athan, Wales; BAC 111 ZH763 forward fuselage to Southampton, Hampshire, via a short spell at St Athan, Wales, 24-11-23. As *W&R* closed for press Varsity T.1 WJ945 was due to make the trek to St Athan, Wales – in anticipation, it's been listed there. Airframes known to have been removed, but with no known 'forwarding address' are: Schiebe SF.28A G-CCIS; Fisher Celebrity N8205H; V-1 replica BAPC.344; Venom FB.50 cockpit J-1649.

Serial	Code	Type	Year	History	Note
❑ 'VN799'		EE Canberra T.4 WJ874 G-CDSX	54	ex CAF, G-CDSX (de-reg 6-11-14), WJ874, Marham, 39, Gaydon SF, Binbrook SF, Coningsby SF, 231 OCU, FRADU, FRU, 231 OCU, Wyton SF, 231 OCU, 39. Arrived 30-7-13. Prototype colours	# 12-23
❑ XN494	'43'	Hunting Jet Provost T.3A	60	ex Pool, Bruntingthorpe, Charlwood, Crawley, B'thorpe, M Wallop, Halton 9012M (10-3-90), 1 FTS, RAFC	# 10-23
❑ 'XS935'	'AK'	EE Lightning F.53 ZF580	67	ex 'XR768', Gateguards UK (11-3-13), Samlesbury, ZF580, Saudi AF 204, 53-672, G-27-42. Last flown 14-1-86. Acquired by 9-14. 5 Sqn colours by 9-22	# 1-24

Defence Survival, Evasion, Resistance, Extraction Training Organisation: Operates as an RAF enclave within the airport. Sea King XV700 was airlifted by Chinook to Gosport, Hants, in June 2023.

Serial	Code	Type	Year	History	Note
❑ XZ587	'C'	Westland Sea King HAR.3	78	ex Gosport, 202 'E' Flt, 22, 202, 22, 202, 1564 Flt, 202, SKTU. Arrived 19-1-16	10-23

Joint Aircraft Recovery and Transport Squadron (JARTS): Based at Boscombe Down, Wilts, the unit uses the airport as a sub-site for training exercises. Also on site is the centre section and starboard wing of Canberra TT.18 WK124, last in use with the fire school at Manston, Kent. Its cockpit is to be found at Gilberdyke, East Yorks. Hawk T.1 XX240 moved to Boscombe Down, Wilts, by October 2023.

Serial	Code	Type	Year	History	Note
❑ XZ607		Westland Lynx AH.7	81	ex Manston, Arborfield, Fleetlands, 657, 847, 657, 672, 662, 663, 671, 653, 654. Cabin. First noted 12-18	10-22
❑ ZA398		Panavia Tornado GR.4	82	ex Manston, Warton, 2. SOC 14-1-14. *Second to None*	[1] 10-22
❑ ZD704		HSA HS.125 CC.3	83	ex Manston, Hawarden, St Athan, 32. Damaged Kandahar 23-4-13. First noted 9-18	10-23
❑ ZH553	'RT'	Panavia Tornado F.3	93	ex Manston, Shawbury, Leuchars, 56, 11, 56, 11, 56, 29	10-22

■ **[1]** ZA398 is fitted with the fin from ZD739, hence the 'mis-matched' code.

Replica Aircraft Fabricators: As well as creating full-size replicas, refurbishing used versions for onward sale, and industrial projects, the company occasionally has *real* airframes on its books, often as the basis for moulds.

◆ **Private** *workshop, prior application* **only** | **www.gateguardsuk.com**

Serial	Code	Type	Year	History	Note
❑ WL332		Gloster Meteor T.7	52	ex Long Marston, Cardiff-Wales, Croston, Moston, FRU, Lossiemouth SF, Ford SF. SOC 11-3-69. Arrived 13-10-20	10-22
❑ WL349*	'Z'	Gloster Meteor T.7	52	ex Staverton, Kemble, 1 ANS, 2 ANS, CFE, 229 OCU. SOC 22-6-76. Arrived 8-22	10-23
❑ A-125		Pilatus P.2-05 G-BLKZ	48	ex Duxford, Spanhoe, Duxford, Swiss AF A-125, U-125. Crashed 31-5-08, de-reg 22-8-08. Forward fuselage, f/n 7-20	6-21

Also: St Mawgan's well-known Shackleton is under restoration in its own compound. *W&R28* (p41) reported the departure of Spitfire FSM 'PL279' with no 'forwarding address'. It migrated to Blackpool, Lancs, by mid-2023.

❑	WL795	'T'	Avro Shackleton AEW.2	53	ex RAF side, 8753M, 8, MR.2, 205, 38, 204, 210, 269, 204. Last flown 24-11-81. Moved on site 4-12-15. Dismantled	1-24

PREDANNACK AIRFIELD off the A3083 south of Helston

Fleet Air Arm School of Flight Deck Operations Fire School: From 2021 the real airframes here were cleared out. The status of the school and the complex purpose-built burning rigs that were employed here, is uncertain.

Froghall, Staffs-based Agility offered several airframes previously in use here during an online auction in April 2022 as part of a clear-out of 'real' airframes: **Dominie** T.1 XS738 removed for scrapping 8-21; **Jaguar** T.4 XX845 and **Harrier** GR.3 XZ969 to St Athan, Wales, 7-7-22; **Jetstream** T.2 XX479 scrapped 8-21; **Lynx** AH.9As ZG915 and ZG919 to Chew Valley Lake, Somerset, 7-12-22; **Sea King** HAS.5 XZ570 to Chew Valley Lake, Somerset, by early 2023; Sikorsky SH-3D XV371 left by road 16-9-22, reportedly to Glastonbury, Somerset. The following fates/destinations unknown: Sea King HAS.6 XV654 departed by road 21-7-22; Sing King HAS.5 XV657; Jetstream T.2 ZA111; Sea Harrier F/A.2 ZD581.

ST AGNES on the B3277 southwest of Newquay

The Swift continues to be kept at a *private* location in the locality.

❑	G-ABTC		Comper Swift	32	ex Lelant. CoA 18-7-84, de-reg 22-2-99. *Spirit of Butler*	7-20

TORPOINT on the A374, west of Plymouth, across the Tamar

HMS *Raleigh*: Large initial training base. Sea King HC.4 ZF118 returned to Gosport, Hampshire, on 13th December 2022, but migrated to Yeovilton, Somerset, 26th January 2024.

❑	XZ726	'316'	Westland Lynx HMA.8SRU	80	ex M Wallop, 815, HAS.3, 702, 815. Arrived 3-12-15	3-17

TRELONK on minor roads west of the A3078, northwest of Varyan

Parnall Engineering Advanced Ltd: Within the Trelonk Estate. Following the Spitfire FSM, a Parnall Panther replica is reported to be on the cards. Spitfire V BL688 became G-LFVE in July 2022 to ARC and is now listed under Duxford, Cambs.

◆ *Prior arrangement* **only** | **www.parnall.net**

❑	'BL709'		V-S Spitfire Vb FSM	20	*St Ives - Cornwall*. Unveiled 6-21	6-21

CUMBRIA

BACKBARROW on the A590 northeast of Ulverston, near Newby Bridge

Lakeland Motor Museum: As well as the aeronautical exhibits, highlights include full-size replicas of Sir Malcolm Campbell's 1935 Bluebird car, his 1939 Bluebird K4 boat and the Bluebird K7 in which son Donald was killed in 1967. As regards the *W&R* 'Scoff Squad', 'Cafe Ambio' is a must!

◆ *Old Blue Mill, LA12 8TA* | **015395 30400** | **info@lakelandmotormuseum.co.uk** | **www.lakelandmotormuseum.co.uk**

❑	'G-ADYV'		Mignet HM.14 'Flea'	94	BAPC.243, ex Malvern Wells, 'A-FLEA', Leigh-on-Sea Bill Francis, Leigh-on-Sea-built.	1-24
❑	G-BNDV		Cameron N-77 balloon	87	CoA 9-5-93, de-reg 18-3-14. *English Lake Hotels*. Basket etc	1-24
❑	G-MBCG		Solar Wings Typhoon	r81	ex Blackburn. De-reg 6-9-94	1-24

CARLISLE LAKE DISTRICT AIRPORT or Crosby-on-Eden EGNC

Solway Aviation Museum: While the impressive airframe collection might draw the eye, the displays charting the incredible aviation heritage of the airport and the region are particularly pleasing. There is a workshop – available for inspection by prior arrangement. The shop and the cafe are both well stocked!

STOP PRESS: See under Paull, E Yorks, for a drop of Cumbrian no guts, no glory and a scheme to save Beverley XB259.

The forward fuselage of Chipmunk T.10 WB584 was delivered to Hooton Park, Cheshire, by July 2023 in an exchange that brought WG303 northwards to be re-united with its rear end. The cockpit of Chipmunk T.10 WB670 was disposed of to a collector at Dumfries, Scotland, in early 2022. *W&R28* (p43) mentioned Solway stalwart David Price's 'lockdown' project Spitfire FSM 'PV144' and it being offered for sale in mid-2021; it was delivered to Hooton Park, Cheshire, in April 2023.

◆ *Crosby-on-Eden, CA6 4NW* | **01228 573823** | **email** via website | **www.solway-aviation-museum.co.uk**

❑ 'G-ADRX'		Mignet HM.14 'Flea'		36	BAPC.231, ex Millom, Torver, Ulverston. Arrived 7-9-10	[1]	1-24
❑ G-APLG		Auster J5L Aiglet Trainer		58	ex Maryport, Bletchley, Romsey, Southend, Rettendon, Corringham. CoA 26-10-68, de-reg 11-2-99. Arrived 4-95		1-24
❑ G-ARPP		HS Trident 1C		65	ex Dumfries, Palnackie, Glasgow, Heathrow, BA, BEA. CoA 16-2-86, de-reg 10-3-83. Arrived 19-8-09. Cockpit		1-24
❑ G-BDTT		Bede BD-5 Micro		r76	ex Haverigg, Barrow, Tattershall Thorpe, Bourne. De-reg 2-2-87. Arrived 2012. On show in the 'terminal' by 6-23		1-24
❑ G-BNNR		Cessna 152 II		81	ex N40SX, N40SU, N6121Q. CoA 15-11-08, de-reg 8-9-11. Arrived 2011		1-24
❑ G-BRHL		Bensen B-8M		89	CoA 26-8-03, de-reg 19-10-10. Arrived 2012		1-24
❑ G-BSEG		Ken Brock KB-2		91	ex Newcastle, Marham. CoA 2-7-02, de-reg 23-5-12. F/n 12-21		1-24
❑ –*		HiWay Scorpion C		~	BAPC.648. Hang-glider, first noted 6-23		1-24
❑ WG303*		DHC Chipmunk T.10		51	ex Hooton Park, Stamford, Bicester 8208M (4-8-72), Shawbury, Kemble, Oxf UAS, Gatow, Wittering, Marham SFs, Birm UAS, 5 RFS, 2 BFTS. Hawarden-built. Cockpit, arrived 8-2-23; since fitted with original tail – see note above		1-24
❑ WE188		EE Canberra T.4		53	ex Samlesbury, 231 OCU, 360, 231 OCU, 360, 100, 56, 231 OCU, Upwood SF, 231 OCU, Upwood SF, Waddington SF, Hemswell SF. SOC 19-11-81. Arrived 4-88		1-24
❑ WP314	'573'	Percival Sea Prince T.1		53	ex Preston, Hull, Syerston, Halton 8634M (8-8-79), Kemble, 750, Sydenham SF, 750, Lossiemouth SF, Shorts FU, Brawdy SF, Lossiemouth SF, 750. Arrived 8-98		1-24
❑ WS832	'W'	Gloster Meteor NF.14		54	ex RRE Pershore, RAE Llanbedr, AWOCU. AWA-built. SOC 24-4-69. Arrived 15-1-77		1-24
❑ WV198	'72'	Sikorsky Whirlwind HAR.21	G-BJWY	52	ex Firbeck, Warmingham, Chorley, Blackpool, Heysham, Carnforth G-BJWY (de-reg 23-2-94), Gosport, Lee-on-Solent A2576, Arbroath, 781, 848, USN 130191. Last flown 9-56. Arrived 13-11-92		1-24
❑ WZ515		DH Vampire T.11		53	ex Duxford, Staverton, Woodford, Chester, St Athan, 4 FTS, 8 FTS, 56, 253, 16. Hawarden-built. SOC 4-12-68. Arr 5-90		1-24
❑ 'WZ792'		Slingsby Grasshopper TX.1		52	ex 'WZ784', arrived 2001	[2]	1-24
❑ XA459	'E'	Fairey Gannet AS.4		56	ex White Waltham, Woodlands St Mary, Lambourn, Cirencester, Cardiff, Culdrose SAH-7 A2608, Lee-on-Solent, 831. SOC 18-11-70. Arrived 12-2-20		1-24
❑ XJ823		Avro Vulcan B.2		61	ex 50, Wadd Wing, 35, 27, 9/35, Wadd W, 230 OCU. Flew in 24-1-83		1-24
❑ 'XP748'		EE Lightning F.53	ZF583	68	ex Warton, Saudi AF 53-681, G-27-51. Last flown 14-1-86. Arrived 8-1-89. 11 Sqn colours		1-24
❑ XS209	'29'	Hunting Jet Provost T.4		64	ex Bruntingthorpe, Kemble, Staverton, Halton 8409M (7-10-74), St Athan, Kemble, Shawbury, CAW. Arr 24-6-06		1-24
❑ XV406	'D'	McD Phantom FGR.2		68	ex 14 MU Longtown 9098M (14-11-91), St Athan, 228 OCU, 111, 43, 228 OCU, 56, 23, 111, 54, 41, 54, 228 OCU, HSA, A&AEE. Arrived 22-4-98. 111 Sqn colours		1-24
❑ XX146*	'GT'	SEPECAT Jaguar T.2		74	ex Bradwell on Sea, Bentwaters, St Athan, 54, T.2, SAOEU, 54, 16, 41, Shawbury, 54, 41, 6, Coltishall SF, 6, 226 OCU, JOCU. Last flown 7-3-05. Arrived 21-7-22		1-24
❑ XX477		HP Jetstream T.1	G-AXXS	73	ex Sunderland, Askern, Finningley 8462M, Little Rissington, CFS, G-AXXS (de-reg 2-5-73). SAL-completed. Crashed 1-11-74. Fuselage. Arrived 27-11-19		1-24
❑ –*		V-S Scimitar CIM		c58	ex Norwich. Cockpit, first noted 10-23	[3]	1-24
❑ E-425		Hawker Hunter F.51		56	ex 'XG190', Coventry, Dunsfold, G-9-446, Danish AF Esk.724, E-425. SOC 28-2-76. Arrived 26-11-08. Danish c/s by 11-21		1-24

■ **[1]** 'Flea' built by Ronnie Jolly at Ulverston; several attempts at flight ended in damage and storage. Restoration carried out at HMP Haverigg, Millom, initial funding came from the Flying Flea Archive. **[2]** Composite, with the port wing *thought* to be from WZ824 - see Bridge of Weir, Scotland. The fin fillet is marked WZ792 and the starboard wing is also marked WZ792. There is *another* 'WZ784' at Felixstowe, Suffolk. **[3]** On loan from City of Norwich Aviation Museum.

Also: Following the rationale outlined on page 7, *all* of the light aircraft given in *W&R28* have been deleted: AA-5 G-BBBI; Cessna 152s G-BHFC and G-BOIO; Cessna 310 G-BJMR; Cessna 172 G-BLHJ; Wilga G-BXBZ.

HOLMESCALES south of the B2654, west of the M6, southeast of Kendal

The Outdoor Adventure Company: ◆ *Prior arrangement* **only** | **www.theoutdooradventurecompany.co.uk**

	Reg	Code	Type	Year	History	Note	Seen
❑	TC-MBE		Fokker Friendship 500	81	ex Coventry, MNG Cargo, D-ACCT, G-JEAG, D-ADAP, G-JEAG. Damaged 18-1-07		8-23

KIRKBRIDE AERODROME south of the B5307, west of Carlisle

Among the active gyros is a long-out-of-use Bensen.

	Reg	Code	Type	Year	History	Note	Seen
❑	G-BHEM		Bensen B-8MV	85	CoA 5-10-00, de-reg 8-4-16		5-23

MILLOM on the A5093 west of Ulveston

Millom Heritage and Art Centre: Among the many superb displays is John Nixon's incredible section on aviation in the area, particularly the former RAF Millom. A 'star' item is an outer wing from a Blackburn Botha, signed by Millom veterans.

◆ *Station Building, Station Road, LA18 5AA* | **01229 772555** | **info@millomhac.co.uk** | **https://millomhac.co.uk**

SPADEADAM FOREST north of the B6318, northeast of Carlisle

RAF Spadeadam: This 'outpost' now boasts a 'gate guardian'.

	Reg	Code	Type	Year	History	Note	Seen
❑	XZ374*	'JC'	SEPECAT Jaguar GR.1	76	ex Cosford 9005M, Shawbury, 14, 20. Last flown 13-8-85. Displayed. First noted 8-23		10-23

Electronic Warfare Tactics Range: The *Hind* is alongside the helicopter operating area, known as the H-7 Complex.

	Reg	Code	Type	Year	History	Note	Seen
❑	XW768	'N' *and* 'POS4'	HS Harrier GR.3	71	ex Manston, Gosport, Cosford, Halton 9072M (10-8-90), 4, 1, 4, 20. Arrived 6-21		10-23
❑	XZ215		Westland Lynx AH.7	79	ex Manston, M Wallop, 9 Regt. Boom of XZ607. Arr 17-6-21		7-22
❑	XZ216		Westland Lynx AH.7	77	ex Manston, Arborfield, Fleetlands, 654, 663, 656, 671, 663, 662. Cabin. Arrived 6-21		7-22
❑	XZ966	'G' *and* 'POS3'	HS Harrier GR.3	73	ex Manston, Cottesmore 9221M (13-10-93), St Athan, 1417 Flt, 4, 1417 Flt, 233 OCU, 1, 1417, 1. Arrived 6-21		10-23
❑	ZA475*		Panavia Tornado GR.1B	83	ex Lossiemouth 9311M, 12, 27, 20, 17, 9, 16, 12. 15 Sqn colours to port, 617 Sqn to stb. Arrived 6-23		10-23
❑	FT-02	'12'	Lockheed T-33A-1-LO	52	ex Prestwick, Belgian AF, 51-4043. Arrived 13-3-80		10-23
❑	FT-06	'10'	Lockheed T-33A-1-LO	52	ex Prestwick, Belgian AF, Netherlands AF M-44, 51-4231 Arrived 19-3-80. Also wears 'AC12'		10-23
❑	FT-07	'70'	Lockheed T-33A-1-LO	52	ex Prestwick, Belgian AF, Netherlands AF M-45, 51-4233. Arrived 27-3-80. Also wears '18' and 'AC11'		10-23
❑	FT-10	'11'	Lockheed T-33A-1-LO	52	ex Prestwick, Belgian AF, 51-6664. Arrived 7-3-80. Also wears '77' and 'AC6'		10-23
❑	FT-11	'01'	Lockheed T-33A-1-LO	52	ex Prestwick, Belgian AF, Netherlands AF M-47, 51-6661. Arrived 3-80. Also wears '80' and 'AC5'		10-23
❑	61	'AC2'	Dassault Mystère IVA	c56	ex Sculthorpe, Fr AF. Last flown 27-7-81, arrived 28-2-82		10-23
❑	64	'AC1'	Dassault Mystère IVA	c56	ex Sculthorpe, Fr AF. Last flown 27-7-81, arrived 3-82		10-23
❑	81	'AC9'	Dassault Mystère IVA	c56	ex Sculthorpe, Fr AF. Last flown 19-1-82, arrived 17-3-82		10-23
❑	139	'AC10'	Dassault Mystère IVA	c56	ex Sculthorpe, Fr AF. Last flown 1-7-81, arrived 3-82		10-23
❑	180	'AC8'	Dassault Mystère IVA	c56	ex Sculthorpe, Fr AF. Last flown 1-7-81, arrived 28-2-82		10-23
❑	184	'AC7'	Dassault Mystère IVA	c56	ex Sculthorpe, Fr AF. Last flown 19-1-82, arrived 17-3-82		10-23
❑	207	'AC4'	Dassault Mystère IVA	c56	ex Sculthorpe, Fr AF		10-23
❑	282	'AC3'	Dassault Mystère IVA	c56	ex Sculthorpe, Fr AF		10-23
❑	98+10	'SU-1'	Sukhoi Su-22M-4 *Fitter*	c86	ex Farnborough, Boscombe Down, Luftwaffe, LSK-LV 820. Arrived 4-95		10-23
❑	09559	'HH1'	Mil Mi-24 *Hind-D*	~	ex Boscombe Down (?), Iraq (?). Arrived by 5-08	[1]	10-23

■ **[1]** To add to the mystery of this *Hind*, it *could* be ex-Afghanistan.

SPARK BRIDGE on the A5092 north of Ulverston

Lakes Lightnings Collection: Neil and Heather Airey's jet 'fleet'. Hunter T.7 XL618 is on loan to the Gutersloh Flugplatz Museum, Germany. See under Coningsby, Lincs, for the status of Lightning F.6 XS897.

◆ *Annual open day over August Bank Holiday. Otherwise* **strictly** *prior permission* **only** | **lakeslightnings@hotmail.co.uk**

❑ WK122		EE Canberra TT.18	54	ex Chipperfield, Bruntingthorpe, Helston, Samlesbury, 7, 15, 61. SOC 10-11-81. Cockpit		1-24
❑ WT711	'833'	Hawker Hunter GA.11	55	ex Coventry, Culdrose A2645, A2731 (23-9-85), Shawbury, Kemble, FRADU, FRU, 764, 738, F.4, 14		1-24
❑ XL609		Hawker Hunter T.7	58	ex South Molton, Yarmouth, Boscombe Down, Firbeck, Elgin, Lossiemouth 8866M (24-7-85), 12, 216, 237 OCU, 4 FTS, 56. Cockpit. 12 Sqn colours. Arrived 4-12		1-24
❑ XM172	'B'	EE Lightning F.1A	60	ex Booker, Coltishall 8427M (10-7-74), 226 OCU, 56		1-24
❑ XN634*	'53'	Hunting Jet Provost T.3	61	ex Ipswich, Scampton, 1 FTS, 7 FTS, RAFC, 6 FTS. Cockpit	[1]	1-24
❑ XS922	'BJ'	EE Lightning F.6	66	ex Stansted, Salisbury, Stock, Wattisham 8973M (14-6-88), Binbrook, 5-11 pool, 56, 5. Cockpit		1-24
❑ ZA327		Panavia Tornado GR.1	80	ex Samlesbury, Warton, Leeming. Cockpit		1-24
❑ ZF596		EE Lightning T.55	68	ex Haverigg, Swinton, Warton, Portsmouth, Stretton, Warton, Saudi AF 233, 55-715, G-27-71. Last flown 22-1-86. Cockpit		1-24
❑ –		HS Harrier two-seater	~	ex Haddington, Long Marston, Dunsfold. Cockpit	[2]	1-24
❑ –		Panavia Tornado F.3 EMU	~	ex Blackpool, Warton		1-24
❑ 5634		Mikoyan-Gurevich MiG-21UM *Mongol*	~	ex '0446', Salisbury, East Tilbury, Farnborough, Egypt AF. *Front* cockpit. Arrived late 2019		1-24
❑ 7735		Sukhoi Su-7BMK *Fitter*	~	ex '7907', Robertsbridge, Farnborough, Egypt AF. Cockpit		1-24

■ **[1]** This 'JP' was written out of *W&R23* (p87) as last physically with Raven Cockpits at Blackpool, Lancs. It was kindly donated to the collection by Raven's Michael Bach. **[2]** A plate on the side declares it to be a Sea Harrier Mk.60 - that would be to the build spec for the Indian Navy T.60s.

Also: Andrew 'Mac' Mackay died in January 2023 and his 'JP' T.4 XS181 cockpit was removed that same month. It initially travelled to 'Cheshire' before settling upon Tetney, Lincs.

WHITEHAVEN on the A595 south of Workington

Whitehaven Academy: Cleator Moor Road. *May* still have a Tomahawk-turned-sim.

◆ *Prior arrangement* **only** | **www.whitehavenacademy.org.uk**

❑ G-BJNN	Piper Tomahawk 112	80	ex Carlisle. CoA 17-8-09, de-reg 19-7-16. Simulator	[1]	4-16

■ **[1]** Converted to a simulator by Creative Cockpits.

WINDERMERE on the A592 north of Bowness on Windermere

Windermere Jetty - Museum of Boats, Steam and Stories: A sensational venue, with views of the lake and trips along it in period vessels. As well as the unique water glider, there are other aviation gems. The Avro-made propeller from the Lakes Flying Company Waterhen biplane of 1912 is mounted above the 1922 motorboat *Canfly* while 'flying' above is a float from a Blackburn-built Sunderland, assembled further up the lake at White Cross Bay. *Canfly* was commissioned by Cooper Pattinson – see the notes on the Falcon, below – and built at Bowness in 1922. Marvel at its engine, a Rolls-Royce Hawk of 1917, one of two that propelled the Submarine Scout Twin 'blimp' SST.3 that patrolled out of Howden, E Yorks, until 1920.

◆ *Rayrigg Road, LA23 1BN* | **info@windermerejetty.org** | **https://lakelandarts.org.uk/ windermere-jetty-museum/**

❑ –	Slingsby T.1 Falcon	36	BGA.266	[1]	1-24

■ **[1]** Modified by Capt T Cooper Pattinson DFC as a flying-boat glider at a workshop in Beresford Road, Windermere. First flown, towed off the lake behind a boat, 3-2-43; *believed* only flown once more, 7-2-43. Readers have asked about the rationale for including the Falcon: Martin Simons writes that it was intended for Air Training Corps usage, which seems a lot to ask a cadet to master.

DERBYSHIRE

Includes the unitary authority of Derby City

ASHBOURNE on the A52 northwest of Derby

One that has long slipped the net; a pair of Bulldogs are stored at a *private* location in the *general* area. Acquired from two separate venues, it is *possible* that these two have been in this area since 2007.

❑ XX539*	SAL Bulldog T.1	73	ex Wellesbourne Mountford, Shawbury, Lpl UAS, CFS, RNEFTS, Glas & S, E Lowlands UASs, RNEFTS, CFS. SOC 12-8-01. First noted 2-22	2-22
❑ XX659*	SAL Bulldog T.1	74	ex Hixon, Shawbury, York, Camb UASs. SOC 12-8-01. F/n 2-22	2-22

BRAILSFORD on the A52 northwest of Derby

Wild Park Derbyshire: ◆ *Prior application* **only** | **www.wildparkderbyshire.com**

❑ XZ235	'630'	Westland Lynx HAS.3S	77	ex Hixon, Fleetlands, 815, *Endurance* Flt, 702, 815, 702, 815, 829, 815, HAS.2, 815. SOC 17-2-10		2-22
❑ XZ237		Westland Lynx HAS.3S	77	ex Hixon, Fleetlands, 702, 815, 702, 815, 702, 829, HAS.2, 829, 815, RAE		2-22
❑ XZ693		Westland Lynx HAS.3S	79	ex Hixon, Fleetlands, 815, 702, 815, HAS.2, 702		2-22

CHESTERFIELD on the A61 south of Sheffield

A car sales centre on the Dronfield Road, has a former Finningley 'JP'.

❑ XM480	'02'	Hunting Jet Provost T.3	60	ex Finningley, Halton 8080M (21-4-70), 6 FTS, 1 FTS		4-22

DERBY

Museum of Making: The rejuvenated museum is devoted to three centuries of industry in Derby and surrounding area. Dominating the Flight Deck hall is a suspended Rolls-Royce Trent 1000 turbofan.

◆ *Silk Mill Lane, off Full Street, DE1 3AF* | **info@derbymuseums.org** | **www.derbymuseums.org**

Rolls-Royce Heritage Trust: Within the Rolls-Royce Learning and Development Centre, the Trust has established an impressive exhibition of engines. On another site, there is the **Derby and Hucknall Branch**'s extensive engine and artefact collection and restoration workshop with additional material from the **Coventry and Ansty Branch**.

The company's airworthy Spitfire PR.19 PS853 (G-RRGN) and Harvard T.2B KF183 (G-CORS) are based at East Midlands Airport, Leics, and ***not*** available for inspection. See also the associated Flight Test Museum at Hucknall, Notts.

Note: As *W&R29* went to press, the Derby and Hucknall Branch's building was closed until further notice.

◆ *Open to groups by prior arrangement* **only** | *PO Box 31, Derby DE24 8BJ* | **heritage.trust@rolls-royce.com** | **www.rolls-royce.com/about/heritage-trust**

❑ WH960		EE Canberra B.15	55	ex Willmore Road, Nottingham, Bruntingthorpe, Cosford 8344M (9-11-72), Akrotiri Wing, 32, 9, 12. Cockpit		1-23

DERBY AERODROME or Egginton, south of the A5132 between Egginton and Hilton — EGBD

Comet Racer Project Group: Maestro Ken Fern is also building – from an off-site workshop – a 100% replica, G-RCSR.

◆ *Prior arrangement* **only** | **derbyaeroclub@btconnect.com** | **www.cometracerproject.co.uk**

❑ G-ACSP		DH Comet	34	ex Stoke-on-Trent, Coventry / Staverton, Bodmin, Chirk, Portugal, CS-AAJ, E-1. *Black Magic*	[1]	1-24
❑ 'G-ACSS'		DH Comet FSM	97	BAPC.257, ex Sywell, London Colney, Hatfield. Acorn Scenery, Feltham-built. *Grosvenor House*. Trailer-mounted. Gale damaged by 10-23	[2]	10-23
❑ G-APNZ		Druine Turbulent	59	ex Lashenden. Dam 2-7-95, CoA 13-12-95. Rollason-built	[3]	1-24

■ **[1]** *Black Magic* was originally registered to James Allan Mollison 21-8-34 and cancelled as sold in Portugal 12-34. **[2]** Best described as *nearly* a full-scale replica! It is seven-eighths scale. **[3]** Registered to the Turbulent G-APNZ Preservation Society.

Also: Cessna 190 G-BTBJ was airworthy by 2022. The following have been deleted: Cessna 177 G-AYPH, Cherokee G-BAFW, Cessna 172 G-BBJY, FRED G-BDBF, Cessna 152s G-BHAV, G-BNMC, G-BNMD and G-BSWH, Cessna 182 G-KWAX.

❑ G-ARAX		Piper Tri-Pacer 150	56	ex N2423A. CoA 3-10-11		7-23
❑ G-ARFB		Piper Caribbean 150	60	ex N3225Z. CoA 19-6-16. First noted 1-18		3-22
❑ G-ASSF		Cessna 182G	64	ex N2492R. Crashed 26-12-07, CoA 10-4-08, de-reg 12-7-11		7-23
❑ G-AVLM		Beagle Pup 160	67	ex Shenstone, Tatenhill, Tollerton, Chippenham. CoA 24-4-69		7-23
❑ G-AXSC		Beagle Pup 100	69	ex G-35-138. CoA 28-4-07		9-23
❑ G-BHZS		SAL Bulldog 120	74	ex Botswana DF OD5, G-BHZS. CoA 20-2-06, de-reg 19-12-12		7-23
❑ G-OFLG		SOCATA Tobago	79	ex G-JMWT, F-GBHF. Crashed 23-7-05, de-reg 15-11-05		3-22
❑ G-SACF		Cessna 152 II	79	ex G-BHSZ, N47125. Crashed 21-3-97, de-reg 11-8-97		10-21

MELBOURNE on the B587 south of Derby

Melbourne Hall - Johnny Vegas Glamping: Within the grounds, the well-known comedian/presenter heads the 'Fields of Dreams' camp site. The Puma, previously in use for spares at the Newark Air Museum, was converted for its new role by Stuart Abbott – Stu-Art, see Durham, D&C – to Johnny's own spec and to prove it, carries his initials on the tail rotor pylon.

◆ *Prior arrangement* **only** | **www.melbournehall.com/johnny-vegas-glamping**

❑ '9L-MLTL'*	'JV'	Sud SA330L Puma	~ 9L-LSG	ex Newark, Horsham, Booker, Sierra Leone, Chilean Army H-259. *Oscar*. See notes above. First noted 2-23		1-24

RIPLEY on the A610 northwest of Nottingham

Iconic World War Two Aircraft: Brothers Mel and Steve Heappey's Spitfire FSM features original undercarriage and much of the cockpit has original fittings. ◆ *Prior arrangement* **only** | **www.iconic-ww2aircraft.co.uk**

❑	'BA377'	'UF-J	V-S Spitfire IX FSM	~	BAPC.377, ex 'EN398', Sleap, Cannock. 601 Sqn colours	1-24
❑	–	'6'	M'schmitt Bf 109E FSM	17	BAPC.376, II/JG 51 colours. Gateguards UK-built	1-24

DEVON

Includes the unitary authorities of Plymouth and Torbay

BARNSTAPLE

Tim Jones: Tim died in October 2023; and is much missed by the preservation 'family'. Cadet TX.3 XN238 had moved to Doncaster, S Yorks, by June 2023.

BERE ALSTON at the end of the B3257 north of Plymouth

Tony Thorne: Keeps his rotorcraft at a *private* location in the area. ◆ *Viewing by prior appointment* **only**

❑	–		Adams-Wilson Hobbycopter	~	ex 'Leicestershire'	1-24
❑	–		Bensen B-7 Gyroglider	~	-	1-24

BIDEFORD on the A39 southwest of Barnstaple

No.**20 (Bideford) Squadron Air Cadets**:

❑	XR747		EE Lightning F.6	65	ex Cubert, Plymouth, Rossington, Binbrook, 5, 11, 5, 11, 5, 111, 23. SOC 24-6-88. Cockpit	3-20

BRAUNTON on the A361 west of Barnstaple

A Hunter is kept on a nearby farm. ◆ *Prior arrangement* **only**

❑	WT744	'868'	Hawker Hunter GA.11	55	ex Ilfracombe, Eaglescott, Yeovilton, FRADU, 738, F.4, 247, AFDS. Last flight 16-3-94. Arrived 15-5-16	9-22

COBBATON north of the A377 / B3227 west of South Molton

Cobbaton Combat Collection: The largest private collection of military vehicles and wartime memorabilia in the southwest.
◆ *Umberleigh, EX37 9RZ* | **01769 540740** | **info@cobbatoncombat.co.uk** | **www.cobbatoncombat.co.uk**

❑	–	'5'	Airspeed Horsa replica	c76	BAPC.351, ex *A Bridge Too Far* (1977)	6-16

DEVONPORT on the A3064, west of Plymouth

Bogey Knights: The military surplus stockist acquired a Hawk cockpit by February 2023.
◆ *Mutton Cove, PL1 4LB* | **01752 562705** | **surplus@bogeyknights.co.uk** | **http://bogeyknights.co.uk**

❑	XX320*		HS Hawk T.1A	80	ex Scampton, Walcott, Scampton, Cranwell, Shawbury, 208, 100, 19, 2 TWU, 1 TWU. Bitteswell-built. Crashed 20-8-08. Front cockpit. 208 Sqn colours. Arrived by 2-23	7-23

DUNKESWELL AERODROME north of Honiton EGTU

Dunkeswell Heritage Centre: Part of the South West Airfields Heritage Trust – see also Upottery, Devon. Dunkeswell gained fame as home to US Navy B-24 Liberators and PB4Y Privateers among other units.
◆ *Close to the Aviator restaurant* | **email** via website | **www.southwestairfields.co.uk**

Aerodrome: Luscombe G-AKUL had moved to Eshott, N&T, by August 2022. The following have been deleted: T.67s G-BJIG and G-BJNG; Cherokee G-BTON; Seneca N21381; AA-5B TC-NLB.

❑	G-AFIN		Chrislea Airguard	38	ex Bury St Edmunds, Wigan, Stoke, Warmingham, Wigan, Finningley, Wigan	[1]	9-20
❑	G-AJON		Aeronca 7AC Champion	47	ex OO-TWH. CoA 10-5-08, de-reg 2-10-23		7-18
❑	G-AOFJ*		Auster 5	56	CoA 9-12-10, de-reg 29-3-12. Arrived 18-8-22		11-22
❑	G-APFA		Druine Turbi	57	ex Exeter area. Britten-Norman built. CoA 22-9-92		12-21

❑ G-BPRV		Piper Warrior II		83	ex N4292G. Crashed 29-3-97, de-reg 20-6-97. Cockpit	8-19
❑ G-BXYU		Cessna F.152 II		80	ex Exeter, Dunkeswell, OH-CKD, SE-IFY. Reims-built. Crashed 2-8-99, de-reg 16-10-99. Cockpit	7-22
❑ I-IJMW		Mooney M.20J		87	crashed 11-1-14. First noted 12-15	5-22
❑ TW501*		T'craft Auster 5	G-ALBJ	45	ex 227 OCU, 43 OTU. CoA 7-8-19. First noted 10-20	11-22

■ **[1]** Under long-term restoration using original parts. De-registered 2-6-45, it was rescued by the Northern Aircraft Preservation Society 7-2-70. A replica fuselage of G-AFIN – BAPC.203 – was completed in 1993 but burnt at Warmingham a couple of years later.

EAGLESCOTT AERODROME west of the A377, north of Ashreigney

EGHU

Tomahawks G-BOLD and G-BTIL have been deleted.

❑ G-AKRP		DH Dragon Rapide	45	ex Coventry, Eaglescott, Sywell, Little Gransden, Germany, CN-TTO, Senegal, F-DAFS, G-AKRP, Dominie RL958. Brush-built. CoA 6-1-08. First noted 7-20	10-22
❑ WB971	FKP	Slingsby Sedbergh TX.1	50	BGA.3324, ex Aston Down	10-22
❑ WZ819	FLB	Slingsby Grasshopper TX.1	60	BGA.3498, ex Halton. Dismantled, in rafters	7-22
❑ XA295	FLB	Slingsby Cadet TX.3	62	BGA.3336, ex Aston Down	10-22

EGGESFORD AERODROME east of Winkleigh and west of the A377

Only long-term restorations and stored airframes are listed at this heavily Auster-flavoured venue. Cub Coupe G-AFZA was flying again by 2024.

❑ G-AMUI		Auster J5F Aiglet Trainer		52	ex Liverpool, Stretton. CoA 15-2-66	8-19
❑ G-AYDW		Beagle Terrier 2		46	ex King's Lynn, Little Gransden, King's Lynn, Camberley, Cranfield, Bushey, G-ARLM, Auster AOP.6 TW568, LAS, AOPS, 227 OCU, 43 OTU. CoA 1-7-73, de-reg 1-7-85	10-23
❑ G-BGKZ		Auster J5F Aiglet Trainer		53	ex Liverpool, Stretton, F-BGKZ. Cr 30-1-93, de-reg 8-8-23	8-18
❑ G-CKXF		Auster J5G Autocar		53	ex 'Home Counties', Saudi Arabia, AP-AHK, VP-KKO. F/n 12-17	8-19
❑ XX561		SAL Bulldog T.1	G-BZEP	74	ex CFS, 3 FTS, St Andrews UAS, Queen's UAS, Southampton UAS, CFS. CoA 25-5-05	10-23
❑ 208*	'IR'	MH Broussard	G-YYYY	60	ex F-GDPZ, ALAT. CoA 24-6-21	10-23

Locally:

❑ G-ASBH	Beagle Airedale	62	CoA 19-2-99	N8-22

EXETER

Arden Family Trust: The late Bertram Arden's airframes are held in careful and *very private* store in the area.

❑ G-AALP	Surrey AL.1	r29	CoA 17-5-40, de-reg 1-12-46	12-97
❑ G-AFGC	BA Swallow II	38	ex BK893, GTS, CLE, RAE, G-AFGC. CoA 20-3-51, de-reg 15-3-10	6-06
❑ G-AFHC	BA Swallow II	38	CoA 20-3-51, de-reg 18-2-59	12-97
❑ G-AJHJ	Taylorcraft Auster 5	44	ex NJ676, 83 GCS, 440. CoA 27-6-49, de-reg 18-2-59	12-97

EXETER AIRPORT

EGTE

HS.146 G-JEAT had gone by April 2022, thought scrapped. Boeing 737 G-JMCY forward fuselage departed by March 2022 – destination unknown, but *possibly* only as far as the Future Skills Centre, see below. Robin G-WYSZ has been deleted.

❑ G-ATSX	Bölkow Junior	66	ex Kirkbride, D-EJUC. CoA 1-7-02, damaged 31-3-13. De-reg 29-10-14		10-21
❑ G-FTIN	Robin DR.400-100	88	crashed 31-8-13, de-reg 4-6-14		10-21
❑ G-ISLH*	ATR 42-320	90	ex Teesside (via Durham), F-HEKF, F-WEKF, OK-VFI, F-WQNE, D-BHHH. Last flight 8-5-22,de-reg 15-6-22. Cockpit, arrived 4-1-24	[1]	1-24
❑ OO-TAQ	HSA HS.146-200	87	ex TNT Airways, G-BNPJ, I-TNTC, G-5-078. Hatfield-built. Arrived 23-7-11		10-23

■ **[1]** Under conversion by Blue Sky Aero Services into a simulator. *May* be bound for the company's Dublin association.

Exeter College – Future Skills Centre: On the eastern edge of the airport, part of the college's multi-site campus.

◆ *Prior application* **only** | **https://exe-coll.ac.uk**

Reg		Type		History		
❑ G-BLKP		BAe Jetstream 3102	84	ex St Athan, Macclesfield, Humberside, Eastern, G-BLEX, G-31-364. CoA 19-4-03, de-reg 7-12-06. Arrived by 5-21		10-23
❑ –*		Boeing 737	~	forward fuselage, f/n 10-23. See note under Airport above		10-23
❑ N121EL*		Learjet 25	~	ex N121GL, N82UH, N10BF, N102PS, N671WM, N846HC, N846GA. De-reg 13-5-03. First noted 9-23		10-23
❑ XP642*		Hunting Jet Provost T.4	62	ex St Mawgan, Welshpool, Lavendon, Luton, Bruntingthorpe, Nottingham, Finchampstead Ridges, Lasham, Shawbury, 2 FTS, CFS. SOC 14-8-72. Cockpit. First noted 10-23	[1]	10-23
❑ –*		HS Nimrod MR.2 SIM	~	ex St Mawgan, Bridlington, 'Lincs', Kinloss. Rediffusion-built. First noted 10-23	[1]	10-23
❑ –*	'AV011'	Panavia Tornado SIM	~	ex St Mawgan, Cosford. Forward cockpit sim. F/n 10-23	[1]	10-23

■ **[1]** On loan from Geremy Britton / Aircraft Preservation Foundation - see Bridlington, E Yorks.

NEWTON ABBOT on the A380 south of Exeter

Andrew Hawkins: Is hard at work on his Firefly cache. He also holds the rear fuselages of Mk.I PP566, AS.5 VT409 and Sea Fury FB.11 VW589. Son, Ben, has joined in with the acquisition of a Widgeon forward fuselage.
◆ *Prior arrangement* **only** | **griffon74@btinternet.com**

Reg	Type		History		
❑ G-APWK	Westland Widgeon	59	ex Harrington, Corby (?), Sywell, *Eye of the Needle*, Yeovil. De-reg 10-7-73. Forward fuselage, arrived 4-21		1-24
❑ WB440	Fairey Firefly AS.6	50	ex Newton-le-Willows, Manchester, Heaton Chapel, Newton, Salford, Failsworth, Anthorn, 737, 826, AS.5. SOC 8-3-57. Fuselage	[1]	1-24
❑ WD889	Fairey Firefly AS.5	51	ex Haverigg, Sunderland, Failsworth, Anthorn, 771, 814. SOC 2-3-57. Cockpit	[1]	1-24
❑ -	Fairey Firefly AS.7	~	ex Quarrywood. Cockpit reconstruction - see above		1-24
❑ WF145	Hawker Sea Hawk F.1	52	ex Ingatestone, Welshpool, South Molton, Salisbury, Torbay, Brawdy, Abbotsinch, RAE, A&AEE. SOC 21-7-59. Cockpit		1-24

■ **[1]** Take a look at Appendix A for the Failsworth yard in its heyday.

Trago Mills: Or the 'The Big Shop' – the Excalibur is on show within. | **www.trago.co.uk**

Reg	Type		History	
❑ G-BDDX	Whittaker Excalibur	76	ex Helston. De-reg 23-6-83	5-23

■ **[1]** Single seat, twin-boom ducted fan pusher, only made one flight, 1-7-76, designed and built at Bodmin, by Mike Whittaker.

UCZ Paintball Park: Poltimore ◆ *Prior arrangement* **only** | **www.ucz.info**

Reg	Type		History	
❑ G-OPNI	Bell JetRanger II	67	ex G-BXAA, F-GKYR, HB-XOR, G-BHMV, VH-SJJ, VH-FVR. Ditched 5-4-99, de-reg 20-1-00	12-21

PLYMOUTH

National Marine Aquarium: Inside this vast – and must-see – venue in the Atlantic Ocean tank is the 'hulk' of a Supermarine Walrus for the sharks to play with. (Shades of the Blackpool, Lancs, Defiant...) Accurate-looking and dramatic it may be, it's an impressive piece of set dressing pure and simple, not remotely an 'airframe' and does not merit a formal listing. ◆ **www.national-aquarium.co.uk**

SOUTH MOLTON The anonymous JetRanger and Harrier cockpit are unaccounted for.

TOPSHAM between the M5 and the A376 south of Exeter

Home to a *private* collection of fast-jets. ◆ *Prior arrangement* **only**

Reg		Type		History	
❑ XV359	'035'	Blackburn Buccaneer S.2B	69	ex Culdrose, A2693 [2] (20-3-94), Predannack, Lossiemouth, 208, 237 OCU, 12, 208, 12, 809, 800. Arrived 23-4-05. 809 Sqn colours	7-20
❑ XZ378	'EP'	SEPECAT Jaguar GR.1A	77	ex Shawbury, 6, 41, 17, 31, 20. Arr 14-11-05. 6 Sqn colours	7-20
❑ ZA353		Panavia Tornado GR.1	80	ex Selby, Boscombe Down, TTTE. First noted 7-20	7-20
❑ ZD612	'731'	HS Sea Harrier F/A.2	85	ex Yeovilton, St Athan, 899, 800, 899, 800, 801, 899. Arrived 2006. 899 Sqn colours	7-20

UPOTTERY east of the A30, northeast of Honiton

Upottery Nissen Hut Heritage Centre: Part of the South West Airfields Heritage Trust - see also Dunkeswell, Devon - is well established on the northeastern edge of the former home of the 439th Troop Carrier Group.

◆ *Cherry Hayes Farm, Slough Lane, EX14 9RD* | **email** via website | **www.southwestairfields.co.uk**

DORSET

Includes the unitary authorities of Bournemouth and Poole

BLANDFORD FORUM on the A350/A354 south of Shaftesbury

A collector at a *private* location in the *general* area has taken on a Lynx cockpit.

❑ ZD264*		Westland Lynx HAS.3	83	ex Old Sarum area, Hixon, Portsmouth, Fleetlands, 815, 702, 702, 815. SOC 5-8-10. Cockpit	6-23

BOURNEMOUTH

The Streetwise Safety Centre closed its doors in December 2020: the fate of Squirrel 'S-WISE' (N354E) is undetermined.

BOURNEMOUTH AIRPORT or Hurn EGHH

Bournemouth Aviation Museum: On the southern perimeter of the airport, co-located with the Adventure Wonderland Theme Park. BAM affords good views of the activity at the airport. During 2023, the museum embarked on expansion of its display area and buildings – aiding the arrival of the former Cosford 'Flea'. Full marks for taking on the former Navy Wings Sea Vixen, which has strong associations with Hurn and nearby Tarrant Rushton and the D.3 drone programme.

Sea Venom FAW.22 WM571 arrived from Southampton, Hants, during April 2023, but moved again on 27th June 2023, to Bruntingthorpe, Leics. AA-1 LX-ARS and 'JP' T.3 XM404 had relocated to the airport site – below – by August 2023.

◆ *Merritown Lane, BH23 6BA* | **01202 473141** | **enquiries@bamhurn.org**| **www.aviation-museum.co.uk**

❑ G-AEEH*		Mignet HM.14 'Flea'	36	ex Cosford, St Athan, Colerne, Bath, Whitchurch. CoA 15-5-38. Acquired 1966	[1]	**due**
❑ G-AZKS		American AA-1A Trainer	70	ex airport, N6134L. CoA 1-6-10. Fuselage, arrived 29-1-20		1-24
❑ G-BAMK		Cameron D96 airship	72	CoA 24-4-90. de-reg 16-8-00. Gondola	[2]	1-24
❑ G-BBFC		American AA-1 Trainer	73	ex N9945L. Crashed 9-6-96, de-reg 14-10-96. Arrived 6-19	[3]	1-24
❑ G-BEYF		HP Herald 401	63	ex Booker, Hurn, Channel Express, RMAF FM1022. CoA 17-3-00, de-reg 18-11-99. Cockpit. Arrived 9-7-15	[4]	1-24
❑ G-BKRL		CMC Leopard	88	ex airport, Old Sarum, Cranfield. CoA 14-12-91, de-reg 25-1-99. Arrived 18-2-05		1-24
❑ G-BOUT		Colomban Cri-Cri	83	ex Eaglescott, Stinsford, N120JN. Arrived 6-19		1-24
❑ G-BWGS		BAC Jet Provost T.5	71	ex N Weald, XW310, 3 FTS, RAFC, 1 FTS. CoA 2-9-08, de-reg 13-7-17. Arrived 8-17		1-24
❑ G-CEAH		Boeing 737-229	75	ex airport, OO-SDG. CoA 14-11-07, de-reg 6-11-13. *The Spirit of Peter Bath*. Forward fuselage. Arrived 8-12-13		1-24
❑ G-OPAS		Vickers Viscount 806	58	ex airport, Duxford, Southend, BWA, BAF, BEA G-AOYN. CoA 26-3-97, de-reg 28-7-97. Arr 5-12-06. Cockpit	[5]	1-24
❑ 'GO-CSE'		American AA-5B G-BFZR	79	ex airport, Fordingbridge, Oxford, EI-BJS, G-BFZR. CoA 24-5-07, de-reg 3-11-05. Travelling exhibit. Arr 9-13		1-24
❑ G-PLAH		BAe Jetstream 31	84	ex Old Sarum, Millom, Blackpool, G-LOVA, G-OAKA, G-BUFM, G-LAKH, G-BUFM, N410MX, G-31-640. CoA 26-7-02, de-reg 22-1-08. Cockpit. Arrived 19-8-20		1-24
❑ –		Vickers Vanguard SIM	~	ex airport, Booker, 'Essex', Hunting, East Midlands. BEA c/s		1-24
❑ 62-APK*		Air Command 582	c98	ex King's Lynn, Belgium. Arrived 23-6-22	[6]	1-24
❑ KF388	'15'	NAA Harvard T.2b	45	ex 'KF488', airport, Wimborne, Sandhurst, 6 FTS, 3 FTS, 1 FTS, 7 FTS. Noorduyn-built. SOC 11-2-57. Arrived 2000	[7]	1-24
❑ WS776	'K'	Gloster Meteor NF.14	54	ex airport, Armthorpe, Sandtoft, North Coates, North Luffenham, Lyneham 7716M (3-5-61), 228 OCU, 60, 72, 85, 25. AWA-built. Arrived 5-2-05		1-24
❑ WT532	'32'	EE Canberra PR.7	55	ex airport, Lovaux, Cosford, 8890M / 8728M, RAE, 13, Wyton SF, 58, 31, 13, 80. Arrived 5-7-99. Cockpit		1-24

	Serial	Code	Type	Reg / ID	Year	History	Note	Date
❑	WT722*	'873'	Hawker Hunter T.8C	G-BWGN	55	ex St Mawgan, G-BWGN (CoA 3-9-97, de-reg 16-3-11), Coventry, Kemble, Exeter, Shawbury, Yeovilton, FRADU, 764, 703, 26, 54. Arrived 2-8-23		1-24
❑	WV381*	'732'	Hawker Hunter GA.11		55	ex Lee-on-Solent, Benson, Culham, Kemble, Farnborough, FRADU, FRU, FWS, 222. Cr 2-11-72. Cockpit. Arr 5-1-23	[8]	1-24
❑	WW450	'P-B'	Percival Provost T.1	G-BZRE	53	ex 'WW421', Booker Armthorpe, Sandtoft, G-BZRE (de-reg 22-5-05), Binbrook, Norwich, Lowestoft, East Kirkby, Tattershall, Lytham, WW450, St Athan '7688M', 7689M (2-11-60), TCCF, 8 FTS, 2 FTS. Arrived 10-10-05	[9]	1-24
❑	XE856	'V'	DH Vampire T.11	G-DUSK	54	ex airport, Henlow, Catfoss, Long Marston, Lasham, Welwyn GC, Woodford, Chester, St Athan, 219, N Weald SF, 226 OCU. Hatfield-built. SOC 30-10-67, de-reg 19-3-09. Arrived 6-9-05. 219 Sqn colours	[10]	1-24
❑	XG160	'U'	Hawker Hunter F.6A	G-BWAF	56	ex airport, Scampton 8831M (2-9-84), 1 TWU, 229 OCU, 111, 43. De-reg 9-12-10. 111 Sqn colours		1-24
❑	XH537		Avro Vulcan B.2MRR		59	ex airport, Bruntingthorpe, Ottershaw, Camberley, Abingdon 8749M (25-3-82), 27, 230 OCU, MoA. Arr 29-10-91. Cockpit		1-24
❑	XL164		HP Victor K.2		61	ex Brize Norton 9215M (11-11-93), 55, 57, 55, 57, MoA. Cockpit, on loan. *Saucy Sal*. Arrived 24-5-13		1-24
❑	XP924*	'134'	DH Sea Vixen D.3	G-CVIX	63	ex Yeovilton, Hurn, Swansea, Llanbedr, RAE, FAW.2, FRL, RAE, Sydenham, 899, RAFHS. Hawarden-built. Accident 27-5-17, de-reg-22-2-23. 899 Sqn colours		**due**
❑	XR346		Northrop Shelduck D.1		61	'Army' titles	[11]	1-24
❑	–*	'PF179'	Folland Gnat T.1	XR541	63	ex North Weald, Bruntingthorpe, USA (?), Humberside, Binbrook, Ipswich, Worksop, St Athan 8602M (17-12-78), CFS, 4 FTS. Arrived 29-3-23	[12]	1-24
❑	XT257		Westland Wessex HAS.3		67	ex airport, East Grinstead, Cosford, Halton 8719M (9-10-81), A&AEE. Arrived 20-1-05. RAF SAR colours		1-24
❑	XT431	'462'	Westland Wasp HAS.1		65	ex 'XS463' Charlwood, Crawley, Ipswich, Weston-super-M, Fleetlands, Wroughton, 829. SOC 10-12-81. Arr 21-12-13	[13]	1-24
❑	XX763	'24'	SEPECAT Jaguar GR.1		75	ex Blackstone, St Athan 9009M, Shawbury, 54, 226 OCU. Arrived 26-9-09. 226 OCU colours	[14]	1-24
❑	ZD620		HSA HS.125 CC.3		82	ex Dunsfold, 32. Last flight 25-3-15. Arrived 29-10-15	[14]	1-24
❑	ZE432		BAC 111-479		73	ex Boscombe Down, ETPS, DQ-FBV. Forward fuselage. Arrived 30-4-14. QinetiQ / ETPS colours	[15]	1-24
❑	'ZF355'*	'633'	Westland Lynx HAS.3(ICE)	XZ238	77	ex White Waltham, Croft, Fleetlands, *Endurance* Flt, 815, HAS.2, 702, 815, 700L, 815, 700L. Arrived 8-8-23		1-24
❑	ZF582		EE Lightning F.53		68	ex Reading, Llantrisant, Luton, Desborough, Portsmouth, Stretton, Warton, Saudi AF 207, 53-676, G-27-46. Last flown 22-1-86. Arrived 21-9-04. Cockpit		1-24
❑	ZJ469*		GEC-Marconi Phoenix UAV		c95	BAPC.408, ex Old Sarum, Larkhill. Arrived 25-10-22	[16]	1-24

■ **[1]** 'Flea' built by Edgar George Davis in Bath, first flew 5-11-36, Authorisation No.68. **[2]** Hot-air airship; envelope stored by the British Balloon Museum and Library. **[3]** On loan, composite airframe. **[4]** *Yankee-Fox* made the last-ever Herald flight, at Bournemouth, on 9-4-99 and was handed over to BAM on loan 26-5-99 but was scrapped 30-6-08 when the museum had to vacate the airport site. The cockpit section returned to Bournemouth in 2015. **[5]** Viscount cockpit on loan from the Duxford Aviation Society. **[6]** Gyro built in Belgium but flown from Arras, France, before entering storage in Belgium. French homebuilds receive exotic-looking 'registrations'. **[7]** Harvard is a composite and carries the serial KF388, which contributed to the amalgam. That being so, it was SOC 11-2-57 and served with 7, 1, 3 and 6 FTSs respectively. **[8]** WV381 loaned by David Webb. **[9]** Provost T.1 has the fuselage of WW450 and the wings of WW421. This exchange occurred during its days at St Athan, when it was even painted up as 7688M (WW421's maintenance serial). **[10]** *Sierra-Kilo* owned by Dick Horsfield and Rod Robinson. **[11]** Shelduck is a composite, including parts of XV383 and XW578. **[12]** 'PF179' from the Gnat's time with the **P**ainting and **F**inishing School at St Athan, Wales. **[13]** Wasp has the boom of XS463. **[14]** Jaguar and HS.125 on loan from Hayward and Green Defence Ltd. **[15]** The 111 is a local product, it first flew from Hurn 16-7-73. **[16]** Apparently merits a heritage identity.

Airport: There is a frequent throughput of so-called 'legacy' airliners here, but only long-termers are listed. **Departures**: Bonanza G-BGSW had been dismantled and removed by 5-23, reportedly bound for a college in China. Warrior II G-BNSY and Cadet 161 G-TLET left by road on 31-3-22 bound for <u>Cotswold</u>, Glos. Seneca 200T G-BPXX and Duchess G-TWNN believed scrapped 2022. Citation G-IKOS was re-registered as N998RH 4-23 and departed in a container mid-23 bound for the USA. Cessna 310 G-MGBG left by mid-2021, for Cotswold, Glos. Cherokee 140 G-SMTH to <u>Evesham</u>, Worcs, 15-2-22. Boeing 737 2-ESKA was sold to Buffalo Airways of Canada as C-FBAE 2-8-23 – replacing a Curtiss C-46, such is progress!

Boeing 737 2-MOVE fuselage departed for China 6-11-23. The following have been deleted: Cherokee G-AVLD, Arrow G-AZDE, Fuji FA.200 G-BBGI, Commander G-BFZM, Duchess G-BRPU; Tomahawk G-BTJL; Duchess G-CBBF; Cessna 172 D-EFUC; Navajo N666AW.

❑ G-BCUV*		SAL Bulldog T.1	75	ex 'XX704', Elstree, Hurn, Ghana AF G-112, G-BCUV. CoA 5-8-14. First noted 5-22		6-22
❑ G-FRAO		Dassault Falcon 20D	69	ex Cobham, N906FR, N33FE, N4400F, F-WNGO. CoA 28-1-18, de-reg 5-5-20		1-22
❑ G-FRBA		Dassault Falcon 20C	70	ex FRA, OH-FFA, F-WPXF. CoA 23-9-11, de-reg 6-12-11		1-22
❑ G-GPFI		Boeing 737-229	74	ex European, VH-OZQ, G-GPFI, VH-OZQ, G-GPFI, F-GVAC, OO-SDA, LX-LGN, OO-SDA. CoA 2-4-09, de-reg 19-6-11. OzJet titles. Forward fuselage, cabin trainer	[1]	1-24
❑ G-TGPG*		Boeing 737-300	89	ex European, OY-JTB, RP-C4010, EI-BZE. Last flight 14-6-22, CoA 20-12-22		1-24
❑ G-VIPP		Piper Navajo 350	79	ex G-OGRV, G-BMPX, N3543D. De-reg 4-5-17. Dismantled mid-23, cockpit. Reported bound for China		7-23
❑ LX-ARS*		American AA-1 Trainer	~	ex BAM, airport, D-EHLD. First noted 8-23		8-23
❑ M-ALUN		HSA HS.125-700A	80	ex N125AM, G-BHKF, G-5-13. Last flown 7-16		1-24
❑ N447FT		Canadair CL-44-O 'Guppy'	61	ex RP-C-8023, 9G-LCA, 4K-GUP, N447T, EI-BND, N447T, CL-44D4. Conroy 'Guppy' conversion. De-reg 6-7-22	[2]	1-24
❑ 2-PSFI		Boeing 737-33	87	ex G-CKTI, OY-JTA, N371FA, N127AW. Arrived 2017		1-24
❑ 9H-PAM*		Boeing 737-33	92	ex N798SQ, HP-1795, F-GIXD, N3213T. Arrived 18-11-17		1-24
❑ XM404*		Hunting Jet Provost T.3	59	ex BAM, Doncaster, Nottingham, Bruntingthorpe, Moreton-in- Marsh, Halton, Newton 8055BM (21-11-69), Shawbury, 3 FTS, 2 FTS. Cockpit. First noted 8-23	[3]	8-23
❑ XW293	'Z'	BAC 'JP' T.5A G-BWCS	71	ex Tatenhill, 6 FTS, CFS. CoA 3-2-09, de-reg 18-10-19		1-24
❑ –		Hawker Hunter T.7	57	ex Biggin Hill, 'G-ERIC', Hurn, Leavesden, Elstree, Hatfield, Danish AF	[4]	1-24

■ **[1]** *Fox-India* is owned and operated on behalf of the airport management by the JARE Airline Training Partnership. **[2]** The Guppy was restored to the US register 23-4-20 only to be cancelled (again) on 6-6-22. **[3]** Wings marked XM404 can also be found at East Wretham, Norfolk. **[4]** Hunter is dedicated as a memorial. The plaque reads: 'Richard Michael Carlton - Aviator'. It is a composite with the cockpit of FGA.9 XJ690 - ex Bitteswell, G-9-451, 20, 14 - the rest is a complex story of ex-Danish T.7(s)!

BOVINGTON off the A352 near Wool, west of Wareham

Tank Museum: Home to the world's finest international collection of armoured fighting vehicles. Walking through the display halls visitors come across what appears to be a packing case with a tank in it: not a bad description of a Hamilcar!

◆ *Linsay Road, BH20 6JG* | **01929 405096** | **visit@tankmuseum.org** | **www.tankmuseum.org**

❑ TK718	GAL Hamilcar I	44	ex Beverley, Christian Malford	[1]	1-24
❑ XM564	Saro Skeeter AOP.12	59	ex Celle, 652, CFS, 12 Flt, 652. 2 RTR colours. Stored	[2]	1-24

■ **[1]** Birmingham Railway Carriage-built; parts of TK718 were used in the creation of the example at Middle Wallop, Hampshire. **[2]** The last Skeeter flown in BAOR; XM564 was presented to the museum by 2 RTR in 3-69.

CANFORD north of the A3049, north of Poole

An ATR 42 fuselage is kept in the locality.

❑ G-ISLG*	ATR 42-320	85	ex Hurn, Greenwich, Hurn, Blue Islands, F-HAAV, F-WKVB, OY-CIG, YU-ALK, VH-AQD. De-reg 3-8-16. Fuselage. 'Convict Airways' titles, *The Cage*. Arrived 23-12-20	12-23

COMPTON ABBAS AERODROME southeast of Shaftesbury EGHA

From 2023 another operating base for Aero Legends – see Lashenden, Kent. Taylorcraft G-BRIJ has been deleted.

❑ G-CBRT	Murphy Rebel	02	de-reg 4-5-21, dumped	[1]	8-21

■ **[1]** Alongside the Murphy is the *cockpitless* hulk of Tomahawk G-RVRB.

FERNDOWN on the A348 north of Bournemouth

A *private* owner is *believed* to be restoring a J4 in the area; with an Alpha held in store.

❑ G-AIJS	Auster J4 Archer	46	ex France, Clothall Common	N1-23
❑ G-APRF	Auster 5 Alpha	58	ex France (?), Felixkirk, Squires Gate, VP-LAF, G-APRF. CoA 14-6-05, de-reg 14-6-05. Stored	12-15

POOLE on the A35 west of Bournemouth

A Short 330 forward fuselage is *believed* to linger at a *private* address in the area.

❑ G-BGNG		Short 330-200	79	ex Hurn, Gill, N330FL, G-BGNG. CoA 14-4-97, de-reg 16-8-96. Fuselage	8-17

PORTLAND

The Sailing Academy: Osprey Quay, displayed within the marina complex is a Lynx.

❑ XZ250	'426'	Westland Lynx HAS.3S	78	ex M Wallop, 702, 815, 702, 815, 702, Fleetlands, 702, 829, HAS.2, 702, 815, 702. SOC 13-10-10	7-21

SWANAGE on the A351 southeast of Wareham

An Auster has arrived at a *private* location in the area for restoration.

❑ G-AGXU*		Auster J1N Alpha	46	CoA 13-8-06	6-23

DURHAM and CLEVELAND

The unitary authorities of Hartlepool, Middlesbrough, Redcar and Cleveland, Stockton-on-Tees and Darlington form the region

DURHAM

Stu-Art Aviation Furniture: Stuart Abbott up-cycles aviation components, fittings, and sections into a wide variety of furniture and decorations. See under Melbourne, Derbyshire, for an example of his handiwork. The cockpit of Boeing 737 G-CELU moved to Blackpool, Lancs, 31st July 2023. Refer to Teesside Airport, D&C (below) for a recent addition to the 'stock cupboard'. ◆ *Prior arrangement* **only** | **www.stu-artaviationfurniture.co.uk**

EDMONDSLEY on the B6532 northwest of Durham

Battlezone Durham : Note change of name. ◆ *Prior application* **only** | **www.battlezonepaintball.co.uk**

❑ ZE368	'R'	Westland Sea King HAR.3	85	ex Colsterworth, Gosport, Fleetlands, 202, 1564 Flt, 202	8-23

Also: The remainder of the former Mini-Moos Sea Kings are held in ***private*** storage and are ***not*** available for inspection.

❑ XV651	'824'	Westland Sea King HAS.5	69	ex Colsterworth, Gosport, Fleetlands, QinetiQ, 771, 706, 826, 814, HAS.1, RAE Thurleigh, RRE, A&AEE	3-23
❑ XZ921	'269'	Westland Sea King HAS.6	79	ex Eastleigh, Bruntingthorpe, Gosport, 820, 814, 810, HAS.5, 706, 820, Falklands, 820, HAS.2	3-23
❑ ZA291	'N'	Westland Sea King HC.4	79	ex Eastleigh, Gosport, Fleetlands, 848, 846, 845, 848, 707, 846, 707, 846, Falklands, 846	7-23
❑ ZA313	'M'	Westland Sea King HC.4	82	ex Eastleigh, Gosport, Fleetlands, 845, 846, 845, 848, 845, 846, Falklands, 846, 707	7-23
❑ ZD625	'P'	Westland Sea King HC.4	84	ex Eastleigh, Gosport, Fleetlands, 848, 846, 848, 846, 845, 846, 707	3-23
❑ ZE425	'WR'	Westland Sea King HC.4	85	ex Eastleigh, Gosport, Fleetlands, 848, 846, 845, 848, 846, 845, 772, 846, 845, 848, 845, 846. 'Arctic' stripes	8-23
❑ ZE428	'H'	Westland Sea King HC.4	85	ex Eastleigh, Gosport, Fleetlands, 845, 846, 845, 846, 845, 846, 845, 848, 772, 845	8-23
❑ ZF121	'T'	Westland Sea King HC.4	86	ex Eastleigh, Gosport, Fleetlands, 846, 845, 846, 845, 846, 845, 772	7-23

FISHBURN AERODROME or Morgansfield, on the B1278, north of Sedgefield

Fishburn Historic Aviation Centre: Run by the **Aircraft Restoration Group** (ARG) Special events are open cockpit days are staged. ◆ *Check details on **Facebook** for availability.* | *Aerodrome details:* **www.fishburnairfield.co.uk**

❑ G-AYTA		MS Rallye Club	71	ex Manchester, Moston, Wickenby. CoA 7-11-88, de-reg 12-5-93. Arrived 19-11-21		1-24
❑ D-IFSB		DH Dove 6 G-AMXR	52	ex London Colney, Hatfield, BFS, D-CFSB, Panshanger, Srs 2A G-AMXR, N4280V. Last flew 24-10-78. Arr 2-2-16	[1]	1-24

❑ –*	'X'	Gloster Meteor F.8 WA984	51	ex Tangmere, 'VZ440', 'WA829', Southampton, Wimborne, Tarrant Rushton, 211 AFS, 19. SOC 4-12-61. Arrived 12-5-22. 609 (West Riding) Sqn colours	[2]	1-24
❑ XG743	'798'	DH Sea Vampire T.22	54	ex Pickhill, Duxford (issued to IWM 15-6-72), Wymondham, Duxford, Brawdy SF, A&AEE, Brawdy SF, 766, 736, 764. Christchurch-built. Arrived on site 3-7-18		1-24
❑ XN458	'19'	Hunting Jet Provost T.3	60	ex Northallerton, Ashington, 'XN594' Cardiff, St Athan, Halton 8334M (21-3-73), Shawbury, 1 FTS. Arrived 7-9-21		1-24
❑ J-1790		DH Venom FB.54 G-BLKA	57	ex London Colney, 'WR410', 'Norfolk', Hurn, Bruntingthorpe, Cranfield, G-BLKA, G-VENM, Swiss AF J-1790. CoA 14-7-95, de-reg 13-10-00. Swiss -built. Arrived 2-2-16. 'Gate guard'		1-24

■ **[1]** Dove is on permanent loan from the DH Aircraft Museum. **[2]** A complex composite, including elements of VZ530.

Workshop and Store: 'Flea' 'G-ADRZ' moved to Cramlington, N&T, on 27th September 2022.

❑ G-APWU	Thurston Tawney Owl	59	ex Masham, Pickhill, Leamington Spa, 'Herefordshire', Stondon, Stapleford Tawney. Crashed 22-4-60, de-reg 15-9-86. Arrived on-site 19-10-19	[1]	1-24
❑ G-CDGT	Montgomerie-Parsons Two-Place	05	ex 'Essex'. *The Flying Scotsman II / Merlin* Arrived 19-1-20		1-24
❑ G-CHTX	Skill Voltair 86	13	ex Sunderland, Eshott, Hartlepool, Newcastle. De-reg 29-3-21. Arrived 29-5-21	[2]	1-24
❑ G-GREG	Jodel DR.220	67	ex Northallerton, Huddersfield, Eversden, F-BOKR. CEA-built. CoA 19-2-91, de-reg 1-4-97. First noted 2-20		1-24
❑ –*	Slingsby Grasshopper	~	ex East Midlands, Doncaster. Arrived 11-22	[3]	1-24
❑ XG775	DH Sea Vampire T.22	55	ex Llandysul, 'Norfolk', London, Southall, Lossiemouth SF, Yeovilton SF, FOFT, 766, 1833, 718. Christchurch-built. SOC 30-1-70. Cockpit, arrived 21-7-21	[4]	1-24

■ **[1]** Tawney Owl was written off on its first flight, at Stapleford Tawney. **[2]** Electric-powered microlight, designed and built by David Skill of Newcastle. "Hopped and skipped" at Eshott in 2013 but made no sustained flight. **[3]** *Possibly* the very similar EoN Primary. **[4]** Under restoration by ARG's Mike Eastman for owner Max Valk.

Aerodrome: The aerodrome is a thriving community, staging special events and the Aviator Bistro is rightly popular. Kraguj G-RADA moved to Eshott, N&T, 27th July 2022. Jodel D.112 G-DAVE has been deleted.

❑ G-AKTP	Piper Vagabond	48	ex Swansea, N4683H. CoA 5-8-03. Arrived 9-21	1-24
❑ G-AVOD	Beagle D5 Husky 180	67	ex Harrogate, Spilsby. Crashed 31-7-92	1-24

HARTLEPOOL

Hartlepool College of Further Education: The Travel, Tourism and Aviation training centre also boasts a 'slice' of former Cathay Boeing 747 passenger cabin. ◆ *Prior application* **only** | **www.hartlepoolfe.ac.uk**

❑ XW309	'ME'	BAC Jet Provost T.5	70	ex Cosford 9179M (11-3-93), Shawbury, 6 FTS, 1 FTS		11-23
❑ XW404	'77'	BAC Jet Provost T.5A	71	ex Exeter, St Athan 9049M (16-8-90), 1 FTS		11-23
❑ XW405		BAC Jet Provost T.5A	71	ex Exeter, Cosford 9187M (5-5-93), Shawbury, 6 FTS, 1 FTS, 7 FTS, 6 FTS, 1 FTS, RAFC. Plinth-mounted		11-23
❑ –	TAD.002	Sud Gazelle CIM	~	ex Colsterworth, Arborfield, M Wallop. Westland-built	[1]	11-23
❑ -	'AV002'	Panavia Tornado SIM	~	ex Sunderland. Cockpit. Built by Environmental Tectonics		11-23

■ **[1]** Inspection of the CIM reveals it to be a transmission, controls and fuel system rig which is labelled '341 Training Aid Unit 1'.

MIDDLESBROUGH

Teesside University: Near Albert Park. ◆ *Prior application* **only** | **www.tees.ac.uk**

❑ G-BAMG	Lobet Ganagobie	r73	ex Yearby. Unfinished homebuilt. De-reg 5-8-91. Arr 12-16	1-24

NEWTON AYCLIFFE on the A167 southeast of Bishop Auckland

Aviator Gin Bar: With seating from a variety of airliners and other elements of aeronautica, the venue invites participants to "Broaden your horizons"! The proprietors claim the Dauphin was acquired for six bottles of 'mother's ruin'!

◆ *Hanger [sic] 18, Northfield Way, DL5 6EJ* | **01325 589076** | **www.the aviatorginbar.co.uk**

❑ G-BLAI	Monnett Sonerai 2L	97	T Simpson, Kirkaldy-built. CoA 12-1-99. Fuselage, f/n 7-20		1-24
❑ G-BTNC	Sud Dauphin II	91	De-reg 26-8-20. Gutted fuselage. Arrived 3-21	[1]	1-24

■ **[1]** Fitted with the tail of G-CEYU.

Also: Stored locally at a ***private*** venue is a Cherokee cockpit, former sim. See under Teesside, below, for more.

❑ G-ATXM*	Piper Cherokee 180C	65	ex Teesside, Godstone (?), Southend, Stapleford, N8809J. CoA 12-10-02, de-reg 25-6-08. Cockpit, stored. Arrived 3-23	3-23

SEAHAM on the A19 north of Hartlepool

The Bunker CQB: Latterly Massive Attack Paintball: CQB is close-quarters battle, of course. At the same time as the 'arena' acquired the Musketeer, it also took delivery of Rallye 120ST G-BGKD: but this was deemed too far gone even for paint-splattering and was scrapped. ◆ *Prior application* **only** | **www.thebunkercqb.co.uk**

❑ G-DHJB*	Beech Musketeer Sport	67	ex G-AZZE. CoA 15-7-02, de-reg 18-10-02. First noted 4-23	1-24

TEESSIDE INTERNATIONAL AIRPORT or Middleton St George, formerly Durham Tees Valley EGNV

The Middleton St George Memorial Association maintains the memorial garden and has a small display of items within the main terminal building. Plans to re-open the heritage room within the former RAF Middleton St George Officers' Mess have yet to materialise. Keep an eye on **www.middleton-st-george-memorial-association.org**

International Fire Training Centre: As well as real airframes, the school has 'synthetic' training rigs, including a 'DC-10' lookalike and the forward fuselage of an 'A380'. ◆ **Strictly** *prior application* **only** | **www.iftcentre.com**

❑ G-AWZS		HS Trident 3B-101		71	ex BA, BEA. CoA 9-9-86, de-reg 18-3-86	1-24
❑ G-AZLS		Vickers Viscount 813		58	ex BMA, SAA ZS-CDV. Hurn-built. CoA 9-6-83, de-reg 19-12-86. Fuselage	1-24
❑ 'G-JON'		Short 330-100	G-BKIE	76	ex Newcastle, G-SLUG, G-METP, G-METO, G-BKIE, C-GTAS, G-14-3005. CoA 22-8-93, de-reg 16-9-97	1-24
❑ XP330		W'land Whirlwind HAR.10		61	ex Stansted, 21, 32, 230, 110, 225. SOC 26-1-76	1-24
❑ XZ360	'FN'	SEPECAT Jaguar GR.3		76	ex Ipswich, St Athan, 41, GR.1, 41. Arrived 28-8-19	1-24
❑ XZ652		Westland Lynx AH.7		81	ex Ipswich, M Wallop. NEA 3-13. Red scheme, Serco logo. Arrived 7-10-14	1-24

Willis Asset Management was establishing here in 2020, carrying out the parting-out of airliners. As with other locations, turnaround is relatively quick and only longer-terms are given here. ATR 42 G-ISLH was ferried in from Jersey 8th May 2022 for parting out. The fuselage departed to Durham, D&C, on 14th December. There the cockpit was removed and trucked to Exeter, Devon, on 4th January 2024. The remainder of the fuselage will be used by Stu-Art for 'up-cycling'.

❑ C-FNWT*	HS HS.146-RJ100	94	ex Norwich, CF-NWT, SE-DSV, N510MM, G-6-250. Last flight 21-12-19. Arrived by road 14-2-23	1-24
❑ DQ-FJF*	Boeing 737-700	98	ex Fiji Airways, N1786B. Cockpit. Arrived 20-9-20	1-24
❑ EC-ELT*	HS HS146-200QT	88	ex TNT, OO-TAQ, EC-ELT, G-BOKZ, G-5-102. Fuselage, arrived 5-5-23	1-24

Others: Cherokee cockpit G-ATXM was in use by AeroSchool as a simulator, but a change of building meant it had to move into storage - see Newton Aycliffe, D&C, above – in March 2023. This was written out of *W&R26* (p60) from Southend, Essex, as going to a dive site at Godstone, Surrey, in August 2016: since then, it has graced the *Submerged* appendix. While it *could* have spent its time drenched, this seems unlikely. Deeply philosophical blockbusters such as 'Did it ever go to Surrey?' and/or 'Where did it *really* go?' *may* spring to mind, or might not...

❑ G-BNGR	Piper Tomahawk 112	79	ex N2492F. CoA 1-8-03, de-reg 18-2-05. Trolley-mounted	1-24
❑ G-CLUE	Piper Seneca 200T	79	ex N8089Z. Damaged 28-7-13, CoA 28-2-14	1-24
❑ N5039Q	ATR 42-300	94	ex Air Ukraine UR-UTA, VP-BLP, D4-CBE, F-WWEA. Arrived 7-12-13. Rescue training	1-24

THORNABY ON TEES west of the A19 and Middlesbrough

Thornaby Aerodrome Memorial: At 'Spitfire Roundabout' on the A1045, is a tribute to the former airfield.

❑ –	V-S Spitfire V FSM	07	BAPC.301, GB-Replicas-built. Pole-mounted	[1]	1-22

■ **[1]** As Mk.V 'BM481' 'YO-T' of 401 Sqn RCAF 1943 (port), and F.22 'PK651' 'RAO-B' of 608 (North Riding) Sqn 1948-1950 (stb).

URLAY NOOK north of the A67, east of Teesside Airport

Great North Air Ambulance: Has a Dauphin training aid. ◆ *Prior application* **only** | **www.greatnorthairambulance.co.uk**

❑ G-BTEU	Sud Dauphin II	90	ex Teesside, Bowburn, Teesside, Newton Aycliffe, Yeadon, Durham. CoA 18-5-15, de-reg 11-6-15. Arr 18-9-19	1-24

YEARBY on the B1269 south of Redcar

A local, and *private*, airstrip. Smith Acro G-BPAA has been deleted. ◆ *Prior application* **only** | **https://acro.co.uk**

	Reg	Type	Yr	Details	Date
❑	G-APYB	Tipsy Nipper III	59	CoA 12-6-96. Avions Fairey-built	1-24
❑	G-BHUO	Evans VP-2	82	CoA 21-12-94, de-reg 23-8-00	7-19
❑	G-MYKY	Mainair Mercury	93	de-reg 27-10-21	12-21

ESSEX

Includes the unitary authorities of Southend and Thurrock

ABRIDGE on the A113, south of the M11/M25 junction

Mayhem Paintball Games: Continues to source 'target' from its next door neighbour, Stapleford Tawney.
◆ *Prior arrangement* **only** | **www.mayhem-paintball.co.uk**

	Reg		Type	Yr	Details	Note	Date
❑	G-AOHL		Vickers Viscount 802	57	ex Stock, Southend, BAF, BA, BEA. CoA 11-4-80, de-reg 27-3-81. Cockpit	[1]	9-23
❑	G-AREE		Piper Aztec 250	60	ex Stapleford. De-reg 16-12-91. Fuselage		3-15
❑	G-BCEF*		American AA-5 Traveler	74	ex Stapleford. De-reg 12-12-15		8-23
❑	G-BEXO*		Piper Apache 160	55	ex Stapleford, OO-APH, N1176P. CoA 10-10-07, de-reg 4-2-09. First noted 4-23		8-23
❑	G-BHGP*		SOCATA Tobago	80	ex Stapleford. CoA 29-5-05, de-reg 4-2-07. First noted 4-23		8-23
❑	G-BOIP		Cessna 152 II	79	ex Stapleford, Tattershall Thorpe, Staverton, N49264. Damaged 11-1-90, de-reg 13-1-06. Tail of C.152 G-BOTB		9-19
❑	G-DFOX*		Aérospatiale Squirrel	82	ex G-NAAS. De-reg 22-2-19. Cobin, first noted 12-22		8-23
❑	G-OBHD		Short 360-100	87	ex Hinstock, Blackpool, G-BNDK, G-OBHD, G-BNDK, G-14-3714. CoA 5-3-06, de-reg 27-1-11. Arrived 1-8-12		9-23
❑	G-OBPL		Embraer Bandeirante	78	ex Stock, Southend, 'G-OBWB', PH-FVB, G-OEAB, G-BKWB, G-CHEV, PT-GLR. De-reg 27-2-04. Fuselage		12-17
❑	XP854		Westland Scout AH.1	63	ex Ipswich, Bedford, Ipswich, Wattisham, M Wallop TAD.043 / 7898M. Crashed 15-5-65		7-23
❑	XT455	'U'	Westland Wessex HU.5	65	ex Hixon, Gosport A2654 [2], Lee-on-Solent A2741 (3-7-86), 845, 707, 845, 846, 845, 707. First noted 3-15		9-23
❑	XX744	'DJ'	SEPECAT Jaguar GR.1	74	ex Ipswich, Coltishall 9251M, Cosford, Shawbury, Warton, 31, 17, 31, 6, 14, 17, A&AEE. 31 Sqn colours		11-21
❑	ZD276		Westland Lynx AH.7	83	ex Yeovilton, 655, 671, 656, 661, 652. Cr 18-3-07. Cabin		8-23
❑	–		Sud Gazelle	-	with a Scout boom	[2]	6-18
❑	776		Westland Sea King Mk.47 G-BDMJ	75	ex Market Drayton, Gosport, Egyptian Air Force, G-BDMJ, G-17-25. Cockpit plus the cabin/rear of HAS.6 ZA136. F/n 9-14		8-23

■ **[1]** Close to the Viscount nose is the centre section of F.27 3C-QSB, from Stock, Essex. **[2]** Gazelle is *very probably* G-TURP.

Short 360 G-OBHD and Squirrel G-DFOX in between bouts of mayhem, August 2023. *Rowland Benbrook*

ANDREWSFIELD AERODROME or Great Saling, north of the A120, west of Braintree EGSL

The Mystère is a reminder of the Rebel Air Museum which was open to the public here 1979 to 1986.

❑ G-BAOB		Cessna F.172M	73	Reims-built. CoA 12-5-07, de-reg 17-12-10		9-23
❑ 319	'8-ND'	Dassault Mystère IVA	c57	ex Sculthorpe, French AF. Last flew 17-10-79, arrived 6-80	[1]	9-23

■ **[1]** Mystère *presumably* held on behalf of the National Museum of the USAF, USA.

AUDLEY END AERODROME off the B1383, west of Saffron Walden

Vintage Fabrics: Clive and Linda Denney and team work wonders transforming aircraft of all eras. Tiger Moth G-BTOG, immaculate in USAAF colours as 'DE-745', flew again on 1st June 2022. Only 'long-termers' are listed, below. Examples of other recent transformations include the following. Nord 1002 G-OTME completed its restoration and was first flown on 19th January 2023 by Clive: it was despatched to White Waltham, Berks, the following month. MS.500 Criquet G-BPHZ arrived from Duxford, Cambs, on 19th January 2023 for refinishing in Luftwaffe 'Green Heart' colours as 'SB+UG': it was moved to St Leonards-on-Sea, E Sussex, 4th October 2023.

◆ ***Private** workshop, prior permission* **only** | **www.vintagefabrics.co.uk**

❑ G-AXUA	Beagle Pup 100	69	ex G-35-150. CoA 5-6-08		1-24
❑ C8996	Royal Aircraft Factory SE.5a G-ECAE	1918	ex Elmsett, Sudbury, Australia, RAAF A2-25, C8996. Austin-built. Crashed 15-7-1927. Arrived 30-11-20	[1]	1-24
❑ WP872*	DHC Chipmunk T.10	52	ex N198DD, C-GBNI, WP872, Bri UAS, 3/4 CAACU, Dur, Queens, S'ton UASs, 1 CAACU, Queens, Lon UASs, 14 RFS. Hawarden-built. Arrived 17-12-21		1-24

■ **[1]** SE.5a registered to Westh Flyg AB of Sweden - see under Elmsett, Suffolk, for the company's Hawker Hart.

Also: By August 2023 Pup 100 G-AXMW was exported to Dublin, Ireland, on 15th December 2021.

❑ G-ACGS		DH Leopard Moth	33	ex ZK-AGS, G-APKH, AX858 1473 Flt, 109, Special Signals Sch, G-ACGH, PH-ALM, G-ACGS	1-24
❑ XF597	'A-H'	P'val Provost T.1 G-BKFW	55	ex Thatcham, CAW, RAFC. CoA 27-7-07. Arrived 7-18. Stored	1-24

BILLERICAY on the A129 east of Brentwood

A collector at a *private* location in the *general* area has amassed a small fleet of airframes.

❑ G-AXDM*		HSA HS.125-400B	69	ex Luton area, Pershore, Farnborough, Edinburgh, BAE Systems, GEC-Marconi. CoA 7-6-03, de-reg 13-11-03. Forward fuselage. First noted 6-22		6-22
❑ WS726*	'H'	Gloster Meteor NF(T).14	53	ex Royton, 7960M (19-6-67), Kemble, 1 ANS, 2 ANS, NF.14, 25. AWA-built. 25 Sqn colours. Arrived 13-4-22		7-23
❑ XL586*		Hawker Hunter T.7	58	ex N' Benfleet, Melksham, Kemble, Ipswich, Colsterworth, Shawbury, BAe Warton, 1 TWU, 2 TWU, 1 TWU, 229 OCU	[1]	7-23
❑ XZ613*		Westland Lynx AH.7	80	ex Belstead, Ipswich, Gosport, Wallop, Arborfield, 655, 665, A&AEE, Yeovil, 657, 654. First noted 6-22	[2]	7-23

■ **[1]** T.7 XL586 is fitted with the rear-end of XL578 *but* carries XL586 to port and XL578 to starboard. **[2]** Fitted with the boom of ZD278 - see Knowsley, Merseyside.

Delta Force Paintball: Last noted in April 2017; Lynx AH.7 XZ606 had moved to Binfield, Berks, by late 2023.

BOXTED between the A134 and the A12, north of Colchester

Boxted's impressive B-26 Marauder exhibit; rear fuselage of *Mr Shorty* to the right. *John Camp*

Boxted Airfield Museum: Run by the Boxted Airfield Historical Group, tells the story of the 386th BG, Gabreski's 56th FG, and the 354th FG. Centrepiece of the new display building is the rear fuselage of B-26C-25-MO 41-35253 *Mr Shorty* plus other Marauder structures, creating a striking tribute to Martin's often maligned but very effective workhorse. The trustees of the Marks Hall Estate at Earls Colne have transferred ownership of *Mr Shorty* to the museum. Boxted is a classic example of how a 'small' museum can be carefully and imaginatively developed to produce a venue that has made the leap from 'local' to 'national' importance. ◆ *Off Langham Lane, Langham, CO4 5NW* | **email** via website | **www.boxted-airfield.com**

BRADWELL ON SEA at the end of the B1021 north of Tillingham

Jaguar T.2 XX146 moved to Carlisle, Cumbria, by August 2022. Lynx HMA.8 ZD266 to North Weald, Essex, by late 2022.

BRAINTREE north of the A120, west of Colchester

B-17 Cockpit Project: Dave Littleton and his brother Paul have created an incredible B-17G cockpit, complete with upper gun turret. The inspiration for this was their late father, John, indefatigable crew chief to *Sally B*. The cockpit is available for film work, set-piece photo sessions etc. Also offered are B-17 parts, component fabrication, and much more.
◆ *Prior arrangement* **only** | b17man@live.co.uk | **www.facebook.com/b17cockpit/**

❑ -	Boeing B-17G Fortress	20	see narrative	1-24

CHELMSFORD

De Havilland Hornet Project: David Collins continues with his exceptional DH Hornet F.1 re-creation. The aim is to make as much of a Hornet as possible and it will be finished in the Medium Sea Grey over PRU Blue colours of 64 Squadron. This is a fitting scheme as some components from PX250 - which served with 64 from new - are to be incorporated.
◆ *Visits* **not** *possible, but appearances at events are made.* | **www.facebook.com/dehavilland.hornet.F1/**

❑ -	DH Hornet F.1	06	BAPC.349, cockpit project – see above	1-24

Also: A *private* collector in the locality *may still* have the cockpit of a Pucará.

❑ A-533	FMA Pucará	c81 ZD486	ex Boscombe Down, Salisbury, St Mary Bourne, M Wallop, Boscombe D', Abingdon, Finningley, ZD486, Arg AF. Cockpit	2-16

CLACTON AERODROME EGSQ

Classic Wings: Has its maintenance base here and its main site of operation at Duxford, Cambs.

❑ G-ANFV	DH Tiger Moth	42	ex DF155, 25 RFS, 28 EFTS. Morris-built. Crashed 12-8-12	3-19
❑ G-ANPE	DH Tiger Moth	40	ex Duxford, G-IESH, G-ANPE, F-BHAT, G-ANPE, T7397, 19 RFS, 18 EFTS. Morris Motors-built. CoA 9-8-12	N9-18
❑ G-BJTB	Cessna A.150M	75	ex N9818J. CoA 27-11-07, de-reg 27-1-23	N10-18
❑ G-CFII	DH Tiger Moth	42	ex N90277, VT-DKN, Indian AF HU726, SAAF 4613, DE630. Morris Motors-built	9-22
❑ DF112	DH Tiger Moth ✈	43 G-ANRM	ex Duxford, 202 AFS, 1 GU, 2 GU, 11 RFS, 22 RFS, 22 EFTS, 16 PFTS, 22 EFTS. Morris-built. Accident 30-6-18, CoA 20-5-19	9-22

CLACTON ON SEA

East Essex Aviation Museum (EEAM) and **Museum of the 1940s**: Located within a Martello tower.
◆ *Orchards Holiday Camp at Point Clear, St Osyth CO16 8NG* | **www.facebook.com/EastEssexAviationSociety/**

❑ 44-14574	NAA P-51D-10-NA Mustang	44	ex 479th FG, 436th FS *Little Zippie*. Inglewood-built. Crashed off-shore 13-1-45. Recovered 16-8-87	8-23

Also: Terrier G-TIMG moved to Maidstone, Kent, by early 2022.

COGGESHALL off the A120, east of Braintree

At a *private* location, the Jungmeister owner also has Jungmann G-JMNN under restoration at Northampton, Northants.

❑ G-MEIS	Bücker Jungmeister	42	ex Rayleigh, USA, Spanish AF ES.1-36. CASA-built	10-23

COLCHESTER

Charleston Aviation Services ◆ *Private workshop,* **strictly** *viewable by prior application* **only**

❑ LA546	V-S Seafire F.46	46 G-CFZJ	ex Newport Pagnell, Newark, Charnock Richard, Carlisle, Anthorn, Lossiemouth Stn Flight. SOC 29-6-51 [1] [2]	N3-23

❑ 854	Messerschmitt Bf 109E-3	G-CLBX	c40	ex Russia, JG5. Shot down 19-4-42. Erla-built. Salvaged 1994 [2]	N3-23
❑ 8347	Messerschmitt Bf 109F-4	G-CLFN	41	ex Hungary, Colchester, Sussex, Russia. Erla-built. Force landed 13-3-42 [3]	N6-23

■ **[1]** See also Old Sarum, Wilts. **[2]** Registered to Craig Charleston. **[3]** Registered to Fighter Aviation Engineering.

Merville Barracks: The Dakota 'guards' 'the **16 Air Assault Brigade** HQ.

❑ 'KG374' 'YS-DM'	Douglas Dakota C.4	KP208	45	ex N Weald, Aldershot, Kemble, AFNE, New Delhi, AFNE, HCCF, 24, MEAF, USAAF C-47B-35-DK 44-77087. Oklahoma City-built. SOC 18-5-70	1-24

No.**308 (Colchester) Squadron Air Cadets**:

❑ ZE556	Grob Viking T.1	84	ex Wethersfield, Syerston, Stapleford, Beeston, Syerston, BGA.3031, CGHF, Arbroath, 662 VGS, 636 VGS, 631 VGS, 661 VGS, 622 VGS. Crashed 12-4-02. Cockpit	3-18

Locally: Proctor IV RM169 (G-ANVY) travelled to Hooton Park, Cheshire, in October 2023.

DANBURY on the A414 east of Chelmsford

A *Flogger* is stored at an industrial estate locally.

❑ 20+45	Mikoyan-Gurevich MiG-23BN *Flogger*	80	ex Germany, Luftwaffe, E German AF. Stored	7-23

EARLS COLNE south of Earls Colne, east of Halstead

A Texan project is *believed* current at a *private* location in the area.

❑ G-BRBC	NAA T-6G Texan	52	ex It AF MM54099, USAF 51-14470. Off-site	N3-23

EAST TILBURY on a minor road east of Tilbury

Whitley Project: Elliott Smock's ambitious project is based locally. The venture does not, as yet, merit a 'formal' listing. Salvaged elements of two Kinloss-based 19 OTU Whitleys, one of which is Mk.V EB384, form the bulk of the project. The centre section of Mk.V N1498, which crashed south of Inverness on 6th January 1942, was acquired from RAF Museum holdings. ◆ *Prior arrangement* **only** | **elliott1940@yahoo.com**

GREAT DUNMOW on the A120 west of Braintree

Paul and **Andrew Wood**: Keep a Hunter at a *private* location in the area. See also Shuttleworth, Beds, for their Sopwith Dove G-EAGA, DH Moth G-ABAG and Puss Moth G-AEOA. ◆ *Prior application* **only**

❑ WP185	Hawker Hunter F.5	55	ex Abingdon, Hendon, Henlow 7583M (30-10-58), 1, 34. AWA-built	9-18

GREAT OAKLEY AERODROME off the B1414 south of Harwich

Percival Aircraft: Mike Biddulph and friends have established a centre of excellence for all things Proctor.
◆ **Private** *workshop, prior application* **only**

❑ G-AHTE	Percival Proctor V	46	ex Nayland, Clacton, Llanelli, Cardiff, Swansea, Llanelli, Hereford (?), Walsall. CoA 10-8-61. Fuselage	4-22
❑ G-AKEX	Percival Proctor III	43	ex Sweden, SE-BTR, G-AKEX, LZ791, ATA, CFE. Hills-built. Crashed 11-1-51	7-23
❑ G-ANPP	Percival Proctor III	42	ex Thruxton, HM354, BCCF, 21 EFTS, BCCF, Digby SF, 34 Wing CF. Hills-built. De-reg 3-4-89	7-23

Also: As part of the 'tidy up' (see page 7) Jodel G-AWVE has been deleted.

❑ G-ARUY*	Auster J1N	62	ex Andrewsfield. CoA 15-10-79	10-23
❑ G-BCMD	Piper Super Cub 95	52	ex OO-SPF, Netherlands AF R-70, L-18C 52-2455. CoA 31-7-15	9-23

HADLEIGH west of Southend-on-Sea

Carvair Cockpit Restoration: Restoration of Marc Wilmott's former Halesworth Carvair is under way in the *general* area.
◆ *Prior arrangement* **only** | **contact@carvaircockpit.co.uk** | **www.carvaircockpit.co.uk**

❑ CF-EPV*	ATEL Carvair	43	ex Halesworth, Beccles, Thorpe Abbotts, Fritton Lake, Woodbridge, LN-MDA and LN-MAB ntu, Southend, EI-AMR, N88819, C-54D 42-72343. Last flown 1973, scrapped 9-78. Flightdeck. Off-site for restoration	[1]	9-23

■ **[1]** C-54 N88819 re-flew as a Carvair on 19-4-63.

HALSTEAD on the A12 northeast of Braintree

An Auster is *believed* to be in the area at a *private* location.

❑ G-AJUL	Auster J1N Alpha	47	CoA 11-9-81, de-reg 23-8-22	N4-18

INGATESTONE on the A12 southwest of Chelmsford

Stuart Gowans: Stuart's Spitfire IX reproduction, with a Merlin and many original parts, is *believed* to be in the general area.

❑ –	V-S Spitfire IX rep	-	see above	10-13

LAINDON north of the A127, near Basildon

A ***private*** strip in the area holds a Luton Minor. Currie Wot G-BKCN has been deleted.

❑ G-ARXP	Luton Minor	65	CoA 17-10-95. Fuselage	10-23

LONDON SOUTHEND AIRPORT once Southend Airport, or even Rochford EGMC

Vulcan Restoration Trust (VRT): Great strides have been made by the team. The keys to Hangar 6, signifying a lease to this huge facility plus adjacent hangar and offices at the rear, were handed over in June 2022. An incredible amount of work ensued and on 15th October 2022, XL426 rolled in to her former home. A 'Back to Hangar 6' appeal raised a large chunk of the £30,000-plus needed to set-up engineering facilities and to make the hangar fit for the public to visit Southend's Vulcan. The taxi runs on 27th August 2022 celebrated the delta's 60th birthday in fine style; the airport fire crews providing a water arch. ◆ *Regular open days and special events* | **info@avrovulcan.com** | **www.avrovulcan.com**

❑ XL426	Avro Vulcan B.2	62 G-VJET	ex Scampton, Waddington, VDF, VHF, Wadd SF, 50, 617, 27, 617, 230 OCU, 617, 230 OCU, 617, 230 OCU, 617, 230 OCU, Scampton, 83. 617 Sqn colours to port, 50 Sqn to stb	[1]	1-24

■ **[1]** XL426 factoids: Replaced with the Vulcan Display Flight by XH558, it made its last flight 19-12-86, clocking up 6,236 flying hours.

Airport: Airliner storage is mostly transient: only long-termers are given here. **Departures/demises**: Airtourer G-ATEX was flying again by later 2021. Terrier 1 VX113 (G-ARNO) was air tested on 28th February 2022; but suffered an accident 7th June 2022. It was trucked to St Athan, Wales, in August 2022. Maintaining the trend, Husky G-AXBF was airworthy by June 2023. Seneca G-BVEV has been deleted.

❑ G-ATPN	Piper Cherokee 140	66	accident 11-2-18, de-reg 3-8-18	1-23
❑ G-ATRP	Piper Cherokee 140	66	damaged 16-10-81, de-reg 10-11-86	1-23
❑ G-BGAF	Cessna FA.152	78	Reims-built. CoA 25-6-74, accident 2-6-14, de-reg 28-3-17	10-22
❑ G-BOZR*	Cessna 150	80	ex N6083M. De-reg 21-12-21	1-23
❑ G-BPEL	Piper Warrior 151	74	ex C-FEYM. CoA 8-2-92, de-reg 28-2-02	1-23
❑ G-FLTY	Embraer Bandeirante	79	ex G-ZUSS, G-REGA, N711NH, PT-GMH. CoA 5-8-06, de-reg 11-4-06. Rescue trainer from 24-8-18	1-23
❑ G-JOTC	HSA HS.146-300QC	74	ex EC-MHR, OO-TAD, G-TNTM, RP-C480, G-TNTM, G-BSLZ, G-6-166. Woodford-built. Arrived 16-5-18	1-24
❑ D-CSAL	Swearingen Metro III	86	ex I-FSAH, N90AG, OY-BPJ, N3117K. Arrived 19-10-18	1-24
❑ FAB-108	HSA HS.146-RJ70	96	ex Bolivian Air Force - not delivered, VT-MDM, G-CDNB, TC-THJ, G-6-230. Woodford-built. Arr 19-1-18. Engine test rig	1-24

Skylark Airport Hotel: Aviation Way, opposite what was the Historic Aircraft Museum.

❑ VH-AHL	HS HS.748-2/228	69	ex airport, RAAF A10-606	1-24
❑ VH-AMQ	HS HS.748-2/228	68	ex airport, RAAF A10-603. Hulk, damaged by fire 28-1-21	1-24

LONDON STANSTED AIRPORT EGSS

❑ CN-SHS*	Embraer ERJ-190 Lineage	11	ex PT-XUZ. Arrived 26-10-16	9-22
❑ SU-MWC	Boeing 737-683	99	ex Kemble, G-CDKT, SE-DNT. Last flight 4-5-10. Fuselage, Ryanair training school	4-21

Stansted Airport College: Near the Runway 04 threshold, a Challenger provides 'Learning on a Jet Plane'.
◆ *Prior arrangement* **only** | **www.stanstedairportcollege.ac.uk**

❑ G-CIAU	Canadair Challenger 600	82	ex Inflite, M-IFES, N240AK, N800AB, N50928, C-GBZE. De-reg 24-4-18, rolled in 14-11-18		12-20

NORTH BENFLEET on the A130 and east of Basildon

Bonville Farm: By June 2022 Hunter T.7 XL586 had moved to Billericay, Essex. ◆ *Prior arrangement* **only**

❑ G-BODX	Beech Duchess	79	ex N67094. CoA 3-9-09, de-reg 22-10-09, fuselage		1-22

NORTH WEALD AERODROME off the A414, junction 7, M11 east of Harlow EGSX

North Weald Airfield Museum: Based at 'Ad Astra' House, located at the former main gate of the station. In the grounds is a very impressive memorial dedicated to all those who served at 'Weald and another to the Norwegians that were stationed there. The museum spearheaded the Hurricane 'gate guardian' - see below.
◆ *Off Hurricane Way, from North Weald village - ie the B181 -* **not** *via the aerodrome. 'Ad Astra House', 6 Hurricane Way, CM16 6AA* | **01992 523010** | **email** via website | **www.nwamuseum.co.uk**

❑ 'V7313'	'US-F'	Hawker Hurricane FSM	08	BAPC.346. 56 Sqn colours, *Spirit of North Weald* Plinth-mounted, 'guarding' the aerodrome entrance		1-24

Note: The site is extensive: aircraft are listed below under their nominal 'keepers'. Airworthy aircraft are not listed: coverage is restricted to long-term restorations and stored types.

Aero Legends: Carries out some maintenance to the flight experience fleet here but comings and goings are fluid. The main operating base is Lashenden, Kent, plus the Vintage Aero restoration centre at Hythe, Kent - which see.
◆ **Private** *working fleet - prior arrangement* **only** | **www.aerolegends.co.uk**

Hangar 11 Collection: Airworthy Spitfires IX PT879 (G-PTIX) and PR.XI PL965 (G-MKXI) and P-51D G-SIJJ *Tall in the Saddle* remain based. ◆ **Strictly** *prior appointment* **only** | **www.hangar11.co.uk**

Heritage Aircraft Trust | Gnat Display Team: Operates Gnat T.1s XR538 (G-RORI) and 'XR992' (G-MOUR - XS102) from 'Weald. Gnat T.1 'PF179' (XR541) moved to Bournemouth, Dorset, 29th March 2023.
◆ **Strictly** *prior appointment* **only** | **www.facebook.com/gnatdisplay/**

❑ N513X		Folland Gnat T.1	XP513	63	ex USA, *Hot Shots* (1991), XP513, RAE, 4 FTS. F/n 4-16		7-22
❑ XR537		Folland Gnat T.1	G-NATY	63	ex Hurn, Cosford 8642M (10-10-83), 'Red Arrows', 4 FTS. CoA 13-7-16, de-reg 4-4-18. Arrived 12-12-17		7-22
❑ XX841	'EW'	SEPECAT Jaguar T.4	VH-UXB	75	ex Tunbridge Wells, Ipswich, Shawbury, 6, 16, T.2, 6, ETPS, 41, 226 OCU. SOC 15-8-05. 6 Sqn colours. Arrived 27-9-18	[1]	4-23
❑ E296		Folland Gnat F.1	G-SLYR	67	ex N296PS, USA, Indian AF E296. Hindustan-built. Arrived 1-5-14. Taxying by 9-18	[2]	6-22

■ **[1]** Registered to Miltek Aviation Pty, Melbourne. **[2]** Registration derived from the nickname 'Sabre Slayer', from victories in the Indo-Pakistan conflicts of 1965 and 1971.

C-54 Skymaster Trust: ◆ *Prior arrangement* **only** | **info@C54skymaster.com** | **www.facebook.com/savetheskymaster/**

❑ 56498	Douglas C-54Q	N44914	45	ex US Navy R5D-3, USAF MAC, BuNo 56498, USAAF C-54D 42-72525. Arrived 27-9-02. Air Transport Cmd colours	1-24

Weald Aviation Services: Jet warbirds, historic helicopters and others operate out of the 'North Weald Heritage Hangars' and extensive ramp. Only 'long-termers' only are given here. Scout AH.1 XP884 (G-WDST) was in permit by 2022; Scout AH.1 XV130 (G-BWJW) moved to Maidstone, Kent, by late 2021; Lynx AH.7 XZ179 (G-NCKS) gained its permit in April 2022 and, while maintained here, is based in Suffolk; Wasp HAS.1 NZ3909 (G-CMBE) flew after restoration on 30th March 2023. SBLim-5/MiG-17 1211 (G-MIGG) left by truck during October 2023, bound for Poland. The cockpits of Lightning F.6 XR759 and T.55 ZF595 were returned to their owner, Glenn Edwards, by October 2022. ◆ **Strictly** *prior appointment* **only**

❑ G-BVSP		Hunting Jet Provost T.3A		59	ex XM370, 1 FTS, 7 FTS, 1 FTS, 2 FTS. First noted 5-18		8-23
❑ WN149*	'AT'	BP Balliol T.2		54	ex St Mawgan, Cosford, Wolverhampton, Bacup, Salford, Failsworth, RAFC. SOC 26-6-57. Arrived 6-7-23	[1]	11-23
❑ WV322		Hawker Hunter T.8M	G-BZSE	55	ex Exeter, Kemble, Cranwell 9096M (11-5-72), WV322, Kemble, 237 OCU, 764, 736, 809, 764, F.4 92. CoA 19-11-11	[2]	2-23

	Serial	Code	Type	Reg	Year	History	Note	Date
❑	WV798*	'147'	Hawker Sea Hawk FGA.6		54	ex St Mawgan, Wycombe, Lasham, Chertsey, Culdrose A2557, FRU, 801, 803, 787. SOC 25-5-67. 803 Sqn colours. Arrived 6-7-23		11-23
❑	WZ450*		DH Vampire T.11		52	ex St Mawgan, Sleap, Corscombe, Lashenden, N Weald, Birmingham, Sealand, Wrexham, Woodford, Hawarden, Shawbury, RAFC, 233 OCU, 202 AFS. SOC 7-1-69. Christchurch-built. Arrived 6-7-23		7-23
❑	'XD693'	'Z-Q'	Hunting Jet Provost T.1	G-AOBU	55	ex Cranfield, Winchester, Thatcham, Old Warden, Loughborough, Luton, XM129, G-42-1. CoA 13-3-07. 2 FTS colours	[3]	8-23
❑	XT140*		Bell Sioux AH.1		64	ex Malmesbury, Kemble, Perth, Middle Wallop. Agusta-built. SOC 29-3-76. Arrived 8-11-23	[4]	1-24
❑	XT634		Westland Scout AH.1	G-BYRX	66	ex Thruxton, M Wallop. Crashed 29-12-15. De-reg 12-7-16. First noted 5-18		8-19
❑	XZ188		Westland Lynx AH.7		78	ex Lyneham, Arborfield, Fleetlands, 654, 662, 655, 665, 655, LCF, 651. Arrived 20-10-21		2-23
❑	XZ678		W'land Lynx AH.7	G-NCKY	82	ex Ipswich, Fleetlands, M Wallop. Arrived 13-10-21		4-22
❑	ZD252*		Westland Lynx HMA.8SRU	G-NCKZ	98	ex Portsmouth, Yeovilton, 815, Fleetlands, 702, 815, HAS.3, 815. Arrived 22-3-22	[5]	2-23
❑	ZD266*	'673'	Westland Lynx HMA.8		83	ex Bradwell-on-Sea, Bentwaters, 815, 702, DERA, HAS.3, DERA, A&AEE. First noted 7-22		2-23
❑	ZD462*	'52'	BAe/McDD Harrier GR.7		89	ex Malmesbury, Ipswich, Cosford, St Athan, Cosford 9302M, St Athan, 1. Ditched 25-1-97. First noted 2-23		12-23
❑	126922	'H-503'	Douglas AD-4NA Skyraider	G-RADR	48	ex G-RAID, F-AZED, La Ferté Alais, Gabon AF, Fr AF No.42, USN 126922. CoA 19-6-17. VA-155, colours	[3]	2-23
❑	2100884	'L4-D'	Douglas C-47A-75-DL Skytrain	N147DC	42	ex Dunsfold, N Weald, Dunsfold, N Weald, G-DAKS, Duxford, '10884', 'KG374', *Airline* 'G-AGHY', Dakota III TS423, RAE, Ferranti, Airwork, Gatow SF, 436, 1 HGSU, 42-100884. Long Beach-built. 439th TCG, 91st TCS c/s, last flown 10-19	[6]	1-24

■ **[1]** Balliol is described as 'half restoration, half replica' by its previous owners, the Boulton Paul Association. **[2]** Hunter registered to Canfield Hunter Ltd. **[3]** Registered to Tim Manna - see Shuttleworth, Beds. **[4]** Written out of *W&R28* (p68) as having left Kemble, Glos, 20-4-16. **[5]** Registered to Bury St Edmunds-based Graham Hinkley. **[6]** The famous 'G-DAKS' is owned by Aviation Filming – previously Aces High – based at Dunsfold, Surrey.

Also: Seminole G-SEMI has been 'tidied' and deleted.

	Reg	Type	Year	History	Date
❑	G-AHUN	Globe GC-1B Swift	46	ex Thurrock, EC-AJK, OO-KAY, N77764. CoA 4-8-95	4-23
❑	G-AKUP	Luscombe Silvaire 8E	48	ex N2774K	N1-23
❑	G-APTU	Auster 5 Alpha	59	ex Leicester, Sywell, Leicester. CoA 8-6-98	N7-23
❑	G-BDXX	Nord NC.854	54	ex airfield, F-BEZQ. CoA 3-7-96. Off-site	N2-20
❑	G-BIVV	American AA-5	79	ex 'G-PRAT', Elstree, N26979. CoA 18-7-05, de-reg 3-10-08. Rescue training	6-17
❑	G-LUND	Cessna 340 II	73	ex G-LAST, G-UNDY, G-BBNR, N69452. CoA 17-9-06, de-reg 12-4-11	11-23
❑	G-TINY	Zlin Z.526F	72	ex OK-CMD. CoA 1-4-09, de-reg 15-2-21	4-23
❑	G-VDIR	Cessna 310R II	75	ex N5091J. Crashed 4-9-05, de-reg 3-6-06	11-23

PURFLEET on A1090 west of the Dartford Bridge

Purfleet Heritage and Military Centre: Incorporating the **Hornchurch Wing** and housed in the incredible Royal Gunpowder Magazine 18th century arsenal, the centre holds an incredible wealth of aviation artefacts.

◆ *Just off the A1090, in Centurion Way, off Tank Hill Road* | **www.purfleet-heritage.com**

RAYLEIGH on the A1095 northwest of Southend-on-Sea

The Cockpit Collection: Sadly, hopes to keep the V-force cockpits as a single entity did not transpire. Victor K.2 XH669 departed to Duxford, Cambs, 8th December 2022 with Valiant BK.1 XD826 following the next day: donated to IWM by Nigel Towler. Vulcan K.2 XH560 moved to St Athan, Wales, 9th December 2022, via a brief stay at Neatishead, Norfolk. Victor B.2 XH670 departed to St Athan, Wales, 9th December 2022. Vampire T.11 cockpit WZ608 is unaccounted for.

RIDGEWELL on the A1017 southeast of Haverhill

Ridgewell Airfield Memorial Museum: Run by the Ridgewell Airfield Commemorative Association and housed in USAAF Station 167's former hospital Nissen huts, this superb museum – which includes the Tony Ince Collection – honours the 381st Bomb Group and the airfield's illustrious past. ◆ *CO9 4RG* | **email** via website | **www.rafcamuseum.co.uk**

SOUTHEND-ON-SEA

Adventure Island: Marine Parade, Lost City Adventure Golf has a novel putting hazard and the R22 adorns the pay-booth!

❑	G-AZRX	Gardan Horizon 160	63	ex Great Yarmouth, Tattershall Thorpe (?), F-BLIJ. Crashed 14-8-91, de-reg 21-10-91	1-24
❑	G-BOEX	Robinson R22	88	ex Rochester. Crashed 13-8-02, de-reg 11-10-02	1-24

Also: Restoration of the Brochet continues while a Europa is kept in a garden. Both are in *separate* and *private* locations.

❑	G-AVKB	Brochet Pipistrelle	48	ex F-PFAL. CoA 30-10-96	10-23
❑	G-JERO	Shaw Europa XS	02	CoA 21-5-07, de-reg 4-5-23. Fuselage, first noted 6-20	1-24

STAPLEFORD AERODROME or Stapleford Tawney, on the A113 south of the M11/M25 junction EGSG

The hulks of Apache G-BEXO and Tobago G-BHGP had both moved to new careers 'next door' at Abridge, Essex, by April 2023. Excel Helicopters' Gazelle AH.1 cache continues to find customers: XX456 was exported to South Africa by 2021.
◆ ***Not*** available for public inspection.

❑	XW848	'D'	Sud Gazelle AH.1	72	ex Colsterworth, Shawbury, M Wallop, 671, 670, ARWS, AETW. Arrived by 8-12	[1]	10-22
❑	XW913*		Sud Gazelle AH.1	74	ex Colsterworth, Shawbury. Arrived 17-7-12	[1]	10-22
❑	XX394*		Sud Gazelle AH.1	76	ex Colsterworth, Shawbury. Arrived by 6-12	[1]	10-22
❑	XX398*		Sud Gazelle AH.1	74	ex Colsterworth, Shawbury. Arrived 5-10	[1]	10-22
❑	XX437		Sud Gazelle AH.1	76	ex Colsterworth, Shawbury, Wattisham, 669, 664, 651, 652, 661, 663, 12 Flt, 661, 12 Flt, 669. Last flown 2-3-05. Arrived 10-12	[1]	9-21
❑	XX438	'F'	Sud Gazelle AH.1	76	ex Colsterworth, Shawbury, 666, 663, 665, 664. Last flown 26-2-09. Arrived 5-12	[1]	10-22
❑	XX455		Sud Gazelle AH.1	80 G-GRAK	ex Colsterworth, Shawbury, Fleetlands, 652, 661, 655, 663, 669, 659. Last flown 24-1-05. Arrived 5-12	[1]	10-22
❑	XX462	'W'	Sud Gazelle AH.1	76	ex Colsterworth, Shawbury, 658, 669, 661, 652, 661, 662, GCF. Arrived by 8-12	[1]	10-22
❑	XZ292*		Sud Gazelle AH.1	76	ex Colsterworth, Shawbury. Arrived 5-10	[1]	10-22
❑	XZ314*	'A'	Sud Gazelle AH.1	77	ex Colsterworth, Shawbury. Arrived 5-10	[1]	10-22
❑	XZ324*		Sud Gazelle AH.1	77	ex Colsterworth, Shawbury. Arrived 5-10	[1]	10-22
❑	XZ344	'Y'	Sud Gazelle AH.1	78	ex Colsterworth, Shawbury, 658, 3 Flt, 658, 656, 657, 670, 3 Flt, 656, 3 Flt, 655. Arrived by 8-12	[1]	10-22
❑	ZA726*		Sud Gazelle AH.1	79	ex Colsterworth, Shawbury. Arrived 5-10	[1]	10-22
❑	ZA776		Sud Gazelle AH.1	81	ex Colsterworth, Shawbury, Yeovilton, 847, 3 CBAS. Last flown 29-6-05. Arrived 5-12	[1]	10-22

■ **[1]** All Westland-built.

STOW MARIES AERODROME north of the B1012 east of South Woodham Ferrers

Stow Maries Great War Aerodrome: Described as "Europe's most complete surviving Great War aerodrome" is an active flying field, stages regular events, has an expanding museum and an exceptional 'feel'. The site serves as a memorial to aircrew lost from 37 Squadron at Stow Maries, Rochford and Goldhanger. The Airmen's Mess consistently gets votes of approval from the *W&R* cake test pilots! There might well have been a large delivery here by the time of *W&R30*...

Airco DH.2 scale replica '9753' (BAPC.407) and the rear fuselage of a Sopwith Camel replica moved to their owner's home on 26th April 2022.

◆ *Hackmans Lane, Purleigh, CM3 6RN* | **info@stowmaries.org.uk** | **www.stowmaries.org.uk**

❑	G-ABAA	Avro 504K	c1918	ex Manchester, 'H2311', 9244M, Henlow, Heathrow, RAeS, Hendon, Nash, Brooklands. CoA 11-4-39, de-reg 1-1-39. Arrived 20-1-22	[1]	1-24
❑	-	American AA-5B	77	BAPC.546, ex Hendon, 'G-ROWL', Cabair, Elstree. Cockpit. Arrived 10-19		1-24

The impressive Handley Page O/400 forward fuselage replica, May 2022. *Paul Middleton*

Reg		Type	Built	History	Note	Last noted
❑ '168'*		Sopwith Tabloid replica G-BFDE	80	ex Stafford, Hendon, Cardington, Hendon, Cardington, G-BFDE (CoA 4-6-83, de-reg 8-12-86). Arrived 16-5-23	[1]	1-24
❑ 'A653'		Sopwith Pup replica	76	BAPC.179, ex 'A7317', Northampton, Coventry, Waltham Abbey, N Weald, *Wings* (1976). 37 Sqn colours	[2]	1-24
❑ 'A2943'		Royal Aircraft Factory BE.2e replica ✈ G-CJZO	14	ex Old Warden, Bicester, New Zealand, ZK-TFZ. Vintage Aviator-built. Arrived 9-9-17	[3]	1-24
❑ 'F235'	'B'	Rep' Plans SE.5a ✈ G-BMDB	88	ex Boscombe Down. Arrived 12-13		1-24
❑ ZE686		Grob Viking T.1	85	ex Hendon, Syerston, BGA.3099. Cockpit. Arrived 10-19	[4]	1-24
❑ –		Sopwith Camel rep	14	BAPC.414, ex South Africa. Arr 30-4-15. Stored	[5]	1-24
❑ –		'Rocking Nacelle' rep	16	Piloting/gunnery simulator, locally built. Kept off-site	[6]	1-24
❑ –*		HP O/400 replica	20	ex Dereham. The Paralyser Group-built, c/n TPG.2. Forward fuselage. Arrived 26-4-22		1-24
❑ 'D2263'		Albatros D.Va rep ✈ G-WAHT	16	ex Old Warden, ZK-ALB. Vintage Aviator-built. Arrived 15-10-19	[3]	1-24
❑ –*		Fokker F.I replica	21	LAA project 238-15542, construction on display	[7]	1-24
❑ –		Gotha G.V rep	16	BAPC.412. Cockpit. Stow Maries-built. First noted 5-16		1-24

■ **[1]** On loan from the RAF Museum. **[2]** Built by Charles Boddington at Sywell for the TV series *Wings*. **[3]** BE.2 and Albatros on loan from Oliver Wulff / World War One Aviation Heritage Trust (WAHT). **[4]** Viking cockpit *may* be from ZE655. Whichever, it was tested to destruction in mid-1986 in a fatigue rig at Syerston. **[5]** On loan from Bianchi Aviation Film Service Ltd. **[6]** 'Rocking Nacelle' built by local volunteers using Tiger Moth forward fuselage frames to Major Lanhoe George Hawker's scheme for crew familiarisation simulator. Owned by WAHT and used as travelling demonstrator. **[7]** Will be finished as '103/17' as flown by Werne Voss; one of three F.I triplanes (also designated V.5) built prior to production of the only slightly different Dr.I.

Locally: Despite the best intentions of *W&R28* (p65) the MW-7 is still resident: it makes occasional forays into the daylight for events on the aerodrome.

Reg	Type	Built	History	Last noted
❑ G-BPHK	Whittaker MW-7	90	CoA 23-6-04, de-reg 17-6-14	10-23

WESTCLIFF-ON-SEA on the A13, south of Southend-on-Sea

Milton Hall Primary School: A Citation fuselage serves as a classroom. ◆ *Prior arrangement **only**.*

Reg	Type	Built	History	Last noted
❑ G-DWJM	Cessna 550 Citation	81	ex Southend, G-BJIR, N6888C. CoA 18-10-10, de-reg 26-2-14. Fuselage. Arrived 3-16	1-24

WETHERSFIELD on the B1053 west of Halstead

The RAF Police enclave closed in April 2022: the airfield site has been designated as a refugee detention centre.

Wethersfield Airfield Museum: Ross Stewart has been working on this project since 2012 and has assembled an impressive collection of material on the former airfield, which celebrated its 80th anniversary in 2023. So far, the archive is *only* available virtually. ◆ *Building 301, CM7 4AZ* | **www.facebook.com/wethersfieldairfieldmuseum/**

Locally: A 'JP' is kept at a *private* location in the area.

Reg	Type	Built	History	Last noted
❑ XM473	Hunting Jet Provost T.3A	60	ex Ipswich, Bedford, Norwich Airport 'G-TINY', Halton, 8974M (9-6-88), 7 FTS, 1 FTS, 7 FTS, 1 FTS, CFS, 3 FTS, 1 FTS	4-21

WICKFORD on the A129 north of Basildon

Bedlam Paintball: ◆ *Prior arrangement* **only** | **www.bedlampaintball.co.uk**

❑ XT467 'BF' Westland Wessex HU.5 65 ex Layer Marney, Hadleigh, Ipswich, Bramley, Odiham, Laarbruch, Brüggen, Gütersloh, 'XR504' 8922M (8-1-87), Wroughton, 848, 771, Wroughton, 707, 781, 845. F/n 5-20 7-23

❑ XZ175 Westland Lynx AH.7 77 ex Barby, Ipswich, Fleetlands, 25 Flt, 661, 671, LCF, ARWF, 1 FTU. First noted 7-18 7-23

GLOUCESTERSHIRE

Includes the unitary authorities of Bristol and South Gloucestershire

ALVESTON on the A38 north of Bristol

St Helen's Primary School: To honour Frank Sowter Barnwell, designer of such icons as the Bristol F.2B, Bulldog and Blenheim, who lived in the village and is buried in the churchyard, the school has launched its 'Flying High' project. The forward fuselage of an RJ100 is to be turned into a reference library. The initial prep work for the fuselage was carried out at Filton: fuselage 'barrels' of '146s were built there. ◆ *Prior arrangement* **only** | **www.sthelensprimary.org.uk**

❑ 5A-FLA* HSA HS.146 RJ100 93 ex Filton, Kemble, Cranfield, G-CEIH, TC-THA, G-6-232. Woodford-built. Arrived 6-1-23 1-24

ASTON DOWN AIRFIELD south of the A419 west of Cirencester

Cotswold Gliding Club: Grasshopper WZ796 was airworthy by mid-2023. ◆ **www.cotswoldgliding.co.uk**

❑ XP493 Slingsby Grasshopper TX.1 61 ex Syerston. Last flight 9-8-84 7-23

BRISTOL

Bristol's City Museum and Art Gallery: In Queen's Road, the Bristol Boxkite 'flies' within the museum.

◆ *Queen's Road, BS8 1RL* | **0117 9223571** | **email** via website | **www.bristolmuseums.org.uk**

❑ – Bristol Boxkite replica 64 BAPC.40, ex Old Warden, Ford, *Those Magnificent Men...* F G Miles-built 1-24

M-Shed: There are buses, boats, locos and lorries that go 'on steam', a 'Flea' and an observation gallery provides panoramic views of the incredible 'Floating Harbour'. **L-Shed** contains many treasures from the former Bristol Industrial Museum: behind-the-scenes tours can be arranged by prior application.

◆ *Princes Wharf, Wapping Road, BS1 4RN* | **0117 3526600** | **email** via website | **www.bristolmuseums.org.uk**

❑ G-AEHM Mignet HM.14 'Flea' 36 ex Wroughton, Hayes, Sydenham (ie Crystal Palace, London), West Byfleet, Whitchurch, Bristol. *Blue Finch*. De-reg 12-38 [1] 1-24

■ **[1]** Built by Harold Dolman of Bristol - no permit issued. On loan from the Science Museum: acquired 9-38.

Bristol Activity Centre: Cribbs Causeway. ◆ **Only** *by prior permission* | **www.bristolactivitycentre.co.uk**

❑ G-BODW* Bell JetRanger II 72 ex Weston-super-Mare, Lyneham area, G-LOCK. Crashed 13-3-89, de-reg 5-4-94. First noted 4-22 [1] 9-23

❑ G-MCMS* Aero Designs Pulsar 93 de-reg 2-12-15. First noted 4-22 9-23

❑ G-PASA* Bölkow Bö 105D 72 ex Weston-super-Mare, G-BGWP, F-ODMZ, G-BGWP, HB-XFD, N153BB, D-HDAS. CoA 17-1-94, de-reg 20-4-93. Pod. First noted 4-22 [1] [2] 9-23

❑ G-PASB* Bölkow Bö 105D 74 ex Weston-super-Mare, Bourn, VH-LSA, G-BDMC, D-HDAS. De-reg 9-4-94. Pod. First noted 4-22 [1] [3] 9-23

❑ S-882 Sikorsky S-55C ~ ex Weston-super-Mare, Panshanger, Elstree, Dan AF Esk.722 9-23

■ **[1]** JetRanger and Bölkows written out of *W&R24* (p206) at Weston-super-Mare, Somerset, having been disposed: it is likely the hulks have been here ever since. **[2]** Original pod, airframe rebuilt as G-BUXS. **[3]** Original pod, airframe rebuilt as G-WMAA.

Bristol Golf Centre: At the junction of the M32 and A4174. Within is **Caddy Gilmore's Adventure Golf Park** for those who don't find golf daring enough. A helicopter provides an impediment to one of the holes.

◆ **Only** *by prior permission* | **www.caddygilmores.co.uk**

❑ G-OHMS* Aérospatiale Squirrel 82 ex N367E. CoA 4-12-21. Cab/boom 12-23

City of Bristol College: **Advanced Engineering Centre** at New Road, near the Parkway Centre. Last noted in December 2015, the fuselage of HS.125-700A is believed to have been removed. ◆ *Prior application* **only** | **www.cityofbristol.ac.uk**

❑ G-AVDR Beech Queen Air B80 67 ex Hurn, Shobdon, Exeter, A40-CR, G-AVDR. CoA 30-6-86, de-reg 18-5-90. 12-23

❑ N309LJ Learjet 25 69 ex Kemble, Staverton, N309AJ, N19FN, N17AR, N3UC, N6GC, N242WT, N954FA, N954GA. Arrived 11-2-16 12-23

❑ – SAL Bulldog ~ fuselage, all-white colours. First noted 1-23 13-23

Pytch: Brislington Trading Estate. The 727 fuselage has received a radical repaint, courtesy of three local artists. ◆ *Prior application* **only** | **https://pytch.co.uk**

❑ VP-CMN Boeing 727-46 67 ex Kemble, VR-CLM, VR-CBE, N4245S, D-AHLQ, JA8325. Last flown 2011. Fuselage, arrived 27-2-21 12-23

University of Bristol, Faculty of Engineering: Lynx AH.7 XZ649 moved to Weston-super-Mare, Somerset, by August 2023.

Vanguard Storage: Dramatically mounted within the atrium of the Russell Town Avenue facility, on the A420 east of the city centre, is a Lightning. See also Greenford and Neasden, both Gtr Lon. | **www.vanguardstorage.co.uk**

❑ XP745 'H' EE Lightning F.3 64 ex Greenford, Boulmer 8453M (25-9-75), Leconfield, 29, 56. 56 Sqn colours. Arrived 5-19, unveiled 9-19 1-24

CHELTENHAM

In the area, **Nick Parker** has a Scimitar cockpit at a *private* location.

❑ XD215 V-S Scimitar F.1 57 ex Ottershaw, Foulness, Culdrose A2573 (9-10-67), 764B, 800, 803, A&AEE. Cockpit 1-19

CHIPPING CAMPDEN on the B4081 north of Stow on the Wold

Mike Pyment: At a *private* location, the Comet cockpit/flight sim is *believed* extant. ◆ *Prior permission* **only**

❑ XV814 DH Comet 4 G-APDF 58 ex Boscombe D, RAE, MSA, Air Ceylon, BOAC G-APDF. Hatfield-built. Last flown 28-1-93, acquired 13-8-97. Cockpit 10-15

COLEFORD on the B4228 east of Monmouth

An Auster is under restoration in the locality at a *private* workshop.

❑ G-BDFX Taylorcraft Auster 5 45 ex Oaksey Park, Kemble, Oaksey Park, F-BGXG, TW517, 661. Crashed 10-10-93. First noted 7-17 4-21

COTSWOLD AIRPORT or Kemble, on the A429 southwest of Cirencester EGBP

Note: The site is extensive; aircraft are given under nominal 'keepers'.

Bristol Britannia XM496 Preservation Society: Regular open days allow visitors to see how much XM496 is cherished. ◆ *On the airport site, follow the signs marked 'XM496'* | **email** via website | **www.XM496.com**

❑ XM496 Bristol Britannia C.1 G-BDUP 60 ex Lanseria, EL-WXA, 9Q-CJH, CU-T120, Afrek, G-BDUP, Kemble, XM496 99/511. Short-built. Last flight 14-10-97. *Regulus*, RAF colours [1] 1-24

■ **[1]** Factoids: First flown at Sydenham, 24-8-60, delivered to Lyneham 17-9-60; made last-ever flight by a 'Brit', into Kemble, 14-10-97 – the arrival footage on the website is incredible!

British Phantom Aviation Group (BPAG): Consolidation continues: the hardstanding was complete by March 2023; a workshop is next. F-4J(UK) ZE360 is presently undergoing restoration at Manston, Kent - which see.
◆ *At present* **only** *by prior arrangement – keep an eye on the website* | **contact@bpag.co.uk** | **www.bpag.co.uk**

❑ XT597 McD Phantom FG.1 66 ex Wymeswold, Bentwaters, Boscombe Down BDAC, DERA, A&AEE, Bedford, NATC Patuxent River, USN. Last flight 28-1-94. Arrived 21-7-21 [1] 1-24

❑ XT905 'P' McD Phantom FGR.2 68 ex Wymeswold, Bentwaters, North Luffenham, Coningsby 9286M (7-5-00), 74, 228 OCU, 31, 17, 31, 14, 17, 228 OCU. Arrived 29-6-21 [2] 1-24

■ **[1]** XT597 made the last-ever flight by a British Phantom; it is owned by Mark Abbott. **[2]** Owned by BPAG's chairman, Paul Wright.

The Buccaneer Aviation Group: (TBAG, pronounced, lovingly, as Tea-Bag!) Both 'birds' are up and running as is the supporters' group – the Buccaneer Buddies Club. ◆ *Regular events, otherwise* **only** *by prior arrangement* | **thebuccaneeraviationgroup2020@gmail.com** | **www.the-buccaneer-aviation-group.com**

❑ XW544	'O'	Blackburn Buccaneer S.2B	72	ex Bruntingthorpe, Shawbury, Cosford 8857M (21-5-85), Shawbury, 16, 15. 16 Sqn c/s. Arr 21-8-20, first taxi 3-7-21	[1]	1-24
❑ XW550		Blackburn Buccaneer S.2B	73	ex Bridgnorth, B'thorpe, West Horndon, Stock, St Athan, 16, 15. SOC 18-8-80. Cockpit. 16 Sqn c/s. Arrived by 9-21	[2]	1-24
❑ XX894	'020'	Blackburn Buccaneer S.2B	75	ex Bruntingthorpe, Farnborough, Kemble, Bruntingthorpe, St Athan, 208, 16, 12, 208, 12. Last flown 7-4-94. 809 Sqn colours, *Norma*. Taxiable. Arrived 21-8-20	[3]	1-24

■ **[1]** XW544 owned by Rob Goldstone. **[2]** XW550 owned by Francis Wallace and TBAG. **[3]** XX894 owned by Colin Robinson; on 27-2-91 it destroyed an An-12 *Cub* on the ground at Shaykh Mazhar, Iraq.

Resource Group: Instructional airframe fleet. ◆ *Prior arrangement* **only**. | **https://training.resourcegroup.co.uk**

❑ G-BIBG		Sikorsky S-76A II+	80	ex Aberdeen, Norwich, 5N-BCE, G-BIBG. CoA 18-8-09, de-reg 8-12-09. Arrived 13-8-13.		4-20
❑ D-ASDB		VFW-Fokker 614	77	ex St Athan, Copenhagen, Muk Air OY-RRW, D-ASDB, Luftwaffe 17+03, D-BABS		1-24
❑ N19EK	'K'	HS Dominie T.1	66	ex Cranwell, XS737, 55, 6 FTS, 1 ANS, HS. Arrived 14-5-11		1-24
❑ N19UG	'H'	HS Dominie T.1	65	ex Cranwell, XS730, 55, 3 FTS, 6 FTS, 1 ANS. Arrived 14-6-11		1-24
❑ 80+55		Bőlkow Bő 105M	~	ex St Athan, HEER		1-24
❑ 80+77		Bőlkow Bő 105M	~	ex Hoofddorp, HEER		1-24

Negus 747: After much preparation and planning Boeing 747 G-CIVB was officially opened on 11th February 2022 and a series of public tours dates was launched. To help earn its keep, it is also available for hire for functions and film use.
◆ *Public tour days, see* **www.negus747.com**

Also: Storage and parting out of airliners is Kemble's forte: most of this done by **Air Salvage International** and too transitory for *W&R*; only long-term items are listed here. The **AV8 Cafe** is well worth visiting. The plaudits in 'social media' sound over the top but are *underplaying* the service and quality on offer!

Departures: During 2022 Canberra PR.9 XH135 was offered up for disposal. A crowd-funding campaign to save the entire airframe failed, but the cockpit, rear fuselage and engines moved to West Raynham, Norfolk, 1-8-22. The cockpit of 747-436 G-BYGA was trucked to Manchester City (aka Barton), Gtr Man, 11-8-22. The cockpit of G-EMBC, lasted noted 12-21 is believed to have been scrapped 3-22. Part of the scenery since its arrival 17-5-09, Boeing 747 G-MKGA was scrapped late November 2022. Warrior G-WFFW has been deleted. The 'forward fuselage' of CRJ-900 PH-ADO is less its cockpit and has *also* been deleted.

❑ G-EMBC		Embraer EMB-145EP	97	ex Exeter, PT-SYU. De-reg 13-4-17. Cockpit, first noted 9-19		12-21
❑ G-BRIA		Cessna 310L	67	ex N2210F. CoA 29-6-08, de-reg 12-12-10. Fire/rescue tnr	[1]	1-23
❑ G-CIVB		Boeing 747-436	93	ex Heathrow, BA. 'Retro' BA colours. Arrived 8-10-20. De-reg 30-10-20. See notes above	[2]	1-24
❑ G-CIVN		Boeing 747-436	97	ex Heathrow, BA. Arrived 16-4-20, de-reg 21-1-21. Scrapped 12-23, flightdeck extant		1-24
❑ G-COTH*		MD 900 Explorer	01	ex Kidlington, N3ND. De-reg 31-5-23		6-23
❑ G-JRSL		Agusta 109E	98	CoA 22-12-01, de-reg 6-7-00. Hulk, rescue training		4-19
❑ G-TLET*		Piper Cadet 161	89	ex Hurn, Shoreham, G-GFCF, G-RHBH, N9193Z. Cr 21-7-12, CoA 18-10-12, de-reg 10-6-13. Arrived 31-3-22	[3]	5-22
❑ EZ-A107		Boeing 717-200	05	ex Turkmenistan AL. Arr 3-10-18, broken up 3-21. Cockpit		7-23
❑ LY-SPC*		Airbus A320-200	94	ex EI-ETM, LY-COS, EI-ETM, SX-SMV, N301LF, ZA-RED, N415MX, EI-TLT, B-HYV, VR-HYV, F-WWBL. Toulouse-built. Arrived 22-12-19		1-24
❑ M-FTOH		Boeing 727-269	80	ex N169KT, 9K-AFA. Arrived 29-6-16, de-reg 11-7-16		1-24
❑ N19CU	'E'	HS Dominie T.1	65	ex Cranwell, XS728, 55, 6 FTS, RAFC, 6 FTS, 1 ANS. Arr 13-6-11		6-23
❑ 2-MMTT		Boeing 727-76	66	ex M-FAHD, VP-BAB, N682G, N10XY, N8043B, VH-TJD. Arrived 7-12-18		1-24
❑ LZ844	'UP-X'	V-S Spitfire V	43	ex Australia, 'R6915', Auckland, New Guinea, cr 12-12-43, RAAF A58-213, LZ844 n/s. CBAF-built. Arr 11-7-11. Stored		8-13
❑ XE665	'876'	Hawker Hunter T.8C G-BWGM	55	ex Exeter, G-BWGM (CoA 24-6-98, de-reg 16-3-11), Shawbury, Yeovilton, FRADU, 764, Jever SF, 118. Squires Gate-built. Displayed at the AV8 Cafe		1-24

	Serial	Code	Type	Built / Reg	Details	Note	Last noted
❑	XH134		EE Canberra PR.9	59 G-OMHD	ex Midair, Marham, 39, 1 PRU, 39, 58, MoA. Short-built. Arrived 31-7-06. CoA 13-8-15. 'Silver' scheme	[4]	1-23
❑	'XR540'		Folland Gnat T.1	62 XP502	ex Ipswich, St Athan 8576M, 4 FTS. 'Red Arrows' colours. Displayed		1-24

■ **[1]** Erroneously omitted from *W&R28*. **[2]** *Victor-Bravo* owned by Kemble Air Services. **[3]** *Echo-Tango* was the test-bed for the Thielert TME 125 diesel. **[4]** XH134 registered to Kemble Airfield Estates 9-16: reported bound for Indian Air Force Vintage Flight.

DURSLEY on the A4135 southwest of Stroud

Retro Track and Air Ltd: Specialist engine overhaul and airframe company equally at home with historic Grand Prix cars. Spitfire IX TE566 (VH-IXT) was sold and is undergoing restoration in two-seat form at an undisclosed venue.

◆ **Strictly** *prior arrangement only* | **www.retrotrackandair.com**

	Serial	Code	Type	Built / Reg	Details	Note	Last noted
❑	N5719		Gloster Gladiator II	38 G-CBHO	ex Narvik, 263. Abandoned in Norway 22-5-40	[1]	N7-23
❑	P8208		V-S Spitfire IIb	41 G-RRFF	ex Oxford, Severn estuary, 52 OTU, 1 CACU, 1 CACF, 303. CBAF-built. Crashed 26-1-43	[1]	N6-21
❑	WP859	'E'	DHC Chipmunk T.10	52 G-BXCP	ex Kemble, 8 AEF, 4 AEF, Lpl UAS, PFS, AOTS, 1 ITS, Bri UAS, 4 SoTT, 663, RAFC. Hawarden-built. De-reg 18-4-17		6-18
❑	GA-43		Gloster Gamecock II	28 G-CGYF	ex Finland, Finnish AF	[1]	N7-23
❑	E.1B-46*		Bücker Jungmeister	42 G-CMMH	ex Spanish AF. CASA-built	[1]	N2-23

■ **[1]** Registered to Retro Track and Air.

Chris Wiltshire: Keeps a Vampire cockpit in the locality. ◆ *Prior arrangement* **only**

	Serial	Code	Type	Built	Details	Last noted
❑	XD452	'66'	DH Vampire T.11	54	ex Chester, Whixhall, Whitchurch, London Colney, Shawbury, 7990M (19-2-68), 3 FTS, 7 FTS, 1 FTS, 8 FTS, 5 FTS. Hawarden-built. Cockpit	12-23

FILTON south of the M5 at Patchway, north of Bristol

Aerospace Bristol / Bristol Aero Collection Trust: While the purpose-built hall that houses *Alpha-Fox* dominates the site it is the coupled World War One era aircraft sheds that provide the greatest interest and a perfect backdrop for the collection.

◆ *Hayes Way, Patchway, BS34 5BZ* | ***Note****: Occasionally, the Concorde Hangar – and sometimes the whole site – is closed for private events: keep an eye on the website to see if the champagne-swilling elite have made way for you!* **info@aerospacebristol.org** | **www.aerospacebristol.org**

	Serial	Code	Type	Built / Reg	Details	Note	Last noted
❑	'G-EASQ'		Bristol Babe III replica	72	BAPC.87, ex Kemble, Banwell, Stoke, Hemswell, Cleethorpes, Selby. Acquired 11-94, arrived by 12-12		1-24
❑	G-ALRX		Bristol Britannia 101	53	ex Kemble, Banwell, Boscombe Down, WB473 / VX447. Crashed 4-2-54, de-reg 5-4-54. Cockpit. Acquired 23-12-13, arrived by 12-12		1-24
❑	G-BOAF		BAC/Sud Concorde 102	79	ex BA, G-N94AF, G-BFKX. CoA 11-6-04. De-reg 11-6-04. Flew in 26-11-03. Rolled in 7-2-17	[1]	1-24
❑	–		BAC/Sud Concorde EMU	~	ex Kemble, Brooklands. Test shell, nose. Acquired 1997		1-24
❑	'A1742'		Bristol Scout replica	62	BAPC.38, ex Old W', Solihull, Norwich, Lowestoft, Duxford, St Mawgan, St Athan, Colerne, Weeton. Arrived by 3-17	[2]	1-24
❑	'A7288'	'7'	Bristol F.2B replica	10	BAPC.387. Unveiled 10-7-10	[3]	1-24
❑	–		Bristol F.2B	~	BAPC.386. Ex conservation centre, USA. Acquired 2013, arrived 2-10-20. Suspended over 'A7288', unveiled 18-10-22. Uncovered fuselage frame and and wings	[4]	1-24
❑	–		Bristol Beaufighter	c42	BAPC.463, ex Hendon, East Fortune, Hendon, Duxford, Hendon, Cranfield. Cockpit. First noted 7-16	[5]	1-24
❑	XF785		Bristol 173 Srs 1	52 G-ALBN	ex Kemble, Cosford, Henlow 7648M (10-7-60), G-ALBN (de-reg 21-7-60). Arrived 8-1-13		1-24
❑	XL824		Bristol Sycamore HR.14	57	ex Stafford, Manchester, Henlow 8021M (11-6-68), Wroughton, CFS, 1564 Flt, 103, 284. Oldmixon-built. Arr -15		1-24
❑	ZD610	'000' *and* '126'	HS Sea Harrier F/A.2	85	ex Bruntingthorpe, Dunsfold, Yeovilton, 800, 899, 801, 800, 899, 801, 899. Arrived 30-9-15, airlifted on site 3-17. 801 Sqn colours to stb, 800 to port	[6]	1-24

■ **[1]** *Alpha-Fox* factoids: Last UK Concorde built, first flown at Filton 20-4-74 and made the type's last-ever flight, back to its birthplace, on 26-11-03. Withdrawn from British Airways service 24-10-03, total hours 18,257, landings 6,045. It is on long-term loan from British Airways. **[2]** Scout 'A1742' is a fine static replica restored by Keith Williams and Mike Thorne. **[3]** F.2B replica built by GKN-Aerospace and Rolls-Royce apprentices for the BAC 100 celebrations, 2010. **[4]** Fuselage frame *reputed* to be a former Weston-on-the-Green example, but the author doubts this. Replica wings built near Boston, USA, by Andy Crumpholt. May, or may not, *also* be BAPC.496... **[5]** Beaufighter cockpit on loan from RAF Museum; thought to be from a 1941-1942-built Merlin XX Mk.IIf. **[6]** 'SHAR' on loan from Gary Spoors - see also his main reference at St Athan, Wales. It was airlifted across the former airfield from the Brabazon hangar storage site by an RAF Chinook 3-17. Its Dunsfold origins might seem at odds with the 'Bristol' theme, but its exceptional Bristol Siddeley Pegasus engine is 100% Filton.

Conservation-in-Action Workshop: Hangar 16M, a 1916 structure last used by the Western Air Ambulance, was inaugurated on 15th July 2021. The anonymous F.2B was moved to the main display hall – above – in 2022.

❑ 9048	'YO-T'	Bristol Bolingbroke IV	41	ex Kemble, USA, RCAF, 7 BGS, 3 BGS, 8(BR). SOC 21-8-46. Fairchild Canada-built. Arrived 25-7-06, acquired 11-19	[1]	1-24
❑ NZ5911	G-AMPK	Bristol 170 Mk.31M	53	ex Ardmore, NZ ZK-EPG, RNZAF NZ5911, ZK-BJP, NZ5911, G-AMPK. Last flight 31-8-78. Arrived 28-12-17		1-24

■ **[1]** Donated by Graham Kilsby in honour of his late father W K Kilsby.

Rolls-Royce Heritage Trust - Bristol Branch: The **Sir Roy Fedden Heritage Centre** keeps an exceptional array of engines, and supportive material, large and small. As well as Bristol and Bristol Siddeley and Rolls-Royce (from 1966), de Havilland and Blackburn powerplants are also represented. ◆ *Prior arrangement* **only** | **www.rolls-royce.com/about/heritage-trust**

No.**2152 (North Bristol) Squadron Air Cadets**: Pine Grove. Last noted in June 2016; the cockpit of Archer II G-BOXY had turned up at Enstone, Oxfordshire, by April 2022.

GLOUCESTER

Gloster Aviation Club: Clive Davies and friends are hard at work on the collection of cockpits. The interior XG331 has been transformed from an empty void and is nearing completion. (Clive is a part owner of Canberra WT333 at 'Brunters' - aka Bruntingthorpe, Leics - which see.) ◆ **Not** *available for public inspection*

❑ XE339	'149'	Hawker Sea Hawk FGA.6	55	ex Dunsfold, Lee-on-Solent, Culdrose A2635, Halton 8156M (19-1-71), FRU, 801, 803, 800. AWA-built. Cockpit	1-24
❑ XF383		Hawker Hunter F.6	56	ex Kidlington, North Scarle, Wittering 8706M (19-1-82), Kemble, 12, 216, 237 OCU, 4 FTS, 229 OCU, 65, 111, 263. AWA-built. 65 Sqn colours. Cockpit	1-24
❑ XG331		EE Lightning F.1(DB)	59	ex Quedgeley, Staverton, Hucclecote, Barton, Chelford, Long Marston, Innsworth, Staverton, Foulness, Warton, A&AEE. Last flight 28-9-66. Cockpit	1-24
❑ ZF590		EE Lightning F.53	68	ex Upwood, Binbrook, Lewes, *Wing Commander* (1999), Portsmouth, Warrington, Warton, Saudi AF 220, 53-679, G-27-49. Last flown 22-1-86. Cockpit	1-24

Also: A Hunter cockpit is *believed* kept at a *private* location in the general area.

❑ XX466	'830'	Hawker Hunter T.7	59	ex Guernsey, Predannack A2651 [2], Culdrose SAH A2738 (15-5-86), FRADU, 1 TWU, Jordan AF, Saudi AF 70-616, HSA, XL620, 74, 66. Cockpit. Arrived 9-6-16	9-16

GLOUCESTERSHIRE AIRPORT or Staverton

EGBJ

Jet Age Museum: Seems like only yesterday, but in July 2023 JAM celebrated a decade open to the public at Staverton. Operated by the **Gloucestershire Aviation Collection**, the museum tells the story of the jet engine, Gloster aircraft and the aerospace industry of the region. A fabulous example of community support took place in the spring of 2022. Runway resurfacing was greatly facilitated by the museum allowing the contractor's plant to access via its premises. This required Jet Age to close over several weekends but earned a goodly number of 'brownie points' in the process.

As foretold in *W&R28* (p71) Canberra TT.18 WK126 did indeed move to St Athan, Wales, making the trip on 17th August 2022. Javelin FAW.4 XA634 made the trek to Binbrook, Lincs, 30th September 2022.

◆ *Meteor Business Park, GL2 9QL* | **01452 260078** | **email** via website | **https://jetagemuseum.org**

❑ G-AWZU	HS Trident 3B-101	71	ex Basingstoke, Stansted, Heathrow, BA, BEA. CoA 3-7-85, de-reg 18-3-86. *Tina*. Forward fuselage, BEA colours to port, BA to stb. Arrived 28-11-13	[1]	1-24

❑ –*		Electro-Flight P1e FSM	16	ex Brimscombe. Full-size engineering model		**due**
❑ 'J7904'		Gloster Gamecock reproduction	97	BAPC.259, ex Staverton, Dursley, Staverton. Unveiled 9-8-98, arrived 10-13. 43 Sqn colours	[2]	1-24
❑ N5914		Gloster Gladiator II	40	ex Dursley, Norway, 263. Shot down 2-6-40. Recovered 12-98, arrived on-site 20-11-13. Restoration project	[3]	1-24
❑ 'V6799'	'SD-X'	Hawker Hurricane FSM	68	BAPC.72, ex 'V7767', Hurn, Brooklands, N Weald, Baginton, Stoneleigh, *Battle of Britain* (1968). Acq 2-7-97. 501 Sqn c/s		1-24
❑ –		Airspeed Horsa replica	16	BAPC.383. Cockpit, built on site		1-24
❑ -		Hawker Typhoon I	c42	BAPC.363, ex Staverton, Twyford, Chippenham. Gloster-built. Cockpit, arrived 26-8-17	[4]	1-24
❑ 'W4041/G'		Gloster E28/39 FSM	05	BAPC.331, on site 2003	[5]	1-24
❑ EE425		Gloster Meteor F.3	45	ex Yatesbury, Earls Colne, Andrewsfield, PEE Foulness (16-2-56), 206 AFS, 210 AFS, 206 AFS, 63, 266, 1, 222. Cockpit. Acquired 1-00. Moved back on site 5-4-12		1-24
❑ VW453		Gloster Meteor T.7	49	ex Innsworth 8703M, Salisbury Plain -CDE, A&AEE, 604, 226 OCU, 203 AFS. SOC 12-6-57. Arrived 22-4-13	[6]	1-24
❑ WH364	'A'	Gloster Meteor F.8	52	ex Kemble 8169M (23-8-71), 85, Takali C&TTS, Idris SF, Takali SF, 601. Arrived 10-9-03. 601 Sqn colours		1-24
❑ 'WM366'		Gloster Meteor TT.20 WM234	52	ex Bruntingthorpe, Enstone, Lasham, Aborfield, FRL, NF.11, 68, 264. AWA-built. Suez stripes. Arrived 16-4-14	[7]	1-24
❑ WS807	'N'	Gloster Meteor NF(T).14	54	ex Kemble, Staverton, Bentham, Staverton, Yatesbury, Watton 7973M (6-7-67), Kemble, 1 ANS, 2 ANS, NF.14, 46. AWA-built. Arrived 7-97. 46 Sqn colours		1-24
❑ XE664		Hawker Hunter F.4	55	ex Marlborough, ?, HSA, 26. SOC 14-4-59. Squires Gate-built. Cockpit. Acquired 21-2-99. Moved on site 5-4-12	[8]	1-24
❑ XH903	'G'	Gloster Javelin FAW.9	58	ex Bentham, Staverton, Hucclecote, Innsworth 7938M (10-8-67), Shawbury, 5, 33, 29, 33, FAW.7, 23. Acquired 19-5-93. 33 Sqn colours	[9]	1-24
❑ XM569		Avro Vulcan B.2	63	ex Bentham, Staverton, Enstone, Cardiff, 44, Wadd Wing, 27, Cott Wing, 27. SOC 21-1-83. Arrived 6-2-97. Cockpit	[10]	1-24
❑ XW264		HS Harrier T.2	69	ex Hucclecote, Innsworth, Dowty, Boscombe D, HSA. Damaged 11-7-70. Acquired 28-6-94. Cockpit	[11]	1-24
❑ -		Folland Gnat T.1 CIM	c62	ex Innsworth. Procedures trainer, forward cockpit. Folland-built. Arrived circa 2014	[12]	1-24

■ **[1]** Donated by Gary Spoors - see also St Athan, Wales. **[2]** Gamecock is fitted with a Jupiter IV, on loan from the RAF Museum. **[3]** On 2-6-40, flown by P/O J L Willkie, N5914 was shot down by a 1/ZG 76 Bf 110 flown by Lt Helmut Lent; Willkie was killed. **[4]** Typhoon salvaged from a yard in Chippenham in 1998, the Typhoon's restoration is dedicated to the memory of Michele Clarke. **[5]** E28/39 FSM used the mouldings for the Farnborough, Hampshire, and Lutterworth, Leics, examples. **[6]** VW453 acquired for JAM in 2013 by Tony Mackinnon and Martin Clarke. **[7]** A complex composite, with the centre section, wings and tailplane from ex Israeli DF/AF 1953-built NF.13 4X-FNA / 5616, ex RAF WM366, A&AEE and RRE; the cockpit from TT.20 WM234 (service history quoted above); and rear fuselage of F.8 VZ462 from Biggin Hill. Previously owned by Gary Spoors, title was transferred to Jet Age in exchange for Meteor WF784 in 8-21. **[8]** Hunter F.4 XE664, original nose, on loan from Bob Kneale. The remainder of XE664 was refurbished in 1959 as a T.8 for the FAA with a new cockpit. In 1969 it was rebuilt for the Singapore ADC as T.75 514 (G-9-293 allocated) and is preserved in New Zealand. **[9]** Previously on loan from the RAF Museum, XH903 was gifted to Jet Age in 2023. **[10]** Vulcan cockpit is on loan from Gary Spoors and David Price, via JAM. **[11]** The wings of XW264 are on XV798 at Hucknall, Notts. **[12]** One that got away, with thanks to Paul Griffiths. This came from 2342 (Innsworth) Sqn, Air Training Corps.

Airport: Robin G-BGBA was written out of *W&R28* (p71) but is still present. The comments below about 'see above' are doubly meaningful – it's stacked on top of a hangar office! Airtourer G-ATHT has been deleted; Tomahawk G-TMHK was flying by 2022; Navajo N477PM left by road for St Athan, Wales, 3rd November 2022; Meteor T.7 WL349 moved to Newquay, Cornwall, during August 2022.

❑ G-BGBA		Robin R2100A Club	78	ex F-OCBA. CoA 23-10-12, de-reg 9-4-14. Fuselage, see above		5-23
❑ N936CT*		Cirrus SR-22	~	crashed 6-6-13. Cockpit, first noted 8-22		5-23
❑ XZ132*	'C'	HS Harrier GR.3	76	ex Selby, Cranwell 9168M, St Athan, 4, 1, 1351 Flt, 1, 233 OCU, 1, 3. Arrived 15-4-19	[1]	8-23

■ **[1]** Harrier kept by a private owner. This was written out of *W&R27* at Selby, N Yorks, as departing for 'Gloucestershire' – which turned out to be staggeringly accurate!

MARSHFIELD Jodel D.150 G-BMEH has been deleted.

A pair of Tornados, 'airliner' burning rigs amid the complex Fire Service College site, July 2023. *David Collier*

MORETON-IN-MARSH on the A44 northeast of Cheltenham

Wellington Aviation Museum: The collection deals in depth with RAF Moreton-in-Marsh but its displays take in a fascinating sweep of wartime artefacts and details. ◆ *Bourton Road, GL56 0HB* | **www.wellingtonaviation.org**

The Fire Service College: Purpose-built rigs are the teaching aid of choice at the site, including a helicopter (referred to as a 'Merlin') and a jetliner (called a '737'). *W&R28* (p72) wrote out 172 G-AZDZ but it was extant in the summer of 2023, semi-hidden in the treeline. ◆ *Prior arrangement* **only** | **www.fireservicecollege.ac.uk**

Reg		Type		History	Date
❑ G-AZDZ		Cessna 172K	69	ex Firbeck, Fownhope, Warmingham, Southend, 5N-AIH, N1647C, N84508. Crashed 19-9-81, de-reg 5-12-83	7-23
❑ XP680		Hunting Jet Provost T.4	62	ex St Athan 8460M (21-12-75), CAW, 6 FTS. 'Crash' scene	1-22
❑ XZ187		Westland Lynx AH.7	78	ex Lyneham, Arborfield, Fleetlands, 655, 667, 655, 667, 655, 651, 654. Arrived 3-21	6-22
❑ XZ207		Westland Lynx AH.7	79	ex Lyneham, Arborfield, Fleetlands, 652, 669, 655, 654. Crashed 17-4-00. Cabin. Arrived 24-8-21	6-22
❑ ZE165	'GE'	Panavia Tornado F.3	86	ex Manston. Shawbury, 43. Arrived 30-11-20	7-23
❑ ZG773		Panavia Tornado GR.4	92	ex Boscombe Down, Warton, BAE Systems/BAe, GR.1. Last flown 20-1-16. Arrived 2020	7-23
❑ TAD.013	'A'	Westland Lynx HC.28 G-BFDV	77	ex Lyneham, Arborfield, Fleetlands, Almondbank, Wroughton, Qatar Police QP-30, G-BFDV, de-reg 18-7-78. Arr 24-8-21	6-22

STONEHOUSE on the A419 west of Stroud

Tile Trader: On the Reyford Industrial Estate displays an unflown VP-2. **www.tiletraderstroud.co.uk**

Reg	Type		History	Date
❑ G-BEFV*	Evans VP-2	c89	de-reg 6-12-95. First noted 6-20	8-21

TETBURY on the A433 southwest of Cirencester

Military Mementos: The cockpit of Venom FB.50 J-1573 moved to Ledbury, Herefordshire, on 28th January 2022 and was followed by March 2022 by Vampire T.11 cockpit XE982, to Port Talbot, Wales.

TEWKESBURY on the A38 north of Gloucester

A *private* yard in the *general* area holds a cache of WG.30s. ◆ **Strictly private** *site - no public access.*

Reg	Type		History	Note	Date
❑ VT-EKE	Westland WG.30-100-60 G-BLPR	84	ex Biggin Hill (?), Redhill, India, Pawan Hans, G-BLPR. First noted 6-00		6-20
❑ VT-EKG	Westland WG.30-100-60 G-BLTY	85	ex Biggin Hill (?), G-BLTY (31-8-04 to 2-2-11), Redhill, India, Pawan Hans, G-BLTY, G-17-9. First noted 6-00		6-20
❑ VT-EKK	W'land WG.30-100-60	86	ex Redhill, India, Pawan Hans, G-17-13. First noted 6-00		6-20
❑ VT-EKL	W'land WG.30-100-60	86	ex Redhill, India, Pawan Hans, G-17-14. First noted 6-00		6-20
❑ VT-EKM	W'land WG.30-100-60	86	ex Redhill, India, Pawan Hans, G-17-15. First noted 6-00		6-20
❑ VT-EKN	W'land WG.30-100-60	86	ex Redhill, India, Pawan Hans, G-17-16. First noted 6-00		6-20
❑ VT-EKX	W'land WG.30-100-60	87	ex Redhill, India, Pawan Hans, G-17-27. First noted 6-00		6-20
❑ VT-EKY	Westland WG.30-100-60	87	ex Redhill, Biggin Hill (?), India, Pawan Hans, G-17-28. First noted 6-00		6-20
❑ N112WG	W'land WG.30-100-60	84	ex WSM, Yeovil (?), PanAm. De-reg 8-6-13	[1]	6-20
❑ N118WG	W'land WG.30-100-60	84	ex WSM, Yeovil (?), PanAm. De-reg 4-1-13	[1]	6-20
❑ N5820T	W'land WG.30-100-60	84	ex WM, Yeovil (?), Airspur. De-reg 4-11-13	[1]	6-20

■ **[1]** *Believed* arrived 14-6-11.

THORNBURY west of the A38, north of Bristol

Delta Force Paintball: Gloucester Road. ◆ *Prior arrangement* **only** | **www.paintballgames.co.uk**

❑ XZ723 '672' Westland Lynx HMA.8 80 ex Ipswich, Fleetlands, 815, 702, 815, HAS.3, 815, HAS.2. First noted 6-16 2-19

TODENHAM east of the A429, south of Shipston on Stour

A Hunter is held at a *private* location in the area.

❑ WT804 '831' Hawker Hunter GA.11 55 ex Moreton-in-Marsh, Culdrose A2646, A2732 (22-10-85), Shawbury, FRADU, Lossiemouth, 247. Arrived 10-17 9-22

HAMPSHIRE

Includes the unitary authorities of Portsmouth and Southampton

ALTON on the A339 southwest of Farnham

Iron Curtain Museum: With the masthead 'A trip through some of our most dangerous years', a collection of military hardware – mostly tracked – has been assembled from late 2018. As W&R29 goes to press, the collection was due to open to the public on 4th May 2024.◆ *Keeper's Lodge, GU34 4AB* | **www.facebook.com/the ironcurtainmuseum/**

❑ –* Bell JetRanger ~ first noted 4-21 7-22

❑ 7811 M-G MiG-21MF *Fishbed* 68 ex Polish AF. Arrived 26-1-20 6-22

Flying Without Fear: The One-Eleven fuselage is used as a teaching aid: 'Nothing to lose and a whole world to gain'. ◆ *On the A339 at GU34 4BH* | **www.flyingwithoutfear.com**

❑ G-AWYV BAC 111-501EX 69 ex Hurn, European, BA, BCAL, Caledonian, BUA. CoA 24-6-04, de-reg 17-12-04. Forward fuselage 5-22

BASINGSTOKE on the A33 southwest of Reading

Centerprise International: A former Danish Hunter is displayed outside this IT and 'solutions' specialist at the Hampshire International Business Park. ◆ **www.centerprise.co.uk**

❑ '349' [٣٤٩] Hawker Hunter F.51 E-408 56 ex 'WT720', Lee-on-Solent, Caerphilly, North Scarle, Sealand, Cranwell 'XF979', Brawdy 8565M, Dunsfold, G-9-436 (10-7-76), Esk.724, Dan AF E-408. Iraqi AF c/s, arrived 5-19 6-23

Also: At a *private* venue in the locality, an Auster is under restoration.

❑ TJ672 'TS-D' Taylorcraft Auster 5 G-ANIJ 44 ex Netheravon, Eggesford, Hurn, 227 OCU, 657. CoA 5-5-71 4-20

BLACKBUSHE AERODROME on the A30 west of Yateley EGLK

Blackbushe Heritage Trust: The very act of bringing *Vagabond* back from Austria to a 'Nissen-like' workshop at Blackbushe is an exceptional achievement. Fundraising and restoration are going on hand-in-hand towards a visitor centre that will tell this airfield's incredibly varied history. ◆ *Occasional special events for members; otherwise by prior arrangement* ***only***. | **team@blackbusheheritagetrust.com** | **www.blackbusheheritagetrust.com**

❑ G-AGRW* Vickers Viking 1 46 ex Vienna, Soesterberg, Autair, Overseas, Hunting, Airwork, trooping XF640, BEA *Vagabond*. De-reg 19-2-68. Arr 2-5-23 1-24

Others: Disabled flying charity **Aerobility** acquired a new simulator in the shape of a Cessna 172 during the summer of 2022. Its predecessor is stored under an impressive layer of dust. Aerobility is managing former RAF Vigilant T.1s, reconfigured and designated G.109 Ables to provide air experience for disabled people. While the work is being carried out at Membury, Berks, airframes are held in store at an unspecified site (ie *not* at Blackbushe). **www.aerobility.com**

❑ G-BDFW Rockwell Commander 112 75 ex N1308J. CoA 22-11-08, de-reg 5-4-11. *This is it!* Spares 7-22

❑ G-KITE Piper Archer II 84 ex N4338X. Cr 3-5-08, de-reg 12-28-08. Cockpit, stored 8-22

❑ G-NIUS* Cessna F.172N 78 ex Netherthorpe, Morgansfield, EI-BSC, G-NIUS. Reims-built. Damaged 29-1-16, de-reg 12-6-20. Cabin, simulator 8-22

❑ N9432B Cessna 175C 58 ex Seething. Arrived 2-15. Poor state 7-22

BORDON and LONGMOOR CAMP on the A325 south of Farnham

A pair of Lynx *may* still serve as targets/waypoints.

❑ XZ190		Westland Lynx AH.7	78	ex M Wallop, AH.1. Arrived 2012	7-19
❑ XZ677		Westland Lynx AH.7	82	ex M Wallop, AH.1. Arrived 2012	7-19

BRAMLEY southeast of Tadley, east of the A340

Army Training Estate Home Counties: Although mostly dated, the airframes are *thought* current.

❑ XK970		Westland Whirlwind HAR.10	56	ex Odiham 8789M, Akrotiri, 84, 230, CFS, Khormaksar SAR Flt, 228, JEHU. Poor state		9-21
❑ XZ300	'L'	Sud Gazelle AH.1	76	ex Fleetlands, M Wallop, 670, 664, 662. Crashed 14-2-97. Westland-built		4-14
❑ 'XZ654'		Westland Lynx AH.7 XZ219	79	ex M Wallop, Fleetlands, 847, 656, SFOR, 654, 669, 654, 669, 662, 653, 662	[1]	9-21
❑ XZ661	'V'	Westland Lynx AH.7	81	ex M Wallop, 671, 653, 1 Rgt, 655, 671, 652, 651		8-16
❑ -	TAD.900	Sud Gazelle AH.1 XW900	74	ex Aborfield, M Wallop SEAE, 660. Crashed 25-5-76		4-14

■ **[1]** XZ219 is painted as 'XZ654' or more likely wears its boom - the rest of it is at Shannon, Ireland.

CALSHOT at the end of the B3053, southeast of Fawley

Calshot Castle and Heritage Area: The former flying-boat base hosted the last Schneider Trophy races, in 1929 and 1931. The last Sunderland flew away in October 1953 and the RAF station closed in May 1961. The massive 'H' shed, now known as the Sunderland Hangar, is 600ft long and houses the Calshot Activities Centre. There are plenty of displays on Calshot's aviation days within the castle and great views of the Solent. **www.english-heritage.org.uk**

DURLEY east of the B3354, between Horton Heath and Bishop's Waltham

A *private* airstrip in the *general* area holds an eclectic variety of 'retirees'. Stampe SV-4C G-AYDR was flying again by 2023. Stampe SV-4A G-STMP was exported to Belgium, as OO-GIV, in March 2023.

❑ G-AFJB*	Foster Wickner Wicko GM1	38	ex DR613 ATA, G-AFJB. CoA 21-7-20	3-23
❑ G-AXSV	Jodel DR.340 Major	68	ex F-BRCC. CEA-built. De-reg 2-1-97	12-22
❑ G-AYDY	Luton Minor	74	CoA 7-1-16	12-22
❑ G-BPZE	Luscombe Silvaire	46	ex Hardwick, N1177K. Dam 8-7-07, CoA 2-5-08, de-reg 19-5-23	12-22
❑ G-BVMD	Luscombe Silvaire	47	ex 9Q-CGB. Crashed 28-7-06, de-reg 6-2-07	12-22

FAREHAM on the A27 west of Portsmouth

No.**1350 (Fareham) Squadron Air Cadets**: Farm Road. Jaguar GR.1A cockpit XX745 moved to Maidstone, Kent, by 2012.

FARNBOROUGH

Whittle Memorial: Dramatically displayed on the roundabout to the north of the airfield, the E28/39 is a tribute to Sir Frank Whittle. This and the one at Lutterworth, Leics (qv), were financed and built by the Sir Frank Whittle Commemorative Trust.

❑ –	Gloster E28/39 FSM	03	BAPC.285, unveiled 28-8-03	1-24

Prince's Mead Shopping Centre: The SE.5a provides 'top cover' for the shoppers. ◆ **www.princesmead.co.uk**

❑ 'D276'	'A'	Royal Aircraft Factory SE.5a replica	90	BAPC.208, AJD Engineering-built. 74 Sqn, 'A' Flt, Edward 'Mick Mannock, colours	12-23

FARNBOROUGH AIRFIELD east of the A325, north of Aldershot EGLF

Farnborough Air Sciences Trust (FAST): Within The Old Balloon School, renamed as Trenchard House in honour of one of its earliest 'bosses', is a truly innovative museum. The incredible Cody is housed within its own pavilion. It is a replica of the British Army Aeroplane No.1A which made the first sustained flight by a British-built aircraft on 16th October 1908, just a stone's throw from FAST's site. In a great piece of 'reverse technology' a mock-up Cody pilot's position - it can't really be called a cockpit - forms the basis of a simulator.

Andrew Lee and his dedicated team have restored *Zulu-India* as a 'live' exhibit. Autoland development with the Trident was a major occupation of Royal Aircraft Establishment, hence its highly appropriate placing at FAST. The cockpit is open every weekend. | **trident3bzi@gmail.com** | **www.facebook.com/tridentgawzi/**

◆ *Farnborough Road, GU14 6TF* | **01252 375050** | **secretary@airsciences.org.uk** | **www.airsciences.org.uk**

❑ G-AWZI		HS Trident 3B-101	71	ex Lasham, Alton, Reigate, Heathrow, BA, BEA. CoA 5-8-85, de-reg 9-7-87, arrived 15-12-04. Flightdeck	[1]	1-24
❑ –		Cody Army Aeroplane No.1A replica	07	BAPC.359. Unveiled 16-10-08, in Cody pavilion. See notes above	[2]	1-24
❑ –		Airbus Zephyr 6	07	BAPC.531, handed over 6-3-17, in Cody pavilion	[3]	1-24
❑ WT309		EE Canberra B(I).6	55	ex Booker, Boscombe Down, Farnborough, B' Down, A&AEE, HS. Arrived 2-98. Cockpit		1-24
❑ WV383		Hawker Hunter T.7	55	ex Boscombe D, DERA, RAE, 28, Jever SF, Gütersloh SF, F.4, RAFFC. *Hecate–Lady of the Night.* Arrived 13-4-00	[4]	1-24
❑ XL563		Hawker Hunter T.7	57	ex South Moor, Hereford 9218M (9-6-95), Kempton, Farnborough, IAM. Last flown 9-7-93. Arrived 4-14		1-24
❑ XP516	'16'	Folland Gnat T.1	63	ex DS&TL, RAE, 8580M (8-2-78), 4 FTS. Arrived 8-6-04	[4]	1-24
❑ XP848		Westland Scout AH.1	62	ex M Wallop, Arborfield, M Wallop, Wroughton, 662, 651, A&AEE. Arrived 3-9-15		7-22
❑ XS420		EE Lightning T.5	65	ex Walpole St Andrew, West Walton Highway, Narborough, Binbrook, LTF, 5, LTF, 226 OCU. SOC 16-6-88, arrived 3-9-03. 226 OCU colours	[5]	1-24
❑ XV631		Westland Wasp HAS.1	69	ex RAE site, Wroughton, 829, *Cleopatra* Flt, *Eskimo* Flt. SOC 19-3-84, arrived 11-2-10. Cabin, off-site		3-18
❑ XW241		Sud SA.330E Puma	68	ex DS&TL, RAE Bedford, F-ZJUX. SOC 10-11-88. Arrived 29-8-07	[4]	1-24
❑ XW566		SEPECAT Jaguar B.08	71	ex DS&TL, RAE, A&AEE. Last flown 17-6-85. Arrived 8-6-04	[4]	1-24
❑ XW934	'Y'	HS Harrier T.4	73	ex DS&TL, 20, 233 OCU, 1. Arrived 29-8-09. 20 Sqn colours		1-24
❑ XZ166		Westland Lynx HAS.2	75	ex QinetiQ, RAE site, A&AEE, Rolls-Royce G-1-2, A&AEE. SOC 18-12-80, arrived 10-09. Cabin, off-site		3-18
❑ ZD280		Westland Lynx AH.7	83	ex Fleetlands, M Wallop, AH.1, 671. Last flown 31-7-15. Arrived 5-12-17	[6]	1-24
❑ ZG631		Northrop Chukar D.2	96	ex Aberporth, Fleet Target Group. Last sortie 15-5-01. Arrived 10-08. Off-site		9-19
❑ ZJ496		GAF Jindivik 104A	c83	ex Boscombe Down, Llanbedr, A92-901. Arr 10-5-05	[4] [7]	1-24
❑ –		EE Lightning	~	procedure trainer	[8]	3-20
❑ –		Short MATS-B	~	(SBAS-029)	[9]	3-20

■ **[1]** Cockpit is on loan from Andrew Lee – see above. **[2]** The incredible Cody is housed in its own pavilion. It is a replica of British Army Aeroplane No.1A which made the first sustained flight by a British-built aircraft on 16-10-08, just a stone's throw from FAST's site. This has *also* been allocated BAPC.394. There is also a replica Cody centre section used as a simulator. **[3]** Zephyr 6 sub-scale development prototype of the Airbus Defence and Space Zephyr S and T 'pseudo-satellites'. (At 39ft 5in span, sub-scale is a relative phrase!) Built at the Airbus facility within the Cody Technology Park at Farnborough. In 2-08 a Zephyr 6 reached 60,000ft and stayed aloft for 82 hours on a sortie from Yuma, Arizona. **[4]** Airframes on loan from DS&TL / QinetiQ. **[5]** Lightning T.5 on loan from Richard Hall – **www.xs420.com** **[6]** ZD280 on loan from the Army Flying Museum, Middle Wallop, Hampshire. **[7]** Jindivik carries 12 mission markers. **[8]** Procedures trainer fitted with ejector seat marked XM171. **[9]** This was deleted during the UAV 'cull' in *W&R26*, but as it has a build number, and the hunt is on for a serial, it's back!

Royal Aircraft Establishment Heritage Quarter: Within the Farnborough Business park, which occupies much of the former RAE site, are several listed buildings reflecting the significance of the airfield. The skeletal 1911 balloon hangar has been erected close to its original location and serves as a unique symbol of the Balloon Factory and Royal Aircraft Factory days. The Grade I-listed Building Q121 is the famous wind tunnel and a local landmark. The former Weapons Testing Building, Q134, is now called **The Hub** and includes a display entitled 'The Secret Factory' and the Aviators Cafe. Also within The Hub is the **National Aerospace Library**, which is open to the public. **www.aerosociety.com**

Defence Science and Technology Laboratory / **QinetiQ**: Displayed within the facility.

❑ XV344	Blackburn Buccaneer S.2C	67	ex Boscombe Down, RAE, 809, 800, 809. Last flight 28-9-94. *Night bird*. Displayed, since 31-3-98	12-23
❑ ZF622*	Piper Navajo 350	~	ex Boscombe Down, St Mawgan, Boscombe Down, DERA, RAE, N35487. SOC 25-1-16. Fuselage. First noted 8-23	8-23

Also: A Canberra cockpit is kept in the *general* area.

❑ WJ775	EE Canberra B.6RC	54	ex Upwood, Bodney, St Athan, Swanton Morley 8581M (5-5-74), 51, 192. Cockpit. Arrived 26-4-15	12-19

FLEETLANDS east of the A32, south of Fareham

StandardAero Aviation Holdings: Helicopter maintenance and storage contractor-run facility. The last remnants of the long-serving Gazelle fleet 'drew-down' in late October 2023. Numbers are migrating here, from Aldergrove and Middle Wallop, but it is too early to say if they will turn out to be 'long-termers': that must await *W&R30*. To keep the pot boiling, the following had arrived by early November 2023 (confirmed dates in brackets): XW846, XW865, XZ290, XZ320 (23-10-23), XZ326 (26-10-23), XZ334 (18-10-23), XZ340, ZA731, ZA736, ZA766, ZA772 (23-10-23), ZA775 (23-10-23), ZB665 (3-10-23), ZB669, ZB674 (23-10-23), ZB678, ZB679 (20-10-23), ZB690 (26-10-23), ZB693 (3-10-23).

	Serial	Code	Type	Year	History	Note	Date
❑	XS539	'435'	Westland Wasp HAS.1	64	A2640 [2], ex A2718 [2] (7-1-92), Lee-on-Solent, Portland, 829, 703, 829, 848, 829. Displayed, since 1992	[1]	12-23
❑	XW844	'GAZ.4'	Sud Gazelle AH.1	72	ex Wroughton. 659. Westland-built. Displayed, since 2002		12-23
❑	XZ697	'313'	Westland Lynx HMA.8SRU	80	ex 702, 815, HAS.3, 815, HAS.2, 815. Arrived 3-18		12-23
❑	ZD480		Westland Sea King HC.4	84	ex Gosport, 846, 845, 846, 845, 846. Arrived by 8-15. 'Zebra' stripe camo. Displayed by 12-15		12-23

■ **[1]** Wasp XS539 attacked the Argentine submarine *Santa Fe* with missiles off South Georgia 25-4-82.

GOSPORT north of the B3333 south of Brockhurst

HMS *Sultan*: Defence School of Aeronautical Engineering (DSAE): The school is a sub-set of the Defence College of Technical Training at Lyneham, Wilts. Also here are the **Defence School of Marine Engineering**, the **Royal Naval Air Engineering and Survival Equipment School** and **764 Initial Training Squadron**, 'operating' the airframes here. The instructional airframe fleet continues to expand.

Departures: **Gazelle**s HCC.4 XW852, AH.1s XX412 and XZ305 to Cosford, Shropshire 29-3-22; **Sea King** HAS.6 ZD634 to Culdrose, Cornwall, by 7-19. **Sea King**s, the following, all last noted 4-19, believed to have been scrapped/reduced to produce by 4-22: HU.5 ZA167, HAS.6s ZD630, ZG816 and ZG818. HU.5 XZ920 to HeliOps at Portland, it was struck off charge 9-11-22 and was part of the gift to Ukraine 11-22. The following slipped the net, most last noted 4-15 and scrapped circa 2016/2017: **Wessex** HC.2 XR518; HU.5s XS514, XT484, XT485 and XV724; **Sea King** HAS.6 XV696; HAS.5 ZA170.

	Serial	Code	Type	Year	History	Note	Date
❑	XP110	'55'	Westland Wessex HAS.3	62	ex A2636, A2714, A2728 (25-4-85), Lee-on-Solent, Fleetlands, 737, 706, HAS.1, 737, 706, 737. *Humphrey*	[1]	4-22
❑	XS568	'441'	Westland Wasp HAS.1	64	ex A2637, Fleetlands A2715 (18-5-83), 829, 771		4-22
❑	XT453	'B'	Westland Wessex HU.5	65	ex Culdrose, Gosport A2666, Lee-on-Solent A2756 (22-7-86), Yeovilton, 845, 707, 845, 707		4-22
❑	XV370	'260'	Sikorsky SH-3D Sea King	G-ATYU	ex A2682, Lee-on-Solent A2771 (8-1-90), ETPS, A&AEE, Yeovil, G-ATYU de-reg 25-10-66		4-22
❑	XV642	'259'	Westland Sea King HAS.2A	69	ex A2614, Lee-on-Solent A2613 (20-3-91), Yeovil, A&AEE, Yeovil, A&AEE, Yeovil		4-22
❑	XV643	'262'	Westland Sea King HAS.6	69	ex Cosford 9323M, St Athan, Gosport A2657 (24-3-00), Culdrose, 819, 849, 819, 814, 820, 819, 824, 814, A&AEE. Arrived 30-3-16		4-22
❑	XV649	'180'	Westland Sea King ASaC.7	69	ex Culdrose, 857, 849, AEW.2, 849, HAS.2, 706, Falklands, 824, HAS.1, 706, 737, 826, 700S. First noted 9-18		4-22
❑	XV653	'63'	W'land Sea King HAS.6	69	ex Cosford 9326M, Gosport, 810, 706. Arrived 17-9-20		4-22
❑	XV655	'270'	Westland Sea King HAS.6	69	ex A2805 (10-12-01), 814, 819, 826, 814, 824, 826, 814, 826, 819, 737, 824		4-22
❑	XV659	'62'	Westland Sea King HAS.6	70	ex Cosford, 9324M, Gosport, Fleetlands, 810, 814, 819, 706, 826, 824, 819, 814, FTU, 824. First noted 10-20		4-22
❑	XV660	'269'	Westland Sea King HAS.6	70	ex A2810 (10-12-01), Culdrose, 819, 814, 810, 706, 810, 819, 810, 824, 706		4-22
❑	XV665	'07'	W'land Sea King HAS.6	70	ex A2812 (10-12-01), 810, 820, 810, 824, 706, 819, 826		4-22
❑	XV672	'187'	Westland Sea King ASaC.7	70	ex Culdrose, 857, 849, AEW.2, 849, HAS.2, 824, 826, HAS.1, 814, 819. First noted 9-18		4-22
❑	XV675	'701'	Westland Sea King HAS.6	71	ex A2622 (1-5-02), 819, 706, 824, A&AEE, 814, 819, 814, 819, 737, 819, A&AEE, 819		4-22
❑	XV676	'ZE'	Westland Sea King HAS.6CR	71	ex 845, 846, Fleetlands, 771, 810, 819, A&AEE, 819, 824, 814, 706, 826, 706, 819, A&AEE, 819		4-22
❑	XV699	'823'	Westland Sea King HU.5	71	ex Gannet SAR Flt, 771, Gannet SAR Flt, 771, 819, HAS.1, Wroughton, 826, 814, 826, 846, 826, 824, A&AEE, 824		4-22

❑ XV700*	'ZC'	Westland Sea King HAS.6CR	71	ex St Mawgan, Gosport, 824, 814, 819, 814, 706, 814, 819, 814, 825, 706, 820, 810, 849, 846, 845. Flown in by Chinook 6-23		6-23
❑ XV701	'64'	Westland Sea King HAS.6	71	ex Cosford, Gosport, Cosford, Gosport A2809 (10-12-01), 814, 820, 810, 819, A&AEE, 819, 706, 824. *Lulabelle*		4-22
❑ XV703	'ZD'	Westland Sea King HAS.6CR	71	ex Fleetlands, 845, 846, 771, 819, 820, 819, 826, 706, 814,826, 706, 820, 824		4-22
❑ XV706	'01'	Westland Sea King HAS.6	71	ex Culdrose, 9344M *and* A2656 (28-2-02), 810, 706, 810, 810, A&AEE, 706, 810, 706, 814, 819	[2]	4-22
❑ XV707	'184'	Westland Sea King ASaC.7	71	ex Culdrose, 849, AEW.2, 849, HAS.2, 819, 706, HAS.1, 819, 814, 819. First noted 9-18		4-22
❑ XV708	'501'	Westland Sea King HAS.6	71	ex A2643 [3], A2635 (1-5-02), 810, 819, 706, 819, 706, 820, 826, 737		4-22
❑ XV711	'515'	Westland Sea King HAS.6	72	ex A2808 (25-3-02), 810, 819, 814, 824, 814, 706, 820, 706, 824, 706, 814, 819, 814, 819		4-22
❑ XV713	'018'	Westland Sea King HAS.6	72	ex A2804 (19-5-00), Fleetlands, 820, 810, 706, 826, 824, 826, 810, 814, 820		4-22
❑ XX431	'43'	Sud Gazelle HT.2	75	ex M Wallop, Shawbury, 9300M, 705, FONA, 705	[3]	5-23
❑ XZ576		Westland Sea King HAS.6	76	ex A2806 (1-5-02), Boscombe Down, A&AEE, A&AEE, 824, 820		4-22
❑ XZ579	'707'	Westland Sea King HAS.6	77	ex A2843 (25-7-07), Brize Norton, Gosport, 819, 820, 814, 820, 819, 826, 824, 706, 814		4-22
❑ XZ580	'ZB'	Westland Sea King HAS.6CR	77	ex Fleetlands, 846, 845, 846, Boscombe D, Gosport, 819, 814, 810, 706, 737, 706, 825, 814		4-22
❑ XZ581	'269'	Westland Sea King HAS.6	77	ex A2638, A2627 (1-5-02), Fleetlands, 814, 810, 826, 819, 824, A&AEE, 826, 706, 814		4-22
❑ XZ692	'764'	Westland Lynx HAS.8SRU	72	ex 702, 815, 702, HAS.2, 815, 702, 815. Arrived 13-8-15. Displayed. 'Black Cats' c/s to port, 764 ITS c/s to starboard		10-23
❑ XZ725*	'415'	Westland Lynx HMA.8SRU	80	ex Yeovilton, Fleetlands, 815, 702, HAS.3, 702, HAS.2, 702, Falklands, 702. SOC 23-9-18. First noted 4-22		4-22
❑ XZ729*	'452'	Westland Lynx HMA.8SRU	80	ex St Athan, Fleetlands, 702, HAS.3, 815, HAS.2, Falklands 1982, 815. First noted 4-22		4-22
❑ XZ922	'ZA'	Westland Sea King HAS.6CR	79	ex 846, 845, 846, Boscombe Down, Gosport, 819, 810, 826, 810, 826, 814, 706		4-22
❑ XZ930	'Q'	Sud Gazelle HT.3	78	ex A2713 (17-11-00), Shawbury, 2 FTS, CFS. Displayed	[3]	4-19
❑ ZA128	'010'	Westland Sea King HAS.6	81	ex Cosford, Gosport (10-10-02), 820, 706, 820. Arr 17-9-20		4-22
❑ ZA131	'271'	Westland Sea King HAS.6	81	ex Cosford, Gosport A2639[3], Cosford, Gosport, A2628 (19-6-02), 814, 820, 826, 810, 826		4-22
❑ ZA133	'831'	Westland Sea King HU.6	81	ex Fleetlands, Gosport, 771, 820, 810, 819, 820, 826, 810, 829, 826. SOC 3-4-06		4-22
❑ ZA168	'830'	W'land Sea King HU.6	82	ex A2844 (12-3-09), 771, 820, 849, 820, 810, 819, 826, 814		4-22
❑ ZA169	'515'	Westland Sea King HAS.6	82	ex Cosford, Gosport A2844 (12-3-09), 820, 771, 810, 814, 820, 819, 820, 706, 820. First noted 10-20		4-22
❑ ZA323		Panavia Tornado GR.1	83	ex Cosford, 9339M, St Athan, 15, TTTE. Arrived 25-4-19		4-22
❑ ZD254	'305'	Westland Lynx HAS.3S	82	ex A2840 (14-1-09), 815, 702. Recruiting airframe		5-23
❑ ZD465*	'55'	BAe/McDD Harrier GR.9	90	ex Cosford, Gosport, Cosford, Gosport, Wittering, Cottesmore, BAE Warton. First noted 5-21		4-22
❑ ZD479	'WQ'	Westland Sea King HC.4	83	ex 848, 845, 848, 707, 846, 707		4-22
❑ ZD636	'182'	W'land Sea King ASaC.7	85	ex Fleetlands, 857, 854, 849, AEW.2, 849, HAS.5, 771, 819		4-22
❑ ZD637	'700'	W'land Sea King HAS.6	85	ex A2811 (15-11-02), 819, 771, 819, 814, 810, A&AEE, 819		4-22
❑ ZE418	'186'	Westland Sea King ASaC.7	86	ex Culdrose, 849, 854, 849, HAS.5, 706, 819, 810, 819. First noted 9-18		4-22
❑ ZE420*	'189'	Westland Sea King ASaC.7	86	ex Portland, Gosport, 849, 857, AEW.2, 849, HAS.5, 706, 826, 819, 820	[4]	4-22
❑ ZE426	'WX'	Westland Sea King HC.4	85	ex 848, 845, 848, 707, 846, 848, 845, 846		4-22
❑ ZF115	'WV'	Westland Sea King HC.4	86	ex Yeovilton, 848, 845, 848, Gosport A2815, A&AEE		5-23
❑ ZF119	'WY'	Westland Sea King HC.4	86	ex 848, 846, 707, 846		4-22

❑ ZF649		EHI EH 101 PP5	89	ex A2714 (9-4-01), Weston-super-Mare, Yeovil		4-22
❑ ZG817	'702'	Westland Sea King HAS.6	90	ex A2814 (19-6-02), 819, 810		4-22
❑ ZG819	'265'	Westland Sea King HAS.6	90	ex A2654, A2641 [4] (19-6-02), 814, 820		4-22
❑ ZH830*	'88'	EHI Merlin HM.1	98	ex Boscombe Down, QinetiQ, Yeovil, DERA. Arr by 12-22		12-22
❑ ZH838*	'70'	EHI Merlin HM.1	99	ex Boscombe Down, Culdrose, 824, 700M, 824. Arr by 12-22		12-22
❑ ZH848*		EHI Merlin HM.1	00	ex Boscombe Down, 820, 829, 824, DERA. Arrived by 12-22		12-22
❑ ZH849*	'14'	EHI Merlin HM.1	00	ex Boscombe Down, 829, 824, 814		11-22
❑ ZH852*		EHI Merlin HM.1	01	ex Boscombe Down, Cerebus (ie AEW) test-bed, Culdrose, 829, 824. Arrived 15-11-22		11-22
❑ ZH855*	'68'	EHI Merlin HM.1	01	ex Boscombe Down, Culdrose, 814, 824. Arrived by 12-22		12-22
❑ ZH858*		EHI Merlin HM.1	01	ex Boscombe Down. Arrived 27-1-22		4-22
❑ ZH863*	'67'	EHI Merlin HM.1	02	ex Boscombe Down, Culdrose, 820, 814, 700M. Arr by 12-22		12-22
❑ ZJ117*	'A'	EHI Merlin HC.2	98	ex Boscombe Down, QinetiQ. Arrived 9-6-22		6-22
❑ ZZ402		Westland Wildcat AH.1	10	ex Yeovil. Handed over 12-10-16		4-22
❑ -*		HS Sea Harrier	~	cockpit, first noted 4-22		4-22

■ **[1]** Another *Humphrey*, of much greater fame, is to be found at Yeovilton, Somerset. **[2]** XV706 has a rare distinction; its 'M' number was allocated on 2nd May 2003 and was the *last ever*. For good measure, it had been given an 'A' number a year earlier... **[3]** Gazelles, of course, built by Westland. **[4]** Listed in error under Somerton, Somerset, in *W&R28*.

HAMBLE southeast of Southampton

Hamble Aerostructures: Part of the Spanish-based Aernnova Aerospace, is guarded by a Gnat at the former Folland plant.

❑ XM693	Folland Gnat T.1	60	ex Abingdon, Bicester 7891M (10-8-65), A&AEE. Last flight 22-10-64. Displayed from 10-80	1-24

LASHAM AERODROME west of Golden Pot, northwest of Alton EGHL

Gliding Heritage Centre: Whether you like gliders or not, it is a certainty that this wonderful venue will fascinate. Many of these wonders were donated to the centre and the incredibly informative website pays tribute to the donors. As well as the 'core' collection, there is an impressive list of other types that have been 'volunteered' for occasional loan and flying: we will stick to the 'regulars' for the list below, but details are given on the website. As befitting the world of silent flight, the emphasis is on informality and the 'best time' to visit is quoted as Sunday afternoons when 'there *might* be some flying'.

Grasshopper TX.1 XA225 moved to Bellarena, N Ireland, by September 2023. The following have left the 'core' collection: Scheibe Zugvogel G-CFYE; Cadet TX.3 FFQ (XE800); Cadet TX.1 FCC (XN243); Swallow 'XS651' (BYB).

◆ *Follow signs for the Gliding Centre. Alton, GU34 5SS* | **enquiriy@glidingheritage.org.uk** | **www.glidingheritage.org.uk**

❑ G-AEKV	DZQ	Kronfeld Drone		36	BGA.2510, ex Brooklands, CoA 6-10-60, de-reg 14-1-99. Arrived 1-9-13	[1]	4-23
❑ –		Mignet HM.14 'Flea'		c05	BAPC.302, ex Shoreham. Arrived 7-5-15	[2]	9-22
❑ G-ALJR	ACF	Abbott-Baynes Scud III		36	BGA.283, ex Dunstable, G-ALJR, BGA.283. Donated by Laurie Woodage. Arrived 18-7-13		10-21
❑ G-ALLF	ARK	Slingsby Prefect		36	BGA.599, ex PH-1, BGA.599, G-ALLF, BGA.599. CoA 10-9-20. Prototype Prefect. Arrived 2-10-18		9-22
❑ G-ALRU	ASR	EoN Baby	G-ALRU	49	BGA.628, ex Shoreham, Aston Down, G-ALRU. Cr 28-5-71		9-22
❑ G-APWL	BRK	EoN 460 Srs 1A ✈		59	BGA.1172, ex Kidlington, Eaglescott, BGA.1172, G-APWL, RAFGSA.268, G-APWL (de-reg 18-2-10). Arrived 15-7-20	[3]	12-23
❑ G-CFYE		Scheibe Zugvogel 3b		63	BGA.3624. CoA 25-2-17		10-21
❑ G-DBJD*		SZD Bocian 1d ✈		61	BGA.998. Arrived 13-1-22		9-22
❑ G-DBSA		Slingsby Dart 15		63	BGA.1187. Prototype Dart. Arrived 7-5-19, last flown 9-7-21		9-22
❑ G-DCBP		SZD Foka C ✈		63	BGA.1414, ex Sutton Bank. Arrived 27-3-14		9-22
❑ G-DCHJ*	'717'	Bölkow Phoebus 17cl		69	BGA.1553. Arrived 13-2-22	[4]	9-22
❑ G-DCKD		PZL Pirat 30 ✈		70	BGA.1596. Arrived 18-5-21, CoA 10-9-22		9-22
❑ G-DCXV		Yorkshire Sailplanes YS-53		74	BGA.1897. *The Beast*. Arrived 10-11-16		9-22
❑ G-DHOC		Scheibe Bergfalke 2 ✈		63	BGA.4111. CoA 18-6-20		9-22
❑ G-DRRT*	'D17'	Slingsby Dart 17R		67	BGA.1313, ex G-DBXH. Last flew 7-19		10-21
❑ G-KSIX		Schleicher Ka.6E		63	BGA.1452. De-reg 19-8-19		10-21
❑ –		Manuel Willow Wren		32	BGA.162, ex Brooklands, Bishop's Stortford. *The Yellow Wren*. Arrived 7-13	[1] [5]	9-22
❑ –		Abbott-Baynes Scud II	G-ALOT	35	BGA.231, ex Old Warden, G-ALOT, BGA.231. Slingsby-built. CoA 1-6-06, arrived 6-10-17		9-22

	Reg	Code	Type		Year	Details	Note	Seen
❑	AHU		Scott Viking 1	G-ALRD	38	BGA.416, ex G-ALRD, BGA.416. CoA 20-5-18, *Lou the Glue*		9-22
❑	ALR		Slingsby T.8 Tutor	G-ALPE	46	BGA.485, ex Germany, G-ALPE, BGA.485. Arrived 19-6-19		9-22
❑	ATH		Slingsby Gull III		39	BGA.643, ex Brooklands, TJ711. CoA 20-6-04. Arr 18-7-13	[1]	9-22
❑	–*	'G46'	Slingsby Sky		51	BGA.698. Arrived 2-2-22		9-22
❑	AWX		Slingsby Skylark 2		55	BGA.729, CoA 3-6-22. Arrived 9-10-19		10-21
❑	BAN		Slingsby Prefect ✈		58	BGA.815, ex Brüggen. Arrived 4-11-14		9-22
❑	BCV	'155'	Slingsby Skylark 3b ✈		59	BGA.870, ex Handley Page GC. Arrived 4-14		9-22
❑	BGR		EoN Olympia 2b ✈		58	BGA.962. Arrived 10-14		9-22
❑	BJK		Slingsby Skylark 3f ✈		61	BGA.1004. Arrived 4-16		9-22
❑	–*	'597'	Slingsby Dart 15		64	BGA.1198. Arrived 10-3-16. Displayed up hangar wall		9-22
❑	BZM		Slingsby Swallow ✈		67	BGA.1365, ex Arbroath. CoA 4-6-05. Arrived 8-12		9-22
❑	BZV		EoN Olympia 463		65	BGA.1373. Arrived 2-14, last flown 21-8-19		9-22
❑	–		Manuel Hawk		69	BGA.1778, ex Fairoaks. Arrived 26-8-13		9-22
❑	DJF	'500'	Halford JSH Scorpion		77	BGA.2146, ex Doncaster, Wroot, Firbeck. Arrived 1-18	[6]	9-22
❑	DPG		München Mü 13D-3		57	BGA.2267, ex D-1327. Scheibe-built. Last flew 7-9-14, Arr 1-13		9-22
❑	EHB		Kaiser Ka 3 ✈		58	BGA.2689, ex RAFGSA/GGA 559. Arrived 6-4-16		9-22
❑	ELV		Scheibe Zugvogel 3b ✈		64	BGA.2779, ex F-CCPX. Arrived 1-20		9-22
❑	HFS		Vogt Lo 100 Zwergreiher		53	BGA.3915, ex D-6040. Hirth-built. Fuselage, used as simulator		9-22
❑	HFZ		Abbott-Baynes Scud I rep		94	BGA.3922, ex Brooklands. Arrived 18-7-13	[1]	9-22
❑	–		Clarke Chanute		1910	BAPC.100, ex Stafford, Hendon, Wyton, Hendon, Cardington, Hayes, South Kensington. Arrived 18-1-28	[7]	9-22
❑	–		Colditz Cock replica		11	BAPC.347, ex *Escape from Colditz* – unflown	[8]	9-22
❑	–		Manuel Crested Wren rep		86	BAPC.405, 'BGA.178' – unflown		9-22
❑	–*		Weiss Olive scale replica		08	Andrew Jarvis-built 5/8th replica		9-22
❑	'CK-8592'		Zlin Z24 Krajanek	G-ALMP	46	BGA.655, ex 'OK-8592'. CoA 13-1-23. Arrived 6-14		9-22
❑	'D-11-875'	'17'	Jacobs Schweyer Weihe	G-ALJW	43	BGA.448, ex G-ALJW, BGA.448, Luftwaffe LO+WQ. Damaged 20-7-79		5-23
❑	'D-6932'	KFW	DFS Grunau Baby IIB		52	BGA.5066, ex D-6932, D-1932. Segelflugzeubau Buller built		9-22
❑	HB-357		Spalinger 21h		43	'Canada Dry' titling. Arrived 21-12-17		10-21
❑	OE-0324	ERZ	Steinadler Mg 19a ✈		55	BGA.2903, ex OE-0324. Oberlerchner-built. Arrived 2011		9-22
❑	WB990	'993'	Slingsby Sedburgh TX.1		52	BGA.3148 / FCF. Martin Hearn-built		5-23
❑	WP270		EoN Eton TX.1		51	ex Stafford, Manchester, Henlow, Hendon, 8598M, Maidstone CCF. Last flight 12-7-62. Arrived 25-1-17		5-23
❑	XE762		Slingsby Cadet TX.2		46	ex TX.1 VM594. Fuselage. Arrived 21-12-17		5-23
❑	'XP463'	JBA	Slingsby G'hopper TX.1 ✈		61	BGA.4372, ex Rufforth. Arrived 7-8-19	[9]	5-23
❑	42-53027		Laister-Kaufmann TG-4		42	C-FRAH, ex Canada, USAAF - no service. Arr 13-4-18		5-23
❑	252983*		Schweizer TG-3A		45	ex Duxford, N66630. Arrived 4-5-22		5-23

■ **[1]** On loan from Brooklands Museum, Surrey. **[2]** 'Flea' built by Tony Short circa 2005 and modelled on the example Henri Mignet brought to Shoreham 17-8-35 at the start of his British tour. **[3]** EoN 460 prototype, donated by Jeremy Pratt, via Crécy Publishing associate AFE. **[4]** The first 'glass' glider in the 'core' fleet' – the website notes that for all its modernity, it's still 55 years old. **[5]** Wren is the oldest known original British glider. **[6]** Scorpion is a rebuild by John Halford of Holmes KH.1 BGA.1666 of 1971 and was donated by the South Yorkshire Aircraft Museum. **[7]** Chanute biplane glider on loan from the Royal Aero Club Trust via the Science Museum; acquired 1914: transferred to the RAF Museum 1983. **[8]** Cock on loan from its builder, South East Aircraft Services, used in *Escape from Colditz*. **[9]** Grasshopper is a complex hybrid, assembled by McClean Aviation. Identity taken from one of the wings - see under Rufforth, N Yorks, for possible duplication.

Airfield: There is a healthy in-and-out of airliners here: only long-termers are listed. Boeing 737 5U-BAG was scrapped during late 2023; its cockpit travelling to St Athan, Wales, 21st November 2023. One that missed the net was 'Super 7' conversion 727-81 2-SEVN, present since at least July 2018. It was broken up in mid-2022, at least its forward fuselage travelling to Cotswold, Glos, 27th October 2022.

	Reg	Type	Year	Details	Seen
❑	EI-DOO	Boeing 737-400	87	ex KD Avia, D-AGEB, N222DZ. Arrived 3-4-09. 'Fire Trainer'	12-14
❑	VP-CMO	Boeing 727-212/RE	80	ex N31TR, VR-COJ, N310AS, 9V-SGJ	9-22
❑	VP-CZY	Boeing 727-200	78	ex A7-AAB. Arrived 27-11-11	9-23

LIPHOOK south of the A3 west of Haslemere

UCAP GreenOps: Airsoft arena. ◆ *Prior arrangement* **only** | **www.ucap.co.uk/greenops-liphook**

	Reg	Code	Type	Year	Details	Note	Seen
❑	XS149*	'61'	Westland Wessex HAS.3	63	ex Weston-s-M, Manadon, Wroughton, Templecombe, Lee-on-Solent, 737, HAS.1, 819, 845, 706. Arrived 6-23	[1]	6-23

■ **[1]** XS149 is fitted with the rear fuselage of Srs 60 G-17-6.

MIDDLE WALLOP AIRFIELD on the A343 southwest of Andover EGVP

Army Flying Museum: As a further sign of the importance of this collection, GKN Aerospace announced that it was entering into a corporate partnership with the museum in November 203. Don't forget to visit the 'Apache Cafe' which offers views of the activity on the airfield.

Aircraft on loan: Duxford, Cambs: Auster XP281; Farnborough, Hampshire, Lynx ZD280; Southampton, Hampshire: Skeeter XL770; Flixton, Suffolk, Pucará A-528; Newark, Notts: Gazelle XW276. See under 'Headquarters', below, for a potential new exhibit. ◆ *Middle Wallop, SO20 8FB* | **01264 781086** | **info@armyflying.com** | **www.armyflying.com**

❑ G-AXKS		Bell 47G-4A	69	ex Bristow, ARWF, G-17-8. Westland-built. CoA 21-9-82, de-reg 9-9-82. Acquired 22-4-82		1-24
❑ 'G285'	'E'	Slingsby Kirby Kite ACH	36	ex Ulster G/C, G-ALNH (de-reg 11-1-63), BGA.285. Acquired 1989		1-24
❑ 'B-415'		AFEE 10/42 replica	82	BAPC.163, ex Wimborne. Acquired 7-82	[1]	1-24
❑ P-5		Hafner Rotachute III	43	8381M, ex Henlow. Acquired 1983	[2]	1-24
❑ N5195		Sopwith Pup G-ABOX	1916	ex Redhill, Lincoln, RNAS War School Manston, 3, 8, 3, 2 (Naval) Sqns. Acquired, on loan, 1985. CoA 22-4-93	[3]	1-24
❑ 'KJ351'		Airspeed Horsa II	45	BAPC.80. Acquired 1968. Fuselage/centre section	[4]	1-24
❑ 'HH268'		GAL Hotspur II replica	95	BAPC.261. Acquired 13-12-01	[5]	1-24
❑ TJ569		Taylorcraft Auster 5 G-AKOW	45	ex PH-NAD, PH-NEG, TJ569, 652, 660, 659. CoA 26-6-82, de-reg 5-8-87. Acquired 10-81		1-24
❑ TK777		GAL Hamilcar I	44	ex Christian Malford. Birmingham Railway Carriage and Wagon Co-built. Forward fuselage/centre section	[6]	1-24
❑ WG432	'L'	DHC Chipmunk T.10	51	ex AFWF, LAS, Bristol UAS, 19 RFS, Cam UAS, 4 BFTS. Hawarden-built. Acquired 1997		1-24
❑ WJ358		Auster 6A Tugmaster G-ARYD	52	ex Perth, AOP.6 WJ358, 651, 657, 1913 Flt. De-reg 5-8-87. Acquired 7-80		1-24
❑ WZ721		Auster AOP.9	55	ex Life Guards Air Sqn, 4 RTR, 16 Flt, 14 Flt, 7 Flt, 11 Flt, 6 Flt, 652. SOC 1-9-66. Acquired 1969. *Dragon*, 4 RTR c/s		1-24
❑ XG502		Bristol Sycamore HR.14	55	ex 'gate', Wroughton, MCS, CFS, 118, 72, TCCF, Op *Musketeer*, JEHU. SOC 29-8-72		1-24
❑ XK776		ML Utility Mk 1	57	ex Cardington, M Wallop, A&AEE. Acquired 7-82	[7]	1-24
❑ XL813		Saro Skeeter AOP.12	59	ex ARWF, 4 Regt, 9 Flt. SOC 25-3-68		1-24
❑ XP821	'MCO'	DHC Beaver AL.1	61	ex Shawbury, Kemble, St Athan, Defence Attaché Laos, 130 Flt, 30 Flt RASC, 656. Acquired 2-10-85. White/grey c/s		1-24
❑ 'XP822'		DHC Beaver AL.1 XP806	61	ex Arborfield, Sharjah, 668, 13 Flt, 15 Flt, 131 Flt, 6 Flt. Crashed 16-9-70. Acquired 1990. Displayed outside	[8]	1-24
❑ XP847		Westland Scout AH.1	61	ex AETW, Wroughton, Yeovil. Acquired 1984		1-24
❑ XP910	'D'	Westland Scout AH.1	63	ex SEAE. Cr 13-9-89, acquired 2002. Displayed outside		1-24
❑ XR232		Sud Alouette AH.2	60	ex Historic Flight, Wroughton, A&AEE, M Wallop, EW&AU, 656, A&AEE, 16 Flt, 6 Flt, F-WEIP. Acquired 5-92		1-24
❑ XT108	'U'	Bell Sioux AH.1	64	ex Duxford, Yeovilton, M Wallop, D&T Flt, M Wallop. Agusta-built. Acquired 6-84		1-24
❑ XV127		Westland Scout AH.1	67	ex Fleetlands, Chelsea, Wroughton, 655. Acquired 1995		1-24
❑ XX153		Westland Lynx AH.1	72	ex Yeovil, Wattisham 9320M, Foulness, Westland. Acquired 28-10-03, handed over 13-11-03		1-24
❑ XZ675	'H'	Westland Lynx AH.7	81	ex Yeovilton, M Wallop, 671, 4 Rgt, 671, 652. Acq 7-8-11		1-24
❑ ZA737		Sud Gazelle AH.1	80	ex 1 Rgt, 847, Fleetlands 'hack', 670, ARWS. Westland-built. Acquired 12-99		1-24
❑ ZE410		Agusta 109A	80	ex 7 Rgt, Yeovilton, M Wallop, 846, Arg Arm CAB.601, AE-334. Workshop, first noted 12-14		1-24
❑ ZG993		BN Islander AL.1 G-BOMD	88	ex Shawbury, 1 Flt, G-BOMD (de-reg 19-3-90). Last flight 1-7-10. Arrived 25-11-15	[9]	1-24
❑ AE-409	'656'	Bell UH-1H Iroquois	72	ex Duxford, M Wallop, 656, Stanley, Argentine Army, 72-21506. Acquired 7-82		1-24
❑ 111989		Cessna L-19A Bird Dog	51	N33600, ex Fort Rucker, Alabama. Acquired 1982		1-24
❑ '243809'		Waco CG-4A Hadrian	44	BAPC.185, ex Burtonwood, Shrewsbury. Acquired 1985. Fuselage		1-24
❑ 70-15990		Bell AH-1F Cobra	70	ex US Army. Acquired 2003		1-24

■ **[1]** AFEE 10/42 is centred on an original Willys Jeep and on loan from the Wessex Aviation Society. **[2]** Rotachute III on loan from the RAF Museum. **[3]** N5195, with an 80hp Le Rhone, was the second Pup restored by Lt Cdr K C D St Cyrien - G-ABOX being registered 12-9-84. Acquired by a Lincoln owner on 'demob' in 1919, the remains were apparently acquired by St Cyrien in Lincoln in 1963 for £25. See under Hendon, Gtr Lon, for his first, N5182 (G-APUP). **[4]** Largest Horsa airframe on show is 'KJ351' (a Thunderbolt II serial) which is an amalgam of TL659, LH208 and 8569M. TL659 was used until salvaged in 1969 as a sports changing room in Abingdon jail. There are two other substantial Horsa sections on display, other sections are in store. **[5]** Hotspur re-creation has adopted the identity and colours of an example that flew with the Shobdon-based 5 Glider Training School. **[6]** Hamilcar (made up of parts from NX836 and TK718 - see also Bovington, Dorset). **[7]** ML Utility inflatable had three wing options, 'Clouy', 'Delta' and 'Gadfly'; all are in store. **[8]** When XP822 left the 'gate' at Middle Wallop in 1990, XP806 was prepared to take over this duty and appeared in October 1990 marked 'XP822'. Already a composite, with the wings of XP815, XP806 took on *some* parts from XP822, the most significant being the constructor's plate (1486 - XP806 being 1455). Apparently, XP806 had lost its plate at some stage... perhaps in the accident in the UAE. **[9]** Operational sorties in Northern Ireland, the Balkans and the 1st Gulf War.

Deep Store: *Not* available for inspection. Magister 'T9707' (T9708) had moved to Cosford, Shropshire, by March 2022.

	Serial		Type	Reg	Year	History	Note	Date
❑	'XM819'		EP Prospector		59	ex Durrington, M Wallop, Blackbushe, Lympne. Composite. Acquired 14-5-81	[1]	4-19
❑	XZ795		Northrop Shelduck D.1		84	ex Fleet Target Group. Last sortie (of just two!) 29-9-85		3-18
❑	ZA209		Short MATS-B Mk.1A		c78	-		10-21

■ **[1]** Largely G-APXW, which crashed 9-73, but also has rear fuselage of G-ARDG (see Blackburn, Lancs) and elements of G-APWZ.

Historic Aircraft Flight Trust: The flight's badge carries a Latin motto which translates as 'Let Their Glory Not Fade'; its aircraft attend a variety of events. Tiger Moth EM840 (G-ANBY) moved to Hooton Park, Cheshire, 28th January 2023.

◆ **Not** *available without prior permission* | **email** via website | **www.historicarmyaircraft.co.uk**

	Serial		Type	Reg	Year	History	Note	Date
❑	LB312		T'craft Plus D ✈	G-AHXE	42	ex Auster I LB312, 234 Sqn, 3 TEU, 43 OTU, 653, 651	[1]	4-22
❑	WD325	'N'	DHC Chip' T.10 ✈	G-CLWK	51	ex BFWF, LAS, 12 GCF, 17 RFS	[1]	4-22
❑	XL812		Saro Skeeter AOP.12	G-SARO	59	ex Wattisham, Saxmundham, M Wallop. SOC 28-5-69. CoA 30-10-06, de-reg 14-4-10		12-19
❑	XL814		Saro Skeeter AOP.12		59	ex 1 Wing, 2 Wing, 651. Stored		3-18
❑	XP820		DHC Beaver AL.1 ✈	G-CICP	61	ex 7 Regt, 667, 132 Flt RCT, 130 Flt RCT, 30 Flt RASC, 11 Flt, 656	[1]	11-22
❑	XR244		Auster AOP.9 ✈	G-CICR	62	ex AFWF. With AAC HAAF from 11-9-81	[1]	7-21
❑	XT131	'B'	Bell Sioux AH.1 ✈	G-CICN	64	ex D&T Flight. Agusta-built. Flown again 22-5-15	[1]	7-22
❑	XT151		Bell Sioux AH.1		65	ex ARWF. Westland-built. Spares		10-20
❑	XT626	'Q'	Westland Scout AH.1 ✈	G-CIBW	66	ex 666, Wroughton, 656, BATUS, 656, 663 Flying by spring 2015	[1] [2]	4-22

■ **[1]** Registered to the Historic Aircraft Flight Trust. **[2]** 'Written out' of *W&R28* (p82) as taken to North Weald for onward sale: no so.

Headquarters, Army Air Corps (AAC): Several airframes serve in the ground instructional role in Stockwell Hall. The **Multi-Platform Support Unit** (MPSU) is working on the wind-down of the now retired Gazelle fleet. Gazelle AH.1 XX392 moved to Wattisham, Suffolk, for refurbishing prior to re-locating to Bury St Edmunds, Suffolk, by June 2023.

	Serial		Type	Reg	Year	History	Note	Date
❑	WZ724		Auster AOP.9		55	ex gate 'WZ670', 7432M (22-5-57), LAS. Off-site	[1]	12-18
❑	'XT123'	'D'	Bell Sioux AH.1	XT827	67	ex Wroughton, Yeovilton, Coypool, 3 CBAS. Westland-built. Displayed, since 1997	[2]	3-23
❑	XT638	'N'	Westland Scout AH.1	z	66	ex Fleetlands, 666. 666 Sqn badge. Displayed, since 1994		3-23
❑	XX452		Sud Gazelle AH.1		76	Westland-built. Rescue trainer	[3]	7-21
❑	XZ181		Westland Lynx AH.7		78	ex MPSU, Fleetlands, AH.1. Fire/rescue airframe		11-22
❑	XZ184	'B'	Westland Lynx AH.7		78	ex MPSU, Fleetlands, 9 Regt, 671, AH.1. Displayed by 6-16		3-23
❑	XZ212		Westland Lynx AH.7		79	ex MPSU, Fleetlands, AH.1. Dumped by 11-19		11-22
❑	XZ298		Sud Gazelle AH.1		77	cockpit, training aid	[3]	1-17
❑	XZ327		Sud Gazelle AH.1		77	ex Fleetlands. Travelling recruiting aid	[3]	3-21
❑	XZ346		Sud Gazelle AH.1		78	ex Netheravon, Shawbury, M Wallop, 665, A&AEE, Yeovil, 3 CBAS, ARWS, 656, 655. Arr by 3-14, displayed	[3]	3-23
❑	XZ672		Westland Lynx AH.7		81	ex 671, 653, 655, 656, 662, 659, 669, 659. Dump. F/n 1-13		11-22
❑	ZD265	'302'	Westland Lynx HMA.8SRU		83	ex 668 Sqn inst (12-2-16), 702, HAS.3, 815, 829, 815. Dumped		11-22
❑	ZG917		Westland Lynx AH.9A		92	SOC 3-10-18. Displayed within the camp	[4]	7-23
❑	ZG918		Westland Lynx AH.9A		92	SOC 3-10-18. Crewman training airframe		6-21

■ **[1]** Restoration required grafting on another, identity unconfirmed, fuselage frame in late 2018. Frame *reported* to be the original from the airworthy XP254 (G-ASCC). **[2]** The plate in the Sioux's cockpit gives it as WA-S-179, which makes it XT827, latterly with the Historic Flight. **[3]** Gazelles all Westland-built. **[4]** AH.9A reported held on behalf of the Army Flying Museum.

NEW MILTON on the A337 east of Christchurch

Sammy Miller Motorcycle Museum: Nearly 400 'bikes' in four galleries and, obviously, a Rallye.
◆ *Bashley Cross Roads, BH25 5SZ* | **01425 620777** | **https://sammymiller.co.uk/**

❑ G-EISO		MS Rallye 150	66	ex D-EISO, F-BNSO. CoA 29-10-13, de-reg 4-3-17	2-22

ODIHAM AIRFIELD on the A32 south of Odiham EGVO

RAF Odiham:

❑ XR453	'A'	Westland Whirlwind HAR.10	62	8873M, ex Foulness, 2 FTS, CFS, 230, 1563 Flt, CFS. Displayed since 9-86. 230 Sqn colours	6-22
❑ ZA678	'EZ'	Boeing Chinook HC.1	81	9229M, ex Fleetlands, 7, N37023. Crashed 24-7-89. Inst	10-16
❑ 86-1677		Boeing CH-47D Chinook	86	ex US Army. Training aid	10-16
❑ 03-08003	'DT'	Boeing YCH-47F Chinook	02	ex US Army. Displayed, unveiled 9-5-12	9-22

Locally: SIPA 903 G-AWLG, last noted in 2009, has been deleted.

PETERSFIELD on the A3 north of Portsmouth

A *private* house in the *general* area is reported to have been offered for sale in December 2023 *with* its Harrier thrown in.

❑ ZG509	'80'	BAe/McDD Harrier GR.7A	91	ex Ipswich, Cottesmore, Wittering, St Athan. Damaged 31-7-01	12-23

PORTSMOUTH

Royal Navy Dockyard: A Sea Harrier is displayed within the BAE Systems-operation **Queen Elizabeth Class Centre of Specialisation** in the north corner - where the 'flat tops' dock. Trials unit **1710 Squadron** occasionally takes airframes, mostly on a short-term basis. Lynx HMA.8 ZD252 moved to North Weald, Essex, by April 2022. Last noted in May 2018, Apache ZJ177 returned to Gosport, Hampshire, by June 2022 before settling upon Wattisham, Suffolk, by August 2023.

❑ ZD611		HS Sea Harrier F/A.2	85	ex Culdrose, St Athan, 899, 801, 899, 800, 899, 800, 899, 800, 899, 801. SOC 29-8-02. Displayed, 899 Sqn c/s. F/n 5-17	5-22

ROMSEY or Farley, on the A27 northwest of Southampton

Delta Force Paintball: Lee Lane ◆ *Prior arrangement* **only** | **www.paintballgames.co.uk**

❑ XZ645		Westland Lynx AH.7	83	ex Upminster, Ipswich, M Wallop. First noted 8-17	1-22

Also: A strip in the locality *should* hold a variety of *W&R* inmates. In accordance with the 'tidy up' outlined on page 7, Monsun G-AVKR has been deleted.

❑ G-ARUO	Piper Comanche 180		61	ex Bruntingthorpe, N7251P. Cr 19-3-00, de-reg 18-7-00		5-18
❑ G-ASYK	Piper Twin Comanche 160		64	ex Eshott, Bruntingthorpe, N7543Y. Crashed 11-5-96, de-reg 30-10-96. Fuselage. First noted 10-17		5-18
❑ G-AVPS	Piper Twin Comanche B		67	ex N8393Y. Crashed 30-11-04, de-reg 6-7-05		5-18
❑ G-AZBB	Bölkow Monsun 150FF		71	ex D-EFJO. CoA 3-5-08, de-reg 20-6-23		5-18
❑ G-AZOB	Bölkow Monsun 150FF		72	ex D-EAAZ. Crashed 21-8-83, CoA 9-7-84, de-reg 20-6-23		5-18
❑ G-BJDO	American AA-5A Cheetah		79	ex N26936. CoA 6-8-08, de-reg 27-10-08		5-18
❑ G-BYDX	American AG-5B Tiger		91	ex N374SA. CoA 5-5-08, de-reg 29-11-05		5-18
❑ G-JNAS	American AA-5A Cheetah		78	ex SE-GEI. CoA 9-3-07, de-reg 19-10-18		5-18
❑ G-RROD	Piper Twin Comanche		66	ex Henstridge. CoA 25-8-09, de-reg 11-4-11	[1]	5-18
❑ EC-AOZ	Piper Pacer	G-BXBB	52	ex N1133C. De-reg 22-4-03		5-18

■ **[1]** Registered in the USA as N7967Y 4-11.

SOLENT AIRPORT, or Lee-on-Solent, east of the B3385, south of Fareham EGHF

The Hovercraft Museum: Offers an incredible array of rubber-skirted exhibits. SRN.4 GH-2007 *The Princess Anne* is so big that its capacious car deck *doubles* as an exhibit hall. The cockpit of Hunter GA.11 WV381, held in store for its owner, moved to Bournemouth, Dorset, by January 2023.
◆ *Marine Parade West, PO13 9NS* | **02392 552090** | **email** via website| **www.hovercraft-museum.org**

Britten-Norman: The phase-out of the Defender fleet took place at Aldergrove – Belfast Airport – in July 2021 with the bulk ferried to Solent where their stay was thought to be short-term. They have since clocked up sufficient time in store to merit inclusion. See also Bembridge, Isle of Wight. ◆ **Strictly** *prior arrangement* **only**

Serial	Type	Reg	Year	History		Date
❑ ZG995*	BN Defender R.2	G-SURV	94	ex Aldergrove, G-SURV, G-BVHZ. SOC 9-7-21. Arrived 27-5-20		1-24
❑ ZG996*	BN Defender R.2	G-BWPR	97	ex Aldergrove, G-BWPR. SOC 9-7-21. Arrived 2-6-21		1-24
❑ ZG997*	BN Defender R.2	G-BWPV	98	ex Aldergrove, G-BWPR. SOC 9-7-21. Arrived 8-7-21		1-24
❑ ZG998*	BN Defender R.2	G-BWPX	04	ex Aldergrove, G-BWPX. SOC 9-7-21. Arrived 8-7-21		1-24
❑ ZH001*	BN Defender R.2	G-CEIO	07	ex Aldergrove, G-BWPX. SOC 9-7-21. Arrived 1-3-21		1-24
❑ ZH002*	BN Defender R.2	G-CEIP	07	ex Aldergrove, G-BWPX. SOC 9-7-21. Arrived 8-7-21		1-24
❑ ZH003*	BN Defender R.2	G-CEIR	07	ex Aldergrove, G-BWPX. SOC 9-7-21. Arrived 11-6-21		1-24
❑ ZH004*	BN Defender T.3	G-BWPO	97	ex Aldergrove, G-BWPO, VH-YVH, 9M-TPS. SOC 9-7-21. Arrived 28-6-21		1-24
❑ ZH005*	BN Defender R.2	G-CGVB	11	ex Aldergrove, G-CGVB. SOC 9-7-21. Arrived 4-5-20		1-24

■ **[1]** All registered to BN as BN-2T-4S Islanders. Other than ZG995, which is denoted as Pilatus-BN built, all BN-built.

Fareham College Centre for Engineering and Manufacturing Advanced Skills Training (CEMAST, no less): Sea King HC.4 ZA296 was exported to Slovakia in late 2022. ◆ *Prior arrangement* **only** | **www.fareham.ac.uk**

Reg	Type	Year	History		Date
❑ G-CIBB	Cessna F.172H	66	ex OY-EGZ, N17013, Reims-built. De-reg 14-7-21		12-21

Others: By late 2022 Curtiss Robin G-BTYY had moved to Coventry, Warks.

Reg	Type	Year	History		Date
❑ G-AALY	DH Moth	29	ex F-AJKM, G-AALY. CoA 15-5-05		N3-22
❑ G-ACLL	DH Leopard Moth	34	ex Jurby, AW165, AFEE, 7 AACU, 6 AACU, Ringway SF. CoA 6-12-95		N2-19
❑ G-ASEO*	Piper Comanche 250	62	CoA 6-3-16, de-reg 15-12-22		12-23
❑ G-RLON	BN Trislander	75	ex Aurigny, G-ITEX, G-OCTA, VR-CAA, DQ-FCF, G-BCXW. Flew in 5-4-17. De-reg 9-12-19	[1]	5-21

■ **[1]** *Oscar-November*'s total time came to 32,604 hours with a staggering 105,130 landings. Held in store for Solent Sky, Southampton, Hampshire - which see.

SOPLEY on the B3347 north of Christchurch

New Forest Airfields Heritage Centre: Based on the former back-up generator building of post-war RAF Sopley, Southern Radar. It also covers the USAAF advanced landing ground of Winkton.

◆ *Mosquito Way, Bransgore, BH23 8AU.* | **email** via website | **https://fonfasite.wordpress.com/the-education-centre**

SOUTHAMPTON

Solent Sky: If it isn't already, this museum should be one of the reader's 'must visits', after which it should be placed firmly on the 'must visit regularly' list. This under-spoken venue is exceptional, whatever time you have put by to view it, treble it and be absorbed in the variety and depth of its presentations. Here is a 'national' collection labelled as a 'regional'. The 'Romance of the Flying-Boat' exhibition is worth the trek its own right: the Sandringham's sumptuous interior is breathtaking and - by prior arrangement and if staffing levels permit - the flightdeck can be inspected.

During March 2022 approval was granted for a £5m extension. With this in mind, the arrival of the 60ft forward fuselage of BAC 111 ZH763 hits at least three 'ticks' for the museum: a taste of an airliner (with respect to the Sandringham); homage to manufacturing just down the coast at Hurn; and it will serve as the new cafe venue.

At the back of the Southampton and the Blitz exhibition, visitors can take a glimpse of progress on the Swift's restoration. The restored extreme nose/bow section of a Supermarine Seagull, previously used as a garden shed, is displayed in the lee of the S.6A. While a precious survivor, it does not merit a formal listing.

Dominating the outside of the building is the Calshot Spit Light Vessel, rescued by the Southampton Heritage Foundation and destined for a long-term restoration. Co-sited is the superb Hampshire Police and Fire Museum: **www.hampshirepolicefireheritage.co.uk**

BN Trislander G-RLON is stored at Lee-on-Solent, pronounced Solent, Hampshire. The museum has an excellent relationship with **424 Squadron (City of Southampton) Air Cadets** - see below. The cockpit of Sea Vixen FAW.1 XJ476 is on loan to BDAC at Boscombe Down, Wilts.

◆ *Albert Road South, SO14 3FR* | **02380 635830** | **aviation@spitfireonline.co.uk** | **www.solentskymuseum.org**

Reg	Type	Year	History		Date
❑ 'G-ADZW'	Mignet HM.14 'Flea'	94	BAPC.253, ex Sandown, Lake, Isle of Wight. Built by Howard Shore. Arrived 5-00		1-24
❑ G-ALZE	Britten Norman BN-1F	51	ex Cosford, Kemble, Bembridge. De-reg 12-6-89. Arr 1985		1-24
❑ G-APOI	Saro Skeeter Mk.8	57	ex M Wallop, Wattisham, Saxmundham, M Wallop, Inverness, Blackpool, East Cowes, Eastleigh. CoA 2-8-00, de-reg 14-4-10. Acquired 3-8-08		1-24
❑ –	SUMPAC man powered	61	BAPC.7, ex Old Warden, Southampton. Arrived 1984 Also, mock-up of the drive train	[1]	1-24

			Type	Yr	History	Note	Date
❑	–		Airwave hang-glider	80	BAPC.215, prototype. Arrived 1987		1-24
❑	VH-BRC		Short Sandringham 4 JM715	43	ex Lee-on-Solent, N158C, VP-LVE *Southern Cross*, N158C, VH-BRC, ZK-AMH, JM715. Rochester-built. Last flown 2-2-81, arrived 2-3-83. *Beachcomber*	[2]	1-24
❑	'C4451'		Avro 504J replica	91	BAPC.210, partially sectioned. AJD Engineering-built		1-24
❑	N248		Supermarine S.6A	29	ex Cowes, Southampton, Henlow, Southampton Pier, 'S1596', Eastleigh, Calshot, S.6, RAFHSF. Acquired 7-2-76		1-24
❑	'N546'		Wight Quadruplane rep	87	BAPC.164, ex Wimborne. Wessex Av Soc-built. Arrived 1988		1-24
❑	–	'AL-K'	Hawker Hurricane FSM	15	volunteer-built, travelling exhibit		6-18
❑	BB807		DH Tiger Moth G-ADWO	35	ex Wimborne, Valley SF, 6 FTS, 22 EFTS, 4 FIS, Cam UAS, 510, 510, 24, 20 EFTS, 12 EFTS, G-ADWO. De-reg 15-9-58. Arrived 1988	[3]	1-24
❑	PK683		V-S Spitfire F.24	46	ex Kingsbridge Lane, Kemble, Colerne, Changi 7150M, Singapore Aux AF. CBAF-built. Accident 29-9-52. Acquired 7-2-76	[4]	1-24
❑	TG263		Saro SR.A/1	46	ex Duxford, Staverton, Cranfield, G-12-1, TG263. Arrived 1993	[5]	1-24
❑	WK570		DHC Chipmunk T.10	52	ex Hurn, Thorney Island 8211M (4-8-72), RAFTC, 663, Hull UAS, 663, RAFC. Hawarden-built. Cockpit	[6]	1-24
❑	XF114		V-S Swift F.7 G-SWIF	57	ex Bicester, Scampton, Hurn, Connah's Quay, Aston Down, CS(A), Cranfield. De-reg 19-7-04. Acquired 2005. Fuselage in conservation workshop		1-24
❑	XJ571	'242'	DH Sea Vixen FAW.2	60	ex Brooklands, Dunsfold, Southampton, Cosford 8140M (30-5-71), Halton, Sydenham, 892, FAW.1, 899, 893. Christchurch-built. Arrived 5-2-03. 893 Sqn colours	[7]	1-24
❑	XK740		Folland Gnat F.1	57	ex Hamble, Cosford 8396M (2-8-61), Bicester, Church Fenton, MoS, Filton. SOC 13-2-61. Acquired 6-3-87	[4]	1-24
❑	XL770		Saro Skeeter AOP.12	58	ex M Wallop, Shrivenham 8046M, Wroughton, 652, 654. SOC 23-5-68. Arrived 1987	[8]	1-24
❑	XV760		HS Harrier GR.3	69	ex Dunsfold, Y'ton A2605 [2] A2614 (30-5-91), Culdrose, St Athan, 3, 4, GR.1, 233 OCU. Cockpit. Arr 2010	[7] [9]	1-24
❑	ZH763*		BAC 111-539GL G-BGKE	80	ex St Mawgan, Boscombe Down, QinetiQ, DRA, Ferranti, G-BGKE British AW. Last flight 26-4-13. Forward fuselage, arrived 24-11-23	[10]	1-24
❑	–		V-S Swift FR.5 CIM		forward fuselage	[11]	1-24
❑	'U-1215'		DH Vampire T.11 XE998	55	ex Farnborough, Wisbech, Huntingdon, Horley, Charlwood, Biggin Hill, Warmingham, Wigan, Woodford, Chester, St Athan, 8 FTS, 4 FTS, 8 FTS. Hatfield-built. SOC 11-12-67. Arrived 2005. Swiss Air Force colours	[7]	1-24

■ **[1]** SUMPAC - Southampton University Man-Powered Aircraft. **[2]** On loan from the Science Museum, South Kensington, Gtr Lon. **[3]** Tiger Moth is a composite, parts from G-AOAC and G-AOJJ. **[4]** Spitfire F.24 and Gnat F.1 are on loan from the RAF Museum, Hendon, Gtr Lon. **[5]** On loan from the Imperial War Museum, Duxford, Cambs. **[6]** On loan from 424 Sqn ATC – see below. **[7]** Sea Vixen, Harrier and Vampire on loan from the Hallett Collection/MCA Aviation USA. **[8]** Skeeter on loan from the Army Flying Museum, Middle Wallop, Hampshire. **[9]** Much of XV760 was consumed in the Sea Harrier FRS.1 composite XZ493, see Yeovilton, Somerset. **[10]** As G-BGKE *County of West Midlands*, carried out the last British Airways 111 service on 30-3-91 and its flight into St Mawgan as ZH763 was the last of the type in the UK. **[11]** 'Favourite' for this is FR.5 XD903 – a life of test and trials, last reported at Wisley, 1956.

Deep Store: Sea Venom FAW.22 WM571 made the move to Bournemouth, Dorset, in April 2023, only to relocate again on 27th June 2023, to Bruntingthorpe, Leics. ◆ ***Not*** *available for inspection*

			Type	Yr	History	Note	Date
❑	XD332	'194'	V-S Scimitar F.1	66	ex Helston, Culdrose SAH-19, Lee-on-Solent A2574 (6-10-67), 764, 736, 807, 804. Arrived 10-3-99		6-20

No.**424 (City of Southampton) Squadron, Air Cadets:** HQ within the Blighmont Army Reserve Centre in Millbrook Road West. Some airframes are held at Solent Sky - see above. ◆ *Prior application* **only**

			Type	Yr	History	Note	Date
❑	XD596		DH Vampire T.11	54	ex Calmore, St Athan 7939M (14-2-67), CATCS, CNCS, 5 FTS, 4 FTS. Hatfield-built		4-12
❑	XP542	'42'	Folland Gnat T.1	63	ex Hamble, Southampton, Shrivenham, St Athan 8575M (5-1-78), 4 FTS. 'Red Arrows' c/s stb, red/white to stb		3-23
❑	–		Hunting Jet Provost CIM	~	marked 'CRAN 22/2'	[1]	4-12

■ **[1]** 'JP' cockpit *may* be wholly 'synthetic' but *perhaps* owes its origins to a Mk.3 or Mk.4, although it is marked 'T Mk 5-A' (sic).

Aero Antiques and **AeroTech**: The classic light aircraft craftsmen continue their magic, mostly with a de Havilland flavour. Airframes are held at a couple of venues – all ***private*** – this heading is used as a 'port of convenience'. Moth Minor G-AFOJ had moved to Challock, Kent, by September 2023. Tiger Moth G-AJOA has moved on, believed to 'Scotland'. Tiger Moth G-AOBH was airworthy by 2022 and Jackaroo G-AOEX was back in the air the following year. Brochet MB.50 G-BADV is more accurately listed under 'Locally' – below. ◆ **Strictly** *prior application* **only**

❑ G-AAZG*	DH Gipsy Moth	30	ex EC-AAE, EC-MMA, Spanish AF, M-CMMA, G-AAZG. Crashed 12-8-13, CoA 7-7-14. First noted 11-22		11-22
❑ G-ABIH*	DH Puss Moth	31	ex N770N, G-ABIH. First noted 11-22		11-22
❑ G-ABNX	Robinson Redwing 2	32	ex Redhill, Old Sarum, Shoreham. CoA 12-5-03		11-22
❑ G-ABWD*	DH Fox Moth	32	ex CH-344. First noted 11-22		11-22
❑ G-ACNS*	DH Moth Major	34	ex New Zealand, G-ACNS. CoA 21-5-12. First noted 11-22		11-22
❑ G-ACYZ	Miles Hawk Major	34	ex Canada, C-FAUV, CF-AUV, VH-ACC, RAAF A37-4, VH-ACC, G-ACYZ. Phillips & Powis-built		11-22
❑ G-ADNL	Miles Sparrowhawk	06	ex Hatch, Bury	[1]	11-22
❑ G-AFJA	Watkinson Dingbat	38	ex Berkswell, Headcorn. Crashed 19-5-75		11-22
❑ G-AFSW	Chilton DW.2	r39	ex Chilton Manor. Unflown. De-reg 1-12-46		11-22
❑ G-AMVS*	DH Tiger Moth	40	ex OO-SOJ, G-AMVS, R4852, FAA n/s, 7 EFTS. F/n 11-22		11-22
❑ G-ANOD	DH Tiger Moth	41	ex T6121, 19 RFS, 10 RFS, Lon UAS, 24 EFTS, Northolt SF, 60 OTU. Morris Motors-built. First noted 4-18		11-22
❑ G-ASEA*	Luton Minor	66	ex Liphook. First noted 11-22		11-22
❑ G-AYSK*	Luton Minor	71	CoA 24-5-05. First noted 11-22		11-22
❑ G-ECDF	DH Fox Moth	47	ex G-CGUO, ZK-AQM. DH Canada-built. First noted 4-18		11-22
❑ G-EUJG*	Avro Avian III	28	ex VH-UJG, G-AUJG. First noted 11-22		11-22
❑ G-EUKS	Westland Widgeon III	28	ex Australia, VH-UKS		11-22
❑ G-FAGK	DH Gipsy Moth	29	ex USA, C-FAGK, CF-AGK. Moth Aircraft Corp-built		11-22

■ **[1]** Much-travelled, much raced Sparrowhawk G-ADNL was morphed in 1952 into the jet-powered Sparrowjet, which was burnt out at Upavon in the summer of 1964. This is a replica of the 1935-era G-ADNL, using Magister wings and a "handful" of metal components discarded during the creation of the jet version,

Hampshire and Isle of Wight Air Ambulance: *Should* still have a Bölkow travelling fund-raiser. | **www.hiowaa.org**

❑ G-ESAM 'AM'	Bölkow Bö 105DB	92	ex G-BUIB, G-BDYZ, D-HDEF. De-reg 26-6-03. Cockpit	[1]	4-11

■ **[1]** Original cockpit from 'DBS-4 upgrade in the early 1990s. G-ESAM, became G-WAAS and was exported to South Africa in 2018.

Locally:

❑ G-BADV	Brochet MB.50	53	ex Ludlow, Dunkeswell, F-PBRJ. CoA 9-5-79	N6-22

SOUTHAMPTON AIRPORT or Eastleigh

Gentle reminder, the Spitfire on a plinth at a roundabout is a large piece of sculpture and not an airframe or even FSM.

SOUTHWICK on the B2177 north of Portsmouth

Defence College of Policing, Security and Guarding: Within historic Southwick Park. *May* still have its Lynx.

❑ XZ174	Westland Lynx AH.7	77	ex Gosport, Brize Norton, 3 Regt, 655, 662, 655, 652, 651. Cabin. First noted 12-11	3-16

STOCKBRIDGE on the A30 south of Andover

Mike Draper: Author of the brilliant *Sitting Ducks and Peeping Toms* on British UAVs has long-held a MATS-B at a *private* location in the area. With an 11ft span, this aerial target is smaller than some radio-controlled *models*. Mike also owns similar device 'ZA220' on loan at Old Sarum, Wilts. ◆ *Prior application* **only**

❑ 'ZA535'	Short MATS-B	82 ZB535	ex Chandler's Ford, Larkhill, Manorbier. Last flight 9-12-82, SOC 5-6-84. Acquired 5-6-84	[1]	8-19

■ [1] Serial incorrectly painted from delivery and never amended. Conducted just six flights, total time 3 hours, 8 minutes.

SWANWICK northwest of Junction 9 of the M27, north of Locks Heath

National Air Traffic Services: Swanwick Centre, in Sopwith Way.

❑ XW917	HS Harrier GR.3	71	ex Boscombe Down, Cottesmore 8975M, Laarbruch, 3, 4, 3. SOC 3-4-88. Displayed since 2012	12-23

THRUXTON AERODROME north of the A303 west of Andover EGHO

Tobago G-HALP moved out, by road, 13th September 2022, destined for 'Wiltshire'.

❑ G-ANWX		Auster J5L Aiglet Trainer	54	ex Chislet. Crashed 1-8-93, de-reg 24-9-93	6-14
❑ G-ASAX		Beagle Terrier 2	46	ex Chislet, Auster AOP.6 TW533, 652, LAS, AOPS, 663. CoA 1-9-96. Off-site	N6-23
❑ G-ASEF		Auster 6A Tugmaster	48	ex Bicester, AOP.6 VW985, 664. De-reg 13-1-67	5-21
❑ G-BGZJ*		Piper Tomahawk 112	79	de-reg 25-2-97. Rescue trainer, fuselage	8-23
❑ G-DISK		Piper Comanche 250	59	ex Turweston, G-APZG, EI-AKW. CoA 27-10-10, de-reg 14-6-16. Arrived 2016. Rescue trainer	8-23
❑ XW799		Westland Scout AH.1 G-BXSL	72	ex Chiseldon, M Wallop, 657, 656, 658. CoA 19-8-02, crashed 19-11-01, de-reg 7-5-02. Rescue trainer	8-23

WINCHESTER east of the M3, north of Southampton

Westland Wasp Historic Flight: Also owns XT434 – see Higher Purtington, Somerset.

◆ *Prior arrangement* **only| https://www.historicwasp.com**

❑ XT780	'636'	Westland Wasp HAS.1	66	ex Lee-on-Solent, Fareham, Fleetlands, A2638 [2], A2716 (17-8-83), Fleetlands, 703, 706, 829. Arrived 20-8-20	9-21

Army Training Regiment, Sir John Moore Barracks: A Gazelle is displayed opposite the guardroom,

❑ ZB672		Sud Gazelle AH.1	84	ex Shawbury, Fleetlands, 651, 663, 654, 672, 662, 657, 664, 3 Flt, Garrison Air Sqn. Westland-built. Arr 27-7-00	12-20

Also: Another transformation to feature in *George Clarke's Amazing Spaces* programme. The former Chichester college 737 has been turned into a 'man-cave' by a *private* owner in the *general* locality. It was said to have cost "around £5k" to purchase and another £3k to transport. ◆ *Prior arrangement* **only**

❑ F-GCSL*		Boeing 737-222	68	ex Chichester, Air Mediterranee, Euralair, United N9028U. Forward fuselage. First noted 4-22	8-22

HEREFORDSHIRE

BICTON west of the B4361, northwest of Leominster

Oaker Wood Leisure: ◆ *Prior arrangement* **only** | **www.oakerwoodleisure.co.uk**

❑ XP360	'V'	Westland Whirlwind HAR.10	62	ex Upper Hill, Sunderland, Warmingham, Lasham, Fawkham Green, CFS, 225. SOC 31-3-76. Red overall	7-21

CREDENHILL north of the A438, west of Hereford

Stirling Lines: Named after Colonel David Stirling, the man who set up the Special Air Service. See also Ewyas Harold, below.

❑ ZE412		Agusta 109A	88	ex Middle Wallop, Arborfield. 8 Flt. SOC 12-6-09. Displayed, first noted 10-17	4-23

EWYAS HAROLD on the A465 southwest of Hereford

Pontrilas Army Training Area: Exercise area for the Herefordshire Gun Club, sorry, SAS - see Credenhill, above.

❑ TF-AME		Boeing 747-312	94	ex Kemble, Air Atlanta, F-GSEA, SIA N121KG. Arr 7-2-15	9-20
❑ 9M-MMI		Boeing 737-4H6	92	ex Kemble, Malaysia Airlines. Fuselage. Arrived 24-2-13	9-20

KINGTON west of Leominster, on the A44

Martin Aubrey - Classic Ultralight Heritage Collection: The fleet is *believed* current. ◆ *Prior arrangement* **only**

❑ G-ADPJ	BAC Drone II	35	ex Selby, Breighton, Wigan, Bristol, Benson, Thetford. Damaged 3-4-55	[1]	N11-22
❑ G-ARIF	Ord-Hume OH-7 Coupe	61	ex Breighton, Wigan	[2]	N11-22
❑ G-ASDF	Edwards Gyrocopter	r62	ex Innsworth, Woking, Coulsdon. De-reg 3-10-63		3-02
❑ G-BXIY	Blake Bluetit	30	ex N Weald, Old Warden, BAPC.37, Winchester	[3]	N11-22
❑ G-MBEP	Aerolights Eagle 215B	80	ex Caernarfon. CoA 8-4-96		3-18
❑ G-MBWI	Microlite Lafayette 1	r82	ex Selby, Leeds, Leigh. De-reg 13-6-90		N12-14

■ **[1]** Also held are parts of fellow G-AEKU. **[2]** OH-7 – or even O-H-7 – is a version of the Luton Minor developed and built by Arthur Ord-Hume, Chiswick. **[2]** Devised by the Blake brothers at Winchester. Cut-down wings from an Avro 504K and the rear fuselages of Simmonds Spartan Two Seater G-AAGN and Spartan Three Seater G-AAJB used in the construction. Flew, unhampered by 'paperwork' from 1930 for about two years.

Also: Auster RT610 (G-AKWS) moved to Shobdon, Herefordshire, by November 2021.

LEDBURY on the A449 southwest of Great Malvern

Ray Challis: Acquired a former Swiss Venom cockpit during January 2022; it is kept in the locality at a *private* venue.
◆ *Prior arrangement* **only** | **rwchallis@hotmail.com**

❑ J-1573*		DH Venom FB.50	55	ex Tetbury, Newbridge, Portarlington, Hurn, HB-RVB,	
		G-VICI		G-BMOB, Swiss AF. Swiss-built. CoA 24-11-99, de-reg 5-3-13. Arrived 28-1-22. Cockpit	1-24

SHOBDON AERODROME north of the A44 west of Leominster

EGBS

Cherokee G-ARVV was flying again by 2022. Agusta 109 G-TGRA has been deleted.

❑ G-AFGD	BA Swallow II	37	ex BK897, GTS, CLE, RAE, G-AFGD. CoA 10-7-14	11-23
❑ G-AWDU	Brantly B2B	68	CoA 3-1-14	6-21
❑ G-BAOU*	American AA-5 Traveller	73	de-reg 13-5-21. First noted 4-23	6-23
❑ RT610*	Taylorcraft Auster 5A-160	44	ex Kington, 657, SOC 9-12-47. CoA 10-6-13.	
	G-AKWS		Lycoming O-320 conversion. First noted 11-21	11-23

HERTFORDSHIRE

BOVINGDON on the B4505 southwest of Hemel Hempstead

Delta Force Paintball: On part of the former airfield. ◆ *Prior arrangement* **only** | **www.paintballgames.co.uk**

❑ XZ612	'UDF'	Westland Lynx AH.7	79	ex Upminster, Ipswich, M Wallop. First noted 1-18	1-18

ELSTREE AERODROME north of Junction 4, M1

EGTR

A clear out of long moribund airframes during the autumn of 2022 involved the removal of: Cessna 150 cockpit G-AWTJ; Seneca G-BORH; Cougar G-BOXR and Cessna 152 G-ENTW; all *probably* to a parts reclamation business. Bulldog T.1 'XX704' (G-BCUV) had returned to Bournemouth, Dorset, by mid 2022. The following have been deleted: Cessna 172 G-ASFA; Cougar G-CYMA; Cessna 150 N23103.

❑ G-AWOE	Aero Commander 680E	59	ex N3844C. CoA 22-6-10, de-reg 21-12-15	5-23
❑ G-PIKK	Piper Cherokee 140	67	ex G-AVLA, N11C. CoA 17-12-16, de-reg 29-12-20	5-23
❑ C-FQIP	Lake LA-4-200	~	ex N1068L	5-23

HARPENDEN on the A1081 north of St Albans

No.**795 (Harpenden) Squadron Air Cadets**: The unit *should* still have a Cessna fuselage employed as a simulator.

❑ G-OPJC	Cessna F.152 II	79	ex Stapleford Tawney, N68354. Reims-built. CoA 17-10-07, de-reg 25-4-08. Fuselage, simulator	10-18

HATFIELD

University of Hertfordshire: The School of Engineering and Technology is *believed* to still keep a Musketeer: its fin fillet carries the quaint title 'Beechcraft Musketeer BE XXIII'. ◆ *Prior arrangement* **only** | **www.herts.ac.uk**

❑ G-NRIA	Beech Musketeer	63	ex I-MIFA, N2373J. De-reg 5-7-12. First noted 5-19	7-19

HEMEL HEMPSTEAD on the A414 west of St Albans

The Vampire Collection: Alan Allen's airframes are kept locally. ◆ *Prior arrangement* ***only*** | **alanwz581@gmail.com**

❑ WZ581	'77'	DH Vampire T.11	53	ex Ruislip, Bushey, Keevil, Exeter, 3/4 CAACU, 229 OCU, 233 OCU, 25. SOC 16-12-71. Hawarden-built. Cockpit	1-24
❑ XT439	'605'	Westland Wasp HAS.1	65	ex King's Lynn, Bruntingthorpe, Cranfield, Wroughton, 829, 703, 829, 845. Crashed 25-3-86. Arrived 10-5-02	1-24

HITCHIN on the A505 northeast of Luton

Philip Leaver: *Should* still have his cockpit-cum-sims. ◆ *Prior arrangement* **only**

❑ G-KAYT		Robinson R22	88	ex G-EIST, N9081H. Crashed 31-8-94, de-reg 18-1-95. Sim	3-12
❑ XV759	'O'	HS Harrier GR.3	69	ex Bruntingthorpe, South Molton, Welshpool, Llantrisant, Pendine, St Athan, 233 OCU, 1417 Flt, 233 OCU, 1, 233 OCU 1, GR.1, 233 OCU. SOC 10-7-89. Cockpit, simulator	3-12

Also: An Auster is under long term rebuild at a *private* location in the *general* area.

❑ G-AOZL	Auster J5Q Alpine	57	ex Earls Colne, Southend. CoA 28-5-88	10-23

KING'S LANGLEY on the A41 north of Watford and J20 of the M25

Great Westwood Equestrian Park: off Old House Lane. Within this woodland site are/were two airframes, used as jumps.
◆ *Prior permission only* | **https://greatwestwoodequestrianpark.weebly.com/**

❑ G-BFBB	Piper Aztec 250E	73	CoA 4-8-10, de-reg 6-4-17	11-18
❑ N519MC	Piper Cherokee 140	~	ex Elstree. De-reg 24-10-17. Fuselage	11-18

LONDON COLNEY south of the A414, southeast of St Albans

De Havilland Aircraft Museum: Pioneering since 1958, the site includes the impressive **Sir Geoffrey de Havilland Hangar**, opened on 16th February 2020. Although not meriting a formal entry, the rear fuselage of Sea Hornet NF.21 VX250 should get an honorary mention. Reduced to produce at St Davids, Wales, in December 1956, its hulk languished on the dump until salvaged by Tony Agar – he of Mosquito HJ711 at East Kirkby, Lincs – in 1972 and later presented to London Colney. Also of note is the rudder and outer wings of an Airco DH.10 Amiens.

Several airframes are in store off-site and are listed separately.

Dove D-IFSB is on loan at Fishburn, D&C. Humming Bird J7326 (G-EBQP) moved to Shuttleworth, Beds, by July 2022.

◆ *Access from the B556, paralleling the M25. AL2 1BU* | **01727 826400** | **museum@dehavillandmuseum.co.uk** | **www.dehavillandmuseum.co.uk**

❑ G-ABLM		Cierva C.24	31	ex Hatfield, Sydenham (ie Crystal Palace, London), West Byfleet. CoA 16-1-35, de-reg 12-39. DH-built. Arr 7-80	[1]	1-24
❑ 'G-ACSR'	'19'	DH Comet FSM	90	BAPC.216, ex 'G-ACSS', St Albans, Kings Langley, Wroughton, Australia. Arrived 2001	[2]	1-24
❑ G-ADOT		DH Hornet Moth	35	ex Hatfield, Old Warden, Stoke Ferry, Stapleford, Houghton-on-the-Hill, X9326, 5 GCF, 23 OTU, 24 GCF, 6 AONS, Halton SF, 2 CPF, G-ADOT. CoA 5-10-59, de-reg 18-9-63. Arrived 1977		1-24
❑ G-AKDW		DH Dragon Rapide	45	ex Amsterdam, F-BCDB, G-AKDW, YI-ABD, Dominie NR833, n/s. Brush-built. Arr 1994. *City of Winchester*		1-24
❑ G-ANAV		DH Comet 1A	52	ex Wroughton, S Kensington, Farnborough, BOAC G-ANAV, CPA CF-CUM, G-ALZA. Hatfield-built. De-reg 1-7-55. Arrived 2016. Cockpit	[3]	1-24
❑ G-ANRX		DH Tiger Moth	39	ex Belchamp Walter, N6550, SLAW, 25 EFTS, 18 EFTS, 241, 14 EFTS, 56 E&RFTS. CoA 20-6-61, de-reg 8-6-67. Arrived 1976. Crop duster. *Border City*		1-24
❑ G-AOTI		DH Heron 2D	56	ex Biggin Hill, Exeter, G-5-19. CoA 24-6-87, de-reg 17-10-95. Arrived 19-8-95		1-24
❑ G-AREA		DH Dove 8	61	ex Hatfield. CoA 8-9-87, de-reg 19-9-00. Arr 2000. BAe c/s		1-24
❑ G-ARYC		HSA HS.125 Srs 1/521	63	ex Hatfield, Filton, R-R, BSE. CoA 1-8-73, last flight 7-9-73, de-reg 31-3-76. Hatfield-built. Acquired 3-76, arrived 1979. Rolls-Royce colours (stb), Bristol Siddeley (pt) colours		1-24
❑ G-AVFH		HS Trident 2	71	ex Heathrow, BA, BEA. Forward fuselage. De-reg 12-5-82. Arrived 7-82. BEA colours	[4]	1-24
❑ G-AWZP		HS Trident 3B-101	71	ex Manchester, Heathrow, BA, BEA. CoA 14-3-86, de-reg 27-6-86. Cockpit. Arrived 10-2-22	[4]	1-24
❑ G-JEAO		HSA HS.146-100	83	ex Filton, Air France Express/JEA, G-UKPC, C-GNVX, N802RW, G-5-512, PT-LEP, G-BKXZ, PT-LEP. Hatfield-built. CoA 4-6-05, de-reg 2-11-09. Arrived 27-7-09. Fuselage	[5]	1-24

Replica of the original Tiger Moth, the DH.71 monoplane of 1927, July 2023. *Ian Humphreys*

Reg	Code	Type		History	Note	
❑ –*		DH Tiger Moth replica	20	fuselage, construction began 2020	[6]	1-24
❑ –		DH Comet 2	53	ex Wroughton, Dan-Air, BOAC, Crawley, Hatfield. Arrived 14-6-96. Simulator. BOAC Comet 4 colours	[7]	1-24
❑ F-BGNX		DH Comet 1A G-AOJT	53	ex Farnborough, G-AOJT (de-reg 9-7-56), Air France F-BGNX. Hatfield-built. Last flight 27-6-56. Arrived 20-3-85. Fuselage, Air France colours	[8]	1-24
❑ W4050		DH Mosquito prototype	40	ex Hatfield, Chester, Hatfield, Panshanger, Hatfield, RR, DH, A&AEE, E-0234. Last flown 12-43. Arrived 9-58	[9]	1-24
❑ LF789	'R2-K'	DH Queen Bee	43	BAPC.186, ex 'K3584', Hadfield, Droylesden, Redhill, St Athan, Pilot-less Aircraft Unit, Manorbier, St Athan, Scottish Aviation-built. SOC 26-11-46. Arrived 13-4-86		1-24
❑ –		Airspeed Horsa I / II	c44	BAPC.232, composite fuselage, rear of Mk.II TL615, latter arrived 7-10-78		1-24
❑ TA122	'UP-G'	DH Mosquito FB.6	45	ex Soesterberg, Delft, 4, 2 GCS, 48, 4, 605. SOC 30-6-50. Arrived 26-2-78. 605 Sqn and/or 4 Sqn colours: rolled-out 17-4-22	[10]	1-24
❑ TA634	'8K-K'	DH Mosquito TT.35 G-AWJV	45	ex Speke, G-AWJV (de-reg 19-10-70) *Mosquito Squadron* (1968), Speke G-AWJV, Aldergrove, 3 CAACU, APS Schleswigland, APS Ahlorn, APS Sylt, 4 CAACU, B.35. Last flown 16-7-68. Arrived 29-9-70. 571 Sqn colours		1-24
❑ WP790	'T'	DHC Chipmunk T.10 G-BBNC	52	ex Rush Green G-BBNC (de-reg 23-9-74), WP790, Birm UAS, Wales UAS, PFTS, AOTS, 1 ITS, RAFC, Man, Glas, Leeds UASs, 24 GCF, Binbrook SF, 5 RFS, 17 RFS. SOC 5-11-73. Hawarden-built. Arrived 1976. Birm UAS c/s		1-24
❑ XG730	'438'	DH Sea Venom FAW.22	57	ex Southwick, Portsmouth, Lee-on-Solent, ADS, Sydenham, 893, 894, 891. Hawarden-built. Last flight 7-7-70, SOC 13-7-70. Arrived 28-10-78. 891 Sqn colours		1-24
❑ XJ565	'127'	DH Sea Vixen FAW.2	60	ex RAE, 899, 893, 766B. Christchurch-built. SOC 29-7-76. Arrived 31-10-76. 899 Sqn colours		1-24
❑ XJ772	'H'	DH Vampire T.11	55	ex Brooklands, Wisley, Shawbury, CATCS, 1 FTS, 8 FTS, RAFC, Norway AF 15018 'PX-G'. Christchurch-built. SOC 3-2-71. Arrived 29-3-94		1-24
❑ XK695		DH Comet C.2(R) G-AMXH	56	ex Stock, Newton 9164M (10-11-92), Duxford, Wyton, 51, 216, Srs 2 G-AMXH (de-reg 2-3-55). Hatfield-built. Last flown 10-1-75. Arrived 17-12-95. Cockpit		1-24
❑ J-1008		DH Vampire FB.6	49	ex Hatfield, Swiss AF. Hatfield-built. Last flown 20-8-74. Arrived 11-5-75		1-24

■ **[1]** C.24 is on loan from the Science Museum, acquired 9-35. **[2]** DH.88 Comet FSM was built in Australia for use in the film *The Great Air Race*. Owned by Ralph Steiner. **[3]** Comet cockpit acquired by the Science Museum 21-5-62, gifted to DHAM upon arrival. **[4]** Tridents being restored with major input from a team from HPT - see Feltham, Gtr Lon. **[5]** The 146 first flew at Hatfield 8-11-83 and made its last flight, into Filton, on 7-1-03. **[6]** DH.71 Tiger Moth - the *monoplane* of 1927. **[7]** Comet 2 sim was built at the same time as the cockpits for the first two prototypes and was used for structural tests. It then went to the DH Servicing School and was later converted into a simulator, fitted with Mk.4 instrumentation. It served with BOAC and then Dan-Air, retiring in 1983 with a total of 10,660 training hours. **[8]** Comet 1A registered as G-AOJT for ferry flight to Farnborough 27-6-56 in the hands of John Cunningham.

[9] 'Mossie' prototype W4050 built at Salisbury Hall and first flown on 25-11-40 by Geoffrey de Havilland Jnr at Hatfield. W4050 broke its back in a taxying accident at A&AEE. on 24-2-41. The fuselage was replaced by the one intended for the photo-recce prototype, W4051, and fitted at Boscombe Down. (W4051 was completed with a production fuselage.) **[10]** FB.6 TA122 rebuilt using the wing of TR.33 TW233 acquired in Israel. The codes 'UP-G' relate to TA122's days with 605 Squadron in May 1945 and with its use with 4 Sqn in Germany 1949-1950. (And *possibly* during its time in between with 2 Group's comms unit at Evere.)

Store: Airframes *not* available for inspection.

❑ TJ118	DH Mosquito TT.35	45	ex Elstree/Borehamwood, *Mosquito Squadron* (1968), *633 Squadron* (1963), Exeter, 3/4 CAACU, 3 CAACU, B.35. SOC 18-9-61. Cockpit, arrived 1973: rear fuselage arrived (from Oxford) by 6-92	[1]	6-20
❑ VV217	DH Vampire FB.5	48	ex Sunderland, Barnham, Bury St Edmunds, 'VV271', 7323M (23-3-56), Oakington, DH. EE-built. Arrived 12-8-09		6-20
❑ WM729	DH Vampire NF.10	52	ex 'Glos', London Colney, Ruislip, Bingley, Bradford, Church Fenton, CNCS, 2 ANS, 25, 151. Hawarden-built. SOC 30-11-59. Arrived 22-6-94. Cockpit,		6-20
❑ WR539	DH Venom FB.4	56	ex Staverton, London Colney, Fownhope, Rhoose, Cosford 8399M, Sek Kong, Kai Tak, 28, 60. Fairey-built. SOC 4-7-62. Arrived 11-92		6-20
❑ WX853	DH Venom NF.3	55	ex Debden 7443M (10-7-57), Shawbury, 23. Hawarden-built. Arrived 1-68		6-20

■ **[1]** TJ118's cockpit was used for studio shots for both films, sectioned allowing unlimited access to the port side. Stripped rear fuselage displayed at the Victoria and Albert Museum, London, 2017 as part of a moulded wood exhibition.

NUTHAMPSTEAD east of the village and the B1368, southeast of Royston

Nuthampstead Airfield Museum: Located in a series of huts alongside the 'Woodman Inn', the collection charts the history of USAAF Station 131 and the resident 55th Fighter Group and 398th Bomb Group.

◆ *South of Bell Lane and Park Farm Lane, SG8 8NB* | **email** via website | **www.nuthampteadmuseum.com**

RYE PARK on the A1170 north of Hoddesdon

Despite *W&R28*, the Cessna 421 is still atop an ISO container at an industrial yard.

❑ N41098	Cessna 421B	~	ex North Weald. Accident 2-12. First noted 5-17	3-23

ST ALBANS

The Paralyser Group (TPG): As foretold in *W&R28* (p90) the HP O/400 replica forward fuselage migrated to Stow Maries, Essex, on 26th April 2022. For the record, construction was carried out under the guidance of Graham Curtis in far-flung Dereham, Norfolk. Without a supporter of substance, the flying replica project (G-BKMG 'TPG.1') remains in abeyance.

ISLE OF MAN

The Island is a self-governing British Crown Dependency - part of the British Isles, but not part of the UK

ANDREAS AERODROME on the A9 northwest of Ramsey

Jodel D.18 G-BSYA is returning to airworthiness and has been deleted.

❑ G-BMFI	SZD-45A Ogar	76	CoA 30-5-08, de-reg 22-5-19	12-18

DOUGLAS

A Super Skymaster is *thought* to still be kept at a *private* location in the area.

❑ G-BOYR	Cessna F.337G	74	ex RA-04147, G-BOYR, PH-RPE. Reims-built. CoA 30-4-09, de-reg 18-11-11	12-17

ISLE OF MAN AIRPORT or Ronaldsway EGNS

Manx Aviation and Military Museum: Run by the Manx Aviation Preservation Society, the superb displays chart the island's varied aviation history and occupies former wartime buildings on the airport site. Part of the exhibition is the **Museum of the Manx Regiment** which has extensive displays on anti-aircraft artillery.

◆ *South of the airport on the Castletown road, IM9 2AT* | **01624 829294** | **airmuseum@manx.net** | **www.facebook.com/mamm.iom** | **www.maps.org.im**

❑ G-BGYT	Embraer Bandeirante P1	79	ex Keenair, N104VA, G-BGYT, PT-SAA. CoA 12-1-06, de-reg 26-9-06. Manx Airlines colours		1-24
❑ 'G-MAUD'	BAe ATP	89	ex airport, West Atlantic, LX-WAN, SE-LHX, LX-WAN, SE-LHX,		
	SE-LHX		N851AW, G-WISS, G-11-20, G-WISS. Last flight 19-6-15. Manx Airlines colours	[1]	1-24
❑ 9019	Bristol Bolingbroke IVW	41	ex Nanton, Canada, RCAF. Fairchild Canada-built. Arrived 21-6-04. Cockpit	[2]	1-24

■ **[1]** Restored by Terry Liddiard / ATP Preservation Project. **[2]** The 'W version was powered by P&W Wasp Juniors.

Airport: Lancair G-JBAS has been 'tidied up'/deleted. ATPs SE-MHD and SE-MHK were broken up on site in December 2022. The last revenue flight by a West Atlantic ATP took place on 24th February 2023.

❑ –	Eider Duck	c66	BAPC.282, displayed within the terminal	[1]	8-23
❑ SE-MEX	BAe ATP	89	ex West Air, CS-TFJ, ES-NBB, G-MANG, G-LOGD, G-OLCD.		
	G-MANG		Arrived 30-4-18		8-23
❑ SE-MHF	BAe ATP	89	ex West Atlantic, G-BTPF, EC-HCY, G-BTPF, N383AE. Last flight 19-9-18. Rescue training by 2-21		8-23

■ **[1]** Single-seat pusher-configured homebuild, unflown.

Also: The Spitfire FSM has been used for the 'Island at War' celebrations, held each August.

❑ 'P7966' 'D-B'	V-S Spitfire FSM	88	BAPC.283, ex Jurby, Farnsfield, Newtown, Kettering, *Piece of Cake.* Feggans Brown-built	9-16

JURBY on the A14 west of Andreas

Isle of Man Motor Museum and TT Museum: On the northern perimeter of the former airfield is the incredible museum: over 500 wheeled exhibits from cycles to tanks, and a 'JP'.

◆ *Ballamenagh Road, IM7 3BD* |**01624 888333** | **email** via website | **www.isleofmanmotormuseum.com**

❑ XN586 '91'	Hunting Jet Provost T.3A	61	ex Ipswich, Brooklands, Weybridge, Cosford 9039M (10-5-90), 7 FTS, 1 FTS, CFS, 2 FTS, RAFC. Arrived 3-20	4-22

SURBY north of Port Erin

A *private* location in the area *should* still be home to an ATP cockpit.

❑ SE-LGV	BAe ATP	91	ex Ronaldsway, West Air Cargo, N857AW, G-11-034. Last flight 28-2-10. Cockpit. Arrived mid-17	12-18

Former West Atlantic ATP SE-MHF serves the Isle of Man Airport rescue services. *Ian Greenhalgh*

ISLE OF WIGHT

ARRETON on the A3056 west of Sandown

Amazon World Zoo Park: Watery Lane ◆ **01983 867122** | **www.amazonworld.co.uk**

❑ G-OPUS	Jabiru SK		98	ex Sandown. De-reg 30-10-15. First noted 4-19	6-22

BEMBRIDGE AERODROME southwest of Bembridge EGHJ

Britten-Norman: The Islander is back in production here; all basic assembly having been previously carried out in Romania. A pair of former Army Islanders are/were undergoing spares recovery. See also Solent, Hampshire, – aka Lee-on-Solent.

◆ **Private** *location, prior arrangement* **only**

❑ G-BLNE	BN Islander R.1	G-BLNE	87	ex ZG844, Shawbury, 1 Flt, G-BLNE. First noted 5-21	[1]	6-21
❑ G-BLNV	BN Islander R.1	G-BLNV	87	ex ZG847, Shawbury, 1 Flt, G-BLNV. First noted 6-21	[1]	6-21

■ **[1]** Both registered as BN-2T Islanders and denoted as Pilatus Britten-Norman-built.

COWES on the A3020, north of the island

Sir Max Aitken Museum: An 18th century sail-maker's loft was the home of Sir Max Aitken from 1947 until his death in 1985. Most of the exhibits are maritime, but there are items from his night-fighting days and 601 Squadron.

◆ *83 High Street, PO31 7AJ* | **01983 293800** | **email** via website | **www.sirmaxaitkenmuseum.org**

Cliftongrade Ltd: The scrap dealers keep a Phantom cockpit at the yard.

❑ XT863	'AS'	McD Phantom FG.1	68	ex Abingdon, 43, 111, 892, 767. SOC 24-2-89. Cockpit	5-21

ISLE OF WIGHT (SANDOWN) AERODROME north of the A3056, west of Sandown EGHN

Wight Aviation Museum: After necessarily limited viewing, WAM celebrated full opening to the public in April 2022. This venue punches well above its weight: the scope and presentation of artefacts large and small is a joy to behold. To mark the 70th anniversary of the maiden flight (voyage?) of the incredible Saro Princess flying boat (22nd August 1952) the museum marked its outline span 209ft 6in, length 148ft in the lawn outside the museum.

The Bulldog is part of the exceptional collection of Richard Holleyman; his archive and other collections are fascinating. Adrian Brimson and John Phillips handed over their beautifully restored Skeeter in May 2023. Built at East Cowes, flight tested at Eastleigh, it is displayed with the cowlings removed, revealing the Gipsy Major: a nice touch. A full-size replica of a Saro Black Arrow R3 rocket is on show and Cushioncraft CC.7 (aka Britten-Norman) hovercraft XX102, built in 1969 at Cowes, has been acquired.

◆ *Hangar 2, well signed* | **07949 704052** | **wightaviationmuseum@gmail.com** | **www.wightaviationmuseum.org.uk**

Former Ghana Air Force Bulldog 'G-AXEH' and virtual pilots, July 2023. *Ken Ellis*

❑ 'G-AXEH'	SAL Bulldog 122 G-CCOA	75	ex Yarmouth, Ghana AF G-111, G-BCUU. Damaged 22-8-01, de-reg 16-6-02. Fuselage, simulator. Arr 2-18	[1]	1-24
❑ G-BOGK*	ARV Super 2	89	ex Ipswich. Monewden Flying Group-built. CoA 22-3-13. Stored	[2]	1-24
❑ XL765*	Saro Skeeter AOP.12	58	ex Melksham, Brackley, Clapham, Leverstock Green, Ipswich, Leamington Spa, Leeds, Rotherham, Tattershall Thorpe, Enfield (damaged 1-12-68), Odiham, Wroughton, 17F, 654, 651. SOC 27-5-68. Arrived 16-10-22, handed over 19-5-23		7-23

■ **[1]** The *real* G-AXEH can be found at East Fortune, Scotland. **[2]** Owned and under restoration by Stuart Allen. ARV Aviation was based at Sandown 1984-1988.

Airframe Assemblies (AA): The Spitfire specialists work on entire projects and in conjunction with other Spitfire workshops on major sub-assemblies, eg fuselages or wings. The latter tend to be short-term enough not to merit inclusion here: only 'long-termers' are listed. Spitfire IX MJ444 (G-LEGD) had moved to Duxford, Cambs, by late 2023.

The company is also engaged in the early phases of the Typhoon project - see under ARC at Duxford, Cambs. Additionally, AA was signed up as the build partner for the **Spitfire P8331 Restoration Project** in June 2020. This is in its formative days and will resurrect Mk.II P8331, registered as G-KOSC – flown by Wg Cdr Piotr Laguna of 303 Squadron and shot down on 27th June 1941 – **www.lagunasspitfirelegacy.org** ◆ **Private** *premises* - **strictly** *prior permission*

❑ PK664	V-S Spitfire F.22	45	ex Old Warden, N Weald, Stafford, South Kensington, Stafford, Cosford, Wyton, Cardington, St Athan, Binbrook, Waterbeach 7759M, 615. CBAF-built. SOC 4-2-54.		5-21
❑ TB382	V-S Spitfire XVI G-CMSF	44	ex Coningsby, EP&TU, 'MK673', 'X4277', 7244M, Abingdon, Bicester, Henlow, Ely, Middleton St George, Thornaby, 602. CBAF-built. Arrived 2002	[1]	5-21
❑ TP298	V-S Spitfire FR.XVIII N41702	44	ex USA N41702, Duxford, India inst, IAF HS662, RAF TP298 n/s. Crashed 19-5-94. Stored		12-13

■ **[2]** TB382 was 'consumed' as a source of spares for the rebuild to flying condition of Mk.XVI TE311 of BBMF. It passed on to Airframe Assemblies in return for the new wings for TE311. It is registered to AA's leading light, Steve Vizard.

Also: Taylor Mini-Imp G-BLWW is *believed* to have moved to Sussex by the beginning of 2022 and then *known* to have been cancelled as sold in the USA in July 2022. A Tornado ADV cockpit is kept on the aerodrome, near the café.

❑ –*	Panavia Tornado ADV	~	procedure module/simulator. First noted 7-23	7-23

NEWPORT on the A3054, middle of the island

Windmill Campersite: Froglands Lane, south of Carisbrooke Castle. Among the 'glamping' options is 'Galahad the Helicopter' – kip in a Falklands veteran! ◆ *Prior permission* **only** | **www.windmillcampersite.com**

❑ XT469	Westland Wessex HU.5	65	ex Weeton, Bowgreave, Kirkham, Stafford, 8920M, Wroughton, 771, 847, 772, 846, 848, 847, 848. SOC 27-9-07	12-23

Also: Kept in *separate* and *private* locations *should* be two homebuilds.

❑ G-AZJE	Gardan GY-20 Minicab	74	ex Sandown. CoA 7-7-82	N12-22
❑ G-BCMF	Levi Go-Plane	74	flown only once, 16-11-74, de-reg 5-12-83	12-13

NORTHWOOD on the A3020, south of Cowes

Wight Military and Heritage Museum: Among the vehicles is an icon of the Island. After a painstaking, decade-long, restoration by the Britten-Norman Aircraft Preservation Society (BNAPS), *Charlie-November* was unveiled in April 2023. The port cowling has been cleverly 'lowered' to allow inspection of the Lycoming. Recognising the importance of this exceptional project, the National Transport Trust awarded BNAPS 'Preservationist of the Year' in September 2023.

◆ *Newport Road, PO31 8QU* | **01983 305555** | **enquiries@wmahm.org.uk** | **www.wmahm.org.uk**

❑ G-AVCN	BN Islander	67	ex Ryde, Bembridge, Puerto Rico, N290VL, F-OGHG, G-AVCN, Aurigny. De-reg 4-6-15. Aurigny colours. Arrived 17-12-20, unveiled 22-4-23	[1]	1-24
❑ VQ-SAC	BN Islander	71	ex Ryde, Lee-on-Solent, Bembridge, East Preston, Shoreham, 5Y-ANU, G-51-287. Crashed 4-9-76. Forward fuselage. Arrived 7-1-21. Stored	[2]	1-24

■ **[1]** *Charlie-November* is the oldest surviving Islander: first flown at Bembridge, IoW, on 24th April 1967. It carried out Aurigny's first passenger service, Alderney to Guernsey, on 1st March 1968. It was restored by, and is on loan from, the Britten-Norman Aircraft Preservation Society – **www.bnaps.org.uk** **[2]** Also on loan from BNAPS, under conversion to flight simulator.

KENT

Includes the unitary authority of Medway

ASHFORD on the M20 west of Folkestone

Although the entry is long-in-the-tooth, the Buccaneer is *believed* extant at a *private* address in the locality.

❑ XV165		Blackburn Buccaneer S.2B	66	ex Spanhoe, Bruntingthorpe, Farnborough, Staverton, Bentham, Staverton, Hucclecote, Heathrow, Stock, Shawbury, 12. Cockpit. 12 Sqn colours	11-11

BRENZETT on the A2070 northwest of New Romney

Romney Marsh Wartime Collection: Throughout the season the volunteers offer a range of special events and commemorations. ◆ *Ivychurch Road, TN29 0EE* | **01797 344747** | **www.rmwcollection.co.uk**

❑ G-AMSM		Douglas Dakota 4	43	ex Booker, Brenzett, Duxford, Brenzett, Lydd, Skyways, Eagle, Starways, KN274, TCDU, 77, St Eval SF, Azores SF, C-47B-20-DK 43-49948. Damaged 17-8-78, de-reg 11-9-78. Oklahoma City-built. Cockpit. Acquired 1979. Air Freight c/s		1-24
❑ 'R6599'	'DW-J'	V-S Spitfire I FSM	c19	BAPC.539, first noted 5-21		1-24
❑ V7350		Hawker Hurricane I	40	ex Robertsbridge, 85. Cr 29-8-40. Acquired 1989. Cockpit	[1]	1-24
❑ VR192		Percival Prentice G-APIT	47	ex Hailsham, Lasham, G-APIT (de-reg 8-11-79, CoA 7-9-67), Biggin Hill, Southend, VR192, 1 ASS, 6 FTS, CFS, 2 FTS. Storm damaged 18-2-22	[2]	1-24
❑ WH657		EE Canberra B.2	52	ex Godalming, Cranfield, RAE, 231 OCU. SOC 29-11-77. Acquired 1987. Cockpit		1-24
❑ XH136	'W'	EE Canberra PR.9	59	ex Spanhoe, Bruntingthorpe, Cosford 8782M (8-2-83), 1 PRU, A&AEE, 39, 13, 58, MoA. Short-built. Acquired 2014. Cockpit		1-24
❑ XK625		DH Vampire T.11	56	ex Firbeck, N Weald, Southend, Woodford, St Athan, 4 FTS, 1 FTS, 7 FTS. Hawarden-built. SOC 4-12-68. Acquired 11-89		1-24

■ **[1]** Sgt Frank Walker-Smith was shot down by Bf 109s and he successfully baled out of V7350 and it crashed at Etchington, Kent. **[2]** Prentice on loan from David Bird –see Hailsham, E Sussex.

CANTERBURY

War and Peace - Battle of Britain Experience: The organisation has replicas available for hire. Its notional headquarters is in the Canterbury area, but the airframes may well be kept elsewhere.

◆ *Prior arrangement* **only** | **email** via website | **01304 813337** | **email** via website | **www.warandpeace.uk.com**

❑ –	'F-4L'	Mignet HM.280	98	BAPC.260, ex Wickenby, Millom. RAF colours	[1]	12-23
❑ 'P7370'	'ZP-A'	V-S Spitfire II FSM	~	74 Sqn colours		12-23
❑ 'V6555'	'DT-A'	Hawker Hurricane I FSM	09	257 Sqn colours		12-23
❑ –		Messerschmitt Bf 109 FSM	~			12-23

■ **[1]** Faithful replica of a 'Pou Maquis' built under the supervision of the South Copeland Aviation Group at HM Prison Haverigg.

CAPEL LE FERNE on the B2011 northeast of Folkestone

National Battle of Britain Memorial: The deeply moving statue of a pilot sitting, contemplating the English Channel, is set against a huge three-bladed propeller akin to the ancient chalk figures found on the South Downs. The Christopher Foxley-Norris Memorial Wall carries the names of all who took part in the Battle.

By June 2022 a 'Junkers Ju 87 sculpture' in crashed pose was on show; this does not deserve a formal mention.

◆ *Signed from B2011* | **01303 249292** | **enquiries@battleofbritainmemorial.org** | **www.battleofbritainmemorial.org**

❑ 'P2970'	'US-X'	Hawker Hurricane I FSM	03	BAPC.291. GB Replicas-built. 56 Sqn colours. *Little Willie*	1-24
❑ 'R6775'	'YT-J'	V-S Spitfire I FSM	04	BAPC.299. GB Replicas-built. 65 Sqn colours	1-24

CHALLOCK AERODROME on the A252 north of Ashford.

Kent Gliding Centre: A Moth Minor has arrived for completion of its restoration.

◆ *Prior arrangement* **only** | **www.kent-gliding-club.co.uk**

- ❑ G-AFOJ* | DH Moth Minor | 39 | ex Southampton, Navestock, London Colney, Navestock, E-1, E-0236, G-AFOJ. CoA 27-8-69. First noted 9-23 | 9-23
- ❑ WB986* | FHC | Slingsby Sedbergh TX.1 | 50 | BGA.3265, ex E Kirkby, WB986, Syerston, 614 VGS. SOC 9-9-86 | [1] | 8-21

■ **[1]** Written out of *W&R17* (p138) at East Kirkby as ready to fly by 9-98.

CHATHAM east of Rochester

The Historic Dockyard Chatham: A huge number of naval attractions await, including a Dragonfly.

◆ *North of the A231. Chatham ME7 1UR* | **01634 823800** | **info@chdt.org.uk** | **www.thedockyard.co.uk**

- ❑ WG751 | '710' | Westland Dragonfly HR.5 | 52 | ex Gosport, Condover, Ramsgreave, Ancoats, Wisbech, Blackbushe, Fleetlands, RAF Handling Sqn, Lossiemouth SF, HR.3, Yeovilton SF, 705. SOC 16-9-65. 705 Sqn colours | 1-24

Royal Engineers Museum and Library: Has a superb catch-line: 'Local Heritage - Global Impact'. Among the exhibits are the medals etc of James McCudden. The former Chattenden, Kent, V-1 is in deep store,

◆ *On the B2004. Prince Arthur Road, ME7 1UR* | **email** via website | **www.re-museum.co.uk**

- ❑ – | Military gas balloon | ~ | basket only. RAF Museum loan | 3-12
- ❑ XZ964 | 'D' | HS Harrier GR.3 | 80 | ex St Athan, 1417 Flt, 233 OCU, 3, 233 OCU, 1. *Ninja One*, 1417 Flt colours | 1-22
- ❑ – | Fieseler Fi 103 (V-1) | c44 | BAPC.158, ex Chattenden. Stored, off-site, from circa 2013 | 1-20

DOVER

Dover Museum: Within the varied collection is a 'Doodlebug'.

◆ *Market Square, CT16 1PH* | **01304 201066** | **museumenquiries@dover.gov.uk** | **www.dovermuseum.co.uk**

- ❑ – | Fieseler Fi 103 (V-1) FSM | c00 | BAPC.290 | 1-24

EASTCHURCH Isle of Sheppey

Eastchurch Aviation Museum: Located within the HM Prison Standford Hill, to the south of the town: the site of the pioneering Eastchurch aerodrome, established in 1910. There are extensive displays and plans to restore a former hangar as a heritage centre. The memorial in the middle of the town is a 'must visit'.

◆ *Wrights Way, off Brabazon Road, ME12 4AA* | **email** via website | **https://eastchurchaviationmuseum.org.uk**

GRAVESEND on the A226 east of Dartford

A Buccaneer S.1 cockpit and a test rig are *believed* to be kept by a collector at a *private* location.

- ❑ XN928 | Blackburn Buccaneer S.1 | 62 | ex Manston, Bruntingthorpe, Rhoose, St Athan 8179M (10-9-74), 736, 809, 801. Pink, *Glenfiddich*, *Jaws / Liz*. Cockpit | 1-22
- ❑ – | Blackburn Buccaneer EMU | ~ | test rig | 7-18

HAWKINGE on the A260 north of Folkestone

Kent Battle of Britain Museum: Occupies buildings used during the Battle of Britain by the famous RAF station. The depth and intensity of the displays is exceptional, as the website says this is: "The worlds [sic] largest Battle of Britain collection of memorabilia, artefacts from over 700 crashed aircraft are on display." In front of the externally displayed Spitfires and Hurricanes is the impressive 'Spirit of the Few' monument. There are plans to acquire adjacent land and to build a display hall to accommodate the 'real' airframes that are currently kept outside.

See under East Kirkby, Lincs, for an exchange benefiting the Bolingbroke and helping Lancaster *Just Jane*. In another exchange – for a vehicle exhibit – DH Moth replica 'G-AAAH' went north to Sunderland, N&T, on 17th January 2023.

◆ *Signed off the A260 to the west of the town. Aerodrome Road, CT18 7AG* | **Note**: *Photography in any form is* ***not*** *permitted within the museum* | **01303 893140** | **info@kbobm.org** | **www.kbobm.org**

- ❑ 'K5054' | V-S Spitfire rep | c88 | BAPC.297, ex Luton, Lowestoft, Luton | [1] [2] | 9-23
- ❑ 'K5054' | V-S Spitfire rep | G-BRDV | 84 | ex Southampton, Sandown, Keevil. CoA 18-2-95, de-reg 19-5-00 | [2] [3] | 9-23
- ❑ 'L7005' | 'PS-B' | BP Defiant replica | 02 | BAPC.281, ex Cosford, Wolverhampton. 264 Sqn colours. Arrived 28-2-15 | [4] | 9-23
- ❑ 'L9446' | 'LA-N' | Bristol Bolingbroke IVT | 42 | BAPC.603, ex Duxford, BAM, OHB, Canada. Fairchild Canada-built. Composite. 235 Sqn colours | [5] | 9-23

	Identity	Code	Type	Year	History	Note	Date
❑	'N2532'	'GZ-H'	Hawker Hurricane FSM	99	BAPC.272. 32 Sqn colours	[6]	9-23
❑	'N3289'	'DW-K'	V-S Spitfire FSM	68	BAPC.65, ex Chilham Castle, *Battle of Britain* (1968). 610 Sqn colours		9-23
❑	'N3317'		V-S Spitfire FSM	68	BAPC.71, ex Flixton, 'N8140', Chilham Castle, 'P9390' and 'N3317', Croydon, *Battle of Britain* (1968)		9-23
❑	'N3842'		Miles Magister	c00	first noted 10-21	[7]	9-23
❑	'N7033'	'K'	NAA Harvard T.2B	44 FX442	ex Hurn, Fordingbridge, B'mouth, Sandhurst, Hullavington, 501, 226 OCU, 203 AFS, 61 OTU. SOC 14-12-56		9-23
❑	'N9181'		DH Tiger Moth	~	ex Bedford area	[8]	9-23
❑	'P2921'	'GZ-L'	Hawker Hurricane FSM	99	BAPC.272, 32 Sqn colours	[6] [9]	9-23
❑	'P3059'	'SD-N'	Hawker Hurricane FSM	68	BAPC.273, ex Chilham Castle, *Battle of Britain* (1968), 501 Sqn colours		9-23
❑	'P3208'	'SD-T'	Hawker Hurricane FSM	68	BAPC.63, ex 'L1592', Higher Blagdon, *Battle of Britain* (1968). 501 Sqn colours		9-23
❑	'P3679'	'GZ-K'	Hawker Hurricane FSM	99	BAPC.278, 32 Sqn colours	[6]	9-23
❑	-	'KV-H'	Hawker Hurricane FSM	68	ex *Battle of Britain* (1968). Foreshortened fuselage		9-23
❑	'P7056'		Westland Whirlwind I FSM	10	forward fuselage. Westland Whirlwind Fighter Project built, with additional 're-engineering' on-site		9-23
❑	'P9398'	'KL-B'	V-S Spitfire FSM	68	BAPC.69, ex 'N3313' (?), Higher Blagdon, Stoneleigh, *Battle of Britain* (1968), 54 Sqn colours		9-23
❑	'X4255'	'LZ-J'	V-S Spitfire FSM	c90	fuselage. 66 Sqn colours	[6]	9-23
❑	'X4321'	'LZ-X'	V-S Spitfire FSM	c90	fuselage. 66 Sqn colours	[6]	9-23
❑	'MK356'	'2I-V'	V-S Spitfire IX FSM	~	on Queen Mary trailer. 443 Sqn colours	[10]	9-23
❑	'425/17'		Fokker Dr.I FSM	78	BAPC.133, ex Winthorpe, Higher Blagdon	[11]	9-23
❑	–		Fokker Dr.I replica	05	BAPC.565, ex Manston, Halton, *Flyboys* (2006)		9-23
❑	–		Gotha G.IV replica	05	BAPC.564, ex Manston, Halton, *Flyboys* (2006). Forward fuselage		1-22
❑	'D-3-340'		DFS Grunau Baby	~	ex Ramsgate		1-22
❑	'14'	1480	Messerschmitt 'Bf 109' FSM	68	BAPC.67, ex Coventry, N Weald, Newark, *Battle of Britain* (1968). JG52 colours	[12]	9-23
❑	–		Messerschmitt 'Bf 109' FSM	68	BAPC.66, ex '1480', Chilham Castle, Langley, *Battle of Britain* (1968)	[12]	9-23
❑	'6'		Messerschmitt 'Bf 109' FSM	68	BAPC.74, ex '6357', '6', Higher Blagdon, *Battle of Britain* (1968)	[12]	9-23
❑	–	'EP'	Messerschmitt Bf 110 FSM	c02	BAPC.566, ex Aviemore, *Monarch of the Glenn*. Fuselage, first noted 6-18		9-23
❑	–*	'1Z+LP'	Junkers Ju 52/3m	54	ex Cosford 'G-AFAP', Spanish AF, CASA 352L T.2B-272, CASA 352A T.2-272. CASA-built. Last flew 31-5-78. Arrived 19-11-22, Luftwaffe colours by 5-23		9-23
❑	'3140'	'A1+DA'	Heinkel He 111	52 B.2I-103	ex Duxford, OFMC, Tablada, Spanish AF B.2I-103, B.2H-51. SOC 4-71. CASA-built C2.111. Arrived 14-3-20. Luftwaffe colours by 5-20	[13]	9-23
❑	–		Fieseler Fi 103 (V-1) FSM	64	BAPC.36, ex Old Warden, Duxford, Old Warden, *Operation Crossbow* (1964)		1-22
❑	–		Fieseler Fi 103 (V-1) FSM	c90	ex Lowestoft. Stored		1-22

■ **[1]** *This* 'K5054' is an unfinished all-metal reproduction by Barry Gennard in Luton. **[2]** There is *another* 'K5054' at Tangmere, W Sussex. **[3]** *This* 'K5054' is full-scale, but with wooden airframe, powered by a converted Jaguar V-12; built 1984 by Viking Wood Products. **[4]** Defiant re-creation uses an original turret and parts from salvaged remains. **[5]** Duxford components, which arrived 6-12-17, comprised the fuselage, centre section and outer wings of RCAF 9893 (the cockpit section of this machine is held in store by the IWM at Duxford). The cockpit of a Mk.IVT and other elements, arrived from Canada in 2019. Elements also supplied via LAHC East Kirkby, Lincs, late 2022, said to be from IVT 9980 ex USA/Canada. Why this machine was given a heritage register identity is beyond the author... **[6]** Built by Terry Arlow of Lowestoft. **[7]** Magister described as "part replica/part original". **[8]** Composite of two accident-damaged airframes. **[9]** There are *other* 'P2921s' at Bentley Priory, Gtr Lon, and *two* at Biggin Hill, Gtr Lon. **[10]** 'MK356' has a real counterpart, at Coningsby, Lincs, and there is *another* 'MK356' at Boscombe Down, Wilts The *real* MK356 served as a gate guardian at Hawkinge 1951-1962. **[11]** Triplane built by Gp Capt A Wilson at Brixham. **[12]** Styled as Merlin-engined Hispano Buchones to match the airworthy examples used in the film, *Battle of Britain*. **[13]** The museum claims this to be Heinkel-built, as covered in two leading aviation magazines, both of which should know better. CASA Seville built, initially fitted with Jumo 211Fs - as a B.2H - and issued to service in 5-52. It was re-engineered 1957-1959 with Merlin 500s - as a B.2I. Bulk is from B.2I-103, with the tail from B.2I-27. Painted as a He 111H-2 of Stab/KG 53 shot down on 15-9-40, raiding London: parts of the original 3140 are on show.

HYTHE on the A259 west of Folkestone

Vintage Aero Ltd: The restoration arm of Aero Legends. The main Aero Legends operating base is at Lashenden, Kent, and its line maintenance operation is at North Weald, Essex. Aero Legends Spitfire Tr.IX project MJ444 (G-LEGD) is at Sandown, Isle of Wight. ◆ *Prior arrangement* **only**

❑ EN179	V-S Spitfire Tr.IX	G-TCHO	43	ex Exeter, 316, 306, Northolt SF, 315. FTR 19-8-43, salvaged	[1]	1-20
❑ '21' white	Yakovlev Yak-3	G-CDBJ	03	ex RA-44553. Accident 5-7-08, CoA 12-5-09	[2]	4-21

■ **[1]** Registered to Martin Phillips – see also Biggin Hill, Gtr Lon. **[2]** Allison V-1710 engined new build by Yakovlev under the Opytno-Konstruktorskoyr Byuro Imeni A S Yakovleva OAO.

Also: Jungmann G-BECU had moved to 'Gloucestershire' by 2021. Jungmann G-BECW and Cub G-RIXA were flying again by 2022. The Firefly cache *should* be held at a *private* location in the *general* area.

❑ G-BLTW	Slingsby T.67B Firefly	85	CoA 15-9-06	N8-23
❑ G-BLUX	Slingsby T.67M Firefly	85	ex G-7-145, G-BLUX, G-7-113. CoA 27-4-07	N8-23
❑ G-BOCL	Slingsby T.67C Firefly	86	CoA 26-2-07	N10-22
❑ G-BONU	Slingsby T.67B Firefly	86	ex Hinton-in-the-Hedges. CoA 29-6-00	N8-23

LANGLEY HEATH southeast of Maidstone

A Hunter is at a *private* location in the *general* area.

❑ 'WB188'	Hawker Hunter GA.11	G-BZPC	55	ex Melksham, Kemble, Exeter, Shawbury XF300, Yeovilton, FRADU, F.4, 130, 234, 71. Squires Gate-built. De-reg 16-3-11. Red scheme. Arrived 7-7-17	[1]	1-22

■ **[1]** See under Tangmere, W Sussex, for the *real* one.

LASHENDEN AERODROME or Headcorn, on the A247 south of Headcorn EGKH

Lashenden Air Warfare Museum: The depth of presentation of the displays is breath-taking and the warmth of the welcome from volunteers is a tribute to the team. During late 2020 Chris Samson donated the extreme nose – about 5ft, ie forward of the cockpit – of Short Sturgeon TT.3 TS482 '592'.

◆ *Ashford, TN27 9HX. Hangar tours are available for a small additional fee, subject to staffing levels.* | **01622 891810** | **info@lashendenairwarfaremuseum.co.uk** | **www.lashendenairwarfaremuseum.co.uk**

❑ 100549	Focke Achgelis Fa 330A-1 Bachstelze	44	ex Manchester, Liverpool, Blackpool, Lavenham, Hullavington, Biggin Hill, Farnborough. Weser Flug-built		1-24
❑ 6/2080	Fieseler Fi 103R-IV	44	BAPC.91, ex Germany, Lashenden, Rochester, Horsham, Farnborough, Dannenberg. Arrived 4-3-13	[1]	1-24

■ **[1]** Almost certain to have originated at Dannenberg and captured 23-4-45; this is a piloted V-1 'Reichenberg'.

Aerodrome: The aerodrome is home to **Aero Legends** offering the public flights in a growing and varied fleet of classic aircraft – full details at **www.aerolegends.co.uk** The organisation operates from several aerodromes and has a workshop at Hythe, Kent. There is no public access to the Aero Legends Lashenden facility, but a public viewing area and the museum - see above - offer great vantage points.

❑ G-ARNI	Auster J1N Alpha	61	CoA 15-6-98, de-reg 24-9-03. First noted 9-18	9-18
❑ G-BFMR	Piper Pacer	50	ex N7025K. Crashed 15-7-03, CoA 6-3-06	7-21
❑ G-BJOV	Cessna F.150K	70	ex PH-VSD. Reims-built. Crashed 1-10-20, de-reg 4-11-20	7-21
❑ G-BVYK	Team MiniMax 91A	95	ex Rochester. De-reg 19-11-14	7-21
❑ G-PVML	Robin DR.400-140B	74	ex F-BVML. CoA 27-8-12, de-reg 24-10-18	9-23

LONDON ASHFORD AIRPORT or Lydd EGMD

Wessex Aviation relocated from Biggin Hill from August 2023 onwards bringing along most of its eclectic airframes.

❑ G-BUCS	Cessna 150F		65	ex N3568L. CoA 1-4-04, de-reg 16-3-11. Rescue training	7-19
❑ G-DAZY	Piper Seneca 200T		77	ex N953A. CoA 2-6-11, de-reg 14-12-11. Rescue training	11-17
❑ N114WG*	Westland WG.30-100-60	G-EFIS	84	ex Biggin Hill, Weston-super-Mare, Yeovil, G-EFIS, G-17-8. Forward fuselage. Arrived 8-23	8-23
❑ VT-EKT*	W'land WG.30-100-60		87	ex Biggin Hill, Redhill, Biggin Hill, India, G-17-23. Imported to UK 7-00. Arrived 8-23	8-23

MAIDSTONE on the A229 south of Chatham and the M20

Chris Bennett: Acquired a Scout by late 2021 and has restored it to an exceptional standard. Its Nimbus turboshaft is regularly run, but not coupled to the rotors. ◆ **Private** *location, prior arrangement* **only**

❑ XV130*	'R'	Westland Scout AH.1 G-BWJW	67	ex North Weald, Thruxton, Babcary, Lee-on-Solent, Thruxton, XV130, 656, Falklands, *Who Dares Wins* (1982), 656, 655, 665. SOC 5-95. CoA 25-1-06, de-reg 13-11-12. Ground runner. First noted 11-21.		6-23
❑ XX720	'FL'	SEPECAT Jaguar GR.3A	74	ex Ipswich, Shawbury, 41, 54, GR.1, 54, 6, A&AEE, 54, Indian AF JI003, G-27-319, Abingdon, A&AEE. Arrived 2018		4-22
❑ XX745*	'GV'	SEPECAT Jaguar GR.1A	74	ex Fareham, Boscombe D, Shawbury, St Athan 9340M, 54, 16, 6, 16, 6, 226 OCU, 54, 6, 20, 226 OCU. Damaged 31-5-00. Cockpit. First noted 11-21		5-23
❑ 163423		BAe/McDD AV-8B Harrier II	88	ex Ipswich, Basingstoke(?), St Athan, USMC VMA-211, VMA-513, VMA-311. Arrived 2018	[1]	6-23

■ **[1]** Cockpit removed circa 1999 when imported to UK; reported for use by QinetiQ at Boscombe Down, Wilts, or Farnborough, Hampshire. Much of the rear fuselage and the cockpit required refabricating to a very high standard.

Also: The Dove and Cessna 120 are part of a nascent collection of transport aircraft, presently at a *private* location in the *general* area and not available for inspection. The anonymous Terrier fuselage and AusterAOP.6 wings are being restored to AOP.6 status at a local, equally *private* venue.

❑ G-ARHX*	DH Dove 8	61	ex Doncaster, Sunderland, Doncaster, Sunderland, Booker, Southgate, Leavesden. CoA 8-9-78, de-reg 6-12-78		6-21
❑ G-BRJC*	Cessna 120	46	ex Doncaster, N1833N. Fuselage	[1]	6-21
❑ G-TIMG*	Beagle Terrier 3	01	ex Clacton-on-Sea area. See above	[2]	2-22

■ **[1]** *Original* fuselage; *Juliet-Charlie* was rebuilt circa 2017 with a 'new' fuselage and is airworthy in Buckinghamshire. **[2]** Unfinished Terrier being completed under LAA aegis, hence 'build' date.

MANSTON on the A253 west of Ramsgate

Will it, won't it – attempts to revive the airport site back into, well, an airport continued as *W&R* went to press.

Spitfire and Hurricane Memorial Museum: The superb Hurricane and Spitfire are both examples of the workmanship of Medway APS, Rochester. There is a wealth of other material to see and the superb 'Merlin Cafeteria' to sample. There is a synthetic Spitfire simulator in the same colours as TB752 which is available on a pre-bookable basis.

◆ *Manston Road, CT12 5DF* | **01843 821940** | **enquiries@spitfiremuseum.org.uk** | **www.spitfiremuseum.org.uk**

❑ 'BN230'	'FT-A'	Hawker Hurricane IIc LF751	44	ex Rochester, Bentley Priory, Waterbeach 5466M (21-7-45), 24 OTU, 1681 BDTF. Unveiled 22-4-88	[1] [2]	1-24
❑ TB752	'KH-Z'	V-S Spitfire XVI	45	ex Rochester, 8086M, Manston 7256M / 7279M, SOC 28-9-55. Lyneham, 5 CAACU, 103 FRS, 102 FRS, 403, 66. CBAF-built. Unveiled 13-6-81. *Val*, 403 Sqn colours	[2] [3]	1-24

■ **[1]** 'BN230' is a composite, with parts from Mk.II Z3687 and Mk.IIc PG593. Colours of Sqn Ldr D A R G Le Roy du Vivier, CO 43 Sqn 8-42. **[2]** Both on loan from RAF Museum. **[3]** While serving with 403 Sqn RCAF, between 21-4-45 and 3-5-45 four different pilots shot down a Bf 109, an Fw 189, a long-nosed Fw 190 and a He 111.

RAF Manston History Museum: From 2020 the entrance area was regenerated, the shop extended, a café introduced and new displays – including a Great War exhibition – established.

◆ *Manston Road, CT12 5DF* | **01843 825224** | **events@rafmanston.co.uk** | **www.rafmanston.co.uk**

❑ 'SE-XZS'		Pitts S-1S FSM	~	installed 8-21, suspended in main hall	6-22
❑ –		Huntair Pathfinder 2	c82	BAPC.466, ex Indonesia. Arrived 2003	1-24
❑ 'A213'	'A'	Nieuport 17 replica	05	BAPC.467, ex Halton, *Flyboys* (2005). Arrived 2005	6-22
❑ –		Nieuport 17 replica	05	BAPC.469, ex Halton, *Flyboys* (2005). Arrived 2005. Forward fuselage	6-22
❑ 'B619'		Sopwith 1½ Strutter rep	04	BAPC.468, ex Halton, *Flyboys* (2005). Arrived 2005	1-24
❑ RT486		Taylorcraft Auster AOP.5 G-AJGJ	44	ex Old Sarum, RT486, 43 OTU. De-reg 10-10-19 Arrived 9-1-18	1-24
❑ 'WD615'		Gloster Meteor TT.20 WD646	51	ex N Weald, Elmdon, Cosford 8189M (10-12-71), 5 CAACU, 3/4 CAACU, NF.11, CSE. AWA-built. Arr 15-11-97. 85 Sqn, c/s	1-24

Manston continues after the photo-spread, on page 113

BEDFORDSHIRE
EE Wren G-EBNV
Shuttleworth, May 2023
Richard Hall

CAMBRIDGESHIRE
Jet Provost T.3 XN554
Abbots Ripton, Feb 2022
Paul Marsh

CAMBRIDGESHIRE

P-51D Mustang FSM '413410'
Bottisham, Aug 2023
Steve Richards

Firefly TT.1 Z2033
Duxford, Aug 2023
Steve Richards

Valiant BK.1 XD826 and Victor K.2 XH669
Duxford, Dec 2022
Paul Middleton

CORNWALL

Lynx HMA.8 ZD566
Lizard, Apr 2023
Steve Hobden

BAC 111-539 ZH763
Newquay, en route
Southampton, Nov 2023
Ian Haskell

CUMBRIA

Friendship 500 TC-MBE
Holmescales, Jul 2022
Pete Tasker

CUMBRIA

Harrier GR.3 XW768
Spadeadam, Aug 2022
Pete Tasker

Slingsby Falcon BGA.266
Windermere. Mar 2023
Ken Ellis

DURHAM

Dove 6 D-IFSB
Fishburn, Oct 2022
David S Johnstone

'Flea' 'G-ADRZ' and Jet Provost T.3 XN458
Fishburn, Sep 2022
David E Thompson

ESSEX

Meteor NF(T).14 WS726
Billericay, Oct 2022
Paul Middleton

GLOUCESTERSHIRE

Buccaneer S.2B XX894
Cotswold, Nov 2023
Jake Wallace

Britannia 101 G-ALRX
Filton, Jun 2022
Ken Ellis

GLOUCESTERSHIRE

Bristol 173 XF785
Filton, Jun 2022
Ken Ellis

Gamecock rep 'J9704'
Gloucestershire Airport,
Nov 2023
Mark Roberts

HAMPSHIRE

Viking 1 G-AGRW
Blackbushe, Jun 2023
Mark Roberts

HAMPSHIRE

Lynx AH.7 XZ184
Middle Wallop, Mar 2023
John Wickenden

'Flea' 'G-ADZW'
Southampton, Jun 2023
Ken Ellis

Skeeter Mk.8 G-APOI
Southampton, Jun 2023
Ken Ellis

HAMPSHIRE

Gnat T.1 XP542
Southampton, Jun 2023
Richard Hall

Boeing 737-222 F-GCSL
Winchester, Jun 2023
Richard Hall

ISLE OF MAN

BAe ATP 'G-MAUD'
Isle of Man Airport, Sep 2022
Tony McCarthy

ISLE OF MAN

Jet Provost T.3A XN586
Jurby, Apr 2022
Ian Greenhalgh

ISLE OF WIGHT

Skeeter AOP.12 XL765
Sandown, Jul 2023
Ken Ellis

LEICESTERSHIRE

Canberra B(I).8 WT333
Bruntingthorpe, Jun 2023
Richard Hall

LEICESTERSHIRE

F-104G Starfighter 22+35
Bruntingthorpe, Nov 2023
Hugh Trevor

Hunter GA.11 WV382
East Midlands, Jul 2022
Ken Ellis

LINCOLNSHIRE

Lightning F.6 XR753
Coningsby, Mar 2023
Brian Downs

TB-25N Mitchell '34037'
East Kirkby, Aug 2023
Richard Hall

Jet Provost T.4 XP629
Hemswell, Nov 2023
Nigel Price

LINCOLNSHIRE

Jetstream 31 G-JXTA
Swinderby, Mar 2023
Mark Whitnall

Buccaneer S.2 S.2B XX895
Tattershall Thorpe, Apr 2022
Ken Ellis

GREATER LONDON

Heron 2D 'G-AOXL'
Croydon, Aug 2023
Brian Downs

GREATER LONDON

Fw 190F-8/U1 584219
Hendon, Jul 2023
Ian Humphreys

Spitfire and Hurricane FSMs
Uxbridge, Apr 2023
Steve Hobden

WEST MIDLANDS

Hunter PR.11 WT723
Birmingham, Jun 2023
Jake Wallace

NORFOLK

Robin R2160
Clenchwarton, Jun 2022
John Wickenden

Hunter F.1 WT660
West Raynham, Sep 2023
Mark Whitnall

Phoenix UAV ZJ385
Weybourne, Apr 2023
Mark Whitnall

NORTHAMPTONSHIRE

Lockheed 12A G-AFTL
Northampton, Mar 2023
Nigel Bailey-Underwood

Tempest II 'PR533'
Northampton, Apr 2023
Nigel Bailey-Underwood

NORTHUMBERLAND

Lynx HMA.8 'ZD249'
Seaton Burn, Apr 2023
David E Thompson

❑ WP772	'4'	DHC Chipmunk T.10	52	ex St Athan, Lyneham, Colerne, Abingdon, St Athan, Middle Wallop, BFWF, QUAS, Hull UAS, 17 RFS. Hawarden-built. Crashed 4-5-90. Arrived 1999. 1 AEF colours		1-24
❑ WT205		EE Canberra B.15	55	ex Eastwood, Foulness, MoA, 9. SOC 31-8-72. Short-built. Arrived 14-10-00. 9 Sqn colours. Cockpit		1-24
❑ XA231		Slingsby Grasshopper TX.1	53	ex Stockport, 'Sealand', Cosford 8888M, Warwick, Kimbolton, Petersfield. Arrived 1999		1-24
❑ XA312		Slingsby Cadet TX.3	53	ex 'VM791', Kenley 8876M, 636 GS, 634 GS, 2 GC, GIS. SOC 22-4-68. Arrived 1999		1-24
❑ XG226		Hawker Hunter F.6A	56	ex Faversham, Manston, Faygate, Catterick 8800M (15-2-83), 1 TWU, TWU, 229 OCU, 92, 66, 92. Arr 23-1-03. Cockpit	[1]	1-24
❑ XL190		HP Victor K.2	61	ex St Mawgan 9216M (27-9-93), 55, 232 OCU, Witt Wing, 139. Arrived 6-2-99. Cockpit		1-24
❑ XR658		Hunting Jet Provost T.4	63	ex Prees Heath, Connah's Quay, Hurn, Wroughton, Abingdon 8192M (29-12-71), RAFEF, 6 FTS, CAW, 7 FTS. Crashed 26-10-71. Arrived 1-10-16		1-24
❑ XR770	'AA'	EE Lightning F.6	65	ex Waddington, Grainthorpe, New Waltham, Laceby, Binbrook, 11, 5-11 pool, 56, 23, 74. SOC 10-6-88. Arrived 3-3-15. 5 Sqn colours		1-24
❑ XS482		Westland Wessex HU.5	63	ex DSFCTE Manston, Farnborough, A&AEE, 848. SOC 20-2-86. Arrived 2000. SAR colours		1-24
❑ XV229		HS Nimrod MR.2	69	ex DFTDC Manston, Kinloss, Kin Wing, St Mawgan Wg, Kin Wg, 42, A&AEE, MR.1, Kin Wg. Flew in 26-5-10. Forward fuselage, plus fin/rudder. Arrived 17-12-20	[2]	1-24
❑ XV352		Blackburn Buccaneer S.2B	67	ex Gravesend, Manston, Stock, St Athan, Lossiemouth, 237 OCU, 208. Arrived 1999. Cockpit		1-24
❑ XV864		Blackburn Buccaneer S.2B	68	ex DFTDC Manston 9234M (28-3-94), 12, 237 OCU, 16. Arrived 14-5-20. 208 Sqn colours		1-24
❑ XZ106	'FR'	SEPECAT Jaguar GR.3A	76	ex Ipswich, St Athan, 2, 41, SAOEU, GR.1, 41, 16, 54. SOC 3-5-05. Arrived 21-11-08. 'Snow' camouflage		1-24
❑ ZA325		Panavia Tornado GR.1	80	ex St Athan 9338M, Cosford, St Athan, 15, TTTE. SOC 13-8-03. Arrived 2010. Cockpit		1-24
❑ –		Fieseler Fi 103 (V-1) rep	c04	BAPC.465, pole-mounted		1-24
❑ –	'4'	PZL Iskra TS-11 G-BXVZ	77	ex airfield, Shoreham, SP-DOF. De-reg 24-4-09. Arrived 8-13. 'Sparks' team colours		1-24
❑ '117415'	'TR-415'	Lockheed T-33AN Silver Star Mk.3	54	ex N Weald, G-BYOY (de-reg 8-6-05), N36TH, N333DV, N134AT, N10018, RCAF 21231. Canadair-built. Arrived 3-2-10. 512th FBS, 406th FBW colours		1-24

■ **[1]** The centre section of XG226 is at East Midlands, Leics, and a wing is at Charlwood, Surrey. **[2]** XV229's delivery to Manston was the last-ever Nimrod MR.2 flight.

Also: RAF Manston History Museum volunteers are restoring the former Paull Hunter on behalf of Lyndon Davies, CEO of Margate-based Hornby Hobbies. The final venue for XF509 has yet to be announced, but Hornby's base is at nearby Margate and includes a flourishing visitor centre. ◆ *Prior arrangement* **only**

❑ XF509		Hawker Hunter F.6	56	ex Paull, Marfleet, Chivenor 8708M (21-12-81), Thurleigh, 4 FTS, AFDS, 54. Arrived 18-6-21		1-24

British Phantom Aviation Group: Members are restoring ZE360 on the former airfield site. When finished it will migrate westwards to BPAG's base, Cotswold, Glos - which see.

◆ *Prior arrangement* **only** - *for more see under Cotswold, Glos* | **contact@bpag.co.uk** | **wwww.bpag.co.uk**

❑ ZE360	'O'	McD F-4J(UK) Phantom	c67	ex Manston 9059M, 74, USN 155574. Last flown 22-2-91. Acquired 25-4-21	[1]	1-24

■ **[1]** Acquired by BPAG with assistance from the 74 Squadron Association.

Others: The former Pitstone Lancaster cockpit gravitated to Manston. With no specific arrival destination, it has been placed here for the time being. JetRangers G-SUER and G-SUEZ have been deleted.

❑ TF-AMC		Boeing 747-2B3F	79	ex Air Atlanta, F-GBOX. Flightdeck	5-19
❑ '154761'	'18'	Bell AB.204B MM80279	~	ex -?-, Hayes, Cormano, It AF. Agusta-built. USMC colours. Travelling exhibition airframe	6-23
❑ –*		Avro Lancaster FSM	10	BAPC.425, ex Pitstone. Forward fuselage, *My Round*. F/n 2-23	1-24

PADDOCK WOOD Super Cub G-PCUB had moved on to 'Somerset' by May 2022.

POSTLING on minor road southwest of Lyminge

No further details on the Dove at a *private* location in the locality.

❑ G-ARHW	DH Dove 8	61	ex Coventry. CoA 19-5-06, de-reg 4-1-19		7-19

ROCHESTER AERODROME on the A229 south of Rochester EGTO

Medway Aircraft Preservation Society Ltd: Having settled in to their new workshop from late 2022, the craftsmen have returned their attention to the rapidly-completing Scion and the Hurricane project.

◆ *East side of the aerodrome, ME5 9SD* | **email** via website | **www.mapsl.co.uk**

❑ G-AEZF	Short Scion II	37	ex Redhill, East Tilbury, Southend, M5. Pobjoy-built. CoA 5-5-54, de-reg 22-1-70. Arrived 13-6-13	[1]	1-24
❑ BH238	Hawker Hurricane IIb	42	ex Sandown, Russia, Soviet AF. Gloster-built. Arrived 12-22		1-24
❑ –*	GEC-Marconi Phoenix UAV	~	BAPC.356, ex Old Sarum, Rochester. Arrived 13-7-22	[2]	1-24

■ **[1]** Pobjoy Airmotors-built at Rochester, first flying 9-12-37 as a floatplane from the nearby Medway. It will return to floatplane status. **[2]** Composite, based on an engineering trials installation fuselage –'Tooling Trial F.A.I.R.' – wings etc from surplus stocks.

Also: 'Tidying up' (see p7), has deleted the following: Robin G-BFBE, Jodel G-BHOL, Yak-18s G-VYAK and HA-JAB (G-UYAK).

❑ G-BXVC	Piper Turbo Arrow IV	79	ex Redhill, D-ELIV, N2152V. Crashed 22-8-98, de-reg 22-1-03. Rescue training		6-16

BAE Systems: The Phoenix is stored within the factory on the A229.

❑ ZJ303	GEC-Marconi Phoenix UAV	c95	ex MAPS. 'Army' titles		6-19

SELLINDGE See under Gatwick, W Sussex, for a predictable outcome.

SEVENOAKS

At a *private* location in the *general* area a pair of Wessex are *thought* to remain.

❑ XV722	'WH' Westland Wessex HC.2	68	ex Hixon, Shawbury, 2 FTS, CATCS, 18, 72, 18		1-19
❑ XV731	'Y' Westland Wessex HC.2	68	ex Redhill area, Fleetlands, 72, WTF, 240 OCU, 18, 78		1-19

Also: Auster J1N Alpha G-APJZ had migrated to 'Norfolk' by 2021.

SHOREHAM west of the A225 north of Sevenoaks

Shoreham Aircraft Museum (SAM): This superb museum is centred upon an extensive number of 'digs'; all beautifully researched and presented. Included in the incredible selection of artefacts is the rear fuselage skin from Bf 109 *Black 6* - which exists in the 'full' at Cosford, Shropshire. The tea room is exceptional!

◆ *High Street, TN14 7TB* | **01959 524416** | **geoff@aviartnutkins.com** | **www.shoreham-aircraft-museum.co.uk**

❑ P3860	Hawker Hurricane I	c40	ex 607. Crashed 17-9-40. Acquired 1986. Cockpit	[1]	1-24
❑ -	Junkers Ju 88A-1	40	ex Norway, USSR. Acquired 2008. Cockpit. *Traudl*, KG 54 colours		1-24

■ **[1]** Hurricane is a substantial exhibit, Merlin, firewall, forward cockpit area, windscreen, and canopy, not all from Sgt John Landsell's machine, but the majority so. The serial for Landsell's Hurricane is also quoted as P3933.

SITTINGBOURNE on the A2 east of Gillingham

A *private* collector has taken delivery of a Jaguar cockpit in the *general* area.

❑ XX140*	SEPECAT Jaguar T.2	73	ex Selby, Charlwood, Faygate, Brough, Cosford 9008M, 226 OCU, 54, 226 OCU, JOCU. Cockpit. First noted 3-23		3-23

WINGHAM on the A257 west of Sandwich

Wingham Wildlife Park: ◆ *North of the A257, east of the town, CT3 1JL* | **www.winghamwildlifepark.co.uk**

❑ G-MVIO	Noble Hardman Snowbird	89	de-reg 14-1-19. First noted 8-20		8-20

LANCASHIRE

Includes the unitary authorities of Blackburn with Darwen, and Blackpool

BANKS on the A565 north of Southport

A *private* workshop in the general area holds a former French Army Bell 47.

❑ F-BJDC		Bell 47G-2	56	ex ALAT 052, F-MBDL, F-MBCS. Arrived 12-3-14		7-23

BLACKBURN

A *private* collector *may* still have a Prospector cockpit in the locality.

❑ G-ARDG		EP Prospector	61	ex Haverhill, Redhill, Washington, Durrington, Middle Wallop, Shoreham, Lympne. De-reg 28-5-82. Cockpit	[1]	7-14

■ **[1]** At least the rear end of EP.9 G-ARDG is incorporated within the composite at Middle Wallop, Hampshire.

BLACKPOOL

Blackpool Zoo: East Park Drive, near Stanley Park. A Cherokee, previously used by the Squires Gate airport fire crews, is at the camel (non-Sopwith variety) enclosure. ◆ **www.blackpoolzoo.org.uk**

❑ –		Piper Cherokee	~	ex Squires Gate. Arrived 10-20		5-22

Manor House Touring and Helicopter Glamping Park: Kitty Lane, FY4 5EG. Bannered as an 'adults only' site, took delivery of a Lynx in late 2021 which includes a hot tub for anti-submarine exercises. A 737 cockpit and a Sea Prince followed.

◆ *Prior arrangement* **only** | **www.manorhousetouringpark.co.uk**

❑ G-CELU*		Boeing 737-377	86	ex Durham, Kemble, Jet2, VH-CZE. Last flight 8-12-14, de-reg 29-6-15. Cockpit, arrived 31-7-23		1-24
❑ WF118*	'569'	Percival Sea Prince T.1	51	ex St Athan, Charlwood, Staverton, G-DACA (de-reg 15-12-09), Kemble, 750, A&AEE, 727, A&AEE, RAE. SOC 1-8-80. Arrived 6-6-23		6-23
❑ 'XZ648'*	'365'	Westland Lynx HMA.8SRU ZD258	83	ex Ipswich, 815, 702, 815, HAS.3, 702, Gib Flt. NEA 8-14. First noted 11-21	[1]	1-24

■ **[1]** Fitted with the boom of XZ689, last recorded dismantled for spares at Woodmancote, West Sussex, 2019.

Sea Life Blackpool: Within the 'walk through' tank is the forward fuselage, including gun turret and parts of the tail, of a Boulton Paul Defiant, complete with staggeringly pristine codes 'YL' amid very real sharks. See narrative in *W&R28* (p117) for additional comment and Plymouth, Devon, for a kindred spirit. It is not a replica, it's a 'lookalike' and does not merit a formal listing. ◆ **www.visitsealife.com**

BLACKPOOL AIRPORT, or Squires Gate, on the B6430, south of Garstang, west of the M6 EGNH

Spitfire Visitor Centre: The Spitfire and Hurricane FSM are available for hire and regularly travel to venues far and wide. There are occasional 'guesting' examples. The centre hosts the ambitious restoration/recreation of an Airspeed Oxford based on the centre section of former Canadian Mk.V EB518 and DH-built Mk.I AT605.

◆ *Hangar 42, FY4 2QS* | **01253 341902** | **enquiries@spitfirevisitorcentre.co.uk** | **https://spitfirevisitorcentre.co.uk**

❑ 'V7752'	'JZ-L'	Hawker Hurricane FSM	89	BAPC.223, ex 'V7467', St Mawgan, High Wycombe, Coltishall. HFL-built. 57 OTU colours. Arrived 7-15	9-21
❑ 'W3442'	'FY-D'	V-S Spitfire IX FSM	~	BAPC.325, ex 'PL256'. 611 Sqn colours by 9-21	9-21
❑ 'X4253'	'FY-N'	V-S Spitfire II FSM	~	BAPC.326, ex 'N3290'. 611 Sqn colours, *Vicky*	9-21
❑ 'BS435'	'FY-F'	V-S Spitfire IX FSM	~	BAPC.324, ex Lytham St Anne's, Delabole, 'RB159', Hooton Park. TDL Replicas-built. 611 Sqn c/s, *Lucy*. Arrived 1-16	8-22
❑ 'PL279'* *and* 'MK464'		V-S Spitfire IX FSM	00	BAPC.268, ex St Mawgan, 'OU-Z', 'MH978', 'N3317', Duxford, *Dark Blue World*. 'MK464' 'Y2-Y' to port, 'PL279' 'ZF-Z' to stb. First noted 6-23	6-23
❑ -		V-S Spitfire IX SIM	~	first noted 7-18. *Lucy*	9-21

Airport: Chipmunk G-APPA moved to Husbands Bosworth, Leics, by February 2023. Diplomate G-AZIB, Osprey G-BVGI and Seneca G-HMJB have been deleted.

❑ G-BBEV	Piper Cherokee 140D	71	ex LN-MTM. CoA 8-9-01, de-reg 16-5-07. Rescue trainer	6-22
❑ G-BLLP	Slingsby T.67B Firefly	84	CoA 4-12-00. Trailer-mounted	N12-23
❑ G-BRPL	Piper Cherokee 140	72	exN15771. CoA 6-11-05, de-reg 18-9-23. Rescue tnr by 6-21	6-21
❑ G-OOGS	American GA-7 Cougar	79	ex G-BGJW, N737G. CoA 27-3-08, de-reg 21-5-18. Rescue tnr	6-22

No.**177 (Blackpool Airport) Squadron Air Cadets**: *Probably* still have a Tornado FSM; but also refer to King's Lynn, Norfolk.

❑ –	Panavia Tornado F.3 FSM	c85	ex Chester, Pant Glas, Hooton Park, Elvington, BBC *Fighter Pilot*		8-19

BURNLEY on the M65, northeast of Blackburn

Despite the somewhat 'historic' last noted date, **David Stansfield** is *believed* to be at work on an Albemarle. The Waco Hadrian elements do not merit a formal listing. ◆ **Not** *available for public inspection*

❑ –	AW Albemarle	~	ex Bacup, Carlisle, Westnewton. Cockpit section etc		5-08

COCKERHAM on the A588 between Lancaster and Fleetwood

Black Knights Parachute Centre: *Should* still have its para-trainer. ◆ *Prior arrangement* **only** | **www.bkpc.co.uk**

❑ G-BKPC	Cessna A.185F Skywagon	79	ex N4599E. CoA 11-11-07		N6-23

ECCLESTON on the B5250 south of Leyland

Bygone Times Antique Warehouse: This huge emporium occasionally offers airframes among the piles of Poole pottery.
◆ *Grove Mill, The Green, PR7 5TZ* | **www.bygonetimes.co.uk**

❑ 'A4850'	RAF SE.5a scale rep	c68	BAPC.176, ex Chorley, Barton, Firbeck, Pontefract		11-23

LYTHAM ST ANNE'S south of Blackpool

Lytham Motive Power Museum: An incredible museum within **Helical Technology**'s headquarters on Dock Rock pays homage to transport technology. Drawing the eye is the working Blue Bird Project's replica of the BSE Orpheus-powered boat *Bluebird K7* in which Donald Campbell met his fate on Lake Windermere on 4th January 1967.
◆ *Prior application* **only** | **www.helical-technology.com/about-us/heritage/**

❑ G-BBTL	Piper Aztec 250C	68	ex Blackpool N6525Y. De-reg 7-2-03		4-21
❑ G-MMJA	Mitchell Wing B-10	83	de-reg 13-1-90		4-21
❑ G-LORT	Avid Speedwing IV	92	de-reg 18-3-13. Stored		8-19
❑ XM708	Folland Gnat T.1	61	ex Bruntingthorpe, Kings Langley, Locking, Halton 8573M 4 FTS, CFS, HS. Last flight 2-12-77	[1]	4-21

■ **[1]** This Gnat was the donor of the engine in the Bluebird K7 replica.

Also: On the inner Promenade a Spitfire FSM is displayed at Fairhaven Lake.

❑ 'W3644' 'QV-J'	V-S Spitfire Vb FSM	12	BAPC.323, unveiled 21-6-13. *Lytham St Anne's*, 19 Sqn c/s		9-21

PRESTON

Phil Elsden: Is *thought* to still have his 'JP' cockpit. ◆ *Prior arrangement* **only**

❑ XW315	BAC Jet Provost T.5A	70	ex Wolverhampton, Long Marston, 'Lincs', CFS, 3 FTS, CFS. Damaged 5-7-84. Cockpit. Arrived 27-6-12		2-14

SAMLESBURY on the A59 east of Preston

BAE Systems: The **Academy for Skills and Knowledge** (ASK) has a former Indonesian Hawk as an instructional airframe, while another is stored. The *proper* Lightning and the F-35B FSMs – the author refuses to call this a Lightning II, especially here! – are mounted alongside each other at the main gate on the A59.

❑ 'XS921' 'BA'	EE Lightning F.6 FSM	14	BAPC.357. Gateguards UK-built. 5 Sqn c/s. Displayed by 2-15		12-22
❑ ZA328	Panavia Tornado GR.1	81	ex Preston, BAe trials fleet. Last flight 12-12-02. Arrived 12-2-05. Stored		11-21
❑ ZK532	HS Hawk T.53	c80	ex Warton, Brough, Warton, Indonesian AF LL-5315. Last flight 10-4-02. Stored		11-21
❑ ZK533	HS Hawk T.53	c80	ex Humberside, Finningley, Brough, Warton, Indonesian AF LL-5317. Arrived 14-9-18. RAF colours		2-22
❑ –	Lockheed-Martin F-35 FSM	17	BAPC.455. Gateguards UK-built. Installed 20-5-17		12-22

WARTON AIRFIELD on the A584 west of Preston EGNO

BAE Systems: Most of the references are tending towards 'elderly' but are *believed* extant.

❑ XS928 'AD'	EE Lightning F.6	67	ex Binbrook, 5-11, 56, 11, 56, 74, 5, 11. SOC 13-6-88. Last flown 31-3-92, unveiled 7-8-99. 5 Sqn colours		1-24

❑ ZG969		Pilatus PC-9	89	ex Brough, HB-HQE. *Percy*. Stored since at least 1-16	6-19
❑ ZJ801		Eurofighter Typhoon T.3	04	ex Coningsby. Fuselage, fatigue tests, arrived 12-6-19	6-19
❑ ZJ922	'QO-C'	Eurofighter Typhoon FGR.4	06	ex Coningsby, 3. Arrived 10-16, SOC 21-2-19	8-19
❑ ZJ951		HS Hawk Mk.120D	02	last flight 5-6-18. SOC 21-6-19	8-19

Locally: An owner at a *private* address in the *general* area has taken on a Canberra cockpit project.

❑ WT486*		EE Canberra T.4	55	ex Westbury, Newtownards, Belfast, Aldergrove 8102M (20-8-70), Wildenrath, 14, 17, 88, Wildenrath SF. Short-built. Cockpit. First noted 6-23	6-23

WEETON on the B5260 east of Blackpool, north of the M55

Ream Hills Holiday Park: Ream Hills Farm in Mythorp Road. Among the attractions is a Lynx that sleeps up to four.
◆ *Prior arrangement* **only** | **www.reamhills.co.uk**

❑ XZ676		Westland Lynx AH.7	77	ex Hixon, M Wallop, 671, 661, 656, 671, 657, 656, 652, 9 Flt, 671, LCF. F/n 4-14	1-24

Ream Salvage: An associated salvage business has a cache of Lynx 'cabs'. ◆ *Prior arrangement* **only**

❑ XZ173	'6'	Westland Lynx AH.7	77	ex Hixon, Fleetlands, 9 Rgt, 659, 4 Rgt, 3 Rgt, 1 Rgt, 669, 661, 669, 663, 656, 3 Rgt, 1 Rgt, 651, ARWF, IFTU. Cabin	7-18
❑ XZ673	'5'	Westland Lynx AH.7	80	ex Fleetlands, M Wallop, 671, 655. Cabin	7-20

LEICESTERSHIRE

Within the administrative county boundaries of Leicestershire are the unitary authorities of Leicester - and far from a county - the People's Republic of Rutland!

BRUNTINGTHORPE between the M1 and the A50 south of Leicester

Cold War Jets Collection (CWJC): *W&R28* related the transformation of the main airfield site from vibrant multi-use to vast vehicle storage facility under Cox Automotive. All airframes held in that area were scrapped and removed: VC10 K.4 ZD241 (N241Z<u>D</u>) was the last to succumb, on 22nd April 2022.

The aeronautical endeavours of David Walton and his family plus associated friends and organisations have since established a heritage area in the northeast corner of the former airfield. Much work has gone on, and continues, to allow increasing access to CWJC's aircraft, and those of other resident institutions. Corners are being turned, those that know this community will appreciate never to write them off: where's there's a will, there's a way. Stay tuned!

Three aircraft are held in the southern 'dispersal' – noted in the listing below – and are effectively 'marooned' at least for now. (David Walton owns Buccaneer S.2 XX900 – see Tatenhill, Staffs.)
◆ *Occasional open days, otherwise* **strictly** *prior permission* **only**

❑ G-BBTG		Cessna F.172M		73	Reims-built. Stored		N2-22
❑ G-PLOW		Hughes 269B		67	ex G-AVUM. Stored		N7-20
❑ XM715		HP Victor K.2		63	ex 55, 232 OCU, 543, 232 OCU, 100, 139. Flew in 19-11-93. *Teasin' Tina*. Southern 'dispersal'	[1]	1-24
❑ XS235		DH Comet 4C	G-CPDA	63	ex XS235, Boscombe D, DTEO, A&AEE, BLEU. Hawarden-built. *Canopus*. Flew in 30-10-97. De-reg 27-3-08. Southern 'dispersal'	[2]	1-24
❑ XV226		HS Nimrod MR.2		68	ex Kinloss, MR.1, Kinloss/St Mawgan Wing. Last flew 27-4-10. Southern 'dispersal'		1-24
❑ XZ382		SEPECAT Jaguar GR.1		77	ex Coltishall, Halton 8908M (29-10-86), Shawbury, 14, 17. Arrived 22-2-99		1-24
❑ 85	'8-MV'	Dassault Mystère IVA		c56	ex East Midlands, Sculthorpe, French AF. Last flown 15-5-79. Arrived 11-84. 'Desert' colours	[3]	1-24
❑ 1018		PZL Iskra 100	G-ISKA	78	ex Polish AF. Flew in 5-7-96. De-reg 24-5-10		1-24

■ **[1]** Shedloads of material on *Teasin' Tina* on **www.victorxm715.co.uk [2]** Made last ever Comet flight; total flying hours as at 14-3-97 came to 8,281. Details of how you can help support the Comet on **www.facebook.com/dh comet xs235(Canopus)project [3]** Mystère held on behalf of the National Museum of the USAF, USA.

Venom FB.50 'WR470', June 2023. *Richard Hall*

Classic British Jet Collection (CBJC)**:** One of the many sayings of Dave 'Mr Shifter' Thomas is 'Adapt, Improve, Overcome' – certainly that was the case with the re-opening of his collection on the northeast site. Two more jets have joined the fold. See under Lubenham, Leics, for the CBJC's Sea Hawk.

◆ *Prior permission* **only** | **mrshifter2009@hotmail.co** | **www.facebook: Classic British Jets Collection Supporters**

Serial	Code	Type	Built	History	Note	Date
❑ WM167		Gloster Meteor TT.20 G-LOSM	52	ex Coventry, St Mawgan, Coventry, Hurn, Blackbushe, RAE Llanbedr, NF.11, 228 OCU, Colerne CS, 228 OCU. SOC 9-1-76. AWA-built. Flew in 5-1-19		1-24
❑ WM571*		DH Sea Venom FAW.22	54	ex Hurn, Southampton, Wimborne, Staverton, ADS, 831, RAE, FAW.21, 891, A&AEE/ Hdg Sqn. Christchurch-built. Last flown 30-4-69. Arrived 27-6-23		1-24
❑ 'WR470'		DH Venom FB.50 G-DHVM	54	ex Coventry, G-GONE, Hurn, Chester, Hurn. Swiss AF J-1542. Swiss-built. CoA 29-4-16, de-reg 8-2-18. *Little Beauty*, 208 Sqn FB.4 colours. Arrived 3-9-18		1-24
❑ WT806		Hawker Hunter GA.11	55	ex Shoreham, Ipswich, Shawbury, Abingdon, Chivenor, FRADU, CFS, 14. SOC 26-11-94. Arrived 12-10	[1]	1-24
❑ XF994*	'873'	Hawker Hunter T.8C G-CGHU	56	ex Scampton, Boscombe D, Shawbury, Yeovilton, FRADU, 759, F.4, 229 OCU, AFDS, 66. Squires Gate-built. SOC 17-3-98. Arrived 25-4-23		1-24
❑ XJ494	'121'	DH Sea Vixen FAW.2	59	ex Kings Langley, Farnborough, FRL, A&AEE, HSA, Sydenham, 899, Sydenham, 892. Christchurch-built. SOC 4-12-83. Arrived 6-99		1-24
❑ XM365		Hunting Jet Provost T.3A G-BXBH	59	ex N Weald, Norwich, G-BXBH (CoA 31-8-01, de-reg 10-10-02) Binbrook, SOC 29-1-97, Shawbury, 1 FTS, 3 FTS, 2 FTS, Arrived 5-10		1-24
❑ XP540	'62'	Folland Gnat T.1	63	ex N Weald, Cambridge, Bruntingthorpe, Halton 8608M (12-10-78), 4 FTS. Arrived 30-1-18		1-24
❑ XW290	'MA'	BAC Jet Provost T.5A	69	ex Cosford, 9199M (6-7-93), Shawbury, 3 FTS, RAFC, CFS. Arr 11-12-14. Moved from 'southern dispersal' by 12-23.	[2]	1-24

■ **[1]** Coded '838' WT806 was part of the Airwork-operated 'Blue Herons' aerobatic team, 1979-1981 and 1986. **[2]** XW290 was part of the CFS 'Red Pelicans' team at Little Rissington, 1971 to 1973, prior to conversion to T.5A.

Lightning Preservation Group: .The team that 'Protects the Protectors' staged a fabulous come-back on 12th November 2022 with an open day and 'fire ups'. ◆ *Prior permission* **only** | **email** via website | **www.lightnings.org.uk**

Serial	Code	Type	Built	History	Note	Date
❑ XP703		EE Lightning F.3	63	ex Norwich, Coltishall, Bruntingthorpe, Warton, MoD, 29, 56, 74. Last flown 23-5-75. Arrived 7-10. Cockpit		1-24
❑ XR713 *and* 'XR718'	'C'	EE Lightning F.3	64	ex Leuchars 8935M (9-3-87), LTF, 5, 11, 5, LTF, 11, LTF, 5, 111, Wattisham TFF, 111. Arrived 5-15, unveiled 23-7-17. 111 Sqn c/s to port, 56 Sqn c/s as 'XR718' to stb	[1]	1-24
❑ XR728	'JS'	EE Lightning F.6	65	ex Binbrook, 11, LTF, 5, 56, 23, 11, 23. Last flown 24-6-88		1-24
❑ XS904	'BQ'	EE Lightning F.6	66	ex BAe Warton, Binbrook, 5-11 pool. Last flown 21-1-93. 11 Sqn colours		1-24

❑ XV328	'BZ'	EE Lightning T.5	66	ex Cranfield, Binbrook, LTF, 5, LTF, 5, 29. SOC 29-6-88. Cockpit. Acquired 25-5-14		1-24

■ **[1]** The *real* XR718 is at Dinsdale, N Yorks.

Also: Several private owners keep airframes at Bruntingthorpe. Clive Davies, co-owner of Canberra WT333 has an appeal that will chime with all in the preservation 'community': "We are facing a manpower shortage due to the great age of the owners and the loss of some crew. We really need to attract some keen new blood to continue operating this jet. If you can help please contact: **canberrawt333@aol.com**" ◆ *All* **strictly** *by prior permission* **only**

❑ WT333		EE Canberra B(I).8 G-BVXC	56	ex Farnborough, Bedford, RAE, C(A). Flew in 28-1-95. De-reg 22-4-03	[1]	1-24
❑ XL565	'Y'	Hawker Hunter T.7	58	ex Kemble, Ipswich, Colsterworth, Shawbury, Lossiemouth, FRADU, 237 OCU, 4 FTS, 208, 8, W' Raynham SF, 8, 1417 Flt, 8, Hawker. SOC 10-10-93. Arrived 21-3-02	[2]	1-24
❑ XL587*	'Z'	Hawker Hunter T.7 G-HPUX	58	ex Scampton, Duxford, Scampton, 8807M (2-3-84), 208, 237 OCU, 1 TWU, 229 OCU. Arrived 25-4-23	[3]	1-24
❑ ZA147*	'F'	Vickers VC10 K.3 N147ZA	66	ex 101, 10, East African 5H-MMT. Flew in 25-9-13. Scrapped by 1-22. Flightdeck, on southern 'dispersal'	[4]	10-22
❑ ZD948		Lockheed Tristar KC.1 N304CS	78	ex Brize Norton, 216, British Airways G-BFCA, N48354. Flew in 25-3-14, scrapped 3-22. Flightdeck, held on southern 'dispersal'	[5]	10-22
❑ 22+35		Lockheed F-104G Starfighter	62	ex Lasham, Manching, JbG34, KE+413, DD+105. Messerschmitt-built. Arrived 28-5-10	[6]	1-24
❑ '53'		Aero L29 Delfin	c66	ex Rosehill, Market Drayton, Boboc, Romanian AF, 395189. Arrived 11-2-10	[7]	11-23

■ **[1]** Roger Wintle, Steve Reglar, Clive Davies and Tony Waller own WT333. Built as a B(I).8 but later fitted with the cockpit of B.2 WK135. Clive Davies is the leading light in the Gloster Aviation Club, see under Gloucester, Glos. **[2]** XL565 owned by David and Amanda Dacre. **[3]** Registered in honour of Hawker's famous demonstrator, T.66 G-APUX, 1959-1967. **[4]** Touched down 25-9-13, making the last flight by an RAF VC10 and the whole breed: total time around 50,000 hours. **[5]** ZD948 was the last RAF Tristar to bow out, 25-3-14. **[6]** 22+35 owned by Geoffrey Pool. **[7]** Delfin owned by Jacek Beben, Mark Boffin and Graham Smith.

Off-site: Adrian Marshall and team have a ***private*** workshop in the region, which is listed here as a 'flag of convenience'.
◆ *Prior arrangement* **only**

❑ L5331	Fairey Battle	39	ex Bruntingthorpe, Canada, RCAF, RAF 98. Austin-built	[1]	3-22
❑ 51-14700	NAA T-6G-NT Texan G-TOMC	42	ex Bruntingthorpe, Stoke-on-Trent, Eccleshall, N Weald, Coventry, *Empire of the Sun*, La Ferté Alais, FAF, USAF, USAAF 42-44514. *Texan Tomcat*. De-reg 1-9-23	[2]	3-22

■ **[1]** Cockpit, centre section, engine mount and 1½ wings. [2] The French called armed Texans 'Tomcats' because of their growl.

EAST MIDLANDS AIRPORT or Castle Donington

EGNX

Aeropark: Run by the **East Midlands Airport Volunteers Association**. A major coup has been the acquisition of several engines from surplus RAF Museum stocks, including Adder, Python, Spectre. There are occasional special 'themed' events and the refreshment area is well recommended. There are two viewing mounds, close to the runway 09 threshold, that provide a superb vista of the comings and goings at the airport.

The anonymous EoN Primary/Slingsby Grasshopper moved to Fishburn, D&C, during November 2022.

◆ *On northern perimeter, signed from terminal, DE74 2PR* | **01332 850591** | **aeropark@eastmidlandsaeropark.org** | **www.eastmidlandsaeropark.org**

❑ G-ANUW	DH Dove 6	55	ex Long Marston, Welshpool, N Weald, Stansted, CAFU. CoA 22-7-81, de-reg 5-6-96. Arrived 31-10-09		1-24
❑ G-APES	Vickers Merchantman	61	ex Hunting, ABC, BEA. *Swiftsure*. CoA 2-10-95, de-reg 28-2-97. BEA 'square' colours. Cockpit		1-24
❑ G-ARBE*	DH Dove 8	66	ex Cricklade, Little Rissington, Kemble, Old Sarum, BAe, HSA, DH. CoA 3-10-02. Fuselage. Arrived 13-12-22. BAe c/s		1-24
❑ G-ARRM	Beagle 206-1X	61	ex Brooklands, Farnborough, Shoreham, Kemble, Banwell, Brooklands, Shoreham, Brighton, Duxford, Shoreham. CoA 28-12-64, de-reg 24-1-68. Arrived 2-3-19. Workshop	[1]	1-24
❑ G-ASDL	Beagle Terrier 2	50	ex Long Eaton, Eccleshall, G-ARLN, Auster AOP.6 WE558, LAS. CoA 18-5-07, de-reg 17-8-04. Arrived 1-12. Frame	[2]	8-23

John Britten's last design: the unflown Sheriff, G-FRJB. *Ken Ellis*

❑ G-BEOZ		AW Argosy 101	60	ex ABC, N895U, N6502R, G-1-7. CoA 28-5-86, de-reg 19-11-87. Arrived 6-87. Elan colours, *Fat Albert*		1-24
❑ G-CSZB		Vickers Viscount 807	57	ex Coleorton, Southend, N141RA, G-CSZB, VQ-GAB, ZK-NAI, SP-LVC, G-AOXU. *Viscount Scotland*. CoA 24-1-97, de-reg 19-8-98. Arrived 4-03. Cockpit	[3]	1-24
❑ G-FRJB		Aircraft Designs Sheriff	82	ex Sandown. De-reg 6-2-87. Unflown. Arrived 1-7-86	[4]	1-24
❑ –		Schleicher K.8	~	Stored		1-22
❑ –		Siebert Sie-3	~	ex Camphill, stored		1-22
❑ VR-BEP		Westland Whirlwind Srs 3 G-BAMH	55	ex Cuckfield, Bristow VR-BEP, G-BAMH, Redhill, HAR.3 XG588, 705, 701, *Warrior* Flt, *Albion* Flt. SOC 10-10-69. Arrived 13-5-86. Bristow colours, sampling probe to port		1-24
❑ WH740	'K'	EE Canberra T.17	53	ex Cosford 8762M, 360, B.2, RNZAF, Upwood SF, 40, 18. SOC 1-12-82. Arrived 8-12-91. 360 Sqn colours		1-24
❑ WL626	'P'	Vickers Varsity T.1 G-BHDD	53	ex Coventry G-BHDD (de-reg 21-11-09), 6 FTS, 1 ANS, 2 ANS, 201 AFS. SOC 12-4-76. Hurn-built. Last flown 14-11-79	[5]	1-24
❑ WM224	'X'	Gloster Meteor TT.20	52	ex N Weald 'WM311', E Dereham, Swanton Morley 8177M (15-10-71), 5 CAACU, 3 CAACU, 3/4 CAACU, NF.11, 29, 228 OCU. AWA-built. Arrived 12-1-03		1-24
❑ WM367		Gloster Meteor NF.13	53	ex Long Marston, Firbeck, N Weald, Powick, Boscombe Down, A&AEE. SOC 17-8-72. AWA-built. Arrived 11-10-08. Cockpit, workshop	[5]	1-24
❑ WP266		EoN Eton TX.1	51	BAPC.423, ex Pickhill, RAFGSA.337. SOC 13-12-66		1-22
❑ WP784	'RCY-E'	DHC Chipmunk T.10	52	ex Long Marston, Hemel Hempstead, Booker, Boston, Holbeach, Wellingborough, Reading, Benson, Abingdon, 6 AEF, Leeds UAS, Aber UAS, 8 FTS, Man UAS, QUAS, Air Attaché Paris, 5 RFS, 17 RFS. Hawarden-built. SOC 21-6-72. 5 RFS colours. Arrived 11-10-08	[6]	1-24
❑ WS760		Gloster Meteor NF(T).14	54	ex Yatesbury, Loughborough, Cranfield, Bushey, Duxford, Brampton, Upwood 7964M (23-8-67), 1 ANS, NF.14, 64, AWOCU. AWA-built. Arrived 11-11-06		1-24
❑ WT914		Slingsby Cadet TX.3	52	BGA.3194 / FED, ex Stamford, Tibenham, Kenley. CoA 7-2-87 Arrived 6-14. Fuselage, above snack bar, wings stored	[5]	1-24
❑ WV382	'830'	Hawker Hunter GA.11	55	ex Long Marston, Smethwick, A2724, Lee-on-Solent A2730 (5-2-85), Shawbury, Kemble, FRADU, FRU, 738, F.4, 67. Arrived 24-1-09. FRU colours		1-24
❑ WW442	'P-D'	Percival Provost T.1	54	ex Charlwood, Kings Langley, Leverstock Green, Cranfield, Booker, St Merryn, Houghton-on-the-Hill, Kidlington, Halton 7618M (10-10-59), CNCS, 3 FTS. Arr by 9-13	[2] [7]	1-24
❑ XD447	'50'	DH Vampire T.11	54	ex L Marston, E Kirkby, Tattershall, Woodford, Chester, St Athan, 8 FTS, RAFC, 5 FTS. SOC 1-12-67. Arrived 3-10-09		1-24
❑ XD534	'L'	DH Vampire T.11	54	ex 'XD382', Welshpool, Barton, Chelford, Hadfield, Wythenshawe, Cheadle, Woodford, Chester, Shawbury, 7 FTS, CFS, 9 FTS, 10 FTS. Hawarden-built. SOC 30-10-67. Arrived 2004	[8]	1-24

❑	XG737	'438'	DH Sea Venom FAW.22	58	ex Long Marston, Rhoose, Yeovilton, FRU, 894, 893, RAE, 891. Hawarden-built. SOC 27-3-69. Arrived 31-10-09. 891 Sqn colours, dismantled in display hangar		1-24
❑	'XJ714'	'B'	Hawker Hunter 'FR.10'	56	BAPC.548, ex '272', 'XJ714', Long Marston. Arrived 23-5-09. 4 Sqn colours by 7-22	[9]	1-24
❑	XL569	'85'	Hawker Hunter T.7	58	ex Abingdon, Cosford 8833M (2-9-84), 2 TWU, 1 TWU, 12, 216, 237 OCU, Laarbruch SF, 15, 237 OCU, 12, 2 TWU, 1 TWU, TWU, 229 OCU. Arrived 20-2-93		1-24
❑	XM575		Avro Vulcan B.2 G-BLMC	63	G-BLMC ntu, ex 44, Wadd Wing, Scampton Wing, 617. SOC 25-1-83, last flight 21-8-83		1-24
❑	XN492		Hunting Jet Provost T.3	60	ex Linton-on-Ouse, Redhill, Haydock, Levenshulme, Firbeck, Stock, Odiham, Cosford, Halton 8079M (18-3-70),6 FTS, RAFC. Cockpit. Arrived 6-15		1-22
❑	XP568	'85'	Hunting Jet Provost T.4	62	ex Long Marston, Faygate, Hatfield, Shawbury, RAFC. SOC 1-10-71. Arrived 25-10-08. RAFC 'silver' colours		1-24
❑	XT604		Westland Wessex HC.2	66	ex Hixon, Colsterworth, Fleetlands, 22, 103, 78, Muharraq SAR Flt, 78. SOC 16-3-00. Arrived 11-7-02	[10]	1-24
❑	XV108	'Y'	Vickers VC10 C.1K	68	ex Bruntingthorpe, 10. *William Rhodes-Moorhouse VC*. Last flight 7-11-12. Arrived 16-11-13. Forward fuselage. Air Support Command titles and 10 Sqn colours	[11]	1-24
❑	XV350		Blackburn Buccaneer S.2B	67	ex Shawbury, Warton, RAE. Arrived 11-12-93		1-24
❑	XW664		HS Nimrod R.1	71	ex 51, Falklands (Chile) 5-82, 51. Last flown 12-7-11	[12]	1-24
❑	XX494	'B'	HP Jetstream T.1	75	ex Bruntingthorpe, Retford, Ipswich, Shawbury, Cranwell, 45, 3 FTS, 45, 6 FTS, METS. SAL-completed. Last flown 22-3-04. Arrived 2-18	[11]	1-24
❑	XZ369	'AP'	SEPECAT Jaguar GR.3A	76	ex Brinklow, Upminster, Ipswich, St Athan, 6, GR.1, 6, Shawbury, 17, 14. Arrived 18-10-20	[13]	1-24
❑	XZ721	'426'	Westland Lynx HMA.8	80	ex Hixon, Fleetlands, 815, HAS.3S, 815. Arrived 3-16	[14]	1-24
❑	ZD477	'E'	Westland Sea King HC.4	84	ex Bruntingthorpe, Gosport, 845, 846, 845, 846, 845, 846, 845, 846, 845, 846. Arrived by 3-18	[11]	1-24
❑	ZF588		EE Lightning F.53	68	ex Warton, Saudi AF 53-693, G-27-63. Last flown 14-1-86. Arrived 8-1-89. 74 Sqn colours		1-24
❑	TAD.001	'Z'	Sud Gazelle AH.1 XX457	76	ex Long Marston, Arborfield TAD.001, 2 Flt, 662, 656, ARWF, GCF. Arrived 11-10-08		1-24
❑	–*		Panavia Tornado GR.4	~	ex Morayvia, Kinloss. Cockpit, simulator. First noted 4-22	[15]	7-22

■ **[1]** Prototype, first flown at Shoreham 15-8-61. On loan from the Brooklands Museum, Surrey. **[2]** Terrier and Provost on loan from Dave Warren. **[3]** Viscount owned by Colin Jacobs. **[4]** G-FRJB's initial design was carried out by Forrester Robin John Britten (he of the Islander) who was High Sheriff of the Isle of Wight at the time. **[5]** Varsity, Meteor NF.13 and Cadet on loan from Graham Vale. **[6]** WP784 is a complex composite. **[7]** Provost was fitted with the wings of IAC T.51 161. **[8]** XD534 owned by Chris Fairhall; and fitted with the wings and tail of XD382. **[9]** A complex beast; with an unused F.6 cockpit from Stafford, the centre section of F.6 XG226 - cockpit at Manston, Kent - the rear end of Danish T.7 ET-272 - cockpit at Flixton, Suffolk - and the wings from PH-NLH. **[10]** XT604's rear fuselage is fitted to XT760 - see Portsmouth in Appendix D. **[11]** VC10, Jetstream and Sea King on loan from Gary Spoors - see St Athan, Wales. **[12]** XW664 was the first R.1; it retired with a total flying time of 21,466 hours. It took part in Operation ACME, Elint/Sigint sorties, from St Félix island, coast of Chile during Falklands conflict. **[13]** Inspection of the build plates on XZ369 notes that it was laid down as fuselage S138 in 11-75 but was completed as S136 11-76. **[14]** Lynx owned by Mark Lindsey. **[15]** GR.4 sim donated by Thales UK.

Airport: Rolls-Royce bases Spitfire PR.19 PS853 (G-RRGN) and Harvard T.2B KF183 (G-CORS) at 'EMA'. This facility is ***not*** available for public inspection, but the PR.19 is a regular at airshows. See Derby, Derbyshire, and South Kensington, Gtr Lon, for more on RR. Fire-rescue trainer Boeing 727-230 TC-CLM was reduced to rubble by June 2022. Rallye G-BBED was written out of *W&R28* (p124) but it has proved far more resilient.

❑	G-BBED	MS Rallye 220	73	ex Aeropark, King's Croughton. CoA 13-9-87. Rescue trainer	6-22

HINCKLEY southwest of Leicester

Steve Milnthorpe's phenomenal project has been fitted out to Boston IIIA configuration. Other items held include port inner mainplane, fully restored turret, landing gear, Boston-fit Wright Cyclone, etc. ◆ *Prior arrangement* **only**

❑	'BZ264'	'B'	Douglas Boston IIIA	43	88 Sqn colours, *XXX Beer is Best*. Forward fuselage	[1]	1-24

■ **[1]** Based upon the forward fuselage of A-20G-30-DO 43-9628 *Lady Constance* of the 388th BS, 312th BG, which crashed in New Guinea 16-4-44. The restoration includes elements of Boston IIA Z2186 ex 418 Sqn RCAF which crashed in Snowdonia 17-10-42.

HUSBANDS BOSWORTH on the A4304/A5199 west of Market Harborough

Armourgeddon Military Collection: ◆ *On the A5199 - look for the tank 'gate guardian'* | **www.armourgeddon.co.uk**

❑ G-ARXH Bell 47G 47 ex Cranfield, N120B, Model 47D-1, 47B. De-reg 3-1-84 12-21

HUSBANDS BOSWORTH AERODROME south of the A427, south of the village

The Gliding Centre: Robin G-BVYG had moved on to 'Nottinghamshire' by mid-2022. Grasshopper TX.1 XK790 has also vacated – no known 'forwarding address'. ◆ *Prior arrangement* **only** | **www.theglidingcentre.co.uk**

❑ G-APPA* DHC Chipmunk T.10 52 ex Squires Gate, Exeter, Shoreham, Kemble, Wellesbourne M', Carlisle, Glasgow, N5703E, G-APPA, WP917, Glasgow UAS, 11 RFS, 8 RFS. Hawarden-built. CoA 14-7-85. First noted 2-23 8-23

KEGWORTH east of J24 of the M1, on the A6

Delta Force Paintball ◆ *Prior arrangement* **only** | **www.paintballgames.co.uk**

❑ XZ177 Westland Lynx AH.7 77 ex Upminster, Ipswich, Fleetlands, M Wallop. 'Marines' titles 4-21

■ **[1]** A *Gazelle* marked 'XZ177' is at Sunderland, N&T.

LEICESTER

Leicester Aircraft Restoration Workshop: As well as the Provost Max (son) and Ritch Blood (dad) are hard at work on their Provost. Their instrument facia and controls of a Brasov IS-28M2A motor glider, designed for 'small people' and disabled access was passed on to Scarborough-based Cameron Adams in 2022. ◆ *Prior arrangement* **only**

❑ 'XF545' Percival Provost T.1 55 BAPC.574, ex Thatcham, Linton-on-Ouse, Swinderby, Finningley 7957M (16-6-67), Shawbury, 6 FTS, 2 FTS. Fuselage, 6 FTS badge [1] 6-23

■ **[1]** Utilises some 'new-old' stock, elements from Alan House's Thatcham shelves and much 'scrounging'. The cockpit side carries an original 6 FTS badge and elements of XF545 and, for the time being, that serial will serve as its 'handle'.

Leicester College: Painter Street. Not noted since December 2016, K&S Cavalier G-BAJV has been deleted.

Leicestershire Museums: The aircraft are stored at *different* venues in the locality. ◆ *Prior arrangement* **only**

❑ G-AFTN Taylorcraft Plus C2 39 ex Coalville, Heavitree, HL535, 43 OTU, 652, 651, G-AFTN. CoA 1-11-57, de-reg 31-1-99. [1] 6-19

❑ G-AGOH Auster J1 Autocrat 45 ex C'ville, Winthorpe, Leicester. CoA 24-8-95, de-reg 7-8-08 6-19

❑ G-AIJK Auster J4 Archer 46 ex Coalville, Leicester, Stratford, Hemswell. CoA 24-8-68, de-reg 8-8-68. Acquired 1980. Frame [2] 8-21

❑ XP280 Auster AOP.9 61 ex Coalville, Leicester, St Athan, 6 Flt, 651. SOC 6-11-74 6-19

■ **[1]** *Tango-November* is the oldest surviving Auster type. **[2]** The firewall backwards to the windscreen of a J4 is displayed at Loughborough, Leics - see below - which *may* be from *Juliet-Kilo*.

Also: The Aeronca is *believed* current at a *private* site locally.

❑ G-BRFI Aeronca 7DC Champion 46 ex Londonderry, Ballymoney, N1058E. CoA 19-2-91, de-reg 4-7-23 N4-19

LEICESTER AERODROME or Leicester East or Stoughton, southeast of Leicester EGBG

T.67C G-BOCM had moved on to 'East Anglia' by the autumn of 2022.

❑ G-ARDJ Auster D6/180 60 crashed 30-5-86. CoA 7-7-88. Off-site N10-22

❑ 'G-FIRE' Grob G.115A EI-CAE 90 ex Swiftair. Trailer mounted, fire rescue trainer. F/n 9-20 8-22

LOUGHBOROUGH on the A6 north of Leicester

Charnwood Museum: The 1956 King's Cup-winning Auster commemorates the wonders worked at nearby Rearsby. Within a display cabinet devoted to Auster are the firewall, Perspex windscreen and a couple of inches behind that of a cockpit from a J4 Archer, *possibly* from G-AIJK, see Leicester, above - but it's more wall plaque than airframe.

◆ *Granby Street, LE11 3DU* | **01509 233754** | **museum@charnwood.gov.uk** | **www.charnwoodmuseum.co.uk**

❑ G-AJRH '7' Auster J1N Alpha 47 ex Leicester, Harrogate, Wigan. CoA 5-6-69, de-reg 18-1-99 1-22

Loughborough University: Department of Aeronautical and Automotive Engineering.

◆ *Prior arrangement* **only** | **www.lboro.ac.uk**

❑ ZH200 HS Hawk 200 87 ex Brough, Warton. Arrived 5-12 12-21

LUBENHAM on the A4304 west of Market Harborough

A Sea Hawk and a 'JP' are held at a *private* location in the *general* area.

❑ XE368	'200'	Hawker Sea Hawk FGA.6	55	ex Barrow-in-Furness, Market Drayton, Bruntingthorpe, Helston, Culdrose SAH-3, Shotley A2534 (28-5-66), 738, 806, 803, 899. AWA-built. First noted 5-21	[1]	7-23
❑ XM405	'42'	Hunting Jet Provost T.3A G-TORE	59	ex Drakelow, Bruntingthorpe, London, Ipswich, G-TORE, (CoA 5-5-95, de-reg 2-2-04), Cranfield, XM405, 1 FTS, RAFC, 1 FTS, 2 FTS. First noted 4-21		7-23

■ **[1]** Classic British Jet Collection airframe – see Bruntingthorpe, Leics.

LUTTERWORTH

Lutterworth and District Museum: Includes much Sir Frank Whittle and Power Jets material and an incredible archive.
◆ *Wycliffe House, Gilmorton Road, LE17 4DY* | **07906 303643** | **email** via website | **www.lutterworthmuseum.org**

Whittle Memorial: Dramatically displayed to the south of the town, on the A426 roundabout, is a superb tribute to Sir Frank Whittle. Static tests of Whittle's engine began at the Ladywood Works, to the north of the town, in 1938. See also Farnborough, Hampshire, for another E28/39 'monument'.

❑ –	Gloster E28/39 FSM	02	BAPC.284. Sir Frank Whittle Commemorative Trust- built	1-24

NORTH LUFFENHAM north of the A6121, southwest of Stamford

St George's Barracks: On the southern perimeter of the former airfield, is the hulk of a Whirlwind.

❑ XP344	Westland Whirlwind HAR.10	62	ex Cranwell 8764M (11-10-82), Finningley, Chivenor, 22, SAR Wing, CFS	6-23

STANFORD northeast of Rugby, near Swinford

Stanford Hall and **Percy Pilcher Museum**: In the Stable Courtyard is a display to Percy Pilcher who crashed in the grounds on 30th September 1899 flying the Hawk and died of his injuries. (The original craft is on show in Edinburgh, Scotland.)
◆ *North of Stanford on Avon. LE17 6DH* | **01788 860250** | **enquiries@stanfordhall.co.uk** | **www.stanfordhall.co.uk**

❑ -	Pilcher Hawkreplica	58	BAPC.45, ex Coventry, Bitteswell. AWA apprentices-built	1-24

WIGSTON southeast of Leicester

Graham Smith: Is *thought* to still have his Harrier. ◆ *Prior arrangement* **only**

❑ XW763	HS Harrier GR.3	71	ex Bruntingthorpe, Wigston, Bruntingthorpe, Duxford, St Athan 9041M, 9002M, 4, GR.1, 1453 Flt, 1, A&AEE, 1, 233 OCU. SOC 22-3-89. Cockpit	6-10

WYMESWOLD on the A6006 northwest of Leicester

A Scout is *thought* to still be kept at a *private* location in the area.

❑ XP883	Westland Scout AH.1	63	ex Bruntingthorpe, Oaksey Park, Boscombe Down, 658, 655, 652. Arrived 8-12-16	[1]	12-16

■ **[1]** The boom of XP883 is to be found on another Scout - see Moy, N Ireland.

LINCOLNSHIRE

Includes the unitary authorities of North Lincolnshire and North East Lincolnshire

BECKINGHAM north of the A17 east of Newark

The military exercise area hosts a Puma.

❑ XW225	Sud Puma HC.1	72	ex Newark, Wallingford, 18, 230, 240 OCU, 230, 240 OCU, 230, 240 OCU, 230, 240 OCU, 230, 240 OCU, 230. Crashed 15-2-97. Arrived 10-12-20	6-22

BINBROOK on the B1203 northeast of Market Rasen

Charles Ross: Keeps an F.6 and a cockpit at a *private* location and owns F.1A XM192 at Tattershall Thorpe, Lincs. Charles' Lightnings come under the 'umbrella' of the Lightning Association – see below. ◆ *Prior arrangement* **only**

❑ XR725	'BA'	EE Lightning F.6	65	ex Rossington, Binbrook, 11, F.3, 11, 5, LTF, 5, 56, 74, 5, 23. SOC 24-6-88	12-23
❑ XS899	'E'	EE Lightning F.6	66	ex Norwich, Coltishall, Bruntingthorpe, Cranfield, Binbrook, 11, 5-11 pool, 23, 5. SOC 24-6-88. Cockpit. 23 Sqn c/s. Off-site	12-23

BINBROOK AIRFIELD north of the B1203, north of the village

Lightning Association (LA): On 25th June 2023 XR724 was rolled into its new, QRA-like, shed. See above for the airframes held by LA founder Charles Ross. ◆ *Prior permission* **only** | **email** via website | **www.lightning.org.uk** and **Facebook**

❑ XR724		EE Lightning F.6 G-BTSY	65	ex G-BTSY (de-reg 26-5-92), Shawbury, BAe Warton, 11, F.3, 11, 5, 11, 5, LTF, 11. Arrived 23-7-92	1-24

Also: Several individuals also keep jets on the site. Darren Swinn and friends are restoring the cockpit of XN728. As *W&R29* closed for press a new organisation – perhaps to be called the English Electric Lightning Museum – was reported to be forming up. The former Cape Town Mk.6 is due to be joined by T.5 ZU-BBD (XS452). Other airframes are also thought to be involved. Stay tuned! ◆ *For all of those given below - prior permission* **only**

❑ ZU-BEY*		EE Lightning F.6 XP693	62	ex South Africa, Thunder City, G-FSIX, Exeter, XP693, Warton, RAE Thurleigh, A&AEE, Hdg Sqn, A&AEE. Arrived 10-7-23	[1]	7-23
❑ XA634*	'L'	Gloster Javelin FAW.4	56	ex Staverton, Leeming, Shawbury, Colerne, Melksham 7641M (2-6-60), Gloster. 228 OCU colours. Arrived 1-10-22		3-23
❑ XN728	'V'	EE Lightning F.2A	61	ex Lincoln, Balderton, Coningsby 8546M (4-4-77), Wildenrath, 92. Cockpit. Arrived 4-14	[2]	8-21
❑ XN795*		EE Lightning F.2A	63	ex Neatishead, Rayleigh, Foulness, RAE, A&AEE, BAC. SOC 10-3-77. Cockpit. Arrived 16-12-23		12-23
❑ XS416	'DU'	EE Lightning T.5	64	ex Holton cum Beckering, New York, Grainthorpe, New Waltham, Rossington, Binbrook, 5, LTF, 11, 74, 226 OCU. SOC 24-6-88. First noted 8-21		3-23
❑ XS457		EE Lightning T.5	65	ex Grainthorpe, North Coates, New Waltham, Laceby, Binbrook, 5, 11, 5, LTF, 11, 226 OCU. SOC 21-9-87. Cockpit	[3]	11-22
❑ XS459	'AW'	EE Lightning T.5	65	ex West Walton Highway, Narborough, Binbrook, 5, LTF, 56, 29, 226 OCU. SOC 21-6-88. Arrived by 5-21	[4]	3-23
❑ XS933*		EE Lightning F.6	67	ex Farnham, Langport, Terrington St Clement, Narborough, Binbrook, 5, 11, BAC, 5, 56, 11. SOC 21-6-88. Cockpit	[5]	10-21

■ **[1]** XP693 completed as an F.3, converted to F.6 in 'increments' 1963 to 1965. **[2]** XN728 owned by Darren Swinn – see notes above. **[3]** Owned by Roy Whitleley / Lincair **[4]** XS459 owned by well-known Lightning 'jockey' Ian Black. **[5]** See under Sunderland, N&T, for *another* 'XS933'.

BOSTON

A cache of Austers is held at *private* locations in the locality. Brochet MB.100 F-BBGH had moved to 'Norfolk', by 2022.

❑ G-AHAP	Auster J1 Autocrat	46	ex March. CoA 20-2-91	12-21
❑ G-AMRF	Auster J5F Aiglet Trainer	52	ex VT-DHA, G-AMRF. *Grey Dove*. CoA 31-3-07	12-21
❑ NJ673	T'craft Auster 5D G-AOCR	44	ex EI-AJS, G-AOCR, NJ673, 26, 174, 137, 182, 247, 430	12-21

COLSTERWORTH on the A1 north of Stamford

Witham Specialist Vehicles Ltd: Vast numbers of military vehicles are dealt with, all with a rapid throughput. The same is true of most of the helicopters handled. Increasingly many do not travel to the yard, being 'hammered' at the point of disposal, or at storage sites in the south of England. All of the Gazelle 'stock' mentioned in *W&R28* (p127) moved on: AH.1s XX378, XX442, XZ311, XZ325 to 'Oxfordshire' by December 2022; AH.1 XX447 untraced; HCC.4 XZ935 became G-CMFO May 2022; AH.1 TAD.017 (XW888) to an owner in 'Yorkshire'. ◆ **Strictly** *prior arrangement* **only** | **www.mod-sales.com**

CONINGSBY AIRFIELD south of the A153, southeast of Woodhall Spa EGXC

Battle of Britain Memorial Flight (BBMF) and **Visitor Centre**: A partnership between the RAF and Lincolnshire County Council provides the public access to the Flight. The **RAF Memorial Flight Club** offers free entry to the Visitor Centre and other goodies: **www.memorialflightclub.com**

In the listing below, the TOC - taken on charge - date applies to the joining of the flight, no matter what its designation (Historic Aircraft Flight 1957-1958, Battle of Britain Flight 1958-1969, BBMF from 1969) was at the time.

Note: As well as attending air events all over the country, BBMF aircraft are overhauled by civilian contractors, and may be away on maintenance, sometimes for lengthy periods. For example, Dakota ZA947 with ARC at Duxford, with Aero Legends' G-ANAF filling in for training from November 2022.

◆ *South of the A153. Access to the BBMF hangar is via guided tour* **only | 01522 782040 | bbmf@lincolnshire.gov.uk | www.lincolnshire.gov.uk/history-heritage/battle-britain-memorial-flight-visitor-centre**

❑	P7350	'KL-B'	V-S Spitfire IIa ✈	G-AWIJ	40	ex *Battle of Britain* (1968), G-AWIJ (de-reg 29-2-84), Colerne, 57 OTU, CGS, 64, 616, 603, 266. CBAF-built. TOC 5-11-68. 54 Sqn colours, *Kiwi III*		1-24
❑	AB910	'SH-F'	V-S Spitfire Vb ✈	G-AISU	41	ex *Battle of Britain* (1968), G-AISU (de-reg 22-8-55), RWE, 527, 53 OTU, 402, 242, 133, 130, 222. CBAF-built. TOC 16-9-65. *Peter John I*. 64 Sqn colours		1-24
❑	'EN398'	'JE-J'	V-S Spitfire IX FSM		~	BAPC.541, ex Duxford. GB Replicas-built. Displayed	[1]	10-19
❑	LF363	'RF-J'	Hawker Hurricane IIc ✈		44	ex Audley End, Coningsby, *Battle of Britain* (1968), *Reach for the Sky* (1955), *Angels One Five* (1951), Biggin Hill SF, 41 GCF, Waterbeach SF, Odiham SF, Thorney Island SF, FCCS, M Wallop SF, 61 OTU, 41 OTU, 62 OTU, 26, 63, 309, 63. TOC 11-7-57. 303 Sqn colours by 3-22		1-24
❑	MK356	'QJ-3'	V-S Spitfire IX ✈		44	ex St Athan, Henlow, *Battle of Britain* (1968), Bicester, Hawkinge, Halton (5690M 2-10-45), 443. CBAF-built. TOC 7-11-97. 92 Sqn colours	[2]	1-24
❑	PA474	'AR-L' *and* 'VN-T'	Avro Lancaster I ✈		45	ex 44, Wroughton, Cranfield College, RAE, FRL, 82 (as PR.1). Hawarden-built. TOC 20-11-73. 460 Sqn (AR-L) *Leader* to port, and 50 Sqn colours, stb		1-24
❑	PM631		V-S Spitfire PR.19 ✈		45	ex Martlesham Heath SF, N Weald SF, Biggin Hill SF, THUM Flt, Buckeburg SF, 206 OCU, 203 AFS. TOC 11-7-57. 541 Sqn colours. On 18-month 'major' with BBMF engineers		1-24
❑	PS915		V-S Spitfire PR.19		45	ex Samlesbury, Preston, Brawdy, St Athan, Coningsby, Brawdy, Leuchars 7548M/7711M, W' Malling, Biggin Hill, THUM Flt, 2, PRDU, 541. TOC 11-7-57. 81 sqn c/s. Stored		1-24
❑	PZ865	'ZY-V'	Hawker Hurricane II ✈	G-AMAU	44	ex 'P2619' 'US-B' *Angels One-Five*, Hawker G-AMAU (de-reg 19-12-72). TOC 29-3-72. 247 Sqn colours		1-24
❑	TE311		V-S Spitfire XVI ✈		45	ex EP&TU, 7241M, 'MK178' 'X4474', France, Abingdon, Henlow, Wattisham, 2 CAACU, 103 FRS, 102 FRS, 83 GSU. CBAF-built. TOC 10-99. Due to have 322 Sqn c/s '3W-M'	[3]	1-24
❑	WG486	'E'	DHC Chipmunk T.10 ✈		51	ex Newton, Gatow SF, ARWF, 3 AEF, Bristol UAS, 3 AEF, Bristol UAS, Liv UAS, PFS, 1 FTS, ITS, AOTS, ITS, RAFC, MECS, 114, 651, 657, 2 FTS, 63 GCF, 9 RFS, 5 BFTS. Hawarden-built. TOC 1995. Bristol UAS colours	[4]	1-24
❑	WK518	'D'	DHC Chipmunk T.10 ✈		52	ex Newton, 1 AEF, Lon, Hull, Leeds, Hull UASs, Coltishall SF, FWS, Cam, Hull, Cam, Man, L'pool UASs, 63 GCF, RAFC. Hawarden-built. TOC 4-83. London UAS colours	[4]	1-24
❑	ZA947	'UK'	Douglas Dakota 3 ✈		42	ex DRA, RAE, Farnborough, West Freugh, 'KG661', RCAF 661, C-47A-60-DL 42-24338. Long Beach-built. TOC 6-93. *Kwicherbichen*, 233 Sqn colours		1-24

■ **[1]** *Other* 'EN398s' can be found at: Taunton, Somerset; Salisbury, Wilts; Pyle, Wales. **[2]** See under Boscombe Down, Wilts, and Hawkinge, Kent, for 'other' MK356s! **[3]** TE311's restoration consumed elements of TB382 - see Sandown, Isle of Wight - as spares. **[4]** WG486 taken on RAF charge 31-12-51, WK518 taken on RAF charge 28-1-52: they are the last of the breed in UK military service.

RAF Coningsby: The resident Typhoon units tend to allocate weapons loading trainers – WLTs – for short periods and then rotate them back into operational service: so *W&R* will avoid them, unless they are seriously long term.

The Lakes Lightnings (see Spark Bridge, Cumbria) F.6 'XP765' (XS897) is due to move to pastures new during 2024.

❑	'XP765'	'A'	EE Lightning F.6	XS897	66	ex Doncaster, Firbeck, Rossington, Binbrook, 5, 11, 5, 11, 56, 74. SOC 5-2-88. 29 Sqn colours. Displayed since 2009. See note above	[1]	1-24
❑	XR753	'XI'	EE Lightning F.6		65	ex Leeming 8969M (25-5-88), Binbrook, 11, 5-11 pool, FCTU, F.3. Arrived 17-11-05. 11 Sqn c/s, displayed	[2]	1-24

Serial	Code	Type	Year	History	Note	Date
❑ XT891	'Z'	McD Phantom FGR.2	68	9136M (10-6-92), ex 74, 228 OCU, 56, 228 OCU, 29, 228 OCU, 29, 228 OCU, 29, 228 OCU, 56, 228 OCU, 6, 54, 228 OCU, 54. Displayed, since 1992. 41 Sqn colours	[3]	1-24
❑ XW924	'G'	HS Harrier GR.3	71	ex Cottesmore 9073M, Laarbruch, Halton, 3, 4, 1, 233 OCU, GR.1, 4, 20, 4. 3 Squadron, displayed, since 2006		1-24
❑ XX962		SEPECAT Jaguar GR.1B	75	ex Pembrey, Cosford, Cranwell 9257M (2-10-96), Coltishall, 6, 17, 20, 17. Arrived 4-7-19. Cockpit		12-21
❑ ZE760	'AP'	Panavia Tornado F.3	88	ex St Athan, ItAF MM7206, RAF, 5. 229 OCU colours. Displayed, since 2003		1-24
❑ 'DJ666'		Eurofighter Typhoon FGR.4 ZJ940	07	SOC 11-6-19. Typhoon Training Flight First noted 10-19		12-21

■ **[1]** Only F.3s were flown by 29, so it was given a small ventral tank, but retains the F.6's conical camber wings. **[2]** XR753 is displayed outside 11 Sqn's Typhoon HQ on the southern perimeter - see under Tangmere, W Sussex, for its doppelgänger. **[3]** Careful study of the fin on XT891 reveals that it is not an RWR example; this was taken from F-4J(UK) ZE354, scrapped at Coningsby in 2001.

CRANWELL AIRFIELD on the A17/B1429 northwest of Sleaford

EGYD

Cranwell Aviation Heritage Centre: Located close to but *not* at, the airfield, the centre charts Cranwell's heritage. With a souvenir shop, 'JP' simulator and archive film show, it is an excellent stop-off when visiting Cranwell - the circuit is in sight.

◆ *Off the A17, near North Rauceby, NG34 8QR* | **01529 488490** | **cranwellaviation@n-kesteven.gov.uk** | **www.heartoflincs.com/cranwell**

Serial	Code	Type	Year	History	Note	Date
❑ XE946		DH Vampire T.11	55	ex Cardington, Henlow, Bicester 7473M (25-9-57), Habbaniya SF, Nicosia SF. Hatfield-built. Cockpit		1-24
❑ XP556	'3'	Hunting Jet Provost T.4	61	ex Bruntingthorpe, Halton 9027M (15-2-90), Shawbury, CATCS, SoRF, 6 FTS, RAFC. Arrived 4-97		1-24

RAF Cranwell: The Spitfire 'guards' the Selection Centre, the Dominie and 'JP' are along the B1429 through the camp.

Serial	Code	Type	Year	History	Note	Date
❑ 'P8448'	'DO-R'	V-S Spitfire FSM	90	BAPC.225, ex Swanton Morley. Displayed since 1995		1-24
❑ XS710	'O'	HS Dominie T.1	65	ex Cosford 9259M (7-10-96), Cranwell, 3 FTS, 6 FTS, CAW. Rescue training		1-23
❑ XS727	'D'	HS Dominie T.1	65	ex 55, 3 FTS, 6 FTS, 1 ANS. Displayed by 9-13		1-24
❑ XW353	'3'	BAC Jet Provost T.5A	71	ex 9090M (18-7-91), 3 FTS, RAFC, CFS, 3 FTS, RAFC. Displayed, unveiled 18-7-91		1-24
❑ TAD.009		W'land Lynx 1-03 XW838	72	ex Lyneham, Aborfield, M Wallop, Yeovil. First noted 2-21	[1]	3-23
❑ ZE378		Westland Lynx AH.7	86	ex M Wallop. Arrived 8-20, instructional		8-20

■ **[1]** A plaque on the instrument panel reads: "Lynx Mk.7 [sic] Reg. XW838. Formally a test and evaluation aircraft. Acquired by Fg Off Ben Southern, ASTC Instructor. Presented to the ASTC on 30 March 2021 for use in training for Aircraft Crash Immediate Action Drills". ASTC is: Aircrew SERE Training Course; SERE is: Survive, Evade, Resist, Extract.

RAF Exhibition, Production and Transportation Unit (EP&TU): The airframes are based on a former airfield close by and run by a contractor. EP&TU is 'parented' by the Cranwell-based Directorate of Recruitment and Selection and for that reason the 'fleet' is listed under this heading. EP&TU also has two Eurofighter Typhoon cockpit mock-ups, both of which include interactive segments. These, 'Chinook' 'IR808' (BAPC.361) and a 'Hercules' – the latter owing more to Crane Fruehauf than to Lockheed Georgia – are *not* considered as deserving of a 'formal' listing. Hawk T.1 FSM 'XX227' (ex 'XX226') had moved to Scampton, Lincs, by 2022. Tornado GR.1 'ZA556' is *believed* to have been disposed of.

◆ *Access* **not** *possible. Airframes spend their time in 'transit camps' elsewhere to minimise vehicle usage.*

Serial	Code	Type	Year	History	Note	Date
❑ 'XX308'		HS Hawk T.1 FSM	81	BAPC.171, ex 'XX227', 'XX253', St Athan, 'XX297', Abingdon, 'XX262'. 'Red Arrows' colours	[1]	7-21
❑ 'IR206'	'IR'	Eurofighter Typhoon FSM	c02	BAPC.360, trailer-mounted. 17 Squadron colours		6-18
❑ –		Lockheed F-35B FSM	c18	first noted 6-18. 617 Sqn colours by 6-23		6-23

■ **[1]** The *real* XX308 is at East Fortune, Scotland.

CROWLAND AERODROME on the A1073 south of Spalding

Darren Speechley: ◆ *Prior arrangement* **only** | **djs1944@hotmail.co.uk**

Serial	Code	Type	Year	History	Note	Date
❑ G-ATDB		Nord Noralpha	48	ex Prestwick, Edinburgh, Skelmorie, Prestwick, F-OTAN-6, Fr mil 186. CoA 22-11-78, de-reg 11-10-10		1-22
❑ G-BAYV		Nord Noralpha	48	ex W' Waltham, St Mawgan, Crowland, Barton, Chelford, 'F-OTAN-6', Sevenoaks, Booker, Hawkinge, Maidstone, Ford, F-BLTN, French AF. Cr 23-2-74, de-reg 28-4-83. Cockpit.		1-22

❑ –	BP Sea Balliol T.21	~	ex Quarrywood. Cockpit	1-22
❑ –	BP Sea Balliol T.21	~	ex Quarrywood. Cockpit	1-22

DIGBY east of the B1188 north of Sleaford

RAF Digby World War Two Sector Operations Room within the **Joint Service Signals Organisation Digby** site.

◆ *Guided tours **only**, by prior arrangement – photo ID required* | 01526 327429 frequently a message line | **www.raf.mod.uk/our-organisations/raf-digby/contact-us/**

❑ 'MJ832' 'DN-Y'	V-S Spitfire FSM	89	BAPC.229, ex 'L1096', Church Fenton. *City of Oshawa*, 416 Sqn colours. Displayed, unveiled 28-3-93	1-24

EAST KIRKBY AERODROME on the A155 west of Spilsby

Lincolnshire Aviation Heritage Centre (LAHC): A section of the former bomber airfield is run by the Panton family as a memorial to Christopher, who was killed on the horrific Nürnberg raid of 30-31st March 1944, and as a tribute to Bomber Command as a whole. The codes on either side of *Just Jane* pay tribute to the late Fred Panton and his brother, Harold, both of whom rescued NX611 and brought it to life.

The long-term project to put *Just Jane* back into the air - and hopefully carry passengers - makes significant and ingenious progress. A major concern was that the restoration would negate the vital income-stream from the very popular taxi rides. Over at le Bourget, France, Les Ailes Anciennes (AA) has been working for a long time on a stable mate of NX611, former Aéronavale NX664. This is also a long-term venture, but '664 is for static display, hopefully at the Musée de l'Air et de l'Espace. The first phase of the plot is to 'bolt on' the outer wings of NX664 to NX611 so that it can continue to take paying 'crews' for taxi rides, while NX611's 'outers' are restored in a jig to CAA flight-worthy standards. Eventually those sections will go back on NX611 and AA will get its 'outers' back pristinely engineered to the highest of static standards. Other sections of NX611 and NX664 will play a similar shuffle in the years to come. Also in the mix is the rear fuselage of former Canadian Mk.10 KB976 from the South Yorkshire Aircraft Museum - see under Doncaster, S Yorks, for notes on its pedigree - which will join the replace-as-you-restore scheme.

Another example of Lancaster co-operation involves the newly arrived Bolingbroke from the Pima Air and Space Museum. As well as the kit-of-parts that comprises 10074, another set of wings was shipped, arriving at 'EK' on 22nd October 2022. These were bound for the Kent Battle of Britain Museum's (KBBM) Bolingbroke project - see Hawkinge, Kent. KBBM has been able to supply parts for NX611's renaissance and the Bolingbroke wings complete the exchange.

Tony Agar's exceptional Mosquito also regularly makes taxi runs. The story of this incredible project is exceptional. Achieving a 'live' Mosquito from such modest, yet challenging, beginnings ranks this 'Wooden Wonder' as one of the most significant 'one man' British restorations of all-time. Tony began his endeavours with the purchase of Mosquito NF.II cockpit HJ711 for £7 at the auction winding down the woeful Reflectaire museum enterprise at Squires Gate on 29th April 1972. In an amazing co-incidence, the 'star' of that sale was Lancaster VII NX611.

Acting in support of the upwardly mobile Lancaster is the **East Kirkby Lancaster Association** – details on the website. Two other groups are based within LAHC: **Lincolnshire Aircraft Recovery Group** (LARG): 'Prize' exhibit is the very substantial Spitfire BL655. **Lincolnshire Aviation Preservation Society** (LAPS): Main project is the painstaking restoration of AE436, the Brian Nicholls Hampden Project and Proctor IV NP294.

◆ *PE23 4DE* | **01790 763207** | **email** via website | **www.lincsaviation.co.uk** | **www.mossie.org/HJ711**

Hampden I AE436 makes progress in the workshop, September 2023. *Terry Dann*

Identity	Code	Type	Built	History	Notes	Noted
❑ –		Druine Turbulent	62	BAPC.154, ex Tattershall, Friskney, Nottingham. Fuselage in workshop rafters. Arrived 12-85	[1]	3-20
❑ AE436	'PL-J'	HP Hampden I	41	ex Coningsby, Henlow, Sweden, 144. Crashed 4-9-42. EE-built. Arrived 11-88. Forward fuselage, etc	[2] [3]	1-24
❑ BL655		V-S Spitfire Vb	41	ex Dorrington Fen, 416, 129, 341, 164, 602, 416. Crashed 1-7-43. Arrived 1993. Substantial remains	[4]	1-24
❑ HJ711	'VI-C'	DH Mosquito NF.II		BAPC.434, ex Elvington, Huntington (York), Squires Gate, Enfield, Chingford, 169, 14. Arrived 30-7-17. Rolled out 30-7-18. 169 Sqn c/s, *Spirit of Val*. Taxying by mid-2020	[5]	1-24
❑ NP294		Percival Proctor IV	44	ex Tattershall, Friskney, Poynton, Andover, Cosford, 4 RS, 2 RS. Hills-built. SOC 22-3-55. Arrived 12-85	[2] [6]	1-24
❑ NX611	'DX-F' *and* 'LE-H'	Avro Lancaster VII G-ASXX	45	ex Scampton, 8375M, Squires Gate, Hullavington, Lavenham, Biggin Hill, Aéronavale, WU-15, St Athan, Llandow. Austin Motors-built. *Just Jane*, 57 Sqn colours to stb, 630 Sqn to port. Arrived 5-88. Taxiable	[7]	1-24
❑ WH957		EE Canberra E.15	55	ex Bruntingthorpe, Cosford 8869M, 100, 98, B.6, 98, Akrotiri Wing, 32, Hemswell SF, Upwood SF, 21, 542, 617. Short-built. Arrived 12-85. Cockpit		1-24
❑ –*		Bristol Bolingbroke IVT	44	ex Pima, Chino, Hartney (Manitoba), RCAF 10073. SOC 20-8-46. Arrived 14-11-22	[8]	1-24
❑ –*		HP Halifax replica	c20	cockpit, first noted 3-22		1-24
❑ –		Heinkel He 111 mock-up	68	BAPC.389, ex New Zealand, East Kirkby, others, *Battle of Britain* (1968). Arrived 3-93. Cockpit, blitz display		1-24
❑ '34037'*		NAA TB-25N-20-NC Mitchell	44	ex Hendon, 8838M, Blackbushe, N9115Z, *Hanover Street* (1978), *Catch-22* (1969), USAAF 44-29366. Arrived 9/10-11-22. *Felix the Cat / Always Dangerous*, USAAF colours		1-24

■ **[1]** Turbulent is unfinished project PFA.1654. **[2]** Hampden and Proctor with LAPS. **[3]** See fellow P1344 at Cosford, Shropshire, lost on the same night. **[4]** Spitfire Vb with LARG. **[5]** Mosquito on loan from Tony Agar is a complex composite, using the cockpit of HJ711 (and the history of HJ711 is charted above), rear fuselage of TT.35 RS715 from Elstree; centre section from Mk XVI PF498 from Leyland; and the outer wings of T.3 VA878 from St Davids. **[6]** Proctor starboard wing from Mk.IV G-ANYR. **[7]** NX611's individual codes are 'F' for Fred Panton, 'H' for Harold. NX611 was acquired by Fred and Harold 1-9-83 while it was still on the 'gate' at Scampton. **[8]** Bolingbroke is a complex composite, *perhaps* up to four donor airframes; assembled at Chino from the famed Wes Agnew 'boneyard'; 10073 is the majority identity.

ELSHAM west of the A15, northeast of Brigg

RAF Elsham Wolds Association Memorial Garden and Memorial Room: A poignant commemoration housed in the premises of the Anglian Water Treatment Plant at the end of one of the old runways.

◆ *Prior arrangement* **only** | **curator@elshamwolds,org.uk** | **www.elshamwolds.org.uk**

FENLAND AERODROME west of the B1168 and Holbeach St Johns

EGCL

Identity	Type	Built	History	Noted
❑ G-BSDL	SOCATA Tobago	80	CoA 1-11-13, de-reg 24-5-17	3-16
❑ G-BSUW	Piper Seneca 200T	77	ex N2360M. CoA 7-9-10, de-reg 30-10-18	8-23

FLEET HARGATE on the A17, east of Holbeach

Harold Payne: WT680 is within the 'Anglia Motel' grounds and looked after by **2430 (Holbeach) Squadron, Air Cadets**.

Identity	Type	Built	History	Noted
❑ WT680	Hawker Hunter F.1	54	ex Aberporth, Weeton 7533M (22-1-57), Rolls-Royce, DFLS, West Raynham SF. Arrived 26-7-04	1-24

FREISTON on minor roads east of Boston

Martin and **Lynn Tydeman**: Great progress on the Gazelle project: engine, tail and rotors all fitted.

◆ *Prior arrangement* **only** | **martin401@btinternet.com**

Identity	Code	Type	Built	History	Notes	Noted
❑ XZ337	'Z'	Sud Gazelle AH.1	77	ex Colsterworth, M Wallop, Abbey Wood-Bristol, M Wallop, Shawbury, 658, 6 Flt, 3/4 Rgt, 664, 667, 656, 657, 658, 659, 669, Aérospatiale F-WXFX. Westland-built. Arr 2-6-21	[1]	1-24

■ **[1]** Many thanks to Martyn for filling in the early history of XZ337. Along with XZ333 (see Lyneham, Wilts) it was freighted to Marignane, France, in 2-78, returning in 1-79 having best test flown with a French experimental category registration.

FREISTON SHORE on even more minor roads east of Freiston and Boston

We'll Meet Again – WW2 Homefront Museum: Opened in August 2017 this is an extensive and very family-friendly venue: the scope of the exhibits is incredible. The Hurricane, a genuine *Battle of Britain* film veteran was displayed atop the Odeon in Lincoln to 'plug' the movie in 1968, has been painstakingly restored. There is also a Lancaster cockpit replica offering 'VR' flights, the Ration Book Cafe and access to the adjacent coastal defence bunkers.

◆ *Shore Road, PE22 0LY* | **paulandlindab@hotmail.co.uk** | **www.wma-ww2museum.co.uk**

❑ –*	'J'	Hawker Hurricane FSM	68	BAPC.68, ex Delabole, H' Park 'P2725', Lincoln, Wembley, Great Bridge, Coventry 'H3426', *Battle of Britain*, 'P3975', Pinewood Studios-built. Unveiled 15-11-23	[1]	1-24

■ **[1]** This was written out of *W&R23* (p34) as Gateguards UK, moved from Delabole to St Mawgan, circa 7-11.

GRANTHAM east of the A1, south of Newark-on-Trent

A veteran glider is kept at a *private* location in the *general* area.

❑ BGA.492	ALZ	Hawkridge Dagling	47	BAPC.81, ex Eaton Bray, Dunstable, Duxford, Warton	10-21

GRIMSBY

John Mallett: Acquired his Chipmunk in June 2023 and celebrated the debut of his project with attendance at *CockpitFest* that same month. ◆ *Prior arrangement* **only** | **johnmallettscartho@hotmail.com**

❑ WG362*	DHC Chipmunk T.10	51	ex Linton, Ely, Newton 8630M, Swinderby, Filton 8437M (30-1-75), Birm, Wales, Oxf UASs, Swanton Morley SF, Carlisle SF, Mildenhall CF, 100, Edin UAS, 3 BFTS, 16 RFS, 3 BFTS, 7 RFS. Hawarden-built. Cockpit, arrived 6-23	6-23

Locally: A Vampire is kept at a *private* location in the *general* area.

❑ WZ584*	'K'	DH Vampire T.11	53 G-BZRC	ex Grimsby, Cantley, Armthorpe, Sandtoft, North Coates, G-BZRC (de-reg 22-2-05), St Albans, Hatfield, CATCS, 1 FTS, 2 CAACU, 32. Hawarden-built. SOC 11-12-70	[1]	5-20

[1] There is *another* 'WZ584' - a Meteor - at Weston Zoyland, Somerset.

HALTHAM on the A163 south of Horncastle

An Aztec is held at a *private* location in the area.

❑ G-BBTJ	Piper Aztec 250E	73	ex Wickenby, N40369. CoA 8-9-10, de-reg 7-6-18. Arr 4-2-17	9-23

HEMSWELL on the A631 east of Gainsborough

The famous bomber base, 'set' for much of the ground-based sequences in *The Dam Busters*, home to the Bomber County Aviation Museum 1989 to 2003 is now host to a cluster of antique centres. **Antiques & Retro** keeps a 'JP.

❑ XP629	'P'	Hunting Jet Provost T.4	62	ex Market Rasen, Layer Marney, Hadleigh, Ipswich, North Luffenham, Halton 9026M (15-2-90), Shawbury, CATCS, SoRF, CAW, 2 FTS	[1]	2-24

■ **[1]** Fitted with the wings of fellow T.4 XP686, last recorded at Layer Marney, Essex.

HIBALDSTOW AERODROME on the B1206 south of Brigg

❑ G-ANHR	Taylorcraft Auster 5	44	ex MT192, 662. CoA 20-7-86, frame	11-21
❑ G-ASDK	Beagle Terrier 2	48	ex G-ARLM, Auster AOP.6 VF631, 654, 652, 656. CoA 4-11-10. Frame	8-22
❑ G-BWCO	Dornier Do 28D-2	79	ex EI-CJU, N5TK, 5N-AOH, D-ILIF. CoA 19-5-99, de-reg 30-1-09	5-21
❑ G-BZHL 'TM-13'	NAA Harvard IIB	44	ex Wickenby, Egypt, FT118 n/s. SOC 11-7-46	8-22
❑ CC-CRI	Dornier Do 28D-2	~	ex WGAF 58+23. Spares - first noted 3-17	5-21
❑ 117	Dornier Do 28D-2	~	ex Kenyan Air Force	5-21

HUMBERSIDE AIRPORT or Kirmington EGNJ

BAE Systems R J Mitchell Aircraft Maintenance Academy: Delete Hawk Mk.102D ZJ100; it is held at Brough, E Yorks.

◆ *Prior arrangement* **only**

❑ N19CQ	HS Dominie T.1	65	ex Kemble, Cranwell, XS712, 55, 3 FTS, 6 FTS, 1 ANS, HS	11-20
❑ N19UK	HS Dominie T.1	66	ex Kemble, Cranwell, XS739, 55, 3 FTS, 6 FTS, 1 ANS	11-20

❑ ZA549	Panavia Tornado GR.4	81	ex Marham, 15, 13. SOC 9-11-11. Arrived 30-5-18. Fuselage	11-20
❑ ZJ800	Eurofighter Typhoon T.3	03	ex Coningsby RTP, 29. Arrived 13-9-18	11-20
❑ ZK531	HS Hawk T.53	80	ex Warton, Brough, Warton, Hurn, Indonesian AF LL-5306, G-9-471. Last flown 31-1-02. F/n 3-15, displayed from 22-9-17	7-23
❑ ZK535	HS Hawk T.53	c80	ex Finningley, Brough, Warton, Indonesian AF LL-5320	11-20
❑ 1129	BAC Strikemaster Mk.80A	76	ex Global Av, Saudi AF, G-27-295. Moved across 7-17. Displayed from 22-9-17	7-23

Also: The Jetstream 41s have been changing status. As predicted, G-MAJK was back in service by July 2020, while G-MAJD and G-MAJL returned to 'ops' in May 2023. The following have been reduced to produce: G-MAJE (January 2023); G-MAJF and 'JI (by May 2021); G-CIHD (November 2022); G-CIHE (January 2023). Last noted in September 2017, the fuselage of Strikemaster Mk.80A 1115 has been deleted.

❑ G-AVMP	BAC 111-510ED	68	ex Iver Heath, Hurn, European, BA, BEA. Forward fuselage. CoA 6-4-01, de-reg 12-11-02. Rescue trainer	3-23
❑ G-CDYI	BAe Jetstream 4100	93	ex N305UE, G-4-019. De-reg 21-217. Fuselage	11-20
❑ G-GCJL	BAe Jetstream 4100	91	ex Woodford, Prestwick. CoA 29-4-95, de-reg 15-11-02. Fuselage, rescue trainer	3-23
❑ G-MAJG	BAe Jetstream 4100	93	ex Eastern, G-LOGL, G-4-009. wfu 5-10-18, CoA 20-9-19	10-20
❑ G-MAJH	BAe Jetstream 4100	93	ex Eastern, G-WAYR, G-4-010. wfu 3-8-16, de-reg 10-2-20. Rescue trainer, blue colours	3-23
❑ G-MAJJ	BAe Jetstream 4100	93	ex Eastern, G-WAFT, G-4-024. wfu 8-12-17, CoA 21-1-19	3-23
❑ G-MAJW*	BAe Jetstream 4100	93	ex Eastern, N303U, G-4-015. Last flight 16-8-18	3-23

INGHAM also known as Cammeringham, west of the B1398, northwest of Scampton

RAF Ingham Heritage Group: In the autumn of 2023 the centre was granted a King's Award for Voluntary Service. Dubbed 'Home of the Polish Bomber Squadrons'. The display hall, reception area, shop and workshop are all based on existing wartime buildings, or contemporary structures re-erected on site. There is a very moving memorial.

◆ *Middle Street, Fillingham, DN23 5BU* | **07787 805978** | **rafingham@hotmail.co.uk** | **www.rafingham.co.uk**

KIRTON IN LINDSEY on the B1206 northeast of Gainsborough

A Vampire and Sedbergh are kept at separate *private* locations in the *general* area.

❑ XD595	DH Vampire T.11	54	ex Glenham, Altrincham, Woodford, Chester, St Athan, 1 FTS, Oakington SF, 7 FTS, 4 FTS. Hatfield-built. SOC 6-11-67. Cockpit	5-20
❑ XN185*	Slingsby Sedbergh TX.1 HNS	56	BGA.4077, ex Scampton, Stafford, Syerston 8942M, CGS, 643 VGS, 4 MGSP, 633 VGS, 635 VGS. CoA 12-4-04	12-22

LINCOLN

International Bomber Command Centre: In the autumn of 2023 the centre was granted a King's Award for Voluntary Service. The site is dominated by a spire as tall as the wingspan of a Lancaster. The 'Wall of Names' wraps around the spire, honouring the Bomber Command aircrew who did not return. The outlines of 53 airmen – representing those who lost their lives in the 'Dams' raid, were unveiled in 2023.

◆ *Canwick Hill, Lincoln, LN4 2HQ* | **01522 514755** | **info@internationalbcc.co.uk** | **www.internationalbcc.co.uk**

LOUTH As part of the 'tidy-up' mentioned at the beginning, TSR.3 G-AWIV and Sportsman G-VJZZ have been deleted.

MARKET RASEN on the A46 north of the town

Fir Park Transport Museum: Enthusiasts have established an eclectic fleet of transport items, many in running condition. The Suzuki/AA-1 hybrid was written out of *W&R26* at Sandtoft, Lincs, (p151) as moved on by mid-2016. Then it was carrying a DVLA registration – 'D164 MBH'. Since it has changed from blatant pink to yellow and gained a false CAA-like registration.

◆ *Regular 'Wings and Wheels' open days: otherwise by prior arrangement* **only** | **https://firparktm.weebly.com**

❑ G-BVLP*	Piper Tomahawk 112	81	ex N91355. De-reg 18-2-15. First noted 9-20	9-20
❑ 'G-FLAP'*	American AA-1 hybrid	~	ex Sandtoft. Fuselage and tail mounted on a Suzuki 4x4. Yellow colours, 'Wings and Wheels' titles. See notes above	6-23
❑ G-FOSY*	MS Rallye Club	69	ex G-AXAK. CoA 17-5-04. Fuselage, 'Fir Park' titles. F/n 6-23	6-23

MESSINGHAM on the A159 south of Scunthorpe

A gathering of AOP.9s is at a *private* location in the *general* area.

❑ WZ711	Auster AOP.9(mod) G-AVHT	54	ex Doncaster, Spanhoe, AOP.9, St Athan, 656, LAS. CoA 1-7-16, de-reg 23-2-18. Arrived 13-8-21		8-21
❑ XK417	Auster AOP.9 G-AVXY	56	ex Melton Mowbray, Tattershall Thorpe, Wisbech, Henstridge, Thruxton, 652, LAS. SOC 7-11-67. CoA 9-7-00		8-21
❑ XP242	Auster AOP.9 G-BUCI	61	ex M Wallop, AFWF, Shrivenham, 653. CoA 19-5-00, de-reg 5-3-01. Arrived 2-21		8-21

METHERINGHAM on the B1191 west of Woodhall Spa

Metheringham Airfield Visitor Centre: Based in what was part of the bomber base's communal site is an excellent presentation showing life at the station and 106 Squadron. 'JP' T.4 XS186 moved to Fishlake, S Yorks, by September 2022.

◆ *Westmoor Farm, LN4 3WF* | **email** via website | **www.metheringhamairfield.co.uk**

❑ KG651 *and* 2108962	Douglas Dakota 3 G-AMHJ	42	ex N Weald, Shawbury, Coventry, SU-AZI, G-AMHJ, ZS-BRW, KG651, 1333 CU, 1383 CU, 24, 109 OTU, C-47A-25-DK 42-108962. Oklahoma City-built. CoA 5-12-00, de-reg 23-1-03. KG651 to stb, 2108962 to port. Arr 16-11-15		1-24

Locally: Dennis Staniland has his 'JP' at a *private* location in the area.

❑ G-BYED	BAC Jet Provost T.5 XW302	70	ex Sleaford, Market Drayton, Chester, Londonderry, N166A, XW302, 6 FTS, 3 FTS, RAFC, 1 FTS. Crashed 12-2-01, de-reg 30-12-04. Cockpit. First noted 8-17		6-23

NEW YORK on the B1192 south of Coningsby

A Tornado is kept at a *private* location in the *general* area.

❑ ZA362 'TR'	Panavia Tornado GR.1	81	ex Inverness, Lossiemouth, 15, TTTE. Arrived 14-12-20		4-21

NORTH COATES AERODROME north of the A1031, south of Humberston

North Coates Heritage Collection: Artefacts covering the history of the airfield 1914 to 1992 are displayed at the flying club. A reminder of its last RAF role, a Bloodhound Mk.1, is on show. Cessna 172 N259SA has been deleted.

◆ **www.northcoatesflyingclub.com**

❑ CEK	Slingsby T.21B(T)	59	BGA.1482, ex RAFGSA.369, XN147. CoA 7-5-05	[1]	9-23

■ **[1]** Motor-glider conversion.

NORTH SOMERCOTES on the A1031, north of Mablethorpe

A trio of Whirlwind HAR.10s is stored at a *private* location in the *general* area.

❑ XJ407	Westland Whirlwind HAR.10 N7013H	54	ex Tattershall, G-BKHB (de-reg 15-6-88), XJ407, Northolt, 32, 103, 110, HAR.4, 22, 155. SOC 27-4-82. First noted 4-21		4-23
❑ XP328	Westland Whirlwind HAR.10 G-BKHC	61	ex Tattershall, Northolt, 32, 21, 28, 110, 225, 110, 225. Crashed 22-8-88, de-reg 4-6-90. Cabin. First noted 4-21		4-23
❑ XP329 'V'	Westland Whirlwind HAR.10	61	ex Shawbury, Lee-on-Solent, Akrotiri 8791M (10-7-82), 84, 230, 110, 225. First noted 4-21		4-23

SANDTOFT AERODROME south of the M180, between Sandtoft and Westgate EGCF

The following, all registered to the same individual, have been 'tidied up' from this edition and deleted: Cherokees G-BIFB and G-BULR; Cessnas G-BIHI, G-BLVS and G-BORY; Mooney G-BSXI.

❑ N131MP	Piper Navajo P	74	ex Warlingham, Shoreham, G-BWDE, G-HWKN, HB-LIR, D-IAIR, N7304L		10-23

SCAMPTON AIRFIELD on the A15 north of Lincoln EGXP

On 27th March 2023 a £300m plan for the site of the now former RAF Scampton was announced. This included housing, leisure, *heritage,* and lots of jobs. The word 'heritage' is highlighted because the all-seeing plan did not include the **RAF Scampton Heritage Centre**, which closed in November 2022. The adage 'the first casualty of war is the plan' certainly applies to Scampton. *Two days after* the wheeze was launched, the Home Office declared that Scampton was to become a refugee accommodation centre as part of the 'world-class' 'Stop the boats' campaign. You couldn't make it up...

Departures: **Airco DH.2** replica '5964' (G-BFVH) roaded to Wickenby, Lincs, by 12-22 and airworthy there by 2023. **Swallow** BRC (BGA.1165) returned to its Lincolnshire-based owner. **Chipmunk** cockpit WG477 departed for sale by GPSV Auctions at Froghall, Staffs, on 28-1-23 it moved to Hooton Park, Cheshire. **Sedbergh** TX.1 XN185 migrated to Kirton in Lindsey, Lincs. **Gnat** T.1 XR571 departed for sale by GPSV Auctions, Leyburn, N Yorks, 25-1-23; successfully 'hammered' for £24,250 all in, it moved to Tangmere, W Sussex, 28-2-23. **Hawk** T.1 FSM 'XX227' had arrived from EP&TU, Cranwell, by 2022; it departed for GPSV at Leyburn 25-1-23 and was reported 'hammered' for £77k; by 6-23 it had arrived at Wickenby, Lincs. **Hawk** T.1A XX266, which had been 'guesting' within the centre, was moved by road to Waddington, Lincs, 27-9-22. **Hawk** T.1A cockpit XX320 left for the GPSV sale by 12-22 and moved to Devonport, Devon, by 2-23. The anonymous **Canberra** T.4 cockpit left circa 2-23 for storage locally before moving to Waddington, Lincs, 31-8-23. The following are unaccounted for: Vulcan K.2 cockpit XL445 'returned to owner'; Harrier GR.3 cockpit XZ138; Vulcan B.1 cockpit drill trainer.

RAF Scampton: The 'Red Arrows' departed for their new home, a challenging cross-country to Waddington, on 27th September 2022. Former gate guardian Hawk T.1A XX306 departed during 27th March 2023 for Leyburn, N Yorks, prior to auction; it then moved the short distance to Leeming Bar, N Yorks, 10th July 2023. Former 'guardian' Hawk T.1A XX253 moved to Leeming, N Yorks, in 2022. The hulk of rescue trainer Hawk T.1W XX349 is believed to have been scrapped.

Hawker Hunter Aviation: The last sortie was flown from Scampton on 31st August 2022 and T.72 XE688 and F.58 ZZ190 were ferried to the new base at Leeming, N Yorks, 21st September 2022. Several airframes have been placed into at least one ***strictly private*** **off-site storage site**. The following Hunters were trucked to Leeming, N Yorks: F.58 ZZ191 8-11-22; F.58 ZZ194 12-22; F.58A J-4110 14-12-22. Hunter GA.11 XE685 moved to Wickenby, Lincs, by 8-23; Hunter T.8C XF994 and T.7 XL587 (G-HPUX) to Bruntingthorpe, Leics, 25-4-23.

❑ XF995	Hawker Hunter T.8B	G-BZSF	56	ex Exeter, Kemble, G-BZSF, Cranwell 9237M (11-9-94), 208, 12, Laarbruch SF, 237 OCU, Honington SF, 237 OCU, 764, F.4, 245, 247. Squires Gate-built. SOC 11-3-19. Stored	10-23
❑ XX885	Blackburn Buccaneer S.2B	G-HHAA	74	ex Lossiemouth 9225M (25-11-93), 12, 208, 12, 208, 216, 16. Stored	6-23
❑ 37+89	McD F-4F Phantom		72	ex Luftwaffe, 72-1199. Arrived 13-6-15. Stored	10-23
❑ 37+91	McD F-4F Phantom		72	ex Luftwaffe, 72-1201. Arrived 6-15. Stored	10-23
❑ 98+14	Sukhoi Su-22M-4 *Fitter*		~	ex WTD-61 Manching, Luftwaffe, East German AF. Stored	10-23

SKEGNESS northeast of Boston

RAMCO: With the byline 'Giving new life to old assets', the company has a wide portfolio with regular auctions that includes MoD surplus airframes and what-have-you. Recent aeronautical activity has included the handling of Hawk carcasses from the reduce to produce programme at Valley, Wales, and the long-term store at Shawbury, Shropshire. Turn-over is rapid with nothing 'lingering'. ◆ *Prior arrangement* **only** | **www.ramco.co.uk**

SKEGNESS (WATER LEISURE PARK) AERODROME or Ingoldmells, on the A52 north of Skegness

Craig Wise's superb Lightning T.5 dominates the horizon at the aerodrome.

❑ XS456	'DX'	EE Lightning T.5	65	ex Wainfleet, Binbrook, LTF, 11, 56. SOC 13-7-88. Arr 7-10	1-24

Also: Adhering to the guidelines on page 7, Apache G-ARCW and Cessna 172 G-AVPI have been deleted.

SPALDING west of the A16, north of Peterborough

Skycraft: The 'Chop Shop' swiftly processes light aircraft for spares. ◆ *Prior arrangement* **only** | **www.sky-craft.co.uk**

SPILSBY on the B1195 west of Skegness

Of the Auster store at a *private* venue in the locality, J1N G-AHSO has been disposed of.

❑ G-AHAR	Auster J1 Autocrat	46	ex North Weald, F-BGRZ. De-reg 31-12-50	10-21
❑ G-AIPV	Auster J1 Autocrat	46	CoA 7-2-05	N8-23

STAMFORD

Martyn and **Aiden Steele's** *CockpitFest* award-winner is *thought* to be kept locally. ◆ *Prior arrangement* **only**

❑ XP757	EE Lightning F.3	64	ex Boston, Woodhall Spa, Keighley, Siddal, Binbrook, 29, 23. SOC 13-11-75. Cockpit	6-15

Also: Chipmunk T.10 cockpit WP978 moved to Hooton Park, Cheshire, 10th April 2022. ◆ *Prior arrangement* **only**

❑ MM52-2420	Piper L-18C Super Cub	52	ex Spanhoe, Lakenheath, Embry-Riddle, N917CS, It AF, USAF	6-23

STURGATE AERODROME southeast of Gainsborough, near Heapham EGCS

Tiger Moth N9372 (G-ANHK) was flying again by May 2023. Last noted in December 2019, Cessna 152 G-BWEU has been deleted, along with Jodel G-BDDG and Emeraude G-BGVE.

SWINDERBY or Norton Disney, south of the A46 northeast of Newark

South of the former airfield is the site of the **Lost Village Festival**. The website declares: "The woods are waiting..." Visitors are invited every August to "navigate through a network of winding pathways, derelict houses, overgrown courtyards, dilapidated streets *and an abandoned airport*"... and hear some music to boot. The Jetstream has been joined by dilapidated Pacer, and a pair of airliner cockpits. The Pacer has had an 'active' life within the pages of *W&R*. It was written out of *W&R23* at Rooks Bridge, Somerset, in late 2011. It made a resurgence at Evesham, Worcs, in *W&R25*, but bowed out from there in *W&R27* as bound for a location in Wales in the spring of 2014.

Also noted in April 2023 was what is best described as a "heap" of light aircraft in varying degrees of upset. The nature of this site is such that these do not – as yet – merit a formal listing. So here goes, with de-registration dates thrown in: Cessna 150E G-ASZB (31-7-23); Jodel D.117 G-AWFW (23-2-21); Cessna 140 G-BRUS (16-9-94 no less); Zenair CH-601 G-BUTG (14-12-22); Jabiru UL-450 G-CBGR (18-9-22); Groppo Trail Mk.2 – no, me neither... – G-RJIT (10-9-20).

◆ *Prior arrangement* **only**. Details of the event at the weird: **https://lostvillagefestival.com/explore**

❑ G-BHMO*	Piper Pacer	50	ex 'Wales', Evesham, Rooks Bridge, Little Gransden, F-BDRO. Crashed 20-8-89, de-reg 1-4-97. Fuselage		3-22
❑ G-JXTA	BAe Jetstream 3103	83	ex Humberside, Inverness, D-CNRY, SE-KHC, OY-EDB, SE-KHC, D-CONI, G-31-50. CoA 15-9-09, de-reg 17-8-16. Fuselage, trailer-mounted. First noted 11-21		4-23
❑ G-MONK*	Boeing 757-200	88	ex Teesside, Icelandair, Monarch. Last flight 4-4-15, De-reg 91-19. Cockpit		4-23
❑ N503ZT*	ATR 42-300	94	ex UTAir, UR-UTB, D4-CBF, F-WWEK. Cockpit		4-23

TATTERSHALL on the A153 southwest of Coningsby

W&R28 (p157) noted the departure of Djinn FR-150 by 2018, destination unknown. It turned up at Ipswich, Suffolk.

TATTERSHALL THORPE on the B1192 southeast of Woodhall Spa

Thorpe Camp Visitor Centre: The former No.1 Communal Site (or 'Thorpe Camp') of RAF Woodhall Spa is a superb venue with a warm welcome. Themes include life in Lincolnshire during World War Two, the history of Woodhall Spa, including its resident units: 97, 617, 619 and 627 Squadrons. A new exhibition hangar was officially opened on 16th April 2022. The **Hodgson Hangar** honours the late and dearly missed Mike Hodgson, the centre's founding father. There is a small, viewable, workshop area and a great cafe. Among the exhibits is the massive arrester gear salvaged from the end of one of Woodhall's runways. This was intended to stop a Lancaster, fitted with a special hook, from over-runs and the airfield prototyped the operational version. The flight training 'simulator' designed and built by Geoff Parker in 1942-1943 for the cadets of the Holbeach and Spalding-based 1406 Squadron is also impressive.

◆ *Woodhall Spa Road, LN4 4PL* | **07396 288655** | **secretary@thorpecamp.org** | **www.thorpecamp.org**

❑ 'G-AEXF'		Percival Mew Gull replica	11	BAPC.367	[1]	1-24
❑ G-ANFU		Taylorcraft Auster 5	45	ex Doncaster, Sunderland, Newcastle, Sunderland, Bristol, TW385, 663, 227 OCU, 13 OTU. Damaged 2-1-76. De-reg 3-8-76, CoA 25-8-76. First noted 11-20	[2]	1-22
❑ 'G-JHAW'		DH Tiger Moth replica	11	BAPC.409. Ex 'G-ANNN'	[3]	1-24
❑ 'B7270'		Sopwith Camel replica	18	locally built, completed 2020. Cpt Roy Brown's colours	[4]	1-24
❑ 'EV771'		Fairchild Argus replica	c97	BAPC.294, ex Southampton. Arrived 2005		1-24
❑ -	'D'	Avro Lancaster replica	c08	forward fuselage. First noted 7-10		1-24
❑ RT520		Taylorcraft Auster 5 G-ALYB	44	ex Doncaster, Firbeck, Bristol, White Waltham, AOP.V RT520, 85 GCS, 84 GCS. CoA 26-5-63, de-reg 29-2-84		1-24
❑ XM192	'K'	EE Lightning F.1A	61	ex Hemswell, Binbrook, Wattisham 8413M (28-5-74), Wattisham TFF, Binbrook TFF, 226 OCU, 111. Arrived 3-12-05. 111 Sqn colours	[5]	1-24
❑ XS887	'403'	Westland Wessex HAS.1	66	ex Doncaster, Helston, Culdrose A2690 (29-5-80), Wroughton, 772, Yeovilton SAR Flt, 829. F/n 12-21		1-24

❑ XX895		Blackburn Buccaneer S.2B	75	ex Kidlington, Woking, St Athan, Lossiemouth, 208, Iraq 1991 - 10 'ops', 208, 12, 237 OCU, 16, 15, 12. SOC 13-1-95. Arrived 29-12-15. Cockpit	[6]	4-23
❑ -		Panavia Tornado F.3 SIM	c82	ex Chester, Leeming. 229 OCU colours. F/n 10-16		4-22

■ **[1]** Mew Gull built in-house by a team led by John Lord. See Shuttleworth, Beds, and Hendon, Gtr Lon, for *other* G-AEXFs. **[2]** Composite, with G-ANFU's forward fuselage, a 'spare' rear AOP.6 frame, stb wing of G-AKPH and port from an AOP.6. **[3]** Built in-house using many original parts by John Horn and the late Anthony 'Tony' Wyatt, hence the 'registration'. **[4]** There's *another* 'B7270' at Brooklands, Surrey. **[5]** XM192 loaned by Charles Ross of Binbrook, Lincs. **[6]** Owned and under restoration by Matt Johnson.

TETNEY on the A1031 south of Cleethorpes

Chris Goossens: At a *private* venue in the locality, Chris has a 'JP' cockpit and makes good progress on its restoration.

❑ XS181*	'F'	Hunting Jet Provost T.4	63	ex 'Cheshire', Spark Bridge, Spanhoe, Bruntingthorpe, Market Harborough, North Weald, Bletchley, Desborough, Bruntingthorpe, Halton 9033M (15-2-90), Shawbury, CATCS, RAFC, 3 FTS. Cockpit. Arrived by 6-23	6-23

WADDINGTON AIRFIELD on the A607 south of Lincoln EGXW

RAF Waddington Heritage Centre: Volunteers have created a superb exhibition in a building that in World War Two housed the catering squadron headquarters. Among the many exhibits are remains of 463 Squadron Lancaster I PD259 which crashed in Scotland on a training detail on 31st August 1944, with the loss of all seven crew.

◆ *Prior arrangement* **only | WAD-heritagecentre@mod.gov.uk | www.raf.mod.uk/rafwaddington**

❑ –*	EE Canberra T.4	~	ex 'Lincs', Scampton. Cockpit. Arrived 31-8-23	[1]	8-23

■ **[1]** Carries a plate marked EEP.71673. *Possibly* 1955-built T.4 XH583. Sold to BAe 12-10-81, allocated G-27-274 and destined for Argentina as a T.94; embargoed and stored at Samlesbury, Lancs. Written out of *W&R16* (p139) as scrapped 1991.

RAF Waddington: The 'Red Arrows' joined the circuit at their new home on 27th September 2022, having found their way from the other side of Lincoln - Scampton. Usurped by the 'Red Arrow's' Hawk; Hunter F.6A 'XE620' (XE606) moved to Sunderland, N&T, 17th October 2022, pending full-time accommodation at Boulmer, N&T.

Gone is the image of a 'boneyard'; the Sentries and Sentinels are no more. **Sentry AEW.1**s ZH105 was scrapped 10th October 2023 and ZH107 fell to the metal grinder on 5th October 2023; ZH101, ZH102, ZH105 and ZH107 gave up the ghost later in October. ZH103 and ZH106 flew off to Chile on 25th and 26th July 2022, respectively. It is criminal that at least a *portion* of such an important type in RAF history should not become a museum piece. Perhaps we can feel less nostalgic about the **Sentinel R.1**... For completeness, they moved out to the USA as follows: ZJ690 became N690BD and was the last to depart, on 21st March 2023; ZJ691 (N691BD) in July 2021; ZJ692 (N692BD) on 7th June 2022; ZJ693 (N693BD) on 27th September 2022 and ZJ694 (N694BD) during July 2022.

❑ XM607	Avro Vulcan B.2	63	8779M, ex Wadd Wing (9/44/50/101 Sqns) Cott Wing (9/12/35 Sqns),Con Wing (35). Last flight 17-12-82. Displayed from 19-1-83	[1]	2-24
❑ XX266*	HS Hawk T.1A	79	ex Scampton, Shawbury, 'Red Arrows'. SOC 18-8-15. Arrived 27-9-22		1-24
❑ –	BAE Systems Tempest FSM	18	BAPC.529, ex Warton. Travelling demonstrator	[2]	7-21

Sentinel R.1 N693BD (ZJ693) ready for migration to the USA, June 2022. *Ian Humphreys*

■ **[1]** Became the primary on BLACK BUCK 1 out of Wideawake, Ascension, 30-4-82-to 1-5-82 dropping 21 x 1,000lb bombs on Stanley airfield, Falklands - 15 hours, 45 min sortie - then the longest bombing raid in history. Also primary on BLACKBUCK 2 and 7. Upon retirement, had clocked 5,514 hours, 40 mins total time. **[2]** The Future Combat Air System, now pronounced Global Combat Air Programme. Nominally based with the RAF Rapid Capabilities Office. Fitted with modified Tornado undercarriage.

Also: Lincolnshire Fire and Rescue Service has a Jaguar for exercises: it is kept in the old bomb dump site.

❑ XX818	'DE'	SEPECAT Jaguar GR.1	75	ex Cosford, Halton 8945M (4-11-87), Shawbury, 31, 20, 17. Arrived 8-10-19	1-24

WAINFLEET southwest of Skegness

Former **Aerial Application Collection**: ◆ *Dispersed stores, by prior arrangement* **only**

❑ G-AOGI		DH Tiger Moth	42	ex OO-SOA, G-AOGI, Mk.II DF186, 608, Valley SF, 21 EFTS. Morris Motors-built. CoA 23-8-91	N9-22
❑ G-AWLX		Auster J2 Arrow	46	ex Gloucester, F-BGJQ, OO-ABZ. CoA 23-4-70	N9-22
❑ G-BFBP		Piper Pawnee 235D	77	ex Rush Green. Crashed 11-5-78, de-reg 21-6-78. Cockpit	7-18
❑ G-BFEY		Piper Pawnee 235D	77	ex Old Buckenham. CoA 19-1-87, de-reg 17-7-90. Frame	7-18
❑ G-NRDC		NDN Fieldmaster	81	ex Sandown, Old Sarum. CoA 17-10-87, de-reg 3-2-95. Fuselage	7-18
❑ –		NDN Fieldmaster EMU	c81	ex Sandown, Old Sarum. Fuselage	7-18

The Tower Friskney: At the range observation tower of the former RAF Wainfleet, at the end of Sea Lane, three airframes are available as holiday cottages. ◆ *Prior arrangement* ***only*** | **https://rafwainfleet.uk**

❑ XX499	'G'	HP Jetstream T.1	76	ex Ipswich, Brooklands, Ipswich, Shawbury, Cranwell, 45, 3 FTS, 45, 6 FTS, METS. SAL-built. Arrived 10-10-19	1-24
❑ ZG822*	'WS'	Westland Sea King HC.4	90	ex St Athan, Bruntingthorpe, Gosport, Yeovilton, 848, 846, 845, 846, 845, 846, 848, 846, 848, 846. Arrived 14-10-23	10-23
❑ ZG914		Westland Lynx AH.9A	91	ex Ipswich, M Wallop. First noted 5-18	1-24

WALCOTT on the B1189 south of Woodhall Spa

Richard and **Kevin Scarborough**: ◆ *Private location, prior arrangement* ***only***.

❑ XS932		EE Lightning F.6	67	ex Market Drayton, Farnborough, Shoreham, Bruntingthorpe, Rossington, Binbrook, 5, 11, 56, 11. SOC 24-6-88. Cockpit	6-22
❑ XV810		HS Harrier GR.3	71	ex Wigston/Bruntingthorpe, St Athan, Abingdon 9038M, St Athan, 233 OCU, 4, GR.1 4, 20. SOC 16-1-89. Acquired 5-13. 233 OCU colours. Cockpit.	6-23
❑ ZD614	'122'	HS Sea Harrier F/A.2	86	ex Lymington, Hurn, Ipswich, St Athan, Yeovilton, 800, 801, 800, 801, 800, 801, FRS.1, 800, 801, 800. Crashed 8-10-01 (into the River Yeo). Acquired 14-10-18. Cockpit	6-23
❑ ZE697	'006'	HS Sea Harrier F/A.2	88	ex Binbrook, Charlwood, St Athan, 801, 899, 800, 899, 800, 801, 899, FRS.1, 801, 800. First noted 4-20	4-20

WALTHAM on the B1203 south of Grimsby

Waltham Windmill Trust and Preservation Society: An element of the extensive site surrounding the windmill is the excellent **RAF Grimsby Exhibition**. This is dedicated to the personnel and Lancasters of 100 Squadron and other units that flew from Waltham, or Grimsby. The A16 cuts through the former airfield's eastern perimeter.

◆ *Signed off the B1203* | *Brigsley Road, DN37 0JZ* | **www.facebook.com/WalthamWindmill1666/**

WICKENBY (LINCOLN) AERODROME north of the B1399, northeast of Lincoln EGNW

The former wartime tower acts as both a **Visitor Centre** and the **RAF Wickenby Memorial Collection**. The Wickenby Register – 12 and 626 Squadron Association – has its archives here.

◆ **01673 885000** | **info@wickenbyairfield.com** | **https://wickenbyairfield.com**

Vintage Skunk Works: The name and logo pay homage to Lockheed's famed research and development centre at Palmdale, California. Tiger Moth G-ACDJ and NAF N3N G-CFXT were flying by 2023. ◆ *Visits are* **not possible**.

❑ G-ANNN		DH Tiger Moth	45	ex Tattershall Thorpe, Eccleshall, Hatch, Southend, Ipswich, T5968, Wattisham SF, 61 GCF, 3 RFS, 28 EFTS, 57 OTU. Morris Motors-built. De-reg 6-11-00. Spares	6-20

❑ G-BZVW		Ilyushin Il-2M3		42	ex Lancing, Russia. Stored	[1]	3-23
❑ G-BZVX		Ilyushin Il-2M3		42	ex Lancing, Russia. Stored	[1]	3-23
❑ G-CJSB		Republic Seabee		47	ex N11NW, CF-JBN, N6513K. CoA 27-3-19. Dismantled		7-23
❑ G-SHOW		MS Alcyon		56	ex Spanhoe, -?-, Bruntingthorpe, Cranfield, Booker, F-BMQJ, FAF 125. CoA 24-5-83		N11-19
❑ N9606H		Fairchild PT-26 Cornell	G-CRNL	42	ex Thruxton, G-CEVL, Wickenby, Martham, Earls Colne, Andrewsfield, Southend, USA, FJ662, 42-15491	[2]	7-23
❑ N6537		DH Tiger Moth	G-AOHY	39	ex Dyce SF, Ringway SF, 11 RFS, 11 EFTS, 35 ERFTS. Crashed 17-7-06, CoA 24-11-16		2-19
❑ WK622		DHC Chipmunk T.10	G-BCZH	52	ex York, Breighton, G-BCZH, Yeovilton, 2 FTS, Wattisham TFF, Bristol UAS, 3 AEF, Bristol, Leeds UASs, 24 GCF, Oxford UAS, 18 RFS, 22 RFS. Hawarden-built. Crashed 6-9-87, de-reg 8-5-19. Arrived 3-19		9-19
❑ XE624	'G'	Hawker Hunter FGA.9		56	ex Metheringham, Leicester, B'thorpe, Brawdy 8875M (4-10-85), 1 TWU, 2 TWU, TWU, 229 OCU, W Raynham SF, 1		1-24
❑ XE685*	'861'	Hawker Hunter GA.11	G-GAII	55	ex Scampton, St Athan, Exeter, Yeovilton, Hurn, FRADU, FRU, 764, Yeovilton SF, 764, 738, F.4 98, 93. Squires Gate-built. Last flight 22-5-12, CoA 15-8-12. Arrived by 8-23, displayed		1-24
❑ 'XX227'*	'74'	HS Hawk T.1 FSM		78	BAPC.152, ex Scampton, EP&TU Cranwell, 'XX226', St Athan, 'XX262', Abingdon, 'XX162'. First noted 6-23, displayed	[3]	9-23
❑ 'C8500/16'		DH Tiger Moth	G-ANKV	40	ex Booker, Croydon, Redhill, T7793, 1 GU, 2 GS, 14 RFS, Ox UAS, 8 RFS, 8 EFTS, 22 EFTS, Ox UAS, 3 EFTS, 21 EFTS.	[4]	4-23
❑ C-558		EKW C-3605	G-CCYZ	48	ex Spanhoe, N31624, Norwich, Little Gransden, Booker, Swiss AF	[5]	8-21

■ **[1]** Registered to Leeds-based Steven Swallow 2-20. **[2]** Cornell previously assumed to be ex FH678, 42-14361. Current thinking quoted above: It is registered to CRNL Aviation. **[3]** See notes under Scampton, Lincs; *real* XX227 is at Cosford, Shropshire. **[4]** G-ANKV will be a 'Rumpler C' lookalike. It was not converted (at Croydon?) and cancelled in 9-56. **[5]** Registered to C W Tomkins Ltd.

Others: Two airframes are off-site, at *separate* and *private*, locations.

❑ G-LUFT		Putzer Elster C	60	ex Rufforth, Humberside, North Coates, G-BOPY, D-EDEZ. De-reg 12-7-07. Off-site	1-12
❑ XK632	'67'	DH Vampire T.11	56	ex Greenham, Denham, Leavesden, H' Hempstead, Bushey, Keevil, Exeter, 3/4 CAACU, CFS. Hawarden-built. SOC 6-1-72. Cockpit. First noted 7-20	1-22

WOODHALL SPA on the B1191 and B1192 southwest of Horncastle

At the junction of the B1191 and B1192 is the impressive 'Dam Busters' memorial and 617 Squadron commemoration. Another 'must' is the 'Petwood Hotel' which was the Officers' Mess for, in turn, 97, 619 and 617 Squadrons. The 'Squadron Bar' has loads of memorabilia. **www.petwood.co.uk**

Locally: At a *private* workshop in the general area Jon Davidson is at work on an Auster cache.

❑ G-AMJM	Taylorcraft Auster 5		45	ex F-BBSO, Newark, Taunton, G-AMJM, TW452, 62 GCF		6-20
❑ 'XP282'	Auster AOP.9	G-BGTC	61	ex -?-, Baxterley, Cranfield, Middle Wallop 7895M (14-7-64), XP283, 654	[1]	2-20

■ **[1]** *Tango-Charlie* utilises the fuselage of XP283; the original frame having been passed on to Doncaster, S Yorks.

GREATER LONDON

Greater London constitutes the following boroughs: Barking and Dagenham, Barnet, Bexley, Brent, Bromley (including Biggin Hill), Camden, City of Westminster, Croydon, Ealing, Enfield, Greenwich, Hackney, Hammersmith and Fulham, Haringey, Harrow, Havering, Hillingdon, Hounslow, Islington, Kensington and Chelsea, Kingston upon Thames, Lambeth, Lewisham, Livingston, Merton, Newham, Redbridge, Richmond upon Thames, Southwark, Sutton, Tower Hamlets, Waltham Forest, Wandsworth
...which leads us, of course, to Mornington Crescent

BATTERSEA on the south bank of the Thames, near Chelsea Bridge

Battersea Children's Zoo: ◆ *Chelsea Bridge Gate, SW11 4NJ* | **www.batterseaparkzoo.co.uk**

	Serial	Type	Year	Notes	Date
❑	XZ727	Westland Lynx HAS.3S	80	ex Ashurst, Hixon, M Wallop, Fleetlands, 815, 702, 815, 702, HAS.2, 815. All-yellow, first noted 8-19	8-23

BENTLEY PRIORY between the A409 and A4140 north of Harrow

The Bentley Priory Museum: Administered by the Bentley Priory Battle of Britain Trust, tells the story of the magnificent country house's role as the HQ of Fighter Command.

◆ *Mansion House Drive, Stanmore, HA7 3FB.* | **020 8950 5526** | **email** via website | **www.bentleypriorymuseum.org.uk**

	Serial	Code	Type	Year	Notes	Ref	Date
❑	'P2921'	'GZ-L'	Hawker Hurricane FSM	89	BAPC.218, ex 'BN230', St Mawgan, Bentley Priory, 'P3386'. 32 Sqn colours, pole-mounted	[1]	1-24
❑	-	'DW-O'	V-S Spitfire FSM	11	610 Sqn colours, pole-mounted		1-24

■ **[1]** There are *other* 'P2921s', at Hawkinge, Kent and Biggin Hill, Kent.

BIGGIN HILL AIRPORT EGKB

Biggin Hill Heritage Hangar Ltd / Spitfire Company (Biggin Hill) Ltd: As well as Peter Monk's collection, other warbirds are looked after and under restoration. The airworthy based 'fleet' varies, with aircraft 'detached' to other operators/locations, so those listed below may not be present during the open days, hangar tours, Spitfire factory tours, 'sit-in-a-Spit' and flight experiences that are staged at 'Biggin'. New Zealand-based Mosquito recreators AvSpecs has been commissioned to work their magic on the remains of former RNZAF Mosquito FB.VI NZ2345 (RAF TE881) which were discovered at Mapua in 2020.

Airworthy aircraft registered to Peter Monk, the Heritage Hangar, etc are listed below; examples owned by others and 'lodging' are not: eg Martin Phillips' Spitfire Tr.IX BS410 (G-TCHI) first flew on 8th April 2022; Simpson Marine Ltd Harvard II 'FE788' (G-CTKL); Mark Bennett's Spitfire IX LZ842 (G-CGZU) first flew 2nd June 2021; Peter Freedman's Spitfire XVI TE184 (G-MXVI); Isle of Man resident 517 Ltd's Spitfire IX TE517 (G-RYIX) first flown 5th April 2023. Associate company Warbird Experiences airworthy machines are nominally based but 'work' across several locations: Hurricane 'P2921' (G-CHTK); Spitfire Tr.IX MJ627 (G-BMSB); Spitfire Tr.IX 'A58-606' (G-AWGB); P-51D Mustang 413779 (G-CMDK), operational by December 2021; Hispano Buchón 'White 9' (G-AWHH).

Two-seat Hurricane II 'BE505' (G-HHII) registered to Hurriback Ltd, was working out of White Waltham, by December 2021; Spitfire IX ML925 (G-CLXB) first flew 14th January 2022, migrated to Duxford in April 2023 for the Great British Aircraft Co; Spitfire XIV RM927 (G-SXIV) first flew 6th June 2022 and de-registered 22nd September 2023 ready to join its French owners as F-AVXX; The Suffolk Spitfire Ltd's Mk.IX RW382 (G-PBIX) was based at Duxford from mid-2021.

◆ *Special events staged, otherwise **strictly** prior arrangement* **only** | **01959 576767** | **office@flyaspitfire.com** | **www.bigginhillheritagehangar.co.uk** | **www.flyaspitfire.com**

	Serial	Code	Type	Reg	Year	Notes	Ref	Date
❑	P9372		V-S Spitfire I	G-CLIH	39	ex Tonbridge, 92. Shot down 9-9-40. Salvaged 1996, arrived 2011	[1]	9-23
❑	X4276		V-S Spitfire I	G-CDGU	40	ex Breighton, 54. Crashed 28-12-40. Salvaged 9-87		N11-22
❑	EN570		V-S Spitfire IX	LN-AOA	43	ex Sandown, G-CISP (de-reg 29-4-16), France, 611. Shot down 18-4-43, St Pol, France. Excavated 2012. Arr by 6-21		10-23
❑	MA764		V-S Spitfire IX	G-MCDB	42	ex off-site, Haverfordwest, Ipswich, 122. CBAF-built. Shot down 25-11-43, St Omer. Excavated 9-05. Arr 2-21		11-21
❑	MJ306*		V-S Spitfire IX	G-HBOX	43	ex 412, crashed 4-3-44. *Hot Box*. Project, registered 10-23		10-23
❑	MK912	'SH-L'	V-S Spitfire IX	G-BRRA	44	ex Canada CF-FLC, Duxford, Audley End, Paddock Wood, G-BRRA, Brussels, Belgian AF SM-29, Netherlands AF H-59, H-119, MK912, 341, 312. CBAF-built. 64 Sqn c/s, *Borough of Bromley*. Accident 1-8-15, CoA 26-9-15. Stored	[2]	9-23
❑	MT818		V-S Spitfire Tr.VIII ✈	G-AIDN	44	ex Booker, Kemble, USA N818MT, Tillamook N58JE, G-AIDN, Supermarine N32, MT818, RAE. Arrived 31-3-16	[3]	9-23
❑	PT989*		V-S Spitfire IX	G-CWIX	44	ex Russia, Sov AF (from 13-10-44), PT989 n/s. Collided with Mk.IX PT879 near Murmansk 18-5-45. Salvaged 9-14. Stored	[4]	N11-22

❑ RM689		V-S Spitfire XIV	44 G-ALGT	ex Castle Donington, Filton, Sandown, Filton, Hucknall, Castle Donington, 'RM619', Hucknall, 443, 350. Crashed 27-6-92, de-reg 14-9-23. F/n 6-20		6-20
❑ RM694		V-S Spitfire XIV	44 G-DBKL	ex High Wycombe area, Booker, Bitteswell, Southend, Henlow, Charnock Richard, Hoylake, Dishforth, Bicester, Hornchurch, Locking 6640M (28-2-49), CFE, 402, 91. Arrived 10-2-21	[5]	9-23
❑ TA805	'FX-M'	V-S Spitfire IX ✈	44 G-PMNF	ex Duxford, Sandown, Oxford, SAAF Museum, SAAF, TA805, 234, 183. CBAF-built. *Spirit of Kent*, 234 Sqn colours		1-24
❑ TE356		V-S Spitfire XVI	45	ex N356TE, N356VE, G-SXVI, B' Hill, Bitteswell, Leeming, Little Rissington, Kemble, Henlow, Bicester. Arrived 1-19		11-21
❑ 3579	'14'	Messerschmitt Bf 109E-4	39 G-CIPB	ex Canada CF-EML, USA N81562, Colchester, Lancing, Russia, JG77, shot down 2-8-42. Arado-built. Arrived 6-1-15. CoA 20-11-19		9-23
❑ UB441		V-S Spitfire IX	43 G-SDNI	ex Booker, N94149, Sedlescombe, Rochester, USA, Burma AF UB441, Israeli AF/DF 20-20, Czech AF A-719, ML 119, 1. CBAF-built. Arrived 9-21	[5]	9-23
❑ 42-29854	'44-R'	Piper L-4H Cub ✈	43 G-BMKC	ex F-BFBA, USAAF 43-29854. *Little Rock-ette* First noted 2-12		10-21
❑ '47092'*		Curtiss TP-40N Warhawk ✈	42 N293FR	ex USA, Evergreen, N67253, P-40K 42-104721 Arrived 10-6-21, first flown in UK 8-6-21	[6]	9-23
❑ 493424*		NAA T-6G Texan	49	ex Tatoi, Greece, Hellenic AF, USAF 49-3424. Arrived 6-22		12-23

■ All registered to Peter Monk, Peter Monk Ltd, or Biggin Hill Heritage Hangar, unless noted. **[1]** Registered to Netherlands-based owners. **[2]** Registered to Lilham Aviation. **[3]** Two-seater prototype, first flown 9-9-46. **[4]** Registered to Greg Davis. **[5]** Registered to Paul Andrews. **[6]** Also quoted as 42-9749.

Also: While biz-jets and warbirds are the main 'flavour' of Biggin Hill these days, there is also a varied – if diminishing - light aircraft population, a large number of which are sufficiently long-term flightless to merit listing. Although the Prentice and Civilian Coupe (spares for the airworthy G-ABNT) are long-in-the-tooth, both are *believed* to still grace the airfield.

During August 2023 Wessex Aviation began to move out and relocate to Lydd, (sorry, London Ashford) Kent, taking with them: WG.30s N114WG and VT-EKT, Wessex HC.2 XV726 departed by road in May 2023 for Barton Seagrave, Northants. Messenger 4B G-AKVZ was flying again by early 2023. Baron G-ASOH, Warrior G-BHVB and Cessna 172L G-BRCM have been deleted.

❑ G-AMZI	Auster J5F Aiglet Tnr	53	CoA 30-9-16, de-reg 31-10-22	5-21
❑ G-AOGE	Percival Proctor III	42	ex BV651, Halton SF, 2 GCS, FAA 755, 756. Hills-built CoA 21-5-84, de-reg 19-1-99	6-22
❑ G-AOKH	Percival Prentice 1	48	ex VS251, 3 FTS, CFS, 2 FTS. Blackburn-built. CoA 2-8-73, de-reg 17-6-92	4-01
❑ G-APPL	Percival Prentice 1	48	ex VR189 RAE Bedford, Parachute Test Unit, Winter Exp Est Flight, Canada. CoA 27-4-17	5-21

Long-term resident, Proctor III G-AOGE, June 2022. *Col Pope*

	Reg		Type	Yr	History	Notes	Date
❑	G-ATXN		Mitchell-Procter Kittiwake	69	CoA 16-6-10. First noted 9-20		5-21
❑	G-BFYA		Bölkow Bö 105DB	77	ex Norwich, D-HJET. CoA 25-5-09		9-20
❑	G-BHJA		Cessna A152	79	ex N4954A. De-reg 8-4-02. First noted 8-20		3-21
❑	G-BYRC		Westland Wessex HC.2	69	ex Redhill, XT671, 60, 72		7-22
❑	G-CKTO		HSA HS.146-RJ300	98	ex Southend, OO-DWE, G-6-327. Woodford-built. De-reg 29-6-18. Forward fuselage. Arrived 21-2-21		12-22
❑	G-IFTE		HSA HS.125-700B	78	ex G-BFVI, G-5-18. De-reg 15-5-18. First noted 9-20		5-23
❑	G-LTEE		Cessna F.172N	78	Reims-built. De-reg 14-2-17. First noted 3-21		5-23
❑	–		Civilian Coupe	32	BAPC.404, unfinished airframe, No.7		10-95
❑	N181WW		Beagle Basset CC.1	75	ex G-BCJF, N181WW, G-BCJF, XS773, 26, TCCF, NCS		7-22
❑	2-WESX		Westland Wessex HC.2	68	ex 9G-AEL, G-HANA, XV729, 22, 72, 103, 78		10-21
❑	XS674	'R'	Westland Wessex HC.2	65	ex Redhill, Hixon, Ipswich, Fleetlands, 60, 72, 18, 78, 72		10-21
❑	XX414		Sud Gazelle AH.1	75	ex Sevenoaks, Hurstbourne Tarrant, Gosport, 671, Fleetlands, 651, 661, 662, 663, 660. Westland-built. Arr 31-1-17		7-23

St George's Chapel of Remembrance / Biggin Hill Memorial Museum: Famed for its 17 stained glass windows and a vast amount of memorabilia, the chapel was built in 1951 in the style of the original RAF Biggin Hill Station Chapel which opened in 1943, but burned to the ground in 1946. The slab-sided museum building is right alongside the church, ruining the atmosphere that existed beforehand. The 'guardians' are well cosseted, both wear cockpit covers during the winter. Sadly, both were damaged by gales 18th February 2022.

◆ *Signed off the A233* | **01959 422414** | **email** via website | **www.bhmm.org.uk**

	Reg		Type	Yr	History	Notes	Date
❑	'K9998'	'QJ-K'	V-S Spitfire FSM	10	BAPC.431. Displayed, 92 Sqn colours	[1]	1-24
❑	'P2921'	'GZ-L'	Hawker Hurricane FSM	10	BAPC.477. Displayed, 32 Sqn colours, *Blue Peter*	[1] [2]	1-24

■ **[1]** Both GB Replicas-built. **[2]** See also Heritage Hangar – above. Still *other* 'P2921s' at Hawkinge, Kent, and Bentley Priory, Gtr Lon.

No.**2427 (Biggin Hill) Squadron Air Cadets:** Close to St George's Chapel; has a Chipmunk.

	Reg		Type	Yr	History	Notes	Date
❑	WZ846	G-BCSC	DHC Chipmunk T.10	53	ex Chatham, G-BCSC (de-reg 21-1-75), Bicester 8439M (10-3-75), Manston, Wales UAS, AOTS, 202, 228, CFE, W Raynham SF, Glas UAS, Bristol UAS, 1 AEF, St Athan, Nott UAS, 63 GCF, Edin UAS, S'ton UAS. Hawarden-built		12-23

CATFORD south of Greenwich, on the South Circular, A205

Catford Independent Air Force: Alan Partington's collection of badges, insignia, Flying Clothing, uniforms and "all types of paperwork" continues to expand. ◆ *Prior arrangement* **only** | **little_fat_al@hotmail.com**

	Reg		Type	Yr	History	Notes	Date
❑	–		Mignet HM.14 'Flea'	33	BAPC.401, unfinished fuselage	[1]	1-24
❑	XH783		Gloster Javelin FAW.7	58	ex Booker, Sibson, Aylesbury, Halton 7798M (31-7-63), 64, 25, GWTS, A&AEE. Cockpit	[2]	1-24
❑	–		V-S Spitfire V FSM	~	built by Feggans Brown for *Piece of Cake*. Cockpit		1-24
❑	–		HS Harrier GR.1	~	cockpit	[3]	1-24

■ **[1]** 'Flea' has a plaque that reads 'Made at Capel'. **[2]** Javelin runs from halfway through the rear cockpit forwards. **[3]** Harrier is an unused cockpit section and *may* have come from Richmond Air Cadets. It is 41H/729048 which puts it between GR.1s XV810 and XW630. Is this the only remaining 'stock' GR.1 cockpit?

CHELSEA north bank of the Thames, near Chelsea Bridge, no less

National Army Museum: The depth of material on show here has to be experienced.

◆ *Royal Hospital Road, SW3 4HT* | **020 7730 0717** | **info@nam.ac.uk** | **www.nam.ac.uk**

	Reg		Type	Yr	History	Notes	Date
❑	ZG921		Westland Lynx AH.9A	92	ex M Wallop, Odiham, AH.9. SOC 3-10-18. First noted 6-21		1-24
❑	–	'B023'	GEC-Marconi Phoenix B	c87	ex Larkhill	[1]	1-24

■ **[1]** Part of the pre-production batch; believed used only for classroom instruction and not flown.

CHESSINGTON on the A243 north of J9 of the M25

World of Adventures: The Sea Life giant aquarium contains sharks, rays, parrot fish and, probably still, a Cessna. The penguin enclosure has a Rallye. ◆ *Off Leathergate Road, KT9 2NE* | **www.chessington.com**

	Reg		Type	Yr	History	Notes	Date
❑	G-BBLM		MS Rallye 100S	73	ex Fishburn, E' Midlands, Sandtoft. De-reg 30-11-10. Arr 1-22		1-22
❑	–		Cessna 150 / 152	~	*Azteca*, fuselage and wings		8-21

CROYDON on the A23 in south London

Croydon Airport Visitor Centre: Within the former terminal building (Airport House) run by the **Historic Croydon Airport Trust** in association with the **Croydon Airport Society**. The pole-mounted Heron stands guard.

◆ *Purley Way. CR0 0XZ* | **info@historiccroydonairport.org.uk** | **www.historiccroydonairport.org.uk**

❑ 'G-AOXL' DH Heron 2D G-ANUO 54 ex Biggin Hill, Exeter. CoA 12-9-86, de-reg 9-8-96 [1] 1-24

■ **[1]** The *real* G-AOXL made the last passenger flight from Croydon, on 3-9-59.

DARTFORD at the southern end of *that* bridge, west of Gravesend

An Auster is *thought* to still be kept at a *private* location in the *general* area.

❑ XN437 Auster AOP.9 G-AXWA 59 ex Rush Green, N Weald, Lashenden, Welling, B' Hill, Luton, Odiham, Maghull, Hoylake, St Athan, 653, 8 Flt. SOC 28-11-67 N5-22

DULWICH As predicted in *W&R28*, Chipmunk T.10 fuselage WB627 moved to Flixton, Suffolk, 9th November 2023.

FELTHAM on the A312 southeast of Heathrow

Heathrow Trident Collection (HTC): Kevin Bowen's incredible collection is well worth a visit. Along with Les Rawlins, Kevin was instrumental in the relocation of Trident 3B G-AWZP cockpit from Manchester, Gtr Man, to London Colney, Herts – qv – where it joined Srs 2E G-AVFH. Both *Zulu-Papa* and *Fox-Hotel* are being restored with the help of HTC members. Large exhibits continue to arrive; the nose landing gear from G-AWZP being a notable example. An ongoing project is the construction of a flightdeck, comprising items from many sources. HTC has a large archive and can offer knowledge and support to other museums, organisations and individuals. ◆ *Prior appointment* **only** | **g-awzk@msn.com**

GREENFORD on the A40 west of the city

Vanguard Holdings: Appleton Lane, off the A40. After 'refreshing' at North Weald, Hunter F.1 WT555 moved to Neasden, Gtr Lon, by May 2022 for display at Vanguard's self-store centre. See also Bristol, Glos, for the Vanguard Storage HQ.

◆ *Prior arrangement* **only** | **www.vanguardholdings.co.uk**

❑ XV123 'V' Westland Scout AH.1 67 ex Ipswich, Shawbury, Thruxton, Ipswich, Weston-super--Mare, Fleetlands. Arrived 5-19. Royal Marine c/s, displayed 1-24

GREENWICH east of the A102 Blackwall Tunnel Approach, just south of the 'Dome'

Emirates Aviation Experience: An impressive full-scale mock-up of an Airbus A380 allows access to the flightdeck; this is more a part of the building than an 'airframe' and is not listed formally. There are two A380 and a pair of Boeing 777 fixed-base simulators, all synthetic. Guests can travel to the venue via the Emirates cable car across the Thames.

◆ *In East Parkside, east of the A102* | **email** via website | **www.aviation-experience.com**

HENDON northwest London, near the end of the M1

Royal Air Force Museum: London (to use the new-fangled jargon – that would be Hendon, then). *W&R28* dealt at length with the pros and cons of the disposal of a significant number of airframes from the collection. Much of this was to create space for a major new display at Cosford, Shropshire, and under that heading the reader will find discussion of the plan.

To mark the 80th anniversary of the 'Dam Busters' raid, a new and permanent exhibition - **Strike Hard, Strike Sure: Bomber Command 1939-1945** - was opened in May 2023. Included are sections of Short Stirling III LK488 of 1651 CU, crashed 19th October 1944 and recovered from Mickle Fell, Yorks, 31st August 1977 were put on display; they were previously at Stafford, Staffs. Although impressive, they do not merit of formal listing. There is more of LK488 to see at Cosford. (Some parts of this are also on show at Cosford, Shropshire.)

Present loans are as follows **Brooklands**, Surrey: Valiant cockpit; **Chatham**, Kent: military gas balloon basket; **Duxford**, Cambs, Canberra WH725, Fi 103; **Filton**, Glos, Beaufighter cockpit; **Manston,** Kent, Hurricane and Spitfire: **Middle Wallop**, Hampshire, Rotachute; **Old Sarum**, Wilts Avro 707A, EE P.1A; **South Kensington**, Gtr Lon, P.1127; **Southampton**, Hampshire, Gnat F.1, Spitfire F.24; **Stow Maries**, Essex, Avro 504K; **Tangmere**, W Sussex: Hunter, Meteor, Phantom, Swift; **Woodford**, Gtr Man, Shackleton AEW.2; **Yeovilton**, Somerset, P.1052, Dragonfly VX595, Supermarine 510. Cadet

Sedbergh TX.1 XN185 previously at Scampton, Lincs, has been disposed of, see Kirton in Lindsey, Lincs.

As well as Hendon, there is the RAF Museum: Midlands and conservation centre at **Cosford, Shropshire**, and the storage site at **Stafford, Staffs**. There is also the **Society of Friends of the RAF Museum** - contact via the website. In the sections below, 'RAeS' denotes the Royal Aeronautical Society's former collection, largely based on the former Nash Collection.

◆ *Grahame Park Way, NW9 5LL* | **020 8205 2266** | **london@rafmuseum.org** | **www.rafmuseum.org**

Lancaster I R5868 beautifully framed by the centre section of Stirling III LK488. *RAF Museum*

'Gate guardians': The Hurricane and Spitfire, with new 'personas', are back on duty.

❑ 'P2725'	'TM-B'	Hawker Hurricane FSM	90	BAPC.205, ex 'Z3427', 'BE421'. 504 Sqn colours		1-24
❑ 'TB288'	'HT-H'	V-S Spitfire FSM	90	BAPC.206, ex 'MH486'. 20 Sqn colours		1-24

Hangar 1: RAF First 100 Years – 1918-2018: The museum's main entrance and the famed/infamous 'Marmite' hall – you either like it or you don't.

❑ F1010	'C'	Airco DH.9A	1918	ex Cardington, Krakow, Berlin, 110. Force-landed 5-10-1918 and captured. Westland-built. Acquired 15-6-77.	[1]	1-24
❑ BL614	'ZD-F'	V-S Spitfire Vb	42	ex Rochester, Manchester, St Athan, Colerne, Wattisham, 'AB871' Credenhill, Bridgnorth, '4353M' Hednesford, Cosford 4354M (23-11-43), 118, 64, 222, 242, 611. CBAF-built. Acquired 27-9-72, on site 27-10-97. 222 Sqn colours		1-24
❑ ML824	'NS-Z'	Short Sunderland MR.5	44	ex Pembroke Dock, French Aéronavale, 330, 201. Acquired 11-1-71. 201 Sqn colours		1-24
❑ XR977	'3'	Folland Gnat T.1	64	ex Cosford, Hangar 1, 2 SoTT 8640M, Red Arrows, 4 FTS. Last flown 5-10-79. Red Arrows colours. Arrived 3-12-17		1-24
❑ XZ585	'A'	Westland Sea King HAR.3	77	ex Gosport, 203, 22, 203, 202, 202, 203, 22, 202, A&AEE. Last flown 23-4-15, Arrived 6-12-17	[2]	1-24
❑ –		Fieseler Fi 103 (V-1)	45	BAPC.92, ex Cardington, St Athan		1-22
❑ –		Lockheed-Martin F-35 FSM	10	BAPC.341, installed 9-11		1-24

■ **[1]** 'Ninak' was the 13th of 18 donated to 110 Sqn and a panel reads: 'Presented by His Highness the Nizam of Hyderabad No.12A' - the potentate was clearly superstitious. The fuselage was acquired from Krakow, wings and much else created/acquired in-house. **[2]** Factoids: Total flying time 14,472 hours; undertook 533 operational winch lifts.

Hangar 2: World War One in the Air 1914-1918: Centred on the re-sited and re-modelled Grahame-White Factory.

❑ No.433	Blériot XXVII	1911	BAPC.107, ex Stafford, Cosford, Wyton, Hendon 9202M, Cardington, Heathrow, RAeS, Hendon, Nash, Brooklands. Acquired 5-63	1-24
❑ '687'	Royal Aircraft Factory BE.2b replica	88	BAPC.181, ex Cardington. John MacKenzie-built, original fittings. Acquired 6-92	1-24

❑ '2345'		Vickers FB.5 Gunbus replica G-ATVP	66	ex Cardington, Hendon, Abingdon, Brooklands, G-ATVP (CoA 6-5-69). Acquired 10-6-68, last flight 14-6-68,	[1]	1-24
❑ '3066'		Caudron G.3	1916	ex 9203M, Henlow, Stradishall, Heathrow, RAeS, Hendon, Nash, Brooklands, G-AETA, OO-ELA, O-BELA. Acquired 1964		1-24
❑ 'A3930'	'B'	Royal Aircraft RE.8 replica	12	ex New Zealand, ZK-TVC. The Vintage Aviator-built. Acquired 28-8-12. 9 Sqn colours	[2]	1-24
❑ 'A6526'		Royal Aircraft Factory FE.2b	1917	BAPC.400, ex main halls, Cosford, Stafford, Wyton, Cardington, Leiston. Acquired 4-76	[3]	1-24
❑ 'C3988'		Sopwith 5F1 Dolphin	1918	BAPC.353, ex Cosford, 'D5239', Wyton, Cardington. Acquired 6-67	[4]	1-24
❑ 'E449'		Avro 504K	1918	ex 9205M, Henlow, Abingdon, Heathrow, RAeS, Nash, Brooklands. Acquired 3-63	[5]	1-24
❑ 'E2466'	'I'	Bristol F.2B	1918	BAPC.165, ex main halls, Cardington, Weston-on-the-Green. Acquired 1965. Semi-skeletal		1-24
❑ F938		Royal Aircraft Factory SE.5a G-EBIC	1918	ex Henlow 9208M, Biggin Hill, Heathrow, Brooklands, Wroughton, Brooklands, 'B4563', Colerne, RAeS, Brooklands, Hendon, Nash, Savage Skywriting, G-EBIC (CoA 3-9-30, de-reg 31-12-38), F938, 84 Sqn. Wolseley-built. Acquired 12-64		1-24
❑ F6314	'B'	Sopwith F1 Camel	1918	ex 'Milestones', Cosford 9206M, Wyton, Hendon, Heathrow, Colerne, Hendon, RAeS, Hendon, Nash, Brooklands, 'H508', Tring, Waddon. Acquired 9-1-64		1-24
❑ N5912		Sopwith Triplane	1917	ex 8385M, Henlow, 49 MU, 5 MU, Cardington, School of Air Fighting, Redcar and Marske. Oakley-built. Acquired 1964		1-24
❑ 'D7343/17'		Albatros D.Va replica	12	ex New Zealand, ZK-TVD. Acquired 28-8-12	[7]	1-24
❑ 8417/18		Fokker D.VII	1918	ex 'Milestones', Cardington, Hendon 9207M, Cardington, Hendon, Cardington, Heathrow, RAeS, Hendon, Nash, Brooklands, Versailles, OO- ?, Belgian AF (?), Jasta 71. Ostdeutsche Albatros Werke-built. Acquired 3-66		1-24

■ **[1]** Gunbus built by the Brooklands-based Vintage Aircraft and Flying Association, first flying 14-6-66. **[2]** RE.8 fitted with a 'reverse-engineered' RAF 4a; unveiled at Old Warden 28-8-12; part of the exchanged for Farman F-HMFI and Hanriot HD-75. Original rudder, wing and fuselage parts found in a garage in Coventry by the Northern Aircraft Preservation Society. **[3]** FE.2 based on an unfinished nacelle built by sub-contractor Richard Garrett and Sons of Leiston and stored at its factory for close on 60 years. Much of the work creating the rest of the airframe was carried out by John MacKenzie of Aircraft and Weapon Reproductions of Southampton 1987 to 2007, with completion by Guy Black's Retrotec. **[4]** Dolphin uses many original parts. Rear fuselage comes from C3988 and this has been adopted as its identity. **[5]** Avro 504K 'E449' is a composite of G-EBJE (fuselage) and Type 548A G-EBKN (wings) – both of which used to ply their joy riding trade from Shoreham – it was originally with the Nash Collection. **[7]** D.Va built by The Vintage Aviator Ltd, fitted with original Mercedes D.III from RAFM stocks; unveiled at Old Warden 28-8-12; part of Farman and Hanriot exchange.

Hangars 3, 4, and 5: War in the Air 1918-1980: Previously known as the Historic Hangars and Bomber Command Hall. From the autumn of 2023 also included was the special exhibition: **Strike Hard, Strike Sure: Bomber Command 1939-1945**. This is the subsidiary of the major revamp at Cosford – which see. Another 'special' – **Higher, Faster, Further** – will feature several of the inter-war types.

W&R28 pre-empted the migration of EH.101 ZJ116 (G-OIOI) to Weston-super-Mare, Somerset: for the record this was not achieved until August 2022. That edition also moved Grasshopper TX.1 WZ791 to Montrose, not so! Jet Provost T.3A XM463 travelled to Cosford, Shropshire, 25th May 2022. TB-25N '34037' (N9115Z) made the trek to East Kirkby, Lincs, on 9th November 2022 having been transferred by gift.

Two-seat Fw 190F-8/U1 584219 finally departed by road, bound for long-term loan at the Berlin, Gatow-based Militarhistorisches Museum der Bundeswehr on 23rd October 2023. It's likely never to return, and rightly so although its departure has made several readers incandescent. The British 'national collection' boasts a 'classic' 'Butcher Bird' – Fw 190A 733682 – at Cosford. That is no field-modified fast courier, it was the upper element of a Mistel combo, no less.

❑ 'G-AEXF'*		Percival Mew Gull replica	08	BAPC.366, ex Stafford, Hendon, Sudbury. AJD Eng-built. Acquired 17-4-08. First noted 12-23	[1]	1-24
❑ G-FAAG		AW R.33 airship	1921	Barlow-built. Dismantled 5-28. Control gondola		1-22
❑ 'E6655'	'B'	Sopwith 7FI Snipe	11	BAPC.348, ex New Zealand. Acquired 10-8-12. 1 Sqn colours, Hinaidi, Iraq, 1926	[2]	1-24
❑ 'J9941'		Hawker Hart G-ABMR	35	ex HSA, 'J9933', G-ABMR. CoA 11-6-57, de-reg 2-2-59. Acquired 1972. 57 Sqn colours		1-24

	Serial	Code	Type	Year	History	Notes	Date
❑	'K2227'		Bristol Bulldog IIA G-ABBB	30	ex Hatch, Cardington, Old Warden, Henlow, Filton, G-ABBB, (de-reg 22-9-61), Science Museum, R-11. Crashed 13-9-64 (with Shuttleworth). Acquired 31-3-99. 56 Sqn 'A' Flight c/s		1-24
❑	K4232		Cierva Rota I	34	ex Spain (1996-98), Cardington, Sweden, SE-AZB, Cierva, 529, 1448 Flt, Cal Flight, 5 RSS, Old Warden, Cardington, SAC, A&AEE, 2, SAC, K4232. Avro-built C.30A. Acquired14-6-78		1-24
❑	K6035*		Westland Wallace II	35	ex Stafford, Hen<u>don</u>, Hatch, Henlow, Newark, Cranwell, 2361M, EWS, 502. Acquired 4-77, arrived 19-9-23. Fuselage		1-24
❑	L5343		Fairey Battle I	39	ex Cosford, Rochester, Hendon, St Athan, Henlow, Leeming, Iceland, 98, 266. Cr13-9-40. Acquired 21-11-72. 98 Sqn colours	[3]	1-24
❑	N5628		Gloster Gladiator II	39	ex 263. Lost in Norway 4-40. Acquired 8-68. Forward fuselage		1-24
❑	N9899		Supermarine Southampton I	1925	ex Cardington, Henlow, Felixstowe (as houseboat), wrecked at moorings, Calshot, 23-11-28, 480 Flt, MAEE, 480 Flt. Acquired 9-67. Fuselage		1-24
❑	P2617	'AF-F'	Hawker Hurricane I	40	ex 8373M, 71 MU, 9 FTS, 9 SFTS, 1, 607, 615. Acquired 5-72. 607 Sqn colours		1-24
❑	R5868	'PO-S'	Avro Lancaster I	42	ex Scampton 7325M, 467, 83. Metropolitan-Vickers-built. Acquired 3-72. 467 Sqn colours	[4]	1-24
❑	R9125*	'JR-M'	Westland Lysander III	40	ex Cosford, Hendon, 8377M, Cosford, Wroughton, Stanmore Park, Wroughton, 161, Mk.IIISD, *School for Danger*, 161, Mk.III, CNS, 7 OTU, CGS, 225. Acquired 3-61. Arrived 22-2-22. 161 Sqn colours		1-24
❑	W1048	'TL-S'	HP Halifax II	42	ex 8465M, Henlow, Lake Hoklingen, Norway, 35, 102. EE-built. Force-landed 27-4-42. Acquired 25-8-73. 35 Sqn c/s		1-24
❑	W2068	'68'	Avro Anson I	39	ex Duxford, 9261M, Australia, VH-ASM, W2068, 4 SFTS, 3 SFTS. Acquired 19-4-96. Fuselage on 'Queen Mary' trailer		1-24
❑	X4590	'PR-F'	V-S Spitfire I	40	ex Cosford 8384M, Finningley, 53 OTU, 303, 57 OTU, 66, 609. Acquired 1-72. 609 Sqn colours		1-24
❑	'DD931'	'L'	Bristol Beaufort VIII	44	BAPC.436, ex 9131M, Cardington, Chino, New Guinea, RAAF. DAP-built. Acquired 1991. 42 Sqn colours	[5] [6]	1-24
❑	FE905		NAA Harvard IIB	43	ex Cardington, Winthorpe, Cardington, Royston, London Bridge, Southend, LN-BNM, Danish AF 31-329, RCAF, 41 SFTS, FE905, 42-12392. Noorduyn-built. Acquired 3-85		1-24
❑	'FX760'	'GA-?'	Curtiss Kittyhawk IV	43	ex Cosford 9150M, Stafford, Wyton, Cardington, Hendon, USA, Hawkins, Chino, New Guinea, 80 Sqn RAAF A29-556, USAAF 42-106101. Acquired 29-5-92. 112 Sqn colours	[6] [7]	1-24
❑	'KK995'	'E'	Sikorsky Hoverfly I KL110	44	ex 'Milestones', Bicester, Henlow, Cranfield, 705, King's Flt, TCDU, 43 OTU, USAAF 43-46596. Acquired 14-1-66	[8]	1-24
❑	'KL216'	'RS-L'	Republic P-47D-40-RA Thunderbolt	45	ex Cosford 9212M, Duxford, Cardington, Bitteswell, Yugo AF 13064, USAAF 45-49295. Acquired 7-86. 30 Sqn SEAC c/s		1-24
❑	KN751	'F'	Consolidated Liberator VI	44	ex Cosford, Colerne, Ind AF 6 Sqn HE807, RAF KN751, 99. Ford-built. Acquired 1-7-74. 99 Sqn, Cocos Islands, c/s	[9]	1-24
❑	LB264		Taylorcraft Auster I G-AIXA	42	ex Cosford, Plus D G-AIXA (CoA 21-2-<u>03</u>, de-reg 13-12-02), Spanhoe, 22 EFTS, 1 EFTS, A&AEE. Acquired 23-10-02		1-24
❑	MN235	'I8-T'	Hawker Typhoon Ib	44	ex Coningsby (7-18 to 10-18) Canada, Hendon, Shawbury, Smithsonian, USAAF FE-491, RAF n/s. Gloster-built. Acquired 19-11-68, arrived 18-10-18. 440 Sqn RCAF colours		1-24
❑	MP425	'G'	Airspeed Oxford I G-AITB	43	ex Cardington, Winthorpe, Cardington, G-AITB (CoA 24-5-61, de-reg 31-10-61), Shawbury, Perth, MP425, 7 FTS, 18 (P)AFU, 1536 (BAT) Flt. Standard Motors-built. Acquired 3-69. 1536 Flt colours		1-24
❑	NV778		Hawker Tempest TT.5	44	ex 'Milestones', Cosford, Wyton, Cardington, Hendon, 8386M (5-9-73), Leeming, 'SN219', Middleton St George, N Weald, Foulness, 233 OCU, Napier. Last flown 12-7-55. Acquired 8-65. 233 OCU colours		1-24
❑	PK724		V-S Spitfire F.24	46	ex Finningley, Gaydon, <u>Norton</u> 7288M (4-11-55), n/s. CBAF-built. Acquired 20-2-70, arrived 2-4-71		7-22

	Serial	Code	Type	Yr	History	Note	Date
❑	RD253		Bristol Beaufighter TF.10	44	ex St Athan 7931M, Portuguese AF BF-13, RD253. Acquired 1965		1-24
❑	'TB675'	'4D-V'	V-S Spitfire XVI RW393	45	ex Stafford, Cosford, Stafford, Cosford, St Athan, Turnhouse 7293M (27-3-56), 602, 3, CAACU, 31, FCCS, 203 AFS. CBAF-built. Arrived 9-15. 74 Sqn colours		1-24
❑	TJ138	'VO-L'	DH Mosquito TT.35	45	ex St Athan, Swinderby, Finningley, Colerne, Thorney Island, Bicester 7607M (8-7-59), Shawbury, 5 CAACU, B.35, 98. Last flight 8-5-59. Acquired 6-67. 98 Sqn colours		1-24
❑	VT812	'N'	DH Vampire F.3	47	ex Cosford, Wyton, Hendon, Cosford, Shawbury, Colerne 7200M (20-4-55), Cardington, 602, 601, 614, 32. EE-built. Acquired 9-6-64. 601 Sqn colours		1-24
❑	WE139		EE Canberra PR.3	53	ex 8369M, Henlow, 231 OCU, 39, 69, 540, Air Race Flt. Acquired 23-4-69	[10]	1-24
❑	WH301		Gloster Meteor F.8	51	ex Henlow 7930M, Kemble, 85, CAW, 609, DFLS. Acquired 17-2-67. 609 Squadron colours		1-24
❑	WP962	'C'	DHC Chipmunk T.10	53	ex 9287M, Newton, 3 AEF, Bristol UAS, AAC, London UAS, 61 GCF, 662. Hawarden-built. Acquired 5-5-00		1-24
❑	WV783		Bristol Sycamore HR.12 G-ALSP	50	ex Rochester, Wyton, Cardington, Fleetlands, Henlow 7841M (1-4-64), HDU Old Sarum, CFS, ASWDU, G-ALSP (de-reg 26-3-52). Acquired 1995. CFS colours		1-24
❑	WZ791		Slingsby Grasshopper TX.1	52	8944M, e Syerston, Halton, High Wycombe, Hove. Acquired 8-8-91. See notes above		7-22
❑	XA302		Slingsby Cadet TX.3	52	ex Syerston, BGA.3786 / HAK, 622 GS, 661 GS, CGS, 2 GC, 671 GS, 615 GS, 613 GS, 126 GS, 123 GS, 22 GS. CoA 24-5-96, acquired 5-5-05	[11]	1-24
❑	XG154		Hawker Hunter FGA.9	56	ex 8863M, St Athan, 1 TWU, 229 OCU, 54, 43, 54. AWA-built. Acquired 30-5-85. 8 *and* 43 Sqn colours		1-24
❑	XG474	'O'	Bristol Belvedere HC.1	62	ex 8367M, Henlow, 66, 26, 66. Oldmixon-built Acquired 7-8-69. 66 Sqn colours		1-24
❑	XL318		Avro Vulcan B.2	61	ex 8733M, Scampton, 617, 230 OCU, Wadd Wing, 617, 230 OCU, Scamp Wing, 617. Acquired 1-1-82, arrived 12-2-82		1-24
❑	XM717		HP Victor K.2	63	ex Cardington, Marham, 55, 57, 55, 543, Witt W, 100. Acquired 2-3-94. *Lucky Lou*. Cockpit		1-24
❑	XP299		Westland Whirlwind HAR.10	61	ex Cosford 8726M, 22, 230, 1563F, Queen's Flt, 230, CFS. Acquired 30-11-81. 22 Sqn colours		1-24
❑	XS925	'BA'	EE Lightning F.6	67	ex 8961M, Binbrook, 11, 5-11 pool. Last flown 21-7-87. Acquired 26-4-88, arrived 28-4-88. 11 Sqn colours		1-24
❑	XV424	'I'	McD Phantom FGR.2	69	ex 9152M, St Athan, Wattisham, 56, 228 OCU, 29, 92, 228 OCU, 29, 228 OCU, 111, 29. Acquired 12-11-92		1-24
❑	XV732		Westland Wessex HCC.4	69	ex Shawbury, 32, Queen's Flt. Last flight 31-3-98. Acquired 26-3-02		1-24
❑	XW323	'86'	BAC Jet Provost T.5A	70	ex 9166M (23-10-92), Shawbury, 1 FTS, RAFC. 1 FTS c/s		1-24
❑	XW855		Sud Gazelle HCC.4	73	ex Shawbury, Fleetlands, 32. Westland-built. Acquired 1-4-03		1-24
❑	ZE887	'GF'	Panavia Tornado F.3	88	ex Leuchars, 111, 43, 25, 11, 5, 11, 43, 229 OCU. Last flown 4-3-10, acquired 18-10-10. 43 Sqn colours	[12]	1-24
❑	A16-199	'SF-R'	Lockheed Hudson IIIA G-BEOX	42	ex Strathallan, G-BEOX (de-reg 12-12-81), VH-AGJ, VH-SMM, 3 Comms Unit, 2 Sqn, 13 Sqn, RAAF A16-199, FH174 n/s, 41-36975. Acquired 14-7-81. RAAF 13 Sqn c/s		1-24
❑	920	'QN'	Supermarine Stranraer	40	ex Queen Charlotte Airlines CF-BXO, RCAF 920. Canadian Vickers-built. Acquired 7-70		1-24
❑	4101	'12'	Messerschmitt Bf 109E-4	40	ex St Athan 8477M, Henlow, Biggin, Fulbeck, Wroughton, Stanmore, Pengam Moors, Stafford, DG200, 1426 Flt, A&AEE, DH Hatfield, Hucknall, RAE, JG51, JG52,JG51. Erla-built. Force-landed 27-11-40. Acquired 9-69		1-24
❑	120227	'2'	Heinkel He 162A-2	44	ex St Athan 8472M, Colerne, Leconfield, VN679, AM.65, Farnborough, Leck, JG1. Acquired 1961. JG1 colours		1-24
❑	191614*	'14'	Messerschmitt Me 163B-1 Komet	44	ex Cosford, 8481M, Biggin Hill, Westcott, Brize Norton, Farnborough, Hussum, II/JG400. Acquired 1975. Arrived by 4-22	[13]	1-24

	Serial	Code	Type	Year	History	Note	Date
❑	494083	'RI+JK'	Junkers Ju 87G-2 'Stuka'	c44	ex St Athan 8474M, Henlow, St Athan, Biggin Hill, Fulbeck, Wroughton, Stanmore, Eggebek. Acquired 9-69		1-24
❑	701152	'NT+SL'	Heinkel He 111H-20/R1	44	ex St Athan 8471M, Henlow, Biggin Hill, Fulbeck, Stanmore Park, RAE, 56th FG USAAF, Luftwaffe. Acquired 9-69		1-24
❑	730301	'D5+RL'	Messerschmitt Bf 110G-4/R6	44	ex St Athan 8479M, Biggin Hill, Stanmore Park, 76 MU, RAE, AM.34, Karup, I/NJG3. Acquired 8-73		1-24
❑	MM5701	'13-95'	Fiat CR-42 Falco	40	ex St Athan 8468M, Biggin Hill, Fulbeck, Wroughton, Stanmore Park, AFDU, RAE, BT474, 95 SCT. Force-landed Orfordness 11-11-40. Acquired 1968		1-24
❑	16336*	'24'	Kawasaki Ki-100-1b	c44	BAPC.83, ex Cosford, Hendon, Cosford, St Athan 8476M, Cosford, Henlow, Biggin Hill, Fulbeck, Wroughton, Stanmore, Sealand, Japanese Army. First noted 12-22		1-24
❑	5439*		Mitsubishi Ki-46-III *Dinah*	44	BAPC.84, ex Cosford, St Athan 8484M, Biggin Hill, Fulbeck, Wroughton, Stanmore, Sealand, ATAIU-SEA. Arrived UK 8-46. 3 Sqn, 81st HQ Rec Group, colours. First noted 12-22		1-24
❑	'10461'*		Yokosuka Ohka 11	c45	BAPC.99, ex Cosford, St Athan 8486M, Cosford, Westcott. First noted 12-22		1-24
❑	'413317'	'VF-B'	NAA P-51D-30-NA Mustang	44	ex N51RT, N555BM, YV-508CP, N555BM, N4409, N6319T, 44-74409. Inglewood-built. Acquired 18-11-03. 4th FG, 336th FS colours, *The Duck*	[14]	1-24
❑	44-83868	'N'	Boeing B-17G-95-DL Flying Fortress	45	ex Stansted, N5237V, USN PB-1W 77233. Douglas-built Acquired 13-10-83. 94th BG, 332nd BS colours		1-24

■ **[1]** See under Shuttleworth, Beds, for the flying G-AEXF and Tattershall Thorpe, Lincs, for another replica. **[2]** Snipe reconstructed by The Vintage Aviator Ltd, with original wings, fuselage, tailplane, and Bentley; exchanged for Farman F-HMFI and Hanriot HD-75. **[3]** Original restoration of L5343 included substantial elements of the centre fuselage of a former RCAF Battle I, believed to be L5340, and other parts from P2183. **[4]** See also Woodford, Gtr Man, for a cockpit replica of 'R5868'. **[5]** Beaufort is a composite: forward fuselage A9-557, rear A9-559, centre section A9-591, all salvaged from Tadji, Papua New Guinea. **[6]** Beaufort and Kittyhawk were part of a package exchange for two 'stock' Spitfire XVIs. **[7]** Kittyhawk restored by RJ Aviation at Hawkins, Texas, and was based on the fuselage of A29-556. A replica starboard wing and tail section were constructed. **[8]** Majority of the Hoverfly is KL110 despite it wearing 'KK995'; the latter was delivered to Cranfield 5-51 and there was probably some exchange of parts. **[9]** Liberator carries 'SNAKE' alongside its serial number, denoting it was destined for Air Command South East Asia and not to be diverted to other taskings or theatres. **[10]** Winner London-Christchurch Air Race, 8-10-53. **[11]** Cadet donated by Bill Walker. **[12]** Tornado F.3 factoids: During its first stint with 43 Sqn, it was deployed to Dhahran for Operation GRANBY, 8-90 to 1-91. Last flight 4-3-10, total time 4,966 hours. **[13]** Komet is marked '191461' on the port fin. **[14]** P-51 donated by Bob Tullius of Group 44 Inc, Sebring, Florida.

Hangar 6: The RAF in an Age of Uncertainty: Previously the Milestones of Flight hangar - aka 'The Time Tunnel'.

	Serial	Code	Type	Year	History	Note	Date
❑	–		V-S Spitfire FSM	03	BAPC.293, built by Concepts and Innovations. Lobby		1-22
❑	XW547	'R'	Blackburn Buccaneer S.2B	72	ex Cosford 9169M, Shawbury, 9095M, Gulf Det, 12, 237 OCU, 208, 12, 216, 12, 237 OCU, 12. Acquired 20-1-93 *Guinness Girl / Pauline / The Macallan*. Pink colours		1-24
❑	XX824	'AD'	SEPECAT Jaguar GR.1	75	ex Cosford, Halton 9019M (10-1-90), Shawbury, 14, 17, 14. Arrived 20-2-18		1-24
❑	ZA457	'AJ-J'	Panavia Tornado GR.1	83	ex St Athan, 2, 617, RAF Gulf Det, 17, 15, 9, 617, 9, TOEU. Acquired 28-7-03		1-24
❑	ZG477		BAe/McDD Harrier GR.9A	90	ex Cosford, Cottesmore, 1, 4, 800, QinetiQ, GR.7/A, 3, 1, 3, 4. Acquired 19-12-01, arrived 21-2-18	[1]	1-24
❑	ZH588		Eurofighter Typhoon DA2	94	ex Brize Norton, Coningsby, Warton, BAE Systems. Acquired 22-1-08	[2]	1-24
❑	64-0553		Lockheed WC-130E	64	ex Pima, Davis-Monthan 53rd WRS, 815th TAS, 53rd WRS, 54th WRS, C-130A. Cockpit. Arrived 14-6-18.	[3]	1-24
❑	83-24104	'BN'	Boeing CH-47D Chinook	84	ex Boeing, CH-47A, 190th Av Co, Vietnam 1966-1971, US Army. Fuselage. Acquired 12-1-07. 18 Sqn, RAF c/s		1-24
❑	03-33119		General Atomics MQ-1B Predator	05	ex USAF, deployments: Kuwait/Iraq (2005-2012), Djibouti (2012), 15th RS. Last flown 13-1-16. Acquired 13-4-18	[4]	1-22

■ **[1]** GR.9 factoids; Operation WARDEN, Turkey, 1993-1994; Operation ALLIED FORCE, Gioia del Colle, Italy, 1999; Operation HERRICK, Afghanistan, 2008-2009. Made final departure from HMS *Ark Royal* 24-11-10 and took part in the 'Farewell to Harrier' formation 15-12-10. Completed 4,191 flight hours and 3,969 landings. **[2]** DA2 data: First flown at Warton, Lancs, 14-8-93; last flight into Coningsby, Lincs, 29-1-07 for spares. **[3]** Herk on loan from the Pima Air and Space Museum, Tucson, Arizona. **[4]** General Atomics MQ-1B Predator, on loan from the National Museum of the USAF

Locally: The Canberra cockpit was virtually auctioned on 9th March 2021 – outcome unknown.

❑ WJ731	EE Canberra B.2T	53	ex Dunstable, Willington, Wyton, Wyton SF, 231 OCU, 7, 231 OCU, 50, 90. Cockpit, trailer-mounted		1-21

HORNCHURCH on the A124 northeast of Dagenham

RAF Hornchurch Heritage Centre: Run by the Hornchurch Aerodrome Historical Trust, the centre is based upon Suttons House, used by the RAF 1939-1946. It is packed with items from this airfield's rich history, and it has a cafe.

◆ *Suttons Lane, RM12 6RU* | **email** via website | **http://rafhornchurch.com**

Hornchurch Country Park: A short walk away from the Heritage Centre is parkland that occupies the site of the former airfield. The **Ingrebourne Nature Discovery Centre** includes more aviation material.

◆ *Squadrons Approach, RM12 6DF* | **email** via website | **www.essexwt.org.uk/nature-reserves/ingrebourne**

KENLEY south of Kenley, west of the A22 at Whyteleafe

Kenley Revival Project: The **Kenley Airfield Friends Group** continues to refine the site, working on the remaining blast pens, rifle range and the fuel depot. ◆ *Not yet open to the public,* occasional *special events* | **www.kafg.org.uk**

KINGSTON-UPON-THAMES

Kingston University: School of Engineering, Roehampton Vale, Friars Avenue. Learjet 25 N121EL relocated to Exeter, Devon, by September 2023. The anonymous HS.146 cockpit and sections, last noted in December 2014, have been deleted.

Also: A Hunter cockpit is *thought* to be extant in the general area.

❑ XG209 '66'	Hawker Hunter F.6	56	ex Chelmsford, Stock, Halton, Cranwell, Halton 8709M (17-11-81), 12, DFLS, 111, 14. Cockpit		1-14

LONDON HEATHROW AIRPORT EGLL

British Airways Heritage Collection - **Speedbird Centre**:

◆ *Prior arrangement* **only** | *Waterside (HDGA), PO Box 365, Harmondsworth, UB7 0GB* | **020 8562 5777** | **email** via website | **www.britishairways.com/travel/museum-collection**

BA Engineering Base: A campaign group calling itself 'Concorde on the Thames' began stirring the idea of re-locating *Alpha-Bravo* somewhere along the riverside as a visitor attraction in early 2024. Both the Brooklands and East Fortune 'hot rods' have moved by surface transport: who knows?

❑ G-BOAB	BAC/Sud Concorde 102	76	ex BA, G-N94AB. CoA 19-9-01, de-reg 4-5-04	[1]	1-24

■ **[1]** *Alpha-Bravo* factoids: Withdrawn from BA service 15th August 2000, total hours 22,297, landings 7,810.

LONDON MEMORIALS

Memorials are not generally part of the remit of *W&R*, but those of national status escape that rubric. **Bomber Command Memorial** at Green Park, Hyde Park Corner: **www.rafbf.org/bomber-command-memorial Battle of Britain Memorial** on the Embankment, opposite the London 'Eye': **www.bbm.org.uk Royal Air Force Church St Clement Danes** at Temple Bar Gate: **www.raf.mod.uk/our-organisation/units/st-clements-danes-church/**

NEASDEN on the A406 south of Hendon

Vanguard Self Storage: Opened in May 2022, Vanguard's new building houses the dramatically posed WT555 and a Spitfire FSM. See also Bristol, Glos, for the Vanguard Storage HQ and Greenford, Gtr Lon, for Vanguard Holdings.

◆ *Staples Corner, North Circular, NW2 7AH* | *Prior arrangement* **only** | **www.vanguardstorage.co.uk**

❑ 'V1964'* 'MA-C'	V-S Spitfire FSM	21	Replica Aircraft Fabricators, St Mawgan-built	[1]	1-24
❑ WT555*	Hawker Hunter F.1	55	ex Greenford, Cosford, Locking 7499M (22-11-57), A&AEE, Dunsfold. Arrived 26-4-22		1-24

■ **[1]** Vanguard was formed in 1964, hence the 'serial'; the code honours founding director 'Mac' McCullagh.

NORTHOLT AIRFIELD on the A4180 northwest of Northolt EGWU

RAF Northolt:

❑ 'L1684'	Hawker Hurricane FSM	89	BAPC.219, ex 'L1710', Biggin Hill. Northolt Stn Flt c/s	7-19
❑ 'MH314' 'SZ-G'	V-S Spitfire FSM	89	BAPC.221, ex 'EN526', 'MH777' 'RF-N'. 316 Sqn colours	3-23
❑ ZD621	HSA HS.125 CC.3	83	ex 32. Last flight 3-15, unveiled 16-7-15	1-24

SHEPHERD'S BUSH south of the A40, west of the A3220

KidZania: An educational centre with the spine-chilling catch-line: 'An indoor city, run by kids'.
◆ *In the Westfield Centre, Ariel Way, W12 7SL* | **www.kidzania.co.uk**

	Reg	Type	Year	Details	Note	Date
❑	EI-DFA	Airbus A319-200	00	ex Kemble, D-ANDI, F-WQQG, OO-SSJ. Hamburg-built. Last flight 15-1-13. BA c/s. Forward fuselage, arrived 4-10-14		12-23

SIDCUP on the A271, southeast London

Lost Island Encounter – World of Golf: ◆ *Off the A20 to the south of the town* | **www.worldofgolf.co.uk**

	Reg	Type	Year	Details	Note	Date
❑	G-BOSU	Piper Cherokee 140	73	ex N55635. Crashed 6-06, de-reg 12-7-07. Zebra stripes		9-21

SOUTH KENSINGTON on the A4 west of Westminster

Science Museum: The **Flight Gallery** holds some of the UK's most iconic airframes. The engine 'stacks' are a work of art, allowing close inspection of an incredible array of powerplants, including the original Whittle unit that was fitted to W4041/G when 'Gerry' Sayer first flew it at Cranwell on 15th May 1941.

On the lower floor is the **Making of the Modern World** exhibition. Aircraft in this exhibition are marked #. The **Winton Gallery** is devoted to the story of mathematics and containing the long reclusive Gugnunc.

The 'large object' store is at **Wroughton**, Wilts. Other ScM airframes can be found at: **Bristol**, Glos ('Flea' G-AEHM), **Lasham**, Hampshire (Clarke Chanute); **London Colney**, Herts (C.24 G-ABLM), **Southampton**, Hampshire (Sandringham VH-BRC) **Yeovilton**, Somerset (Concorde G-BSST, Ohka, Vampire LZ551).

◆ *Exhibition Road, SW7 2DD* | **033 0058 0058** | **email** via website | **www.sciencemuseum.org.uk**

	Reg		Type	Year	Details	Note	Date
❑	G-EBIB		Royal Aircraft Factory SE.5a	1918	ex 'F939', Hendon, Savage Skywriting G-EBIB, F937, 84 Sqn. Wolseley-built. CoA 6-6-35, de-reg 1-12-46. Acquired 24-7-39		1-24
❑	G-AAAH		DH Moth	28	CoA 23-12-30, de-reg 12-31. *Jason*. Acquired 21-1-31. Amy Johnson's Australian flight machine, 5-30	[1]	1-24
❑	G-AACN		HP Gugnunc	29	ex Wroughton, Hayes, Sydenham, West Byfleet, K1908 RAE. De-reg 12-30. Acquired 7-34, Winton Gallery	[2]	1-24
❑	G-ASSM		HSA HS.125-1/522	65	ex Wroughton, Chester, Southampton, 5N-AMK, G-ASSM. Acquired 16-3-89	[3]	1-24
❑	G-AZPH		Pitts S-1S	70	ex Meppershall, Chessington, N11CB. Damaged 10-5-91, de-reg 8-1-97. Acquired 10-91. *Neil Williams*	[4]	1-24
❑	G-NXTE*		ElectroFlight NXTE	20	de-reg 21-9-22. *Spirit of Innovation*. Unveiled 1-11-23	# [5]	1-24
❑	DFY		Schempp-Hirth Cirrus	c75	BGA.2091, ex Army Gliding Assoc. Acquired 1992		1-24
❑	–		Frost Ornithopter	1902	wings, flapping mechanism etc. Acquired 1925	[6]	1-24
❑	–		Roe Triplane	1909	BAPC.50, ex Newton Heath. Last flown 10-09. Acquired 1925	[7]	1-24
❑	–		Blériot XI	1909	BAPC.429, cockpit. Acquired 1920	[8]	1-24
❑	–		JAP-Harding Mono	1910	BAPC.54, Blériot-based, presented by JAP Ltd in 1930		1-24
❑	–		Antoinette Monoplane	1910	BAPC.55, ex Brough, Colwyn Bay. Acquired 1926. Minus starboard wing, port wing uncovered	[9]	1-24
❑	–		Vickers Vimy IV	1918	BAPC.51, Alcock and Brown's transatlantic machine Acquired 15-12-1919. Starboard fuselage uncovered		1-24
❑	–		Wright Flyer replica	48	BAPC.53, Hatfield-built. Acquired 1948		1-24
❑	–		Lilienthal replica	76	BAPC.124, Shawcraft (Models) Ltd, Uxbridge-built	[10]	1-24
❑	NC5171N		Lockheed 10A Electra G-LIOA	35	ex Wroughton, G-LIOA (de-reg 26-4-02), N5171N, NC243 Boston-Maine AW, N14959 Eastern. Acquired 21-6-82	#	1-24
❑	304		Cody Military Biplane	1912	BAPC.62, ex Farnborough, 4 Squadron, wrecked 31-3-1913. Handed over to the museum 26-11-1913		1-24
❑	D7560		Avro 504K	1918	ex M Wallop, South Kensington, Sydenham, West Byfleet, Hull, Waddon, 3 TDS. Acquired 22-1-1920	# [2]	1-24
❑	J8067		Hill Pterodactyl I	1925	ex Yeovil, Sydenham, West Byfleet, Farnborough, RAE, Westland, RAE. Acquired 1951. Stbd wing uncovered	[2]	1-24
❑	L1592	'KW-Z'	Hawker Hurricane I	38	ex 9 PAFU, 5 PAFU, 9 AOS, SDF, 615, 43, 17, 43, 17, 56. Acquired 16-12-54. 615 Sqn colours		1-24
❑	P9444	'RN-D'	V-S Spitfire Ia	40	ex Sydenham, 53 OTU, 61 OTU, 58 OTU, 72. SOC 10-8-44. Acquired 16-12-54. 72 Sqn colours	[2]	1-24

❑ S1595	'1'	Supermarine S.6B	31	ex RAFHSF. Acquired 18-4-32. Schneider winner 1931	[11]	1-24
❑ W4041/G		Gloster E28/39	41	ex RAE, Gloster. Acquired 28-4-46	[12]	1-24
❑ AP507	'KX-P'	Cierva C.30A Rota	34	ex Halton, Sydenham, 76 MU, 5 MU, 529, 1448 Flt, Duxford Calibration Flt, RAE, G-ACWP (de-reg 1-6-40). Avro-built. Acquired 24-5-46. 529 Sqn colours	[2]	1-24
❑ XG900		Short SC.1	57	ex Wroughton, Yeovilton, Wroughton, Hayes, South Kensington, RAE Bedford. Acquired 22-6-71	#	1-24
❑ XJ314		R-R Thrust Measuring Rig 'Flying Bedstead'	53	ex Wroughton, Yeovilton, East Fortune, Strathallan, Hayes, S' Kensington, crashed 16-9-57, RAE Bedford and Farnborough, Rolls-Royce. Acquired 9-1-61	# [13]	1-24
❑ XN344		Saro Skeeter AOP.12	60	ex M Wallop 8018M, 654, 652. SOC 27-5-68		1-24
❑ XP831		Hawker P.1127	60	ex Hendon 8406M, RAE Bedford, Dunsfold. Arr 31-5-92	[14]	1-24
❑ –		Short Bros gas balloon	1910	basket. Acquired c1912		1-24
❑ –		Balloon Factory Airship	1910	BAPC.430, No.17, *Beta II*, gondola. Acquired c1917		1-24
❑ –	'448'	Douglas Dakota 4	44	ex Ottawa, RCAF, KN448, 436, 10, USAAF C-47B-30-DK 44-76586. Oklahoma City-built. Acquired 1976. Cockpit		1-24
❑ 210/16		Fokker E.III	1916	BAPC.56, captured 1-4-16 and allocated XG4. Acquired 27-2-1918. Stripped airframe	[15]	1-24
❑ 191316	'6'	Messerschmitt Me 163B-1a Komet	43	ex Halton, 3 MU, 47 MU, 6 MU, Farnborough, Husum, II/JG.400. Acquired 1958		1-24
❑ 442795		Fieseler Fi 103A-1 (V-1)	44	BAPC.199, sectioned		1-24

■ **[1]** Replicas of *Jason* at Sunderland, N&T and Kingston upon Hull, E Yorks. **[2]** In this case the 'Sydenham' is not near Belfast, but the museum's long since former store at Crystal Palace, Sydenham, London. **[3]** HS.125 wears UK markings, these were cancelled when it was exported to Nigeria, 28-5-80. Upon return to the UK, it was not restored to the UK register. **[4]** Pitts was flown by the aerobatic master, Neil Williams, and in his honour is displayed *inverted.* **[5]** Modified, electric-powered, Nemesis NXT. Flying from Boscombe Down, Phil O'Dell clocked two world records for an electric aircraft: top speed of 387.4mph, time-to-climb 3 min 22 sec to 3,000m. **[6]** Second machine built by E P Frost, 3hp engine, wings covered with artificial feathers; there is evidence of 'flight'. First example was presented to Richard Shuttleworth in 1925 - assumed broken up. **[7]** Alliott Verdun Roe made the first sustained flight by a British national in a British designed and built aeroplane 23-7-09 at Lea Marshes. **[8]** Blériot was the first aircraft to fly the Irish Sea 22-4-12 - Denys Corbett Wilson piloting. **[9]** Almost certainly owned by North Wales-based Vivian Hewitt. Co-incidentally, Hewitt was *second* across the Irish Sea, on 26-4-1912 in a Blériot. Robert Blackburn – aviation pioneer and founder of the company that carried his name, bought it for £60 in 1916 and kept it at Brough until presenting it to the museum. **[10]** Lilienthal original held at Wroughton, Wilts. **[11]** S1595, piloted by Flt Lt J Boothman at Calshot, 13-9-31 secured the Schneider Trophy for the UK at 340.05mph. **[12]** First British jet, first flew at Cranwell 15-5-41, pilot P E G 'Gerry' Sayer. **[13]** Official name Rolls-Royce Thrust Measuring Rig, but universally known as the 'Flying Bedstead'. **[14]** P.1127 prototype - first tethered hover 21-10-60 - on loan from the RAF Museum. **[15]** 'Eindecker' was being ferried from Valenciennes to Wasquehal to start its operational career when it force-landed behind the lines. Evaluated at Upavon and retrospectively given the captured aircraft serial XG4, but probably never wore it.

Andrew Martin International: The famous Knightsbridge store. **www.andrewmartin.co.uk**

❑ XS100		Folland Gnat T.1	64	ex Fyfield, Hurn, Ipswich, Halton 8561M (14-11-77), 4 FTS. Forward fuselage, stored, off-site	1-20

SOUTH LAMBETH on the A3203 east of Lambeth Palace

Imperial War Museum London: Runs several sites. From a *W&R* point of view the other dominant one is Duxford, Cambs, but there is also IWM North at Manchester, Gtr Man. For completeness, there are two other London-based venues: HMS *Belfast* and the Churchill War Rooms – both brilliant, but non-aviation, venues.

◆ *Lambeth Road, SE1 6HZ* | **0207 416 5000** | **email** via website | **www.iwm.org.uk**

❑ N6812		Sopwith 2F1 Camel	1918	ex Duxford, South Lambeth, 'F3043', Yeovilton, Honington, Cardington, South Kensington (store), South Lambeth. Beardmore-built. Acquired 1920, returned by 7-2014	[1]	1-24
❑ R6915		V-S Spitfire I	40	ex Duxford, South Lambeth, Cardiff, RNDU, 57 OTU, 61 OTU, 609. SOC 21-6-47. Arrived 15-1-14		1-24
❑ DV372	'POF'	Avro Lancaster I	43	ex Duxford, South Lambeth, Croydon, 1651 CU, 467. SOC 4-1-45. Acquired 1960. Metropolitan-Vickers built. *Old Fred*. Cockpit		1-24
❑ ZD461	'51A'	BAe/McDD Harrier GR.9A	89	ex Duxford, Cottesmore, 4, 20, GR.7, 1. Damaged 26-1-10, SOC 14-12-10. Acquired 14-3-12, arrived 2-12-13		1-24
❑ 477663		Fieseler Fi 103F-1 (V-1)	44	BAPC.198, ex Duxford, South Lambeth. World War Two and Holocaust gallery		1-24

❑ 3685 'Y2-176'	Mitsubishi A6M3 *Zeke*	c43	ex Duxford (arrived 1986), Boise, USA, Taroa, Marshall Islands. Arrived by 7-14		1-24
❑ –	Yokosuka Ohka 11	45	BAPC.159, ex Duxford, Chattenden. Acquired 4-11. Arrived 2-3-20, 'hung' 6-3-20	[2]	1-24

■ **[1]** Flown by Lt S D Culley off a lighter towed by HMS *Redoubt* on 11-8-18 to intercept, and shoot down, the Zeppelin L53. **[2]** Restoration of the Ohka revealed it to be composite, from at least two examples. The fuselage bears the number '1100' while the nose/warhead section carries '1174'.

UXBRIDGE on the A4020 south of the town

Battle of Britain Bunker and Visitor Centre: Fantastic amount to see above ground: guided tours of 11 Group's command bunker, 60ft below and in use from 1939 to 1958, are available by prior booking *only*.

◆ **01895 238154 | bunker@hillingdon.gov.uk | www.battleofbritainbunker.co.uk**

❑ 'L1035'	'SH-D'	V-S Spitfire FSM	~	BAPC.500. GB Replicas-built. 64 Sqn colours	1-24
❑ 'P3873'	'YO-H'	Hawker Hurricane FSM	~	BAPC.499. GB Replicas-built. 401 Sqn colours	1-24
❑ 'P3901'	'RF-E'	Hawker Hurricane FSM	10	BAPC.475. GB Replicas-built. 303 Sqn colours, outside	1-24
❑ 'BS239'	'5R-E	V-S Spitfire FSM	10	BAPC.222. GB Replica-built. 64 Sqn colours, outside. Gale damaged by 4-23	1-24

GREATER MANCHESTER

Includes the unitary authorities of Bolton, Bury, Manchester, Oldham, Rochdale, Salford, Stockport, Tameside, Trafford and Wigan

APPELY BRIDGE on a minor road north of the A5209, west of the M6

Charity Farm: Camping and glamping site. ◆ *Prior arrangement* **only | www.charityfarm.co.uk**

❑- G-BVKB	Boeing 737-59D	94	ex Bruntingthorpe, British Midland. Last flight 23-5-13, de-reg 19-7-13. Forward fuselage	12-20

ASHTON-UNDER-LYNE on the A635 east of Manchester

No.**247 (Ashton-under-Lyne) Squadron Air Cadets**:

❑ XM474	Hunting Jet Provost T.3	60	ex South Reddish, Levenshulme, Firbeck, Heaton Chapel, Warrington, Shrewsbury 8121M (15-12-70), Shawbury, BSE, 6 FTS, CFS. Cockpit, first noted 12-18	12-18
❑ XN466 '29'	Hunting Jet Provost T.3A	60	ex Manchester, Radcliffe, 1 FTS, 7 FTS, 1 FTS. Crashed 29-1-63. Cockpit	6-23

BOLTON

Steak Out: Across the fuselage is the legend 'Steaks-on-a-Plane', a pun based on the puerile 2006 movie *Snakes on a Plane*. The steak house in Deane Road looks to be much more entertaining than the film. **Facebook** and the usual suspects

❑ VP-BRU	Boeing 737-500	91	ex Kemble, Yamal Airlines, F-GJNA. Last flight 6-10-14. Arrived 18-9-15. Forward fuselage	3-23

LEVENSHULME on the A6 southeast of Manchester

No.**1940 (Levenshulme) Squadron Air Cadets**: St Oswald's Road. Chipmunk PAX WG418, last noted as far back as January *2006*, was to be found at Syerston, Notts, by November 2023.

MANCHESTER

Imperial War Museum North: The building is designed to represent a shattered globe, and three 'shards' of this 'Air', 'Earth' and 'Water'. IWM, of course, runs a series of sites: from a *W&R* point of view the two dominant ones are Duxford, Cambs, and South Lambeth, Gtr Lon.

◆ *The Quays, Trafford Wharf Road, M17 1TZ* | **0207 416 5000** | **email** *via website* | **www.iwm.org.uk**

❑ 159233	'CG'	HS AV-8A Harrier	74	ex Yeovilton, VMA-231, USMC	1-24

Former **Science and Industry Museum Aviation Gallery**: Of the airframes unaccounted for in the great diaspora recounted in *W&R28* (p154); the following had been secreted away at Wroughton, Wilts: EoN 460 BQT / BGA.1156; Volmer BAPC.175; Flexiform BAPC.252 and the anonymous Skyhook. Spectrum BAPC.251 was fleetingly in Wiltshire before moving to St Athan, Wales, in January 2022. Mainair Tri-Flyer G-MJXE travelled to the British Hang-Gliding Museum at Weston-super-Mare, Somerset, via a brief sojourn at Hooton Park, Cheshire.

MANCHESTER AIRPORT or Ringway EGCC

Runway Visitor Park: Viewing platforms allow great photographic possibilities of the airliners taxying by and the eatery has huge windows allowing all-weather eating and ogling. The RJX is open to inspection all week, Concorde/Nimrod/Trident are pre-bookable. ◆ *Wilmslow Old Road, WA15 8XQ* | **0161 4893932** | **runwayvisitorpark.enquiries@manairport.co.uk** | **www.runwayvisitorpark.co.uk**

❑ G-AWZK	HS Trident 3B-101	71	ex Heathrow, BA, BEA. CoA 14-10-86, de-reg 29-5-90 Arrived 11-9-05. BEA colours	[1]	1-24
❑ G-BOAC	BAC/Sud Concorde 102	75	ex BA, G-N81AC. CoA 16-5-05, de-reg 4-5-04. Arr 31-10-03	[2]	1-24
❑ G-DMCA	Douglas DC-10-30	80	ex Monarch, N3016Z. CoA 11-3-03, de-reg 3-11-03. Arrived 19-12-03. Cockpit		1-24
❑ G-IRJX	HSA HS.146 RJX 100 T2	01	ex Woodford, G-6-378. de-reg 20-2-03. Arrived 6-2-03	[3]	1-24
❑ XV231	HS Nimrod MR.2	71	ex Kinloss, Kin Wing, Kin & St M Wing, 42, 203, 236 OCU. Arrived 21-4-10		1-24

■ **[1]** For details of the saving of this aircraft at Heathrow see **www.zulukilo.org.uk** **[2]** *Alpha-Charlie* factoids: Withdrawn from BA service 30-8-03, total hours 22,260, landings 7,730. It is on long-term loan from British Airways. **[3]** *Juliet-Xray* first flew 23-9-01 and last flew 6-2-03 when it arrived with a total of 198:23 hours and 135 landings.

Airport:

❑ –	BAe ATP	94	ex Woodford, Chadderton. Arrived 8-8-11. Rescue trainer	4-23

■ **[1]** Unfinished fuselage, very likely, c/n 2071.

◆ On the northern boundary of the airport, close to the threshold of Runway 24 Right, is the HQ of *W&R*'s publishers, **Crécy Publishing**, and its sister company Airplan Flight Equipment. The well-stocked shop is always well worth a visit. ◆ *1a Ringway Trading Estate, Shadowmoss Road, Manchester, M222 5LH* | **0161 4990024** | **www.crecy.co.uk**

MANCHESTER BARTON AERODROME (Note yet another change of name.) EGCB

The Deck 747: (Previously Manchester Flight Sim) Also has a wholly synthetic A320 simulator. The Commander is believed to be up for disposal. ◆ *Prior arrangement* **only** | **www.thedeck747.com**

❑ G-BYGA*	Boeing 747-436	98	ex Kemble, Heathrow, BA. De-reg 21-1-21. Flight deck, arrived 11-8-22		6-23
❑ N9AC	Rockwell Commander 112TC		cockpit as sim, first noted 1-21	[1]	5-23

■ **[1]** The Commander's tail *had* been displayed as a sign, including the legend 'Alpine Commander'.

Also: Sherwood Ranger G-GKFC has been deleted.

OLDHAM Last noted in June 2019 at Oldham College, the fuselage of Boeing 737 EI-CKR was scrapped, circa 2020.

ROYTON on the A671 north of Oldham

No.**1855 (Royton) Squadron Air Cadets**: *W&R28* recorded the departure of long-termer Meteor NF(T).14 WS726 in December 2021: it moved to Billericay, Essex, ending 54 years 'on duty' with the cadets.

STALYBRIDGE on the A6018 east of Ashton-under-Lyne

Top Gun Flight Simulator Centre: Waterloo Court. ◆ *Prior permission* **only** | **www.topgunflightsimulator.co.uk**

❑ XK637	'56'	DH Vampire T.11	56	ex Millom, Royton, Woodford, Chester, St Athan, 4 FTS, 7 FTS. Hawarden-built. SOC 30-11-67. Cockpit	1-20
❑ '47'	692147	Aero L29 Delfin	~	ex Ashton-under-Lyne, Market Drayton, Romanian AF. Cockpit, simulator	1-20

STOCKPORT on the A6 southeast of Manchester

Roger Light: The collection also includes a couple of 'mini' balloons. Campbell-Bensen B-8 G-ASNY is on loan to the Newark Air Museum at Newark, Notts. Bensen B-8 G-BJZY is the tail section only and has been deleted.

◆ **Private** *collection, prior arrangement* **only**

❑	G-ATLH	Fewsdale Tiger Mk.1	r65	ex Thornaby-on-Tees. De-reg 10-2-82	10-23
❑	G-AXIY	Bird Gyroplane	r69	de-reg 9-8-91	10-23
❑	G-AXVK	Campbell Cricket	70	CoA 27-4-05, de-reg 15-10-18	10-23
❑	G-AXYZ	WHE Airbuggy	75	CoA 22-12-92, de-reg 8-9-06	10-23
❑	G-AXZB	WHE Airbuggy	80	de-reg 8-9-06	10-23
❑	G-BIFN	Bensen B-8MR	80	de-reg 24-2-10	10-23

Peter and **Mike Rolfe**: The cockpit of Sea Venom FAW.22 XG692 travelled to Kinloss, Scotland, 4th June 2023.

WOODFORD between the A5102 and A523 southwest of Poynton

Avro Heritage Museum: The collection has a pleasing accessibility policy: as well as the Vulcan, other cockpits can be 'sampled'– best enquire before a visit for availability. Special events are staged throughout the 'season'.

◆ *Chester Road, Woodford, SK7 1AG* | **01625 877534** | **avroheritage@gmail.com** | **www.avroheritagemuseum.co.uk**

❑	G-AGPG		Avro XIX Srs 2	45	ex Liverpool, Market Drayton, Hooton Park, Chadderton, Brenzett, Lympne, Southend, Ekco, Skyways, Avro. CoA 13-12-71; de-reg 5-11-75. Arr 5-12-16. Forward fuselage	[1]	1-24
❑	G-ORAL		HS HS.748-2A/334	77	ex Speke, Hooton Park, Blackpool, Reed, Emerald, Janes, G-BPDA, G-GLAS, 9Y-TFS, G-11-8. CoA 12-11-07, de-reg 15-6-09. *Paper Plane*. Cockpit. Arrived 8-17		1-24
❑	–		Avro Type F replica	10	BAPC.328, ex Manchester. Roe Heritage Group-built. Arrived 6-3-18	[2]	1-24
❑	'R5868'	'PO-S'	Avro Lancaster replica	15	BAPC.471, ex Scampton, North Coates. Forward fuselage. Arrived 13-11-17. 467 Sqn colours	[3]	1-24
❑	WK118	'CQ'	EE Canberra TT.18	54	ex Worcester, Stock, Wyton, 100, 7, B.2. 59, 103. Avro-built. Cockpit. Installed 11-8-16		1-24
❑	XM602		Avro Vulcan B.2	63	ex Swinton, Bruntingthorpe, Woodford, St Athan 8771M (16-3-83), 101, Wadd Wing, 35, 230 OCU, Wadd Wing, Cottesmore Wing, 12. Cockpit. Arrived 20-4-13		1-24
❑	XM603		Avro Vulcan B.2	63	ex 44, 101, Wadd Wing, Scampton Wing, 9. Flew in 12-3-82		1-24
❑	XV106		Vickers VC10 C.1K	67	ex Bruntingthorpe, 101, 10. Last flight 17-12-12. Arrived 8-9-16. Cockpit	[4]	1-24
❑	XV235		HS Nimrod MR.2	69	ex Scampton, Kinloss, Kin Wing, Kin & St M Wing, 42, Kinloss, St M, 236 OCU. Forward fuselage. Arrived 8-9-16		1-24

■ **[1]** Among other work, 'Aggie-Paggie' served as the test bed for the E320 weather radar for Concorde. Total time on retirement 1,948 hours.**[2]** On loan from Science and Industry Museum, Manchester. **[3]** Lancaster replica built by Martin Willoughby, using many original parts. It is finished in 467 Sqn colours, R5868 - see Hendon, Gtr Lon. Martin's father, Ted, worked as ground crew on the original. Previously on loan from Martin, the replica was acquired by the museum in late 2020. **[4]** On loan from Gary Spoors. The centre fuselage of XV106 is displayed at the South Wales Aviation Museum, St Athan, Wales. If the VC10 seems out of place, BAe Woodford inherited design authority for the tanker programme from Filton after the denationalisation of the consortium in 1986.

Store: *Not* available for inspection.

❑	G-CFTF	Roe Triplane I replica	09	ex Bicester, Brooklands, Manchester. De-reg 28-8-16, arrived 16-1-19. Stored	[1]	1-24
❑	TX235	Avro Anson C.19/2	46	ex Hooton Park (temporary), Baginton, Caernarfon, Higher Blagdon, Andover, Shawbury, SCS, FCCS, CTFU, OCTU, 64 GCS, 2 GCS. SOC 11-10-65. Arrived 8-9-20		1-24
❑	WR960	Avro Shackleton AEW.2	54	ex Manchester, Cosford, 8772M (28-11-82), 8, 205, A&AEE, 210, 42, 228. Arrived 17-1-22	[2]	1-24
❑	WZ744*	Avro 707C	53	ex Cosford, Topcliffe, Finningley, Colerne 7932M, RAE. Bracebridge Heath-built. Last flown 7-6-66. Arrived 14-11-22		1-24
❑	–*	HP Victor SIM	~	ex Neatishead, Newark, Ashby de Launde, Elvington, Marham, Warton. Arrived 3-22	[3]	1-24

■ **[1]** Triplane on loan; built by the Roe Heritage Group, on loan from Eric Alliott Verdon-Roe, grandson of 'AV'. Fitted with a 9hp JAP, it commenced flight trials in October 2009, achieving only limited 'hops'. **[2]** On loan from the RAF Museum. **[3]** Victor owned by Geremy Britton / Aircraft Preservation Foundation – see Bridlington, E Yorks.

MERSEYSIDE

Includes the unitary authorities of Knowsley, Liverpool, St Helens, Sefton, and Wirral

BIRKENHEAD Wirral

The planned Battle of the Atlantic Experience, to be sited close to the Woodside Ferry terminal, took delivery of the former IWM Duxford Avenger in April 2023. It is temporarily stored at the nearby premises of the Wirral Transport Museum and Heritage Tramway: it is ***not*** available for inspection.

❑	'46214'*	'X-3'	Grumman TBM-3E Avenger	44	ex Duxford, CF-KCG, RCN 326, USN 69327. General Motors-built. 'Lt George Bush' titling. *Ginny*. Arrived 5-4-23		4-23

KNOWSLEY on the B5194, north of J3 on the M57

Delta Force Paintball: At the Safari Park. ◆ *Prior arrangement* **only** | **www.paintballgames.co.uk**

❑	ZD278		Westland Lynx AH.7	83	ex Upminster, Ipswich, M Wallop	[1]	9-22

■ **[1]** The boom of ZD278 is fitted to XZ613 - see Billericay, Essex.

LIVERPOOL

Crowne Plaza Hotel: With the blessing of the hotel management, the **Speke Aerodrome Heritage Group** (SAHG) nurtures its collection. On the 'old' airport site, the superb hotel is a development of the 1930s terminal building. During late 2023 HS.748 G-BEJD was craned up and sits on its undercarriage and supports. Sharing the apron is the **Britannia Aircraft Preservation Trust** (BAPT) which continues with the challenging restoration of *Charlie-Fox*.

◆ *On the A561 | Occasional special events, otherwise by prior arrangement* **only** | *SAHG:* **bookings@spekeaero.org** | **www.facebook.com/SpekeAero** | *BAPT:* **www.facebook.com/britanniatrust**

❑	G-AMLZ		Percival Prince 6E	52	ex Haverigg, Caernarfon, Coventry, VR-TBN, Shell G-AMLZ. CoA 18-6-71, de-reg 9-10-84. Arr 23-11-08. Shell c/s	[1]	1-24
❑	G-ANCF		Bristol Britannia 308F	59	ex Kemble, Banwell, Brooklands, Manston, 5Y-AZP, G-ANCF, LV-GJB, LV-PPJ, G-ANCF, G-14-1, G-18-4, N6597C, G-ANCF. CoA 12-1-81, de-reg 21-2-84. Short-built. Arrived 7-3-07. British Eagle colours, *New Frontier*. BAPT		1-24
❑	G-BEJD		HS 748-1/105	61	ex Squires Gate, Emerald, LV-HHE, LV-PUF. CoA 29-3-06, de-reg 8-4-10. Arrived 20-10-11	[2]	1-24
❑	G-JMAC		BAe Jetstream 4100	92	ex Woodford, Prestwick, G-JAMD, G-JXLI. CoA 6-10-97, de-reg 21-5-03. Arrived 29-1-03. *Spirit of Speke*		1-24
❑	G-SEXY		American AA-1 Yankee	70	ex G-AYLM. Damaged 11-2-94, de-reg 15-11-00. Arrived 2006. Dismantled		7-22
❑	WH291		Gloster Meteor F.8	51	ex Booker, Lasham, Kemble, 229 OCU, 85, CAW, 257. SOC 10-2-76. Arrived 3-11. 79 Sqn colours	[3]	1-24

■ **[1]**. *Lima-Zulu* factoids: last flown 13-11-73, total time 2,858 hours. **[2]** The only Srs 1 (15 built) surviving; so it's the oldest 748 extant; and the only complete civilian 748 preserved in the UK. **[3]** Meteor on loan from Mike Davey - see below and Newark, Notts.

Jordan and **Robbie Burgess**: Are *thought* to *still* keep the award-winning AV-8B locally ◆ *Prior arrangement* **only**

❑	162730		BAe/McDD AV-8B Harrier II	86	ex Peterborough, Charlwood, St Athan, Wyton, St Athan, USMC VMA-231. *Lucy*. Forward fuselage, trailer-mounted		12-17

Mike Davey - F-4 Phantom Preservation Society / Mike Davey Aero Collection: As well as his Meteor at the Crowne Plaza – see above – Mike has other airframes and here serves as a good place under which to list them. Having restored the cockpit of Avro XIX G-AGPG – now at the Avro Heritage Museum, Woodford – Mike has taken on one of 'Aggie-Paggie's' Cheetah XV complete with full nacelle and *retractable* main undercarriage. This is available for running at events. See also Newark, Notts, for Mike's *other* Phantom and Hooton Park, Cheshire.

◆ *Airframes held at dispersed locations,* **not** *available for inspection*

❑	XT895		McD Phantom FGR.2	68	ex 'Rayleigh', Foulness, Valley 9171M, 74, 228 OCU, 92, 228 OCU, 111, 6, 228 OCU, 6, 228 OCU. Damaged 10-10-92. Cockpit. Arrived by 11-20	[1]	6-23
❑	ZE352	'G'	McD F-4J(UK) Phantom	67	ex Hooton Park, Haverigg, Preston, Hooton Park area, Stock, Foulness, Pendine, Laarbruch 9086M (30-8-84), 74, Wattisham, 74, USN 153783, VX-4, VMFA-333. Cockpit		12-20

❑ -		McD Phantom SIM	~	ex Leuchars. Redifon-built		12-20

■ **[1]** XT895 was involved in trials over Cardigan Bay, out of Valley, on 10-10-92 when an errant Skyflash missile impacted the starboard intake: leaving a small hole visible to this day. That was sufficient to have it struck off charge and issued to the Valley fire crews.

Liverpool University: Last noted in June 2013, the cockpit of Tomahawk G-LSFD has been deleted.

LIVERPOOL (JOHN LENNON) AIRPORT or Speke – *Above Us Only Sky*

EGGP

❑ G-BGSH	Piper Tomahawk 112	79	de-reg 31-7-17		6-21
❑ G-BNYK	Piper Tomahawk 112	82	ex N2376V. De-reg 14-12-18. Cockpit		7-20

NEW BRIGHTON on the A554 north of Birkenhead

Fort Perch Rock: Home of the **Warplane Wreck Investigation Group** since 1977. Displays include the 'Luftwaffe over Merseyside' exhibition and a section dedicated to 610 (County of Chester) Squadron.

◆ *Marine Promenade, CH45 2JU* | **info@fortperchrock.org.uk** | **www.fortperchrock.org.uk**

❑ XE584	Hawker Hunter FGA.9	56	ex Hooton Park, Woodford, Barton, Chelford, Macclesfield, Bitteswell, G-9-450, 208, 8, 1. SOC 12-2-76. 111 Sqn colours. Cockpit. Arrived 5-22	[1]	10-23
❑ –	Hawker Sea Hawk	~	BAPC.352, ex Hooton Park, Peasedown St John, Cardiff-Wales. Red scheme. Cockpit, arrived 5-22	[1]	10-23

■ **[1]** During 2022 Grahame Sparkes transferred ownership to Dougie Darroch.

WOODVALE AIRFIELD on the A565 north of Formby

RAF Woodvale: A Hawk 'guards' the resident Tutor fleet.

❑ XX247	HS Hawk T.1A	78	ex Shawbury, 19, 100, 1 TWU, 2 TWU, 1 TWU. Last flight 7-4-11. SOC 5-12-17. Arrived 27-11-17		1-24

WEST MIDLANDS

Within the administrative regional county boundaries can be found the unitary authorities of Birmingham, Coventry, Dudley, Sandwell, Solihull, Walsall and Wolverhampton

BIRMINGHAM

Thinktank - Millennium Discovery Centre, the former Birmingham Science Museum.

◆ *Curzon Street, B4 7XG* | **0121 3488000** | **email** via website | **www.birminghammuseums.org.uk/thinktank**

❑ 'P3395'	'JX-B'	Hawker Hurricane IV	43 KX829	ex Loughborough, 631, 1606 Flt, 137. SOC 8-3-46. Acquired 1961. 1 Sqn colours		1-24
❑ ML427	'HK-A'	V-S Spitfire IX	44	ex Castle Bromwich, St Athan 6457M (15-10-47), FLS. CBAF-built. Acquired 1958. Fighter Leader School colours		1-24

Also: A Hunter is plinth-mounted outside **Specialist Computer Centres Technology Campus** at the junction of Westwood Avenue and Battery Way in Tyseley.

❑ WT723	'692'	Hawker Hunter PR.11	55 G-PRII	ex St Athan, 'XG164', N723WT, A2616 [3] (19-3-93) Culdrose, WT723, FRADU, 764, GA.11, 764, F.4 14. CoA 9-6-16, de-reg 8-2-21. Plinth-mounted by 9-21		12-23

BRIERLEY HILL on the A461 southwest of Dudley

Mason Metals: Disposed of the cockpit of Andover E.3A XS643 to a private owner in the Coventry, Warks, area in September 2020; it moved on the Bramcote, Warks, by August 2022.

COVENTRY

Coventry University: The faculty of Engineering and Computing, Aerospace Workshop in Gulson Road has a Harrier.

◆ *Prior arrangement* **only** | **www.coventry.ac.uk**

❑ XW270	HS Harrier T.4	70	ex Ipswich, Bruntingthorpe, Cranfield, Wittering, 4, 1, 233 OCU, 1, 233 OCU. SOC 10-2-92	[1]	1-24

■ **[1]** Fitted with the wings of XV748 - which is to be found whole at Elvington, N Yorks. The cockpit is fitted out as a flight sim.

Also: The Heath Parasol is at a *private* location in the area.

❑ G-AFZE		Heath Parasol	39	ex Horley. De-reg 1-5-66, restored 17-7-74	8-21

HOCKLEY HEATH east of junction 4, M42, south of Solihull

Delta Force Paintball Solihull: ◆ *Prior arrangement* **only** | **www.paintballgames.co.uk**

❑ G-SHIP		Piper Aztec 250F	76	ex -?-, Hockley Heath, Coventry, Birmingham, N62490. Crashed 4-12-83, de-reg 13-2-89	1-20
❑ XX739	'I'	SEPECAT Jaguar GR.1	74	ex Upminster, Ipswich, Syerston, Cosford 8902M (27-5-86), Halton, Shawbury, Gib Det, 6, 226 OCU. First noted 12-18	3-23

SOLIHULL

Solihull College: At Woodlands Campus, Auckland Drive. The college needs wiring diagrams for its Jetstream – can readers help? (Replies via the website.) ◆ *Prior arrangement* **only** | **www.solihull.ac.uk**

❑ XX478	'564'	HP Jetstream T.2	73	ex Ipswich, Culdrose, 750, RAF T.1 CFS, G-AXXT SAL-completed. De-reg 5-12-83, last flown 31-3-11. F/n 5-16	1-24

Also: A local *private* owner may still have the cockpit of a HS.146 converted into a summerhouse.

❑ HB-IXX		HSA HS.146 RJ100	95	ex Sunderland, Kemble, Swiss, Crossair, G-6-262. Woodford-built. Cockpit	8-17

TETTENHALL south of the A41 northwest of Wolverhampton

Tettenhall Transport Heritage Centre: Based in a former Great Western Railway goods depot, the centre concentrates on the motive transport heritage of Wolverhampton and locality. ◆ *Henwood Road, WV6 9NX.* | **alecbrew@hotmail.co.uk** | **Facebook.com/p/Tettenhall-Transport-Heritage-Centre/**

❑ G-MJIA		Flexiform Striker	82	ex Penkridge. CoA 20-9-96, de-reg 5-11-13. First noted 6-12		1-24
❑ G-MMFS		MBA Tiger Cub 440	83	ex Baxterley, Abbots Bromley, Wolverhampton, Otherton. *Black Adder*. CoA 27-7-01, de-reg 11-3-10. Travelling exhibit		1-24
❑ G-MVJM		Microflight Spectrum	88	ex Baxterley. De-reg 22-8-12. *Poppy*. First noted 4-15		1-24
❑ –	'20'	S-D Demoiselle replica	64	BAPC.194, ex Stafford, Wyton, Cardington, Brooklands, Henlow, Gatow. First noted 8-16		1-24
❑ –		Breen hang-glider	~	BAPC.432, ex Stafford. First noted 8-16	[1]	1-24
❑ 'PD685'		Slingsby Cadet TX.1	~	BAPC.355, ex Penkridge, W'hampton, Stoke. Fuselage	[2]	1-24
❑ 'RG907'		Miles Martinet replica	18	BAPC.514. Cockpit	[3]	1-24
❑ WJ576		EE Canberra T.17	53	ex Baxterley, Wolverhampton, Bruntingthorpe, Cardiff, St Athan, 360, *Swifter* Flight, 231 OCU. HP-built. SOC 9-3-83. Cockpit. Arrived 11-4-15		1-24
❑ WK576		DHC Chipmunk T.10	52	ex W'hampton, Lichfield, 8357M (10-8-73), AOTS, 3/4 CAACU, Cam, Oxf, Lon, Cam, Lon, Cam, Hull, Cam, Birm, Cam UASs, 22 RFS. Hawarden-built. Cockpit. Arr 5-14	[4]	1-24
❑ WN516		BP Balliol T.2	53	ex Baxterley, Haverigg, Sunderland, Failsworth, RAFC. Blackburn-built. SOC 26-6-57. Forward fuselage. Arr 11-4-15		1-24
❑ WN534		BP Balliol T.2	54	ex Baxterley, Wolverhampton, Bacup, Salford, Failsworth, Silloth, RAFC. Blackburn-built. SOC 26-6-57. Cockpit		1-24
❑ WT877		Slingsby Cadet TX.3	51	ex Penkridge, W'hampton, Walsall, Swinderby, St Athan GC, Syerston, 621 GS, 625 GS, 643 GS, 22 GS. SOC 21-8-86		1-24
❑ WZ755	FSC	Slingsby Grasshopper TX.1	52	BGA.3481, ex Baxterley, Wolverhampton, Gallows Hill, Brunton, Barnstaple. CoA 30-4-93		1-24
❑ XD445	'51'	DH Vampire T.11	54	ex Baxterley, Abbots Bromley, Hemswell, Cleethorpes, Huddersfield, Woodford, Chester, St Athan, 4 FTS, 5 FTS, Bückeburg SF. SOC 18-3-63. Arrived 11-4-15. Cockpit, 79 Sqn c/s	[5]	1-24
❑ XP494		Slingsby Grasshopper TX.1	61	ex Baxterley, W'hampton, Rattlesden, Breighton, Stoke, Syerston, Stamford, Cosford, Ratcliffe, Syerston		1-24

■ [1] Original design by Gerry Breen and Sqn Ldr Dave Willis made the first-ever flights off Ben Nevis, 1973. The RAF Museum was a sponsor of early Breen ventures; hence it came into the collection. **[2]** Cadet restored to represent an example that served from Walsall with 43 Gliding School. **[3]** Wooden framed and using many original parts, including canopy. **[4]** WK576 on loan from 1046 (Fordhouses) Sqn Air Cadets. **[5]** Vampire flew in 79 Sqn colours when it served as a 'hack' with the Bückeburg Station Flight.

WALSALL

Dinosaur World Adventure Golf: Part of the Calderfields Driving Range. | **www.dinosaurworldadventuregolf.co.uk**

❑ G-BTWX* SOCATA TB-9 Tampico 91 crashed 24-3-16, de-reg 24-1-17 1-24

WILLENHALL on the A454 west of J10 of the M6

Cable and Alloys: Springvale Street. The Lansen was offered for sale during April 2023.

❑ G-BMSG SAAB Lansen 56 ex Cranfield, Swedish AF, Malmslatt, Fv32028. G-BMSG de-reg 20-6-14. Cockpit, wings, and other parts 4-23

❑ ZD281 'K' Westland Lynx AH.1 83 ex Fleetlands, M Wallop. Fuselage, first noted 1-15 12-23

NORFOLK

ATTLEBOROUGH on the A11 southwest of Norwich

Dave Pope: Keeps his Raven at a *private* address in the locality.

❑ G-MTMK Southdown Raven X 87 ex Heckington. CoA 1-8-02, de-reg 11-5-05. Arrived 19-7-18 1-20

BIRCHAM NEWTON between the B1153 and B1155 northeast of Docking

RAF Bircham Newton Heritage Centre: The former RAF station is home of the National Construction College East and, thanks to that institution, volunteers have established a tribute to the airfield (1918-1962) and its satellite at Docking.

◆ *Occasional open days: otherwise* group *tours by prior arrangement* | **www.facebook.com/groups/**

BODNEY CAMP on the B1108 west of Watton

Army Training Estate East: South of the camp is an extensive training area, centred upon Stanford Water and referred to as STANTA, for Stanford Training Area. See also East Wretham, below.

❑ XS872 Westland Wessex HAS.1 65 ex Wroughton, Farnborough, A2666, Leatherhead, Wroughton, *Eagle* SAR Flt, 706, 820. SOC 18-5-78 7-23

CANTLEY on the B1140 south of Acle

Great British Aircraft Spares: Bruce Gordon's treasure trove has been wound down, having helped with many projects over the years. Vampire T.11s XD547 and XH328 moved on to the Cranfield, Beds, area. Bruce's swansong was as a consultant and to restore Vampire FB.9 WL505 for its lead role in the Disney 'short' *The Shepherd* – see West Raynham, Norfolk, for the full story. This rebirth used the wings of T.11 XD624 and other 'Vampire-alia' held by Bruce. As *W&R29* closed for press, the anonymous Pawnee fuselage frame had been offered up for disposal and very likely moved on in one form or another.

CLENCHWARTON on minor roads west of King's Lynn

Along with a huge anchor, the fuselage of a Robin 'guards' the entrance to a reclamation yard.

❑ G-OCFC Robin R2160 02 crashed 27-5-15, de-reg 9-11-16. Fuselage. F/n 12-18 6-22

COLTISHALL or Scottow Enterprise Park, east of the B1150, north of the village

RAF Station Coltishall Heritage Trust: Centred upon the main guardroom of the former and famous RAF station. Pre-booked 'Talk and Tour' events are regularly staged, plus occasional special events.

◆ *Former Main Guardroom, Building 40, NR10 5FB* | **rafscht@btinternet.com** | **www.rafscht.co.uk**

❑ XS421* EE Lightning T.5 65 ex Neatishead, Rayleigh, Foulness, RAE, 23, 111, 226 OCU. SOC 22-10-75. Cockpit, arrived 20-7-23 7-23

Swift Aircraft: As well as developing its own light aircraft, the company supports and overhauls Slingsby T.67s. An unflown example is used for engineering development. ◆ *Prior arrangement* **only** | **www.swiftaircraft.com**

❑ G-BYBX Slingsby T.67M Firefly 98 ex Teversham, Kirbymoorside. De-reg 29-1-15. Arr 18-12-20 12-20

DEREHAM on the A47 west of Norwich

The Moth Minors are at a *private* workshop in the *general* area. Pilatus P.3 A-806 (G-BTLL) was airworthy by early 2022.

❑ G-AFNI	DH Moth Minor	39	ex Stalbridge, Woodley, W7972 100 GCF, Foulsham SF, 241, G-AFNI. CoA 26-5-67	6-20
❑ G-AFOB	DH Moth Minor	39	ex Dorchester, Old Warden, Duxford, X5117 10 OAFU, St Andrews UAS, 513, G-AFOB. CoA 11-5-93	6-20

EASTON on the A47 west of Norwich

Congo Rapids Crazy Golf: Within the Norwich Family Golf Centre is a zebra-striped KR-2. | **www.congorapids.co.uk**

❑ G-WYNN	Rand KR-2	95	de-reg 17-7-04	1-24

EAST WRETHAM east of the A1075 north of Thetford

Thorpe Camp: See also the 'northern' end of this area, listed under Bodney Camp, Norfolk.

❑ XM386 '08'	Hunting Jet Provost T.3	59	ex St Athan, Halton 8076M (2-2-70), Shawbury, 2 FTS, CFS	[1]	5-19
❑ XT643	Westland Scout AH.1	66	ex Waterbeach, Wroughton, 660, 661		5-19

■ **[1]** The wings alongside the fuselage of XM386 are from XM404 - see Bournemouth, Dorset.

FORNCETT ST PETER west of the A140 and Long Stratton

Norfolk Tank Museum: Has an impressive collection of 'Cold War' era hardware; some of it 'in steam'.

◆ *Station Road, NR16 1HZ* | **01508 532650** | **info@norfolktankmuseum.co.uk** | **www.norfolktankmuseum.co.uk**

❑ XL739	Saro Skeeter AOP.12	58	ex Wattisham, Detmold, 15/19 Hussars, 1 Wing, 651, A&AEE,BATUS, A&AEE. SOC 11-10-68. Stored. Arrived c2011	6-23

FRETTENHAM east of the A140, southwest of Coltishall

New Farm Aviation Heritage Group: Material held includes the remains of 458th BG, 754th BS B-24H Liberator 42-50404 *Belle of Boston* which crashed on take-off from Horsham St Faith (Norwich Airport) on 8th May 1944.

◆ *Buxton Road, NR12 7NG. Regular open days, otherwise by appointment* | **www.facebook.com/newfarmaviation**

GREAT YARMOUTH

Vauxhall Holiday Park, Acle New Road. The Aerobat was written out of *W&R28* (p161) but it is still to be found in 'Louie the Lion's Adventure Golf'. ◆ *via* **www.parkdeanresorts.co.uk/**

❑ G-BPRO	Cessna A.150K	70	ex N221AR. CoA 24-3-99, de-reg 23-11-00	8-22

HARDWICK or Shelton Common, east of the A140, west of Bungay

93rd Bomb Group Museum: An incredible museum set in Nissen (sorry, Quonset) huts and the all-important Mess (sorry, that would be Chow) Hall on the former Station 104's Communal Site A. The website is a delight!

◆ *Denton Road / Topcroft Street, NR35 2BA. Regular open days, or by prior arrangement* | **www.93rd-bg-museum.org**

HETHEL north of the B1135, east of Wymondham

389th Bomb Group Memorial Exhibition and **Home for the 466th BG Attlebridge**: As well as two Nissen huts, Station 114's wartime chapel is a unique element of Eighth Air Force history.

◆ *Potash Lane, NR14 8EY. Regular open days, or by prior arrangement* | **www.hethel389th.wordpress.com**

KING'S LYNN

Tornado cockpit at a *private* house. See under Blackpool, Lancs, for a candidate.

❑ -	Panavia Tornado EMU / FSM	~	cockpit – see above	12-20

LANGHAM south of Stiffkey, between Cockthorpe and Langham

Langham Dome: Announcing itself as "small building, big story", the rare anti-aircraft gunnery trainer dome includes exhibitions on the former airfield's heritage and more. The Spitfire comes off its plinth and 'hibernates' for the winter.

◆ *Langham Road, Cockthorne, NR25 7BP* | **01328 830169** | **admin@langhamdome.org** | **www.langhamdome.org**

❑ -	V-S Spitfire FSM	~	'The Silver Spitfire', pole-mounted, unveiled 21-8-20	1-24

LONG STRATTON on the A140 south of Norwich

Stratton Motor Company: Last noted in August 2018, Eurocopter Tiger FSM 'F-ZWWW' has been deleted.

MARHAM AIRFIELD south of the A47 west of Swaffham EGYM

Marham Aviation Heritage Centre: Within the former station church. The cockpits are used for special occasions and are not generally accessible. ◆ *By appointment* **only** | **marham.aviation.heritage@gmail.com**

❑ WH850		EE Canberra T.4	54	ex Narborough, Winthorpe, Barton, Chelford, Samlesbury, St Athan, Laarbruch SF, Wildenrath SF, 14, 88, Marham SF. SOC 26-11-81. Cockpit. Arrived 10-2-16		10-22
❑ XD857		Vickers Valiant BK.1	57	ex Flixton, Manston, Rayleigh, Foulness, 49. SOC 6-3-65. Arrived 5-5-17. Flightdeck	[1]	11-20
❑ XL160		HP Victor K.2	61	ex Flixton, Walpole, Marham 8910M (2-7-86), 57, 55, 57, 55, Witt Wing, 100, Rolls-Royce. Cockpit. Arrived 27-4-18	[1]	11-20

■ **[1]** On loan from Garry O'Keefe.

RAF Marham: Tornado GR.4 ZD744 made the trek to Montrose, Scotland, on 19th May 2022. GR.4 ZG791 was presented to Australia, and was dispatched to Bull Creek, Western Oz, in January 2022.

❑ XH169		EE Canberra PR.9	60	ex 39, 1 PRU, 39, 58. Short-built. *End of an Era*. Unveiled 20-11-07, displayed	1-24
❑ ZA407		Panavia Tornado GR.1	83	ex 9336M, 617, TWCU. Last flown 22-11-01. Removed from its plinth 3-3-20	7-23
❑ ZA614	'076'	Panavia Tornado GR.4	82	ex 9, GR.1, 15.Unveiled on the 'gate' 4-8-21	1-24

NEATISHEAD east of the A1151, north of Hoveton, near Horning

RAF Air Defence Radar Museum Norfolk: Dedicated to every aspect of radar, air defence and battle management and housed in the original 1942 Operations Building, exhibits include a Battle of Britain 'Ops' Filter Room, a 'Cold War' era 'Ops' Room and a ROC Field Post. Don't miss the 'Crumbs' cafe!

The anonymous Victor SIM moved to Woodford, Gtr Man, in early March 2022.

◆ *Off the A1062, Birds Lane, NR12 8YB* | **01692 631485** | **manager@radarmuseum.co.uk** | **www.radarmuseum.co.uk**

❑ XX979	SEPECAT Jaguar GR.1A	75	ex Coltishall 9306M, St Athan, DTEO, A&AEE. Cockpit	1-24
❑ ZE936	Panavia Tornado F.3	88	ex Church Fenton, Bedford, 229 OCU. Arrived 2-8-17. Cockpit	1-24

Carl Lamb: Lightning F.2A cockpit XN795 moved to Binbrook, Lincs, on 16th December 2023. T.5 cockpit XS421 travelled to Coltishall, Norfolk, in July 2023.

NORWICH

Second Air Division Memorial Library: Plenty of memorabilia on show, along with the amazing 'Friendly Invasion' mural, all dedicated to the division's B-24 Liberator-equipped units.

◆ *The Forum, Millennium Plain, NR2 1AW* | **01603 774747** | **americanlibrary@norfolk.gov.uk** | **www.2ndair.org.uk**

County Hall: In Martineau Lane, off the A1054 between Lakenham and Old Lakenham south of the city centre.

❑ XW563	SEPECAT Jaguar S.07	70	ex Coltishall, 8563M (26-1-78), 'XX822', Brüggen. A&AEE, Warton. *Spirit of Coltishall*. Arrived 27-2-07. Displayed	[1]	12-23

■ **[1]** Composite, based upon the majority of S.07 XW563 which first flew 12-6-70.

Jaguar XW563 guarding Norfolk's County Hall, September 2022. *Nigel Price*

Also: **Dave Higgins** *should* continue to work on a Chipmunk locally; he also owns Whirlwind XJ758 at Welshpool, Wales.

❑ WB560		DHC Chipmunk T.10	50	ex S' Molton, Doncaster, Firbeck, Fownhope, St Athan, Oxf UAS, 242 OCU, 2 SoTT, South Cerney SF, ITS, 7 AEF, Nott UAS, 4 AEF. Hatfield-built. Cockpit, composite. Arrived mid-2012		5-16

NORWICH AIRPORT or Horsham St Faith

EGSH

City of Norwich Aviation Museum (CNAM): See under West Walton Highway, Norfolk, for comments on CNAM's magnificent rescue of the former Fenland and West Norfolk Aviation Museum's extensive and important artefact collection. Construction of a new display hall commenced early 2023.

The RAF **100 Group Association** bases its exceptional collection at CNAM and the museum has been 'adopted' by the **74 'Tiger' Squadron Association**; the unit was based at Horsham St Faith and nearby Coltishall. Other displays show the history of RAF Horsham St Faith, Bomber Command, the Eighth Air Force, the role of women in aviation and local aviation pioneers; and there is Friendship Tearoom to sample.

Evans VP-2 G-BTAZ moved to Foxhall, Suffolk, by March 2023. The anonymous Scimitar CIM relocated – on loan – to Carlisle, Cumbria, by October 2023.

◆ *Off the A140, Old Norwich Road, NR10 3JF* | **01603 893080** | **admin@cnam.co.uk** | **www.cnam.org.uk**

❑ G-ASAT		MS Rallye Club	62	ex Defford. CoA 2-8-02, de-reg 18-1-11, arrived 12-6-12	[1]	1-24
❑ G-ASKK		HP Herald 211	63	ex Air UK, PP-ASU, G-ASKK, PI-C910, CF-MCK. CoA 19-5-85, de-reg 29-4-85. Arrived 5-85		1-24
❑ G-AYMO		Piper Aztec 250	65	ex Wellesbourne Mountford, 5Y-ACX, N5845Y. De-reg 27-11-13. Arrived 5-16		1-24
❑ G-BCDN		Fokker Friendship 200	63	ex airport, Air UK, PH-OGA, JA8615, LV-PMR, PH-FDP. CoA 19-7-96, de-reg 28-1-98. Arrived 7-4-17		1-24
❑ G-BHMY		Fokker Friendship 200	62	ex KLM UK, Air UK, F-GBDK, F-GBRV, PK-PFS, JA8606, PH-FDL. CoA 22-5-99, de-reg 27-2-03. Arrived 10-8-00		1-24
❑ G-OVNE		Cessna 401A	69	ex airport, N401XX, N171SF, N71SF, N6236Q. CoA 8-10-92, de-reg 8-2-94. Arrived 2006		1-24
❑ EI-RJN		HSA HS.146-RJ85	99	ex airport, Cityjet, N526XJ, G-6-351. Woodford-built. Last flight 16-2-19. Moved on site 31-10-20		1-24
❑ N30NW*		Piper Twin Comanche	64	ex Old Buckenham. First noted -22		1-24
❑ –		Westland Whirlwind I rep	06	BAPC.433, forward fuselage. *Crikey!*	[2]	1-24
❑ WH984		EE Canberra B.15	55	ex Mold, Sealand, Bruntingthorpe, Hinckley, B'thorpe, Cosford 8101M (6-8-70), Akrotiri Wing (32/73), Handling Sqn, B.6, 9, Binbrook SF, 9. Short-built. Last flown 11-3-69. Arrived 30-11-05. Cockpit. 32 Sqn colours	[3]	1-24
❑ WJ633	'EF'	EE Canberra T.17	54	ex Wyton, St Athan, Wyton, 360, B.2, 231 OCU, 100. HP-built. Arrived 2007. Cockpit	[4]	1-24
❑ WK654	'B'	Gloster Meteor F.8	52	ex 'WL135' Neatishead 8092M, Kemble, 85, CFE, Odiham SF, AWFCS, 247. SOC 9-4-70. Arr 25-11-95. 245 Sqn c/s		1-24
❑ WM267		Gloster Meteor NF.11	53	ex ?, Walpole, Firbeck, Hemswell, Misson, 151, 256, 11. AWA-built. SOC 30-10-67. Arrived 11-9-06. Cockpit		1-24
❑ –		Hawker Hunter F.6	c57	ex Wymondham, Duxford. Cockpit. 74 Sqn c/s, sim	[5]	1-24
❑ XD434*	'25'	DH Vampire T.11	54	ex West Walton Highway, Marham, Barton, Woodford, Chester, St Athan, 5 FTS, 7 FTS. Hawarden-built. SOC 1-12-67. Arrived 12-10-22		1-24
❑ 'XE683'	'G'	Hawker Hunter F.51	56	ex 'XF383' Cardiff-Wales, 'WV309', 'XF383', Dunsfold, G-9-437 (9-12-75), Danish AF Esk.724 E-409. Arrived 7-10-95. 74 Sqn colours		1-24
❑ 'XG168'	'10'	Hawker Hunter F.6A XG172	56	ex N Weald, Ipswich, Scampton 8832M (2-9-84), 1 TWU, 229 OCU, 263, 19. Arrived 2-2-01. 79 Sqn colours	[3]	1-24
❑ XL564		Hawker Hunter T.7	58	ex Aylesbury, South Molton, Yarmouth, Boscombe Down, ETPS, 229 OCU. Crashed 6-8-98. Cockpit. Arrived 7-15	[6]	7-21
❑ XM612		Avro Vulcan B.2	64	ex 44, Wadd Wing, Scampton Wing, 9. SOC 19-1-83. Arrived 30-1-83		1-24
❑ XN967	'233'	Blackburn Buccaneer S.1	63	ex Coltishall, Weybourne, Fleckney, Helston, Culdrose A2627 / SAH-20, Lossiemouth, 736, 809. SOC 23-1-70. Arrived 2006. Cockpit		1-24

❑ XP355 Westland Whirlwind HAR.10 62 ex G-BEBC (de-reg 5-12-83), Faygate, 8463M (6-2-76), 38 GCF, 21, CFS. Arrived 15-6-80. 22 Sqn colours 1-24

❑ XV255 HS Nimrod MR.2 70 ex Kinloss, Kinloss Wing, A&AEE, 42, Kin Wing, 42, St Mawgan Wing. *Brenda*. Arrived 24-5-10 1-24

❑ XV426 'P' McD Phantom FGR.2 69 ex Coltishall, Coningsby, 56, 19, 56, 23, 29, 228 OCU, 56, 111, 31, 31. Arrived 2007. 56 Sqn colours. Cockpit 1-24

❑ XW268 '720' *and* '68' HS Harrier T.4N 70 ex Faygate, Yeovilton, 899, 233 OCU, T.2, 233 OCU. Accident 27-6-94. Arrived 8-5-08. 899 Sqn colours [6] 1-24

❑ XX109 'GH' SEPECAT Jaguar GR.1 72 ex Coltishall 8918M (21-10-86), Warton, A&AEE. Arrived 1-9-04. 54 Sqn colours [7] 1-24

❑ XX830 SEPECAT Jaguar T.2 74 ex Coltishall 9293M, Warton, Shawbury, St Athan, ETPS, A&AEE, 226 OCU. Last flown 29-9-99. Arr 2006. Cockpit [8] 1-24

❑ XZ375 SEPECAT Jaguar GR.1 76 ex Coltishall, St Athan 9255M (20-9-96), Warden Det, 54, Gulf Det, 54, 14, 20. Arrived 2006. *The Avid Guardian Reader*. Cockpit [8] 1-24

❑ 121 '8-MY' Dassault Mystère IVA c57 ex Sculthorpe, FAF. Last flown 27-7-81, arrived 31-1-82 [9] 1-24

❑ 53-686 *and* G-AWON EE Lightning F.53 ZF592 68 ex Portsmouth, Luxembourg, *Wing Commander* (1999), Stretton, Warton, R Saudi AF 223, 53-686, 1305, G-AWON, G-27-56. Last flown 22-1-86, arrived 6-2-02 [3] [10] 1-24

❑ 16718 'TR-999' Lockheed T-33A-5-LO 51 ex Sculthorpe, Turkish AF, FAF. Arrived 31-5-86. USAF colours, 47th BW [9] 1-24

■ **[1]** Rallye has come 'home' having bashed the circuit with the Norfolk and Norwich Aero Club 8-63 to 11-69. **[2]** Built by the late Ray Wood of Thetford as a reminder of an extinct type – W E W Petter's incredible Whirlwind twin-Peregrine fighter. **[3]** Canberra cockpit WH984, Hunter F.6A 'XG168' and Lightning ZF592 / 53-686 on loan from John Sheldrake. **[4]** Canberra cockpit WJ633 on loan from Richy Doel. **[5]** Based on a real Hunter cockpit, 1986 (Wymondham) Sqn Air Cadets superb simulator is *possibly* from F.6 XE612. If so, it is very appropriate, serving only with 74 Squadron, it aborted take-off and hit the barrier at Horsham St Faith 17-5-60 and caught fire. **[6]** Hunter cockpit and Harrier on loan from Dan Lander. **[7]** XX109 is coded 'GH' in honour of Graham Hall. **[8]** Jaguar cockpits are on loan from The Coltishall Cockpit Collection. **[9]** Airframes from the National Museum of the USAF's Loan Program. **[10]** ZF592 carries Saudi markings to port and G-AWON to starboard; it appeared as *Oscar-November* at Farnborough 1968. It is reportedly fitted with the wings of 53-700 (ZF589) – see Charlwood, Surrey.

Airport: Is also used for storage and parting-out of jetliners: most are short term; only long-termers are given. The reference to the Friendship fuselage at the **KLM UK Engineering Training School** is long-in-the-tooth: the 737 may well be a replacement. Fokker F70 VH-NUV was scrapped in November 2020.

❑ G-BCDO Fokker Friendship 200 63 ex Air UK, PH-OGB, JA8621, PH-FEZ. *Lord Butler*. Damaged 19-7-90, de-reg 27-1-95. Fuselage 6-12

❑ G-CELS Boeing 737-377 86 ex Jet2, VH-CZH. De-reg 21-8-19, arrived 21-9-16 6-20

❑ P4-GIU HSA HS.146-RJ85 99 ex YV-2767, EI-RJL, OH-SAQ, EI-RJL, N524XJ, G-6-349. Woodford-built. Arrived 2-11-11 7-21

Offshore Fire and Survival Training Centre: On northern perimeter. ◆ *Prior appointment* **only** | **www.petans.co.uk**

❑ 'G-DRNT' Westland WG.30-100 83 ex N5880T, Weston-super-Mare, Yeovil, Air Spur, G-17-31 7-22

OLD BUCKENHAM AERODROME south of the A11, east of the B1077 near Attleborough EGSV

453rd Bomb Group Museum and **Eighth Air Force Heritage Gallery**: Drive into the aerodrome and the genial face of that great film actor James 'Jimmy' Stewart will greet you. Major James Maitland Stewart DFC arrived at 'Ol Buck' on 30th March 1943, becoming the resident 453rd BG's operations officer. As well as the museums, there is a memorial within a garden of remembrance. A major attraction is 'Jimmy's' cafe and there is an outside area offering views of the comings and goings at this superb aerodrome. ◆ **01953 860806** | **email** via website | **www.453museum.com**

Locally: The biplane cache is *believe*d to be current at a *private* workshop. Stampe SV-4A 156 (G-NIFE) was exported to Belgium, as OO-JST, in March 2023, via Challock, Kent.

❑ G-AOAA DH Tiger Moth 42 ex Turweston, Lavenham, Spanhoe, Manston, Thruxton, Chilbolton, DF159, 24 GCF, 1 RS, 1 GTS, 20 PAFU, 5 GTS. Morris-built. Crashed 4-6-89. 'Super Tiger' variant 2-16

❑ G-AYCG Stampe SV-4C 46 ex Staverton, F-BOHF, F-BBAE, French mil. Nord-built. CoA 19-12-14 N7-20

❑ G-BHFG Stampe SV-4C 46 ex Staverton, F-BJDN, French mil. Nord-built. CoA 17-4-08 N1-22

❑ G-EHLT DH Tiger Moth 41 ex G-BHLT, Turweston, Sywell, ZS-DGA, SAAF 2272, T6697, n/s. Morris Motors-built 1-19

SCULTHORPE on the A148 west of Fakenham

RAF Sculthorpe Heritage Centre: Housed within the Wicken Green Rural Centre, on the northwest edge of the airfield, the centre has exceptional displays on a very distinctive air base. Among the artefacts are the remains of Douglas RB-66 Destroyer 54-433 of the resident 47th BW which was abandoned and crashed on 3rd July 1958. A former Coltishall Jaguar is displayed on farmland nearby.

◆ *Chapel Street, NR21 7RR* | **rshc1955@gmail.com** | **www.rafsculthorpeheritagecentre.org**

❑ XZ394	'FG'	SEPECAT Jaguar GR.3	77	ex Ipswich, Shoreham, Bentwaters, St Athan, 41, GR.1, 54, 6, Shawbury, 17, 20. 'Saint', black colours. F/n 9-19	[1]	1-24

■ **[1]** Jaguar on farmland at Tattersett, west of the B1454: there's an honesty box – make sure it's filled!

SEETHING AERODROME east of the B1332, north of Bungay EGSJ

Station 146 Control Tower Museum: On the southern perimeter of the aerodrome the tower is dedicated to the Liberator-equipped 448th Bomb Group. ◆ *Toad Lane, NR35 2EQ* | **info@448bombgroup.co.uk** | **www.448bombgroup.co.uk**

Aerodrome: Q.6 G-AFFD travelled to Coventry, Warks, 11th October 2023. Off-site, Jodel D.140 G-EGUR has been deleted.

◆ **Strictly** *no access without prior arrangement*

❑ G-FLYP		Beagle 206 Srs 2	67	ex Cranfield, N40CJ, N97JH, G-AVHO, VQ-LAY, G-AVHO. CoA 6-9-18	8-23

SHIPDHAM off the A1075 southwest of East Dereham

Another one bites the dust... The aerodrome closed in November 2023 – redevelopment awaits.

❑ WZ797	FMA	Slingsby Grasshopper TX.1	52	BGA.3359, ex Upwood, Shenington, Locking, Wimborne. CoA 17-8-89. Off-site	8-21

SWAFFHAM on the A1065, northeast of Downham Market

No.**1894 (Swaffham) Squadron Air Cadets**: Keep the frame of an Auster at the TA Centre, Sporle Road.

❑ XK418	Auster AOP.9	56	ex Hardwick, South Molton, Lasham, Basingstoke, Thruxton, Netheravon, Middle Wallop 7976M (24-7-57), 19 MU, 12 Flt, Middle Wallop, LAS. Frame	6-21

SWANTON MORLEY east of the B1110, north of East Dereham

Two Nords are stored at a *private* location in the *general* area.

❑ No.37	Nord 3400	G-ZARA	60	ex Boston, Stixwould, Breighton, Coventry, La Ferté Alais, ALAT F-MMAB. De-reg 30-6-97	6-21
❑ No.124	Nord 3400	G-BOSJ	60	ex La Ferté Alais, ALAT F-MMAB. Damaged 12-6-94	6-21

THETFORD

Combat Paintball: On Roudham Heath. Whirlwind HAR.10 XJ727 was reported here from mid-2018 until August 2021. This was written out of *W&R24* (p92) at Richborough, Kent, as last noted October 2007.

◆ *Prior arrangement* **only** | **www.combatpaintball.com**

❑ G-BMVA	Scheibe SF-25B Falke	72	ex RAFGGA.512. CoA 5-6-08, de-reg 16-4-14. F/n 6-17	7-18

Also: A *private* collection of cockpits is *believed* to be extant in the locality.

❑ WW664		Hawker Hunter F.4	55	ex Spanhoe, Cottesmore, Newark, Winthorpe, Newark, Harrogate, HSA, 26. Squires Gate-built. Cockpit	[1]	3-13
❑ XG325		EE Lightning F.1(DB)	59	ex Rayleigh, Southend, Wattisham, Foulness, Warton, DH Hatfield, A&AEE. Last flight 26-10-64, SOC 23-6-65. Cockpit		3-13
❑ XN650	'456'	DH Sea Vixen FAW.2	61	ex Spanhoe, Bruntingthorpe, Newton Abbot, Welshpool, Bruntingthorpe, Cardiff, Culdrose A2639, A2620, A2612 (3-3-72), RAE, 892. Christchurch-built. Cockpit. Arrived 9-10		3-13
❑ 764		Mikoyan-Gurevich MiG-21SPS *Fishbed*	66	ex Northampton, Booker, East German AF. Cockpit		3-13

■ **[1]** The rest of WW664 became the prototype T.8B in 1958 for the Fleet Air Arm and later went to Singapore as a T.75.

THORPE ABBOTTS off the A140 at Dickleburgh, north of Scole

100th Bomb Group Memorial Museum: Contents of the tower museum are exceptional (as is the website and the archive services), offering poignant insights into the life and times of the men and machines of the 'Bloody Hundredth'.

◆ *Common Rd, Dickleburgh, IP21 4PH* | **01379 740708** | **info@100bgmus.org.uk** | **www.100bgmus.org.uk**

TIBENHAM north of the B1134, north of Diss

Three *separate* restoration projects are at *private* locations the *general* area.

❑	G-ASSV		Kensinger KF		53	ex Deopham Green, Brenchley, Deopham Green, Tonbridge, Bobbington, N23S. Crashed 2-7-69	N4-22
❑	G-MOTW		Myers OTW-145		41	ex Duxford, Breighton, N34301, NC34301. Arrived 24-11-21	12-22
❑	N6965	'FL-J'	DH Tiger Moth	G-AJTW	38	ex N6965, 13 OTU, 16 EFTS, 13 OTU, 418, Northolt SF, 24, 81, 613. Crashed 7-6-99, CoA 9-9-00. 81 Sqn colours	N2-20

WEST RAYNHAM north of the A1065, west of the village

Jon and Shell Booty own the control tower, fire section and immediate surrounds. Hunter WT660 served from February 1955 for two years at 'Raynham with the Day Fighter Leaders School.

◆ *Open days planned; otherwise by prior arrangement **only**.* | **www.westraynhamcontroltower.co.uk**

❑	WT660	'C'	Hawker Hunter F.1	54	ex Inverness, Cullen, New Byth, Kingstown, 71 MU 7421M (11-4-57), 229 OCU, DFLS. Arrived 15-10-20	7-23

Canberra Heritage Trust: Acquired the cockpit, rear fuselage and engines of PR.9 XH135.

◆ *Regular open days reported; otherwise by prior arrangement **only**.* | **info@xh135co.uk** | **www.xh135.shop**

❑	XH135*	EE Canberra PR.9	59	ex Kemble, Marham, 39, 1 PRU, 39, 13, 58, MoA, HS. Last flight 31-7-06. Short-built. Cockpit, arrived 2-8-22	1-24

Naked Kitchens: To emphasise the company's jingle – 'Built for the High Life' – *The Shepherd* Vampire 'climbs away' from a kitchen 'set' in the corner of the hangar/showroom. Restored by a team led by Bruce Gordon – see Cantley, Norfolk - the Vampire arrived at 'Raynham in March 2022 for shooting of the Disney 'short', *The Shepherd*, based upon Frederick Forsyth's 1975 novella of the same name. The FB.9/T.11 composite carries the serial 'WA123' (before you ask that was a 1950-built EE-built FB.5) call-sign *Charlie-Delta* which is involved in a drama-laden sortie out of Celle, West Germany, on Christmas Eve 1957. ◆ *Hangar 4, Blenheim Way – closed weekends* | **www.nakedkitchens.com**

❑	'WA123'* 'R-A' *and* 'K'	DH Vampire FB.9	WL505 G-FBIX	51	ex *The Shepherd*, 'Suffolk', Norwich, Bournemouth, Bridgend, Bruntingthorpe, Cranfield, St Athan 7705M, Ely, 19, RAFC, 73. De-reg 17-5-05. Hawarden-built. Arrived 3-22 [1]	1-24

■ **[1]** Wing from T.11 XD624 – see Cantley, Norfolk. Tail flying surfaces removed. WL505 was written out of *W&R27* (p173), latterly with Classic Aero Services, Norwich. Post-Norwich it moved to a barn in 'Suffolk' and from there to Disney stardom.

WEST WALTON HIGHWAY on the A47 northeast of Wisbech

Fenland and West Norfolk Aviation Museum (F&WNAM): Opened to the public on 20th June 1987, this pioneering and charismatic museum closed its doors on 28th October 2022. By their nature, *W&R* readers tend to be airframe-centric and while the City of Norwich Aviation Museum (CNAM) has a hand in that side of things, the denizens of the northern perimeter of Norwich Airport have a far more vital – but likely unsung – role in the ongoing heritage of F&WNAM. The collection of artefacts, documents, photos and wot-nots has always been the maturity and strength of the West Walton Highway displays: beautifully presented, thoughtfully captioned and... you get the picture. Stepping in and saving the majority of these - and keeping them in much the same geographic area - is a huge feather in CNAM's cap - take a bow!

Disposals: Shackleton MR.3/3 cockpit WR971 and Jet Provost T.3 XM402 to Kinloss, Scotland, on 31-3-23 and 22-3-23, respectively; Vampire T.11 XD434 to Norwich Airport, Norfolk, 12-10-2022; Buccaneer S.2B cockpit XN983, owned by the Terrington Aviation Collection, was offered for sale in March 2022, moving to Stranraer, Scotland; the anonymous Spitfire FSM to Wisbech, Norfolk; the Jet Provost CIM, owned by 1220 Sqn Air Cadets, has been 'lodged' under March, Cambs,

---

WEYBOURNE on the A149 west of Cromer

Muckleburgh Collection: Bannered as Britain's largest working military collection, there is much to fascinate, including 'live' tank demonstrations. ◆ *Military Camp, NR25 7EH* | **01263 588210** | **info@muckleburgh.co.uk** | **www.muckleburgh.co.uk**

❑	'XT581'		Northrop Shelduck D.1	13	BAPC.501. 'Army' titles. Suspended within the cafe [1]	4-23
❑	XZ968	'3G'	HS Harrier GR.3	80	ex Marham 9222M (13-10-93), St Athan, 233 OCU, 1417 Flt, 1, 4	1-24

❑ ZJ385		GEC-Marconi Phoenix UAV	c95	'Army' titles	4-23
❑ –		Fieseler Fi 103 V-1 replica	~	BAPC.550, on ramp	4-23

■ **[1]** The *real* XT581 is at Duxford, Cambs. This Shelduck was created by the Kelling Model Flying Club using an original wing - complete with shrapnel damage - left behind when Weybourne Camp closed in 1958.

WINFARTHING on the B1077 north of Diss

Sound Sleep: The bedding showroom in Mile Road has a 'guardian' | **www.sound-sleep.co.uk**

❑ G-CBCY		Beech Sierra	77	ex Goodwood, N881RS, PH-HLA. CoA 24-3-11, de-reg 17-5-21	8-21

WISBECH off the A47 southwest of King's Lynn

Three airframes, at *separate* venues, each on *private* property and in the *general* area.

❑ N70353		Boeing 737-300	87	ex Continental. Last flown 5-6-08. Cockpit, first noted 8-19	8-19
❑ 'BR404'* *and* 'DU-X'	'RJ-F'	V-S Spitfire IX FSM	~	BAPC.540, ex West Walton Highway, Duxford. *Helen*. 'RJ-F' to stb, 'DU-X' to port. First noted 10-23	10-23
❑ WT534*		EE Canberra PR.7	55	ex Doncaster, South Clifton, Upwood, Doncaster, Boscombe Down, Shirley, Halton 8549M (10-7-78), St Athan, 17. Short-built. Cockpit. Arrived 2019	6-20

NORTHAMPTONSHIRE

BARTON SEAGRAVE north of the A6633 east of Kettering

Kestrel Caravan Park: The collection of light aircraft has been joined by a Wessex, a potential 'glamper'.

◆ *Prior arrangement* **only** | **www.kestrelcaravans.co.uk**

❑ G-APWP		Druine Turbulent	60	de-reg 20-6-18	12-23
❑ G-ATFR		Piper Pawnee 150	60	ex OY-ADJ. De-reg 20-3-18. First noted 7-20	12-23
❑ G-OMAX		Brantly B2B	67	ex G-AVJN. CoA 19-1-10, de-reg 13-3-12	12-23
❑ G-TAMA		Hughes 269D	04	ex -?-, Kelham 'K-HALL', Shoreham. Schweizer-built. CoA 12-6-08, crashed 4-2-08, de-reg 16-6-08	12-23
❑ XV726*	'J'	Westland Wessex HC.2	68	ex Biggin Hill, Hixon, Shawbury, 72, 60, 72, 60, 72, Queen's Flight. Arrived 5-23	12-23

CORBY

Frank and **Lee Millar**: Keep their Vampire in the area. See under Newark, Notts, for their Canberra PR.9 cockpit.

❑ XE849	'V3'	DH Vampire T.11	54	ex Barton, Shobdon, Mildenhall, Long Marston, Yatesbury, Monkton Farleigh, Conington, Ware, St Athan 7928M (13-10-66), 3 CAACU (?),CATCS, CNCS, 5 FTS, 7 FTS, 1 FTS, 4 FTS. Hatfield-built	12-23

HARRINGTON southeast of Market Harborough

'Carpetbagger' Aviation Museum: Centred upon the hardened group operations building of what was once USAAF Station 179 and home of the clandestine 492nd and 801st BGs. Exhibitions on the covert operations of the US from Harrington and by the RAF from Tempsford, Beds. Working in support of the museum is the **Harrington Aviation Museum Society**.

◆ *Sunny Vale Farm Nursery, off Lamport Road, NN6 9PF Note: Photography, via cameras or mobile phones,* not *permitted within the museum*. | **01536 711556** | **enquiries @harringtonmuseum.org.uk** | **www.harringtonmuseum.org.uk**

IRTHLINGBOROUGH on the A6 northwest of Higham Ferrers and Rushden

Rock UK Frontier Centre: Last noted in July 2014 Cessna 150 'G-BMAF' (G-BOWC) has been deleted.

KETTERING

Chariots: Kettering Venture Park | **www.chariotsspecialistcars.com**

❑ 'G-BGEI'		Oldfield Baby Great Lakes	85	G-BGLS, de-reg 12-12-11. Displayed	[1] 12-23

■ **[1]** The Great Lakes masquerades as another of the species, G-BGEI, also out of CoA (27-6-13). One reason for this might be that *Echo-India* was tested at Samlesbury, Lancs, for PFA permit clearance 26-8-80 by none other than Wg Cdr Roland Beamont.

Tresham College: In the campus (main entrance on Windmill Avenue, near Wickstead Park) is a One-Eleven used by the Travel and Tourism courses. ◆ **Strictly** *by prior arrangement* | **www.tresham.ac.uk**

❑ G-AVMJ		BAC 111-510ED	68	ex Watford, Horton, Hurn, Farnborough, Hurn, Filton, BA, BEA. CoA 17-11-94, de-reg 11-5-01. Fuselage	[1]	9-23

■ **[1]** *Mike-Juliet* factoids: First flew 15-7-68, last flew with BA 13-1-92, ferry to Hurn. Final flight Hurn-Filton 25-5-93.

NORTHAMPTON AERODROME or Sywell, northeast of Northampton, off the A43 EGBK

Sywell Aviation Museum (SAM): Charting the history of wonderful Sywell and the entire county, SAM is a landmark among 'small' museums; it's a cliche but this place really does punch well above its weight. The Paul Morgan Hall honours a gifted local engineer and warbird owner who was killed in his Sea Fury FB.11 WH588 (G-EEMV) on 12th May 2001. There is a poignant 'missing man' memorial fountain to Paul in front of the 'Aviator Hotel'. The Jetstream is under restoration for eventual use as a classroom.

◆ *Car parking for the museum (no charge) doubles as a viewing area for the aerodrome. NN6 0BN* | **07968 061708** | **sywellaviationmuseum@gmail.com** | **www.sywellaviationmuseum.org.uk**

❑ G-RAVL	'197'	HP Jetstream 200	69	ex Cranfield, G-AWVK, N1035S, G-AWVK. CoA 26-2-94, de-reg 30-1-01. 'Jenny'. Arrived 23-3-21		1-24
❑ KF650		NAA Harvard T.2B	45	ex Kenilworth, Henlow, 2 FTS, 22 FTS. Crashed 14-5-54. Noorduyn-built. Forward cockpit. Arrived by 10-14	[1]	1-24
❑ WG419		DHC Chipmunk T.10	51	ex Armthorpe, Finningley 8206M (2-8-72), Laarbruch SF, Gütersloh SF, Ahlhorn SF, Oldenburg SF, CFS, Abn UAS, Birm UAS, 15 RFS, 4 BFTS, 6 RFS. Hawarden-built. Cockpit. 'Clare'. Arrived 5-8-07		1-24
❑ WN904 and 'WN921'	'Q' 'S'	Hawker Hunter F.2	54	ex Waterbeach, Duxford, Newton, Melksham, Halton 7544M (31-3-58), 257. AWA-built. Arrived 2-8-12. 'Heidi' 257 Sqn colours to port, 263 Sqn to starboard	[2]	1-24
❑ XD599	'A'	DH Vampire T.11	54	ex Ingatestone, Welshpool, Shobdon, Caernarfon, Hurn, Blackbushe, Staverton, Stroud, CATCS, RAFC, 1. Hatfield-built. SOC 15-12-70. Arrived 10-10-04. Cockpit		1-24

■ **[1]** KF650 on loan from the Midland Aircraft Recovery Group. **[2]** WN904 is dedicated to the memory of 23-year-old Fg Off Dennis R Courtney of 263 Sqn and all others lost by the unit.

Store and off-site: ***Not*** available for public inspection.

❑ G-AOES		DH Tiger Moth	41	ex Baxterley, Redhill, Biggin Hill, Cosford, Mk.II T6056, Waddington SF, Benson SF, 18 EFTS. Morris-built. Crashed 26-9-99, CoA 15-6-02. Fuselage. Arrived 3-13		1-24
❑ WH887	'847'	EE Canberra TT.18	54	ex Upwood, Basingstoke, Llanbedr St Athan, FRADU, B.2, Upwood SF, 21, 542, 1323 Flt, 82, 1323 Flt. Short-built. Cockpit. 'Cindy'. Arrived 25-10-14, off-site from 3-21	[1]	1-24
❑ WZ820		Slingsby Grasshopper TX.1	52	ex Shoreham, Lancing College. Arrived 2001		1-24

■ **[1]** Canberra, owned by Andy Shemans, is being restored and will have the electrics 'live'.

Air Leasing / Ultimate Warbirds: A row of blister hangars, one simply called 'The Spitfire Blister', the site inevitably known locally as 'Graceland', form the home of the Grace family's operational warbird fleet and an incredibly productive restoration centre. Sywell is base of the iconic Spitfire Tr.IX ML407 (G-LFIX), Seafire III PP972 (G-BUAR), Buchón two-seater '11' (G-AWHC), among others. Warbird experience flights are offered, and third-party aircraft are also looked after. As with elsewhere in the book, the active warbirds are not formally covered, *W&R* concentrating on restoration projects.

Plenty of words have been published following tragic news of the death of **Carolyn Grace** in a motor accident in her native Australia on 2nd December 2022. Following the death of her husband, Nick, in 1988 - ironically also in a road accident - Carolyn was determined to keep Spitfire ML407 within the family and she went solo in it two years later. Gifted, determined, always modest, Carolyn's skills and endeavours were the launchpad for the present-day operation at 'Graceland' which stands as a vibrant tribute to her.

Pete Kynsey was at the controls for the first test flight of Fighter Aviation Engineering's (FAE) Tempest II 'PR533' (G-TEMT, Indian HA586, RAF MW763) on 10th October 2023. Bedecked in the colours of 33 Squadron, it was rolled out on 24th May 2021 and staged its first taxi run on 29th June 2023. The first flight ended at Duxford, putting yet another iconic type into the air for a very lucky British audience to appreciate.

Another FAE treasure arrived on 26th March 2022. I'm sure more that a few readers will get their hackles up when I type that this machine has a significance that far outweighs many a UK-based warbird. This is Lockheed 12A G-AFTL, made famous by Sidney Cotton for his audacious private-venture clandestine photo-recces of Hitler's Germany as Europe plunged ever further into war. If you need any persuading, get hold of *The Last Plane Out of Berlin* by Jeffrey Watson: that sortie was out of Berlin's Tempelhof on 24th August 1939 with the cameras in the belly clicking away. The story has it all: derring-do, espionage, power politics and the birth of the RAF's Photo-Reconnaissance Unit. A brilliant import, do I detect a film in the offing? As *W&R* closed for press G-AFTL's 'paperwork' was pending, herewith a brief 'CV': Built late 1936 at Burbank as NC16077, imported into the UK for Sidney Cotton, becoming G-AFTL. Last flight 18th June 1940 from Jersey to its base at Heston. Badly damaged in a bombing raid on Heston 19th September 1940: to Lockheed for rebuild. Sold as VP-TAI 1943; N1161V 1948; N12EJ 1992. Registered to FAE as G-AFTL 29th March 2022.

Warbird Experiences' Hurricane XII 'V6748' (G-ORGI) was test flown on 24th May 2022, departing to Biggin Hill. Former Maurice Hammond P-51D *Janie* (G-MSTG) was test flown (as G-CLNV) on 25th August 2023 and departed for its new home in France on 2nd September. As *W&R* went to press former South African T-28A Trojan G-CMNJ (ZU-FWH), registered to Air Leasing, was being processed, ready to join the 'circuit'.

◆ ***Private*** *workshop,* ***not*** *available for inspection* | **www.ultimatewarbirdflights.com**

❑ G-AYRJ		Le Vier Cosmic Wind	48	ex G-NZOC, N289A, N20C. *Little Toni*. First noted 3-21		N4-23
❑ G-HISP		Hispano HA-1112-M1L Buchón	c52	ex USA, *Battle of Britain* (1968), Pinewood and Spain, Spanish AF C.4K-111. Arrived 2-16	[1]	N5-23
❑ G-TMPV		Hawker Tempest V	44	ex Bentwaters, 4887M (6-10-44), JN768, 3. Spares	[2]	N2-21
❑ EN224		V-S Spitfire XII G-FXII	42	ex Bentwaters, Newport Pagnell, Redbourn, Salford, Cranfield (4-7-46), 595, 41		N5-23
❑ 14798		Messerschmitt Bf 109G-2 G-CLFI	42	ex Australia, VH-EIN, JG 5 *Black 11*, shot down Russia 30-3-44. WNF-built. Recovered 1981	[3]	N6-23
❑ HA604		Hawker Tempest II G-PEST	45	ex Wickenby, Sandtoft, Brooklands, Chichester, India, Ind AF, RAF MW401 n/s (SOC 25-5-48). Bristol-built	[3]	N6-23
❑ C.4K-30	'7'	Hispano HA-1112-M1L	58	ex USA, *Battle of Britain* (1968). Spares. First noted 7-18	[1]	7-18
❑ 22-296		Royal Aircraft Factory SE.5E G-BLXT	1919	ex Bentwaters, Greenham Common, Duxford, M Wallop, Booker, 'B4863', Orlando, Tallmantz, N4488, *Hell's Angels* (1930), USAAS 22-296. CoA 15-9-16. Arrived by 7-16	[4]	N5-23
❑ 42-66841	'153'	Lockheed P-38H-5-LO Lightning	42	ex Bentwaters, Germany, Australia, Papua New Guinea. Crashed PNG 10-6-44. *Scarlet Angel*		6-17
❑ 413668		NAA P-51D-5-NA Mustang G-CLRG	44	ex 338th FS, 55th FG, 44-13668. Crashed 9-10-44. Inglewood-built. Restoration project. First noted 7-20		N4-23
❑ 464005	'E9-Z'	NAA P-51D-20-NA Mustang N51CK	44	ex USA, N51WB, N6339T, RCAF 9561, USAAF 44-64005. Inglewood-built. *Mary Mine*. Arrived 3-17		12-17

■ All registered to Air Leasing, Ultimate Warbirds or members of the grace family unless noted. **[1]** Bf 109 with RR Merlin 500 built by Hispano Aviacion, Spain, -M1L single-seater, -M4L two-seater. With thanks to Paco Rivas please note that the plural of Buchón is Buchones – *without* the accent. **[2]** Registered to the Hawker *Typhoon* Preservation Group – see main entry under Duxford, Cambs. **[3]** Registered to Fighter Aviation Engineering. **[4]** British-built SE.5a re-engined by Eberhart Steel Products Co, at Buffalo, New York. US designation SE.5E - cap 'E'. Registered to Flying A Services.

Matthew Boddington: Super Cub G-ARAM moved to Norfolk, by June 2022. Slingsby SE.5 'C8846' (G-AVOU) took to the air following restoration on 23rd April 2023.

❑ G-ADGT	DH Tiger Moth	35	ex Seething, Headcorn, BB697, 652, 26 EFTS, 6 EFTS. CoA 25-8-12. First noted 1-21	[1]	1-21
❑ G-APVT	DH Tiger Moth	35	ex K4254, Colerne SF, 81 GCF, 60 GCF, 18 RFS, Lon UAS, 6 EFTS, 1 GTS, 101 OTU, 17 EFTS, 7 EFTS, 14 EFTS, 20 E&RFTS, 24. Crashed 29-7-73		9-21
❑ G-JMNN	Bücker Jungmann	50	ex Spanish AF E.3B-335. CASA-built. Arrived 27-12-13	[2]	10-23

■ **[1]** *Golf-Tango* registered to the London Aerobatic Company. **[2]** See under Coggeshall, Essex, for the owner's Jungmeister.

Also: Navajos G-EGLG and G-FILL have been deleted.

❑ G-KSWI	Hughes 369E	86	CoA 18-6-12, de-reg 19-1-12. Fire training ground	1-18
❑ G-SWLL	Aero AT-3 R100	05	ex SP-KAC. CoA 23-11-17, de-reg 15-3-22. Fire training ground	1-18

SPANHOE AERODROME southeast of Harringworth

Windmill Aviation: Desford Trainer VZ728 (G-AGOS) took its final flight, 19th August 2022, to Newark, Notts. Plus D LB375 (G-AHGW) was flying by early 2022. Chipmunk 21 G-ANWB and T.10 WZ872 (G-BZGB) were both flying by mid-2023.

◆ **Strictly** *by prior arrangement* **only**

❑ G-ARNN	Globe GC-1B Swift	46	ex Tatenhill, Leicester, VP-YMJ, VP-RDA, ZS-BMX, NC3279K. Crashed 1-9-73, de-reg 26-1-11. Off-site	2-18

❑ G-BRZK	Stinson 108-2		47	ex N9846K. CoA 18-2-13	7-23
❑ G-CFGE	Stinson 108-1		46	ex Wickenby, Hibaldstow, Little Gransden, ZS-BHW, N97127	7-23
❑ EI-AYL	Beagle Airedale	G-ARRO	63	ex Abbeyshrule, G-ARRO, EI-AVP, G-ARRO. CoA (Irish) 1-2-86. De-reg 22-11-23	3-23
❑ EI-BAL	Beagle Airedale	G-ARZS	62	ex Abbeyshrule, G-ARZS. De-reg 22-11-23	3-23
❑ –* c/n 3705	Auster D6/180		~	ex Newark-on-Trent, White Waltham, Rearsby. Frame	10-23
❑ '43-35943'*	Beech D.18S	G-BKRN	52	ex Langham, Bruntingthorpe, Cranfield, Perth, Prestwick, CF-DTN, RCAF inst A675, RCAF 1500. CoA 26-6-83. US Navy c/s, *Naval Encounter.* Arrived by 4-23	10-23

WEEDON BEC on the A5 west of Northampton

The Depot: A massive heritage development centred upon the extensive, refurbished Georgian Royal Ordnance Factory arsenal buildings with workspaces, shops, antique dealers, you-name-it. A Cessna twin fuselage is on show within Unit 14 – its wings etc are stored outside – by an 'upcycling' organisation, Gasoline Juice: it *may* be very transitory, or it *may* linger... Either way the company produces aviation-related items and – like the whole site – is well worth visiting.

◆ *NN7 4PS* | **01327 226812** | **visitorscentre@thedepot.uk** | **https://the-depot.uk** | **www.gasolinejuice.com**

❑ N401JN*	Cessna 401	~	ex Blackpool. Crashed 21-1-07, de-reg 21-5-15. Fuselage – see notes above. First noted 7-23	11-23

NORTHUMBERLAND and TYNESIDE

The five unitary authorities of Gateshead, Newcastle-upon-Tyne, Sunderland, North Tyneside and South Tyneside comprise the 'counties'

BAMBURGH on the B4130 east of Belford and northwest of Seahouses

Bamburgh Castle: In the West Ward, is the superb **Armstrong and Aviation Museum**. Among the exhibits are sections of 280 Squadron Vickers Warwick I HG136 which crashed near Wooler on 23rd July 1946.

◆ *NE69 7DF* | **01668 214208** | **administrator@bamburghcastle.com** | **www.bamburghcastle.com**

BELSAY on the A696 northwest of Newcastle

Battlezone Paintball Newcastle: ◆ *Prior application* **only** | **www.battlezonepaintball.co.uk**

❑ G-BVTA	Tri-R KIS	95	ex Rowley. CoA 30-1-12, de-reg 30-4-15	1-20

BOULMER east of Alnwick

RAF Boulmer: The Air Surveillance and Control System station is guarded by a Phantom. Hunter F.6A XE606 is due; stored for the time being courtesy of NELSAM at Sunderland, N&T – which see. The former is in the colours of 19 Squadron, which is resident as the Control and Reporting Centre (CRC) unit. The latter will have 20 Squadron markings, which is also resident, acting as the CRC operational conversion unit.

❑ XE606	Hawker Hunter F.6A	56	see notes above	**due**
❑ XV415 'AA'	McD Phantom FGR.2	68	ex 9163M, 56, 74, 228 OCU, 23, 56, 92, 29, 228 OCU, 56, 228 OCU, 31, 228 OCU, 41, 228 OCU, 41, 54, A&AEE. Displayed, since 1993. 19 Sqn colours	1-24

CRAMLINGTON on the A189, north of Newcastle upon Tyne

Gavin Carr: Took delivery of a 'Flea' on 27th September 2022 for long-term restoration.

◆ *Prior application* **only** | **gavncarr@gmail.com**

❑ 'G-ADRZ'*	Mignet HM.14 'Flea'	~	BAPC.481, ex Fishburn, Masham, Pickhill, South Molton, Dunstable, South Molton. Arrived 27-9-22	[1]	1-24

■ **[1]** Exact provenance of the 'Flea' is unknown, it is likely a 'new-build' from the 1980s.

CURROCK HILL northwest of Leadgate, south of Prudhoe

A Cherokee is kept at a *private* house in the locality.

❑ G-AWBH	Piper Cherokee 140	68	CoA 30-12-04, de-reg 16-3-10. First noted 8-15	1-24

ESHOTT AERODROME east of the A1 south of Fenton

Chipmunk T.10 WP860 (G-BXDA) moved to Dumfries, Scotland, 9th October 2022. Tomahawk G-BXZA relocated to Bagby, N Yorks, by March 2022. Arrow G-BMKK has been deleted.

Reg	Code	Type	Other	Year	Details	Note	Noted
❑ G-BDNC		Taylor Monoplane		84	CoA 15-7-16, de-reg 28-5-21		4-19
❑ G-AKUL*		Luscombe Silvaire 8A		46	ex Dunkeswell, Southend, N1462K. CoA 21-5-90. F/n 8-22		12-23
❑ G-ANOK		SAAB Safir		r54	ex Morpeth, Yarrow, Strathallan, East Fortune, SE-CAH. De Schelde-built. CoA 5-2-73		12-23
❑ G-ASWW		Piper Twin Comanche 160		64	ex Skegness, N7531Y. Damaged, CoA 23-1-10, de-reg 12-8-09		12-23
❑ G-BWVR	'52'	Yakovlev Yak-52		87	ex LY-AKQ, Sov AF 134. IAR Bacau-built. CoA 7-12-06		12-23
❑ G-CDET*		Culver Cadet		40	ex N29261. CoA 21-7-11		12-23
❑ G-RADA*	'J-20'	Soko Kraguj		76	ex Fishburn, Linton-on-Ouse, Biggin Hill, Yugoslav AF 30140. CoA 5-9-05. Arrived 27-7-22		12-23
❑ YU-DLG		UTVA 66	G-CLJX	70	ex Morpeth, Linton-on-Ouse, Biggin Hill, Yugoslav AF 51109. First noted 6-20		12-23
❑ –*	'AZ-G'	V-S Spitfire Vb FSM		94	BAPC.242, ex Usworth, 'BL924', Reading, Lower Basildon, Liskeard, Perranporth, Tangmere. TDL Replicas-built. 234 Sqn c/s. Arr 21-3-23. 'Gate guardian' - damaged 4-23	[1]	12-23
❑ 50042*	'72'	SAAB Safir	G-CLSP	53	ex SE-KUA, RSwAF Sk.50B 50042, De Schelde-built. First noted 9-20		12-23

■ **[1]** On loan from the Spitfire Society.

MORPETH or Tranwell, east of the A1, north of Newcastle upon Tyne

The Turbulent and the Taylorcraft are stored at *separate*, and *private*, locations in the *general* area.

Reg	Code	Type	Other	Year	Details	Note	Noted
❑ G-APOL		Druine Turbulent		63	ex Charterhall. Crashed 24-7-93, de-reg 13-9-00		5-23
❑ 42-58687		Taylorcraft DF-65	G-BRIY	43	ex N59687, TG-6 42-58678. CoA 10-7-98		4-21

NEWCASTLE AIRPORT or Woolsington EGNT

Newcastle Aviation Academy ◆ *Prior arrangement* **only** | **www.ncl-coll.ac.uk**

Reg	Code	Type	Other	Year	Details	Note	Noted
❑ G-AZMF		BAC 111-530FX		72	ex Hurn, European, 7Q-YKJ, G-AZMF, PT-TYY, G-AZMF. CoA 22-1-04, de-reg 10-3-06. Forward fuselage		7-21
❑ G-BBYM		HP Jetstream 200		69	ex Cosford, Cranfield, BAe, G-AYWR, G-8-13. Jetstream A/c, Leavesden-completed. CoA 20-9-98, de-reg 7-6-00		7-21
❑ G-CCXI		Thorp T-211		03	de-reg 18-2-10. Unfinished project, first noted 3-12		2-20
❑ C-GWJO		Boeing 737-2A3		69	ex Westjet, HR-SHO, CX-BHM, N1797B, N1787B		7-21
❑ N37LW		Piper Aztec 250		60	ex Fishburn, Kirknewton, G-EEVA, G-ASND, N4800P		1-14
❑ XM355	'D'	Hunting Jet Provost T.3		59	ex Bruntingthorpe, Shobdon, Cambridge, B'thorpe, Halton 8229M (17-10-73), Shawbury, 1 FTS, 7 FTS, CFS. Blue/white colours		4-22
❑ XM419	'102'	Hunting Jet Provost T.3A		60	ex St Athan 8990M (15-3-89), 7 FTS, 3 FTS, CFS, RAFC, CFS, 3 FTS, RAFC, 6 FTS, RAFC, 2 FTS		4-22

SEATON BURN east of the A1, north of Newcastle upon Tyne

The organisation hiring out the anonymous Spitfire FSM simulator is no longer offering the service: no details of the fate or otherwise of the anonymous 'airframe'.

Delta Force Paintball ◆ *Prior arrangement* **only** | **www.paintballgames.co.uk**

Reg	Code	Type	Other	Year	Details	Note	Noted
❑ XZ698*	'316'	Westland Lynx HMA.8		80	ex Kirknewton, Upminster, Ipswich, Fleetlands, 815, 702, HAS.3, 815, 829, HAS.2, 815, A&AEE. F/n 10-22	[1]	11-23

■ **[1]** Fitted with the boom of ZD249 – see Ipswich, Suffolk.

SUNDERLAND site of the former Usworth aerodrome, west of Sunderland

North East Land, Sea and Air Museums (NELSAM): Combining the exhibits and enterprise of the **North East Aircraft Museum**, the **Military Vehicle Museum** and the **North East Electrical Traction Trust** has produced a wonderful selection of exhibits. A look through the website reveals the incredible scope of this venue. Underlining this was the opening of the Made on Wearside car collection in March 2023 – cementing a long-term relationship with Nissan.

Here is yet another example of how time marches on: 2024 is the 50th anniversary of NELSAM's founder organisation – the North East Vintage and Veteran Aircraft Association. The museum has been allocated a Hawk from MoD: due on site in March or April 2024. Spitfire FSM BAPC.242 moved to Eshott, N&T, 21st March 2023.

◆ *Off the A1290 and A19, Old Washington Road, SR5 3HZ* | **0191 5190662** | **info@nelsam.org.uk** | **www.nelsam.org.uk**

❑	'G-AAAH'*		DH Moth replica	81	BAPC.168, ex Hawkinge, Croydon, Gatwick. *Jason*. Arrived 17-1-23	[1]	1-24
❑	'G-ADVU'		Mignet HM.14 'Flea'	93	BAPC.211, ex Stoke-on-Trent. Arrived 1994	[2]	1-24
❑	'G-AFUG'		Luton Minor	44	BAPC.97, ex Stoke-on-Trent, Sunderland, Sibson, Sywell, Sunderland, Stanley. Acquired 1977		1-24
❑	G-APTW		Westland Widgeon	59	ex Helston, Southend, Westland. CoA 26-9-75, de-reg 24-8-72. Arrived 1993		1-24
❑	G-ARAD		Luton Major	60	ex local, Borgue. De-reg 16-10-02. Arrived 4-6-01	[3]	1-24
❑	G-ARPO		HS Trident 1C	65	ex Middleton St George, BA, BEA. CoA 12-1-86, de-reg 18-1-84. Arr 31-7-11, unveiled 11-6-15. Northeast c/s	[4]	1-24
❑	G-ATDD		Beagle 206-1	65	ex Filton, Kemble, Filton, Wroughton, South Kensington, Leeds. Damaged 6-73, de-reg 9-4-74. Cockpit. Arr 16-9-21		1-24
❑	'G-AVYW'		Brooklands Mosquito G-AWIF	69	ex Gloucester, Clitheroe. De-reg 27-11-18. Unveiled 3-19	[5]	1-24
❑	G-AWRS		Avro Anson C.19	46	ex Strathallan, Kemps, TX213, WCS, 22 GCF, OCTU, 18 GCF, 2 TAF CS, 527, CSE, RCCF. SOC 6-9-68. CoA 10-8-73, de-reg 30-5-84. Arrived 6-8-81		1-24
❑	G-BEEX		DH Comet 4C	61	ex East Kirkby, Tattershall, Woodford, Lasham, Dan-Air, Egypt Air/UAA SU-ALM. Hatfield-built. Last flight 15-10-76, de-reg 19-5-83. Arrived 1989. Cockpit		1-24
❑	G-OGIL		Short 330-100	81	ex Woolsington, Gill, G-BITV, G-14-3068. Damaged 1-7-92, de-reg 12-11-92. Arrived 4-93		1-24
❑	–		Brown Helicopter	62	BAPC.96, ex Stanley. Acquired 1977		1-24
❑	–		Bensen B-7	c65	BAPC.119, ex Stanley. Acquired 1977		1-24
❑	–	'AF-'	Hawker Hurricane FSM	19	BAPC.521, under construction	[6]	1-24
❑	'5191'		MS Type 'N' FSM	18	BAPC.472	[7]	1-24
❑	WG724	'932'	Westland Dragonfly HR.5	52	ex Chester-le-Street, Leyburn, Darlington, Blackbushe, Fleetlands, Lossiemouth SF, FRU, Ford SF, Eglinton SF SOC 16-9-65. Acquired 3-75		1-24
❑	WJ639		EE Canberra TT.18	54	ex Samlesbury, 7, B.2, 57. HP-built. SOC 9-12-81. 7 Sqn colours. Arrived 8-88		1-24
❑	WL181	'X'	Gloster Meteor F.8	54	ex Chester-le-Street, Acklington, Kemble, CAW, Tangmere SF, 34. SOC 3-11-71. Acquired 3-5-75. 92 Sqn c/s		1-24
❑	WZ518	'B'	DH Vampire T.11	53	ex Chester-le-Street, Handforth, Pomona Dock, 5 FTS, Oldenburg SF, 2 TAF CF, 14. Hawarden-built. SOC 30-10-67. Arrived 11-10-75. 14 Sqn colours	[8]	1-24
❑	WZ767		Slingsby Grasshopper TX.1	52	ex Halton. Arrived 4-85. On loan		1-24
❑	XG680	'438'	DH Sea Venom FAW.22	56	ex Sydenham, ADS, 891, Merryfield SF. Hawarden-built. SOC 20-1-70. Arrived 7-81		1-24
❑	XJ917	'S-H'	Bristol Sycamore HR.14	57	ex Filton, Kemble, Banwell, Helston, Wroughton, CFS, 275. SOC 12-12-72. Oldmixon-built. Arrived 3-6-21		1-24
❑	XL319		Avro Vulcan B.2	61	ex 44, Wadd W, 35, 230 OCU, 617, 230 OCU, Scamp W, 617. 44 Sqn colours. Flew in 21-1-83		1-24
❑	XM555		Saro Skeeter AOP.12	59	ex Stafford, Hendon, Cosford, Shawbury 8027M, Ternhill, CFS, HQ BAOR, 654. SOC 25-7-68. Arrived 12-5-15		1-24
❑	XN258		Westland Whirlwind HAR.9	59	ex Helston, Culdrose SF, *Hermes* SAR Flt, HAS.7, Lossie' SF / SAR Flt, 705, A&AEE. SOC 27-6-74. Arr 10-93		1-24
❑	XN503		Hunting Jet Provost T.3A	60	ex Old Sarum, Boscombe D, Haverfordwest, Milford Haven, Salisbury, Firbeck, Coventry, Bicester, Kemble, RAFEF, 4 FTS, 2 FTS, 6 FTS, A&AEE. SOC 28-5-76. Cockpit. Arrived 3-11-18		1-24
❑	XN696	'751'	DH Sea Vixen FAW.2	61	ex Flixton, Wisbech, Walpole, Farnborough, RAE, Tarrant Rushton, FRU, 899, 893, FAW.1, 899, A&AEE, 899. Christchurch-built. SOC 10-11-81. Arr 2-3-11. Cockpit	[9]	1-24

❑ XP627		Hunting Jet Provost T.4		62	ex London Colney, Hatfield, Shawbury, 6 FTS, 3 FTS, 1 FTS. SOC 1-10-71. Arrived 25-11-80.	[10]	1-24
❑ 'XS933'		EE Lightning F.53	ZF594	68	ex Warton, ZF594, Saudi AF 226, 1308, 53-696, G-27-66. Last flown 14-1-86. Arrived 4-89. 11 Sqn c/s	[11]	1-24
❑ 'XZ177'		Sud Gazelle 1	G-SFTA	73	ex Carlisle, 'XZ345', G-SFTA, HB-XIL, G-BAGJ, XW858. Westland-built. Crashed 7-3-84, de-reg 21-5-86. Arrived 11-86. 'ARMY' black/green camo	[12]	1-24
❑ ZD582*	'123'	HS Sea Harrier F/A.2		85	ex Aynho, Henley-on-Thames, Shawbury, Colsterworth, Shawbury, 800, 899, 800, 899, FRS.1, 801, 800. Arr 16-3-22		1-24
❑ ZE204	'FC'	Panavia Tornado F.3		86	ex Manston, Shawbury, Leuchars, 25, 23. Last flown 17-3-08. Arrived 28-6-21, handed over 13-9-21	[13]	1-24
❑ –		Panavia Tornado GR.4 SIM		~	ex Filton, Boscombe Down. Arrived 16-9-21		1-24
❑ A-522		FMA Pucará		c80	ex Yeovilton, St Athan 8768M (27-9-82), Stanley, Argentine AF. Arrived 24-7-94	[14]	1-24
❑ E-419		Hawker Hunter F.51		56	ex Dunsfold, G-9-441, Dan AF Esk.724. Last flown 10-4-76. Acquired 12-7-77		1-24
❑ 42157	'11-ML' *and* '11-ER'	NAA F-100D-16-NA Super Sabre		54	ex Sculthorpe, French AF, USAF 54-2147. Last flown 24-5-77, arrived 4-78	[15]	1-24
❑ 16171		NAA F-86D-35-NA Sabre		53	ex Greek AF, USAF 51-6171. Arrived 7-87. *Sabre Knights*, 325th FIS USAF c/s to stb, 512th FIS to port		1-24
❑ 26541		Republic F-84F-40-RE Thunderstreak		53	ex Greek AF, USAF 52-6541. Arrived 9-10-85		1-24
❑ –		HP C-10A Jetstream EMU		c68	ex Doncaster, Sunderland, Booker, Bushey, West Ruislip, Stanmore, St Albans, Radlett. Arr 1993. Cockpit, RAF c/s		1-24

■ **[1]** Other 'G-AAAHs' can be found at Kingston upon Hull, E Yorks, and the *real* thing at South Kensington, Gtr Lon. **[2]** 'G-ADVU' incorporates parts from an original, built at Burns Garage, Congleton, Cheshire, 1936. **[3]** G-ARAD is an unflown project; construction started 1959 at Borgue, Scotland. **[4]** Ownership of *Papa-Oscar* was transferred to the museum during 2023. **[5]** Mosquito is a memorial to Spennymoor-based designer/constructor/pilot Ernie Brooks, killed in the real G-AVYW 9-3-69. **[6]** Hurricane will wear 607 Sqn colours as 'P2874' 'AF-F'. **[7]** The 'N' commemorates Fulwell-born Claude Riley MM, who flew 'Ns' and other types on the Western Front and as CO of 37 Sqn at Stow Maries. Built with a grant from Heritage Lottery Fund is association with local Air Cadets and Sunderland College. **[8]** WZ518 is fitted with the wings of WZ608, the cockpit is at Rayleigh, Essex. **[9]** Sea Vixen cockpit transferred to NELSAM ownership by 2021. **[10]** 'JP4' XP627 has the wings of Mk.3 XN584, see Treforest, Wales, for the fuselage. **[11]** See under Binbrook, Lincs, for the *real* XS933. **[12]** The *real* XZ177 - a *Lynx* - is to be found at Kegworth, Leics. **[13]** F.3 handed over to the Lord Lieutenant of Tyne and Wear who accepted it on behalf of the people of the North East of England. **[14]** Pucará is on loan from the Fleet Air Arm Museum. **[15]** On loan from the National Museum of the USAF's Loan Program.

Also: The museum is looking after Hunter F.6A 'XE620' until its new location at Boulmer, N&T, is ready for it.

❑ 'XE620'*	'B'	Hawker Hunter F.6A	XE606	56	ex Waddington, Barkston Heath, 'XE673', Cottesmore, Laarbruch 8841M (29-11-84), 8737M, 1 TWU, TWU, 229 OCU, 92, 74, 65, 54, CFE. 8 Sqn colours. Arrived 17-10-22	12-23

Deep store: ***Not*** available for inspection.

❑ G-APKM		Auster J1N Alpha	58	ex Doncaster, Spanhoe, Newark. CoA 9-1-89. Arr by 12-18	[1]	1-24
❑ G-BCPK		Cessna F.172M Skyhawk	74	ex Stamford, Spanhoe, Little Staughton, D-ELOB. CoA 12-1-01, de-reg 18-8-14. Fuselage, stored		1-24
❑ G-MBDL		AES Lone Ranger	81	de-reg 13-6-90. Arrived 1989		1-24
❑ DUC		Carmam M.100S	r78	BGA.2383, ex Carlton Moor, F-CCSA. CoA 6-5-88. Arr 2009		1-24
❑ –		Electra Flyer Olympus	c85	BAPC.228. Arrived 1989. Hang-glider, in its bag!		1-24
❑ WB685		DHC Chipmunk T.10	50	ex Leeds, Irlam, Harrogate, Bassingbourn SF, Edin UAS, Lyneham SF, 8 RFS, 1 RFS. SOC 19-7-72. Hatfield-built. Arrived 1986	[2]	1-24
❑ WT913	FGA	Slingsby Cadet TX.1	52	BGA.3239, ex Doncaster, Strubby, 614, 618, 613, 618, 671 203 and 183 GSs. CoA 21-7-96. Arrived 2-7-19, stored	[3]	1-24

■ **[1]** *Kilo-Mike* was based at Newcastle from 1960 to 1969 and leased to the Sunderland Flying Club at Usworth. **[2]** WB685 is a composite, including the rear of WP969 (G-ATHC) and wings of WP833. **[3]** WT913 fitted with the wings of WT917.

NOTTINGHAMSHIRE

Includes the unitary authority of Nottingham

BILSTHORPE east of the A614, south of Ollerton

Paintball Jungle Nottingham: The Lynxes are either reclusive or long gone.

◆ *Prior application only* | **www.paintball-jungle.co.uk**

❑ XZ178	Westland Lynx AH.7	77	ex Hixon, Middle Wallop. Cabin. First noted 4-17	7-17
❑ XZ611	Westland Lynx AH.7	80	ex Hixon, Middle Wallop. Cabin. First noted 4-17	7-17

COLWICK southeast of Nottingham, south of the A612 ring road

St John the Baptist Primary School: ◆ *Prior arrangement* **only** | **www.st-johns-pri.notts.sch.uk**

❑ G-SSWO	Short 360-100	83	ex Millom, Blackpool, Emerald, SE-KLO, N343MV, G-BKMY, G-14-3609. CoA 4-12-04, de-reg 6-6-07. Classroom	12-23

HUCKNALL on the A611 north of Nottingham and south of Hucknall town

Hucknall Flight Test Museum: The former airfield was a famous engine flight test site. Affiliated with the Rolls-Royce Heritage Trust, the 'Wing Hangar' test-bed buildings are intended to form the venue for a visitor centre. As *W&R* closed for press, this had yet to come to fruition – keep an eye on the website. ◆ **www.huflighttestmuseum.co.uk**

❑ XV798	HS Harrier GR.1	70	BAPC.450, ex W'-super-Mare, Kemble, Banwell, Foulness, Dunsfold, 20, 233 OCU. Crashed 23-4-71. Arrived 1-2-20 [1]	12-23

■ **[1]** With wing of T.2 XW264 - see Gloucestershire, Glos. XV798 was used for Pegasus plenum chamber burning (PCB) ground trials.

LANGAR on minor roads south of the A46, north of Harby

The reference to Beech 18 G-BKRN should have referred to *Langham*, Leics (or Rutland if you must...). By April 2023 the project had relocated to Spanhoe, Northants.

MANSFIELD on the A60 north of Nottingham

Vision West Nottinghamshire College: Derby Road. The Travel and Tourism faculty has an A321 fuselage.

◆ *Prior arrangement* **only** | **www.wnc.ac.uk**

❑ YL-LCL	Airbus A320-214	95	ex St Athan, EI-DDL, SP-IAA, EI-DDL, F-GYFK, F-WQSY, B-652L, B-2224, HB-IJA, F-WWIF. Toulouse-built. Last flight 11-10-20. Forward fuselage, arrived 26-8-21	1-24

No.**384 (Mansfield) Squadron Air Cadets**: Botany Avenue. Gave up the long-standing Canberra PR.7 cockpit WT507; it travelled to Kinloss, Scotland, on 20th February 2023.

NEWARK or Winthorpe, on the A46 northeast of Newark-on-Trent

Newark Air Museum: Following the announcement that the museum had been successful in taking on Typhoon DA4 ZH590 from the Imperial War Museum, it had been listed here – since *W&R27* no less – with the caveat 'Due'. Its migration was surely a matter of logistics. No, it won't be coming: the woeful story is to be found under Duxford, Cambs, section.

Canberra PR.7 WH791 arrived, on loan, in November 1998 having spent 26 years slowly decaying on the gate at Cottesmore. As time went by it was clear that the owners were not undertaking significant remedial work on the airframe, as stipulated in the loan agreement. Prior to the loan expiry in March 2022, a thorough inspection by museum personnel revealed a stack of issues that wisely were assessed as beyond the museum's facilities and the skills of its restoration team. The response of the owner of WH791 was to unilaterally transfer WH791 to the museum on 15th May 2023; leaving the Newark team with a 'damned if you do, damned if you don't' responsibility. The museum bit the bullet and began disposal procedures with offers being considered up to 30th June 2023. With no takers of the whole airframe the decision was taken to dispose of WH791, where practical dealing with requests for parts, panels etc from other organisations. This is a mature conclusion: the museum has other priorities and WH791 would consume unwarranted amounts of time and money while starving more deserving exhibits of resources. A tough call, but the correct one.

In Hangar 1's 'Lancaster Corner' is a Lancaster rear fuselage section, presented in March 1974, that had served for decades as a garden shed in Gainsborough. With the 9 Squadron codes 'WS-J' still evident on its sides, it was soon confirmed as Mk.I W4964 *Johnnie Walker - Still Going Strong* which took part in the raid on the German warship *Tirpitz* on 15th September 1944. That was W4964's hundredth 'op': only 36 Lancasters became 'century' bombers.

The museum has hosted the unique *CockpitFest* since its inception in 2000 - see also the Appendix section. At the June 2022 event. resident cockpits scored a 'double': Lightning F.6 XR757 took the 'Cockpiteers' and Buccaneer S.2 XX899 the 'Grand Champion' awards respectively.

After use as spares for XW208, SA.330L 9L-LSG departed in early 2022, eventually bound for Melbourne, Derbyshire.

◆ *Drove Lane, NG24 2NY* | **01636 707170** | **enquire@newarkairmuseum.org** | **www.newarkairmuseum.org**

❑ G-ANXB	DH Heron 1B	53	ex Biggin Hill, BEA, G-5-14. CoA 25-3-79, de-reg 2-11-81. Arrived 27-10-81. BEA colours		1-24
❑ G-APRT	Taylor Monoplane	59	CoA 31-7-12, de-reg 16-4-12. Arrived 10-4-12	[1]	1-24
❑ G-APVV	Mooney M.20A	59	ex Skelmersdale, Barton, N8164E. Crashed 11-1-81, de-reg 3-4-89. Arrived 13-12-95		1-24
❑ G-ASNY	Bensen B-8	c64	ex Stockport, Eccles. De-reg 17-12-91. Arrived 20-4-09	[2]	1-24
❑ G-AXMB	Slingsby Motor Cadet	71	ex Ringmer, BGA.805, VM590 (Cadet TX.1 1946). CoA 9-7-82, de-reg 9-1-92. Arrived 18-8-02		1-24
❑ G-BFTZ	MS Rallye Club	68	ex Firbeck, Hooton Park, Warmingham, Fownhope, Rhoose, F-BPAX. CoA 19-9-81, de-reg 14-11-91. Arr 27-1-96. *Kathy S*		1-24
❑ G-BJAD	Clutton FRED Srs 2	r81	ex Retford. Unfinished project, de-reg 13-3-09. Arr 9-1-02		1-24
❑ G-BKPG	Luscombe Rattler Strike	r83	ex Egginton, Tatenhill. De-reg 31-7-91. Arrived 16-12-00		1-24
❑ G-CCLT	Powerchute Kestrel	93	ex Nantwich. De-reg 9-12-03. Arrived 27-10-03		1-24
❑ 'G-MAZY'	DH Tiger Moth	c41	BAPC.21, ex Innsworth, Staverton, Newark (1967), Thruxton. Arrived 25-6-95. Partially covered	[3]	1-24
❑ G-MBBZ	Volmer VJ-24W	r81	ex Old Sarum. CoA 3-9-93, de-reg 29-11-95. Arr 16-10-98		1-24
❑ G-MBUE	MBA Tiger Cub 440	r82	ex Retford, Worksop. De-reg 6-9-94. Arrived 16-7-94. *The Dormouse Zeitgeist*		1-24
❑ G-MBVE	Hiway Skytrike	r82	de-reg 13-6-90, arrived 21-6-95		1-24
❑ G-MJCF	Maxair Hummer	r82	de-reg 24-1-95, arrived 17-1-06		1-24
❑ G-MJDW	Eipper Quicksilver MX	82	ex Horncastle. CoA 5-5-07, de-reg 13-2-08. Arrived 15-12-07		1-24
❑ G-MNRT	Aviasud Sirocco 377GB	86	ex Mansfield area. CoA 18-8-01. Arrived 28-6-05	[4]	1-24
❑ BDW	Slingsby T.8	c47	BGA.895, ex VM637. CoA 12-6-93. Stored		1-24
❑ CDX	SZD Pirat	68	BGA.1470, ex Darlton. CoA 6-1-07. Arrived 2007. Stored		1-24
❑ –	Lee-Richards Annular rep	64	BAPC.20, ex Shoreham, Winthorpe, *Those Magnificent Men...* Arrived 1975		1-24
❑ –	Mignet HM.14 'Flea'	37	BAPC.43, ex E' Kirkby, Tattershall, Wellingore. Arr 9-3-94	[5]	1-24
❑ –	Mignet HM.14 'Flea'	36	BAPC.101, ex Tumby Woodside, East Kirkby, Tattershall, Sleaford. Arrived 9-3-94. Battered fuselage	[6]	1-24
❑ –	Zurowski ZP.1 helicopter	c77	BAPC.183, ex Burton-on-Trent. Unflown. Arrived 26-4-85		1-24
❑ –	Ward Gnome	c00	BAPC.330, unflown. Citroen 2CV. Arrived 11-07		1-24
❑ –	Slingsby T.67 Firefly CIM	95	ex Barkston Heath. Arrived 1-11. Cockpit procedure trainer		1-24
❑ –	Lockheed TriStar SIM	c75	ex Hendon, British Airways. Arrived 2-16	[7]	1-24
❑ VH-UTH	GAL Monospar ST-12	35	ex Innsworth, Winthorpe, Booker, Croydon, Panshanger, Biggin Hill, Australia, New England Airways. Arrived 18-3-68		1-24
❑ 4X-ARI	DH Dove 1 G-AHRI	46	ex Long Marston, East Kirkby, Tattershall, Little Staughton, 4X-ARI, G-AHRI. De-reg 18-5-72. Arrived 13-5-89. Iraq Petroleum Trans Co colours		1-24
❑ RA897	Slingsby Cadet TX.1	c44	stored. Arrived 2004		1-24
❑ TG517	HP Hastings T.5	48	ex 230 OCU, SCBS, BCBS, 202, 53, 47. Flew in 22-6-77		1-24
❑ VL348	Avro Anson C.19 G-AVVO	46	ex Southend, G-AVVO (de-reg 16-9-72), Shawbury, 22 GCF, 24 GCF, Colerne SF, 62 GCF, HCMSU, RCCF. SOC 15-11-67. Arrived 11-72	[8]	1-24
❑ VR249 'FA-EL'	Percival Prentice T.1 G-APIY	48	ex G-APIY, Laarbruch Fg Club, 1 ASS, RAFC. SOC 17-8-57. CoA 18-3-67, de-reg 19-4-73. Flew in 8-7-67. RAFC colours		1-24
❑ VZ608	Gloster Meteor FR.9	51	ex Hucknall, Shoreham, MoS, RR. RB.108 test-bed. Arr 2-70		1-24
❑ VZ634	Gloster Meteor T.7	48	ex Wattisham 8657M, 5 MU, Leeming SF, Stradishall SF, 41, 141, 609, 247. SOC 15-11-71. Arrived 16-12-85. 234 Sqn c/s		1-24
❑ VZ728*	R&S Bobsleigh G-AGOS (Desford Trainer)	45	ex Spanhoe, Coalville, Perth, Strathallan, Thruxton, RAE, Desford. CoA 28-11-80, de-reg 9-9-22. Flew in 19-8-22	[9]	1-24
❑ WB491	Avro Ashton 2 G-AJJW	51	ex Woodford, Rhoose, Dunsfold, Farnborough, RR, RAE, Tudor 2 G-AJJW (de-reg 10-4-49), TS897. SOC 13-2-62. Arrived 26-2-03. Forward fuselage	[10]	1-24

❑ WB624		DHC Chipmunk T.10	50	ex Hooton Park, Firbeck, Long Marston, Warmingham, East Midlands, Wigan, Dur UAS, Aberdeen UAS, Henlow, St Athan, 22 GCF, Debden, Jurby SF, 8 FTS, 18 RFS. SOC 14-7-72. Hatfield-built. Arrived 14-9-95		1-24
❑ WF369	'F'	Vickers Varsity T.1	51	ex 6 FTS, AE&AEOS, AES, 2 ANS, 201 AFS. SOC 1-4-76, flew in same day. 6 FTS colours		1-24
❑ WH791		EE Canberra PR.7	54	ex 'WH792' Cottesmore 'WH717' 8187M (19-11-71), St Athan 8176M and 8165M, 81, 58, 82, 542. Arrived 29-11-98. 81 Sqn colours. See notes above		1-24
❑ WH863		EE Canberra T.17	53	ex Marham 8693M, 360, A&AEE, B.2, RAE, IAM. Short-built. SOC 29-5-81. Arrived 10-7-90. Cockpit	[11]	1-24
❑ WH904	'K'	EE Canberra T.19	53	ex Cambridge, 7, 85, T.11, W Raynham TFF, 228 OCU, B.2 35, 207. Short-built. SOC 4-6-80. Arrived 1-10-85. 85 Sqn colours by 6-22	[12]	1-24
❑ WK277	'N'	V-S Swift FR.5	55	ex Congresbury, Wisley, Cosford, Leconfield 7719M (9-11-61), 2, F.4, RAE. Arrived 18-8-69. 2 Sqn colours		1-24
❑ WM913	'456'	Hawker Sea Hawk FB.3	54	ex Fleetwood, Sealand 8162M, Culdrose A2510 (14-7-61), Abbotsinch, 736, 700, 895, 897, 806. Arr 1-7-84. 897 Sqn c/s		1-24
❑ WR977	'B'	Avro Shackleton MR.3/3	57	ex Finningley 8186M (3-11-71), 203, 42, 206, 203, 42, 201, 206, 201, 220. Arrived 1-5-77. 42 Sqn colours	[13]	1-24
❑ WS692	'C'	Gloster Meteor NF.12	53	ex Cranwell, Henlow 7605M (8-7-59), 72, 46. AWA-built. Arrived 31-10-81. 72 Sqn colours		1-24
❑ WS739		Gloster Meteor NF(T).14	54	ex Misson, Church Fenton 7961M (12-10-67), Kemble, 1 ANS, 2 ANS, NF.14, 25. AWA-built. Arrived 21-1-84. 25 Sqn c/s		1-22
❑ WT651	'C'	Hawker Hunter F.1	54	ex Lawford Heath, Halton, Credenhill, Weeton 7532M (22-11-57), 229 OCU, 233 OCU, 229 OCU, 222. Arrived 17-1-92. 222 Sqn colours		1-24
❑ WT933		Bristol Sycamore 3 G-ALSW	51	ex Sutton, Strensall, Halton 7709M (18-11-60), A&AEE, G-ALSW (de-reg 26-3-51). Arrived 17-6-80		1-24
❑ WV606	'P-B'	Percival Provost T.1	54	ex Halton 7622M (20-11-55), 1 FTS. Arrived 2-72		1-24
❑ WV787		EE Canberra B.2/8	52	ex Abingdon 8799M (23-12-83), A&AEE, Ferranti, ASM. Arrived 24-11-85. Hefner 'bunny' logo, A&AEE colours		1-24
❑ WW217	'351'	DH Sea Venom FAW.22	55	ex Cardiff, Ottershaw, Culdrose, Yeovilton, ADTU, 891, FAW.21, 890. Hawarden-built. SOC 20-8-70. Arrived 18-12-83. 890 Sqn colours		1-24
❑ WX905		DH Venom NF.3	53	ex Henlow, Hendon, Yatesbury 7458M (14-10-57), 27 MU, 23. Hawarden-built. Arrived 16-5-89. 23 Sqn c/s		1-24
❑ XA239		Slingsby Grasshopper TX.1	53	ex 'Northampton'. Arrived 2004		1-24
❑ XB261		Blackburn Beverley C.1	55	ex Duxford, Southend, A&AEE. SOC 6-10-71. Scrapped 5-89. Arrived 25-5-04. Flightdeck		1-24
❑ XD593	'50'	DH Vampire T.11	54	ex Woodford, Chester, St Athan, 8 FTS, CFS, FWS, 5 FTS, 4 FTS. Hawarden-built. SOC 12-12-68. Arr 30-3-73. CFS c/s		1-24
❑ XH992	'P'	Gloster Javelin FAW.8	59	ex Cosford 7829M (21-2-64), Shawbury, 85. Arrived 22-8-81. 85 Sqn colours		1-24
❑ XJ560		DH Sea Vixen FAW.2	59	ex RAE Bedford, Farnborough, Halton 8142M (29-6-71), 893, 899, 892, 890. Christchurch-built. Arrived 10-8-86		1-24
❑ XL764	'J'	Saro Skeeter AOP.12	58	ex Nostell Priory, Rotherham, M Wallop, Arborfield 7940M (13-3-67), Hayes, A&AEE, MoA, AAC, Saro, AAC. Arr 16-7-80		1-24
❑ XM383	'90'	Hunting Jet Provost T.3A	60	ex Crowland, Scampton, 7 FTS, 1 FTS, RAFC, 6 FTS, BSE, 2 FTS, A&AEE, 2 FTS. Arrived 12-11-94. 7 FTS colours		1-24
❑ XM594		Avro Vulcan B.2	63	ex 44, Scampton Wing, 617, 27. SOC 19-1-83. Flew in 7-2-83. 44 Sqn colours	[13]	1-24
❑ XM685	'513'	Westland Whirlwind HAS.7 G-AYZJ	59	ex Panshanger, Elstree, Luton, G-AYZJ (de-reg 29-12-80), Fleetlands, Lee-on-Solent, 771, *Ark* Ship's Flt, 847, 848. SOC 24-3-71. Arrived 17-6-80. 771 Sqn colours		1-24
❑ XN573	'E'	Hunting Jet Provost T.3	61	ex Blackpool Airport, Kemble, 1 FTS, CFS. SOC 28-5-76. Arrived 15-4-89. Cockpit		1-24
❑ XN819		AW Argosy C.1	61	ex Finningley 8205M (10-7-72), 8198M, Shawbury, Benson Wing, 105, MoA. Arrived 2-84. Cockpit in display hall		1-24

Serial	Code	Type	Reg	Built	History	Note	Date
❑ XN964	'630'	Blackburn Buccaneer S.1		63	ex Bruntingthorpe, E Midlands, Brough (10-10-76), Pershore, RRE, RAE, 803, 736, 801. Arr 26-2-88. 736 Sqn c/s		1-24
❑ XP226		Fairey Gannet AEW.3		62	ex Lee-on-Solent, Southwick, Lee-on-S', A2667 (28-3-79), Lossiemouth, Ilchester, 849. Arr 7-11-82. 849 'D' Flt colours		1-24
❑ XR534	'65'	Folland Gnat T.1		63	ex Dunholme Bridge, Valley 8578M (2-12-77), 4 FTS, CFS. Arrived 2-12-00. 4 FTS colours		1-24
❑ XR757		EE Lightning F.6		65	ex Scampton, Grainthorpe, New Waltham, Rissington, Binbrook, 5-11 pool, 23, 5. SOC 24-6-88. Cockpit. Arrived by 6-15. 11 Sqn colours	[14]	1-24
❑ XS238		Auster AOP.9		62	ex M Wallop, 14/20 Air Sqn, 21 Flt, 651. SOC 15-7-66. Arrived 1999. Fuselage		1-24
❑ XS417	'DZ'	EE Lightning T.5		64	ex Binbrook, LTF, 5, 11, 5, 11, LTF, 56, 23, 11, 23, 226 OCU. SOC 29-7-88. Arrived 5-9-88. LTF colours		1-24
❑ XS726	'T'	HS Dominie T.1		65	ex Ipswich, Cosford 9273M (24-6-97), Cranwell, 3 FTS, 6 FTS, CAW. Arrived 24-9-14. 55 Sqn colours		1-24
❑ XT200	'F'	Bell Sioux AH.1		65	ex M Wallop. Westland-built. Arrived 1978		1-24
❑ XV490		McD Phantom FGR.2		69	ex Nantwich, Bruntingthorpe, Wattisham, 74, 228 OCU, 92, 56, 22, 92, 56, 23. SOC 1-10-92. Cockpit. 92 Sqn c/s	[15]	1-24
❑ XV728	'A'	Westland Wessex HC.2		68	ex Fleetlands, 72, 2 FTS, CFS, 18. Arr 18-8-98. *Argonaut*		1-24
❑ XW208		Sud Puma HC.1		71	ex Cranwell, Shawbury, Boscombe Down, 33, 230, 33, 72, 33, 230, 240 OCU, 1563 Flt, 33, 240 OCU, 33, 240 OCU, 33. Arrived 7-2-18. 33 Sqn colours		1-24
❑ XW276		Sud Gazelle 03		70	ex Sunderland, Wroughton, Southampton, M Wallop, Farnborough, Leatherhead, F-ZWRI. Arrived 4-99	[16]	1-24
❑ XX467	'86'	Hawker Hunter T.7	G-TVII	58	ex Bruntingthorpe, Exeter, Kemble, G-TVII (de-reg 28-7-14) Perth, SOC 13-10-83. 1 TWU, Jordan AF 836, Saudi AF 70-617, G-9-214, XL605, 66, 92. Arrived 3-5-17	[17]	1-24
❑ XX492	'A'	HP Jetstream T.1		75	ex Culdrose, Cranwell, 45, 3 FTS, 45, 6 FTS, METS. SAL-completed. Arrived 9-12-04. 45 Sqn colours		1-24
❑ XX634	'T'	SAL Bulldog T.1		74	ex Wellesbourne M', Shawbury, Liv UAS, Man UAS, E Mids UAS, CFS, 3 FTS, CFS, Cam UAS, 2 FTS. Arr 9-1-06. CFS c/s		1-24
❑ XX753		SEPECAT Jaguar GR.1		75	ex RAF EP&TU, Bottesford, 9087M, St Athan, Abingdon, Shawbury, 54, 226 OCU, 6. Arr 1-5-10. Cockpit. 16 Sqn c/s		1-24
❑ XX829	'GZ'	SEPECAT Jaguar T.2A		74	ex Ipswich, Shawbury, St Athan, 54, 16, 6, 226 OCU, 6, 54. Arrived 21-3-12. 54 Sqn colours		1-24
❑ XX899		Blackburn Buccaneer S.2B		76	ex Coventry, Kidlington, Stock, St Athan, Lossiemouth, 208, 12, Gulf Det, 12, 237 OCU, 16, 15, 208, 12. SOC 10-10-94. Arrived 26-10-18. Cockpit. 12 Sqn colours	[18]	1-24
❑ ZA176	'126'	HS Sea Harrier F/A.2		81	ex Yeovilton, 801, 800, 801, 899, 801, 899, 800, 801, 899, 801, 809, 800, 809, 899. Arr 21-7-04. 800 Sqn c/s		1-24
❑ ZA717		Boeing Chinook HC.1		82	ex Cranwell 9238M, St Athan, Fleetlands, 78, 7, 1310 Flt, 18, N37056. Crashed 25-7-89. Arrived 22-2-18		1-24
❑ –		Hunting Jet Provost CIM		c60	procedures trainer. Arrived 1998		1-24
❑ –		Folland Gnat T.1 CIM		c62	ex Melton Mowbray. Procedures trainer - forward cockpit. Folland-built. Arrived 1994		1-24
❑ –	'DB001'	McD Phantom CIM		69	ex Wattisham. Full-axis simulator. Arrived 1992		1-24
❑ –		EE Canberra PR.9		c52	BAPC.518, ex Corby, Stock, Rhoose, Brough, Boscombe Down, Short-built. Arrived 14-11-00. Cockpit	[19]	1-24
❑ –		SAL Bulldog T.1 CIM		~	ex Newark, Newton	[20]	1-24
❑ A92-708		GAF Jindivik 103B		c75	ex Filton, Kemble. Llanbedr. Lost 28-8-80 on 125th sortie, salvaged. Arrived 28-6-21		1-24
❑ AR-107		SAAB S.35XD Draken		71	ex Scampton, Esk.729, Danish AF. Last flight 25-2-94. Arrived 29-6-94		1-24
❑ 83	'8-MS'	Dassault Mystère IVA		56	ex Sculthorpe, French AF. Last flown 3-5-78, arrived 9-78. ET.1/8 colours	[21]	1-24
❑ QP-31		Westland Lynx HC.28		77	ex Fleetlands, Almondbank, Wroughton, Qatar Police, G-17-21. Arrived 18-12-18	[22]	1-24
❑ 56321		SAAB 91B-2 Safir	G-BKPY	56	ex Norwegian AF. Flew in 14-7-82. De-reg 8-2-02	[23]	1-24

Identity	Type	Year	History	Notes	Date
❑ Fv37918 '57'	SAAB AJSH.37 Viggen	76	ex Cranwell, Swedish AF, F21 and F10 Wings. Last flight 7-2-06, arrived 25-6-06. F21 colours		1-24
❑ '458'	Mikoyan-Gurevich MiG-23ML *Flogger*	c75	ex Chester, Latvia, USSR. (024003607). Imported 1993. Arrived 22-5-02. Polish colours	[24]	1-24
❑ '71'	Mikoyan MiG-27K *Flogger*	c79	ex Chester, Latvia, USSR. (61912507006). Imported 1993. Arrived 22-5-02. Soviet AF colours	[24] [25]	1-24
❑ 42-12417	NAA Harvard IIB	42	ex Earls Colne, Harrington, East Tilbury, Windsor, North Weald, Dutch AF B-163 (SOC 15-11-62), RCAF FE930, 42-12417. Noorduyn-built. Arrived 24-8-10		1-24
❑ '91007' 'TR-007'	Lockheed T-33A-1-LO	51	ex '5547', Sculthorpe, French AF, 51-9036. Last flown 30-5-78. Arrived 1979. 36th FBG colours	[21]	1-24
❑ '0-63008'	NAA F-100D-16-NA Super Sabre 54-2223	54	ex Sculthorpe, French AF, USAAF 54-2223. Last flown 24-5-77. Arrived 5-78. *Last Hun in USAFE* and *Spirit of Liberty*, 494th TFS colours by 8-21	[21]	1-24
❑ '82127' *and* G-APNJ	Cessna 310 G-APNJ	56	ex Shoreham, EI-AJY, N3635D. CoA 28-11-74, de-reg 5-12-83. Arrived 4-3-04. USAF L-27 / U-3A colours, *Blue Canoe*		1-24

■ **[1]** G-APRT is the prototype JT.1 Monoplane, designed and built by John Taylor and first flown at White Waltham 4-7-59. **[2]** *November-Yankee* is on loan from Roger Light - see Stockport, Gtr Man. **[3]** Tiger Moth 'G-MAZY' is a composite; mostly G-AMBB, ex T6801, in which case it is: ex Scampton SF, 6 FTS, 18 EFTS. **[4]** Sirocco was built by Midland Ultralights at Bitteswell, Leics. **[5]** Built by Alan Troop at Wellingore, Lincs - made a few hops in 1938. **[6]** Built by 'Bobby' Earl at Carlight Motors, Sleaford; believed unfinished. **[7]** Simulator built by Atkins and Merrill, Tulsa, Oklahoma. **[8]** Anson has the outer wings of Mk.XI G-ALIH (ex NL229) which was delivered to the museum on 3-9-69 from Southend, but destroyed by fire on 11-5-71. **[9]** Built by Reid and Sigrist at Desford as the RS.3 Desford advanced trainer, first flown 9-7-45. Converted to RS.4 Bobsleigh prone-pilot test-bed VZ728, first flown 13-6-51. Civilianised for aerial survey work in 1958 as Desford Trainer. **[10]** Laid down at Woodford as Tudor 2 G-AJJW, TS897, but completed as an Ashton. **[11]** T.17 cockpit is on loan from Aaron Braid. **[12]** T.19 WH904 was built by Shorts Brothers and Harland as a B.2 and therefore the forward fuselage *should* have a plate reading SHB-0-2388. Inspection found the cockpit to have the plate EEP71123, which would make it WH651. The logic works out like this... WH651 was issued to English Electric for conversion from a B.2 to a T.4 on 5-7-56 and in this process it would have been fitted with a new-build T.4 cockpit. It looks as though the old cockpit passed on to Boulton Paul for use in the B.2 to T.11 conversions. WH904 was issued to BP on 17-10-57 for T.11 fit. It received the cockpit of WH651. (And later was further converted to T.19 status.) **[13]** Shackleton and the Vulcan were transferred from ownership by Lincolnshire's Lancaster Association to the museum 15-12-21. **[14]** XR757 on loan from Trevor Garrod and Scot Bouchard. **[15]** Phantom cockpit on loan from Mike Davey - see also Liverpool, Merseyside. **[16]** Gazelle on loan from the Army Flying Museum, Middle Wallop, Hampshire. **[17]** T.7 on loan from Colin Savill. **[18]** Buccaneer cockpit, a 1991 Gulf War veteran - 19 missions - on loan from Robin Phipps - see also under Steventon, Oxfordshire. **[19]** PR.9 cockpit, owned by Frank and Lee Millar (see also Corby, Northants), is the first of two unflown 'boiler plate' cockpits for development and/or installations trials. It was last used for miniature detonation cord trials at Brough. **[20]** Bulldog CIM is on loan from Higgins Aviation, Newark, Notts. **[21]** From the National Museum of the USAF's Loan Program. **[22]** Lynx donated by Andy Rawdon, see South Clifton, Notts. **[23]** Safir delivered under NATO documentation; UK registration allocated as part of a plan to fly it on the UK airshow circuit for a while. **[24]** *Floggers* on loan from Hawarden Av Svs, Hawarden, Wales. **[25]** Mr Gurevich had been airbrushed out of history by the time the MiG-27 was designated.

NEWARK-ON-TRENT

Austers G-ALNV (front) and G-AOCP (behind) en route to Dumfries, June 2022. *Ken Ellis*

Cliff and **David Baker**: The curtain was rung down on the famous Auster workshop and collection in the area during the summer of 2022 and by November was clear. In their time the members of the Baker family have been vital to the longevity of Austers as a breed; their kind are increasingly rare.

Disposals: Autocrat G-AHHK reduced to spares and scrapped; Auster 5 G-ALNV to Dumfries, Scotland, 26-6-22 along with G-AOCP for spares; Auster B.4 replica 'G-AMKL' moved to Old Sarum, Wilts, 14-10-22; Tugmaster G-ARGB and Terrier 1 G-ARTM to Hooton Park, Cheshire, 25-10-22; Airedale G-AROJ removed circa 2020 to 'Kent'; Plus D EI-AMF to Spanhoe, Northants, 1-7-23 and reverted to G-ARRF; it was back in the air care of Carl Tyers and team - wearing LB286 – before the year was out. Terrier 3 frame c/n B.648 to a Norfolk-based owner and D6/180 c/n 3705 to Spanhoe, Northants, by 9-22. Auster 5D G-ANHW is reported to have gone to 'Doncaster' and from there to somewhere else – no further details.

Air and Space Institute: Friary Road. ◆ *Prior arrangement* **only** | **https://asi-newark.co.uk**

❑	–*		Airbus A318	~	ex Kemble. Fuselage, arrived 10-23	10-23

NOTTINGHAM

University of Nottingham Aerospace Technology Centre: Innovation Park, Triumph Road.
◆ *Prior arrangement* **only** | **www.nottingham.ac.uk/aerospace**

❑	–		Robinson R22	~	first noted 3-21	3-21

Also: The Archaeopteryx is at a *private* location in the *general* area. It is held by the descendants of the Granger brothers, Richard Francis and Richard John, who designed and built light aircraft in the 1920s and 1930s: including G-ABXL.

❑	G-ABXL		Granger Archaeopteryx	30	ex Old Warden, Radcliffe on Trent, Old Warden, Chilwell. CoA 22-9-82	N12-22

NOTTINGHAM CITY AERODROME or Tollerton, south of the A52, east of the city EGBN

❑	G-BGGF		Piper Tomahawk	78	CoA 15-10-94, de-reg 4-12-02. Fuselage	1-23
❑	G-GRAY		Cessna 172N		ex N4859D. Ditched 2-4-93, de-reg 27-9-00. Fuselage, dumped	6-22

SOUTH CLIFTON south of the A57 and west of the A1133, west of Lincoln

Andy Rawden: Airframes are kept at a *private* location in the area. ◆ *Prior arrangement* **only**

❑	5N-AAN	'K'	HSA HS.125-3B/RA	67	ex Newark, Sunderland, Woolsington, Biggin Hill, F-GFMP, G-AVAI, LN-NPA, G-AVAI. Cockpit. Dominie colours		8-20
❑	XT640		Westland Scout AH.1	64	ex Westbury, Ipswich, Arborfield, Lee-on-Solent, M Wallop, 654, 666, 663. Arrived by 7-21		6-23
❑	XZ694		Westland Lynx HAS.3	79	ex Ipswich, Fleetlands, Yeovilton, 815, Gulf War, 815, HAS.2, 815, 702. Arrived by 6-18	[1]	8-20

■ **[1]** Took out an Iraqi tug 15-2-91 care of a Sea Skua missile.

SYERSTON AIRFIELD off the A46 southwest of Newark-on-Trent EGXY

RAF Syerston: Home of the **Air Cadet STEM College**'s Tornados and Tucano, and the **2 FTS** / **Central Gliding School** and the **Central Glider Maintenance Flight.** There are two Viking and two Vigilant 'cockpits' in use, all 'synthetic' and not production-airframe-based.

❑	WG418*		DHC Chipmunk T.10 G-ATDY	51	ex Levenshulme, 8209M (4-8-72), Woodvale, Hamble, Jever SF, London UAS, G-ATDY (de-reg 19-1-68), 61 GCF, Queen's UAS, London UAS, 3 BFTS, 16 RFS. Hawarden-built. Cockpit, for conversion to SIM		11-23
❑	ZA267	'FA'	Panavia Tornado F.2	80	ex Marham 9284M, Boscombe Down. 25 Sqn colours. First noted 2-18. Displayed within base		11-23
❑	ZA357	'TTV'	Panavia Tornado GR.1	81	ex Cosford, 9341M, St Athan, 15. 15 Sqn colours Arrived 25-4-19. Displayed within base		11-23
❑	ZE550	'V'	Grob Viking T.1	84	ex 615, 614, 626 VGSs, CGS, 622 VGS, BGA.3025. Damaged, instructional	[1]	11-23
❑	ZE652*	'YD'	Grob Viking T.1	84	ex BGA.3082. Instructional. Frist noted 1-23		11-23
❑	ZF202		Short Tucano T.1	89	ex Linton-on-Ouse, Shawbury, 72, 1 FTS, 3 FTS, CFS. Arrived 18-8-20. Displayed within base		11-23
❑	ZH185		Grob Vigilant T.1	90	ex D-KGRO, D-KMSN. SOC 10-2-20. Fuselage		11-23

■ **[1]** ZE550 was written out of *W&R26* (p196) as "issued back to service" – clearly not so. Used for assembly/disassembly instruction. The code 'VX' has been truncated to 'V'.

WORKSOP on the A57/A60 east of Sheffield

Phil Jarvis: Took on a Jaguar full-motion simulator in June 2022. ◆ *Prior arrangement* **only**

❑ ZH655	BAe/McDD Harrier T.12	94	ex Doncaster, Ipswich, Cottesmore, Wittering. Crashed 26-7-95. Cockpit	4-18
❑ –*	SEPECAT Jaguar GR.1 SIM	~	ex Ipswich, Cosford, Gosport, Cosford, Cranwell, Selby, Coltishall. Simulator, acquired 6-22	6-23

OXFORDSHIRE

ABINGDON

Lodge Hill Garage: West of the A4183, close to its junction with the A34, has a plinth-mounted Spitfire.

❑ 'N3310' 'AI-A'	V-S Spitfire FSM	~	BAPC.393, ex Wellesbourne Mountford, Winthorpe	2-22

Also: A Chipmunk *should* still be at a *private* location in the *general* area.

❑ WP977	DHC Chipmunk T.10 G-BHRD	52	ex South Molton, Cambridge, Yateley, Crowland, Doncaster, Stamford, Burford, 9M-ANA, VR-SEK, WP977, Malayan Aux AF, Rufforth SF, Man UAS, Liv UAS, 63 GCF, Queen's UAS, Man UAS. Hawarden-built. Crashed 21-1-97, de-reg 19-1-98	12-23

ARNCOTT south of the A41 southeast of Bicester

St George's Barracks: Within is the **Defence Explosive Ordnance Disposal, Munitions and Search School**.

❑ XP855	Westland Scout AH.1	63	ex Arborfield, Wroughton, 652, 651, 655. First noted 6-17	6-23
❑ XW430 'MW'	BAC Jet Provost T.5A	72	ex Cosford, 9176M (20-1-93), 1 FTS, CFS, 3 FTS, Leeming SF, 3 FTS. First noted 6-17	6-23
❑ XX396 'N'	Sud Gazelle HT.3	75	ex Cranwell, 8718M, EPTT, St Athan, Abingdon, Henlow, 2 FTS. Westland-built. Crashed 30-6-81. First noted 6-17	6-23
❑ ZD607	HS Sea Harrier F/A.2	85	ex Gosport, St Athan 9328M, Warton, St Athan, 800, FRS.1, 801, 800, 801, 800, 801, 800, 899. Crashed 2-7-00. Arrived 23-8-12	6-23

BECKLEY north of the B4027, northeast of Oxford

Two helicopters are held at a *private* location in the *general* area.

❑ N260A	Bell JetRanger III	~	gutted cab, first noted 4-21	6-22
❑ ZA135 '705'	Westland Sea King HAS.6	81	ex Hixon, Fleetlands, Gosport, 771, 849, 820, *Gannet* SAR Flt, 819, 820, 819, 810, 706, 820. SOC 7-10-09. Arrived 12-13 [1]	2-23

■ **[1]** The tail end of ZA135 is/was fitted to XV657, last noted at Culdrose, Cornwall.

BENSON AIRFIELD east of the A4074, east of Wallingford EGUB

RAF Benson: The venerable Puma is set to be even more venerable with its retirement date slipping still further into the mid- to late-2020s. Several examples are held in 'deep store', but this situation is bound to be fluid. For the record, the following were in 'deep' store here in late 2021: XW219, XW232, ZA935 and ZA936. The forward fuselage of Chinook 82-23762 had migrated to Boscombe Down, Wilts, by July 2022.

❑ 'PL904'	V-S Spitfire FSM	89	BAPC.226, ex 'EN343'. 541 Sqn c/s, displayed since 1989	8-23
❑ XW223	Sud Puma HC.1	71	ex 33, 230. Westland-built. SOC 31-12-12. Instructional	4-16
❑ ZA937	Sud Puma HC.1	80	ex 230, 33, 230. Westland-built. SOC 31-12-12. Moved to 'gate' 16-1-23	12-23

BICESTER northeast of Oxford

Written out of *W&R27* (p299) from Scarborough, N Yorks, Geoffrey New's incredible 504 makes excellent progress at a *private* location in the *general* area. ◆ *Prior arrangement* **only**

❑ G-EASD*	Avro 504L	1920	ex Scarborough, Woodford, Richmond, Sudbury, S-AHAA, S-AAP, G-EASD [1]	9-22

■ **[1]** Three-seat 504L built by Eastbourne Aviation, exported to Sweden in 1921.

BRIZE NORTON AIRFIELD on the A4095 southwest of Witney EGVN

RAF Brize Norton: The **Defence Movements Training Squadron** (DMTS) and the **Joint Air Delivery Test and Evaluation Unit** (JADT&EU) keep airframes for instruction and trials. Several mock-ups are employed, including the rear end of an A400M. Adding to *W&R28* (p181), Hercules C.1 XV304 was scrapped by August 2020. The Dakota is displayed outside the **47 Air Despatch Squadron** hangar.

❑ 'FZ626'	'YS-DH'	Douglas Dakota 4	G-AMPO	44	ex Lyneham, Coventry, G-AMPO (CoA 29-3-97, de-reg 18-10-01), LN-RTO, G-AMPO, KN566, Oakington SF, 77, 62, Waterbeach SF, 1381 CU, 133 CU, 238, USAAF C-47B-30-DK 44-76853. Oklahoma City-built. Arr 16-9-12. 271 Sqn c/s [1]	1-24
❑ XW236		Sud Puma HC.1		73	ex Benson, 33, 230, 27, 33, 230, 1563 Flt, 33. Westland-built. Forward fuselage. Arrived 16-6-14. JADT&EU	1-24
❑ ZB684		Sud Gazelle AH.1		83	ex 9330M, Fleetlands, 667, 665, 655. Westland-built. JADT&EU. First noted 9-15	1-24
❑ ZJ133*	'R'	EHI Merlin HC.3		01	ex Boscombe Down, Yeovil. Arrived 8-3-22. JADT&EU loading trainer	1-24

■ **[1]** 'Dak' acquired by the Air Despatch Association, by which time it had clocked 25,508 hours, Painted to commemorate Mk. III FZ626 of 271 Sqn, shot down over Arnhem 19-9-44 and courageously flown into a German anti-aircraft gun emplacement; miraculously three of the eight crew survived, becoming PoWs.

CHALGROVE AIRFIELD on the B480 northwest of Watlington EGLJ

Martin-Baker: Flying test-beds Meteor T.7s WL419 (G-JSMA) *Asterix* and WA638 (G-JWMA) are based.

◆ **Strictly** *by prior permission*

❑ EE416	Gloster Meteor III	46	ex Wroughton, South Kensington, M-B. Cockpit [1]	9-23
❑ XX316*	HS Hawk T.1A		ex Valley, 74, 208, 234, 74, 234, 1 TWU. Bitteswell-built. Arrived 21-6-23	6-23

■ **[1]** With a Martin-Baker ejection seat squeezed in behind the pilot, EE416 carried out the first airborne use of a British 'bang seat' on a sortie out of Chalgrove on 24-7-46. The 'ejectee' was Bernard 'Benny' Lynch, a volunteer.

Ejection seat pioneer, Meteor III EE416 is cherished by Martin-Baker, September 2023. *Richard Hall*

CULHAM on the A415 east of Abingdon

Lasergaming Oxford: Located within the former airfield site. ◆ **Strictly** *prior permission* | **https//.outdoorlaser.com**

❑ XV720		Westland Wessex HC.2	68	ex Hixon, Gosport A2701 [2], Fleetlands, SARTU, 22, 18	1-24
❑ XZ643	'C'	Westland Lynx AH.7	80	ex Croft, Middle Wallop. First noted 11-13	1-24

ENSTONE AERODROME on the B4030 east of Chipping Norton EGTN

Some sources quote up to ten, others 'several', 'Stearman' airframes in store off-site, awaiting their turn for restoration. Taylorcraft LB369 (G-AHHY) was airworthy by June 2023. In accordance with the 'tidying up' outlined on page 7, the following have been deleted: Tri-Pacer G-ARET, Cessna F.150K G-AXPF, Quickie G-BNCG, Tomahawk G-BODS, Trinidad F-GDNR, JOB 15 D-ECFE.

❑ G-BHRW	Jodel DR.221 Dauphin	67	ex F-BPCP. CEA-built. De-reg 7-7-17	6-23
❑ G-BOXY*	Piper Archer II	78	ex Filton, Netherthorpe, N3073D. Crashed 24-7-02, de-reg 22-10-02. Cockpit, simulator. First noted 4-22	6-23

❑	G-BTET		Piper J-3C-65	46	ex N98141. Damaged 31-8-13, CoA 4-12-13		7-20
❑	G-BWVL*		Cessna 150M	76	ex N50NA. CoA 18-1-03, de-reg 26-4-05. Fuselage		6-23
❑	G-JIMB		Beagle Pup 100	69	ex G-AWWF, G-35-033. CoA 10-5-12. First noted 11-20		6-23
❑	G-RORY		Piaggio P.149D	58	ex Marshall, G-TOWN, D-EFFY, Luftwaffe 90+06, BB+394. Focke-Wulf-built. CoA 7-1-08. First noted 6-14		6-23
❑	G-SION		Piper Tomahawk 112	81	ex N32661. Crashed 2-7-97, CoA 28-12-00, de-reg 9-9-02		12-21
❑	N66576		Boeing PT-17 Kaydet G-CLLW	41	ex USA, 41-8559. Fuselage. First noted 8-16. See notes above		
❑	XX764	'13'	SEPECAT Jaguar GR.1	75	ex Woodmancote, Small Dole, St Athan 9010M, Shawbury, 226 OCU, 6, 226 OCU, 14. Last flown 3-9-84. Arrived 22-9-17, displayed	[1]	12-23
❑	'3091'		NA Harvard II G-CPPM	41	ex Bruntingthorpe, Canada, Trenton, Uxbridge (Ontario), RCAF 3019, 1 FTS, 1 SFTS, 8 SFTS. RCAF colours		2-23

■ **[1]** Jaguar under restoration by Neil Atterbury – more details on **www.jaguarxx764.co.uk**

GROVE on the A417 northwest of Wantage

Grove Business Park: Located on the western edge of the former airfield.

❑	J-1758	DH Venom FB.54 G-BLSD	57	ex Lambourn, N Weald, N203DM, Cranfield, G-BLSD (de-reg 5-6-96), Swiss AF. Swiss-built. 145 Sqn colours. Badly damaged in storm 28-2-22	4-22

HENLEY-ON-THAMES on the A4155 north of Reading

Fawley Steam Museum: Run by the Fawley Museum Society this enchanting railway-plus-more collection is well worth seeking out. The website poses the question of the 'Flea' "Is it art or aviation?" and notes that "packing cases, newspapers and a teapot" were used in its construction. Built by installation artist Chris Dobrowolski 'to the book' it qualifies in both categories: it is reported to have flown. ◆ *Fawley Hill, limited open days* | **www.fawleymuseum.org**

❑	–*	Mignet HM.14 'Flea'	94	built by Chris Dobrowolski, Citroen 2CV	6-23

Bremont Manufacturing and Technology Centre: The high-tech headquarters in Reading Road for the famous watch maker, opened in 2021, is called 'The Wing'. ◆ *Prior arrangement* **only** | **www.bremont.com**

❑	G-BYGB	Boeing 747-436	99	ex Kemble, St Athan, BA. Last flown 2-9-20. De-reg 5-5-21. Flightdeck	12-23

No.**447 (Henley-on-Thames) Squadron Air Cadets**: Friday Street.

❑	XS218	Hunting Jet Provost T.4	64	ex Woodley, Halton 8508M (23-2-77), Shawbury, 3 FTS. Cockpit	10-23

Also: At separate sites in the *general* area, the Aero and Vampire are at *private* locations.

❑	G-ATBH	Aero 145	65	ex Redhill. LET-built. CoA 26-10-81	12-21
❑	J-1169	DH Vampire FB.6	~	ex Samedan, Swiss AF. Swiss-built	6-20

OXFORD AIRPORT or Kidlington EGTK

Tailwind G-BDBD has been deleted.

❑	G-AHUG	Taylorcraft Plus D	42	ex Turweston, Thame, Panshanger, Auster I LB282, Turnhouse SF, 43 OTU, 653. First noted 11-21	11-21
❑	G-BYKR	Piper Warrior 161	88	ex HB-PLM. Crashed 30-8-06, CoA 11-8-08, de-reg 22-8-07. Rescue trainer, trailer mounted	6-21
❑	2-LCXO*	BAe Jetstream 3102	87	ex Firnas AW, G-LNKS, G-JURA, SE-LDH, OY-SVK, C-FAMU. Last flight 19-5-17. First noted 2-20	6-22

SHRIVENHAM east of Swindon, south of the A420

Defence Academy of the United Kingdom Technology School: Within the vast Joint Service Command and Staff College complex, complete with GCHQ-like 'doughnut' building, several airframes are used for instruction. By March 2022 Scout AH.1 XT621 had moved to Colsterworth, Lincs, but had been sold on – destination unknown – by that July.

❑	XV122	'A'	Westland Scout AH.1	68	ex Almondbank, Wroughton	5-14
❑	ZA556	'047'	Panavia Tornado GR.4	81	ex Marham, 9, GR.1, Warton. Arrived 2-4-19	3-23

❑ ZJ369	GEC-Marconi Phoenix UAV	c95	'Army' titles	8-19
❑ 69-16445	Bell AH-1F Cobra	69	ex US Army, 1/1 CAV, Budingen. Arrived 2-7-96 Technology School. 'IFOR' (Bosnia) markings	3-23

STEVENTON on the B4017 south of Abingdon

Aces High Aviation Gallery: After 28 years at the gallery in Wendover, Bucks, during May 2023 the well-known military fine art dealers opened up at larger premises which has permitted extra display space, including a full-size Spitfire replica, wartime vehicles, memorabilia, and an air strip for wing-borne visitors.

◆ *Skyfall, Church Lane, OX13 6SN* | **01296 625681** | **uk@aces-high.com** | **www.aces-high.com**

❑ 'MK392'* 'JE-J'	V-S Spitfire IX FSM	~	first noted 7-23	1-24

Robin Phipps: Keeps his Gannet and Sea Vixen cockpits at *private* locations in the general area. His Buccaneer cockpit is at Newark, Notts. ◆ *Prior arrangement* **only**

❑ XL449 '044'	Fairey Gannet AEW.3	58	ex Booker, Camberley, Booker, Camberley, Cardiff, Yeovilton, Lossiemouth, GSU, 849, A&AEE. SOC 2-10-78. Cockpit	6-23
❑ XN647 '707'	DH Sea Vixen FAW.2	61	ex Bruntingthorpe, Helston, Culdrose SAH-10, A2610 (25-2-71), 766, 892, FAW.1, 766, 899. Christchurch-built. Cockpit	6-23

UPPER HEYFORD or Heyford Park, north of the B4030, north of Oxford

Upper Heyford Heritage: As part of the plan for a visitor centre, pre-book airfield tours are presently offered.

◆ *Building 103, Camp Road, OX25 5HD* | *Prior arrangement* **only** | **uhheritage@outlook.com** | **www.uperheyfordheritage.co.uk**

SHROPSHIRE

Includes the unitary authority of Telford and Wrekin

BRIDGNORTH

Millington Racing Engines: Roy Millington and friends have lovingly restored a Harrier to 'running' condition.

◆ *Prior arrangement* **only** | **www.millingtonengines.com**

❑ XV808 'DD08'	HS Harrier GR.3	71	ex Gosport, Culdrose, A2687[2] (11-7-94), 9076M, 233 OCU, 3, GR.1 20, 4. Arrived 13-9-12. Engine runs 5-19	6-21

COSFORD AIRFIELD south of Junction 3 of the M54 EGWC

Royal Air Force Museum: Midlands: On 13th December 2022 the museum proudly announced its latest venture under the RAF Museum Midlands Development Programme. With the National Lottery Heritage Fund on board from the first round of funding for what is estimated to be a £22.1 million programme with building work to commence in 2025 and due for completion in the summer of 2027. All of this will include a purpose-built Collections Hub bringing together archival material previously held off-site and including 65,000-plus items large and small from Stafford; a Learning Centre; a woodland area and public 'realm' and a (can't help using curator-speak): "a new innovative nationally relevant exhibition" this last bit is the reason for the off-loading of so many airframes.

In the autumn of 2023, the new exhibition **Strike Hard, Strike Sure: Bomber Command 1939-1945** opened within the reconfigured Hangar 3. This has resulted in a major reshuffle and departures: movements from hangar to hangar are not specified, but transfers into open store are. The sight of highly significant test and trials aircraft outside – be it short or long term is most disturbing. Some airframes have moved on as transfer by gift or outward loan, but others – predictably the Argosy, Varsity et al have yet to find new homes – and it remains to see how this initiative plays out. (Those offered in 2022 for **transfer by gift** are marked ●: those offered for **outward loan** are marked ❖)

As well as the display halls and the external exhibits, there is a cafe within the visitor centre, with views over the active airfield. The **Aerospace Museum Society** provides a vital link in both the restoration of exhibits and the running of the museum and special events. (Royal Air Force Museum: London is, of course, Hendon, Gtr Lon – where there are further comments on the disposal process. See also under Stafford, Staffs.)

◆ *Off Junction 3 of the M54. TF11 8UP* | **01902 376200** | **cosford@rafmuseum.org** | **www.rafmuseum.org**

Hangar 1: Transfers by gift: Junkers Ju 52 'G-AFAP' (T.2B-272) to Hawkinge, Kent, 19-11-22; Auster C4 WE600 to Coventry, Warks, 11-22; Sycamore HR.14 XJ918 to Long Kesh, N Ireland, 9-12-22. As *W&R* closed for press, 'Flea' G-AEEH was due to move to Bournemouth, Dorset, and – fingers crossed – the opportunity has been taken to anticipate the transfer.

	Reg	Code	Type	Alt	Year	History	Note	Date
❑	G-EBMB		Hawker Cygnet		25	ex Hendon, Cardington, Henlow, Lympne No.14. De-reg 30-11-61, acquired 1968		1-24
❑	G-ACGL	'6'	Comper Swift		33	ex Hatch, Stafford, Timperley, Wigan, Stockport, Kinver. CoA 22-3-40, de-reg 1-12-46, arrived 3-11-11	❖	1-22
❑	G-APAS		DH Comet 1XB	XM823	53	ex Shawbury 8351M, XM823, G-APAS, G-5-23, Air France F-BGNZ. Hatfield-built. De-reg 22-10-58, last flown 8-4-68, arrived 17-9-78. BOAC colours		1-24
❑	'T9707'*		Miles Magister I	T9708 G-AKKR	40	ex M Wallop, Cardington, Manchester, Hendon 8378M, Gaydon, Henlow, G-AKKR, 'T9967', T9708, 51 MU, 16 EFTS, 239. Phillips & Powis-built. CoA 10-4-65, de-reg 16-7-69. First noted 9-21		1-24
❑	'FS628'		Fairchild Argus II	G-AIZE	43	ex Rochester, G-AIZE, Cosford, Henlow, Hanwell, G-AIZE, N9996F, 43-14601. CoA 6-8-66, de-reg 6-3-73, acquired 2-73		1-24
❑	PM651	'X'	V-S Spitfire PR.19		45	ex MBCC, Stafford, Middle East 'tour' with name *Bahrain*, Stafford, Cosford, Wyton, Cardington, St Athan, Hendon, St Athan, Benson, Bicester, Andover, Hucknall 7758M (16-7-54), THUM Flt, 6 MU.		1-24
❑	'RG904'	'BT-K'	V-S Spitfire FSM		12	BAPC.333, *Haldane Place*, 441 Sqn colours	[1]	1 24
❑	TX214		Avro Anson C.19		46	ex Henlow 7817M, HCCS, MCS, RCCF, Staff College CF, 1 FU, 16 FU. Acquired 29-8-63		1-24
❑	VP952		DH Devon C.2/2		47	ex St Athan 8820M, 207, 21, WCS, SCS, Upavon SF, TCCF, MCS, BCCS, HCCS, A&AEE, MCCF, AAFCE, Hendon SF, HS. Last flown 5-7-84	●	9-23
❑	WL679		Vickers Varsity T.1		53	ex 9155M, Farnborough, RAE, BLEU, RAE. Hurn-built. Last flown 27-7-92	❖[2]	9-23
❑	WL732		BP Sea Balliol T.21		54	ex store, Henlow, A&AEE, Lossiemouth, Anthorn. Acquired 7-2-69. On show by 7-14	❖	1-22
❑	WP912		DHC Chipmunk T.10		52	ex Hendon 8467M, Man UAS, RAFC, ITS, Cam UAS, CFS, 2 FTS, Lon UAS, FTCCS, HCCS, 8 FTS. Hawarden-built. Acquired 14-12-76	[3]	1-24
❑	WV562	'P-C'	Percival Provost T.1		54	ex MBCC, 'XF688' Oman c/s, Hendon, Cosford, Cranwell, Henlow 7606M (30-6-59), 22 FTS. Acquired 9-79		1-24
❑	WV746		Percival Pembroke C.1		55	ex 8938M, 60, 207, 21, WCS, TCCF, FTCCS, BCCS, Handling Sqn, 2 TAFCF. Acquired 13-4-87. 60 Sqn colours	❖	9-23
❑	XD674		Hunting Jet Provost T.1		54	ex store, St Athan, Swinderby, Finningley, Bicester 7570M, 71 MU, A&AEE, AS Bitteswell, Hunting. Last flown 4-6-57		9-23
❑	XP411		AW Argosy C.1		62	ex 2 SoTT 8442M (22-5-75), 6 FTS, Kemble, 70. Acquired 4-88	❖	9-23
❑	XR525	'G'	Westland Wessex HC.2		64	ex Shawbury, 72, 60, 72, Benson SF, SAR Wing, Benson SF, 72. Acquired 13-5-04. *Sunshine*, 72 Sqn colours		1-24
❑	XS639		HS Andover E.3A		67	ex 9241M, Northolt, 32, 115, C.1, 32, 46. Last flown 13-7-94. 32 Sqn colours		1-24
❑	XX654	'3'	SAL Bulldog T.1		74	ex Shawbury Newton, CFS, 3 FTS, CFS, 3 FTS, Bristol UAS, 2 FTS. Acquired 1993		91-24
❑	XZ997	'V'	HS Harrier GR.3		82	ex Hendon 9122M, 233 OCU, 1453 Flt, 4, 1, 4. Acquired 4-12-91, arrived 10-18. 4 Sqn colours		1-24
❑	ZA718*	'BN'	Boeing Chinook HC.6A		82	ex Odiham, HC.4 (2012), HC.2 (1993), 18, 27, Falklands, HC.1, 18, A&AEE, N37058. *The Survivor*. Arrived 15-3-22	[4]	1-24

■ **[1]** Spitfire, claimed to be the only 1:1 'Airfix' 'kit', was assembled during a James May TV programme called *Toy Story* at Cosford in 2009. It was removed during 2010, going to Gateguards (UK) Ltd at Newquay, Cornwall, for what was termed "maintenance and strengthening". It returned in October 2010 and occupies space that could be taken up by a *real* exhibit. **[2]** WL679 made the last-ever flight by the type, into Cosford, on 27-7-92. **[3]** Chipmunk was used by the Duke of Edinburgh during his flying training. **[4]** Long since earmarked for preservation, *Bravo-November* was airborne on an air test 25-5-82 when the *Atlantic Conveyor* was hit by Argentine Exocets. Suddenly it was the only Chinook the task force had, hence the name *The Survivor*, operating from *Hermes* initially. Among its exploits during its time on the Falklands, it carried 55 tons of cargo, 1,500+ personnel, 650 Argentine PoWs and its pilots earned four DFCs. Lynx XZ183 is marked 'ZA718' at Boscombe Down, Wilts.

Hangar 2: Bizarrely, this hangar is still entitled **Test Flight**, although many of its previous inmates are now out in the cold. The following have been moved outside (listed separately below): Meteor WK935, SR.53 XD145, 'JP' XM351, Hunting 126 XN174, Jaguar XX765.

	Serial	Code	Type	Year	History	Note	Last noted
❑	'A8226'		Sopwith 1½ Strutter replica G-BIDW	80	ex Hendon, Cardington, Land's End, '9382', G-BIDW Westward Airways-built. (CoA 29-12-80, de-reg 4-2-87). Acquired 1-81. Arrived 15-7-14		1-24
❑	'C4994'		Bristol M.1C replica G-BLWM	87	ex Hendon, Cardington, 'C4912', Hucknall, G-BLWM (CoA 12-8-87, de-reg 12-5-88). Don Cashmore-built. Acquired 8-87. Arrived 15-7-14. Up on 'poles'	[1]	1-24
❑	K8042		Gloster Gladiator II	37	ex Hendon, 8372M, Biggin Hill 'K8442', 61 OTU, 5 (P)AFU, A&AEE. Acquired 11-65. 87 Sqn colours. Arrived by 11-16		1-24
❑	K4972		Hawker Hart Trainer	35	ex Hendon, Cosford, Cardington, Hendon, St Athan, 1546 ATC, Carlisle, Wigton 1764M, 2 FTS. AWA-built. Acquired 16-10-63. Arrived 20-4-17. Up on 'poles'		1-24
❑	K9942	'SD-D'	V-S Spitfire I	39	ex Hendon 8383M, Rochester, Hendon, 71 MU Bicester, Fulbeck, Wroughton, Newark, Cardiff, 53 OTU, 57 OTU, 72. Acquired 9-11-71. 72 Sqn colours		1-24
❑	N1671	'EW-D'	Boulton Paul Defiant I	38	ex Hendon, Rochester, Hendon 8370M, Finningley, 285, 307. 307 Sqn colours. Acquired 23-7-68, arrived by 11-16		1-24
❑	'N5182'		Sopwith Pup G-APUP	16	ex 9213M (31-8-93), Hendon, Blackbushe, Old Warden, G-APUP (CoA 28-6-78, de-reg 4-10-84), Musée de l'Air, Dover Defence Flt, Walmer DF, 9, 3, 8 Sqns RNAS, 1 Wing, A8736. Acquired 6-82. Arrived 15-7-14. *Shelia*	[2]	1-22
❑	LF738	'UH-A'	Hawker Hurricane II	44	ex Rochester, Biggin Hill, Melksham, 5405M, 22 OTU, 1682 BDTF. Arrived 16-8-95. 1682 BDTF colours		1-24
❑	WG760		EE P.1A	54	ex Binbrook, Henlow, St Athan, Weeton 7755M (7-6-62), Warton, A&AEE. Last flight 18-2-61. Arrived 23-1-86		1-22
❑	WG768		Short SB.5	52	ex Topcliffe, Finningley 8005M, ETPS, RAE Bedford, RAE Farnboro', A&AEE, RAE Bedford, A&AEE. Last flown 7-3-68	[3]	1-22
❑	WG777		Fairey FD.2	56	ex Topcliffe, Finningley 7986M, RAE Bedford. Acquired 8-9-67		9-23
❑	XF926		Bristol 188	63	ex 8368M, Foulness, RAE. Last flown 12-1-64. Arrived 3-9-72	❖ [4]	1-22
❑	XR220		BAC TSR.2 XO-2	64	ex Henlow 7933M, Boscombe Down, A&AEE. Never flown. Acquired 20-6-67, arrived 4-5-75		1-24
❑	XS695		HS Kestrel FGA.1	65	ex Wyton, Cardington, Yeovilton, Culdrose 'SAH-6', Manadon A2619 (10-5-73), A&AEE, RAE, CFE, Tri-Partite Eval Sqn, A&AEE, RAE. Crashed 1-3-67	[5]	1-24
❑	ZF534		BAe EAP	85	ex Loughborough, Warton. Last flown 1-5-91, Arr 27-3-12	[6]	1-24
❑	–*		Hawker Hind (Afghan)	37	BAPC.82, ex Stafford, Cosford, Hendon, Kabul, Afghan AF, RAF. Acquired 10-1-68, arrived by 9-23		1-24
❑	10639	'6'	Messerschmitt Bf 109G-2 G-USTV	40	ex Hendon, Duxford G-USTV (de-reg 24-9-98), Benson, Northolt, Lyneham 8478M, Henlow, Wattisham, Stanmore Park, Sealand, CFE-EAF, 1426 Flt, RN228, Lydda, 3 Sqn Gambut, III/JG77. Erla-built. Crashed 12-10-97. Acquired 10-3-02, arrived 11-16		1-24

■ **[1]** Don Cashmore also built Hawker Cygnet G-CAMM at Shuttleworth, Beds. **[2]** The story goes that Lt Cdr K C D St Cyrien was permitted to bring this out of museum storage for return to flight and that he did it piece by piece over a series of years! In 2-59 he registered G-APUP as a Pup *replica*, but in 1973 changed this to an *original*. Cyrien was also responsible for G-ABOX, currently at Middle Wallop, Hampshire. **[3]** The T-tail rear fuselage is displayed alongside WG768. **[4]** Only Bristol turbojet-powered design to fly: total flying time came to a mere 26 hours, 11 minutes. **[5]** Kestrel was placed on RAF Museum charge 10-5-74 but went to Manadon on extended loan, before coming back into the fold. **[6]** EAP factoids: first flown at Warton 8-8-86, total time 191 hrs, 21 mins.

Hangar 3 - War in the Air including **Strike Hard, Strike Sure, Bomber Command 1939-1945**: The hangar has received a major reconfiguration and changes of airframes. One of the 'stars' in this is the restored Wellington – another shining example of the capabilities of the team at the Michael Beetham Conservation Centre. Also included are sections of Short Stirling III LK488 of 1651 CU, crashed 19th October 1944 and recovered from Mickle Fell, Yorks, 31st August 1977. Previously at Stafford, Staffs; although impressive, they do not merit a formal listing: there are also elements of this 'fallen warrior' on show at Hendon. Supporting displays include a 'Wall of Reflection' and the inevitable inter-active gizmos.

The following moved to Hendon, Gtr Lon: Me 163B 191614 by April 2022;Kawasaki Ki-100 16336, Mitsubishi Ki-46 5439 and Yokosuka Ohka '10461' all be December 2022.

Serial	Code	Type	Year	History	Note	Noted
❑ 'L8756'*	'XD-E'	Bristol Bolingbroke IVT	42	ex Hendon, Boscombe Down, RCAF 10001. Fairchild Canada-built. Acquired 25-4-66. 139 Sqn colours as Blenheim IV. Arrived by 5-23		1-24
❑ T6296		DH Tiger Moth	41	ex Hendon, 8387M, Yeovilton SF, BRNC, RNEC, Stretton, 7 EFTS, 1 EFTS. Morris-built. Acquired 15-3-72. Arrived 11-16		9-23
❑ MF628		Vickers Wellington T.10	44	ex MBCC, Hendon 9210M, Abingdon, St Athan, Biggin Hill, Hendon, Heathrow, Wisley, Vickers, *Dam Busters* photo-ship (1954), 1 ANS. Squires Gate-built as B.X. Acquired 1964, arrived 1-7-10	[1]	1-24
❑ 'PR536'	'OQ-H'	Hawker Tempest II	46	ex MBCC, Hendon, Duxford, Cardington, Chichester, Indian AF HA457, RAF 5. Acquired 13-11-91, arrived by 10-20. 5 Sqn colours	[2]	9-23
❑ RF398		Avro Lincoln B.2/4A	45	ex 8376M, Henlow, Abingdon, 151, CSE, BCBS. AWA-built. Last flown, and acquired, 30-4-63		1-24
❑ TA639	'AZ-E'	DH Mosquito TT.35	45	ex Henlow, CFS, *633 Squadron* (1963), 'HJ682', CFS 7806M (6-5-63), 3 CAACU, Aldergrove TT Flt, Ballykelly SF, B.35. Last flight 3-10-65. Acquired 5-7-67. 627 Sqn colours	[3]	1-24
❑ 112372	'4'	Messerschmitt Me 262A-2a	45	ex Hendon, Cosford 8482M, St Athan, Cosford, Finningley, Gaydon, '110880', Cranwell, Farnborough, VK893, Twenthe. Acquired 1972, arrived 5-17	[4]	9-23
❑ 360043	'D5+EV'	Junkers Ju 88R-1	43	ex Hendon, St Athan 8475M, Henlow, St Athan, Biggin Hill, Fulbeck, Wroughton, Stanmore, PJ876, 47 MU, CFE, 1426 Flt, RAE. Defected 9-5-43. Acquired 9-69. Arr by 2-17		9-23
❑ 418947		Fieseler Fi 103 (V-1)	c44	BAPC.94, ex 8583M, Westcott		1-22
❑ 420430	'3U+CC'	Messerschmitt Me 410A-1/U2	43	ex MBCC, St Athan 8483M, Cosford, Fulbeck, Wroughton, Stanmore Park, Brize Norton, Farnborough, AM.72, Vaerlose. First noted 11-19		9-23
❑ 475081	'GM+AK'	Fieseler Fi 156C-7 Storch	44	ex St Athan, Coltishall, Bircham Newton, Finningley, Fulbeck, Halton 7362M (3-8-56), VP546, RAE, AM.101, Farnborough. Mraz-built. Arrived 6-4-89		9-23
❑ 733682		Focke-Wulf Fw 190A-8/R6	43	ex South Lambeth, 9211M, ex Duxford, South Lambeth, Biggin Hill, Cranwell, Brize Norton, Farnborough AM.75. Arrived 20-12-12	[5]	9-23
❑ –		Focke Achgelis Fa 330A-1 Bachstelze	44	ex 8469M, Henlow, Farnborough. Weser Flug-built. Acquired 9-67		7-22

■ **[1]** Made almost certainly the last-ever Wellington flight 24-1-55, St Athan-Wisley. **[2]** 'PR536' fitted with wings of an IAF Mk.II and Centaurus donated by IAF 11-78 and rear fuselage of Mk.II 'KB418' from RNEC Manadon 4-87. **[3]** 'M' number nominal as TA639 retained for display flying 30-5-63 to -10-65 when total time was 607 hours. *Loaned* for use in *633 Squadron*, 1963. Last 'Mossie' to fly under RAF aegis. Portrays Mk.XX KB627 in which Wg Cdr Guy Gibson was killed 19/20-9-44. **[4]** History track revised to reflect recent thinking on the Me 262; it is most likely 112372. **[5]** Fw 190A was modified to be the upper component of a Mistel S3B flying-bomb combination and was mounted on a Ju 88H when captured. It joined the collection at Cranwell from 18-9-46 and remained on loan from the RAF Museum during its time at IWM.

National 'Cold War' Exhibition:

Serial	Code	Type	Year	History	Note	Noted
❑ N9050T		Douglas Dakota 3	44	ex Stafford, Hendon, Rochester, Cosford, Fleet, Thruxton, Hal Safi, 5N-ATA, PH-MAG, G-AGYX, KG437, USAAF C-47A-10-DK 42-92648. Oklahoma City-built. Cockpit		1-24
❑ KN645		Douglas Dakota C.4	44	ex 'KG374', 8355M, Colerne, AFN CF, MinTech, AFN CF, MinTech, AFN HQ, SHAPE CF, Malta CF, BAFO CS, 2nd TAF CS, USAAF C-47B-35-DK 44-77003. Oklahoma City-built. Acquired 1-5-74. Transport Command colours		1-24
❑ TG511		HP Hastings T.5	48	ex 8554M, 230 OCU Radar Tng Flt, SCBS, BCBS, Met.1, 202, C.1 Lyneham Wing, Topcliffe Wing, 47. Acquired 16-8-77		1-24
❑ TS798		Avro York C.1	45	ex 'MW100', Shawbury, Brize Norton, Staverton, 'LV633', G-AGNV, Skyways, BOAC, TS798. CoA 6-3-65, last flight 9-10-64. De-reg 7-5-65. Acquired 16-5-72	[1]	1-24

❑ WS843	'J'	Gloster Meteor NF(T).14	54	ex Hendon, St Athan, Henlow 7937M, St Athan, Kemble, 1 ANS, NF.14, A&AEE, 228 OCU. AWA-built. SOC 8-3-66. Acquired 13-3-67. 264 Sqn colours		1-24
❑ XA564		Gloster Javelin FAW.1	54	ex 2 SoTT, Locking 7464M, Filton. Acquired 9-75		1-24
❑ XB812	'U'	NAA Sabre F.4	53	ex Hendon, 9227M, Duxford, Rome, Italian AF MM19666, XB812, 93, 112, RCAF (n/s) 19666. Acquired 31-1-94. 93 Sqn colours		1-24
❑ XD818		Vickers Valiant BK.1	56	ex Hendon, Marham 7894M, 49 'A' Flt. Acquired 25-5-65, arrived 8-05. 49 Sqn colours	[2]	1-24
❑ XE670		Hawker Hunter F.4	55	ex deep store, St Athan 8585M / 7762M, Abingdon, Bicester, 93, 26. Squires Gate-built. Cockpit		1-24
❑ XG337		EE Lightning F.1(DB)	59	ex 2 SoTT 8056M, Warton, A&AEE, Warton. Acquired 10-83		1-24
❑ XH171	'U'	EE Canberra PR.9	60	ex 2 SoTT 8746M, 39, 13, 39, MoA, 58. Short-built. Last flight 13-7-82. 39 Sqn colours		1-24
❑ XH672		HP Victor K.2	60	ex 9242M (26-3-94), Shawbury, 55, 57, 543, MoA. Last flown 30-11-93. *Maid Marion.* 55 Sqn colours	[3]	1-24
❑ XL568	'X'	Hawker Hunter T.7A	58	ex Cranwell 9224M (19-11-93), Lossiemouth, 12, 74, MoA, 74, HS. Acquired 12-2-02. 74 Sqn colours		1-24
❑ XL993		SAL Twin Pioneer CC.1	58	ex Henlow 8388M (6-2-69), Shawbury, 21, 78		1-24
❑ XM598		Avro Vulcan B.2	63	ex 8778M, 44, Waddington Wing, Cottesmore Wing, 12. Arrived 20-1-83. 44 Sqn colours		1-24
❑ 'XN972'		Blackburn Buccaneer S.1 XN962	63	ex Hendon, Cosford, St Athan, 'XN972', Abingdon 8183M, Foulness, 736, 800, 809. Acquired 7-95. Cockpit		1-22
❑ XR371		Short Belfast C.1	67	ex Hucknall, Kemble, 53. Arrived 6-10-78. *Enceladus.* 53 Sqn colours		1-24
❑ XV591	'013'	McD Phantom FG.1	69	ex St Athan, 111, 43, 892. 892 Sqn Trans-Atlantic air race colours. Cockpit		1-24
❑ 503		Mikoyan-Gurevich MiG-21PF *Fishbed* G-BRAM	66	ex Farnborough, Hurn, G-BRAM (de-reg 16-4-99), N610DM, North Weald, Hungarian AF. Acquired 18-10-06. Hungarian AF c/s		1-24
❑ 1120 red		Mikoyan-Gurevich MiG-15*bis Fagot*	55	ex Hendon, Cardington, S Lambeth, Hendon, Middlesbrough, Polish AF. WSK-built Lim-2. Acquired 29-10-86. Polish AF c/s		1-24
❑ 68-8284		Sikorsky MH-53M Pave Low IV	68	ex Brize Norton, Baghdad, *Desert Thunder*, 20th SOS, 67th ARRS, SEA. Acquired 17-12-08		1-24
❑ 74-0177		GD F-111F Aardvark	64	ex Mildenhall, AMARC, 27th TFW, 48th TFW, 366th TFW, 347th TFW. Last flown 10-95, arr 3-11-05. 492nd TFS c/s		1-24

■ **[1]** York made its and the type's last-ever flight on delivery to the Skyfame Museum at Staverton 9-10-64. **[2]** On 15-5-57 XD818 dropped a 'Short Granite' thermonuclear fusion bomb over Christmas Island, SW Pacific. **[3]** Victor XH672 flew during the Falklands conflict, including the BLACK BUCK raids and had the highest sortie score during Operation GRANBY – 52 'ops'. When it landed at Shawbury (for roading to Cosford) on 30-11-93 it made the last flight by a Victor.

External Exhibits:

❑ XG225		Hawker Hunter F.6A	56	ex 8713M (15-2-82), Weapons School, 2 SoTT, Kemble, 237 OCU, F.6, TWU, 229 OCU, 92, 74, 20. 237 OCU colours		1-24
❑ 'XM497'		Bristol Britannia 312F G-AOVF	57	ex Southend, 9Q-CAZ, G-AOVF (de-reg 21-11-84), Stansted, British Eagle, BOAC. Last flown 2-5-84. RAF c/s, *Schedar*		1-24
❑ XR808	'R'	Vickers VC10 C.1K	66	ex Bruntingthorpe, 101, 10. *Kenneth Campbell VC.* Last flew 29-7-13. Arrived 21-6-15, on display by 11-15		1-24
❑ XS709	'M'	HS Dominie T.1	64	ex Cranwell, 55, 3 FTS, 6 FTS, 1 ANS, CAW, 1 ANS, A&AEE, G-37-65 Rolls-Royce. Last flight 11-2-11		1-24
❑ XV202		Lockheed Hercules C.3	67	ex Brize Norton, 47, Lyneham TW, C.1, Lyneham TW, 48, USAF 66-8552. Last flown 12-8-11		1-24
❑ XV249		HS Nimrod R.1	70	ex Kemble, Waddington, 51, MR.2 Kinloss Wing, St Mawgan Wing, 42, MR.1, Kin W, 203, Kin W. 'Nimrod R.1 1974-2011' titles. Last flown 29-7-11, arrived 3-12, unveiled 28-9-12	[1]	1-24

■ **[1]** Nimrod made the last-ever flight by the breed (into Kemble) on 29-7-11, completing 18,488 flying hours.

Michael Beetham Conservation Centre (MBCC): Wellington MF628 trundled across to Hangar 3 – above – in early 2023. Ohka 11 997 was delivered on loan to the Pima Air and Space Museum, Tucson, USA, during 2022. (Note: the Pima website gives this as 1174.)

Leaving long term storage in December 2023 were the outer wing panels of Hasting C.1A TG568, bound for Trenton, Ontario, to help in the restoration of Speke-built Halifax VII NA337. TG568 ended up on the fire dump at RAF Thurleigh in 1974. The wings were salvaged circa 1978 for potential use in the resurrection on Hendon's Mk.II W1048, but not required.

◆ *Annual open event - see website for details. Otherwise by prior arrangement* **only.**

Serial	Code	Type	Year	History	Note	Date
❑ P1344	'PL-K'	HP Hampden TB.I	42	ex 9175M, Wyton, Cardington, Hatch, Petsamo, USSR, 144, 14 OTU. Forced down 4-9-42. Salvaged 1990. Arrived UK 4-9-91.	[1]	1-24
❑ 7198/18		LVG C.VI	1918	ex Old Warden, 9239M, G-AANJ (CoA 8-5-04, de-reg 11-12-03), Stanmore, Colerne, Fulbeck. Last flown 20-9-03, arrived 12-11-03		1-24
❑ 1160	'5K+AR'	Dornier Do 17Z-2	40	ex Goodwin Sands, 7/KG3. Shot down 26-8-40. Hulk, salvaged from sea. Arrived 6-13		1-24

■ **[1]** Hampden is being restored to allow inspection of the interior. The wings will not be restored and will be stored. At some stage in its career P1344 was fitted with the tailboom of Short-built Hereford I L6012. This was SOC on 20-10-41 while serving with the Jurby-based 5 BGS following a collision with an Anson. The Hereford was a Hampden powered by Napier Daggers. See fellow AE436 at East Kirkby, Lincs, lost on the same night.

Outside store: Has swollen with the arrival of some 'Test Flight' refugees: hopefully for the short term. Those offered in 2022 for **transfer by gift** are marked ●: those offered for **outward loan** are marked ❖.

Serial	Code	Type	Year	History	Note	Date
❑ WK935		Gloster Meteor F.8(mod)	53	ex Test Flight, St Athan, Colerne 7869M, Lyneham, Kirkbride, RAE. AWA-built. Prone-pilot test-bed. Last flown 12-6-59. Acquired 12-1-65. Outside by 9-23	❖ [1]	9-23
❑ XD145		Saro SR.53	56	ex Test Flight, Brize Norton, Henlow, Westcott, A&AEE. Last flown 20-10-59, arrived 2-3-82. Outside by 9-23	[2]	9-23
❑ XM351	'Y'	Hunting Jet Provost T.3	58	ex Test Flight, 2 SoTT, Halton 8078M (25-2-70), Shawbury, 3 FTS, 7 FTS, 2 FTS. Acquired 6-96. Outside by 9-23		9-23
❑ XM463*	'38'	Hunting Jet Provost T.3A	60	ex Hendon, 1 FTS, RAFC. Acquired 6-3-91. Fuselage. Arrived 25-5-23		9-23
❑ XN714		Hunting 126/50	63	ex Test Flight, RAE Bedford, NASA Ames and Moffett, Holme-on- Spalding Moor, RAE. Last flown 9-11-67, arrived 30-4-74. Outside by 4-23		9-23
❑ XX496	'D'	HP Jetstream T.1	75	ex 'Cold War', Cranwell, 45, 6 FTS, 3 FTS. SAL-built. Arrived 22-3-04. 45 Sqn colours. Outside by 11-17	❖	9-23
❑ XX765		SEPECAT Jaguar GR.1(mod)	75	ex Test Flight, Loughborough, Warton, BAe, GR.1, 226 OCU, 17, 14. Last flown as GR.1 4-8-78, as ACT 11-84. Arrived 10-11-99. Outside by 9-23	[3]	9-23
❑ L-866		Consolidated PBY-6A Catalina	45	ex 8466M, Colerne, Danish AF Esk.721, 82-866, BuNo 63993. Acquired 29-5-74, moved outside 9-16	❖	9-23
❑ 204		Lockheed SP-2H Neptune	61	ex Dutch Navy, 320 Sqn, Valkenburg, 5 Sqn, 321 Sqn. Last flight 22-7-82. 320 Sqn colours	●	9-23
❑ 853		Hawker Hunter FR.10	57	ex Hendon, Oman, SOAF, Jordan AF 853, XF426, 229 OCU, 2, 208. AWA-built. Acquired 6-9-03. First noted 12-16, by 11-19	[4]	9-23

■ **[1]** Last Meteor to be built by AWA at Coventry; converted as prone pilot test-bed, first flown 10-2-54. Issued to RAE Farnborough 31-8-54. **[2]** SR.53 first flew on 16-5-57 and last flew 20-10-59 with a total time of just under 18 hours in 46 sorties. **[3]** XX765 is much-modified Active Control Technology (ACT) test-bed. It was the world's first to fly with an all-digital quadruplex 'fly-by-wire' control system, on 21-10-81. **[4]** Hunter FR.10 was a gift from the Sultan of Oman.

Deep Stores: Transfers by gift: Meteor T.7(mod) WA634 to Long Kesh, N Ireland, 9-12-22; Avro 707C WZ744 to Woodford, Gtr Man, 14-11-22; Vampire FB.5 VX461 and P-51D Mustang '413573' (N6526D) crated and despatched to Hunter Fighter Collection, Scone, NSW, Australia, 11-22, arriving 4-23; Gnat F.1 XK724 to Coventry, Warks, 1-12-22. Last noted in store 11-16, Spitfire IX FSM 'MK356' had travelled to Boscombe Down, Wilts, by 6-22.

The EE-built Vampire FB.5's identity and unit history was 'nailed' in time for it to go 'down under'. Its pedigree should have read: ex Henlow, Hendon, 'WA346', 7646M (13-6-60), 3/4 CAACU, 8 FTS, 16, 26, At some stage VX461 was painted as 'WA346' while on display at Hendon, and/or with 120 Sqn ATC, both while at Hendon up to acquisition by the museum in 6-69. *OR*... while at 49 MU Colerne in 1960 while being prepared for display at Hendon; it consumed parts from fellow former 3/4 CAACU FB.5 WA346. Other interpretations are available; your statutory rights have not been interfered with.

Those offered in 2022 for **transfer by gift** are marked ●: those offered for **outward loan** are marked ❖.

◆ ***Not*** available for inspection.

	Reg	Code	Type	Built	History		Noted
❑	–	'33'	Avian hang-glider	~	ex Stafford, Hendon. First noted 6-18	●	1-22
❑	DG202/G		Gloster F9/40 Meteor	42	ex Hendon, Cosford, Colerne, Yatesbury, Locking 5758M, Moreton Valance. Acquired 1965. Arrived 5-17	[1]	1-22
❑	RH746		Bristol Brigand TF.1	46	ex Kemble, Sunderland, Failsworth, CS(A), ATDU Gosport, Bristol, ATDU, A&AEE, Bristol. Fuselage; tail at MBCC		1-22
❑	VX573		Vickers Valetta C.2	50	ex 8389M, Henlow, Wildenrath CF, Buckeburg CF. Acquired 7-11-68. *Lorelei*	❖	1-22
❑	WE982		Slingsby Prefect TX.1	50	ex 8781M, Cardington, Henlow, Syerston, Manston, ACCGS, CGS, 1 GC, 621, 612, 644, 643, 166 and 143 GSs	●	1-22
❑	XA893		Avro Vulcan B.1	56	ex Abingdon, Bicester 8591M (10-6-63), A&AEE. Cockpit		1-22
❑	XD515		DH Vampire T.11	54	ex Rugeley, Winthorpe, Misson, Linton-on-Ouse 'X<u>M</u>515', 7998M (5-1-68), 3 FTS, 7 FTS, 1 FTS, 5 FTS, 206 AFS. Christchurch-built. Arrived 2008		2-18
❑	'XL554'	'Z'	SAL Pioneer CC.1 XL703	56	ex MBCC, Hendon, Cosford, Manchester, Henlow 8034M (1-10-68), 209, 230. SOAF colours.		1-22
❑	XT903	'X'	McD Phantom FGR.2	68	ex Wyton, Leuchars, 56, 228 OCU, 92, 228 OCU, 23, 228 OCU, 2, 228 OCU. Cockpit		1-22
❑	XX946	'WT'	Panavia Tornado P.02	74	ex MBCC, museum, Hendon, Honington 8883M (5-2-86), Laarbruch, Honington, Warton. Acquired 16-11-94	❖	1-22
❑	–		Hawker P.1121	58	ex Henlow, Cranfield. Fuselage sections	●	1-22
❑	A-515		FMA Pucará	78	ex museum, 9245M, ZD485, A&AEE, Yeovilton, Stanley, Arg AF, Mauritania AF M4 / 5T-MAB. Last flown (as ZD485) 9-9-83. Gr 3 de Ataque colours. F/n 4-17		6-22
❑	6130		Lockheed Ventura II	42	ex SAAF Museum, Ysterplaat, SAAF, 17, BGANS, 21, 29 OTU, RAF AJ469, n/s. Acquired 1983		2-22
❑	J-1704		DH Venom FB.54	56	ex museum, Greenham Common. Swiss AF. Swiss-built. Acquired 8-6-79. First noted 4-17	❖	1-22

■ **[1]** Prototype Meteor, first flown 24-7-43; Rolls-Royce-built W2B/23 turbojets.

Defence School of Aeronautical Engineering (DSAE): This facility and DSAE Sultan at Gosport, Hampshire, are sub-sets of the Defence College of Technical Training at Lyneham, Wilts. Major element **1 School of Technical Training** was joined by the re-formed **2 School of Technical Training** (SoTT) on 20th July 2023. (History repeating itself, the Cosford-based 2 SoTT was re-numbered from the previously Halton-based 1 SoTT on 24th November 1994.) Prior to the rebirth of 2 SoTT, the following units functioning within 1 SoTT: **Avionics Training Flight**; **Aerosystems Training Wing** - comprising the **Avionics Training Flight** and the **Weapons Training Flight**; the **Airfield Squadron**; and a **Battle Damage Repair Flight**. Some of these are bound to now fall under 2 SoTT domain. No attempt has been made to delineate which airframes are with which of these elements in the listing below. Also here is **1 Radio School**, which does not use airframes and the **Mechanical Training School** in Building 146, which does.

Several airframes on DSAE charge are referred to as 'Non-effective ground display' and are marked #. Some Jaguars are believed to have been allocated to India, almost certainly for spares, as far back as 27th October 2016: these are marked @. See comments under Duxford, Cambs, for the saga of Typhoon ZH590.

Departures: **Harrier** GR.9 ZD465 returned to <u>Gosport</u>, Hampshire, by 4-22; **Jaguar** GR.3A XX119 to <u>Lossiemouth</u>, Scotland, 7-12-23; T.2A XX145 to <u>Old Sarum</u>, Wilts, 24-8-23; GR.1 XX727 to <u>St Athan</u>, Wales, 26-5-23; GR.1 XX743 to <u>Kinloss</u>, Scotland, 22-10-22; GR.1 XZ374 to <u>Spadeadam</u>, Cumbria, by 8-23; GR.1 XZ383 to <u>Elvington</u>, N Yorks, 5-8-23; GR.1 XZ389 arrived at <u>Long Kesh</u>, N Ireland, 18-11-23.

	Reg	Code	Type	Built	History		Noted
❑	XM362		Hunting Jet Provost T.3	59	ex 8230M, Halton, Kemble, Shawbury, 3 FTS, 2 FTS. Arrived 21-3-73. 'Cutaway' and camouflaged		4-19
❑	XR498	'X'	Westland Wessex HC.2	63	ex St Mawgan, Gosport, Cosford 9342M, Shawbury, 72, 60, 72, A&AEE. Arrived 17-5-17. 22 Sqn colours	#	6-22
❑	XW327	'62'	BAC Jet Provost T.5A	70	ex Halton 9130M (9-12-91), CFS, 7 FTS, 6 FTS, 7 FTS, 1 FTS, CFS, RAFC. Parked outside by 10-19, rescue trainer		12-23
❑	XW852*		Sud Gazelle HCC.4	73	ex Gosport, Cosford 9331M, St Athan, Fleetlands, 32. Arrived 29-3-22	[1]	6-22
❑	XX110	'EP'	SEPECAT Jaguar GR.1	74	ex 8955M (3-12-87), Shawbury, 6, A&AEE, BAC. *Baghdad or Bust* (stb). Outside SHQ		10-21
❑	XX112	'EA'	SEPECAT Jaguar GR.3A	73	ex Coltishall, 6, GR.1, 6, A&AEE. Arrived 13-6-07		3-22
❑	XX117	'ES'	SEPECAT Jaguar GR.3A	73	ex St Athan, 16, GR.1, 16, 6, SAOEU, 226 OCU, 54, Indian AF JI004, G-27-317, A&AEE, 6, 226 OCU, JOCU. Last flown 1-7-05		3-22

Serial	Code	Type	Year	History	Note	Date
❑ XX141	'T'	SEPECAT Jaguar T.2A	74	ex Cranwell 9297M, 6, 16, 226 OCU, 6, 226 OCU, JOCU. Arrived 23-4-13	@	6-22
❑ XX168		HS Hawk T.1	77	ex Shawbury, Valley, FRADU, 208, 100, 6 FTS, 74, 4 FTS. NEA 12-19. Arrived 3-3-20		3-22
❑ XX178		HS Hawk T.1	77	ex Shawbury, 208, 19, 92, 234, 4 FTS. NEA 12-19. Arrived 27-2-20		3-22
❑ XX181		HS Hawk T.1	77	ex Shawbury, 208, 19, 208, 100, TWU, 4 FTS. SOC 18-11-20. Arrived 28-10-20		7-23
❑ XX185		HS Hawk T.1	77	ex Shawbury, Marham, 208, 6 FTS, 19, 4 FTS. SOC 18-11-20. Arrived 18-11-20		10-21
❑ XX187	'CO'	HS Hawk T.1A	77	ex 100, 74, 6 FTS, CFS, 4 FTS, 1 TWU, 2 TWU, TWU. Arrived 26-11-21		11-21
❑ XX218		HS Hawk T.1A	78	ex Shawbury, 208, 19, 208, 74, 234, TWU. NEA 12-19. Arrived 10-3-20		3-22
❑ XX224		HS Hawk T.1	78	ex Shawbury, 208, 19, CFS, 4 FTS, CFS, 4 FTS. SOC 18-11-20. Arrived 19-11-20		7-23
❑ XX227		HS Hawk T.1A	78	ex Shawbury, 'Red Arrows', CFS. Arrived 25-2-20	[2]	3-22
❑ XX235		HS Hawk T.1	78	ex Shawbury, 208, 19, 208, 19, 74, CFS, 4 FTS. Accident 28-5-09,SOC 18-11-20. Arrived 17-11-20		6-22
❑ XX236		HS Hawk T.1W	78	ex Shawbury, 208, 19, CFS, 234, CFS, 4 FTS. Arrived 19-3-19		10-21
❑ XX244		HS Hawk T.1	78	ex Shawbury, 'Red Arrows', 208, 74, 208, 234, 4 FTS. Arrived 13-10-21. 'Red Arrows' colours		6-22
❑ XX283		HS Hawk T.1W	79	ex 208, 100, TWU. NEA 12-19. Arrived 5-3-20		3-22
❑ XX335		HS Hawk T.1A	80	ex Shawbury, 208, 100, 19, 2 TWU. Arrived 27-2-18		10-21
❑ XX412*		Sud Gazelle AH.1	75	ex Gosport, Cosford, Shawbury, 847, 3 CBAS. '238 Sqn' c/s, Marines lettering. Arrived 29-3-22	[1]	6-22
❑ XX723	'EU'	SEPECAT Jaguar GR.3A	74	ex Shawbury, 6, 41, 54, DERA, GR.1, 54, 6, 54, 226 OCU. Arrived 24-4-07		7-23
❑ XX724	'EC'	SEPECAT Jaguar GR.3A	74	ex Coltishall, 6, T.2, 54, Shawbury, 54, 226 OCU, A&AEE. *Ecoops* (pt), *Egleno* (stb). Last flown 12-6-07. Retired ground-runner		7-23
❑ XX725	'KC-F'	SEPECAT Jaguar GR.3A	74	ex Coningsby, 41, 54, SAOEU, GR.1, 54, SAOEU, 54, 6, Indian JI010, G-27-235, 54, 226 OCU. Last flown 2-7-07. Desert pink colours. Retired ground-runner		6-22
❑ XX726	'EB'	SEPECAT Jaguar GR.1	74	ex Halton 8947M (9-12-87), Shawbury, 6		3-22
❑ XX729	'EL'	SEPECAT Jaguar GR.3A	74	ex Coltishall, 6, GR.1, SAOEU, 6, 54, 226 OCU, 6, 54, Indian JI012, G-27-326, 6, 226 OCU. *Eliam*. Arrived 18-5-07		3-22
❑ XX738	'ED'	SEPECAT Jaguar GR.3A	74	ex Coltishall, 6, GR.1, SAOEU, 54, 6, Shawbury, 54, Indian AF JI016, G-27-329, 6. Arrived 13-5-07		7-23
❑ XX746	'S'	SEPECAT Jaguar GR.1A	74	ex Halton 8895M (23-5-86), Shawbury, 226 OCU, 14, 17, 6, 31, 226 OCU. Stored	@	6-23
❑ XX748	'EG'	SEPECAT Jaguar GR.3A	74	ex Coltishall, 6, GR.1, 54, 14, 226 OCU. *Egaz*. Last flown 18-5-07. Retired ground-runner		3-22
❑ XX752	'EK'	SEPECAT Jaguar GR.3A	75	ex Coltishall, 6, 41, 16, GR.1, 6, Shawbury, 54, 226 OCU, 54. Arrived 16-6-07		3-22
❑ XX756	'W'	SEPECAT Jaguar GR.1	75	ex 8899M (23-5-86), 14, 20, 226 OCU, 14		3-22
❑ XX766	'EF'	SEPECAT Jaguar GR.3A	75	ex 9257M, St Athan, 6, 16, GR.1, 6, 54, 226 OCU, 17. Arrived 31-1-06		3-22
❑ XX767	'FK'	SEPECAT Jaguar GR.3A	75	ex Shawbury, 41, 54, GR.1, 54, 17, 31, 14, 226 OCU, 14. Last flown 11-4-06		7-23
❑ XX819	'CE'	SEPECAT Jaguar GR.1	75	ex 8923M (19-12-86), Shawbury, 226 OCU, 20, 17	@	6-23
❑ XX821	'P'	SEPECAT Jaguar GR.1	75	ex 8896M (23-5-86), Cranwell, Coltishall, 41, 14, 17. Black colours. Arrived 4-4-12. Retired ground-runner		3-22
❑ XX825	'BN'	SEPECAT Jaguar GR.1	75	ex 9020M, Halton, Shawbury, 17, 31, 14. Stored	@	10-21
❑ XX833		SEPECAT Jaguar T.2A	75	ex Boscombe Down, QinetiQ, DERA, RAE, 41, 14, 20, 226 OCU. QinetiQ titles. Stored	[3]	10-21
❑ XX835	'EX'	SEPECAT Jaguar T.4	75	ex Coningsby, 6, 41, T.2, 41, 6, 54, RAE, 226 OCU. Last flown 1-7-07. Retired ground-runner, 'RAF 100' colours		10-21

Jaguar gathering, June 2023. Left to right: XX959, XX746, XZ374, XZ370, XX976, XX189. *Jake Wallace*

	Serial	Code	Type	Year	History	Note	Date
❑	XX837	'Z'	SEPECAT Jaguar T.2	75	ex Cranwell, Cosford, Halton 8978M (29-9-88), Shawbury, 226 OCU. Black colours. Arrived 7-8-12	@	10-21
❑	XX840	'T'	SEPECAT Jaguar T.4	75	ex Coltishall, 6, 16, T.2, St Athan, Shawbury, 41, 2, 226 OCU, 17. Last flown 12-6-07. Retired ground-runner		7-23
❑	XX847	'EZ'	SEPECAT Jaguar T.4	76	ex Coltishall, 6, 16, T.2, St Athan, 41, Shawbury, 226 OCU, 31, 20, 14, 2, 226 OCU. Last flown 18-5-07. Retired ground-runner		7-23
❑	XX959	'CJ'	SEPECAT Jaguar GR.1	75	ex 8953M, Shawbury, 20, 14. Last flown 4-7-84. Stored	@	6-23
❑	XX965	'C'	SEPECAT Jaguar GR.1A	75	ex Cranwell 9254M (18-9-96), Coltishall, 16, 226 OCU, 54, 14. 16 Sqn colours. Arrived 17-10-12		3-22
❑	XX967	'AC'	SEPECAT Jaguar GR.1	75	ex 9006M, Shawbury, 14, 31. Arrived 2-11-89. Stored	@	7-23
❑	XX968	'AJ'	SEPECAT Jaguar GR.1	75	ex 9007M, Shawbury, 14, 31. Arrived 1-11-89		3-22
❑	XX969	'01'	SEPECAT Jaguar GR.1	75	ex 8897M (23-5-86), 226 OCU, 31		10-21
❑	XX970	'EH'	SEPECAT Jaguar GR.3A	75	ex Coltishall, 6, GR.1, 6, 226 OCU, 17, 31. Arrived 13-6-07		3-22
❑	XX975	'07'	SEPECAT Jaguar GR.1A	76	ex Halton 8905M (23-9-86), Shawbury, 226 OCU, 17, 31. Was with '238 Sqn', stored		10-21
❑	XX976	'BD'	SEPECAT Jaguar GR.1	76	ex Halton 8906M (22-10-86), Shawbury, 17, 31. Was with '238 Sqn', stored		6-23
❑	XZ103	'EF'	SEPECAT Jaguar GR.3A	76	ex Coltishall, 41, SAOEU, GR.1, 41, Shawbury, 2. *Exfoxy 2004-2009*. Arrived 12-6-07		3-22
❑	XZ104	'FM'	SEPECAT Jaguar GR.3A	76	ex St Athan, 41, 6, 2. Arrived 27-10-05		6-22
❑	XZ109	'EN'	SEPECAT Jaguar GR.3A	76	ex Shawbury, 6, SAOEU, GR.1, 6, 54, 2. Arrived 29-8-07		3-22
❑	XZ112	'GW'	SEPECAT Jaguar GR.3A	76	ex Shawbury, 41, 54, GR.1, 54, Shawbury, 2. Last flown 12-4-06		10-21
❑	XZ114	'EO'	SEPECAT Jaguar GR.3A	76	ex Shawbury, 6, 41, GR.1, Shawbury, 41. Last flown 11-4-06		10-21
❑	XZ115	'ER'	SEPECAT Jaguar GR.3A	76	ex Shawbury, 6, 16, GR.1, SAOEU, 41, Shawbury, Gulf Det, 41, 2, 41. Arrived 24-10-06		3-22
❑	XZ117	'ES'	SEPECAT Jaguar GR.3A	76	ex Shawbury, 41, 6, GR.1, Warden Det, 54, 41. Arrived 17-11-09. Retired ground-runner		7-23
❑	XZ305*		Sud Gazelle AH.1	76	TAD.020, ex Gosport, Middle Wallop, Arborfield, 3 Regt, 665, 662, 654, GCF. Arrived 29-3-22	[1]	3-22
❑	XZ358	'L'	SEPECAT Jaguar GR.1A	76	ex Cranwell, 9262M (18-10-96), Coltishall, 41, Warden Det, 41, Gulf Det, 41. 41 Sqn colours		3-22
❑	XZ367	'EE' *and* 'GP'	SEPECAT Jaguar GR.3	76	ex Ipswich, Coltishall 9321M, Shawbury, Warden Det, GR.1, 54, Gulf Det, 54, 2, 226 OCU, 2	[4]	7-23
❑	XZ368	'E'	SEPECAT Jaguar GR.1	76	ex 8900M (23-5-86), Coltishall, 14, 6, 14		3-22
❑	XZ370	'JB'	SEPECAT Jaguar GR.1	76	ex 9004M, Shawbury, 14, 17. Arrived 18-10-89. Stored	@	6-23
❑	XZ371	'AP'	SEPECAT Jaguar GR.1	76	ex 8907M (23-5-86), Shawbury, 14, 17		3-22

❑ XZ377	'EP'	SEPECAT Jaguar GR.3A	77	ex St Athan, 6, GR.1, 6, 16, 6, 54, 226 OCU, 2, 31, 20. Arrived 6-7-07		10-21
❑ XZ384	'BC'	SEPECAT Jaguar GR.1	77	ex 8954M (3-12-87), Shawbury, 17, 31, 20. Stored		10-21
❑ XZ390	'DM'	SEPECAT Jaguar GR.1	77	ex 9003M, Shawbury, 2, 20, 31. Last flown 25-4-85		3-22
❑ XZ391	'ET'	SEPECAT Jaguar GR.3A	77	ex Coltishall, 6, GR.1, 6, 16, 54, 226 OCU, 54, 31. Last flown 12-4-06		7-23
❑ XZ392	'EM'	SEPECAT Jaguar GR.3A	77	ex Coltishall, 16, GR.1, Shawbury, 54, 20, 31. Arr 12-6-07		3-22
❑ XZ398	'EQ'	SEPECAT Jaguar GR.3A	77	ex Coltishall, 6, 41, GR.1, 41, 54, 41, 6, Indian AF J1007, G-27-323, Warton. Arrived 18-5-07		3-22
❑ XZ399	'EJ'	SEPECAT Jaguar GR.3A	76	ex Coltishall, 6, GR.1, 226 OCU, 6, 226 OCU, 6, 14, 6. *Ejordan 2004-2007 - Sleep Well Mighty Cat!* Arr 12-6-07		3-22
❑ XZ941	'B'	Sud Gazelle HT.2	78	ex 9301M, St Athan, Shawbury, 2 FTS, Odiham hack, CFS. Battle damage repair airframe	[1]	6-22
❑ XZ991	'3A'	HS Harrier GR.3	81	ex 9162M, St Athan 9162M, 233 OCU, 4, 1417 Flt, 233 OCU, 1, R-R, 1, 3, 1	#	6-22
❑ ZA320	'CA' *and* 'JG'	Panavia Tornado GR.1	79	ex 9314M (8-4-02), St Athan, 15, TTTE. 17 Sqn 'CA' to stb, 'JG' 27 Sqn to port. Stored	#	7-23
❑ ZA356		Panavia Tornado GR.1	80	ex Marham, St Athan, 15. Cockpit. First noted 4-19		3-22
❑ ZA447	'019'	Panavia Tornado GR.4	83	ex Marham, 12, GR.1, 12. Arrived 14-3-18	[5]	3-22
❑ ZA450	'TH'	Panavia Tornado GR.1	83	ex 9317M, St Athan, 15, 12, 617, 12, 27, 20, 15. Arr 14-5-02		3-22
❑ ZA459	'025'	Panavia Tornado GR.4	83	ex Marham, 617, GR.1, 617. Arrived 7-3-18		3-22
❑ ZA585	'054'	Panavia Tornado GR.4	81	ex Marham, 9, GR.1, 9. Arrived 16-10-18		3-22
❑ ZB615		SEPECAT Jaguar T.2	82	ex Cranwell, Boscombe Down, ETPS. F/n 8-13. Stored		6-22
❑ ZD715	'083'	Panavia Tornado GR.4	84	ex Marham, 617. Arrived 7-9-16		4-23
❑ ZD793	'101'	Panavia Tornado GR.4	84	ex Lossiemouth, Marham, 15. *100 Not Out*. Arrived 4-3-17		4-23
❑ ZD849	'110'	Panavia Tornado GR.4	85	ex Marham, 12. Arrived 8-10-18		3-22
❑ ZE340	'GO'	Panavia Tornado F.3	87	ex 9298M, Coningsby, 56. Rear fuselage of ZE758. Arrived 4-9-01. 43 Sqn colours	#	7-23
❑ ZH590*		Eurofighter Typhoon DA4	97	ex Duxford, Coningsby, Warton trials fleet. Arrived 29-11-23. See notes above	[6]	11-23
❑ ZH796	'001'	HS Sea Harrier F/A.2	95	ex Culdrose, Shawbury, Yeovilton, 801, 899. Arr 4-14	#	6-22
❑ ZJ619		Eurofighter Typhoon CIM	~	fuselage, in classroom. First noted 5-18	[7]	3-20
❑ ZJ695	001	GenFly Mk.2	c02	Typhoon training rig	[8]	3-22
❑ ZJ696	002	GenFly Mk.2	c02	Typhoon training rig	[8]	3-22
❑ ZJ697	003	GenFly Mk.2	c02	Typhoon training rig	[8]	3-22
❑ ZJ698	004	GenFly Mk.2	c02	Typhoon training rig	[8]	3-22
❑ ZK006		Eurofighter Typhoon CIM	c02	cabin conditioner training rig	[9]	3-22
❑ ZK007		Eurofighter Typhoon CIM	c02	unspecified training rig	[9]	10-13
❑ ZK008		Eurofighter Typhoon CIM	c02	pressure refuelling training rig	[9]	4-19
❑ TAD.018		Sud Gazelle AH.1 XW889	74	ex Aborfield, Middle Wallop, ARWF, GCF Corrosion control instruction	[1]	10-21

■**[1]** Gazelles are, of course, Westland-built. **[2]** See Wickenby, Lincs, for 'another' 'XX227'. **[3]** Jaguar XX833 factoids: total flying time 5,335 hours - 1,070 of these since arriving at Boscombe in April 1994; it has had *five* bird strikes, one lightning strike and *nine* different engines. **[4]** XZ367 was supplied in response to a tender issued in 2009, it seems DCAE mis-calculated how many GR.3s it would need. **[5]** See also White Waltham, Berks, for an 'imposter' ZA447. **[6]** DA4 made its first flight on 3-3-97 and its last on 13-12-06. **[7]** Two-seat fuselage resting on its undercarriage, stub wings, canards, stub fin/rudder. Sophisticated training airframe, *perhaps* taken from the production line and modded. See also note [8] regarding serial allocation. **[8]** Four sophisticated Typhoon purpose-built training rigs, called GenFlies. These have the capacity to generate over 100 different faults, to really annoy the trainees. They have been allocated serials not because they are intended to fly, but because they have a full maintenance schedule, just like a live airframe. **[9]** Cockpit-based CIMs. Other 'sims' in use include a barrage of so-called Emulator Test Rigs, AV001 to AV018.

Midlands Air Ambulance: Cosford is one of three bases for the charity; the others being Tatenhill, Staffs, and Strensham, Worcs. This heading suffices as the 'base' for the travelling demonstrator/fund-raiser airframe. The trusty, and anonymous, Bölkow Bö 105 travelling demonstrator/fund-raiser has been replaced by a BK 117.

◆ *Prior arrangement* **only** | **www.midlandsairambulance.com**

❑ 'G-EOFF'*		MBB BK 117	~	ex N508TJ, N177LS, N628MB, D-HBCH. Trailer-mounted cab	6-23

Warped Sports: In a field near Junction 3 of the M54. *W&R28* (p192) 'wrote out' the cab of Robinson G-HERA: it lives on, only just, likewise the mannequin sitting at the controls! ◆ *Prior arrangement* **only** | **www.warpedsports.com**

❑ G-HERA*		Robinson R22	90	ex Halfpenny Green, Blackpool. CoA 15-6-99, de-reg 21-8-99. Cab, poor state – see note above	6-22
❑ XZ318		Sud Gazelle AH.1	77	ex Shawbury, Fleetlands, Yeovil, Fleetlands, 656, 664, 657, 664, 656, 670, ARWS, A&AEE. Westland-built. Damaged 2-1-97. Less boom, poor state	6-22

DONNINGTON south of the A518, northeast of Telford

Defence Fulfilment Centre: This huge logistics base has a Harrier on show.

❑ XZ971	'U'	HS Harrier GR.3	81	ex Shawbury, Benson 9219M (13-10-93), HOCU, 20, 1417 Flt, 20, 233 OCU, 1417 Flt, 233 OCU. Displayed	5-23

NEWPORT on the A41 northeast of Telford

The An-2 is under restoration to ground-running status. ◆ *Prior arrangement* **only**

❑ RA-01641	'3'	Antonov An-2 *Colt*	~	ex Baxterley, Wolverhampton. Crashed 9-99. Fuselage	7-20

REDNAL east of the A5 and Oswestry

Rednal Karting: Centred around the former watch tower. ◆ *Prior arrangement* only | **www.rednalkarting.co.uk**

❑ XT480	'468'	Westland Wessex HU.5	66	ex East Midlands, Hixon, Fleetlands, A2617[2] (13-12-90), A2603[2], Wroughton, 771, 847, 772, 846, 707. Arr 26-9-11	8-21

SHAWBURY AIRFIELD on the B5063 north of Shawbury EGOS

Aircraft Maintenance and Storage Unit (AM&SU) operated on behalf of the Defence Aviation Repair Agency by FB Services. Other than the 'Red Arrow' examples, the magnificent Hawk T.1 bowed out of service in the spring of 2022: both 100 Squadron at Leeming and 736 Squadron at Culdrose disbanded on 31st March with the Centre for Aviation Medicine having withdrawn its pair (XX162 and XX327) by that date. AM&SU expanded its holding while AMRO at Valley, Wales, handles the soon to be completed reduce to produce programme. Hawks held as spares/replacements for the 'Reds' under the RAFAT-2030 programme; are marked #. Aircraft marked NEA – non-effective airframe – have embarked upon the disposal process and are likely to depart.

Departures: **Gazelle** AH.1s ZB677, ZB683, ZB689 all up for sale 4-22 and registered as G-CMKP, G-CMKS (later becoming HA-LFZ), G-CMKT to Yorkshire-based operator 9-22; **Hawk** T.1W XX169 to Leyburn, N Yorks, 26-5-23; T.1 XX238 to Doncaster, S Yorks, 3-10-23; T.1A XX260 to Long Kesh, N Ireland, 15-5-23; T.1A XX286 to Long Kesh, N Ireland, arriving 30-7-22; T.1 XX309 to Caernarfon, Wales, 15-5-23; **departures to AMRO**, Valley, Wales, for reduction to produce: XX199 7-12-22; XX220 6-12-22; XX307 22-2-23; **Sea Hawk** FGA.6 WV908 (G-CMFB) to Yeovilton, Somerset, 27-5-22; **Tucano** T.1 all of the examples held are *believed* to have departed to the USA, via ISO containers, from the summer of 2019, with the last few making the move in the first weeks of 2020 – that *should* be: ZF163, ZF263, ZF268, ZF286, ZF288, ZF315, ZF318, ZF350, ZF372, ZF376, ZF405, ZF408, ZF414, ZF416, ZF418, ZF446, ZF449, ZF486, ZF487, ZF488, ZF490, ZF492, ZF513.

❑ XW198	Sud Puma HC.1	70	ex Benson, 33, 230, 72, 230, 33, 240 OCU, Benson. Westland-built. SOC 31-12-12. Arrived 23-8-17		8-17
❑ XW200	Sud Puma HC.1	71	ex 33, 240 OCU, HOCF. Crashed 9-4-01. Westland-built. Arrived 2-7-01		12-15
❑ XW210	Sud Puma HC.1	71	ex Benson, 33, Boscombe Down, 1563 Flt, 33, 240 OCU, 33, 230, 33, 240 OCU, 33. Westland-built. Arrived 12-8-14		12-15
❑ XW217*	Sud Puma HC.1	71	ex Benson, 33, 230, 33. Westland-built. Arrived 22-1-24		1-24
❑ XW218	Sud Puma HC.1	71	ex 1563 Flt, 33. 230, 72, 33, 72, 18, 230, 33, 18, 230, 33, 230, 240 OCU, 230. Westland-built. Crashed 15-4-07, arrived 5-3-08		12-15
❑ XW226	Sud Puma HC.1	71	ex Benson, 33, 230, 72, 320, 33, 72, 33, 72, 27, 230, 33, 18, 230. Westland-built. Arrived 12-8-14		12-15
❑ XX158	HS Hawk T.1A	76	ex 208, CFS, 208, 19, 2 TWU. Arrived 9-5-16. NEA 12-19		10-21
❑ XX159	HS Hawk T.1A	76	ex 736, FRADU, 208, 19, CFS, 74, 4 FTS, TWU, A&AEE. Arrived 24-7-18	#	10-21
❑ XX160	HS Hawk T.1	77	ex 208, 19, 208, DERA, TEE, RAE. Arr 18-6-07. NEA 12-19		10-21
❑ XX162*	HS Hawk T.1A	77	ex Valley, Centre for Av Med (etc), 74, 4 FTS, CFS. Fuselage, arrived 9-8-22		8-22
❑ XX167	HS Hawk T.1	77	ex 208, 4 FTS, TWU, 4 FTS. Arrived 27-2-12. NEA 12-19		10-21
❑ XX170	HS Hawk T.1	77	ex 100, 736, Llanbedr, 234, CFS, 4 FTS. Arr 25-5-16. NEA 12-19		10-21

❑ XX171		HS Hawk T.1	77	ex 208, 19, 208, 74, CFS, 4 FTS. Arr 20-5-11. NEA 12-19	10-21
❑ XX174		HS Hawk T.1	77	ex 208, 19, 6 FTS, 19, 74, 4 FTS. Arrived 14-1-13. NEA 12-19	10-21
❑ XX176		HS Hawk T.1W	77	ex 208, 100, 92, 19, CFS, 4 FTS. Arrived 14-1-13. NEA 12-19	10-21
❑ XX190	'CN'	HS Hawk T.1A	77	ex 100, 208, 74, 4 FTS, 1 TWU, 2 TWU, 1 TWU, TWU. Arrived 30-6-08	# 10-21
❑ XX191*	'CC'	HS Hawk T.1A	78	ex 100, 208, 234, 1 TWU, TWU. Arrived 28-3-22	3-22
❑ XX194	'CP'	HS Hawk T.1A	78	ex 100, 74, TWU. Arrived 8-5-13. NEA 12-19	10-21
❑ XX195		HS Hawk T.1W	78	ex 208, 4 FTS, 19, 208, 100, 2 TWU, 1 TWU, TWU. Arrived 2-2-10	# 10-21
❑ XX198*	'CH'	HS Hawk T.1A	78	ex 100, 19, 208, 234, 1 TWU, 2 TWU, TWU. Arrived 28-3-22	3-22
❑ XX201	'CQ'	HS Hawk T.1A	78	ex 100, 92, 2 TWU, TWU. Arrived 17-11-16. Fleet spare	10-21
❑ XX203*	'CF'	HS Hawk T.1A	78	ex Leeming, 100, 19, 74, 19, CFS, 4 FTS, 2 TWU, 1 TWU, TWU. Arrived by road 4-3-22	3-22
❑ XX205*		HS Hawk T.1A	78	ex Valley, 92, 2 TWU, TWU. Fuselage, arrived 9-8-22	8-22
❑ XX217		HS Hawk T.1A	78	ex 736, 100, 19, 2 TWU, 1 TWU, A&AEE, TWU. Arr 6-18	# 10-21
❑ XX222	'CI'	HS Hawk T.1A	78	ex 100, 208, 74, TWU. Arrived 15-7-11	# 10-21
❑ XX225		HS Hawk T.1	78	ex 208, FRADU, 208, 19, 4 FTS. Arrived 3-8-07. NEA 12-19	10-20
❑ XX228		HS Hawk T.1	78	ex 208, 100, 2 TWU, 1 TWU. Arrived 8-11-07. NEA 12-19	10-21
❑ XX230	'CM'	HS Hawk T.1A	76	ex 100, 74, 19, TWU. Arrived 2-11-17	# 10-21
❑ XX231		HS Hawk T.1W	78	ex 208, 74, 92, 19, 4 FTS, RAE, 4 FTS. Arr 27-9-11. NEA 12-19	10-21
❑ XX234		HS Hawk T.1	78	ex 208, FRADU, 234, 74, 4 FTS. Arrived 21-7-11. NEA 12-19	10-21
❑ XX239*	'842'	HS Hawk T.1W	78	ex 736/FRADU, 19, 74, 208, 74, 208, 19, CFS, 4 FTS. Arr 2-3-22	3-22
❑ XX248	'CJ'	HS Hawk T.1A	78	ex 100, 1 TWU, 2 TWU, 1 TWU. Arrived 4-10-07. NEA 12-19	10-21
❑ XX250		HS Hawk T.1W	79	ex 208, 100, 208, 100, 6 FTS, 4 FTS, CFS, 4 FTS, CFS. First noted 6-18.	# 10-21
❑ XX255*	'CB'	HS Hawk T.1A	79	ex 100, 736/FRADU, ETPS, 74, 7 FTS, TWU. Arrived 26-1-22	1-22
❑ XX256*	'846'	HS Hawk T.1A	79	ex 736/FRADU, 74, 19, 2 TWU, 1 TWU. Arrived 2-3-22	3-22
❑ XX258	'CE'	HS Hawk T.1A	79	ex 100, 74, 19, CFS, TWU. Arrived 2-5-19	10-21
❑ XX261*	'CJ'	HS Hawk T.1A	79	ex 100, 208, 100, 119, 208, 234, 1 TWU. Arrived 28-3-22	3-22
❑ XX264		HS Hawk T.1A	79	ex 'Red Arrows'. Arrived 6-14. NEA 12-19	10-21
❑ XX265	'CP'	HS Hawk T.1A	79	ex 19, 100, 92, 2 TWU, 1 TWU. Arrived 6-10-10	# 10-21
❑ XX284	'CN'	HS Hawk T.1A	79	ex 100, Shawbury, 100, 208, 100, TWU. Arrived 5-12-17	# 10-21
❑ XX285*	'CK'	HS Hawk T.1A	79	ex 100, 2 TWU, TWU. Arrived 28-3-22	3-22
❑ XX287		HS Hawk T.1A	79	ex 208, 92, 2 TWU, 1 TWU. Arrived 20-4-16. NEA 12-19	10-21
❑ XX289	'CO'	HS Hawk T.1A	79	ex 100, 19, TWU. Arrived 4-7-12	# 10-21
❑ XX294		HS Hawk T.1	79	ex 'Red Arrows', 4 FTS. Arrived 2-6-11. NEA 12-19	10-21
❑ XX296		HS Hawk T.1	79	ex 208, 74, 4 FTS. Bitteswell-built. Arr 21-1-04. NEA 12-19	10-21
❑ XX299		HS Hawk T.1W	79	ex 208, 100, 19, 208, 74, 92, 4 FTS. Bitteswell-built. Arrived 2-4-08. NEA 12-19	10-21
❑ XX301		HS Hawk T.1A	80	ex 100, 19, 92, TWU. Bitteswell-built. First noted 6-18	# 10-21
❑ XX303*		HS Hawk T.1A	80	ex 100, 74, 19, CFS, 74, 1 TWU. Arrived 7-3-22	3-22
❑ XX313		HS Hawk T.1W	80	ex 208, 74, 19, CFS, 19, 4 FTS. Arrived 16-8-12. NEA 12-19	10-21
❑ XX314		HS Hawk T.1W	80	ex Valley, 19, 100, 208, 4 FTS, 2 TWU, 4 FTS. Bitteswell-built. Arrived 18-10-11. NEA 12-19	10-21
❑ XX315		HS Hawk T.1A	80	ex 208, 234, 1TWU. Arrived 19-1-16. NEA 12-19	10-21
❑ XX324*		HS Hawk T.1A	80	ex 736, 19, 208, 234, 4 FTS, 1 TWU. Bitteswell-built. Arrived 24-3-22	3-22
❑ XX327*		HS Hawk T.1	80	ex Centre/Inst Av Med, 2 TWU, RAE, TWU. Bitteswell-built. Arrived 29-3-22	3-22
❑ XX330		HS Hawk T.1A	80	ex 100, 19, 208, 92, 1 TWU, 2 TWU. Bitteswell-built. First noted 6-18	# 10-21
❑ XX331		HS Hawk T.1A	80	ex 100, 2 TWU. Bitteswell-built. Arrived 29-6-11	# 10-21
❑ XX337*	'CM'	HS Hawk T.1A	81	ex 100, FRADU, 100, 92, 2 TWU. Arrived 29-3-22	3-22
❑ XX338		HS Hawk T.1W	81	ex 208, 19, 208, 19, 4 FTS. Arrived 12-9-13. NEA 12-19	10-21
❑ XX339*	'CL'	HS Hawk T.1A	81	ex 100, 19, 208, 74, CFS, 74, 1 TWU. Arrived 29-3-22	3-22
❑ XX345	'CB'	HS Hawk T.1A	81	ex 100, 19, 92, TWU. Bitteswell-built. Arrived 3-12-08	# 10-21
❑ XX348*	'CQ'	HS Hawk T.1A	81	ex 100, 19, 74, 234, 1 TWU, 2 TWU, TWU. Bitteswell-built. Arrived 29-3-22	3-22
❑ XX350	'D'	HS Hawk T.1A	81	ex 100, 74, 1 TWU. Bitteswell-built. First noted 6-18	# 10-21

❑ ZA773	'F'	Sud Gazelle AH.1	80	ex 666, 665, 655, 665, 655. Westland-built. Arr 31-10-05	11-22
❑ ZJ910	'DO'	E'fighter Typhoon FGR.4	07	ex Coningsby, 11. Arrived 24-6-16	6-16
❑ ZJ911	'QO-Z'	E'fighter Typhoon FGR.4	05	ex Coningsby, 11. Arrived 24-8-16	8-16
❑ ZJ912		E'fighter Typhoon FGR.4	05	ex Coningsby. Arrived 12-2-18	6-18
❑ ZJ918		E'fighter Typhoon FGR.4	05	ex Coningsby, 3. Arrived 11-1-18	1-18
❑ ZJ925	'DXI'	E'fighter Typhoon FGR.4	06	ex Coningsby, 11. Arrived 26-5-16	5-16
❑ ZJ927		E'fighter Typhoon FGR.4	06	ex Coningsby, 29. Arrived 11-1-18	1-18
❑ ZJ930		E'fighter Typhoon FGR.4	06	ex Coningsby. Arrived 22-1-18	6-18
❑ ZJ932	'DB'	E'fighter Typhoon FGR.4	06	ex Coningsby, 11. Arrived 26-5-16	5-16
❑ ZJ934		E'fighter Typhoon FGR.4	06	ex Coningsby. Arrived 18-12-17	6-18
❑ ZJ936	'QO-C'	E'fighter Typhoon FGR.4	07	ex Coningsby, 3. Arrived 23-5-16	5-16
❑ ZJ942		E'fighter Typhoon FGR.4	07	ex Coningsby, 29. Arrived 22-1-18	1-18

Also:

❑ XR516	'V'	Westland Wessex HC.2	64	ex Gosport, 9319M, A2709 [2], Shawbury, 2 FTS, 18. Displayed, since 2003	[1] 12-23

■ **[1]** Wessex XR516 has been 'adopted' by the resident 60 Squadron.

SHREWSBURY

Roger Marley: The Demon project includes an RR Kestrel and is a painstaking tribute to Falklands-born Flt Lt Donald Eric Turner who flew Demons from Hal Far with 74 Squadron 1935-1936. While serving with 238 Squadron, Turner was shot down and killed in Hurricane P3823 off the Isle of Wight on 8th August 1940: Roger has Turner's uniform and Demon items from his time on Malta. ◆ *Available* **only** *by prior permission* | **roger.marley@btinternet.com**

❑ 'K4540'		Hawker Demon I	34	Fuselage	[1] 1-24

■ **[1]** Includes parts from an Audax frame from a Shrewsbury scrapyard and Hind K6666, issued to the RNZAF as NZ1529 9-40.

SLEAP AERODROME southwest of Wem EGCV

Wartime Aircraft Recovery Group Aviation Museum: Courtesy of Shropshire Aero Club, the group runs a small exhibition, including artefacts from 'digs' including WARG's 'founder', 61 OTU Spitfire IIa P7304 involved in a mid-air collision near High Ercall on 22nd August 1943, recovered in 1977. A recent recovery is a substantially complete under fuselage/bomb bay pannier from a Halifax/Halton. ◆ **twarg1943@gmail.com** | **www.facebook.com/TWARGM/**

❑ 'K7271'		Hawker Fury II replica	79	BAPC.148, ex Market Drayton, Cosford. Stored	4-21

Locally: Bob Mitchell's former PT Flight is *believed* to be held in store. ◆ *Available* **only** *by prior permission*

❑ G-AEUJ		Miles Whitney Straight	37	ex Cosford, Sutton Coldfield, Marple, East Midlands, Hurn. Phillips & Powis-built. CoA 4-6-70	N9-21
❑ G-AFRZ		Miles Monarch	38	ex Cosford, Sutton Coldfield, Shipdham, G-AIDE, W6463, Kemble, 10 GCF, FTCCF, 13 EFTS, G-AFRZ. Phillips & Powis-built. CoA 29-6-70	N9-21
❑ G-AWIW		Stampe SV-4B	47	ex Cosford, Colerne, F-BDCC. Nord-built. CoA 6-5-73	N9-21
❑ G-AYKZ		SAI KZ-VIII	49	ex Coventry, HB-EPB, OY-ACB. CoA 17-7-81	N9-21
❑ G-RIDE		Stephens Akro	76	ex N81AC, N55NM. CoA 13-8-92	N9-21
❑ N1344		Ryan PT-22 Recruit	41	ex Cosford, 41-20877	10-11
❑ N49272	'23'	Fairchild PT-23-HO	42	ex Cosford, USAAF 42-49413	10-11
❑ N56421	'855'	Ryan PT-22 Recruit	41	ex Cosford, 41-15510	10-11
❑ N58566		Vultee BT-15 Valiant	42	ex Cosford, USAAF 42-41882	10-11

TELFORD

Excellency Midlands: This large wedding venue in Stafford Park, has acquired a Lynx, perhaps for the blushing couple to pretend they arrived by chopper. ◆ *Prior permission* **only** | **https://excellencymidlands.com**

❑ XZ213*		Westland Lynx AH.1	79	ex 'Ipswich', Fleetlands, Wroughton, M Wallop TAD.213, Wroughton, 659. Accident 20-3-86. First noted 5-22	12-23

SOMERSET

Includes the unitary authorities of North Somerset and Bath and North East Somerset

BRIDGWATER south of Weston-super-Mare, on the B3140

Bridgwater and Taunton College: Bath Road. ◆ *Prior permission* **only** | **www.btc.ac.uk**

❑ XT633	Westland Scout AH.1	66	ex Farnborough, M Wallop, Arborfield, Wroughton, 659, 653, 661, 660, Wroughton. Arrived 20-8-20	8-20

BRISTOL AIRPORT or Lulsgate EGGD

Delta Force South Bristol: West of the airport. ◆ *Available* **only** *by prior permission* | **www.paintballgames.co.uk**

❑ G-AWOX	Westland Wessex 60	68	ex Weston-super-Mare, Hurn, W-s-M, G-17-2, G-AWOX, 5N-AJO, G-AWOX, 9Y-TFB, G-AWOX, VH-BHE, G-AWOX, VR-BCV, G-AWOX, G-17-1. CoA 13-1-83, de-reg 23-11-82	2-10

BURNHAM ON SEA on the A38 north of Taunton

Grahame Cox, avid collector of aviation and transport artefacts, died on 3rd September 2022. The anonymous Adams-Wilson was due to make the trek to Weston-super-Mare, Somerset, in January 2024.

◆ *Prior arrangement* ***only*** | **www.silverscouters.co.uk**

❑ 5Y-AYR	Bristol Britannia 307F	57	ex Hurn, African Cargo, G-ANCD, Gemini, Lloyd, BUA, Air Charter, 4X-AGE El Al, N6595C, G-ANCD, G-18-3. Cockpit	1-24

CHEW VALLEY LAKE south of Chew Stoke, north of the A368 west of Bath

The shore of this huge reservoir is the venue for the annual **Valley Fest** food and music jamboree. Several airframes have been gathered: they may only be short-termers. **www.valleyfest.co.uk**

❑ G-BZOS*	Sud Gazelle HT.2	74	ex XW894, 705. Crashed 14-7-02, de-reg 21-11-02	4-23
❑ XZ570*	Westland Sea King HAS.5(mod)	76	ex Predannack, Culdrose, Gosport, A2672, A2686 (11-10-01), Boscombe Down, RAE Bedford, A&AEE. First noted 2-23	8-23
❑ ZG915*	Westland Lynx AH.9A	91	ex Predannack, Middle Wallop. SOC 3-10-18. Arrived 7-12-22	7-23
❑ ZG919*	Westland Lynx AH.9A	91	ex Predannack, Middle Wallop. SOC 3-10-18. Arrived 7-12-22	4-23

FELTON west of the A38, east of Bristol Airport

Park Farm: A 'JP' is kept at the off-airport parking site. **www.parkfarmbristol.co.uk**

❑ XN551	'100'	Hunting Jet Provost T.3A	61	ex St Athan 8984M (6-2-89), 7 FTS, RAFC, 1 FTS, 3 FTS, 6 FTS, RAFC	1-24

HENSTRIDGE AERODROME south of the A30, east of Henstridge Marsh EGHS

Aztec G-BBDO was parted out in mid-August 2023 and the hulk exported. The following have been deleted: Sonerai G-BJLC, Cherokee G-LTFC, Yak-52 G-SPUT.

❑ G-AANO	DH Moth	30	ex Cambridge, S'ton, N590N. Moth Corp-built. Arr 18-12-16		8-23
❑ G-AYLP	American AA-1 Yankee	70	ex EI-AVV, G-AYLP. CoA 15-6-11, de-reg 24-5-21	[1]	6-22
❑ G-BIBB	Mooney M.20C	64	ex OH-MOD. CoA 23-6-08, de-reg 16-12-10		8-23
❑ G-STNR	Yakovlev Yak-52	83	ex LY-ALY. IAR Bacau-built. De-reg 23-11-18. F/n 10-18	[2]	8-23

■ **[1]** AA-1 used as a training aid for the local air ambulance. **[2]** See under Swansea, Wales, for *another* 'G-STNR'.

HIGHER PURTINGTON south of the A30 between Chard and Crewkerne

Historic Helicopters: Andrew Whitehouse and friends. Several airframes were offered for sale via Air and Ground Aviation in mid-2023 – these are marked #. Lynx AH.7 XZ220 moved to White Waltham, Berks, in December 2023.

◆ *Occasional open days, also members-only events, otherwise* **only** *by prior permission* | **email** via website | **www.historichelicopters.com**

❑ G-ANLW	Westland Widgeon 2	54	ex Sywell, Flixton, Sywell, Squires Gate, 'MD497', Wellingborough, Little Staughton, Tattershall Thorpe, *When Eight Bells Toll*, *Eye of the Needle*, Southend. CoA 27-5-81, de-reg 15-11-02. first noted 11-21	12-23

	Serial	Code	Type	Yr	History	Note	Date
❑	XJ729		Westland Whirlwind HAR.10 ✈ G-BVGE	56	ex Mullingar, Finningley 8732M (1-8-84), SARTU, 22, 202, 228, 22, HAR.2, 22. Acquired 28-11-13		1-24
❑	XT434	'455'	Westland Wasp HAS.1 G-CGGK	65	ex Breighton, Ipswich, Fleetlands, A2643 [2], A2723 Lee-on-Solent, 829, 703. *Dobbin*. Arrived 25-10-21	[1]	1-23
❑	XT761		Westland Wessex HU.5 ✈ G-WSEX	66	ex Culdrose, Gosport, Lee-on-Solent, A2678 [2], A2767 (12-4-88), Wroughton, 845, 771, 846, 848, 847, 848, 707. Acquired 5-7-17, first flown 15-2-19		1-24
❑	XT771	'620'	Westland Wessex HU.5	67	ex Culdrose, Gosport A2673 [2], Lee-on-Solent A2761 (11-4-88), 772, 845, 848, 707. Acquired 5-7-17, stored		1-24
❑	XT787*		Westland Wasp HAS.1 G-KAXT	67	ex Middle Wallop, North Weald, Cranfield, Weston-super-Mare, RNZN NZ3905, XT787, 829, 703, Fleetlands. CoA 14-8-20. Stored	[2]	1-24
❑	XV647	'28'	Westland Sea King HU.5 G-CMFN	69	ex Gosport, 771, Gannet Flt, 771, HAS.5, 771, 814, 826, HAS.2, 826, 820, HAS.1, 706, 826, 737, 700S	[3]	1-24
❑	XZ597	'M'	Westland Sea King HAR.3 ✈ G-SKNG	78	ex Colsterworth, 203, 202, 78, 202, SKTU, 202. Arrived 6-12-17, first flown 20-3-20	[3]	1-24
❑	XZ616		Westland Lynx AH.7 ✈ G-LNKX	80	ex M Wallop, AH.1. Arrived 30-4-20. First flown 18-11-21	#	1-24
❑	ZA314	'WT'	Westland Sea King HC.4 ✈ G-CMDO	82	ex Gosport, 846, 848, 845, 846, 845, 846, Bosnia, 846, 845, 707, 846, A&AEE. Arrived 7-1-20	#	12-23
❑	ZF122	'V'	Westland Sea King HC.4 G-CMFM	87	ex Colsterworth, 846, 845, 846, 845, 846, 845, 846, 772, 848, 772. Arrived 6-12-17	# [3]	1-24
❑	RS-02		Westland Sea King Mk.48 G-BDNI	76	ex OO-SEE, Koksijde, Belgian Air Force, G-BDNI, G-17-2. Acquired mid-2020, arrived 20-10-21	[3]	1-24
❑	RS-04		Westland Sea King Mk.48 G-BDNK	76	ex OO-KNG, Koksijde, Belgian Air Force, G-BDNK, G-17-4. Acquired mid-2020, arrived 20-10-21	[3]	1-24
❑	'156112'		Westland Sea King HAR.3 ✈ G-SEAK XZ588	77	ex Fleetlands, 202, 22, 202, SKTF, 202, SKTF, 202. Arrived 30-4-20; first flown 20-6-21. *Marine 1* c/s from TV series *The Diplomat*	# [3]	1-24

■ **[1]** Registered to Aeromedical Training Ltd, operated by Westland Wasp Historic Flight – see Winchester, Hampshire and **https://www.historicwasp.com** **[2]** Written out of *W&R24* (p57) as moving from North Weald to Middle Wallop, c2012. **[3]** Registered to Lift West (Helicopters) Ltd.

MARKSBURY on the A39 west of Bath

Hamburger Hill: ◆ *Prior permission* **only** | **www.hamburgerhill.co.uk**

	Serial	Code	Type	Yr	History	Date
❑	XE668	'832'	Hawker Hunter GA.11	55	ex Predannack, A2647 [2], Culdrose SAH A2733 (8-2-85), Yeovilton, FRADU, 738, F.4, 26, 4. Squires Gate-built	7-22
❑	XT762		Westland Wessex HU.5	66	ex Predannack, A2661 [2], Culdrose A2751 (28-7-87), Lee-on-Solent, Wroughton, RAE Bedford, A&AEE, 848	7-22
❑	S-886		Sikorsky S-55C	~	ex Weston-super-Mare, Panshanger, Elstree, Danish AF	7-21

PORTISHEAD The Bristol Activity Centre airframe(s) is/are to be found at the Bristol, Glos, site – qv.

SOMERTON on the B3153 northwest of Yeovil

HeliOperations: While flying from Portland, Dorset, and Culdrose, Cornwall, the company has established a maintenance and storage site here. *W&R28* (p198) reported Sea King ASaC.7 ZE420 as coming here: it is to be found at Gosport, Hampshire. Sea King HU.5 ZA134 moved on to Portland on 4th January 2023 where it became Ukrainian UR-H034 and was delivered on 13th May 2023. By May 2023 HU.5 ZA137 had made the trek to Portland for return to flight.

◆ ***Strictly not*** *available for inspection* | **www.helioperations.co**

	Serial	Code	Type	Yr	History	Date
❑	XV656	'85'	Westland Sea King ASaC.7	70	ex Gosport, Culdrose, 854, 857, 849, AEW.2, 849, HAS.2, 706, Falklands, 825, 819, HAS.1, 819, 824. F/n 12-20	6-21
❑	XV664	'90'	Westland Sea King ASaC.7	70	ex Gosport, Culdrose, 857, 854, 849, AEW.2, 819, 824, 826, HAS.1, 826. First noted 12-20	6-21
❑	XV670	'17'	Westland Sea King HU.5	70	ex Gosport, Culdrose, 771, 845, 706, HAS.2, 814, 737, HAS.1, 819. Arrived 3-9-20	3-21
❑	XV671	'90'	Westland Sea King ASaC.7	70	ex Gosport, Culdrose, 857, 854, 857, 849, AEW.2, 849, HAS.2, HAS.1, 814, 820, 819. First noted 12-20	6-21

❑ XV697	'81'	Westland Sea King ASaC.7	71	ex Gosport, Culdrose, 849, AEW.2, 849, HAS.1, Falklands, 819, 706. First noted 12-20		6-21
❑ XV714	'88'	Westland Sea King ASaC.7	70	ex Gosport, 849, AEW.2, 857, 849, HAS.2, 826, 824, Falklands, 825, 706, 826, 819, HAS.1, 706, 820. Arr by 10-20		3-21
❑ XZ586		W'land Sea King HAR.3	78	ex Gosport, 22, 78, SKTU, 22, 202, 1564 Flt, 202. F/n 12-20		6-21
❑ XZ590	'F'	W'land Sea King HAR.3	78	ex Gosport, 202, 78, 202, 22, 202. First noted 12-20		6-21
❑ XZ594		Westland Sea King HAR.3	76	ex Gosport, SKTU, 202, 22, 202. Arrived 23-7-20		3-21
❑ XZ596	'L'	Westland Sea King HAR.3	76	ex Gosport, 202, 203, SKTU, 22, 202. Arrived 23-7-20		3-21
❑ ZA105	'Q'	Westland Sea King HAR.3	80	ex Gosport, 22, 20		3-21
❑ ZA126	'191'	Westland Sea King ASaC.7	80	ex Gosport, 849, 854, 849, HAS.6, 810, HAS.5, 706, 820, 706, 820		3-21
❑ ZE422	'92'	Westland Sea King ASaC.7	86	ex Gosport, 854, 857, HAS.6, 771, 820, 810, 819, 814, 706, HAS.5, 826, 814. SOC 26-9-18		3-21

TAUNTON

Army Reserve Centre: Mountway Road, Bishops Hull on the western side of the town.

❑ ZB670		Sud Gazelle AH.1	84	ex Dishforth, Arborfield, 665. Westland-built. Arrived 21-6-16. Displayed		10-23

County Classics Motor Museum: Based on the collection of Patrick Hawkins. Opening was delayed due to the Boris-19 Pandemonium, until 20th November 2023 in the well-known, County Stores shop.

◆ *North Street, TA1 1ND* | **01823 253777** | **www.countyclassicsmotormuseum.co.uk**

❑ G-ARJZ*		Druine Turbulent	61	Rollason-built. CoA 4-9-95, de-reg 11-9-00	[1]	11-23

■ **[1]** Famed as the Tiger Club's 'Sea Turbulent' floatplane in the late 1960s.

Spitfire Spares: Specialising in trading in World War Two artefacts, spares etc, the organisation has a taxiable Spitfire IX, powered by a Rolls-Meteor V-12 tank engine and available for hire. A travelling Typhoon FSM is/was being created. 'Gunbus' BAPC.234 (last noted March 2012) and the anonymous Hurricane FSM (last noted April 2017) have been deleted.

◆ *Available* **only** *by prior permission* | **www.spitfirespares.com**

❑ 'EN398'	'JE-J'	V-S Spitfire IX FSM	~	BAPC.555, see notes above	[1]	12-22
❑ 'JP8xx'	'T'	Hawker Typhoon I FSM	18	BAPC.556, *Tally Ho*, under construction, see notes above		12-19

■ **[1]** Other 'EN398s' can be found at Coningsby, Lincs; Salisbury, Wilts; Pyle, Wales.

Also: A cache of Austers has been gathered at a *private* airstrip in the *general* area.

❑ G-AGYK		Auster J1 Autocrat	46	ex Shobdon. CoA 17-8-07, de-reg 11-2-13		12-21
❑ G-AOBV		Auster J5P Autocar	55	ex Wickenby, Cheshunt, Laindon, Stapleford Tawney, Benington. CoA 7-4-71, de-reg 14-11-91		12-21
❑ G-ASOC		Auster 6A Tugmaster	46	ex AOP.6 VF603, 227 OCU, 1958 Flt, 661. CoA 18-5-02, de-reg 22-5-09		12-21
❑ G-AXMN		Auster J5B Autocar	52	ex F-BGPN. De-reg 9-11-10		12-21

WEDMORE on the B3139 west of Wells

Castle Farm Camping and Caravanning: Neil Banwell, site owner, has a SHAR, displayed outside during the summer.

◆ *Prior permission* ***only*** | **www.castlefarmcampsite.co.uk**

❑ XZ494	'128'	HS Sea Harrier F/A.2	80	ex St Athan, 800, FRS.1, 899, 801, 899, 800, 899, 801, 800, 899. 800 Sqn colours		1-24

WESTON-SUPER-MARE AERODROME on the A371 east of Weston-super-Mare

The Helicopter Museum (THM): In October 2023 Elfan ap Rees stood down as Chairman of Trustees at THM. In one form or another he has presided over this pioneering collection for more than 40 years. Elfan began collecting helicopter memorabilia from the age of 13, adding his first complete helicopter in 1969. He's not escaping THM, he's been elected as Life President and Museum Founder. Explaining his decision as being triggered by a review, to be carried out by an independent consultant to develop a succession plan for ageing key trustees, a process encouraged by The Heritage Lottery Fund as a prerequisite for securing future grant aid.

The helipad is a much-used facility and there is a 500m grass strip. Subject to operational conditions, there are frequent helicopter experience flight days. Regular 'open cockpit' days and loads of special events are staged. Catering is excellent – kick off with a THM breakfast!

Evans VP-2 G-BVPM is on loan at St Athan, Wales.

A one-off abbreviation in the listing below should cause no headaches: WSM = Weston-super-Mare. The **Reserve Collection** is listed separately – below – and the restoration centre can also be viewed.

◆ *Locking Moor Road, BS24 8PP* | **01934 635227** | **contact@helimuseum.com** | **www.helicoptermuseum.co.uk**

Reg	Type		Year	Details	Note	Date
❑ G-ALSX	Bristol Sycamore 3		51	ex Duxford, Staverton, G-48/1, G-ALSX, VR-TBS (1958-1959), G-ALSX. CoA 24-9-65, de-reg 31-1-66	[1]	1-24
❑ G-AODA	Westland Whirlwind Srs 3		55	ex Redhill, Bristow, 9Y-TDA, EP-HAC, G-AODA. *Dorado*. CoA 23-8-91, de-reg 23-9-93. Arrived 7-8-93		1-24
❑ G-AOUJ	Fairey Ultra-Light Helicopter		56	ex Staverton, Innsworth, WSM, Harlow, White Waltham, XJ928. CoA 29-3-59, de-reg 26-2-69. Arrived 2010		1-24
❑ G-AOZE	Westland Widgeon 2		57	ex Cuckfield, Shoreham, 5N-ABW, G-AOZE (de-reg 20-6-62). Arrived 1986	[1]	1-24
❑ G-ASTP	Hiller UH-12C		61	ex Biggin Hill, Thornicombe, 'Wales', Thornicombe, Redhill, N9750C. CoA 3-7-82, de-reg 24-1-90. Arr 12-10-89		1-24
❑ G-ATFG	Brantly B2B		65	ex East Fortune, Newport Pagnell. CoA 25-3-85, de-reg 25-9-87. Arrived 21-1-04	[1]	1-24
❑ G-AVNE *and* G-17-3	Westland Wessex 60 Srs 1		67	ex Hurn, WSM, Redhill, G-17-3, 5N-AJL, G-AVNE, 9M-ASS, VH-BHC, PK-HBQ, G-AVNE. CoA 7-2-83, de-reg 23-11-82. Arrived 1987		1-24
❑ G-AWRP	Cierva Grasshopper Srs.3		69	ex Blackpool, Heysham, Shoreham, Redhill. Servotec-built. CoA 12-5-72, de-reg 5-12-83. Arrived 1993	[2]	1-24
❑ G-AXRA	Campbell Cricket		69	de-reg 25-10-90. Arrived 10-13. Inside the cafe		1-24
❑ G-BAPS	Campbell Cougar		73	CoA 20-5-74, de-reg 21-1-87. Acquired 5-76		1-24
❑ G-BGHF	Westland WG.30-100		79	ex Yeovil, Westland. CoA 1-8-86, de-reg 29-3-89. Acquired 22-12-88	[3]	1-24
❑ G-BIGP	Bensen B-8M		81	ex Shrewsbury. CoA 20-10-07, de-reg 27-11-08		1-24
❑ G-BKGD	Westland WG.30-100		82	ex Bristol, WSM, Yeovil, Penzance, G-BKBJ. CoA 6-7-93, de-reg 15-4-93. Arrived by 4-18		1-24
❑ G-BVWL	Air and Space 18A		66	ex East Fortune, Kinnetties, SE-HIE, N90588, N6152S. De-reg 18-10-00. Arrived 22-11-07		1-24
❑ G-BWCW	Barnett J4B		95	de-reg 3-3-05. Arrived 29-10-15		1-24
❑ G-BYMP	Campbell Cricket		99	ex Cheshire, Newtownards. Arrived 16-1-14		1-24
❑ G-EHIL	EHI EH 101 PP3		88	ex Yeovil, ZH647. De-reg 28-4-99. Arrived 26-11-99	[5]	1-24
❑ G-ELEC	Westland WG.30-200		83	ex Westland, WSM, Yeovil, G-BKNV. CoA 28-6-85, de-reg 27-2-98. Arrived 7-12-01		1-24
❑ G-HAUL	Westland WG.30 TT300		86	ex G-17-22, Yeovil. CoA 27-10-86, de-reg 22-4-92. Arr 1991		1-24
❑ G-LYNX	Westland Lynx Srs.1(mod)		79	ex Yeovil, WSM, Yeovil, ZB500, ZA500 , G-LYNX, De-reg 27-2-98. Arrived 18-1-95	[6]	1-24
❑ G-OAPR	Brantly B2B		65	ex G-BPST, N2280U. CoA 1-10-15	[1]	1-22
❑ G-ORVB	McCulloch J-2	G-HEKY	71	ex G-ORVB (de-reg 30-1-09), G-BLGI, G-BKKL, Bahrain Public Security BPS-3, N4329G. Arrived 21-12-08		1-24
❑ G-OTED	Robinson R22HP		81	ex Elstree, G-BMYR, ZS-HLG. CoA 17-2-02, de-reg 26-3-02		1-22
❑ G-TIGE	Aérospatiale Super Puma		82	ex Gosport, Norwich, Aberdeen, G-BJYJ, F-WTNM. De-reg 8-12-15. Arrived 30-11-15		1-24
❑ G-WBAT	Julian CD Wombat		90	ex Breeqhou, St Merryn, G-BSID. De-reg 29-4-09. Arr 9-7-13		1-24
❑ –	Slingsby T.8 Tutor		~	BGA.1759, ex Keevil, Wolverhampton, Dowty G/C, Pershore, RAFGSA.178. Arr 27-10-16. Fuselage, in Pilot Block		1-24
❑ –	Hafner R-II Revoplane		3<u>0</u>	BAPC.10, ex M Wallop, Locking, WSM, Higher Blagdon, Old Warden, WSM, Heston, Austria. Arrived 1979, donated 1996	[7]	1-24
❑ –	Murray M-1 Helicopter		54	BAPC.60, ex Wigan, Salford. Arrived 10-95		1-24
❑ –	Watkinson CG-4		77	BAPC.128, ex Horley, Bexhill. Arrived 1978.	[8]	1-24
❑ –	Westland WG.33 EMU		78	BAPC.153, ex Yeovil. Arrived 1980	[9]	1-24
❑ –	Bensen B-8M		84	BAPC.264, ex Westbury-on-Trym. Unflown		1-24
❑ –	Bensen B-8M Gyro-Boat		c65	BAPC.289, ex Brooklands, Glasgow. Arrived 11-10-03		1-24
❑ –	Husband Modac Hornet		02	BAPC.339, ex Sheffield. 'Hopped' only. Arrived 13-11-04		1-24
❑ D-HMQV	Bölkow Bö 102		60	ex Bückeburg, Germany	[1] [10]	1-24
❑ DDR-SPY	Kamov Ka-26 *Hoodlum*		73	ex D-HOAY, Germany, Interflug DDR-SPY. Arrived 12-6-95		1-24

❑ F-OCMF	'335'	Sud Super Frelon	67	ex Aérospatiale, Olympic, F-BTRP, F-WKQC, F-OCZV, F-RAFR, F-OCMF, F-BMHC, F-WMHC. Arrived 28-4-93. Olympic colours, *Hermes*	[11]	1-24
❑ F-WGTX		Intora-Firebird Atlas	c98	ex Horsted Keynes, Brentwood, Southend, France. Arrived 19-7-17	[12]	1-24
❑ F-WQAP		Sud Dauphin 2	79	ex Eurocopter, Marignane, F-WZJJ. Acquired 19-3-03	[13]	1-24
❑ N8186E		ATI CH.1 G-BXZN	87	ex Horsted Keynes, Brentwood, Southend, N8186E, Switzerland. De-reg 28-10-05. Arrived 19-7-17	[4]	1-24
❑ OO-SHW		Bell 47H-1 G-AZYB	56	ex Thruxton, G-AZYB, LN-OQG, SE-HBE, SABENA OO-SHW. Crashed 21-4-84, de-reg 22-4-85	[1]	1-24
❑ SP-SAY		Mil Mi-2 *Hoplite*	85	ex Hiscso, ZEUS. PZL-Swidnik-built. Arrived 24-11-97		1-24
❑ AP506		Cierva C.30A G-ACWM	34	ex Staverton, Tewkesbury, AP506, 529, 1448 Flt, 5 RSS, G-ACWM (de-reg 17-3-59), Autogiro Fg Club, Hanworth. Avro-built. Arrived 1986. Frame	[1]	1-24
❑ WG719		Westland Dragonfly HR.5 G-BRMA	52	ex G-BRMA (de-reg 30-3-89), 'WG718', Shawbury, WSM, Yeovilton, Southampton, Fleetlands, Britannia Flt, FRU, Yeovilton SF, HR.3, 705, Hal Far SF. SOC 5-5-70. Acquired 4-76	[1]	1-24
❑ XD163	'X'	Westland Whirlwind HAR.10	54	ex Wroughton, 8645M, CFS, Akrotiri SAR Flt, MoA, 228, 275, 155, MoA. SOC 20-3-80	[1]	1-24
❑ XE521		Fairey Rotodyne Y	57	ex Cranfield, W' Waltham. Sections, acquired 1981	[1] [14]	1-24
❑ XG452		Bristol Belvedere HC.1 G-BRMB	60	ex G-BRMB (de-reg 3-7-96), Ternhill, Cosford 7997M (8-12-67), RR, A&AEE, RR, A&AEE. Oldmixon-built. Arrived 5-11-74		1-24
❑ XG454		Bristol Belvedere HC.1	60	ex Manchester, Henlow, 8366M, Abingdon, A&AEE, Bristol, Old Sarum, Belvedere Trials Unit. Accident 30-8-61. Oldmixon-built. Acquired 2017, arrived 21-1-22		1-24
❑ XG462		Bristol Belvedere HC.1	61	ex Henlow, WSM, 72, 66. Crashed 5-10-63. Oldmixon-built. Cockpit. Arrived 1989	[1]	1-24
❑ XK940	'911'	Westland Whirlwind HAS.7 G-AYXT	57	ex G-AYXT (CoA 4-2-99, de-reg 8-8-00), Tibenham, Redhill, Northampton, Heysham, Carnforth, Panshanger, Elstree, Luton, Blackpool, Fleetlands, 771, Culdrose SF, 705, 825, 824, 845. SOC 24-3-71. Arrived 6-6-00	[1] [15]	1-24
❑ XL811		Saro Skeeter AOP.12	59	ex Stoke-on-Trent, Warmingham, Southend, Peel Green, Wroughton, 17F, 656, 651. SOC 27-5-68. Arrived 1993	[1]	1-24
❑ XL829		Bristol Sycamore HR.14	57	ex Bristol, 32, MCS, Khormaksar SAR Flight. SOC 18-12-71. Oldmixon-built. Arrived 17-10-07		1-24
❑ XM328	'653'	Westland Wessex HAS.3	60	ex Culdrose, A2644 [2], A2727 (9-5-85), Wroughton, Culdrose SAR Flt, 772, 737, A&AEE, HAS.1, A&AEE. Arrived 3-04. *The Sow*		1-24
❑ XM330		Westland Wessex HAS.1	59	ex Farnborough, RAE, ATDU, ETPS, RAE Farnborough, A&AEE, HS. SOC 16-6-83. Arrived 16-5-94		1-24
❑ XP165		Saro P.531-2	60	ex HAM Southend, ETPS, A&AEE, RAE, A&AEE. Last flown 28-5-71. SOC 26-8-71. Acquired 10-5-83		1-24
❑ XR486		Westland Whirlwind HCC.12 G-RWWW	64	ex G-RWWW (CoA 25-8-96, de-reg 10-7-00), Redhill, Tattershall Thorpe, St Athan 8727M (9-12-81), 32, Queen's Flt, HAR.10 Arrived 8-6-00	[1]	1-24
❑ XT190		Bell Sioux AH.1	65	ex Wattisham, Soest, M Wallop, UNFICYP. Westland-built. Arrived 8-6-95		1-24
❑ XT443	'422'	Westland Wasp HAS.1	66	ex Oldmixon, Sherborne, 703. SOC 7-5-87. Arrived 18-1-95. HMS *Aurora* titles		1-24
❑ XV733		Westland Wessex HCC.4	69	ex Shawbury, Queen's Flight. Last Royal sortie 11-3-98, last flight 13-3-98. Arrived 15-11-01	[16]	1-24
❑ XW839		Westland WG.13 00-05	74	ex Yeovilton, A2624 [2], A2657 (1-11-88), A2710, Manadon, BS Eng. Arr 11-1-96. 'HMS *Thunderer*' titles	[17]	1-24
❑ XX910		Westland Lynx HAS.2	74	ex Yeovilton, DERA/RAE Farnborough, Aberporth, A&AEE. Arrived 5-12-00	[18]	1-24
❑ ZB686		Sud Gazelle AH.1	83	ex M Wallop, 9322M, ex Fleetlands, 665, 655. Westland-built. Cockpit, trailer mounted		1-24

Reg	Marks	Type		Year	History	Note	Seen
❑ ZE477		Westland Lynx 3		84	ex G-17-24, Yeovil, Westland. Arrived 1989		1-24
❑ ZJ116*	'IOI'	EHI EH.101 PP8	G-OIOI	90	ex Hendon, Brize Norton, Yeovil, G-OIOI (CoA 5-5-94, de-reg 1-4-96), G-17-01. Last flight 23-10-01. Arr 8-22	[19]	1-24
❑ 'ZS782'		W'land WG.25 Sharpeye		81	ex Yeovil. RPV, Full-scale EMU/wind tunnel model		1-24
❑ A41	'ACB'	Sud Alouette II		67	ex Belgian Army. Arrived 19-2-08		1-24
❑ 622		Piasecki HUP-3 Retriever		54	ex Philadelphia, N6699D, RCN, 51-16622. Arrived 1991		1-24
❑ 9147		Mil Mi-4 *Hound*		c57	ex Prague, Sechov, Tabor, Czech AF. Arrived 1-94		1-24
❑ FR-41	'ARB'	Piasecki H-21C Shawnee		57	ex ALAT F-MARB, F-MBEE, Marine Nationale F-XCAF, ALAT F-MAAY, 56-2025. SOC 4-70. Arrived 27-1-16	[20]	1-24
❑ FR-108	'CDL'	Sud-Ouest Djinn		59	ex ALAT F-MCDL. Arrived 1991		1-24
❑ 81+00		Bölkow Bö 105M		84	ex Heer, D-HZYR. Arrived 3-5-07	[21]	1-24
❑ 96+26		Mil Mi-24 *Hind-D*		81	ex Luftwaffe, East German 421. Arrived 20-2-95		1-24
❑ MM80927		Bell 206C-1	'CC-49'	74	Carabinieri. Agusta-built. Arrived late 2012		1-24
❑ MM81205		Agusta 109A II	'GF-128'	86	ex Guardia di Finanza GdiF-128. Arrived 6-10-10		1-24
❑ 1005	'05'	PZL-Swidnik SM-2		c65	ex Polish Air Force. Arrived 10-6-91	[22]	1-24
❑ 2007	'07' red	Mil Mi-1 *Hare*		59	ex Poland. WSK-Swidnik-built SM-1. Soviet c/s. Arr 2-9-93		1-24
❑ '07' red		Mil Mi-8PS *Hip*	618	c79	ex Polish AF, 37 PST, 36 SPLT. Arr 5-2-10. Soviet c/s	[23]	1-24
❑ DS-1482		Gyrodyne QH-50D		66	ex USA, Lenwood, Fort Irwin, White Sands. Arr 2-10-14	[24]	1-24
❑ 66-16579		Bell UH-1H Iroquois		67	ex US Army, UH-1D. Arrived 29-8-92		1-24
❑ 67-16506		Hughes OH-6A Cayuse		68	ex US Army. Arrived 8-99		1-24

■ **[1]** Airframes on loan from Elfan ap Rees. **[2]** As well as this, the Grasshopper 3 prototype, substantial elements of the unflown second and third examples are held: G-AXFM used as a ground-running rig and the centre section, floor pan and dynamics of G-AZAU. **[3]** WG.30 prototype, first flown 10-4-79. **[4]** Also known as Dragonfly DF.1, single-seat, ultra-light tip-jet-driven helicopter. Powered by the now-banned hydrogen peroxide (H_2O_2), effectively making it steam-driven! Built in the USA by Advanced Technologies Inc for Liteco Helicopter Systems of Switzerland. To the UK by 1998 and marketed by Intora-Firebird. See also [12]. **[5]** EH 101 factoids: First flown at Yeovil 30-9-88, retired 2-99 with 653 hours in 581 flights. **[6]** G-LYNX established a world air speed record in 8-86 of 249.1mph. **[7]** Not a cliché, a truism, this is a national - no, *international* - treasure. The oldest surviving helicopter in Britain, the R-II was designed by Raoul Hafner in association with Bruno Nagler and built and flown at Aspern, near Vienna. It was brought to the UK by 1933 and used by Hafner as a rotor test-bed at Heston before being put into store at Filton. Hafner went on to design the Bristol Sycamore. Initially on loan to the museum, Hafner's widow, Eileen, donated the R-II in 1996. **[8]** CG-4 is a man-powered rotorcraft. **[9]** WG.33 - engineering mock-up of a single-seat ultra-light observation helicopter. **[10]** Although bolted firmly down on to a base-plate, the Helitrainer was capable of flight, but intended as a fully-functioning procedure and flight trainer. **[11]** Frelon started life as SA.321 c/n 116. It is in Olympic Airways colours as worn at the 1969 Paris Salon. **[12]** Two-seat tip-jet helicopter developed from the CH.1 - see [4]. Third airframe, fitted with boom from prototype, F-WGTX. **[13]** First production SA.365N, modified to fly-by-wire test-bed; retired in 2001. Record holder: 6-2-79 Paris-London-Paris (Issy-le-Moulineaux-Battersea and back) 182.84mph; 8-2-79 took it to 200.03mph. **[14]** Rotodyne project was cancelled in February 1962 and XE521 stored at White Waltham and eventually broken up. A couple of times in *W&R* the rules are broken and although there is no cockpit, the fuselage sections and rotor pylon are substantial enough to be formally listed. **[15]** G-AYXT was also allocated to XK907, but not taken up - see Coventry, Warks. **[16]** Last Wessex built for British armed forces, first flew Yeovil 13-5-69. **[17]** Fifth prototype, 'pre-Lynx', first flown 19-6-74. **[18]** During refurbishing at Yeovilton XX910 was fitted with the boom of Danish MK.80 S-142. **[19]** 8th Yeovil-built example; civil variant, to have been marketed as the Heliliner. **[20]** Supplied direct to France, served in Algeria from delivery 5-57, it was loaned to the Marines mid-1958 to 4-60. Based in France from 10-62. **[21]** Bö 105M donated by Eurocopter.**[22]** SM-2 re-engineered Mi-1/SM-1. **[23]** *Hip* is a VIP version - square, not round, windows, delivered to Poland in the 1970s, serving until retirement in 2005. It flew with 37 Air Assault Regiment (PST), Leznica Wielka, Lodz. **[24]** QH-50 a pioneering rotorcraft UAV used mostly by the US Navy.

Reserve Collection: Wessex HAS.3 XS149 travelled to Liphook, Hampshire, in June 2023. In January 2024 WG.30-100 N5840T departed for a new life as a 'glamping' pod – no 'forwarding address' as yet. There is a *possibility* that the former Burnham-on-Sea, Hobbycopter is the example that was many years displayed at car spares business at Sunbury-on-Thames, Surrey. This was written out of *W&R26* (p276) as having gone by August 2017.

◆ Available for inspection ***only*** by special arrangement - check with the contacts given above.

Reg	Type	Year	History	Note	Seen
❑ G-ANFH	Westland Whirlwind Srs 1	54	ex Redhill, Great Yarmouth, Bristow, Autair, BEAH, BEA HEU. CoA 17-7-71, de-reg 2-9-77, acquired 1978	[1] [2]	10-21
❑ G-ANJV	Westland Whirlwind Srs 3	54	ex Redhill, Bristow, VR-BET. De-reg 1-8-74		10-23
❑ G-ARVN	Cierva Grasshopper 1	61	ex Shoreham, Redhill. Servotec-built CoA 18-5-63, de-reg 14-3-77	[3]	3-20
❑ G-ASCT	Bensen B-8M	r62	ex Hungerford. CoA 11-11-66, de-reg 20-9-73. Arrived 1993. Major components		3-20
❑ G-ATBZ	Westland Wessex 60 Srs 1	65	ex Austria, Hurn, G-17-4, WSM. CoA 15-12-81, de-reg 23-11-82. Arrived 1988		10-23
❑ G-AVKE	Gadfly HDW-1	67	ex Southend, Thruxton. De-reg 12-10-81. Arrived 1978	[1]	10-21

❑ –		Bensen B-6 gyroglider	c60	BAPC.212. Major components		3-20
❑ –		Cranfield Vertigo	c82	BAPC.213, ex Yeovil, Cardington, Yeovil	[4]	10-20
❑ –*		Adams-Wilson Hobbycopter	~	ex Burnham-on-Sea, 'West Sussex'. Arrived 1-24 See notes above		1-24
❑ XG596	'66'	W'land Whirlwind HAS.7	57	ex Wroughton A2651 (7-1-76), 705, 829, 771, 705, 737	[1]	10-23
❑ XL736		Saro Skeeter AOP.12	58	ex Saxmundham, Stuttgart, Moordrecht, 1 Flt, 655, M Wallop. Ground accident 25-9-68. Less boom		3-20
❑ XM557		Saro Skeeter AOP.12	59	ex Saxmundham, Stuttgart, Moordrecht, 5 Flt, 652, 17 Flt, 652, 4 Flt, 654, 652, 1 Wing. Less boom		3-20
❑ XN345		Saro Skeeter AOP.12	60	ex Saxmundham, Stuttgart, Moordrecht, 26 Regt, 17 Flt, 652, 17 Flt, 654, 655, 1 Wing. SOC 20-10-69		3-20
❑ XP404		Westland Whirlwind HAR.10	62	ex Finningley, Benson 8682M (10-10-82), 22, SAR Wing, 202, 228. Arrived 1991		10-23
❑ XP886		Westland Scout AH.1	63	ex Yeovil Tech, Arborfield, Wroughton, 652, 660, 651		3-20
❑ XR526		Westland Wessex HC.2	64	ex Yeovil, Sherborne, Farnborough, Odiham 8147M, 72. Damaged 27-5-70. Arrived 26-8-99		10-21
❑ XS486	'F' *and* '524'	Westland Wessex HU.5	64	ex Colerne 9272M (31-5-91), Wroughton, 772, 771, 707, 848, 707, A&AEE, 707, 848, 707, 848. Arrived 13-5-04		8-21
❑ XT472	'XC'	Westland Wessex HU.5	66	ex Hullavington, Netheravon, M Wallop, Lyneham, Wroughton, 845, 847, 845. SOC 10-9-82. Arrived 1987		10-21
❑ XZ649*		Westland Lynx AH.7	80	ex Bristol, Farnborough, Boscombe Down, 657. F/n 8-23	[5]	10-23
❑ -		Westland WG.30-300 EMU	~	ex Yeovil. Transmission rig, based on unfinished c/n 022		10-22

■ **[1]** Airframes on loan from Elfan ap Rees. **[2]** Thanks to Jon Horswell for reminding the author of the vital role played by this machine, in its BEA days, in the final sequence of the 1964 film *A Hard Day's Night* - when the logo on the access door was altered to read 'BEA TLES'. It also appeared in *The Damned* (1961), *Where the Bullets Fly* and *Murderer's Row* (both 1966). **[3]** *Victor-November* is Britain's first co-axial helicopter, first flown 1962. **[4]** Vertigo, a man-powered rotorcraft and nothing to do with Cranfield, Beds; the project was led by Andrew *Cranfield*. **[5]** XZ649 is fitted with the boom of XZ646 – see Boscombe Down, Wilts.

British Hang-Gliding Museum (BHGM): The *nominal* base for the 80-plus 'airframes' held across a series of sites. BHGM is beyond the scope of *W&R* but for those so inclined, its amazing website is **www.british-hang-gliding-museum.co.uk**

WESTON ZOYLAND AERODROME or Middle Zoy, on the A372 east of Bridgwater

The southern element of the former RAF airfield has been substantially developed as the thriving **Middle Zoy** general aviation centre. (The element north of the A372 is a microlight strip.) The intention is to mount the Meteor on a plinth as a reminder of the heady days of 209 AFS and 12 FTS, 1952 to 1955. Vagabond OY-AVW has been deleted.

❑ 'WZ584'	'54'	Gloster Meteor T.7 WL360	52	ex Booker, Yatesbury, Staverton, Hucclecote, Locking 7920M (13-9-66), 229 OCU, 1, Wattisham SF, 211 AFS, 210 AFS, 215 AFS. Arrived 16-11-19	[1]	7-23

■ **[1]** WL360 / 'WZ584' has the wings, tail etc of T.7 WL345 (ex Booker, Hollington, Hastings, Kemble, CAW, etc SOC 1-11-74), its cockpit having been exported to Malta. The *real* WZ584 - a Vampire T.11 - is at Binbrook, Lincs.

Paul Childs makes good progress on Provost *Romeo-Fox* which carries a dedication to his late father: 'Feet on the ground - Head in the clouds - in loving memory of Bernie Childs.' ◆ *Prior application* **only**

❑ WV499	'P3'	Percival Provost T.1 G-BZRF	53	ex Exeter, Booker, Armthorpe, Sandtoft, N Weald, St Athan, Weeton 7698M, 6 FTS	7-23
❑ WW388	'O-F'	Percival Provost T.1	54	ex Audley End, Newport, Sleap, Hemswell, Firbeck, Long Marston, Rhoose, Llanelli, Chinnor, Chertsey, Cuxwold, Chessington, Halton 7616M (13-10-59), 2 FTS. F/n 7-20	7-23
❑ WW453		Percival Provost T.1 G-TMKI	55	ex Clevedon, Cranfield, Thatcham, Strathallan, Perth, Hunting, 1 FTS, 2 FTS. De-reg 3-10-11. Spares	7-23
❑ XF836	'J-G'	Percival Provost T.1 G-AWRY	55	ex Audley End, Thatcham, Popham, Old Warden, 8043M, 27 MU, CATCS, CNCS, RAFC, Man UAS. Damaged 28-7-87. CoA 22-8-88. First noted 7-20, off-site	7-23

YEOVIL AIRFIELD to the west of Yeovil

EGHG

Leonardo Airborne and Space Systems: Pronounced 'Westland'. The Lynx, representing the record-breaking G-LYNX (see Weston-super-Mare, Somerset) is displayed at the Lysander Road gate.

❑ ZD560	Westland Lynx AH.7	87	ex Eastleigh, Boscombe Down, ETPS, AH.5(I). Last flown 28-3-12. Displayed by 8-21	10-22

❑ ZH822		EHI Merlin HM.1	97	ex Shawbury, Culdrose, Fleetlands, DERA. NEA 28-11-18. Arrived 27-7-19. Stored		10-21
❑ ZH825		EHI Merlin HM.1	97	ex Shawbury, Culdrose, Fleetlands, DERA. NEA 28-11-18. Arrived 20-11-19. Stored		10-21

Yeovil College: Mudford Road ◆ *Prior application* **only** | **www.yeovil.ac.uk**

❑ ZT800		Westland Super Lynx 300	99	ex Yeovil. Handed over, on loan, 12-16		1-24

YEOVILTON AIRFIELD on the B5131, south of the A303, north of Yeovil EGDY

A one-off abbreviation used throughout this section: VL = Yeovilton (from the shore station code once worn on the tail).

Fleet Air Arm Museum (FAAM): Part of the **National Museum of the Royal Navy** which encompasses several venues, including Portsmouth Historic Dockyard and HMS *Victory*, among others. Yeovilton is a sure-fire all-absorbing visit, with 'Carrier' representing the best of innovation. An observation window allows visitors to see progress in the conservation workshop and another that overlooks the ramp giving views of activity on the base. The 'Swordfish' restaurant is excellent. There is an active **Friends of the FAAM** – enquiries via the museum website.

FAAM aircraft can be found on loan at: Coventry, Warks, Gannet XA508; Sunderland, Tyneside, Pucará A-522; Woodley, Berks, Gannet XG883, Scimitar F.1 XD220 with the Empire State Aerosciences Museum, New York, USA.

◆ *RNAS Yeovilton, BA22 8HT, sat-nav junkies use BA22 8HW* | **01935 840565** | **fleetairarm.enquiries@nmrn.org.uk** | **www.nmrun.org.uk/visit-us/fleet-air-arm-museum**

Main Halls (1 and 2): Seafire F.17 SX137 joined the newly revamped 'Carrier' (below) by mid-2022.

❑ –		Short S.27 replica	79	BAPC.149, ex Lee-on-Solent. Acquired 1980		1-24
❑ 8359		Short 184	1915	ex Duxford, South Lambeth, Crystal Palace, Buncrana, Rosyth, Dundee, Killingholme. Westland-built. Damaged 31-1-41. Arrived 28-1-76. Forward fuselage	[1]	1-24
❑ L2301		Supermarine Walrus I G-AIZG	39	ex Arbroath, Thame, G-AIZG (de-reg 5-1-49), EI-ACC, IAC N18, L2301 - no service. Acquired 6-12-66		1-24
❑ L2940		Blackburn Skua II	40	ex Lake Grotli, Norway, 800. Crashed 27-4-40. Substantial wreckage, arrived 1974		1-24
❑ N1854		Fairey Fulmar II G-AIBE	40	ex Lossiemouth, Fairey G-AIBE (CoA 6-7-59, de-reg 30-4-59), A&AEE. Acquired 1962		1-24
❑ 'N2078'		Sopwith Baby floatplane	1916	BAPC.442, ex Cobham, Fleetlands, Heathrow, RAeS, Nash, Brooklands. Acquired 5-70. *The Jabberwock*	[2]	1-24
❑ 'P4139'		Fairey Swordfish II HS618	43	ex 'V6105', 'W5984', Manadon A2001, Donibristle, 834. SOC on HMS *Hunter* 5-8-43. Blackburn-built. Acquired 1962		1-24
❑ AL246		Grumman Martlet I	40	ex Loughborough, 768, RAE, 882, 802. Acquired 1963		1-24
❑ EX976		NAA Harvard III	41	ex Portuguese AF 1657, n/s FAA, EX976, 41-33949. Acquired 30-9-80		1-24
❑ KD431	'E2-M'	Vought Corsair IV	44	ex Cranfield, 768, 1835, BuNo 14862. Acquired 1964. 768 Sqn colours		1-24
❑ KE209		Grumman Hellcat II	45	ex Lossiemouth SF, Stretton, Anthorn, BuNo 79779. Last flown 7-54. Acquired 1970		1-24
❑ LZ551/G		DH Vampire 1	44	ex Waddon (Science Museum), DH, RAE, 778, A&AEE, RAE. Hatfield-built. SOC 13-8-47. Acquired 1966	[3]	1-24
❑ VX595		Westland Dragonfly HR.5	49	ex Portland, Gosport, Fleetlands, Henlow, F'lands, ETPS, RAE, ETPS, A&AEE, AFEE, A&AEE, AFEE. Acquired 23-11-98	[4]	1-24
❑ WJ231	'115'	Hawker Sea Fury FB.11	51	ex Wroughton, VL 'WE726', VL SF, FRU. Acquired 1965		1-24
❑ WN493		Westland Dragonfly HR.5	53	ex Culdrose, Culdrose SF, 705, 701, A&AEE. Acquired 19-10-66		1-24
❑ XA127		DH Sea Vampire T.22	54	ex CIFE, 736. Christchurch-built. SOC 12-8-65. Cockpit		1-24
❑ XB446		Grumman Avenger ECM.6	45	ex Culdrose SF, 831, 751, 820, USN 69502, VC-11, VT-87. Acquired 9-4-68. 'Invasion stripes' and 1944 camouflage		1-24
❑ XP142		Westland Wessex HAS.3	62	ex Cobham Hall, Wroughton, VL A2720, 737, 706, 814, 706, 845. Acquired 26-7-82. *Humphrey*	[5]	1-24
❑ XS508		Westland Wessex HU.5	64	ex Cobham, A2677, A2766 (14-4-88), Lee-on-Solent, Wroughton. Acquired 28-6-93; on show from 8-7-15		1-24
❑ XT765	'J'	Westland Wessex HU.5	66	ex Cobham Hall, VL gate 2004-2011, Gosport A2665, A2755, Lee-on-Solent, 845, Lee SAR Flt, 772, 846, 845. Acquired 3-11		1-24

❑ XV663	'18'	Westland Sea King HAS.6	70	ex Gosport, Falmouth, Gosport A2807 (10-12-01), Fleetlands, 819, 810, 820, 819, 737, 706, 825, 706, 826. Arrived 21-5-15	[6]	1-24
❑ XZ699		Westland Lynx HAS.3	80	ex Cobham, VL, Fleetlands, 815, 702. Acquired 11-06		1-24
❑ 100545		Focke Achgelis Fa 330A-1 Bachstelgze	44	ex Wroughton, VL, Higher Blagdon, Cranfield, Farnborough. Weser Flug-built. Acquired 25-8-93		1-24
❑ 1420		Mikoyan-Gurevich MiG-15*bis Fagot* G-BMZF	64	ex N Weald, Gamston, Retford, G-BMZF (de-reg 23-2-90), Polish AF. Aero-built SBLim-2A. Acquired 14-5-87. North Korean colours		1-24

■ **[1]** Short 184 on loan from the Imperial War Museum. It was damaged in a bombing raid while stored at South Lambeth 31-1-41. **[2]** Sopwith Baby 'N2078' is a composite, using parts from the sequential 8214 and 8215. Both, ordered in 1915, were passed on to the Italian government to act as patterns in July 1916, for production by Ansaldo. This would go a long way to explaining the Italian tricolour on the rudder of the components acquired by R G J Nash. **[3]** Sea Vampire prototype on loan from the Science Museum. Piloted by Lt Cdr Eric 'Winkle' Brown, it made the world's first-ever landing by a pure-jet on a carrier - HMS *Ocean* - 3-12-45. **[4]** VX595 on loan from RAF Museum. **[5]** *Humphrey* attacked the Argentine submarine *Santa Fe* with depth charges 25-4-82 off South Georgia. There is another *Humphrey*, see Gosport, Hampshire. **[6]** XV663 is painted in Royal Navy colours to port and RAF SAR rescue yellow to starboard; because of this it is nicknamed 'Banana Split'.

Carrier Experience (Hall 3): A £1m refurbishment of this incredible exhibition was completed during the spring of 2022. In a reshuffle the following moved to Cobham Hall (below) during 2022: Sea Venom WW138, Gannet XA466, Scimitar XD317, Buccaneer XV333. Technically, Wessex XT769 is in Hall 2 - but as the method of 'travel' to 'Carrier', it really belongs here.

❑ 'N6452'		Sopwith Pup replica	83	ex Cobham Hall, museum, Whitehall, G-BIAU (CoA 13-9-89, de-reg 10-3-97). Acquired 10-6-85		1-24
❑ SX137		V-S Seafire F.17	45	ex main halls, Culdrose, 'W9132', VL SF, 764, 759, 1831, Culham. Last flown 16-7-60, acquired 1964		1-24
❑ VR137		Westland Wyvern TF.1	49	ex Cobham Hall, Cranfield, Yeovil. Acquired 2-66	[1]	1-24
❑ WA473	'102'	V-S Attacker F.1	51	ex Abbotsinch, 736, 702, 800. SOC 16-6-58, acquired 1964		1-24
❑ WV856	'163'	Hawker Sea Hawk FGA.6	54	ex RAE, 781, 806.AWA-built. Acquired 7-67		1-24
❑ XN957	'630'	Blackburn Buccaneer S.1	63	ex 736, 809, 801. SOC 10-11-72. Acquired 1974		1-24
❑ XS590	'131'	DH Sea Vixen FAW.2	66	ex 899, 892. Hawarden-built. Acquired 26-11-70. 899 Sqn c/s		1-24
❑ XT482	'ZM'	Westland Wessex HU.5	66	A2656, ex A2745, Lee-on-Solent, Wroughton, 707, 845, 847, 707, 771, 707. Acquired 24-2-94	[2]	1-24
❑ XT596		McD Phantom FG.1	66	ex Scampton, Holme-on-Spalding-Moor, RAE Thurleigh, H-o-S-M, Hucknall, Patuxent River, Edwards. Arr 19-1-88	[3]	1-24
❑ XT769		Westland Wessex HU.5	67	ex Lee-on-Solent, Wroughton, Culdrose, 771, 772, 771, 846, 848. Acquired 3-11	[2]	1-24
❑ XZ499	'003'	HS Sea Harrier F/A.2	81	ex Cobham Hall, St Athan, 801, 800, 801, 899, 800, 801, 800, 809, 801. Arrived 13-11-02		1-24

■ **[1]** Wyvern from a pre-production batch of 20 TF.1s, powered by the 24-cylinder RR Eagle 22: this one did not fly. **[2]** Visitors to 'Carrier' exhibition travel to the flight deck 'on board' Wessex XT769 and disembark from XT482! **[3]** The second YF-4K development airframe, first flown at St Louis, USA, 31-8-66.

Hall 4:

❑ G-BSST		BAC/Sud Concorde 002	69	CoA 30-10-74, de-reg 21-1-87. Flew in 4-3-76	[1]	1-22
❑ N5419		Bristol Scout D replica	90	ex Kemble, Banwell, Cardington, USA. Skeletal airframe. Arrived 30-11-98	[2]	7-23
❑ WG774		BAC 221	64	ex East Fortune, RAE Bedford, Filton, Fairey Delta 2. Last flight 9-6-73. Arrived 1-80	[3]	7-23
❑ XP841		Handley Page HP.115	61	ex Cosford, Colerne, RAE Bedford. Last flown 1-2-74. Acquired 6-6-79		1-22
❑ XP980		Hawker P.1127	63	A2700, ex Culdrose, Tarrant Rushton, RAE Bedford, Cranwell, A&AEE. Acquired 6-3-89		7-23
❑ XZ493	'001'	HS Sea Harrier FRS.1	80	ex Dunsfold, Yeovilton, Lee-on-Solent, 899, 801. Ditched 15-12-94, acquired 1-3-95. 801 Sqn colours	[4]	7-23
❑ XZ720	'410'	Westland Lynx HAS.3GMS	80	ex Cobham Hall, Fleetlands, 815, 829, 815. Handed over 26-4-12. 815 Sqn, 216 Flt c/s, HMS *Gloucester* titles.	[5]	7-23
❑ ZA298	'Y'	Westland Sea King HC.4 G-BJNM	81	ex Cobham, Fleetlands, Camp Bastion, 846, Basrah, 845, 846, 848, 845, Split, 846, 848, 846, Falklands, 846, G-BJNM (de-reg 14-12-81), Westland, 846. Arr 31-3-16	[6]	7-23
❑ ZD433	'45A'	BAe/McDD Harrier GR.9A	89	ex Cobham Hall, Cottesmore, 800. Acquired 20-12-11. On show from 13-6-17	[7]	7-23

■ **[1]** UK prototype Concorde G-BSST is on loan from the Science Museum; it first flew on 9-4-69 and clocked 836 flight hours and 438 landings. **[2]** Scout D is on loan from Sir George White; its 'serial' is actually its US civil registration. **[3]** Build date given is that of its second guise as ogival wing test-bed for Concorde, prior to that is was the first FD.2, first flying 6-10-55 and achieving the world air speed record of 1,132mph on 10-3-56. **[4]** FRS.1 is a composite. Rebuilt for museum purposes by BAe at Dunsfold, the forward fuselage of XZ493 was grafted on to the wings and rear fuselage of Harrier GR.3 XV760. The cockpit of XV760 can be found at Southampton, Hampshire. **[5]** XZ720 served almost from new during the Falklands, but came to fame in the first Gulf War when it attacked - and 'killed' - five Iraqi Navy ships with Sea Skua missiles. **[6]** ZA298 is known as the 'King of Kings' because of its incredible history: *four* combat theatres, Falklands, Croatia, Iraq, Afghanistan. It took part in the rescue operation of the burning HMS *Coventry*, off Pebble Island, 25-2-82. ZA298 was shot at by an Argentine A-4 Skyhawk, a cannon shell hitting a rotor blade on 13-6-82. After a forced landing, it was back in the fray just over 120 minutes later. Two days later, it ferried General Menendez and his entourage off HMS *Fearless* for the surrender. Another war, another country: it was hit by an RPG round which exited - leaving no casualties and some on the spot BDR - in Afghanistan 21-5-10. And it was briefly a civilian for a sales tour to Algeria in late 1981. **[7]** GR.9A is kept in its battle-weary condition and as such has been nicknamed *Dirty Harry*!

Restoration Workshop: At the end of the 'Carrier' tour can be found the workshop area, which is glass-walled to provide visitors with a great view of what's going on.

❑ DP872		Fairey Barracuda II	43	ex Wroughton, VL, Enagh Lough, 769. Boulton Paul-built. Crashed 18-1-44. Remains recovered 5-71	[1]	1-24

■ **[1]** The long-term restoration of Barracuda II DP872 will use the substantial wreckage of Mk.II LS931 from its crash site on the Scottish Isle of Jura 2-1-45. Other crash site components gathered - not necessarily to be incorporated: Mk.II BV739 (crashed 29-9-43); Mk.II DR306 (crashed 15-12-45); Mk.III MD953 (crashed 20-9-45); Mk.II PM870 (crashed 14-7-45).

Cobham Hall: Named after FAAM Trustee Sir Michael Cobham, the building is home of the reserve collection and archive.

Pup replica 'N6452', Wyvern VR137 and Sea Harrier XZ499 joined the revamped 'Carrier' (above) by mid-2022. Wessex HAS.3 XP142 and HU.5 XT765 moved to the main halls (above) by 4-23. Firefly TT.1 Z2033 returned to Imperial War Museum custodianship, travelling to Duxford, Cambs, 17-8-23. Lynx HMA.8 XZ725 moved to Gosport, Hampshire, by 4-22.

◆ *Occasional open days, otherwise* **only** *by prior appointment. Contact details as given above*

❑ 'G-ABUL'		DH Tiger Moth	XL717 G-AOXG	40	ex G-AOXG, Mk.II T7291, 24 EFTS, 19 EFTS. Morris-built. De-reg 31-10-56. Acquired 1972		1-22
❑ G-AZAZ		Bensen B-8M		71	ex Wroughton, Houndstone, VL, Manadon. De-reg 19-9-75. Acquired 2-12-99		3-20
❑ G-BGWZ		Eclipse Super Eagle h-g		79	ex Wroughton, Houndstone, VL. De-reg 5-12-83		1-18
❑ 'B6401'		Sopwith Camel replica	G-AWYY	69	ex 'C1701', N1917H, G-AWYY. CoA 1-9-85, de-reg 25-11-91. Acquired 1985	[1]	1-22
❑ 'N4389'	'4M'	Fairey Albacore	N4172	41	ex museum, Land's End, VL, Wroughton, 828. Crashed 1-4-41. Acquired 1983		2-22
❑ 'N5459'		Sopwith Triplane replica		76	BAPC.111, ex 'N5492', Chertsey. *Black Maria*. Acquired 25-3-87. 10 (Naval) Sqn, 'B' Flight colours		1-22
❑ 'N5579'		Gloster Sea Gladiator II		39	ex workshop, 'N5579', Dursley, Cardington, Norway. Acquired 17-7-02. Frame. Arrived 28-6-17		3-22
❑ 'S1287'		Fairey Flycatcher replica	G-BEYB	79	ex Andover, M Wallop, Duxford, M Wallop, VL, G-BEYB de-reg 12-7-96. Acquired 5-6-96. 405 Flt colours	[2]	1-22
❑ VH127	'200'	Fairey Firefly TT.4		47	ex Wroughton, VL, Culdrose, FRU, 700, 737, 812. Acquired 29-11-72		3-22
❑ VV106		V-S 517		48	ex Wroughton, Lee-on-Solent, Cosford, St Athan, Colerne, Cardington, Halton 7175M (17-1-55), RAE. Acquired 2-90, arrived 24-11-99.	[3] [4]	1-22
❑ VX272		Hawker P.1052		48	ex Wroughton, Lee-on-Solent, Cosford, St Athan, Colerne, Cardington, Halton 7174M (14-1-55), RAE. Acquired 2-90, arrived 24-11-99.	[3]	1-22
❑ WM292	'841'	Gloster Meteor TT.20		53	ex Bruntingthorpe, Cardiff, Yeovilton, FRU, Kemble, NF.11 527. AWA-built. Acquired 4-6-69		1-22
❑ WP313	'568'	Percival Sea Prince T.1		53	ex Wroughton, Kemble, 750, Sydenham SF, 750, Lossiemouth SF, 750. Acquired 1-87		1-22
❑ WS103	'709'	Gloster Meteor T.7		52	ex Wroughton, Crawley, Wroughton, Lee-on-S', FRU, Kemble, VL Standards Sqn, Anthorn. SOC 19-1-71. Acquired 8-1-71		1-22
❑ WT121	'415'	Douglas Skyraider AEW.1		51	ex Culdrose, 849, USN VC-12, VC-11 124121. SOC 22-9-60. Acquired 1962	[5]	1-20
❑ WV106	'427'	Douglas Skyraider AEW.1		50	ex Culdrose, Helston, Culdrose, 849, Donibristle, Abbotsinch, US Navy VC-12 124086. SOC 23-9-60. Acquired 1964. 849 Sqn colours. External store		1-20

	Serial	Code	Type	Year	History	Note	Date
❑	WW138	'227'	DH Sea Venom FAW.22	55	ex Carrier, Cobham, AWS, 831, 809. Christchurch-built. Acquired 9-69. Installed 11-7-17. Suez stripes		7-22
❑	XA129		DH Sea Vampire T.22	54	ex Wroughton, VL, CIFE, 736. Christchurch-built. Acquired 14-7-70		1-20
❑	XA466	'777'	Fairey Gannet COD.4	57	ex Carrier, Wroughton, VL, Lee-on-Solent, Lossiemouth, 849. Acquired 12-12-78		7-22
❑	XA864		Westland Whirlwind HAR.1	53	ex Wroughton, VL, RAE, A&AEE, RAE, G-17-1. Acquired 10-3-70		1-20
❑	XB480	'537'	Hiller HT.1	53	ex Wroughton, VL, Manadon, A2577, 705. Acquired 5-10-71		1-20
❑	XD317	'112'	V-S Scimitar F.1	59	ex Carrier, FRU, RAE, 800, 736, 807. Acquired 18-9-69		7-22
❑	XE340	'131'	Hawker Sea Hawk FGA.6	55	ex Montrose, Strathallan, Wroughton, Staverton, Brawdy, 801, 898, 897, 800. Acquired 21-10-70. External store		1-20
❑	XG574	'752'	Westland Whirlwind HAR.3	55	ex museum, Portland, Wroughton, VL, Wroughton, Lee-on-Solent, A2575, 771, 705, 701. Acquired 12-3-75		1-20
❑	XG594	'517'	Westland Whirlwind HAR.3	57	ex East Fortune, Strathallan, Wroughton, Lee-on-Solent, 771, A&AEE, Fleetlands, 705, 846, 737, 701, RAE Bedford, 700. Acquired 23-5-70		1-20
❑	XJ481		DH Sea Vixen FAW.1	58	ex Fleetlands, Southampton, Ilkeston, VL, Portland, VL, Boscombe D', LRWE. Christchurch-built. Acquired 7-3-74		1-20
❑	XK488		Blackburn NA.39	58	ex Filton, BSE, DHE, Blackburn, RAE, DHE, Blackburn. Acquired 22-7-67	[6]	1-22
❑	XL503	'070'	Fairey Gannet AEW.3	61	ex RRE, 849, A&AEE, RAE, 849, A&AEE. Acquired 26-4-73. 849 Sqn 'D' Flt colours		1-22
❑	XL580	'723'	Hawker Hunter T.8M	66	ex museum, FRADU, FOFT, 764. Acquired 26-11-94. Moved 13-6-17. 899 Sqn colours		1-22
❑	XL853		Westland Whirlwind HAS.7	58	ex Portland, Fleetlands, Southampton, M Wallop, Lee-on-Solent, A2630, Wroughton, VL SF, 824. Acquired 7-12-98		1-22
❑	XN332		Saro P.531 G-APNV	58	ex Portland, Wroughton, VL, Wroughton, VL, Manadon A2579 (6-5-63), 771, RAE, 700, RAE, 700, A&AEE, G-APNV (de-reg 1-10-59). Acquired 7-10-71		1-22
❑	XN334		Saro P.531	58	ex Wroughton, Crawley, Weston-super-Mare, VL, Arbroath, A2525 (13-9-62), RAE, 771, 700, RAE, 700. Ditched 4-3-62. Acquired 22-7-83		1-22
❑	XN462	'17'	Hunting Jet Provost T.3A	60	ex Wroughton, Sharnford, Shawbury, 1 FTS, 2 FTS, CFS, 3 FTS, 7 FTS, 1 FTS. Acquired 25-3-98	[7]	1-22
❑	XS527		Westland Wasp HAS.1	63	ex Wroughton, 829, 703, A&AEE. Acquired 31-7-86. *Endurance* colours	[8]	1-22
❑	XS574		Northrop Shelduck D.1	~	dismantled		1-18
❑	XT176	'U'	Bell Sioux AH.1	65	ex Wroughton, 3 CBAS. Acquired 6-6-94		1-22
❑	XT427	'606'	Westland Wasp HAS.1	65	ex Helston, VL, Wroughton, Lee-on-Solent, 829, 703, 829. Acquired 28-3-84		1-22
❑	XT778	'430'	Westland Wasp HAS.1	66	ex A2642, A2722 (23-3-88), ex Portland, West Moors, Lee-on-Solent, 829, VL, Wroughton, Lee-on-S', A&AEE. Acquired 15-2-99. *Achilles* Flt colours		1-22
❑	XV333	'234'	Blackburn Buccaneer S.2B	66	ex Carrier, 208, 12, 15, 16, FAA, 237 OCU, 12. Arrived 23-3-94. 801 Sqn colours		7-22
❑	XW864	'54'	Sud Gazelle HT.2	73	ex Shawbury, 705, Wroughton. Westland-built. Acquired 21-10-02		1-22
❑	XW994		Northrop Chukar D.1	71	ex Wroughton, VL, Wroughton		7-18
❑	XZ228*	'313'	Westland Lynx HAS.3GMS	76	ex Middle Wallop, Culdrose, VL, 815, 702, HAS.2, 815, A&AEE. SOC 22-6-12		2-23
❑	XZ574		Westland Sea King HAS.6	76	ex Gosport, 771, 810, 820, 819, 810, 820, 826. Acquired 9-6-08, arrived 8-7-15	[9]	1-22
❑	XZ617*		Westland Lynx AH.7	80	ex Lyneham, Middle Wallop. SOC 11-4-15. F/n 2-23		2-23
❑	XZ691	'310'	Westland Lynx HMA.8SRU	79	ex Fleetlands, 702, HAS.3, 815, 702, 815, HAS.2, Falklands, 815, 702. SOC 3-10-18. Arrived 3-4-19		1-22
❑	ZB604	'722'	HS Harrier T.8	83	ex Wittering, Shawbury, VL, 899, T.4, 899. Arrived 29-6-11. 899 Sqn colours		1-22
❑	–		Fairey IIIF	~	fuselage frame		1-18

❑ AE-331		Agusta 109A	ZE411	80	ex 7 Rgt, M Wallop, VL, M Wallop, 846, Arg Army CAB.601, AE-331. Acquired 10-10. Argentine colours		1-22
❑ AE-422		Bell UH-1H Iroquois		74	ex Wroughton, VL, Stanley, Arg Army, 74-22520. Acq 6-6-89		1-22
❑ 0729	'411'	Beech T-34C-1 Turbo-Mentor		78	ex Wroughton, VL, Stanley, Pebble Island, Arg Navy Acquired 7-7-83		1-22
❑ '102/17'		Fokker Dr.I replica		68	BAPC.88. Acquired 1975	[10]	6-19
❑ 15-1585		Yokosuka Ohka 11		c45	BAPC.58, ex Hayes, South Kensington. Acquired 1977	[11]	6-19

■ **[1]** Camel built by Slingsby. **[2]** Flycatcher built by Westward Airways (aka Viv and Rod Bellamy). **[3]** Supermarine 517 and P.1052 are on loan from the RAF Museum. **[4]** On 14-12-52 Supermarine *510* VV106 suffered a wheels-up landing at Farnborough. It was returned to Supermarine on 10-7-53 for repair and to have a hinged rear fuselage fitted. This substantial modification was given the design number 517. **[5]** For reasons best known to someone, Skyraider WT983 was painted correctly as 'WT' but given the 'last-three' of its US Navy serial number and this stuck throughout its career. **[6]** Third prototype Buccaneer - also designated NR/A.39 - with non-folding wings; first flown 10-31-58. **[7]** Jet Provost was donated by a former RN pilot who earned his wings on this very aircraft while with 1 FTS – where Navy pilots received their training. **[8]** XS527 also let rip at the *Santa Fe*, with SS.12 missiles. **[9]** XZ574 factoids: entered service 6-10-76; detached to HMS *Invincible* for Operation 'Corporate' 4-82 to 9-82 and flown by - among others - HRH Prince Andrew; total time upon retirement 9,168 hours. **[10]** Triplane based on a Lawrence Parasol, making it a five-eighths scale replica. **[11]** Ohka on loan from the Science Museum.

Navy Wings Heritage Flight / Navy Wings Associate Collection: The latter comprises private owner aircraft working to help and support the aims of the Trust. These include some based with Navy Wings and others such as Historic Helicopters at Higher Purtington, Somerset, and Kennet Aviation at Old Warden, Beds.

Having made the wise decision not to return Sea Vixen XP924 to airworthiness, *Foxy Lady* was offered for disposal and Bournemouth Aviation Museum was successful. As *W&R* closed for press, the move to Bournemouth, Dorset, was imminent and the opportunity has been taken to pre-empt this. Provost T.1 XF690 (G-MOOS) was moved to Shuttleworth (aka Old Warden), Beds, by December 2022. Looked after by the Flight, Phantom FG.1 XV586 departed by road and arrived at Kinloss, Scotland, 21st February 2023. ◆ *Frequently attend airshows, otherwise by prior arrangement* **only | 01935 842005 | office@navywings.org.uk | www.navywings.org.uk**

❑ G-NWHF		NAA T-6J Texan ✈		52	ex G-BSBG, Moz AF 1753, Port AF 1753, WGAF BF+053, AA+053, USAF 52-8562. CCF-built. Acquired 22-3-21. Yellow scheme and 'Navy Wings' titles by 4-22	[1]	12-23
❑ N9328	'69'	DH Tiger Moth ✈	G-ALWS	39	ex Henstridge, Welshpool, Bromsgrove, Rothesay, Strathallan, Perth, N9328, Upwood SF, 6 FTS, 15 EFTS, 17 EFTS 15 EFTS, 19 EFTS, Duxford SF, Farnborough SF	[2]	12-23
❑ W5856	'4A'	Fairey Swordfish I ✈	G-BMGC	41	ex Brough, Strathallan G-BMGC, Alabama, RCN, Wroughton. Blackburn-built. 820 Sqn c/s, *City of Leeds*	[1] [3]	12-23
❑ LS326	'L2'	Fairey Swordfish II	G-AJVH	43	ex Westland, White Waltham, G-AJVH, Worthy Down, 836, Blackburn-built. 836 Sqn c/s, *City of Liverpool*	[1]	12-23
❑ NF389		Fairey Swordfish III		44	ex Brough, VL, Brough, Lee-on-Solent, 781, ATDU, 4 Ferry Flt. Blackburn-built. Spares		12-23
❑ SX336	'105'	V-S Seafire F.17 ✈	G-KASX	46	ex Old Warden, N Weald, Nottingham, G-BRMG, Cranfield, Twyford, Newark, Warrington, Stretton A2055, Bramcote, 728. Westland-built. Arrived 15-21-21. 766 Sqn colours	[1]	12-23
❑ VR930	'110'	Hawker Sea Fury FB.11	G-CLNJ	48	ex Brough, VL, Boscombe Down, Lee-on-S', Wroughton, VL, 8382M, Colerne, Dunsfold, FRU, Lossiemouth, Anthorn, 801, Anthorn, 802. 802 Sqn colours. Stored	[1] [4]	12-23
❑ WB657		DHC Chipmunk T.10	G-CNVH	49	ex BRNC, Leeds UAS, 16 RFS, 25 RFS, Leeds UAS, 25 RFS. SOC 1-4-19. Hawarden-built	[1]	12-23
❑ WK608	'906'	DHC Chipmunk T.10 ✈	G-CLNI	50	ex BRNC, Bristol UAS, 7 FTS, 3 FTS, Edinburgh UAS, 11 RFS. Hawarden-built	[1]	12-23
❑ WV908*	'188'	Hawker Sea Hawk FGA.6	G-CMFB	55	ex Shawbury, VL, Dunsfold, VL, Dunsfold, VL, Culdrose SF, Halton 8154M, Sydenham A2660, 738, 806, 898, 807. AW-built. Last flown 2010, 806 Sqn c/s. Arrived 27-5-22		12-23
❑ XT420	'422'	Westland Wasp HAS.1 ✈	G-CBUI	50	ex N Weald, Fleetlands, Wroughton, 829, Falklands, 829, 706, 829. SOC 18-4-94. *Aurora* Flt colours	[1]	12-23
❑ 42-46703		Stinson AT-19 Reliant ✈	N69745	43	ex USN 11442, FAA FK877, 703, 740. Arrived 19-12-20	[5]	12-23

■ **[1]** Registered to Fly Navy Heritage Trust / Flight. **[2]** Tiger registered to Jim Norris. **[3]** W5856 in the colours of Lt Hugh de Graaf Hunter, awarded a DSC for the attack on the *Bismarck*, launched from the *Ark Royal*, 5-41. **[4]** After several traumas with Bristol Centaurus-engined 'Furies, *November-Juliet* will feature a P&W R2800 Double Wasp. **[5]** Owned by Paul Kehoe.

Sea Hawk FGA.6 WV911 and Harrier GR.3 XW630, rescue training airframes, December 2022. *Hugh Trevor*

Others: A variety of airframes are used for technical instruction, rescue training, display purposes or are stored.

	Serial	Code	Type	Reg	Year	History	Note	Date
❑	WV911	'115'	Hawker Sea Hawk FGA.6		55	ex RNHF store, Dunsfold, Lee-on-Solent A2622, A2626, Fleetlands, Lee-on-Solent A2526 (31-10-62), 700, 804. AW-built. Rescue training by 7-19		8-23
❑	XS513		Westland Wessex HU.5		64	ex A2681, Gosport, A2770 (14-3-87), Lee-on-S', 772, 845, 772, 845, 707, 846, 845, 846, 845, 707, 846, 848, 845, 848		8-23
❑	XT458	'P'	Westland Wessex HU.5		65	ex Gosport, A2679, A2768 (15-3-88), Lee-on-Solent, 772, 845, 772, 845, 846, 845, 707, A&AEE, 781. 845 Sqn c/s. Displayed outside Command HQ from 14-8-12		10-23
❑	XW630		HS Harrier GR.3		71	ex A2671, Gosport, A2759 (15-5-91) Lee-on-Solent, 3, 4, 3, 20. FAA colours. Rescue trainer		8-23
❑	XW784		M-P Kittiwake I	G-BBRN	71	ex G-BBRN, CoA 15-3-08		6-22
❑	XW890		Sud Gazelle HT.2		74	ex Fleetlands, Wroughton, 705. SOC 17-3-95. Displayed outside Gazelle House, since 1995	[1]	9-22
❑	XZ230		Westland Lynx HAS.3GMS		76	ex Fleetlands, Hixon, 815, 829, HAS.2, 815, 702. SOC 17-5-04. Wildcat avionics trainer, 'WAvT' lettering	[2]	4-21
❑	XZ257		Westland Lynx HAS.3		79	ex Hixon, VL, M Wallop, 815, 702, 815, 702, HAS.2, 815, 702. SOC 13-7-09. Wildcat training aid, 'AST' lettering	[3]	9-21
❑	XZ670	'A'	Westland Lynx AH.7		81	ex M Wallop, Fleetlands, 847, 4 Regt, 847, AAC, 847, 3 Regt. Arrived 20-10-16. At Senior Rates Mess	[4]	8-23
❑	XZ674	'T'	Westland Lynx AH.7		81	ex M Wallop. SOC 3-3-14. Rescue training		12-22
❑	–		Westland Lynx AH.7		~	paint bay, first noted 2019		4-21
❑	XZ719		Westland Lynx HMA.8		80	ex Fleetlands, 815, HAS.3, 702, 815, 702, HAS.2. SOC 3-11-14. Arrived 27-2-15. Rescue training		8-23
❑	XZ728	'326'	Westland Lynx HMA.8DSP		80	ex A2852, Fleetlands, 815, HAS.3, 702, 815, HAS.2, 815. Accident 25-2-97. SOC 20-9-04. Displayed, since 3-7-07		8-23
❑	XZ736		Westland Lynx HMA.8SRU		81	ex M Wallop, 815, 702, HAS.3, 815, HAS.2, Falklands -82. Stored	[5]	4-21
❑	ZD578	'122' *and* '000'	HS Sea Harrier F/A.2		85	ex St Athan, 801, 899, 801, 899, 801, FRS.1, 800, 801, 899, 801, 800, A&AEE, 800, 899. SOC 20-5-02. Displayed from 4-12-02. 800 Sqn colours (port), 801 (stb)		8-23
❑	ZF118*	'O'	Westland Sea King HC.4		86	ex Gosport, Torpoint, Gosport, 845, 846, 845, 846, 845, 846, 772, 846, 707, 846, 845. Arrived 26-1-24		1-24
❑	'ZH800'	'123'	HS S' Harrier F/A.2	ZH801	96	ex Cottesmore, VL, 800, 899, 801, 899	[6]	12-22
❑	'ZH801'	'001'	HS S' Harrier F/A.2	ZH800	96	ex Cottesmore, Greenwich, VL, 899, 801, 800	[6]	12-22
❑	ZZ400		Westland Wildcat AH.1		10	ex Lyneham, Yeovil. Handed over 10-10-16	[7]	8-21
❑	ZZ401*		Westland Wildcat AH.1		10	ex Staverton, Yeovil. Weapons loading tnr, f/n10-22	[7]	1-23
❑	–		Westland Lynx CIM		77	purpose-built at Almondbank		6-12
❑	773		Westland Sea King Mk.47	G-BDMH	75	ex Gosport, Egyptian Air Force, G-BDMH, G-17-17. Rescue trainer, on side		12-22

■ **[1]** XW890 has the boom of AH.1 ZB668 and is Westland-built. **[2]** XZ230 scored multiple ASM strikes, Iraq 1/2-91. **[3]** Training airframe, created from a Lynx HAS.3 by Pennant International. **[4]** While serving with the Royal Marines, 847 Sqn XZ670 hit an Iraqi T55 tank and then destroyed another two on 24-3-03. **[5]** Converted into a mobile bar for the Lynx decommissioning ceremonies, 2017. **[6]** Serials were transposed during repainting at Cottesmore: ZH801 was ready before the other but numerical sequence was employed! **[7]** With Leonardo-run Wildcat Training Centre.

STAFFORDSHIRE

Includes the unitary authority of Stoke-on-Trent

ALREWAS on the A513 east of the town, midway between Lichfield and Burton

National Memorial Arboretum: The scope of the commemorations and landscaping within the 150-acre site is breath-taking. Memorials of an aeronautical nature include: Berlin Airlift, Coastal Command, Operation 'Market-Garden' etc.
◆ *Croxall Road, DE13 7AR* | **01283 245100** | **info@thenma.org.uk** | **www.thenma.org.uk**

BASSETT'S POLE at the junction of the A38 and A453, northeast of Sutton Coldfield

NPF Bassett's Pole: Multi-leisure pursuit site. ◆ *Prior arrangement* **only** | **www.npfbassettspole.com**

❑ XP350 Westland Whirlwind HAR.10 62 ex Bruntingthorpe, Helston, Chivenor, 22, 225. SOC 3-3-82. With boom of XK969 8-22

BIDDULPH on the A527 south of Congleton

A Jaguar cockpit is kept at a *private* location in the *general* area.

❑ XZ385 SEPECAT Jaguar GR.3A 77 ex Selby, Ipswich, St Athan, 41, 16, GR.1, 16, 6, 16, 54, 6, Gib Det, 41, 17, 14. Cockpit. First noted 9-20 9-20

BUCKNALL on the A52 east of Stoke-on-Trent

Kingsland C of E Academy: Eaves Lane ◆ *Prior arrangement* **only**

❑ G-SSWE Short 360-100 86 ex Market Drayton, Coventry, SE-IXE, G-BNBA, G-14-3705. CoA 22-8-05, de-reg 6-6-07. *The King's Wings* 12-22

BURSLEM on the A50 northwest of Stoke-on-Trent

Supermarine Aero Engineering: Spitfire components and structures specialists at the appropriately-named Mitchell Works.
◆ *Prior arrangement* **only** | **https://supermarine.net**

❑ SL611 V-S Spitfire XVI G-SAEA 45 ex Scafell, 603, 111 OTU. CBAF-built. Crashed 20-11-47 N3-23
❑ RW389 'E' V-S Spitfire XVI G-SAEB 45 ex 5 CAACU, 20. CBAF-built. SOC 13-6-56 N4-23

CANNOCK

XH174 is *believed* held at a *private* location in the *general* area.

❑ XH174 EE Canberra PR.9 60 ex South Molton, Welshpool, Staffordshire, Basingstoke, Shawbury, St Athan, 1 PRU, 39, 13, 39, MoS, 39, 58. Cockpit. Arrived 7-10-12 10-12

FROGHALL on the A52 east of Stoke-on-Trent

Agility Defense and Government Services UK Ltd: (Yes, that's defense with an 's'.) Offers vast amounts of former military hardware via tender or auction. Airframes come and go at the warehouse complex here, but these tend to be only fleeting. There is also a storage depot at Leyburn, N Yorks - qv. ◆ **Strictly** *prior arrangement* **only** | **https://agilitystoke.com**

❑ XX169* HS Hawk T.1W 77 ex Shawbury, 19, 92, FRADU, 19, 74, 6 FTS, 234, 4 FTS. NEA 12-19. Arrived 26-5-23 5-23

LICHFIELD northwest of Tamworth

Defence Medical Services: Whittington Barracks.

❑ ZE449 Sud Puma HC.1 c75 ex Shawbury, Boscombe Down, 230, Weston-super-Mare, 9017M, Port Stanley, Argentine Prefectura Naval PA-12. Crashed 9-7-09. Arrived 8-4-14 1-22

LONGTON on the A50 south of Stoke-on-Trent

Motor Clinic: Trentham Road, has a 'JP' on show and is known as 'The Place with the Plane' | **www.motorclinicltd .co.uk**

❑ XM425 '88' Hunting Jet Provost T.3A 60 ex King's Lynn, Bruntingthorpe, Halton 8995M (10-4-89), 7 FTS, 1 FTS, RAFC, 3 FTS, CFS 12-23

STAFFORD

Royal Air Force Museum Reserve Collection: 'Lodges' with the Defence Electronics and Components Agency, on a sub-site to the north of the huge Stafford storage complex - see below. The storage facility is due to relocate; date undisclosed.

As well as the airframes there are countless smaller artefacts. The following provide a taste of what is held: the pilot's seat and immediate surroundings of HP Halifax II R9371 of 10 Squadron, crashed 9th March 1942 and restored by the Cotswold Aircraft Restoration Group; tail section of a HP V/1500 (and parts from an O/400); a float from a Fairey Seafox. Sections of Short Stirling III LK488 of 1651 CU, crashed 19th October 1944 and recovered from Mickle Fell, Yorks, 31st August 1977 had moved to Hendon, Gtr Lon, and Cosford, Shropshire, by March 2023 for display.

Museum airframes offered in 2022 for **transfer by gift** are marked:●: those offered for **outward loan** are marked ❖.

Departures: DH Moth G-AAMX was restored to the register 23-2-23 to the family of the original donor, with a Haywards Heath, W Sussex, address. Mew Gull replica 'G-AEXF' returned to Hendon, Gtr Lon, by late 2023. Dragon Rapide G-AHED to Doncaster, S Yorks, 14-12-22, as transfer by gift. Wallace II K6035 to Hendon, Gtr Lon, 19-9-23. Afghan Hind BAPC.82 to Cosford, Shropshire, by 9-23. BAE Systems HERTI-1 to Elvington, N Yorks, by 10-23. Venom FB.6 J-1172 to Kinloss, Scotland, 20-12-23. ◆ *Viewing possible* **only** *via prior arrangement – occasional,* ***strictly*** *pre-booked, open days.*

❑ G-AEKW	Miles Mohawk	36	ex Hendon, Cosford, Hatch, Cosford, Hatch, Wyton, USA, Spain, HM503, MCCS, Turnhouse SF, G-AEKW. P&P-built		2-22
❑ 'F8614'	Vickers Vimy replica G-AWAU	69	ex Hendon, 'H651', Wisley, Brooklands, G-AWAU. Damaged by fire 14-6-69, de-reg 19-7-73. Acquired 12-70 *Triple First*	[1]	2-22
❑ A301	Morane BB	16	ex Wyton, Cardington, Hendon. Fuselage	●	1-22
❑ P3175	Hawker Hurricane I	40	ex Hendon, 257. Shot down 31-8-40. Acquired 1978. Forward fuselage, wreck		1-22
❑ Z7197	Percival Proctor III G-AKZN	40	ex Hendon 8380M, St Athan, Swinderby, Finningley, G-AKZN, (CoA 29-11-63), AST, 18 EFTS, 1 RS, 2 SS. Hills-built		2-22
❑ HS503	Fairey Swordfish IV	43	BAPC.108, ex Cosford, Wyton, Cardington, Cosford, Henlow, Canada, RCAF (SOC 21-8-46), 754, 745. Blackburn-built. Acquired 10-70		2-22
❑ LA226	V-S Spitfire F.21	45	ex Cosford, Wyton, Cardington, St Athan, Shawbury, Abingdon, Biggin Hill, South Marston, London, South Marston, Little Rissington, Albrighton, 7119M (18-1-54), 3 CAACU, 122, 91. Arrived by 9-02		2-22
❑ SL674	V-S Spitfire XVI	45	ex Cosford, Wyton, Cardington, St Athan, 8392M, Biggin Hill, Little Rissington, 612, 501, 17 OTU. CBAF-built	❖	2-22
❑ VS618	Percival Prentice T.1 G-AOLK	49	ex Hendon, G-AOLK, Southend, Southend, VS618, 9 MU, 22 FTS. CoA 17-9-10, de-reg 9-2-10. Acquired 9-10-09		2-22
❑ VX275	Slingsby Sedbergh TX.1	48	ex Cosford, Wyton, Cardington, St Athan 8884M, 612 GS, 613 GS, 623 GS, 123 GS, BGA.572	●	2-22
❑ XK781	ML Utility Mk.1	57	ex Cardington, M Wallop. Nacelle and other bits		8-13
❑ ZJ493	GAF Jindivik Mk.104AL	c98	ex Llanbedr, QinetiQ/DERA, ATA, RAAF A92-814. *End of an Era*. Last UK Jindivik flight, 26-10-04		1-22
❑ –	Cody Man-Lifting Kite rep	~	BAPC.428. ex Manchester	❖	1-22
❑ –	Balloon Factory Airship replica	~	BAPC.296, ex Hendon. *Nulli Secundus I*. Gondola First noted 10-17	[2]	2-22
❑ No.164	Blériot XI	c1910	BAPC.106, ex Hendon, Cosford 9209M, Cardington, Hendon, Colerne, Hendon, Heathrow, RAeS, Hendon, Nash, Brooklands. Acquired 1964, first noted 10-17		1-22
❑ –	Blériot XI	c1910	fuselage frame	[3]	9-18
❑ –	Curtiss JN-4 'Jenny'	c1922	fuselage frame		1-22
❑ –	Fairchild Cornell II	c42	ex Cosford, Wyton, Cardington, Henlow, Canada. Fleet-built	● [4]	1-22
❑ –	Eurofighter Typhoon FSM	03	BAPC.292, ex Hendon, BAE Systems		10-13
❑ A2-4	Supermarine Seagull V	35	ex Hendon, Cardington, Wyton, VH-ALB, RAAF A2-4. Acquired 5-72. First noted 10-17		2-22
❑ E.3B-521 '781-3'	Bücker Jungmann	56	ex Hendon, Spanish AF. CASA-built. Acquired 23-1-97		2-22
❑ –	Fieseler Fi 103 (V-1)	c44	BAPC.237, ex Soesterberg. Arrived 11-13		2-22

■ **[1]** Vimy built by the Vintage Aircraft and Flying Association, first flying 3-6-69 at Brooklands. Badly damaged by fire at Manchester Airport 14-6-69; it was rebuilt and handed over to the RAFM in June 1972. The name *Triple First* denotes the first Atlantic, Australia and South Africa flights undertaken by Vimys. **[2]** Replica of 1907 airship, built by the Army Balloon Factory, under the supervision of Samuel Franklin Cody. **[3]** Believed part of the Nash Collection cache. Fuselage frame appears to have been lengthened - two-seater? Set of wings also to hand, and short span, leading to the notion that this *may* have been a 'Penguin', a taxi-only 'trainer'. **[4]** PT-26A Cornell II has parts from at least three machines. Port wing is RCAF 15195, starboard from 14590. Fuselage had a plate stamped 'FAL Ser No FV351, BAC Ser No FV351, Eng No R007174'. The RAF serial FV351 corresponds to RCAF 15252. These and several other Cornell 'elements' were acquired from/via Canadian Warplane Heritage as part of an exchange.

MoD Stafford: West of the city and Littleworth. Elements of the sprawling site is being marketed as the **'Aerospace Technology Centre'**. 'Lodger' organisations include the **Tactical Supply Wing** (part of Joint Helicopter Command); the **Defence Electronics Components Agency**; and **Beacon Barracks**, controlling several Army units. Within, the **Staffordshire Wing, Air Cadets** should still have a Phantom cockpit.

❑ XT672	'WE'	Westland Wessex HC.2	66	ex Shawbury, Hixon, Shawbury, 2 FTS, Benson SF, 72. SOC 12-5-99. Arrived 20-10-10. *Aries*, displayed	[1]	1-19
❑ XV581		McD Phantom FG.1	69	ex Aberdeen, Buchan, 9070M (12-9-91), Wattisham, 43, 111, 43. Cockpit, 43 Sqn colours		9-17
❑ XZ987	'C'	HS Harrier GR.3	81	9185M, ex St Athan, 1417 Flt, 3, 4. 1417 Flt colours. Displayed, since 1993		4-21

■ **[1]** XT672 is on loan from Air and Ground Aviation.

STOKE-ON-TRENT

Potteries Museum and Art Gallery: Within the **Spitfire Gallery** Mk.XVI RW388 is the centre piece of many artefacts honouring Reginald Joseph Mitchell – Stoke being his birthplace. The Spitfire is not just a tribute to its designer, but to the craftsmen of the Medway Aircraft Preservation Society. Alongside RW388 is Violet's Cafe which is well worth sampling and honours Canadian-born Violet Milstead who flew Spitfires and other types with the Air Transport Auxiliary. She *may well* have been the pilot that delivered RW388 from the Castle Bromwich factory to Brize Norton on 18th July 1945.

A full-size stainless-steel plinth-mounted Spitfire *sculpture*, built by apprentices of the Newcastle-under-Lyme metal fabrications specialists the KMF Group, was unveiled on 11th January 2023.

◆ *Bethesda Street, Hanley, ST1 3DW* | **01782 232323** | **email** via website | **www.stokemuseums.org.uk**

❑ RW388 'U4-U'	V-S Spitfire XVI	45	ex Rochester, Stoke-on-Trent (acquired 15-2-72), Kemble, 'AB917', 71 MU 6946M (30-9-52), 19 MU, 5 MU, Andover, Benson, Colerne, FCC&RS, 612, 667. CBAF-built. Arrived 6-21. 667 Sqn colours		1-24

STONE on the A34 north of Stafford

Alan Simpson: Still cherishes his Sea Venom.

❑ XG629	'668'	DH Sea Venom FAW.22	56	ex Long Marston, Fleetlands, Higher Blagdon, Culdrose, ADS, 831, Yeovilton SF, 893, FAW.21, 893. Hawarden-built. SOC 3-9-70	3-20

TATENHILL AERODROME south of the B5234, west of Burton-on-Trent

EGBM

❑ G-RHHT	Piper Lance 300	78	ex N36476. De-reg 13-3-12, CoA 2-6-12, crashed 3-6-11. Rescue trainer, poor state		1-17
❑ XX900	Blackburn Buccaneer S.2B	76	ex Bruntingthorpe, St Athan, 208, 12, 208, 216, 12, 208. Arrived 6-11-20. Desert camo (a la Red Flag) by 11-23	[1]	11-23

■ **[1]** Owned by David Walton – see Bruntingthorpe, Leics.

WOLVERHAMPTON AERODROME or Halfpenny Green, east of Bridgnorth

EGBO

The 'JP' 'guards' the flying centre. Jetstream 31 G-PLAJ was removed on 16th April 2022 – no 'forwarding address'. Seneca 200 G-BSDN had been reduced to a set of wings by August 2021 and those had gone by December 2022. Bölkow Bö 105 G-XBLD and Yak-55 RA-01274 have been deleted.

❑ G-ATTK*	'	Piper Cherokee 140	66	de-reg 31-5-23. First noted 6-22	1-24
❑ XW434	'MY'	BAC Jet Provost T.5A	72	ex Selby, Cosford 9091M (1-3-91), Halton, 1 FTS, 7 FTS, 3 FTS, CFS. Arrived 29-5-13, displayed	10-23

SUFFOLK

BAWDSEY at the end of the B1083, on a minor road south of Bawdsey village

Bawdsey Radar: Billed as the world's first operational radar site, the transmitter block at the Manor is the centre of a fascinating museum. ◆ *Bawdsey, IP12 3BA* | **07821 162879** | **info@bawdseyradar.org.uk** | **www.bawdseyradar.org.uk**

BECCLES AERODROME south of the A146 west of Lowestoft — EGSM

Last noted in November 2020, Cessna 150s G-ATMM and G-AVZU have been deleted. The following have been removed under the new exclusion criteria – see *Before You Start...* Apache G-ASMY, Cessna 150s G-ATHZ, G-AWTX, G-BEIG.

	Reg	Type	Year	Details	Last noted
❑	G-AVPH	Cessna F.150G	67	ex Blackpool, Woodvale. Reims-built. CoA 9-4-86, de-reg 26-3-02. Fuselage	6-23
❑	G-BAOP	Cessna FRA.150L	73	Reims-built. Crashed 22-6-01, CoA 11-4-02, de-reg 1-5-14	6-23
❑	G-BWSC	Piper Tomahawk 112	81	ex N23203. De-reg 3-9-14	6-23

BECK ROW on the A1101 north of Mildenhall

Cross Country RV: A Hunter guards the premises on the Mildenhall Industrial Estate.

	Reg	Type	Year	Details	Last noted
❑	XG210	Hawker Hunter F.6	56	ex DRA Bedford, Hatfield, CFE, 19, 14. SOC 11-9-85. RAE c/s	10-23

■ **[1]** XG210 has the starboard wing of XL572 (most of it is at Elvington, N Yorks) and XL623 (Dunsfold, Surrey) to port.

BELSTEAD south of the A14 south of Ipswich

Lynx AH.7 XZ613 left early in 2022, first to Colsterworth, Lincs, before settling on Billericay, Essex, by June 2022.

BENTWATERS AIRFIELD south of the A1152, northeast of Woodbridge

Bentwaters Cold War Museum: Run by the **Bentwaters Aviation Society**. Centred on the Wing Command Post this incredible museum includes the 'Battle Cabin' and the War Operations rooms. Jaguar GR.1A XX741 got the pulses racing on 15th March 2020 with its first taxi run – magnificent!

Some airframes are being worked on in a HAS on the airfield and are *not* available for public inspection.

◆ *Off the A1152 | Building 134, Bentwaters Park, IP12 2TW* | **07588 877020** | **info@bcwm.org.uk** | **www.bcwm.org.uk**

	Reg	Code	Type	Year	Details	Note	Last noted
❑	WH453		Gloster Meteor D.16	51	ex Llanbedr, Tarrant Rushton, West Freugh, F.8, 5 CAACU, 72, 222. SOC 10-10-90. Arrived 18-1-05	[1]	1-24
❑	XE707	'865'	Hawker Hunter GA.11 G-BVYH	55	ex Ashbourne, N707XE, USA, Exeter, G-BVYH, FRADU, 764, 738, RAF F.4, 118, 98, 93. Squires Gate-built. Last flown 21-4-94. Arrived 1-7-10	[2]	1-24
❑	XV401	'I'	McD Phantom FGR.2	68	ex Boscombe Down, BDAC, DERA, Wattisham, 74, 228 OCU, 19, 56, 23, 56, 29, 228 OCU, 56, 111, 41, 228 OCU. Arrived 8-13	[3]	1-24
❑	XX741	'EJ'	SEPECAT Jaguar GR.1A	74	ex Ipswich, Shawbury. 226 OCU, 6, 54, 226 OCU. Acquired 16-8-09. 6 Sqn c/s. First fast taxi 15-3-20	[4]	1-24
❑	ZD667		HS Harrier GR.3	86	ex Predannack, Culdrose 'DD67', A2684[2], 9201M, 1417 Flt, 233 OCU, 4. Arrived 2-13. 4 Sqn colours	[3]	1-24
❑	ZF581		EE Lightning F.53	67	ex Rochester, Portsmouth, *Wing Commander* (1999), Portsmouth, Warton, Saudi AF 206, 53-675, G-27-45. Last flown 14-1-86, arrived 22-5-11. 56 Sqn colours		1-24
❑	'6771'		Republic F-84F-51-RE Thunderstreak	52	ex Cosford, Rochester, Southend, Belgian AF FU-6, 52-7133. Arrived 25-9-19. Will have 81st FBW colours		1-24
❑	51-9252		Lockheed T-33A-1-LO	51	ex Tangmere, Hailsham, Sculthorpe, French AF. Last flown 25-1-78. Arrived 11-7-18. 81st TFW colours		1-24
❑	80-0219		Fairchild GA-10A Thunderbolt II	81	ex Alconbury, 509th TFS, 10th TFW, 81st TFW. Crashed 4-4-89. 10th TFW/TRW, 509th TFS. Arrived 24-5-16. 511th TFS colours, *Phoenix*	[5]	1-24

■ **[1]** Meteor was donated to BCWM in 2012 and will appear in 72 Sqn colours and F.8 guise. **[2]** GA.11 exported to the USA and flown there in 1995, it returned in 2005. Fitted with rear fuselage of Danish F.51 E-410 1981. **[3]** XV401 and ZD667 acquired from Everett Aero using donation from Brian Smee. **[4]** Jaguar, first flown 4-10-74, taken on charge 18-11-74; last flight 31-1-94; total flying time 4,260 hours; disposed of 18-11-05; joined BCWM 16-8-09 thanks to a donation from Brian Smee. **[5]** 'Warthog' on loan from the National Museum of the USAF since 11-2-18.

BROME on the A140 south of Diss

A 'JP' is kept at a *private* location in the area.

❑ XW304	'MD'	BAC Jet Provost T.5		70	ex Colsterworth, Cosford 9172M (17-12-92), 6 FTS, CFS, 1 FTS		7-23

BURY ST EDMUNDS on the A140 south of Diss

Blenheim Camp: TA Centre in Newmarket Road *should* house a Lynx cab'.

❑ XX392*		Sud Gazelle AH.1		75	ex Middle Wallop, Shawbury, 3 Flt, 670, ARWS, 3 CBAS. Westland-built. Recruiting aid. First noted 6-23		6-23
❑ XZ608		Westland Lynx AH.7		80	ex Middle Wallop. Cabin. First noted 10-17	[1]	8-19
❑ ZG923*		Westland Lynx AH.9A		92	ex Middle Wallop. SOC 3-10-18	[1]	6-23

■ **[1]** The tail boom of XZ608 is fitted to XZ680, see East Grinstead, Surrey.

Locally: A Hunter and a Scout arrived at separate *private* locations in the *general* area. ◆ **Strictly** *by prior arrangement*

❑ WV256*	'D'	Hawker Hunter GA.11	G-BZPB	54	ex St Mawgan, 'WB188', G-BZPB (CoA 17-7-03, de-reg 16-3-11), Baginton, Kemble, Exeter, WV256, Shawbury, Yeovilton, FRADU, 738, 229 OCU, 26. 26 Sqn c/s. Arr 1-8-23		9-23
❑ XT624*		W'land Scout AH.1	G-NOTY	66	ex Ipswich, North Weald, Plymouth. CoA 28-10-10, de-reg 15-11-18. Arrived by 6-21		6-21

DEBACH south of the B1078, west of Wickham Market

493rd Bomb Group 'Helton's Hellcats' Museum: Centred on USAAF Station 152's former control tower, the museum has been painstakingly put together – restoration of the barracks building is a current project. As has the website, which includes a vast amount of material: for example, the locals pronounce it 'Deb-idge', while Americans call it 'Dee-bark'.

◆ *Grove Farm, Clopton, IP13 6QS* | **493bgdebach@gmail.com** | **www.493bgdebach.co.uk**

Locally: A Scout is stored at a *private* venue in the *general* area.

❑ XP907*		W'land Scout AH.1	G-SROE	63	ex Wattisham, Ipswich, Middle Wallop, BSE Filton. CoA 20-3-06. First noted 4-22	[1]	4-22

■ **[1]** Registered to Saunders-Roe Helicopter Ltd – the Scout being a much-developed Saro P.531.

ELMSETT AERODROME on minor roads northeast of Hadleigh

AJD Engineering / Hawker Restorations Ltd: ◆ **Strictly** *by prior arrangement* | **www.hawkerrestorations.co.uk**

❑ –		Hawker Hart	G-CIAJ	37	ex St Leonards-on-Sea, Sweden, R Swedish AF B4A F17 Kallinge. AB Gotaverken-built. Arrived by 7-16, off-site 10-21	[1] [2]	10-21
❑ L2005		Hawker Hurricane I		39	ex Sudbury, 151, 56. Shot down 28-8-40	[3]	7-23
❑ P3966*		Hawker Hurricane I	G-LNWZ	40	ex 85. Shot down 26-8-40, Essex. Remains salvaged 2019	[4]	7-23

■ **[1]** Hart registered to Westh Flyg AB of Sweden - see under Audley End, Essex, for the company's SE.5. **[2]** Substantial wreckage discovered in Sweden in the late 1980s One of 42 licence-built and originally fitted with a Nohab-built Bristol Mercury radial. **[3]** Intended restoration as a two-seater. **[4]** Registered to White Waltham Airfield Ltd. See also Swordfish HS554 (G-RNMZ) at White Waltham, Berks: AJD is working on the wings and tail surfaces here.

FELIXSTOWE at the end of the A14, southeast of Ipswich

Glenn Cattermole: XT284 makes good progress. ◆ *Prior arrangement* **only**

❑ XT284	'H'	Blackburn Buccaneer S.2A		65	ex Stock, St Athan, Abingdon 8855M (21-5-85), St Athan, 237 OCU, 15, 208, 809, 803, 736. Cockpit		3-22

Steve Williams: Has a Motor Cadet and Grasshopper at a *private* location in the *general* area.

❑ G-BVFS		Slingsby Motor Cadet III		93	ex Southend. Unflown, stored		N10-23
❑ 'WZ784'		Slingsby Grasshopper TX.1		c52	ex Southend, Thurrock. Composite	[1]	2-10

■ **[1]** There is another 'WZ784' at Lake District Airport, Cumbria.

Suffolk concludes after the photo-spread, on page 225

NOTTINGHAMSHIRE

Tornado F.2 ZA267
Syerston, Aug 2023
Andy Wood

Tornado GR.1 ZA357
Syerston, Aug 2023
Andy Wood

Tucano T.1 ZF202
Syerston, Aug 2023
Andy Wood

SHROPSHIRE

Hart Trainer K4972
Cosford, Apr 2023
Ian Haskell

Wellington T.10 MF628
Cosford, Apr 2023
RAF Museum

Hunting 126 XN714
Cosford, Apr 2023
David Willis

SHROPSHIRE

Chinook HC.6A ZA718
Cosford, Apr 2023
David Willis

SOMERSET

Grasshopper Srs.3 G-AWRP
Weston-super-Mare, Oct 2023
David S Johnstone

EH.101 PP8 ZJ116
Weston-super-Mare, Oct 2023
David S Johnstone

SOMERSET

Provost T.1 WV499
Weston Zoyland, Jul 2023
Andrew Simpson

Swordfish II LS326
Yeovilton, Jun 2022
John Wickenden

Sea Hawk FGA.6 WV911
Yeovilton, Dec 2022
Hugh Trevor

SOMERSET

Sea Harrier F/A.2s 'ZH801'
and 'ZH800'
Yeovilton, Dec 2022
Hugh Trevor

SUFFOLK

Jaguar GR.1A XX741
Bentwaters, May 2023
Jake Wallace

WEST SUSSEX
Hunter GA.11 WW654
Ford, Mar 2022
Tony McCarthy

WARWICKSHIRE
Gnat F.1 XK724
Coventry, May 2023
Ian Humphreys

Flettner Fl 282B 280020
Coventry, May 2023
Ian Humphreys

WARWICKSHIRE

Percival Q.6 X9407
Coventry, Oct 2023
Dave Thomas

Lightning T.4 XL629
Boscombe Down, Mar 2023
John Wickenden

Beagle 206 Z2 XS743
Old Sarum, Nov 2023
Hugh Trevor

WILTSHIRE
Tornado GR.1T ZA319
Old Sarum, Nov 2023
Jake Wallace

WORCESTERSHIRE
Meteor T.7 WH166
Birlingham, Aug 2023
Jake Wallace

Cherokee 140 G-SMTH
Evesham, Apr 2023
Steve Richards

EAST YORSHIRE

Hawk T.55 LL-5313
Brough, Jan 2023
Mark Whitnall

NORTH YORKSHIRE

Halifax 'LV907'
Elvington, Oct 2022
Brian Downs

BAE Systems HERTI-1 UAV
Elvington, Oct 2022
Brian Downs

NORTH YORSHIRE

Hawk T.1A XX306
Leeming Bar, Jul 2023
Dave Thomas

Sea King HAS.3s ZE369, ZE370, XZ589
Scarborough, Aug 2023
Andy Wood

SOUTH YORKSHIRE

Whirlwind HAR.10 XP345
Doncaster, Jun 2022
David S Johnstone

SCOTLAND

Provost T.1 WV493
East Fortune, Oct 2022
Jim Simpson

Herald 201 G-APWJ
Kinloss, Mar 2022
Jim Simpson

Hunter F.1 WT619
Montrose, Jun 2023
Jim Simpson

SCOTLAND

Hunter T.7 N-315
Netherley, Aug 2023
Paul Middleton

Jetstream 41 SX-ROD
Perth, Oct 2023
Jim Simpson

Lightning F.3 XR749
Peterhead, Aug 2023
Paul Middleton

WALES

Hawk T.1 XX309
Caernarfon, May 2023
Ian Doyle

Antonov An-2R CCCP-19733
Hawarden, Apr 2023
Ian Doyle

Jet Provost T.4 XP585
Hawarden, Aug 2023
Ian Doyle

WALES

Hunter T.8C WV396
Newborough, May 2022
Ian Doyle

Tempest II HA580
St Athan, Aug 2023
Chris England

Commando Mk.2C SL-01
St Athan, Sep 2023
Chris England

WALES

Jetstream 31 G-NFLA
St Athan, May 2023
Chris England

Tornado GR.4 ZA607
Sealand, Nov 2023
David S Johnstone

NORTHERN IRELAND

Short 330 G-BSBH
Portadown, Aug 2023
Ian Thompson

IRELAND

Viscount 808 EI-AOH
Dublin, Aug 2023
Ian Thompson

Cessna 337A N19F
Newcastle, Sep 2023
Rowland Benbrook

CYPRUS

Whirlwind HAR.10 XD184
Akrotiri, Oct 2023
John Phillips

FLIXTON on the B1062 west of Bungay

Norfolk and Suffolk Aviation Museum (N&SAM): Within are airframes from the former Boulton Paul Aircraft Heritage Project: the company started its aviation activities at Mousehold, Norwich. As well as aircraft, the company also built industrial buildings and hangars and one of the display halls in based on a B&P structure of 1937. Don't forget to take time to amble down to the River Waveney on the Adair Walk. The remains of the former airfield, home of the B-24s of the 446th BG, lie to the east. Neighbouring is the 'Flixton Buck' public house, dating from the 16th century.

Three substantial items do not merit a 'formal' listing as such: a replica Mosquito night-fighter which was started in 2016 and is essentially an instrument cluster and windscreen; a project to create a Hurricane I fuselage, using many elements from former 257 Squadron P3708, shot down on 18th August 1940; and sections from 9 Squadron Wellington I L4288 which crashed near Honington on 30th October 1939.

Titch G-BABY departed by September 2023 to 'Cornwall'. EoN Primary CDN (BGA.1461) was returned to its owner in March 2022 for restoration to flying condition.

◆ *The Street, NR35 1NZ* | **01986 896644** | **nsam.flixton@gmail.com** | **www.aviationmuseum.net**

Identity	Code	Type	Year	History	Notes	Date
❑ G-APUG		Luton Major	64	ex Wattisham. De-reg 5-8-87. Arrived 17-10-06		1-24
❑ G-ARLP		Beagle Terrier	48	ex Felthorpe, Fakenham, Terrier (1961), AAC College, Auster T.10, AOP.6 VX123, 19 MU, 663, 661. Arrived 5-7-16		1-24
❑ G-ASRF		Gowland Jenny Wren	66	ex Brookmans Park, Panshanger, Brookmans Park. CoA 4-6-71, de-reg 11-12-96. Arrived 11-9-04	[1]	1-24
❑ G-BDVS		Fokker Friendship 200	63	ex Norwich, Air UK, S2-ABK, PH-FEX, PH-EXC, 9M-AMM, PH-EXC, PH-FEX. *Eric Gander Dower*. CoA 5-6-00, de-reg 19-12-96. Arrived 17-12-96. Cockpit		1-24
❑ G-BJZC		Thunder Ax7-65Z HAB	82	ex Lancing. CoA 17-6-94, de-reg 8-7-98. *Greenpeace Trinity*	[2]	1-24
❑ G-CDFL*		Zenair CH-601UL	19	ex Spalding. De-reg 4-10-19. Arr 12-21. Fuselage, simulator		1-24
❑ G-CDFW		Lovegrove Sheffy gyro	04	ex Didcot. De-reg 17-5-10. Arrived 3-4-10. *Sheffy*	[3]	1-24
❑ G-MBUD		Skycraft Super Scout 250	82	de-reg 6-9-94. Arrived 11-11-07		1-24
❑ G-MJSU		MBA Tiger Cub	r83	ex Swanton Morley. CoA 31-1-86, de-reg 23-6-93. Arr 8-8-02		1-24
❑ G-MJVI		Lightwing Rooster 1	r83	ex Littlehampton. De-reg 13-6-90. Arrived 24-2-04	[4]	1-24
❑ G-MMWL		Eurowing Goldwing	83	CoA 20-11-06, de-reg 19-4-10. Arrived 15-7-07		1-24
❑ G-MTFK		Flexiform Striker	r87	de-reg 13-6-90. Last taxi 3-7-94. Arrived 7-94	[2] [5]	1-24
❑ DUD		DFS Grunau Baby III	54	BGA.2384, ex Bristol, BGA.2074, RAFGSA.374, D-9142. CoA 29-3-92. Arrived 2002		1-24
❑ HCG		Maupin Woodstock	92	BGA.3833, ex Happisburgh. CoA 23-3-11. Arrived 25-9-10		1-24
❑ HKJ		Penrose Pegasus 2 rep	93	BGA.4002, ex Littlehampton. CoA 15-9-98. Arr 24-2-02	[4] [6]	1-24
❑ JTA		Colditz Cock replica	00	BGA.4757, ex Duxford. *Spirit of Colditz*. CoA 20-2-00	[7]	3-24
❑ 'X-25'		B&P P.6 replica	01	BAPC.274, ex Cosford, Wolverhampton. Arrived 19-1-15		1-24
❑ –	'LHS-1'	Bensen B-7	66	BAPC.147, ex Loddon, Marham, Coltishall. Arrived 1978		1-24
❑ –		Mignet HM.14 'Flea'	c36	BAPC.115, ex Earls Colne, Andrewsfield, Duxford, London, Porthcawl	[8] [9]	1-24
❑ –		Goldfinch Amphibian 161	96	BAPC.303, ex Old Sarum. Arrived 23-9-08	[8] [10]	1-24
❑ –		Wasp Falcon 4 hang-glider	76	BAPC.372		1-24
❑ –		Antonov C.14 hang-glider	92	BAPC.374		1-24
❑ –		UFM Icarus II	74	BAPC.364, arrived 6-11-05. Biplane, tail-less, hang-glider		1-24
❑ –		Lovegrove Discord gyro	96	BAPC.306, ex Didcot. Arrived 4-10. *The Discord*	[3]	1-24
❑ NC16676		Fairchild 24C8F	36	ex Tibenham, USA, CAP. Arrived 18-3-03. CAP colours	[11]	1-24
❑ –		Felixstowe F.5	18	BAPC.390, ex Felixstowe. Nose section	[12]	1-24
❑ 'K4556'	'F'	B&P Overstrand replica	11	BAPC.358, ex Cosford, Wolverhampton. Forward fuselage, 101 Sqn colours. Arrived 19-1-15		1-24
❑ 'FJ801'		Boeing PT-27 Kaydet	42	BAPC.375, ex Tibenham, USA. Arrived 26-6-12	[13]	1-24
❑ 'TD248'	'8Q-T'	V-S Spitfire XVI	45	BAPC.368, fuselage re-creation. 695 Sqn colours	[8] [14]	1-24
❑ VL349	'V7-Q'	Avro Anson C.19	47 G-AWSA	ex Norwich, N5054, G-AWSA (de-reg 18-8-69), SCS, NCS, North Coates SF, WSF, FCCS, HCCS, HCEU, 116, CSE, 1 FU. SOC 5-3-68. Arrived 1-74. Central Sig Est colours		1-24
❑ VX580		Vickers Valetta C.2	50	ex Norwich, MCS, MEAF CS, Aden SF, 114, Malta CS, HS. Last flight 12-12-68. Arrived (via Chinook) 27-5-83		1-24
❑ WB627*	'N'	DHC Chipmunk T.10	50	ex Dulwich, 9248M (27-3-96), Cambridge, 5 AEF, 1 AEF, Lon UAS, Camb UAS, 2 SoTT, 22 GCF, Debden SF, Jurby SF, 8 RFS, 18 RFS. Hatfield-built. Fuselage. Arrived 9-11-23		1-24

❑ 'WE168'		EE Canberra PR.3	00	cockpit re-creation. Arrived 2002	[15]	1-24
❑ WF128	'676'	Percival Sea Prince T.1	52	ex Honington 8611M (5-2-79), Kemble, Sydenham SF, A&AEE, 750. Arrived 25-9-81. 750 Sqn colours		1-24
❑ WF643	'F'	Gloster Meteor F(TT).8	51	ex Coltishall, Kemble, 29, Nicosia SF, 611, 1, 56. AWA-built. SOC 29-11-71. Arrived 10-5-75. 56 Sqn colours by 9-23		1-24
❑ WG789		EE Canberra B.2/6	52	ex Mendlesham, Booker, Kew, Burgess Hill, RAE Bedford, RRE, 231 OCU. SOC 23-2-82. Arrived 6-3-02. Cockpit	[2]	1-24
❑ WH840		EE Canberra T.4	54	ex Seighford, Locking 8350M, St Athan, Laarbruch SF, A&AEE, 97, 151, 245, 88, 231 OCU, CFS. SOC 3-4-74. Arrived 3-94	[8]	1-24
❑ WV605	'T-B'	Percival Provost T.1	54	ex Henlow, Higher Blagdon, Macclesfield, 6 FTS, 3 FTS, 22 FTS. SOC 31-10-66. Arrived 14-9-78		1-24
❑ WV838	'182'	Hawker Sea Hawk FGA.6	54	ex Warrington, Liverpool, Bruntingthorpe, Chippenham, Fleetlands, 736, 738, 806, 802. Crashed 9-2-59. Arrived 23-8-11. 806 Sqn colours. Cockpit	[2]	1-24
❑ XA226		Slingsby Grasshopper TX.1	53	ex Milton Keynes, Turweston, Ipswich, Halton. Arr 21-4-04		1-24
❑ 'XE531'		Hawker Hunter T.53	58	ex Cosford, Wolverhampton, N Weald, Bruntingthorpe, Hurn, B'thorpe, Bitteswell, Hatfield, G-9-430 (1-12-75), Danish AF Esk.724, ET-272, 35-272. Cockpit. Arr 19-1-15	[16]	1-24
❑ XG254	'A'	Hawker Hunter FGA.9	56	ex Clacton, Coltishall, Weybourne, Coltishall 8881M (9-12-85), St Athan, 1 TWU, 2 TWU, TWU, 229 OCU, 54, Handling Sqn, 54. Arrived 19-2-02. 54 Sqn colours	[8]	1-24
❑ XG329		EE Lightning F.1(DB)	59	ex Swinderby, Cranwell 8050M (8-7-69), A&AEE, Warton. Last flight 2-6-69. Arrived 1993	[8]	1-24
❑ XG518		Bristol Sycamore HR.14	55	ex Sunderland, Balloch, Halton 8009M (7-5-68), Wroughton, Khormaksar SF, El Adem SF, Habbiniya SF, CFS, Amman SF. Arrived 24-2-97	[8]	1-24
❑ XG523	'V'	Bristol Sycamore HR.14	55	ex Sunderland, Hayes, M Wallop, Ternhill 7793M, CFS, JEHU. Crashed 25-9-62. Arrived 25-1-97. Cockpit	[8]	1-24
❑ XH892	'J'	Gloster Javelin FAW.9R	57	ex Duxford, Colerne 7982M, Shawbury, 29, 64, 23. AWA-built. SOC 30-6-67. Arrived 6-5-82		1-24
❑ XJ482	'713'	DH Sea Vixen FAW.1	58	ex Wimborne Minster, Tarrant Rushton, Lee-on-Solent A2598 (3-8-69), 766, Thurleigh, 700Y. Christchurch-built. Arrived 25-11-79. 766 Sqn colours		1-24
❑ XK624	'32'	DH Vampire T.11	56	ex Lytham St Athan, Blackpool, CFS, 3 FTS, 7 FTS, 1 FTS, 23 GCF, CFS, 7 FTS. Hawarden-built. SOC 14-12-71. Arrived 11-4-80		1-24
❑ XM279		EE Canberra B(I).8	59	ex Doncaster, Flixton, Firbeck, Nostell Priory, Cambridge, 16, 3. SOC 19-3-74. Acquired 3-94. Cockpit. 16 Sqn, Shark's mouth colours	[8] [17]	1-24
❑ XN304	'W'	Westland Whirlwind HAS.7	59	ex Bedford, Henlow, Wroughton, Shrivenham, W'ton, 705, JHDU, 848. SOC 7-1-76. Arrived 19-7-82. 848 Sqn c/s		1-24
❑ XN500		Hunting Jet Provost T.3A	60	ex Southampton, Farnborough, East Midlands, Ipswich, Oxford, 7 FTS, RAFC, 3 FTS, RAFC, 3 FTS, RAFC. SOC 26-1-93. Arrived 7-10-07. CSE logo	[8]	1-24
❑ XP743*		EE Lightning F.3	64	ex Wattisham, Burton-upon-Trent, Stafford, Leconfield, 29, 56, 29, 56, Wattisham TFF, 56. SOC 16-10-75. 56 Sqn colours. Cockpit. Arrived 17-3-22	[18]	4-24
❑ XR485	'Q'	W'land Whirlwind HAR.10	63	ex Wroughton, 2 FTS, CFS. SOC 29-1-81. Arrived 19-2-81		1-24
❑ XV497*	'D'	McD Phantom FGR.2	69	ex Bentwaters, Waddington, Coningsby 9295M, 74, 1435 Flt, 23, 228 OCU, 92, 19, 92, 29, 19, 228 OCU, 92, 23, 56, 228 OCU, 17, 228 OCU, 41, 6. 23 Sqn / Falklands c/s. Arrived 28-7-20	[2]	1-24
❑ ZA175		HS Sea Harrier F/A.2	81	ex Yeovilton, 899, 800, 899, 800, 899, 801, 800, 899, 800, 801, 899. Arrived 27-7-04. 899 Sqn colours	[2]	1-24
❑ –		Folland Gnat T.1 CIM	65	ex Cosford, Wolverhampton. Procedures trainer, forward cockpit. Folland-built. Arrived 19-1-15		1-24
❑ A-528		FMA Pucará	79	ex Sunderland, M Wallop, Cosford, Abingdon 8769M, Stanley, Argentine AF. Arrived 24-7-94. *Toto Juan*	[19]	1-24

Identity	Type	Built	History	Note	Date
❑ 79 '2-EG'	Dassault Mystère IVA	54	ex Sculthorpe, FAF, ET.2/8, GE 314, EC.1/5. Last flown 3-5-78, arrived 18-11-78. Suez stripes	[20]	1-24
❑ '157/18'	Fokker D.VIII scale rep	84	BAPC.239, ex '694', Lowestoft. Arrived 1991, stored		1-24
❑ '1972' *and* '3794'	Mikoyan-Gurevich MiG-15*bis Fagot* 3794	56	ex Duxford, Czech AF. Letov-built S-103. Czech AF colours to stb, Polish to pt. Arrived 14-8-07		1-24
❑ 42196	NAA F-100D-11-NA Super Sabre	54	ex Sculthorpe, French AF, 54-2196 USAF 48th FBW, 45th FS. Last flown 22-2-77, arr 18-3-78. 'Skyblazers' c/s	[20]	1-24
❑ 55-4433 '433'	Lockheed T-33A-5-LO	55	ex Sculthorpe, French AF, USAF 803rd ABG. Last flown 25-1-78, arrived 21-7-78. 20th FBG colours	[20]	1-24
❑ 6289 '2W' *and* FG-289	NAA T-28C Trojan N99153	57	ex East Ham, France, N99153, Zaire AF FG-289, Congo AF FA-289, USN 146289. Crashed 14-12-77. Arrived 28-5-81. Fuselage. Zaire AF colours to port, USN VT-3 to stb	[21]	1-24

■ **[1]** Jenny Wren built using the wings of Luton Minor G-AGEP. **[2]** Airframes on loan: Thunder balloon G-BJZC (Mobberley Balloon Collection); Striker G-MTFK; Canberra WG789 (Steve Pickup); Sea Hawk WV838, Sea Harrier ZA175 (IWM, Duxford); Phantom XV497 **[3]** Designed and built by Peter Lovegrove. **[4]** Rooster and Pegasus donated by the widow of the late John M Lee, who also built the wings of the museum's Colditz Cock. **[5]** Striker was the last aircraft to fly from Flixton before the runways were broken up. **[6]** Penrose Pegasus 2 is a reproduction of the original Harald Penrose example. **[7]** See comments under Note [10]. **[8]** Airframes on loan from Ian Hancock. **[9]** Built by, or for, George Pine, proprietor of Pine's Airways of Porthcawl – operators of Fox Moth G-ACEX and Porthcawl's Rest Bay Aerodrome. It appeared at annual displays at Rest Bay, up to 1938, but it's believed not to have flown. Skeletal remains substantially rebuilt by Stan Brett at Andrewsfield 1980-81. **[10]** Goldfinch Amphibian 161 was built by the late Flt Lt Leslie 'Bill' Goldfinch at his home in Wiltshire. His illustrious career included the designing of the Colditz Cock glider during his time 'banged up' - the museum has a replica on show. Unfinished, the Goldfinch was intended as a scale taxiable aircraft, inspired by the Loening OA-1 Air Yacht, using Jodel D.11 wings and other components. The '161' bit comes from the plans number for the D.11 that 'donated' its wings. **[11]** Fairchild 24 (pre-Argus) was the second C8F built and served with the Civil Air Patrol, fitted with bomb racks and flare chutes as a sub 'scarer'. **[12]** The extreme nose section (10ft long) of a Felixstowe flying-boat, once a potting shed, while not fitting our criteria totally, represents a singular survivor. It would be great if it were found to be B&P-built. Another section of Felixstowe, about 8ft long, is on hand from the RAF Museum. **[13]** PT-27 is a composite donated by Tibenham-based Black Barn Aviation. **[14]** Spitfire XVI fuselage is centred on the original skin of TD248 acquired from Historic Flying. The skin, coupled with an original frame No.19, and a fibreglass tail section has created a fuselage containing many original fittings. (TD248 is airworthy as G-OXVI.) After much thought, this is best termed a 're-creation'. **[15]** WE168 was vandalised during its time with its previous owner. Exceptionally well equipped inside, it was stripped out and the battered 'outer' airframe disposed of. N&SAM purchased all of the 'innards' and a completely new 'cutaway' cockpit, including outer skin, was created in wood and metal. Like TD248, it is best termed a 're-creation'. **[16]** Hunter T.53 cockpit is painted as the one-off RAE test-bed T.12 XE531, which was written off 17-3-82. The rear fuselage of ET-272 is at East Midlands, Leics. **[17]** XM279 returned from refurbish at Doncaster by 10-20. **[18]** XP743 owned by Ken Hayward. **[19]** On loan from the Army Flying Museum, Middle Wallop, Hampshire. **[20]** Airframes from the National Museum of the USAF's Loan Program. **[21]** First use of N99153, registration re-allocated to former Zaire FG-576 (140576) after the crash of 14-12-77.

FOXHALL west of the A12, south of Kesgrave

Suffolk Aviation Heritage Museum: On the southern edge of the former Martlesham Heath airfield, close to what was the Runway 04 threshold, the venue is run by the **Suffolk Aviation Heritage Group**. The cavernous building, used by the USAF for communications and known as 'The Roc', was last used by the 2164th Comms Squadron up to the early 1990s. Spares donor Vampire T.11 cockpit XD616 has reached the end of its days and by the time this is read will have been scrapped.

◆ *Off the A12, Foxhall Road, IP10 0AH* | **www.facebook.com/suffolkaviationheritagegroup/**

Identity	Type	Built	History	Note	Date
❑ G-BAXX	Cessna F.150L	73	ex Monewden, Bruntingthorpe, Cambridge, Shobdon, Barnstaple. Reims-built. Damaged 21-9-78, de-reg 8-10-80. Fuselage, arrived 8-7-18		1-24
❑ G-BBXZ*	Evans VP-1	75	CoA 8-3-96, de-reg 20-10-14		1-24
❑ G-BTAZ*	Evans VP-2	88	ex Norwich Unflown project. De-reg 12-3-09. F/n 3-23		1-24
❑ G-MVBB*	CFM Shadow BD	90	CoA 8-10-00, de-reg 7-2-10		1-24
❑ –	Woodhams Sprite	60	BAPC.17, ex Canterbury, Manchester, Hooton Park, Wigan, Irlam, Wigan, Liverpool, Leamington Spa. Unfinished	[1]	1-24
❑ –	Blériot XI replica	18	BAPC.479. Built by Telford 'Tom' Thompson locally	[2]	1-24
❑ WH798	EE Canberra PR.7	54	ex Canterbury, Cardiff-Wales, WAM, CTTS St Athan 8130M, 31, 17, 13, 80, 17, 100, 542. SOC 30-11-81. Cockpit		1-24
❑ XD506	DH Vampire T.11	54	ex Staverton, Bentham, Staverton, Thrupp, Staverton, Pyle, Swinderby, Finningley 7983M (7-9-67), CATCS, CNCS, 5 FTS, 206 AFS. Hawarden-built. Arrived 7-10-17		1-24
❑ XG274* '71'	Hawker Hunter F.6	56	ex Newmarket, Ipswich, Halton 8710M (30-11-81), 4 FTS, 229 OCU, 66, 14. Arrived 11-21		1-24
❑ XK821*	Slingsby Grasshopper TX.1	56	ex ?? 'Fuselage' forward of the 'A' frame. First noted 8-22		1-24

❑ XN629	'49'	Hunting Jet Provost T.3A G-KNOT	61	ex Bentwaters, N Weald, G-BVEG (re-reg 9-6-99), XN629, 1 FTS, 7 FTS, 1 FTS, CFS, RAFC, 3 FTS. CoA 10-10-07, de-reg 21-6-07. Forward fuselage, 'RAF Wilminster' badge	1-24

■ **[1]** All-wood, single-seat twin-boom pusher, designed and built by a team led by Bill Woodhams. Work stopped in 1965 and it joined the Northern Aircraft Preservation Society (today's TAC) on 25-5-69. **[2]** Blériot honours Ipswich-born Edith Maud Cook, Britain's first female pilot. She took instruction at the Blériot School at Pau, France, in late 1909.

FRAMLINGHAM AERODROME or Parham, on the B1116 north of Woodbridge

Parham Airfield Museum: incorporating the **390th Bomb Group Memorial Air Museum** and the **Museum of British Resistance**. The tower houses a superb museum dedicated to the 390th and USAAF Station No.153. The Resistance Museum is dedicated to the work of the Auxiliary Units - the so-called 'Stay Behind' cells in the event of an invasion. On 28th June 2023 the Moller Building, greatly expanding display and catering capacity, was officially opened.

◆ *Off the A12, IP13 9AF* | **01728 621373** | **parhamairfield@yahoo.co.uk** | **www.parhamairfieldmuseum.co.uk**

HALESWORTH on the A144 south of Bungay

Halesworth Airfield Station 365 Memorial Museum: Established on the former Eighth Air Force airfield (also known as Holton); this museum includes an exceptional range of exhibits.

◆ *Sparrowhawk Way, Upper Holton, IP19 8NH* | **01986 875084** | **halesworthairfieldmuseum@outlook.com** | **www.halesworthairfieldmuseum.co.uk**

John Flanagan: Long-term custodian of the flightdeck of Carvair CF-EPV transferred it to Marc Wilmott and it moved to Hadleigh, Essex, by mid-2023.

HONINGTON AIRFIELD on the A1088 southeast of Thetford EGXH

RAF Regiment / RAF Police: The Tornados provide training for airfield patrol at the HAS site on the northern perimeter.

❑ XK526		Blackburn Buccaneer S.2	60	8648M (10-3-80), ex RAE Bedford, RRE, A&AEE, RAE, A&AEE, RAE, A&AEE. Displayed, unveiled 16-2-83	1-24
❑ ZA553	'045'	Panavia Tornado GR.4	81	ex Marham, GR.1, 31. First noted 7-19	9-23
❑ ZA587	'055'	Panavia Tornado GR.4	81	ex Marham, GR.1, 15. SOC 25-6-19	7-21
❑ ZA613	'076'	Panavia Tornado GR.4	81	ex Marham, GR.1, 15. First noted 7-19	9-23
❑ ZD711	'079'	Panavia Tornado GR.4	84	ex Marham, St Athan, GR.1, DARA. Arrived 10-4-18	7-19
❑ ZG752	'129'	Panavia Tornado GR.4	91	ex Marham, GR.1, 13. SOC 25-6-19	7-21
❑ TAD.021*		Sud Gazelle HT.2 XW860	75	ex Lyneham, Middle Wallop, Fleetlands, Wroughton, 705. Westland-built. First noted 11-22	9-23

HORHAM on the B1117 east of Eye

The Red Feather Club: The official museum of 95th Bomb Group, operated and managed by the **95th Bomb Group Heritage Association**, has brought back to life the former NCOs' club at USAAF Station 119, once home to the B-17s of the 95th. Included in the exhibits are the famous murals painted by S/Sgt Nathan Bindler.

◆ *Horham Road, IP21 5DG* | **email** via website | **www.95thbg-horham.com**

IPSWICH

Everett Aero: There are several storage sites, including Bentwaters: 'Ipswich' is a generic label.

Departures: **Harrier** T.12 cockpit ZH665, last noted 9-15, left by 2022, no further details; anonymous GR.5 test rig, last noted 5-19, also departed, no other details; **Jaguar** GR.3A XZ366, last noted 8-18, had moved on by 2022, no further details; **Jet Provost** T.5A XW321 left by 2022, no further details; **Lynx** AH.1 XZ213 to Telford, Shropshire, 5-22; HMA.8 ZD258 to Blackpool, Lancs, by 11-21; HMA.8 ZD566 to Lizard, Cornwall, 16-12-22; AH.9A ZG916 to Aberdeen, Scotland, by 3-23; **Scout** AH.1 XT624 to Bury St Edmunds, Suffolk, by mid-2021; Typhoon fatigue rig 'TR001' moved on by 2016. JetRanger G-OBYT has been deleted. ◆ **Strictly** *private locations - prior arrangement* **only** | **www.everettaero.com**

❑ XG196	'31'	Hawker Hunter F.6A	56	ex Mytchett, Bracknell 8702M (24-11-81), Kemble, 1 TWU, TWU, 229 OCU, 19. 234 Sqn colours. Arrived 27-3-14	10-23
❑ XV460	'R'	McD Phantom FGR.2	69	ex BCWM - Bentwaters, Ipswich, Sunderland, Coningsby, Wattisham, 74, 56, 19, 92, 29, 228 OCU, 92, 228 OCU, 19, 56, 228 OCU, 31. Arrived 4-5-16. Cockpit	10-23

❑ XW267	'SA'	HS Harrier T.4	70	ex Toton 9263M (23-10-96), Boscombe D, SAOEU, RAE, A&AEE, RAE, 233 OCU, 1, 233 OCU, T.2, 233 OCU. Arr 12-3-14		4-22
❑ XW418	'MT'	BAC Jet Provost T.5A	72	ex Cosford, DSAE, 9173M (17-12-92), Shawbury, 1 FTS, 7 FTS, CFS, 3 FTS, Leeming SF, 3 FTS. First noted 4-17		4-22
❑ XX139		SEPECAT Jaguar T.4	73	ex St Athan, 16, T.2, 226 OCU, 6, 226 OCU, JOCU. Arr 27-10-05		4-22
❑ XX144	'U'	SEPECAT Jaguar T.2A	74	ex Shawbury, 16, 226 OCU, 6, 54, 226 OCU, JOCU		4-22
❑ XX836	'ER'	SEPECAT Jaguar T.2A	75	ex Shawbury, 6, 17, 14, 54		4-22
❑ XX838	'FZ'	SEPECAT Jaguar T.4	75	ex St Athan, 41, 16, T.2, Shawbury, 226 OCU, 17, 226 OCU		10-23
❑ XX842		SEPECAT Jaguar T.2A VH-UXB	75	ex St Athan, 41, 16, Warton, T.2, 16, 41, Shawbury, ETPS/RAE, 6, 2, 41, 54, 226 OCU. Arrived 10-8-06		4-22
❑ XZ234	'630'	Westland Lynx HAS.3S	77	ex Staverton, M Wallop, 702, 815, 702, 815, HAS.2, 815, 702, 700L, Westland. SOC 20-12-10. First noted 9-17		4-22
❑ XZ735	'404' *and* '305'	Westland Lynx HAS.3GMS	81	ex Fleetlands, M Wallop, 815, 829, 815, HAS.2, 815. Cabin		4-22
❑ ZD249	'635'	Westland Lynx HAS.3S	82	ex Fleetlands, SOC 20-4-10, 815, 702, A&AEE	[1]	4-22
❑ ZD274	'M'	Westland Lynx AH.7	83	ex Middle Wallop		4-22
❑ ZE375		Westland Lynx AH.9A	85	ex M Wallop. SOC 23-9-16. Arrived 18-11-16		4-22
❑ ZE379		Westland Lynx AH.7	86	ex Dishforth, Arborfield, 655, 657, 655. Cabin, boom of ZD283		4-22
❑ ZG478		BAe/McDD Harrier GR.9	90	ex Yeovilton, Cottesmore. Crashed Khandahar 14-5-09		4-22
❑ ZG884		Westland Lynx AH.9A	90	ex M Wallop. SOC 23-9-16		4-22
❑ ZG885		Westland Lynx AH.9A	91	ex M Wallop. Arrived 24-9-19		4-22
❑ ZG886		Westland Lynx AH.9A	91	ex M Wallop. SOC 23-9-16		4-22
❑ ZG887		Westland Lynx AH.9A	91	ex M Wallop. SOC 23-9-16. First noted 9-17		4-22
❑ ZG888		Westland Lynx AH.9A	91	ex M Wallop. SOC 23-9-16. First noted 9-17		4-22
❑ ZH658		BAe/McDD Harrier T.10	94	ex Cottesmore, St Athan, Wittering, 20. Crashed 16-4-03. Forward fuselage		4-22
❑ ZH806	'730'	HS Sea Harrier F/A.2	98	ex Shawbury, 899, 800, 801, 899. SOC 28-7-05. Arr 2-2-06		4-22
❑ ZH812	'005'	HS Sea Harrier F/A.2	98	ex Shawbury, Y'ton, 801, 899, 801. SOC 29-3-06. Arr 22-6-10		4-22
❑ H-07		Agusta 109BA	92	ex Woodmancote, France, Belgian Army. First noted 9-17		1-18
❑ FR-150*		Sud-Ouest Djinn	59	ex Tattershall, France, F-AZZT, ALAT F-MCDL. F/n 7-21	[2]	4-22

■ **[1]** ZD249's boom is on fellow XZ698 at Seaton Burn, N&T. **[2]** Written out of *W&R28* at Tattershall, Lincs, as moved on by 2018.

KESGRAVE Piper L-21B MM54-2372 had moved on, destination/fate unknown, by 2022.

KESSINGLAND on the A12 south of Lowestoft

Kessingland Beach Holiday Park: Offers 'Helibus Glamping' in a Lynx and promises an 'Airbus A320 pod', sleeping four.

◆ *Prior arrangement* **only** | **www.parkdeanresorts.co.uk**

❑ ZF539	Westland Lynx AH.9	87	ex Ipswich, Middle Wallop. First noted 5-20	8-21

LAKENHEATH AIRFIELD on the A1065 south of Brandon EGUL

USAF Lakenheath, 48th FW – Wings of Liberty Memorial Park ◆ *Prior permission* only

❑ 'BM361'	'XR-C'	V-S Spitfire V FSM	99	BAPC.269, 71 'Eagle' Sqn, colours. Displayed, since 1999	3-20
❑ '65-777'		McD F-4C-15-MC Phantom II 63-7419	63	ex Alconbury, Texas ANG. 48th TFW colours. Unveiled 7-95	6-21
❑ 74-0131		McDD F-15A-12-MC Eagle	74	ex 122 TFS / Louisiana ANG. Unveiled 7-95	6-21
❑ 68-011		GD F-111E-CF Aardvark	68	ex Upper Heyford, 20 TFW. 48th TFW colours, *Miss Liberty*. Unveiled 7-95	6-21

Airfield:

❑ '63319'	'FW-319'	NAA F-100D-16-NA Super Sabre 54-2269	54	ex '54048', French AF. Arrived 30-3-76. Displayed Marked 'A2' on the fin	5-22
❑ 76-0124		McDD F-15B-15-MC Eagle	76	BDR	10-21

LAVENHAM AERODROME on the A1141 north of Sudbury

◆ *Prior permission* **only**

❑ G-AIRK	DH Tiger Moth	39	ex N9241, 8 EFTS, 10 FIS, TTU, 2 CPF, 224. CoA 1-8-07	9-22

LOWESTOFT on the A12 south of Great Yarmouth

Simply Spitfire: The Spitfire is available for hire. ◆ *Prior arrangement* **only** | **www.simplyspitfire.com**

❑ 'MK805' 'SH-B'	V-S Spitfire IX FSM	10	BAPC.426, 64 Sqn colours, *Peter John III*	[1]	12-20

■ **[1]** The *real* MK805 (once MM4084) is preserved in Italy.

MARTLESHAM HEATH southeast of Woodbridge, the A12 runs through the site

Martlesham Heath Control Tower Museum: The vista of a control tower amid a housing estate is quite surreal. Run by the **Martlesham Heath Aviation Society**, the museum contains a vast amount of material on a former airfield with an incredible heritage, 1917 to 1963. The car park for the museum was once revetments where the P-47s and P-51s of the USAAF's 356th FG used to park. Concrete sandbags that made the walls of one of these have been preserved.

◆ *Parkers Place, off Eagle Way, IP5 3UZ* | **secretary@mhas.org.uk** | **www.mhas.org.uk**

MILDENHALL on the A1304 east of Cambridge

Sim2do Flight Simulation Centre: In Gregory Road has a 'synthetic' Boeing 737 and F-35B and a *real* Lynx.

◆ *Prior arrangement* **only** | **www.sim2do.com**

❑ XZ195	Westland Lynx AH.7	79	ex Hixon, Fleetlands, M Wallop, 672. Cockpit	12-23

MILDENHALL AIRFIELD on the A1304 east of Cambridge

USAF Mildenhall: The Cayuse that was issued to the 352nd SOG for loading training is *thought* to be still held, despite an ancient 'last noted' date.

❑ 69-15979	Hughes OH-6A Cayuse	69	ex Hurlburt Field, USA. Training aid	10-14

ROUGHAM, or Bury St Edmunds, north of the A14 east of Bury St Edmunds

Rougham Tower Association: Sadly, the aerodrome is no more, leaving the superbly-preserved tower to honour this B-17 base. Displays are dedicated to the men and the memories of the 322nd and 94th BGs and there are poignant memorials.

◆ *Off A14 east of 'Bury, Rougham Industrial Estate, IP33 7QB* | **07931 971771** | **email** via website | **www.rctam94th.co.uk**

STOWMARKET on the A14 east of Bury St Edmunds

Giles Howell: The EE P.1B is *believed* to still be in the area for restoration and eventual display.

❑ XA847	EE P.1B	57	ex Portsmouth, Southampton, Hendon 8371M, Farnborough, A&AEE, EE. Last flight 21-4-66	8-15

WALPOLE on the B1117 southeast of Halesworth

Former **Blyth Valley Aviation Collection** cockpits: **not** available for public inspection.

❑ WE122 '845'	EE Canberra TT.18	52	ex N Weald, Stock, Llanbedr, St Athan, Llanbedr, FRADU, 7, B.2, 98, 245, 231 OCU. Cockpit	2-16
❑ WE192	EE Canberra T.4	54	ex Long Marston, Firbeck, Winsford, Samlesbury, St Athan, 231 OCU, 360, 231 OCU, 39, 231 OCU, 3, 231 OCU. SOC 26-11-81. Cockpit	2-16
❑ WH953	EE Canberra B.6(mod)	55	ex Lowestoft, Stock, Farnborough, RAE. Short-built. Cockpit	2-16
❑ XH165	EE Canberra PR.9	60	ex Stock, St Athan, 1 PRU, 39, 13, 58. Short-built. SOC 10-4-94. Cockpit	2-16

WATTISHAM AIRFIELD north of the B1078, south of Stowmarket EGUW

Wattisham Station Heritage Museum: Run by the **Wattisham Museum Society**. Situated in the former Station Chapel during the airfield's USAAF days, the displays are dedicated to the airfield's incredible history from 1937 to date. The team has the use of a 'Cold War' hardened aircraft shelter which serves both as a workshop and storage site. Visitors can inspect this as well as the museum on special occasions. The cockpit of Lightning F.3 XP743 moved to Flixton, Suffolk, 17th March 2022. Gazelle AH.1 XX444 returned to the airfield site – see below.

◆ *Within an Army base, **visits must be pre-booked**.* | **wshmuseum@gmail.com** | **www.wattishamstationheritage.org**

❑ WD686* 'S'	Gloster Meteor NF.11	52	ex Defford, Old Sarum, Weybourne, Duxford, RAE Bedford, RRE, Defford, Wroughton, A&AEE, CFE, TRE Defford. AWA-built. SOC 2-11-67. Arrived 8-9-23	1-24

❑ XG194	'N'	Hawker Hunter FGA.9	56	ex North Luffenham, Cosford 8839M (25-10-84), 1 TWU, TWU, 229 OCU, 1, F.6, 92, 111, 43. Arrived 28-11-09. 111 Sqn 'Black Arrows' colours	[1]	1-24
❑ XT617		Westland Scout AH.1	65	ex airfield, Almondbank, Wroughton, 653, 660. F/n 6-15		1-24
❑ XT914	'Z'	McD Phantom FGR.2	68	ex Brampton, Leeming 9269M (5-10-92), 74, 228 OCU, 92, 56, 228 OCU, 92, 228 OCU, 56, 228 OCU, 17, 14, 228 OCU. Damaged 22-5-92. Arrived 8-3-12. 74 Sqn colours		1-24
❑ XZ605	'L'	Westland Lynx AH.7	79	ex M Wallop. NEA 8-13, arrived 28-4-14		1-24

■ **[1]** Restored to F.6 status and 'Black Arrows' colours when it was flown by Sqn Ldr Roger Topp, callsign *Blackjack Red 1*, from the famed 22-ship formations flown at Farnborough and Odiham in 1958.

No.**3 Regiment, Army Air Corps / 24 Air Mobile Brigade / 7 Battalion, REME**: With the arrival of AH-64Es, Apache AH.1s are entering store here during 2023. The situation is too fluid for this edition, but a pair are in use for instruction. Despite *W&R28* Gazelle AH.1 XZ330 *had* departed, with no 'forwarding address' perhaps as far back as 2011. Gazelle AH.1 XX444 travelled to Lyneham, Wilts, 23rd March 2023. By April 2022 Scout AH.1 XP907 (G-SROE) had moved to Debach, Suffolk.

❑ XX380	Sud Gazelle AH.1	74	ex Sunderland, Shawbury, Fleetlands. Westland-built. Displayed, at Gate 1, since 5-14	12-23
❑ ZA729	Sud Gazelle AH.1	80	ex Gütersloh, Shawbury, Fleetlands, 658, 1 Regt. 4 Regt, 661, 652. Westland-built. Dumped	12-23
❑ ZG920*	Westland Lynx AH.9A	92	ex Winterbourne Gunner, M Wallop. SOC 3-10-18. F/n 7-23	12-23
❑ ZJ171*	McDD Apache AH.1	99	ex Middle Wallop, Boscombe Down, N3266T. Instructional	12-23
❑ ZJ177*	McDD Apache AH.1	01	ex Gosport, Portsmouth, Gosport, Wattisham, M Wallop, 9 Regt. Westland-built. Crashed Afghanistan 4-9-08. Arrived 26-7-23. Instructional	12-23

SURREY

ASH on the A323 east of Aldershot

A Jaguar *should* still be kept at a *private* location in the area.

❑ XX751	'10'	SEPECAT Jaguar GR.1	74	ex Ipswich, Syerston, Cosford 8937M (29-5-87), Abingdon, 226 OCU, 14. Arrived 12-5-16	5-16

BROOKLANDS or Weybridge, on the B374 south of Weybridge

Brooklands Museum: The 'Aircraft Factory' – the Bellman hangar that used to sit astride the finishing straight of the historic motor racing circuit - and 'Flight Shed' are the main display halls. Beneath 'Flight Shed' are a workshop, store and archive. The clubhouse – once the design office of Barnes Wallis - the hill climb, the cars, motorcycles and push-bikes all add to the magic. Within the site is the **London Bus Museum** - entry is included with the site ticket - **www.londonbusmuseum.com** There is a very active **Brooklands Members** organisation with plenty of benefits for regular visitors.

See under Dunsfold, Surrey, for the 'VC10; Langley, Berks, for the 'Flea'; the Gliding Heritage Centre at Lasham, Hampshire, for the Gull III, Kronfeld Drone, Scud I and Willow Wren; and East Midlands, Leics, for Beagle 206 G-ARRM.

◆ *Brooklands Road, KT13 OSL* | **01932 857381** | **info@brooklandsmuseum.com** | **www.brooklandsmuseum.com**

Aircraft Factory and Flight Shed:

❑ 'G-EBED'		Vickers Viking replica	74	BAPC.114, ex 'R4', Chertsey, *The Land that Time Forgot* (1974). Arrived 27-10-87		1-24
❑ 'G-AACA'		Avro 504K replica	68	BAPC.177, ex 'G1381', Henlow. Arrived 29-1-87		1-24
❑ G-AZLP		Vickers Viscount 813	58	ex Sunderland, Middleton St George, BMA, SAA ZS-CDT. Hurn-built. CoA 3-4-82; de-reg 19-12-86. Arr 14-11-13. Cockpit, partially sectioned, in primer		1-24
❑ G-CHOI		White 'Baby' Canard rep	13	1912 replica, ground runs. Arrived 2013	[1]	1-22
❑ G-CJAU		White Sports Mono rep	16	1912 replica, ground runs. Arrived 2016. Workshop	[1]	1-22
❑ G-LOTI	'2'	Blériot XI replica	82	ex Bicester, Halton, Brooklands. CoA 19-7-82, de-reg 6-3-09. Arrived 1984, acquired 12-12-89	[2]	1-24
❑ G-VTOL		HS Harrier T.52 ZA250	71	ex ZA250, Dunsfold. CoA 2-11-86, de-reg 13-3-90. Arrived 6-4-89. Skyhook markings	[3]	1-24

	Reg	Code	Type	Year	History	Note	Date
❑	–		S-D Demoiselle XX rep	99	BAPC.256. Arrived 1-99. Ground runs	[1] [4]	3-20
❑	–	'3'	Sopwith Tabloid rep	13	BAPC.354, floatplane, partially covered. Handed over 27-11-13	[5]	1-24
❑	–		Vickers Vanguard EMU	59	ex East Fortune, South Kensington. Flightdeck mock-up, Trans Canada colours	[6]	1-24
❑	'B7270'		Sopwith Camel F1 replica	77	ex Land's End, Duxford, Chertsey, G-BFCZ (CoA 23-2-89, de-reg 23-1-03). Westward Airways-built. Arrived 14-4-88. 209 Sqn colours. Ground-runs	[7]	1-24
❑	'F5475'	'A'	Royal Aircraft Factory SE.5a replica	94	BAPC.250. Arrived 1996. *1st Battalion Honourable Artillery Company*	[8]	1-24
❑	'K5673'		Hawker Fury I replica	94	BAPC.249. Arrived 1996. 1 Sqn 'A' Flt colours	[9]	1-24
❑	N2980	'R'	Vickers Wellington Ia	39	ex 20 OTU, 37, 149. Ditched in Loch Ness 31-12-40. Arrived 27-9-85	[10]	1-24
❑	–		Vickers Wellington	11	BAPC.421. Arrived 2000. Forward fuselage	[11]	1-24
❑	Z2389	'XR-J'	Hawker Hurricane II	40	ex Murmansk, Sov AF, RAF 253, 136, 247, 71, 249. Shot down 20-6-42. Arrived 14-10-97. 71 Sqn colours	[12]	1-24
❑	WK198		V-S Swift F.4	53	ex Millom, Sunderland, Failsworth, Kirkham 7428M (23-7-57), Aldergrove, MoS. Arr 3-2-11. Fuselage, primer	[13]	1-24
❑	XD816		Vickers Valiant BK.1	56	ex Henlow, Abingdon, BAC, 214, 148. Last flown 23-4-68, SOC 26-8-70. Arrived 9-88. Cockpit, 'silver' colours	[14]	1-24
❑	'XF368'	'N'	Hawker Hunter F.51	56	ex 'XF314', Booker, Sandown, Tangmere, Dunsfold, G-9-439 (27-3-76), Danish AF E-412, Esk.724. Arrived 10-9-05. Stb primer / port 4 Sqn		1-24
❑	XP984		Hawker P.1127	64	ex Dunsfold, Lee-on-Solent, Manadon A2658 (12-2-76), RAE Thurleigh, (accident 31-10-75), RAE Farnborough. Arrived 28-9-00	[15]	1-24
❑	XV741		HS Harrier GR.3	69	ex Selby, Gosport, Culdrose, A2608[3], A2607 (25-4-91), Cosford, 233 OCU, 3, 233 OCU, 3. Arrived 2-4-19. 1969 Transatlantic air race colours	[16]	1-24
❑	ZA101		HS Hawk Mk.50 G-HAWK	76	ex Samlesbury, Warton, G-HAWK (de-reg 13-3-90), ZA101, XX155. Last flown 3-2-05, arrived 23-1-19	[17]	1-24
❑	–		BAC TSR.2 EMU	63	ex Newark, Farnborough. Arr 13-8-92. Cockpit, primer	[18]	1-24
❑	E-421		Hawker Hunter F.51	56	ex Brooklands Tech, Kingston, Dunsfold, G-9-443 (16-5-76), Aalborg, Esk.724, Danish AF. Arrived 18-3-89		1-24

■ **[1]** Canard Pusher, Sports Monoplane and Demoiselle built by Julian Aubert. **[2]** Blériot built by Mike Beach. The company L Blériot (Aeronuatics) Ltd was set up at Brooklands, becoming Blériot and Spad Ltd at nearby Addlestone, Surrey. In turn it became the Air Navigation and Engineering Co (ANEC) in 1919. **[3]** G-VTOL on loan from BAE Systems. **[4]** Demoiselle built on site 1996-1999 and based on the 1909 version with wing-warping and the original method of construction, bamboo. **[5]** Tabloid built under the leadership of Steve Green; representing the Schneider Trophy winner, flown by Howard 'Picky' Pixton at Monaco, April 1914, at 86mph. **[6]** Wooden ergonomics mock-up, built in the very same hangar it is now displayed in. **[7]** There's *another* 'B7270' at Tattershall Thorpe, Lincs. **[8]** SE.5a built on site. **[9]** Fury built on site. There is *another* 'K5673' - see Morpeth, N&T. **[10]** *R-for-Robert* factoids: First flown, at Brooklands, by 'Mutt' Summers 16-11-39; with 149 Sqn took part in the ill-fated 'Battle of Heligoland Bight' 18-12-39; total time 330:20. **[11]** Wellington based on an unidentified Hawarden-built centre section acquired from a site in Shropshire, circa 1986 - and best classified as a recreation. **[12]** Hurricane was shot down by a Bf 109F of JG5, near Murmansk. **[13]** Swift is on loan from Unimetals Industries Ltd. Piloted by Mike Lithgow in Libya, WK198 took the world speed record to 735.7mph on 25-9-53; sadly an F4D-1 Skyray raised it to 752.9mph just 48 hours later! **[14]** Valiant on loan from RAF Museum. XD816 was the last of the type to fly. **[15]** P.1127 - the 6th prototype - on loan from BAE Systems and fitted with an unidentified Harrier GR.3 wing. **[16]** On loan from Paul Griffith. Returned to GR.1 status, including nose profile. XV741 was flown by Sqn Ldr Tom Lecky-Thompson out of a yard near St Pancras railway station on 5-5-69 as the RAF entrant in the *Daily Mail* transatlantic air race, landing in New York 5 hours and 57 mins later. Back-up was GR.1 XV744 - see Tangmere, W Sussex. **[17]** Circa 2015 ZA101's one-piece wing was fitted to Indian AHP structural/ergonomic airframe Mk.102D ZJ100 and ZA101 was given ZJ100's original wing. By 2020, ZA101's original wing, wearing Indian AF markings, was moved from Brough to Brooklands for eventual re-fitting to ZA101. **[18]** TSR.2 a 'boiler plate' built for ejection seat trials.

Aircraft Park and other areas:

	Reg	Type	Year	History	Date
❑	G-AGRU	Vickers Viking 1	46	ex Cosford, Soesterberg, Channel, Kuwait Oil, BWIA, VP-TAX, G-AGRU, BEA. CoA 9-1-64, de-reg 9-6-64. Arr 27-6-91	1-24
❑	G-APEJ	Vickers Merchantman	61	ex Hunting, ABC, BEA. *Ajax*. CoA 29-1-93, de-reg 15-11-96. Arrived 26-8-95. Cockpit, in 'Strat Chamber'	1-24
❑	G-APEP	Vickers Merchantman	61	ex Hunting, ABC, BEA. *Superb*. CoA 1-10-98, de-reg 28-3-97. Flew in 17-10-96	1-24

	Reg		Type		Yr	History	Note	Date
❑	G-APIM		Vickers Viscount 806		58	ex Southend, BAF, BA, BEA. Damaged 11-1-88, de-reg 1-3-91. Arrived 11-2-90. *Viscount Stephen Piercey*		1-24
❑	G-ARVM		Vickers VC10 Srs 1101		64	ex Cosford, BA, BOAC. CoA 5-8-80, de-reg 9-11-79. Arrived 19-10-06. BA colours. Fuselage		1-24
❑	G-ASYD		BAC 111-475AM		65	ex Filton, BAe, BAC. CoA 13-7-94, de-reg 25-7-94. Flew in 14-7-94. 'Fly By Light Technology'.		1-24
❑	G-BBDG		BAC/Sud Concorde 202		74	ex Filton. CoA 1-3-82, de-reg 10-8-84. Last flight 24-12-81. Arrived 5-6-04	[1]	1-24
❑	–		Roe I Biplane replica		85	BAPC.187. Unveiled 5-6-88. In 'Avro' shed	[2]	1-24
❑	–		Vickers Vimy replica		97	BAPC.420. Arrived 2008. Cockpit, centre section, engine nacelles, displayed as 'mural'. Vickers building		1-24
❑	–		Vickers VC10 EMU		~	test shell, cockpit. BOAC colours		1-24
❑	–		BAC/Sud Concorde SIM		72	ex Filton; in its own building		1-24
❑	A4O-AB		Vickers VC10 1103		64	ex Sultan of Oman, G-ASIX, BCAL, BUA. Flew in 6-7-87		1-24
❑	NX71MY		Vickers Vimy replica		94	ex Dunsfold. Flew in 15-11-09. Vimy pavilion. Ground runs	[3]	1-24
❑	WF372	'T'	Vickers Varsity T.1		52	ex Sibson, 6 FTS, 1 ANS, RAFC, 201 AFS. SOC 25-3-76. Arrived 7-11-88		1-24
❑	XT575		Vickers Viscount 837		60	ex Bruntingthorpe, DRA Bedford, OE-LAG. SOC 10-7-93. Arrived 14-1-96. Cockpit		1-24

■ **[1]** *Delta-Golf* factoids: total hours 1,282, landings 633. **[2]** Roe Biplane largely built on-site by Mike Beach. **[3]** Vimy was officially handed over to the museum by Peter McMillan on 26-8-06.

Deep Stores: ◆ **Not** *available for inspection.*

	Reg		Type		Yr	History	Note	Date
❑	G-BJHV		Voisin scale replica		r81	ex Redhill, Brooklands, Old Warden. De-reg 4-7-91. Arr 1987		3-20
❑	G-ROEI		Roe I Biplane replica		08	ex off-site, Filton, Brooklands. Built on site. Arr 2017	[1]	3-20
❑	–		Rogallo hang-glider		73	*Aerial.* On loan		3-18
❑	–		'hang-glider'		~	-	[2]	3-18
❑	–		BAC 111 EMU		~	flightdeck mock-up		1-21
❑	F-BGEQ		DH Tiger Moth		44	ex Hungerford, Brooklands, Chessington, Brooklands, French mil, Mk.I NL846, n/s. Morris-built	[3]	3-18
❑	WP921		DHC Chipmunk T.10	G-ATJJ	52	ex Croydon, Wallingford, Benson, G-ATJJ (de-reg 19-1-68), WP921, Colerne SF, Oxford UAS, HCMSU, 10 RFS. SOC 16-7-73. Hawarden-built. Cockpit. Arrived 1995.	[4]	3-20

■ **[1]** Roe registered to Brooklands Museum. **[2]** Unidentified hang-glider, previously in the 'Balloon' Hangar. **[3]** Tiger stored off-site from 30-1-14 by BAE Systems. **[4]** Chipmunk on loan from Peter Smith.

CATERHAM west of the A22, north of Junction 6 on the M25

Nalson Aviation: The long established business continues to process light aircraft types for spares. Turn-around is swift.

◆ *Prior arrangement* **only** | **www.nalsonaviation.com**

CHARLWOOD west of the A23/A217 junction, north of Gatwick Airport

Gatwick Aviation Museum: Mostly housed in an impressive, purpose-built, display hall. Several aircraft are maintained in ground running condition. For those of such a mind, the grounds offer great views of Gatwick's traffic!

By late 2020 the cockpit of Lightning F.53 ZF589 had moved on – no 'forwarding address'.

◆ *Lowfield Heath Road, Charlwood, RH6 0BT* | **01293 862294** | **hello@gamc.org.uk** | **www.gamc.org.uk**

	Reg		Type		Yr	History	Note	Date
❑	'G-RAFM'		Robinson R22	G-OTHL	87	ex Hendon, Redhill. CoA 2-3-00, de-reg 8-2-00		1-24
❑	–		BN Islander		~	ex Crawley, Bristow. Cockpit. First noted 8-17	[1]	1-24
❑	VZ638		Gloster Meteor T.7	G-JETM	49	ex N Weald, Hurn, Southampton, G-JETM (de-reg 15-12-09), Southend, Kemble, CAW, RAFC, 237 OCU, 501, Biggin Hill SF, FCCS, 85, 54, 25, 500. SOC 12-1-72. Arrived 7-88. Black c/s		1-24
❑	WK146		EE Canberra B.2		54	ex Hull, Wroughton, Abingdon, Bicester, 59, 102. Avro-built. SOC 12-5-67. Arr 2001. Cockpit, sectioned		1-24
❑	WP308	'572'	Percival Sea Prince T.1	G-GACA	52	ex Staverton, G-GACA (de-reg 15-12-09), Kemble, 750, Sydenham, 750, Lossiemouth, 750. SOC 16-9-80. Arrived 12-11-89. 750 Sqn colours		1-24
❑	WR982	'J'	Avro Shackleton MR.3/3		58	ex Cosford 8106M (28-9-70), 201, 206, MoA, 205, 203, 206. Arrived 7-89		1-24

	Serial	Code	Type	Other id	Year	History	Note	Last noted
❑	'XE489'	'485'	Hawker Sea Hawk FB.3	G-JETH	54	ex Jet Heritage, Hurn G-JETH (de-reg 15-12-09), WM983, Chilton Cantelo, Culdrose, 'SAH-6', A2511, FRU, 806, 811. SOC 1-9-61. Arrived 10-10-87. 899 Sqn colours	[2]	1-24
❑	XL591	'82'	Hawker Hunter T.7B		58	ex Kemble, Ipswich, Colsterworth, Shawbury, 237 OCU, 208, 237 OCU, 208, 237 OCU, 4 FTS, RAE, 4 FTS, 229 OCU, FCS. SOC 11-10-93. Arrived 2002. 4 FTS colours		1-24
❑	XN923		Blackburn Buccaneer S.1		62	ex Boscombe Down, West Freugh, A&AEE, RAE, A&AEE, RAE, A&AEE, RAE, A&AEE, 700Z. SOC 17-5-54. Arrived 23-3-90		1-24
❑	XS587		DH Sea Vixen FAW.2(TT)	G-VIXN	65	ex Hurn G-VIXN (de-reg 15-12-09), FRL, 8828M, RAE, FRADU, FRU, 899, 893. Hawarden-built. Last flown 6-6-84, SOC 4-2-85. Arrived 9-90		1-24
❑	XV751	'AU'	HS Harrier GR.3		69	ex Bruntingthorpe, Charlwood, Lee-on-Solent A2672, A2760, 3, 1, 3, 20, 233 OCU. Arrived 4-10-95. 3 Sqn c/s		1-24
❑	–		Hawker Hunter F.51	E-430	56	ex Charlwood, Faygate, Chertsey, Dunsfold, G-9-448, Esk.724, Dan AF. FAA colours, GA.11-style	[3]	1-24
❑	53-671		EE Lightning F.53	ZF579	67	ex Portsmouth, Luxembourg, *Wing Commander* (1999), Stretton, Warton, Saudi AF 203, 53-671, G-27-41. Last flown 14-1-86. Arr 18-4-00. Saudi AF colours		1-24
❑	J-1605		DH Venom FB.50	G-BLID	52	ex Duxford, G-BLID (de-reg 15-12-09), Swiss AF. Swiss built. Arrived 27-10-89		1-24

■ **[1]** The Islander is a full-motion simulator created by Thales; but looks *very* un-Islander-ish – so wholly 'synthetic'? **[2]** When Jet Heritage was restoring FGA.6 XE489 (G-JETH) to flight it was found that the spar attachments had been cut - very probably when it was moved by road to Southend, Essex, 5-67. To get around this FB.3 WM983 was borrowed from the Sea Scouts at Chilton Cantelo, Somerset, 8-85 and its *entire* fuselage was used in G-JETH, along with the wings of XE489. By 3-87 the Sea Scouts got 'their' Sea Hawk back. It constituted the fuselage of XE489 plus the wings of 'WM983', which came from FGA.4 WV909 which had been fitted as far back as the mid-1960s when it was in service on the 'deck' at SAH Culdrose. Chilton Cantelo disposed of 'WM983' (but in the majority XE489) on 8-8-89 when it was sold in the Netherlands. **[3]** Presented by Adrian Wright of Aerospace Logistics - see below. Fitted with wings of XF418 and XG226 - for the latter see also East Midlands, Leics, and Manston, Kent.

Aerospace Logistics: Has a storage site here, while the main base is Horsham, W Sussex: there is some 'shuffling' of stock between the two. Sea King HAR.3 ZE369 migrated to Scalby, N Yorks, on 20th January 2022.

◆ **Strictly** *by prior arrangement* **only** | **www.asl-uk.com**

	Serial	Code	Type	Year	History	Last noted
❑	XZ497	'126'	HS Sea Harrier F/A.2	82	ex St Athan, 801, A&AEE, FRS.1, 899, 801	8-22
❑	XZ595		Westland Sea King HAR.3	78	ex 202, 22, 202. First noted 7-18	11-21
❑	ZA130	'19'	Westland Sea King HU.5SAR	81	ex Gosport, 771, *Gannet* Flt, 706, 819, 824, Falklands, 826. First noted 7-18	11-21
❑	ZA312		Westland Sea King HC.4	81	ex Gosport, QinetiQ, 848, 707, 845, 846, 707, 846. F/n 7-18	8-22
❑	ZE698	'123'	HS Sea Harrier F/A.2	88	ex St Athan, 800, FRS.1, 800, 801,899, 801	8-22

CHERTSEY northeast of Junction 12 of the M25 and Junction 2 of the M3

Thorpe Park: Last noted in August 2014, Agusta 109A 'G-SARD' (G-DNHI) is believed to be long gone.

COBHAM north of the M25, east of Woking

Delta Force Paintball: Surrey: ◆ *Prior arrangement* **only** | **www.paintballgames.co.uk**

	Serial	Type	Year	History	Note	Last noted
❑	–	Westland WG.30	~	Displayed at site entrance	[1]	1-20
❑	XZ217	Westland Lynx AH.7	79	ex *Edge of Tomorrow*, Barby, Ipswich, Fleetlands, 655	[2]	1-22

■ **[1]** Believed to be WG.30-100 G-BIWY which was last noted at Weston-super-Mare, Somerset, in *W&R18* (p190) as being exported to Italy for Agusta in November 2000. **[2]** Identity confirmed.

DUNSFOLD AERODROME or even Dunsfold Park, on the A281 south of Guildford EGTD

During the spring of 2023 construction of a new roundabout and access road to the site began, bringing the reality of 'Dunsfold Park - A New Surrey Village' with up to 1,800 houses nearer.

See under Balcombe, West Sussex, for a plan for a museum at Dunsfold Park.

Brooklands Museum: In co-operation with the museum the **Hawker Association** is restoring the last Kingston-built Hunter T.7, XL623. When completed it will be displayed on a pole near to the former Hawker plant at Kingston.

◆ *Prior arrangement* **only** | **www.brooklandsmuseum.com**

❑ ZA150 'J'	Vickers VC10 K.3 N150ZA	70	ex Brize Norton, 101, 5H-MOG East African AW. Arrived 24-9-13. Taxiable	[1]	12-23
❑ XL623	Hawker Hunter T.7	59	ex Woking, Newton, Cosford 8770M (31-12-82), 1 TWU, 74,19, 1, 43, 92, 208, 65. Arrived 22-7-18		12-22

■ **[1]** Last of 54 VC10s built.

Reg Day Memorial Museum: (Also known as the Dunsfold Airfield Museum): A volunteer crew maintains a fascinating museum devoted to the airfield's wartime and Hawker heritage. ◆ **Note**: *Prior arrangement* **only**. *Within the security compound:* ***no*** *access to other areas is permitted* | **https://regdaymuseum.co.uk**

Aviation Filming Ltd (previously Aces High): Much of the hardware used in filming is transitory and only long-term 'stars' are included here. C-47A N147DC has been kept at North Weald, Essex, since late 2019.

Jetstream T.3 N437TH departed by road to St Athan; Commando Mk.2C SL-01 left 23rd April 2022, reported for export to China. Instead, it was stored at Lee-on-Solent, Hampshire, before travelling to St Athan, Wales, arriving 11th May 2023.

◆ **Strictly** *prior arrangement* **only** | **www.aviationfilming.com**

❑ G-BDXJ	Boeing 747-236B N88892	80	ex *Casino Royale*, Air Atlanta Europe, BA G-BDXJ (de-reg 12-1-11), N1792B. Flew in 25-5-05		1-24
❑ G-BNLY	Boeing 747-436	93	ex Rhoose, BA, N60659. De-reg 16-12-20. *City of Swansea*. Arrived 5-12-20	[1]	1-24
❑ G-CIVW	Boeing 747-436	98	ex Rhoose, Hurn, BA. CoA 18-4-21, de-reg 30-10-20 Arrived 22-10-20	[2]	1-24
❑ 'OE-FZO'*	BN Islander	~	ex *Spectre*. Fuselage, first noted 11-22		11-22
❑ N797EL	Boeing 737-500	93	ex Hurn, European, Braathens LN-BRX. Last flown 21-1-15. Arrived 16-9-18. Forward fuselage		8-22
❑ WV795	Hawker Sea Hawk FGA.6	54	ex Farnborough, Bruntingthorpe, Cranfield, B'thorpe, Hurn, Rhoose, Culdrose A2661, Halton 8151M, Sydenham, 738, 806, 700. SOC 17-3-71. 806 'Ace of Diamonds' colours		12-22
❑ XL621	Hawker Hunter T.7 G-BNCX	59	ex Brooklands, Hurn, G-BNCX (de-reg-1-3-93), RAE, 238 OCU, RAE. SOC 10-12-86. ETPS colours		12-22
❑ ZE395	HSA HS.125 CC.3	93	ex Northolt, 32. Flew in 25-3-15		11-22
❑ 72+59	Bell UH-1D Iroquois	70	ex HEER. Dornier-built. First noted 12-18	[3]	11-22
❑ '335'	Mil Mi-24 *Hind-D*	~	ex Leavesden, '03 red', N Weald, Chester, Latvia, USSR (3532461715415) Hungarian colours. Off-site		5-19
❑ 'RA-914B11'	Mil Mi-8 *Hip*	~	first noted 8-20		12-22

■ **[1]** *Lima-Yankee* joined BA on 1-2-93 and carried out its last service 22-3-20, amassing 122,358 hours. **[2]** *Victor-Whisky* joined BA on 15-5-98; last service 17-7-20, amassing 90,617 hours. **[3]** Composite, includes elements of 73+01.

EGHAM on the A30 west of Staines

Air Forces Memorial - Commonwealth War Graves Commission: "He is not missing, he is here." This is a quote from Field Marshal Lord Plumer when he opened the memorial at Ypres in 1927, but it sums up beautifully the role of the famed Runnymede memorial. Here is a tribute to the aircrew of RAF, Commonwealth and allied forces that have no known grave. Currently 20,291 souls are commemorated. ◆ *Cooper's Hill Lane, TW20 0LB* | **www.cwgc.org**

Jeremy Hall: Has created the forward fuselage (all 21ft of it) of a Lancaster, using as many original parts as possible. It 'does the rounds' of shows and events.

❑ –	Avro Lancaster replica	~	ex Woodford. *Hi Ho!, Hi Ho!* to port and *Maggie's Murderous Mission* to stb. Forward fuselage	11-19

FARNHAM on the A31 southwest of Aldershot

Despite the date, the Terrier is *believed* extant. Lightning F.6 cockpit XS933 moved to Binbrook, Lincs, by October 2021.

❑ G-ASYN	Beagle Terrier 2	47	ex Doncaster, Bruntingthorpe, Derby, Southend, Sibson, Auster AOP.6 VF519, 661. Damaged 2-1-76, de-reg 26-10-78	2-12

GODALMING on the A3100, southwest of Guildford

Restoration of a former Soviet Spitfire is *believed* to make progress in the area.

❑ SM639	V-S Spitfire IX G-CKYM	44	ex Norwich, Colchester, Milden, Russia, USSR, Sov AF, RAF no service. CBAF-built. Recovered 1993. Arrived 5-05	N3-23

GODSTONE Last noted in February 2013, Scout AH.1 XV124 has been deleted.

PIRBRIGHT on the A324 west of Woking

Army Training Centre, Pirbright Camp:

❑ XZ651	'O'	Westland Lynx AH.7	80	ex Middle Wallop, AH.1. Arrived 24-6-20	6-20
❑ ZE380		Westland Lynx AH.9A	86	ex Middle Wallop. SOC 1-2-18. Arrived 9-12-19	7-22

REDHILL AERODROME south of South Nutfield, southeast of Redhill EGKR

Cessna 152s G-BRNE and G-BRUM have been deleted.

❑ G-NOIL*		BN Islander	73	ex 4X-AYR, G-BJWO, 4X-AYR, SX-BBX, 4X-AYR, G-BAXC. FBN-built. CoA 116-1-16, arrived 29-6-21	11-22

SUTTON

Simon Balch: ◆ *Prior arrangement* **only**

❑ XP853		Westland Scout AH.1	61	ex Dunkeswell, Bramley, Arborfield, Middle Wallop, 655	12-22
❑ XW796	'X'	Westland Scout AH.1	65	ex Layer Marney, Hadleigh, Ipswich, Wattisham, Middle Wallop, Wroughton, 660, 659. Arrived 19-6-20	12-22
❑ ZH766		Northrop Chukar D.2	c94	ex Hemel Hempstead, Aberporth	[1] 12-22

■ **[1]** Not deployed until 2001; one and only launch failed 29-1-01. With parts from ZJ481, ex Culdrose and Manorbier.

WALTON ON THAMES

Adrian Windsor: *Should* have a Hunter cockpit in the area.

❑ E-420		Hawker Hunter F.51	56	ex Marlow, Ascot, Dunsfold G-9-442 (1-5-76), Danish AF E-420. Cockpit	1-14

WHYTELEAFE on the A22 southeast of Croydon

Gary Brown: The Buchón project will appear in the guise of a *Battle of Britain* film 'extra', using as many original parts, including Bf 109, as possible. ◆ *Prior application* **only**

❑ –		Hispano Buchón FSM	~	ex Lingfield, Bf 109G 'FM+BB', Germany	7-17

EAST SUSSEX

Includes the unitary authority of Brighton and Hove

BEXHILL on the A259 west of Hastings

A Swallow is under restoration at a *private* address in the locality.

❑ G-ACXE		Klemm L25cl Swallow	34	ex 'Hastings', Bagshot, Birmingham. CoA 7-4-40	N2-18

BRIGHTON

No.**225 (Brighton No.1) Squadron Air Cadets**: Lewes Road.

❑ WD370		DHC Chipmunk T.10	51	ex Hove, 3 AEF, 2 SoTT, 1 AEF, Hull UAS, 2 BTFS. SOC 12-3-75. Hawarden-built. Cockpit	12-22

CHAILEY on the A275 north of Lewes

A pair of cockpits *should* still be with a *private* collector in the area.

❑ WH964		EE Canberra E.15	55	ex Bruntingthorpe, Cosford 8870M, St Athan, 100, 98, B.15, 98, Akrotiri Wing, 32, B.6, 12. Short-built. Cockpit	12-11
❑ XG195		Hawker Hunter FGA.9	56	ex Sleap, Seighford, Macclesfield, Bitteswell, G-9-453 (12-2-76), 208, F.6, 1, 19. Cockpit	12-11

DITCHLING on the B2112 east of Hassocks

Blackberry Wood: Among a variety of 'dwellings' offered at the venue is a two-berth 'Holicopter' – aka Wessex.
◆ *Prior arrangement* **only** | **www.blackberrywood.com**

❑ XS886	'27'	Westland Wessex HAS.1	66	ex Ipswich, Evesham, Birmingham, Lee-on-Solent A2685 (2-4-80), Wroughton, 771, 706, *Hermes* SAR Flt, 706, 826	12-23

FOREST ROW on the A22 south of East Grinstead

Bullswood Skirmish Paintball Centre: Has closed down: the hulk of Cherokee Six G-BSTV is unaccounted for.

HAILSHAM on the A22 north of Eastbourne

David Bird: Is restoring a Prentice. Fellow VR192 (G-APIT) is on loan at Brenzett, Kent. ◆ *Prior arrangement* **only**

❑ ZS-EUS		Percival Prentice	49	ex South Africa, SAAF Museum, ZS-EUS, G-AOPL, VS609, 7 FTS. Arrived 2010	9-20

HASTINGS

The former Afghan Hawker Hinds are *believed* stored in the locality. ◆ **Strictly private, not** *available for inspection*

❑ K5409	Hawker Hind	36	ex Kabul, Afghan AF, RAF, 211, 218, 57, 52	7-10
❑ K5462	Hawker Hind	36	ex Kabul, Afghan AF, India, RAF 113, 15	7-10
❑ K5554	Hawker Hind	36	ex Kabul, Afghan AF, RAF 211, 113, 12	7-10
❑ K6618	Hawker Hind	36	ex Kabul, Afghan AF, India, RAF 211, 98	7-10
❑ K6833	Hawker Hind	37	ex Kabul, Afghan AF, India, RAF 211, 82	7-10
❑ L7191	Hawker Hind	37	ex Kabul, Afghan AF, RAF ME, 21	7-10

NEWHAVEN east of Brighton on the A259

Newhaven Fort: The fort is undergoing a £7.5 million restoration – reopening in 2025. See Robertsbridge, below. **www.newhavenfort.org.uk**

ROBERTSBRIDGE on the A21 northwest of Hastings

Robertsbridge Aviation Centre: Run by the **Robertsbridge Aviation Society** (RAS); 2024 marks the 60th anniversary of the centre. RAS had provided displays for Newhaven Fort – it is not known if this will be the case when that venue re-opens.
◆ *Annual open day and other events. Bush Barn, Silver Hill, TN32 5PA* | **email** via website | **www.robertsbridgeaviationsociety.com**

❑ WA630	Gloster Meteor T.7	49	ex Newhaven, Robertsbridge, Sevenoaks, Oakington SF, 4 FTS, 205 AFS, RAFC. SOC 16-11-62. Arrived 1991. Cockpit	5-23
❑ WE173	EE Canberra PR.3	53	ex Stock, Coltishall, Farnborough, RAE, 39, 69, Upwood SF, 58, 82. SOC 31-3-81. Arrived 1996. Cockpit	5-23
❑ WN907	Hawker Hunter F.2	54	ex Walpole, Ascot, St Athan, Colerne, Melksham 7416M (1-8-57), 257. AWA-built. Arrived 17-3-02. Cockpit	5-23
❑ XJ488	DH Sea Vixen FAW.1	58	ex Nottingham, New Milton, Portsmouth, Boscombe Down, A&AEE, 22 JSTU, A&AEE, DH, RRE, A&AEE, RAE, DH. Christchurch-built. SOC 23-3-72. Arrived 1997. Cockpit	5-23
❑ XP701	EE Lightning F.3	63	ex High Halden, Hawkinge, Binbrook 8924M (9-2-86), LTF, 5, 11, 56, 29, 111, 29, A&AEE. Arrived 1991. Cockpit	5-23
❑ XR681	Hunting Jet Provost T.4	63	ex Newhaven, Odiham, Abingdon 8588M, RAFEF, CATCS, 6 FTS, RAFC. SOC 1-10-71. Arrived 2002. Cockpit	5-23

ST LEONARDS-ON-SEA west of Hastings

Retrotec / Aero Vintage: See under Duxford, Cambs, for the associated **Historic Aircraft Collection of Jersey** (HAC). Retrotec is involved in The People's Mosquito project, which is in its early stages – **www.peoplesmosquito.org.uk.**
◆ **Strictly private** *location,* **not** *available for inspection* | **www.retrotec-ltd.co.uk**

❑ K5600	Hawker Audax I	G-BVVI	37	ex Kirkham 2015M (18-6-40), SAC, 226. Westland-built. Off-site	[1] N3-23

❑ L7181*		Hawker Hind I	G-CBLK	37	ex Duxford, St Leonards-on-Sea, Rockliffe, Canada, Kabul, Afghanistan AF, RAF, 211. Arrived 4-10-23	[1] 10-23
❑ EF545		V-S Spitfire V	G-CDGY	43	ex New Zealand, ZK-MKV, New Guinea, RAAF A58-149, EF545 n/s. Westland-built. Off-site	[2] N8-21
❑ 1342		Yakovlev Yak-1	G-BTZD	41	ex Sudbury, Audley End, Paddock Wood, USSR	[3] 1-20
❑ 4034		Messerschmitt Bf 109E-1	G-CDTI	39	ex India, JG53, force-landed Kent 11-2-40. Focke-Wulf-built. Salvaged 2002	[1] N1-21
❑ –*	'SB+UG'	MS Criquet	G-BPHZ	46	ex Audley End, Duxford, St Leonards-on-Sea, 'DM+BK', 'TA+RC', Duxford, F-BJQG. French mil. CoA 29-4-09. Arrived 4-10-23	[1] [4] 10-23

■ **[1]** Registered to Aero Vintage Ltd. **[2]** Registered to Warbird Experiences 8-21. **[3]** Yak registered to HAC. **[4]** MS.505 started as Fi 156 airframe (w/nr.1827), completed as a Criquet with a Jacobs R-755A2.

SEDLESCOMBE AERODROME on the B2244 north of Hastings

HM.293 G-AXPG was donated to the PFA... sorry, LAA and moved to Bicester, Oxfordshire, for restoration in 2021 prior to settling on Turweston, Bucks, on 30th March 2022. Jodel G-AWFT has been deleted.

❑ G-BOFL*	Cessna 152		80	ex Little Gransden, Little Staughton, N5457H. CoA 30-11-11, de-reg 4-10-21	8-22
❑ G-BOFM*	Cessna 152		81	ex Little Gransden, Little Staughton, Sibson, N6445M. De-reg 26-2-13	8-21

In the locality a Spitfire restoration project is *believed* to be still current at a *private* location.

❑ BM539	V-S Spitfire V	G-SSVB	42	ex G-CGBI, BM539, 19, 485, 610, 411, 242. CBAF-built. Crashed 9-7-43, excavated 8-07	N12-21

TICEHURST on the B2099 west of Hawkhurst

A *private* site in the *general* area has gained a Wessex.

❑ XR502	'Z'	Westland Wessex HC.2	N486KA	63	ex Sevenoaks, G-CCUP (de-reg 7-1-13), Colsterworth, Fleetlands, 60, 72, WTF, 18, 1 FTU. SOC 16-3-00. F/n 8-21	8-21
❑ ZF587		EE Lightning F.53		68	ex Headcorn, Reading, Portsmouth, *Wing Commander* (1997), Portsmouth, Stretton, Warton, Saudi AF 215, 53-691, G-27-61. Cockpit. Arrived 1-2-20	8-21

WEST SUSSEX

AMBERLEY on the B2139 west of Storrington

Amberley Museum and Heritage Centre: Standard and narrow-gauge railways, vintage road transport of all sorts and much more in the you-name-it category make this a 'must do' even if it doesn't have an aviation 'flavour'. A museum supporter has created a full-size Lancaster forward fuselage, using many original/contemporary instruments and fittings based upon largely a wood structure. The display is ingeniously arranged to that the starboard side of the 'fuselage' is absent, allowing the viewing public an unlimited view of the interior.

◆ *New Barn Road, BN18 9LT* | **01998 831370** | **office@amberleymuseum.co.uk** | **www.amberleymuseum.co.uk**

❑ G-AHWJ*	Taylorcraft Plus D	42	ex Worthing, Auster I LB294, West Raynham SF, Milfield SF, 43 OTU, 653. De-reg 11-11-11. Off-site	8-21
❑ –*	Avro Lancaster FSM	20	forward fuselage - see narrative above	5-23

BALCOMBE on the B2036, south of Crawley

Wings World War Two Remembrance Museum: Run by Daniel and Kevin Hunt and friends. The quality of displays is excellent, including elements of Hampden I P1273 'PL-Q' salvaged from the Russo-Finnish border; the substantial remains of A-20G Havoc 43-21664, also acquired from Russia (and previously formally listed, but it lacks the cockpit). Other crash-site relics are a 51 Squadron Halifax; Hurricane II BD731 salvaged from Murmansk; two Mount Farm-based USAAF F-5B Lightnings and a pair of Nakajima Ki-43 Hayabushas from the Kurile Isles.

Workmaster fuselage G-OJAS on its lofty perch, August 2023. *Brian Downs*

There are plans for a museum at **Dunsfold**, Surrey, dedicated to the former airfield's prolific time as a Hawker/HSA facility and its wartime activity as a Mitchell haven: hence the acquisition of the Kestrel and *Bedsheet Bomber* – see below.

◆ *Not all airframes listed will be on public display. Brantridge Lane, off High Beeches Lane, RH17 6JT* | **info@wingsmuseum.co.uk** | **www.wingsmuseum.co.uk** | **www.facebook.com/wingskestrel**

❑ G-AIUA		Miles Hawk Trainer III	40	ex Redhill, King's Lynn, West Chiltington, Benington, Bushey, Old Warden, Duxford, Felthorpe, T9768, 10 AGS, 7 FIS, 15 EFTS, Wyton SF. Phillips & Powis-built. CoA 13-7-67. Acquired 2003. Fuselage	[1]	1-24
❑ G-OJAS		Auster J1U Workmaster	52	ex Redhill, F-BJAS, F-WJAS, F-OBHT. Acquired 2003		1-24
❑ –		Bristol Beaufighter If	~	ex Australia, South Africa. Cockpit. Arrived 9-15	[2]	1-24
❑ –		Bristol Beaufort VIII	~	ex Australia, Papua New Guinea. Cockpit, arrived 3-20	[3]	1-24
❑ WD377		DHC Chipmunk T.10	51	ex Blackburn, Haverhill, Dumfries, 12 AEF, Glasgow UAS, HCEU, 11 RFS, 2 BFTS. Hawarden-built. Cr 29-7-66. Cockpit	[4]	1-24
❑ –		DHC Chipmunk T.10	51	ex South Molton, Firbeck, Salisbury, Stamford, Blackburn, Radley. Forward cockpit	[5]	1-22
❑ WK127	'FO'	EE Canberra TT.18	54	ex Peterborough, Bassingbourn, Wyton 8985M, 100, 7, B.2, 10. Damaged 13-12-88. Avro-built. Arr 26-1-16. Cockpit		1-24
❑ XM468		Hunting Jet Provost T.3	60	ex Terrington St Clement, King's Lynn, Stock, St Athan, Halton 8081M (6-5-70), Shawbury, 6 FTS, RAFC. Cockpit		1-22
❑ XS694*		HS Kestrel FGA.1	64	ex off-site store, Florida, NASA 520, Langley, USAF 64-18267, TES-CFE XS694. Crashed 27-8-67. Acquired 7-18, moved on site 4-8-22		1-24
❑ 339		Nakajima B5N2 *Kate*	c44	ex Redhill, Kurile Island. Acquired 2003. Front fuselage		1-24
❑ '2100766'	'4U-D'	Douglas C-47A-65-DL Skytrain	42	ex N Weald, Woodley, Kew, Cranfield, 6W-SAF, F-GEFU, Senegalese AF, USAF MAAG Brussels, USAAF 42-100611. Long Beach-built. *Lilly Bell II*. Acquired 9-07. Cockpit and fuselage section	[6]	1-24
❑ 43-4315	'17'	Bell P-63C Kingcobra	43	ex Redhill, Kurile Island. Acquired 2003. *Little Toots*	[7]	1-24
❑ 43-36140		NAA B-25J Mitchell	43	ex Redhill, Kurile Island. Acquired 2003. Front fuselage		1-24
❑ 64-17657		Douglas B-26K Invader N99218	64	ex Redhill, South Molton, Canterbury, Norwich, Ludham, Booker, Canterbury, Southend, Chino, USAF, USAAF 43-22649. Arrived 2-10. *Victory Belle*. Cockpit	[8]	1-24

■ **[1]** See under Magister N3788 at Shuttleworth, Beds. **[2]** Beaufighter discovered in a scrapyard in Cape Town and restored by Peter Sledge, Warbird Restorations Downunder. **[3]** Beaufort is believed to be A9-555, which served with 100 Sqn RAAF. **[4]** Rear fuselage of WD377 can be found under Upper Ballinderry, N Ireland. **[5]** *Likely* bloodline of the Chipmunk is that it is WG319 SOC 18-7-61 at Valley. **[6]** Cockpit of C-47A 6W-SAF has been grafted to the fuselage of C-47B 'FL586' (ex OO-SMA, N99346, Belgian AF K-1 / OT-CWA, 43-49240. **[7]** Also substantial remains of 44-11137, from the same source. **[8]** Heavily re-engineered B-26 Invader by On Mark Engineering at Van Nuys, California, given new USAF serial.

Off-site: Kestrel XS694 moved *on*-site on 4th August 2022 - witness above. Inspection of the B-25 is *not* possible.

❑ 44-30861	NAA VB-25N-NC Mitchell N9089Z	45	ex Crowland, Booker, N Weald, Duxford, 'HD368', Southend, Biggin Hill, N9089Z, B-25J 44-30861. *Bedsheet Bomber*. Acquired 7-19; final sections arrived 3-5-22	1-24

BOGNOR REGIS on the A27 southeast of Chichester

Aviator Bar and Grill: At the Carlton Hotel on the Esplanade, what was the Aviator Bar and Grill is now the Promenade Bar. As of December 2023, the cockpit of Bandeirante G-OHIG had gone – destination/fate undetermined.

BRIGHTON CITY AIRPORT or Shoreham EGKA

Airport Visitor Centre: Offers an array of archives and artefacts, and tours, on the incredible history of this aerodrome.
◆ **01273 467351 | visitorcentre@gmail.com | https://flybrighton.com/home-page/history-museum-tours**

Greater Brighton Metropolitan College: Motor and aero engineering campus.
◆ *Prior arrangement* **only | www.gbmc.ac.uk**

❑	G-AVKL		Piper Twin Comanche	66	ex OY-DHL, G-AVKL, N8284Y. CoA 27-6-08, de-reg 28-9-07	7-21
❑	G-AWKX		Beech Queen Air A65	68	CoA 25-10-89, de-reg 19-12-90. Forward fuselage	7-21
❑	G-AWVJ		HP Jetstream T.2	68	ex Boscombe Down, 750, A&AEE, XX475, N1036S, G-AWVJ. Arrived 20-11-05	12-22
❑	G-SACD		Cessna F.172H	67	ex G-AVCD. Reims-built. CoA 27-7-00, de-reg 29-11-10	2-22
❑	XX491	'K'	HP Jetstream T.1	76	ex Ipswich, Culdrose, Cranwell, 45, 3 FTS, 45, 6 FTS, METS. SAL-completed. Arrived 10-11-05	12-22

Also:

❑	G-APAJ		Thruxton Jackaroo	40	ex Winchester, VH-KRK, G-APAJ, T5616, 63 GCF, 5 RFS, 12 RFS, 23 RFS, 25 RFS, 28 EFTS, 24 EFTS, Church Fenton SF, 10 FIS, 5 FIS. Jackaroo conversion 1958	12-22
❑	'WV514'	'CN'	Percival Provost T.51 G-BLIW	54	ex Baldonnel, Irish Air Corps 177. Accident 16-9-10. CoA 16-5-05	12-22
❑	WW447	'F'	Percival Provost T.1 G-CMIP	55	ex Reading, Exeter, CATCS, CNCS, RAFC. SOC 24-1-69. Fuselage	3-23
❑	115227*	'10'	NAA T-6G Texan G-BKRA	51	ex Sandown, It AF MM63664, USAF 51-15227. CoA 13-8-16. US Navy colours	12-22

Provost T.1 WW447, March 2023. *Ian Haskell*

CHICHESTER

Chichester College: By mid-2022 the college had disposed of Boeing 737 F-GCSL to Winchester, Hampshire.

Jungle Paradise Adventure Golf Course: ◆ *Prior arrangement* **only | www.chichestergolf.com**

❑	OO-MHB	Piper Dakota 236	80	ex Squires Gate, Southend. Accident 20-10-90. F/n 2-15	12-23

Locally: An Airedale and a Safir are kept in the *general* area at a *private* location.

❑	G-AVKP	Beagle Airedale	63	ex Peplow, SE-EGA. CoA 26-9-03	3-21
❑	G-BCFW	SAAB Safir	62	ex Peplow, PH-RLZ. CoA 24-7-06	3-21

CHICHESTER AERODROME or Goodwood EGHR

Spitfire Flight Academy: (Note change of name.) Experience flights and training operations, which are also staged from Solent Airport - Lee-on-Solent, Hampshire, have expanded considerably. The fleet includes Spitfire Tr.IXs BS410 (G-TCHI) SM520 (G-ILDA) and T-6G Texan 'KF402' (G-TEXN).
◆ **Private** *working fleet: prior arrangement* **only | www.spitfires.com**

❑ 'G-IRTY' V-S Spitfire IX FSM 85 BAPC.184, ex 'MK392', 'EN398', Derby, N Weald, Duxford. Specialised Mouldings-built. Displayed, 'silver' c/s by 6-22 [1] 3-23
❑ – V-S Spitfire IX SIM 22 simulator [2] 3-23
❑ MK392* V-S Spitfire IX ~ gale damaged by 3-23 3-23

■ **[1]** Repainted into the scheme of the around-the-world Spitfire G-IRTY - the original having Danish owners since 4-21. **[2]** The website declares this to be "the world's only Spitfire simulator that can be used for training Spitfire pilots. *W&R* would not normally formally list such a device, but it is claimed 50% of parts are genuine wartime; 40% are modern recreations that did not meet airworthiness standards; 10% specifically simulator elements.

Also:
❑ G-FNAV* Piper Navajo Chieftan 77 ex PH-XPI. De-reg 13-12-21. First noted 10-23 10-23

COPTHORNE on the A264 east of Crawley

Driver Wood Activity Centre: Old Hollow. ◆ *Prior arrangement* **only** | **https//driverwoodactivitycentre.co.uk**
❑ XZ205 Westland Lynx AH.7 79 ex High Bradfield, *Edge of Tomorrow* (2014), Hixon, Middle Wallop. First noted 4-20 12-23

CRAWLEY

Last noted at the Central Sussex College in January 2017, AA-5 Traveler G-BBCZ has been deleted. A Scout is under restoration at a *private* location in the *general* area.
❑ XT630 'X' Westland Scout AH.1 G-BXRL 66 ex Wymeswold, Bruntingthorpe, Burbage, G-BXRL. Crashed 16-10-99, de-reg 20-3-00. First noted 4-18 7-19

EAST GRINSTEAD on the A22 east of Crawley

(It's been some time since the author moved an entire location from county to county: East Grinstead was previously listed under Surrey – now amended.) A Lynx is kept in the *general* area.
❑ XZ680 'N' Westland Lynx AH.7 80 ex Ipswich, Weeton, Hixon, M Wallop, 671, 653, 669, 671, 657, 656, 657, 656, 665, Garrison Air Sqn. Cabin 9-19

■ **[1]** Fitted with boom of XZ608 – see Bury St Edmunds, Suffolk.

FAYGATE on the A264 between Horsham and Crawley

Holmbush Paintball Centre ◆ *Prior arrangement* **only** | **www.holmbushpaintball.co.uk**
❑ H255 Sud SA.330L Puma ~ ex Billingshurst (?), Horsham, Kemble, Chilean Army. Arrived 19-11-14 3-21

FORD north of the A259 west of Littlehampton

Atop a lofty plinth on the *Hunter*ford site on the edge of the former airfield is Peter Hague's Hunter. Can't resist noting that there is a cafe outside the nearby prison called 'Serving Thyme' – brilliant!
❑ WW654 '834' Hawker Hunter GA.11 55 ex Oving, Portsmouth, Culdrose A2664, A2753 (11-2-87), FRADU, 738, F.4, 229 OCU, 98, 4, 98. Squires Gate-built. SOC 11-2-87. Refurbished 8-22 12-23

HAYWARDS HEATH on the A272 north of Brighton

No.**172 (Haywards Heath) Squadron, Air Cadets**: Inside the TAVR centre in Eastern Road *should* be a Bulldog.
❑ XX520 'A' SAL Bulldog T.1 73 ex Newton 9288M (1-9-00), damaged 12-10-98, EM UAS, CFS, RNEFTS, 2 FTS 7-23

HORSHAM on the A264 southwest of Crawley

Aerospace Logistics: Also has a sub-site at Charlwood, Surrey. ◆ **Strictly** *prior arrangement* **only** | **www.asl-uk.com**
❑ XV674 Westland Sea King HAS.6 70 ex RAN spares, FAA Gosport A2669, 820, 819, 826, HAS.5, 819, HAS.2, 819, HAS.1 819. Arrived 6-14 12-23
❑ N16-114 '05' Westland Sea King Mk.50 G-BCIA 74 ex RAN, G-BCIA (de-reg 4-10-74), G-17-5. Arrived 6-14 12-23
❑ N16-125 W'land Sea King Mk.50 75 ex RAN, G-17-10. Arrived 6-14 12-23
❑ N16-238 '20' W'land Sea King Mk.50A 83 ex RAN, G-17-12. Arrived 6-14 12-23

	Reg		Type	Yr	History	Notes	Date
❑	N16-239	'21'	W'land Sea King Mk.50A	83	ex RAN, G-17-03. Arrived 6-14		12-23
❑	N16-918		W'land Sea King Mk.50B	79	ex RAN, FAA HAS.2 XZ918, 706, 820, 706, 814. Arrived 6-14		12-23

LONDON GATWICK AIRPORT

EGKK

The UK Heritage Aviation Trust threw in the towel in August 2022 regarding its plans to rescue Herald 209 G-CEXP – at least 26 years mouldering away as a rescue trainer – and it was scrapped on 29th November 2022.

	Reg		Type	Yr	History	Notes	Date
❑	I-DAVA		McDD MD82	86	ex ItAli Airlines. Last flight 21-10-10. Trygon Aviation titles		1-24

STORRINGTON on the A283 north of Worthing

A Luton Minor is stored at a *private* venue in the locality.

	Reg		Type	Yr	History	Notes	Date
❑	G-AFIR		Luton Minor	38	ex Aylesbury, Cobham, Rearsby. CoA 30-7-71, de-reg 22-11-21		11-21

TANGMERE south of the A27, east of Chichester

Tangmere Military Aviation Museum: As well as the aircraft and a staggering collection of memorabilia, there are several simulators, including a modified Link trainer and a fully-fledged Lightning simulator. The Lysander FSM is an impressive commission, commemorating 161 Squadron's association with Tangmere as its forward base. During January 2024 a mezzanine floor was opened, affording more angles on the exhibits.

Meteor F.8 'VZ440' (WA984) moved to Fishburn, D&C, arriving on 15th May 2022.

◆ *Gamecock Terrace, PO20 2ES* | **01243 790090** | **info@tangmere-museum.org.uk** | **www.tangmere-museum.org.uk**

	Reg		Type	Yr	History	Notes	Date
❑	-		Royal A/c Factory SE.5a rep	17	built on site by volunteers. Cockpit and centre sections		1-24
❑	'K5054'		V-S Spitfire prototype FSM	92	BAPC.214, ex Southampton, Hendon, Thruxton, M Wallop, Thruxton, Andover. Arrived 1997		1-24
❑	'L1679'	'JX-G'	Hawker Hurricane I FSM	92	BAPC.241, ex Chilbolton, M Wallop, Thruxton. AeroFab-built. Arrived 8-94. 1 Sqn colours		1-24
❑	P3179		Hawker Hurricane I	40	ex Hove, 43. Shot down 30-8-40. Arrived 1999. Cockpit		1-24
❑	'V9822'	'MA-E'	Westland Lysander III(SD) FSM	15	BAPC.371, ex 'V9875'. Gate Guardians UK-built. 161 Sqn colours. Arrived 16-6-18.	[1]	1-24
❑	-		V-S Spitfire IX SIM	~	cockpit, built on-site		1-24
❑	EE549		Gloster Meteor IV Special	46	ex Cosford, St Athan, Abingdon, Hendon, St Athan, Innsworth, Fulbeck 7008M Cranwell (13-1-53), CFE, FCCS, RAFHSF. SOC 10-6-52. Arrived 19-9-92	[2] [3]	1-24
❑	WB188		Hawker Hunter Mk.3	51	ex Cosford, St Athan, Colerne, Melksham, Halton 7154M (10-11-54), Hawker P.1067. Arrived 19-9-92	[2] [4]	1-24
❑	WE113		EE Canberra B.2	52	ex Woodhurst, Wyton, 231 OCU, 100, 85, 98, 231 OCU. Arrived 6-11. Cockpit	[5]	1-24
❑	WK281	'S'	V-S Swift FR.5	56	ex Hendon, St Athan, Swinderby, Finningley, Colerne, Northolt 7712M (7-3-61), 79. Arrived 1995. 79 Sqn c/s	[2]	1-24
❑	WP190	'K'	Hawker Hunter F.5	55	ex Quedgeley, Hucclecote, Stanbridge 'WP180', 8473M (13-2-76), Upwood, Finningley, Bircham Newton 7582M (10-9-58), 1. AWA-built. Arr 2-6-02. 1 Sqn, Suez, c/s	[6] [7]	1-24
❑	WV332		Hawker Hunter F.4	55	ex Godalming, Dunsfold G-9-406, Halton 7673M (17-1-61), 234, 112, 67. Arr 2003. 234 Sqn c/s. Cockpit	[8]	1-24
❑	WZ876		DHC Chipmunk T.10 G-BBWN	53	ex Goodwood, Yateley, Twyford, G-BBWN (CoA 13-7-96, de-reg 13-3-96), Tattershall Thorpe, Lon UAS, 1 AEF, Lon UAS, Biggin Hill SF, Lon, Oxf, Birm UASs, MCS, 31. Hawarden-built. Cockpit, sectioned. Arrived by 10-14		1-24
❑	XF840		Percival Provost T.1	55	ex Waltham Abbey, -?-, Shawbury, CNCS, RAFC. SOC 29-5-61. Arrived 2014. Cockpit, 'partial' sim		1-24
❑	XH313		DH Vampire T.11 G-BZRD	56	ex Godstone, Booker, Sandtoft, North Coates, St Albans, Hatfield, CATCS, Wattisham SF, 111. Hawarden-built. SOC 17-12-70. De-reg 22-2-05. Arrived 22-10-08. 111 Sqn c/s		1-24
❑	XJ580	'131'	DH Sea Vixen FAW.2	60	ex Christchurch, Hurn FRL, RAE Farnborough, Llanbedr, 899, 766, FAW.1, 899, 893, 892. Christchurch-built. SOC 17-12-84. Arrived 27-6-00. 899 Sqn colours		1-24
❑	XR571*		Folland Gnat T.1	63	ex Scampton, Cranwell, Scampton, Cosford, Kemble, Brampton, 8493M (7-5-76), Kemble, 4 FTS. Arrived 1-3-23		1-24

View from Tangmere's mezzanine, with Hunter WB188 centre stage, January 2024. *Hugh Trevor*

❑ 'XR753'	'A'	EE Lightning F.53	ZF578	67	ex Quedgeley, Rhoose, Warton, Saudi AF 53-670, G-27-40. Last flown 14-1-86. Arr 6-02. 23 Sqn c/s	[6] [9]	1-24
❑ XS511	'M'	Westland Wessex HU.5		64	ex Gosport, A2660 [2], A2750 (18-9-86), Lee-on-Solent, 845. Arrived 2004	[10]	1-24
❑ XV408	'L'	McD Phantom FGR.2		68	ex Fairford, Halton 9165M, Cranwell, Wattisham, 19, 92, 19, 92, 29, 23, 228 OCU, 54, 228 OCU, 6. Arrived 30-11-05. 6 Sqn colours	[2] [11]	1-24
❑ XV744		HS Harrier GR.3		69	ex Shrivenham, St Athan 9167M (10-4-93), 233 OCU, GR.1, 1, 233 OCU. Arrived 14-3-13	[12]	1-24
❑ XZ459	'25'	HS Sea Harrier F/A.2		80	ex Shoreham area, Queensbury, Charlwood, St Athan, 809, 800, 801, 899, 800, 801, 800, 801, 800, A&AEE, 801, 899, 801, 899. Arrived 24-8-20	[13]	1-24
❑ –		EE Lightning SIM		~	ex Haslemere, Farnborough. Arrived 12-08. Cockpit		1-24
❑ –*		Westland Lynx SIM		~	Thales donated, Army variant. Arrived 10-19. Stored		1-24
❑ –*		Short Tucano SIM		~	ex Simuserve, Linton-on-Ouse. Forward cockpit. Arrived 21-6-20. Stored		1-24

■ **[1]** As flown by Fg Off Jimmy 'Mac' McCairns of 'A' Flight 161 Sqn - 25 'ops', many from Tangmere. **[2]** On loan from the RAF Museum. **[3]** EE549, also known as a 'Star Meteor', flown by Gp Capt E M Donaldson, operating from Tangmere, set world airspeed record of 616mph on 7-9-46. **[4]** Hunter prototype and, as the one-off Mk.3, world speed record breaker - Neville Duke, operating from Tangmere, took record to 727mph on 7-9-53. See under Langley Heath, Kent, for another 'WB188'. **[5]** WE113 is on loan from S/L Joe and Pam Marsden. **[6]** Hunter F.5 and Lightning were donated by Raymond and Meryl Hansed and located in the Meryl Hansed Memorial Hall. **[7]** WP190 on charge with 1 Sqn Tangmere 30-8-55 - 11-7-58. **[8]** F.4 cockpit is on loan from 1254 Sqn ATC, Godalming, Surrey. The rest became Swiss T.68 J-4201 and is still extant. **[9]** Lightning is in the markings of F.6 XR753 'A', 23 Squadron. The *real* XR753 can be found at Coningsby, Lincs. **[10]** XS511 is on loan from 2464 Sqn ATC, Storrington, W Sussex. **[11]** XV408 honours Gp Capt David Baron, late Chair of Trustees who flew it in those colours. **[12]** XV744 flown by Sqn Ldr Graham Williams, 2-5-69 on an eastbound practice for the *Daily Mail* Transatlantic Air Race landed at 'RAF St Pancras' on a flight from downtown New York. Winner of the race was GR.1 XV741 - see Brooklands, Surrey. **[13]** 'SHAR' completed 54 combat sorties during the Falklands conflict.

TURNER'S HILL

Tulleys Farm: Among the attractions *should* be a Diplomate | **www.tulleysfarm.com**

❑ G-AYKG	SOCATA ST-10 Diplomate	70	ex Somerford, Turner's Hill. Crashed 4-3-75, de-reg 27-6-75	12-17

WOODMANCOTE on the A281 east of Henfield

Hayward and Green Defence: Lynx parts recycling continues to attract airframes – most very short term. SH-14D Lynx 272 arrived at St Athan, Wales, on 13th August 2022. See also the Bournemouth Aviation Museum, Bournemouth, Dorset.

◆ *Prior arrangement* **only** | **www.haywardandgreendefence.com**

	Serial	Code	Type	Built	History	Date
❑	ZF557*	'426'	Westland Lynx HMA.8	87	ex St Athan, Fleetlands, 702, 815, HAS.3, 815, 702. F/n 6-20	12-20
❑	ZF562*	'353'	Westland Lynx HMA.8	88	ex Middle Wallop, Yeovilton, 815, 702, 815, Mk.3, 815, 829. SOC 1-4-19. Arrived 11-19	8-23

WORTHING By August 2021 Taylorcraft G-AHWJ had moved to Amberley, W Sussex.

WARWICKSHIRE

BIDFORD AERODROME west of Stratford-upon-Avon

Restoration of the Auster T.10-based Terrier continues at a *private* location.

	Serial	Type	Reg	Built	History	Date
❑	WJ404	Beagle Terrier 2	G-ASOI	53	ex Auster T.10, 662, 665. CoA 30-9-16	6-23

BRAMCOTE on the B4114 east of Nuneaton

T&M Aviation: Located on a portion of the former wartime airfield, the company was established in 2019 and specialises in restoration projects and airframes/artefacts/vehicles for hire. The Bulldog was the founder-airframe, with the Andover a recent acquisition. Also held are the wings and booms of Vampire T.11 XE979; the pod was stripped down for spares in 2015 at Cantley, Norfolk – see *W&R25* (p171). ◆ *Prior arrangement* ***only*** | **www.facebook.com/tandmaviation/**

	Serial	Code	Type	Built	History	Note	Date
❑	XS643*		HS Andover E.3A	67	ex Coventry, Brierley Hill, Stock, Manston 9278M, Boscombe Down, 32, A&AEE, 115, 84. Cockpit		1-24
❑	XX655*	'V'	SAL Bulldog T.1	74	ex Coventry, Evesham, Stockport (?), Doncaster, Manston, Colerne 9294M (10-6-00), Bri UAS, 2 FTS. Cockpit	[1]	1-24

■ **[1]** Bulldog cockpit written out of *W&R25* (p302) at Doncaster as disposed of by 5-15, *perhaps* to a Stockport owner.

CORLEY MOOR on minor roads southwest of the M6's Corley Services

A *private* collection of airframes in the area is *thought* unchanged. ◆ *Prior arrangement* ***only***.

	Serial	Code	Type	Built	History	Date
❑	XR506	'V'	Westland Wessex HC.2	63	ex Selby, Greatham, Gosport, Cosford 9343M, Shawbury, 72, 60, 72, 18	5-19
❑	XV783	'DD83'	HS Harrier GR.3	70	ex Ipswich, Predannack, Culdrose A2609[3] (16-3-90), Lee-on-Solent, Culdrose SAH, Cosford, 233 OCU, 4, 3, 233 OCU, 1, 233 OCU, 1, 233 OCU, 1417 Flt, 233 OCU, 4, 20, 4	10-13
❑	ZD284	'K'	Westland Lynx AH.7	84	ex Ipswich, Middle Wallop. Arrived by 12-14	12-14

COVENTRY AIRPORT or Baginton EGBE

In October 2023 the consortium proposing the **West Midlands Gigafactory** – which had outline planning permission granted in January 2022 – announced that the hunt was on for Asian backers and that project was very much still 'on the cards'. Since the original launch of the venture, by Coventry City Council and Coventry Airport Ltd, the airport has taken on what can best be described as a 'planning blight' torpor. As charted below, migrations have begun...

Midland Air Museum (MAM), incorporating the **Sir Frank Whittle Jet Heritage Centre**: In *theory*, the Gigafactory plans will not impinge on the museum site. MAM has taken on two RAF Museum 'trickle down' handouts, the Auster and *another* Gnat F.1. The former, an East Midlands product, is stored pending the mandated covered space: footings for a new building were noted being laid in late 2023. The Gnat's minimal dimensions will have helped its choice. MAM has a *pair* of T-33As, so it may be that both Gnats will stay. Acquired in 1975 and latterly in fanciful Finnish colours, the first F.1 is a composite fuselage. The Flettner and HH-43 have completed lengthy restorations.

Founder of the Midland Aircraft Preservation Society (MAPS), **Roger Smith**, died on 24th June 2022, aged 74. Adverts in local newspapers placed by 19-year-old Roger in 1967 led to the creation of MAPS later that year. Roger, and other MAPS pioneers, went on to establish MAM which opened on its present site on 2nd April 1978. Not content with this, Roger then rounded up regional preservation societies and so the British Aircraft Preservation Council was kick-started. (A former MAPS airframe arrived at Baginton in 2023 – see Q.6 G-AFFD under 'Also', below.

◆ *Rowley Road, CV3 4FR* | **02476 301033** | **enquiries@midlandairmuseum.co.uk** | **www.midlandairmuseum.co.uk**

Airframes held in deep store are listed separately – see below.

❑ 'G-AEGV'		Mignet HM.14 'Flea'	c69	ex Coventry, Knowle, Northampton, Sywell	[1]	1-24
❑ 'G-ALVD'		DH Dove 2 G-ALCU	47	ex airfield, VT-CEH. CoA 16-3-73, de-reg 8-9-78. Acquired 28-3-80. Dunlop colours		1-24
❑ G-APJJ		Fairey Ultra-Light Helicopter	57	ex Heaton Chapel, Coventry, Cranfield, White Waltham, RAE Bedford, CoA 1-4-59, de-reg 2-3-73. Arrived 1975	[2]	1-24
❑ G-APRL		AW Argosy 101	59	ex ABC/Elan, N890U, N602Z, N6507R, G-APRL. *Edna*. CoA 23-3-87, de-reg 19-11-87, flew in 20-2-87		1-24
❑ G-APWN		Westland Whirlwind Srs 3	59	ex Cranfield, Redhill, VR-BER, G-APWN, 5N-AGI, G-APWN. CoA 17-5-78, de-reg 25-6-81, arrived 1984. Bristow colours		1-24
❑ G-ARYB		HSA HS.125 Srs 1	62	ex Hatfield. CoA 22-1-68, de-reg 4-3-69. Hatfield-assembled. Arrived 2-12-93		1-24
❑ G-BRNM		CMC Leopard	89	ex Hurn, Old Sarum. De-reg 31-1-05, arrived 26-3-08		1-24
❑ G-CHNX		Lockheed Electra 188AF	59	ex Pershore, Hurn, Channel Express, EI-CHO, G-CHNX, N5535. CoA 31-10-01, de-reg 12-5-03. Cockpit		1-24
❑ G-MJWH		Chargus Vortex 120 h-g	r83	former microlight. Arrived 1989		1-18
❑ ANW		EoN Olympia 2 G-ALNE	47	ex BGA.538, G-ALNE, BGA.538. CoA 9-3-04. Frame		1-18
❑ –		Humber-Blériot Monoplane replica	53	BAPC.9, ex Birmingham, Yeovilton, Wroughton, Yeovilton, Coventry, *Those Magnificent Men*, Old Warden, Honington. Arrived 12-91	[3]	1-24
❑ –		Slingsby Cadet TX.1	c54	'BGA.804', ex Perranporth. Arrived 12-6-68		8-22
❑ –		Druine Turbulent	c58	BAPC.126, ex Shoreham, Croydon. Rollason-built non-flyer. Acquired 13-9-78	[4]	1-24
❑ F-BGNR		Vickers Viscount 708	54	ex Hatch, Perth, Air Inter. Hurn-built. Last flown 8-10-73. Arrived 6-9-07, acquired 10-7-08		1-24
❑ EE531		Gloster Meteor F.4	46	ex Bentham, Coventry , Birmingham, Weston Park, B'ham, 7090M, RAE Lasham, A&AEE. SOC 25-8-53. Acquired 26-6-73		1-24
❑ VF301	'RAL-G'	DH Vampire F.1	46	ex Stoneleigh, Debden 7060M (10-8-53), 208 AFS, 595, 226 OCU. EE-built. Acquired 11-72. 605 Sqn colours		1-24
❑ VS623		Percival Prentice T.1 G-AOKZ	49	ex Shoreham, Redhill, Southend, VS623, CFS, 2 FTS, 22 FTS. SOC 11-5-56. De-reg 4-10-61, arrived 26-7-82	[5]	1-24
❑ VT935		Boulton Paul P.111A	50	ex Cranfield, RAE Bedford. Arrived 13-7-75	[2]	1-24
❑ VZ477		Gloster Meteor F.8	50	ex Kimbolton 7741M, APS, 245. SOC 22-6-62. Arrived 4-6-92. Cockpit		1-24
❑ WE600*		Auster C4 'Antarctic'	51	ex Cosford, St Athan, Swinderby, Finningley 7602M, Antarctic Expedition 1956-1957, T.7 663. Arr 11-22, stored		1-24
❑ WF922		EE Canberra PR.3	52	ex Cambridge, A&AEE, RRE, A&AEE, Wroughton, BP, 39, 69, 58, 1323 Flt, 82. SOC 23-5-75, arrived 24-6-84. *Stevenson's Rocket*		1-24
❑ WH646		EE Canberra T.17A	52	ex Wyton, 360, B.2 45, RNZAF, 45, 10, 50. Arr 1995. Cockpit		1-24
❑ WS838	'D'	Gloster Meteor NF.14	54	ex Cosford, Manchester, Cosford, Shawbury, Colerne, SOC (to RAF Museum) 9-2-72, RAE Bedford, A&AEE, RRE Pershore, 64, AW OCU. AWA-built. Arr 15-3-86	[6]	1-24
❑ WV797	'491'	Hawker Sea Hawk FGA.6	54	ex Perth, Culdrose A2627, Halton 8155M (12-3-71), Sydenham, 738, 898, 899, 787. AWA-built. Arrived 6-2-86		1-24
❑ XA508	'627'	Fairey Gannet T.2	55	ex Yeovilton, Manadon A2472 (12-4-57), 737. Arrived 26-9-82. 737 Sqn colours	[7]	1-24
❑ XA699		Gloster Javelin FAW.5	57	ex Cosford, Locking 7809M (14-2-64), Shawbury, Kemble, Shawbury, 5, 151. AWA-built. Arrived 19-9-81. 151 Sqn colours by 8-22		1-24
❑ XF382	'15'	Hawker Hunter F.6A	56	ex Brawdy, 1 TWU, TWU, 229 OCU, FCS, 65, 63, 92. AWA-built. SOC 10-7-84. Arrived 1-12-86. 234 Sqn c/s	[8]	1-24
❑ XH592	'L'	HP Victor B.1A	58	ex B'thorpe, Cosford 8429M (17-10-74), St Athan, 232 OCU, TTF, 232 OCU, Honington Wing, 15. Cockpit. Arr by 10-15		1-24
❑ XJ579	'121'	DH Sea Vixen FAW.2	60	ex Farnborough, A&AEE, Llanbedr, 899, 766. Christchurch-built. Arrived 18-8-92. Cockpit		1-24
❑ XK724*		Folland Gnat F.1	56	ex Cosford, Cranwell, Bicester, Henlow 7715M (25-2-61), Folland. Last flight 26-5-56. Arrived 1-12-22		1-24

	Identity	Code	Type	Year	History	Note	Date
❑	XK789		Slingsby Grasshopper TX.1	55	ex Warwick, Cosford, Stamford		1-22
❑	XL360		Avro Vulcan B.2	62	ex 44, 101, 35, 617, 230 OCU, Wadd Wing, 230 OCU, Scamp W, 617. Flew in 4-2-83. *City of Coventry*. 617 Sqn c/s		1-24
❑	XN685	'703'	DH Sea Vixen FAW.2	61	ex Chester, Cosford, Cranwell 8173M (3-8-71), 890, 766, 893, HSA. Christchurch-built. Arrived 14-9-92. 890 Sqn c/s		1-24
❑	XR635		Westland Scout AH.1	65	ex Coventry, Ipswich, Arborfield, Yeovilton, M Wallop, 653, 660. Arrived 10-9-12	[9]	1-24
❑	XR771	'AN'	EE Lightning F.6	66	ex Binbrook, 5, 11, 5, 56, 74. SOC 21-6-88, arrived 15-7-88		1-24
❑	ZA452	'021'	Panavia Tornado GR.4	83	ex Leeming, 12, GR.1, 20, A&AEE. Arrived 9-13. 2 Sqn c/s	[10]	1-24
❑	ZE694	'004'	HS Sea Harrier F/A.2	88	ex Yeovilton, 801, 800, 801, 800, 801, 899, 800, 801, 800. Arrived 16-2-05		1-24
❑	–		Bristol Beaufighter	42	BAPC.398, ex Birmingham, Coventry. Arr 10-89. Cockpit	[11]	1-22
❑	–		Hunting Jet Provost SIM	c60	procedure trainer		1-22
❑	–		BAe/McDD Harrier GR.5	90	procedure trainer		3-18
❑	8449M		Beagle 206-1 G-ASWJ	65	ex Bristol, Halton 8449M (9-8-76), G-ASWJ Rolls-Royce, CoA 30-1-75, de-reg 9-9-75. Acquired 1-93. arrived by 2-13		1-24
❑	'117529'	'TR-529'	Lockheed T-33A-1-LO 51-7473	51	ex Cosford, Sculthorpe, French AF, USAF 51-7473. Last flown 30-5-78, arrived 26-10-93. Italian AF colours	[7]	1-24
❑	R-756		Lockheed F-104G Starfighter	64	ex Aalborg, Danish AF, 64-17756. Arrived 30-4-87	[7]	1-24
❑	'GN-101'		Folland Gnat F.1 XK741	57	ex Leamington Spa, Fordhouses, Dunsfold, Hamble, Boscombe Down, Dunsfold, Folland. Last flight 22-9-61, SOC 10-11-61. Acquired 7-6-75. Fuselage. *Kreivi von Rosen*, Finnish AF colours	[12]	1-24
❑	70	'8-NV'	Dassault Mystère IVA	c56	ex Sculthorpe, French AF. Arrived 1/2-6-79	[7]	1-22
❑	280020	'GF+YF'	Flettner Fl 282B Kolibri	44	ex Coventry, Cranfield, Brize Norton, Travemünde. Arrived 5-75	[2] [13]	7-23
❑	959		Mikoyan-Gurevich MiG-21SPS *Fishbed*	c66	ex Duxford, Cottbus, East German AF. Arrived 25-6-01		1-22
❑	'1706'		PZL Iskra TS-11	c77	ex airfield, Scampton, Duxford, Polish AF 408. On loan. 1 OSL, Deblin colours		10-23
❑	55-713	'C'	EE Lightning T.55 ZF598	67	ex Warton, ZF598, Saudi AF 55-713, G-27-72. Last flown 14-1-86. Arrived 14-1-89. Saudi colours		1-22
❑	'17447'		McD F-101B-80-MC Voodoo 56-0312	56	ex Alconbury, Davis-Monthan, Kentucky ANG, USAF. Arrived 7/8-3-92. RCAF 416 Sqn colours	[7]	1-24
❑	29640	'08'	SAAB J29F 'Tunnen'	c54	ex Southend, F20 R Swedish AF. Arrived 27-4-85		1-24
❑	0-82062		DHC U-6A Beaver	58	ex Mannheim, Berlin Brigade Av Det, US Army, 58-2062. Arrived 10-7-81	[7]	1-24
❑	48-0242	'FU-242'	NAA F-86A-5-NA Sabre N196B	48	N196B, ex Duxford, Chino, 48-0242. Arrived 22-4-05	[14]	1-24
❑	51-4419		Lockheed T-33A-1-LO	51	ex Sculthorpe, French AF. Last flown 25-1-78, arrived 1979. 57th FIS colours	[7]	1-24
❑	54-2174	'SM'	NAA F-100D-16-NA Super Sabre	54	ex Sculthorpe, French AF, USAF 54-2174. Last flown 22-2-77. Arrived 29-3-78. *Carol Anne*. USAF colours	[7]	1-24
❑	63-7699	'CG'	McD F-4C-21-MC Phantom	63	ex Upper Heyford, Fairford, 55th TFS, 356th TFS, 480th TFS, USAF 63-7699. Arrived 7-10-93. 366th TFW c/s	[7] [15]	1-24
❑	62-4535		Kaman HH-43F Huskie	52	ex Woodbridge, Alconbury, 40 ARRS, Det 2, HH-43B. SOC 9-73. Arrived 7-3-81	[16]	1-24
❑	-		Mil Mi-24 *Hind-D*	c77	ex Rochester, Chester, Latvia, USSR. Arrived 15-9-05. BAE Systems colours	[17]	1-24

■ **[1]** 'Flea' has the original wings from G-AEGV coupled with new-build fuselage etc, circa 1969. Original built by East Midlands Aviation Co at Sywell and first flew 24-5-36. **[2]** Airframes on loan from Cranfield University, Beds. **[3]** Thanks to John Berkeley, this machine likely was assembled (or 'created') at 94 MU Honington in 1953 (although 58 MU was also at the base at the time); earliest sighting at Old Warden 1959. Goldsmith provenance *possibly* in doubt... At Coventry, it was fitted with an original Humber engine, loaned from Coventry Museum, to represent a 1911 Humber-Blériot. **[4]** During 1960 (at least), the 'Turb' was with 714 Squadron ATC at Selhurst Grammar School, Croydon. **[5]** VS623 is fitted with the wings from G-AONB (VR244). **[6]** WS838, ownership transferred from the RAF Museum to MAM. **[7]** Gannet T.2 is on loan from FAAM, Yeovilton. **[8]** Airframes from the National Museum of the USAF's Loan Program: a large number of RAF Hunters were MDAP funded. **[9]** Scout is on loan from Coventry University (see Coventry, W Mids) and used as a teaching aid. **[10]** Tornado credited with 32 'ops' during the 1st Gulf War, deployed to Tabuk, Saudi Arabia, from 8-90; carrying the code 'GK', this gave rise to one of the two names it carried on the nose, *Gulf Killer*; the other being *I Luv Gaynor XX*.

[11] Beaufighter cockpit is *possibly* Mk.I T5298. In which case it was previously 4552M and TFU Defford. It was previously with Coventry Technical College and Birmingham Science Museum. **[12]** Gnat fuselage is a composite, rear from XK739, w/o 15-7-58. **[13]** Flettner is *most likely* the V20 series prototype, w/nr 282000020, 'CJ+SN'. **[14]** Sabre is on loan from the IWM, Duxford. **[15]** F-4 37699 crewed by Major Samuel O Bakkel and WSO Capt Robert W Lambery shot down a NVN MiG-17 *Fresco* on 14-5-67. **[16]** HH-43 uses parts from 24538, including the fins. **[17]** *Hind* on loan from BAE Systems and boasts the build number 353246505029.

Deep store: The following are ***not*** available for public inspection.

	Reg	Type	Year	History	Note	Date
❑	G-EBJG	Parnall Pixie III	24	ex Coventry, Stratford, Horley, Dorking, Carlisle (?), Heston, CoA 2-10-36, de-reg 1-12-46. Remains, acquired 8-67		1-14
❑	G-ABOI	Wheeler Slymph	r31	ex Coventry, Old Warden. De-reg 1-12-46. Arrived 4-68	[1]	1-14
❑	–	Crossley Tom Thumb	37	BAPC.32, ex Coventry, Bewdley, Coventry, Banbury. Arrived 29-7-69	[2]	1-14
❑	XD626	DH Vampire T.11	54	ex Bitteswell, Shawbury, CATCS, CNCS, 5 FTS, RAFC, CFS. SOC 19-7-67. Christchurch-built. Arrived 10-8-82. Spares		9-21
❑	XE855	DH Vampire T.11	54	ex Upton-by-Chester, Woodford, Chester, 27 MU, 22 MU, 10 MU, AWOCU. Hatfield-built. SOC 30-10-67. Arrived 28-8-82. Cockpit		9-21
❑	XK907	Westland Whirlwind HAS.7 G-AYXT	57	ex Bubbenhall, Panshanger, Elstree, G-AYXT (de-reg 8-8-00), Luton, ETPS, RRE Pershore, Alvis. Last flown 30-10-68. Arrived 8-3-81. Cockpit, spares recovered	[3]	9-21
❑	57-0270	McD F-101B-80-MC Voodoo	57	ex fire crews, MAM, Woodbridge, Davis-Monthan, Texas ANG, USAF 57-0270. Arrived 4-92. Forward fuselage		9-21
❑	63-7414	McD F-4C-15-MC Phantom	63	ex Woodbridge, New York ANG, USAF 63-7414. Arrived 5-92	[4]	9-21

■ **[1]** On loan from the estate of the late Air Cdre Alan Wheeler. **[2]** Crossley is an unfinished 1930s homebuild, from Banbury. **[3]** See Weston-super-Mare, Somerset, for the *real* G-AYXT. **[4]** F-4C from the National Museum of the USAF's Loan Program.

Former **Classic Air Force Airbase** / **Air Atlantique**: Dakota 4 KK116 (G-AMPY) departed for the USA on 17th May 2022 - the end of an incredible era. ◆ ***Not*** *available for inspection*

	Reg	Type	Year	History	Note	Date
❑	VP959 'L'	DH Devon C.2	48	ex Wellesbourne, Biggin Hill, N959VP, G-BWFB, VP959, RAE. Stored, off-site		9-19
❑	XM223 'J'	DH Dove 7 G-BWWC	57	ex Cumbernauld, West Freugh, DGTE, T&EE, RAE. De-reg 10-1-19. Stored, off-site	[1]	9-19

■ [1] XM223 is fitted with the wings of G-APSO.

Nimrod Preservation Group: Plans to relocate to St Mawgan, Cornwall, were dashed with the collapse of the museum. Engine runs were carried out during 2023 – keep an eye on the website for news of events and future plans.
◆ **www.xv232.com**

	Reg	Type	Year	History	Note	Date
❑	XV232	HS Nimrod MR.2	69	ex Kinloss, Kin Wing, Kin & St M Wing, Kinloss, 203 Flew in 11-5-10		1-24

Shackleton Preservation Group: (SPT): The group elected to join the diaspora, moving to the Yorkshire Air Museum. Work began on dismantling in late autumn 2023 and, in anticipation of the move, WR963 has been listed under Elvington, N Yorks. The cockpit of Shackleton T.4 VP293 made the move northwards to Elvington, N Yorks, on 19th December 2023.

Flight Simulators Midlands: Among the 'sims' – which include a wholly synthetic 'Bf 109' and a 'P-51' – is a former BA A320 real motion cockpit. There is also a 737-800 based upon a former sim built for Sabena in the USA by Atkins and Merryl.
◆ *Prior arrangement* ***only*** | **www.flyfsm.co.uk**

	Reg	Type	Year	History	Note	Date
❑	G-BUSF*	Airbus A320-111	89	ex Lasham, BA. De-reg 11-10-07, CoA 25-5-08. Cockpit		1-24

Also: The Q.6 is an epic, long-term, at times frustrated, restoration; serious work began in 1980. Bear with the writer, but since *Fox-Delta* was acquired by the Midland Aircraft Preservation Society – MAM's founders – from Redhill in November 1973, it's put some land/ferry miles in. Using the trusted AA Route Planner: Redhill-Duxford-Sutton Coldfield (sorry, that's The Royal Town of Sutton Coldfield)-Douglas-Ronaldsway-Seething-Baginton comes to 953 miles. That's six adventures on-and-off trucks.

	Reg	Type	Year	History	Note	Date
❑	G-ACGT	Avro Avian IIIA	28	ex Yeadon, Linthwaite, EI-AAB. CoA 21-7-39. Off-site	[1]	12-22
❑	G-AESE	DH Hornet Moth	37	ex Air Atlantique, W5775, 526, 72 Wing CF, 6 RSS, 4 CPF, G-AESE. *Sheena*. CoA 8-6-16	[1]	12-22
❑	G-AGTM	DH Dragon Rapide	44	ex Air Atlantique, St Mawgan, Coventry, JY-ACL, OD-ABP, G-AGTM, Dominie NF875 n/s. Brush-built. *Sybille*. CoA 30-9-16	[1]	12-22

	Registration	Code	Type	Other ID	Year	History	Note	Date
❑	G-BTYY*		Curtiss C-2 Robin		29	ex Lee-on-Solent, N348K. CoA 1-9-97		12-22
❑	G-BXJA		Cessna 402B		73	ex N5753M. CoA 17-10-07, de-reg 13-10-20. F/n 8-20		12-22
❑	G-LOFB		Lockheed L.188CF Electra		61	ex Atlantic, N667F, N133AJ, CF-IJW, N131US. Damaged 28-1-10. CoA 8-2-11, de-reg 29-9-16		10-23
❑	G-GRRC		Piper Warrior II		89	ex G-BXJX, HB-POH, D-EJTB, N9149X. CoA 8-1-09, De-reg 12-2-09. Cockpit in Coventry Flying Club building	[2]	1-22
❑	SE-LPU		BAe ATP		98	ex West Air, LX-WAM, SE-LPU, LX-WAM, SE-LPU, G-OBWO, G-11-060. Arrived 9-9-15. Rescue trainer		12-23
❑	N308SF		Douglas C-47A-65-DL Skytrain		43	ex N98BF, Aéronavale '18984', N45V, N65384, 42-100521, 436th TCG USAAF. Long Beach-built. *Night Fright*. F/n 9-16	[3]	12-22
❑	N8041B		Douglas C-47A-50-DL Skytrain	G-AJAZ	42	ex USA, Spanish AF, EC-ADR, G-AJAZ, Dakota III FL517, 1381 CU, 511, 512, USAAF 42-24238. Cockpit, off-site	[4]	5-23
❑	X9407*		Percival Q.6	G-AFFD	38	ex Seething, Ronaldsway, Douglas (IoM), Sutton Coldfield, Duxford, Redhill, G-AIEY, X9407, MCS, 510, Old Sarum SF, Halton SF, Heston SF, Northolt SF, 6 AACU, G-AFFD. CoA 31-8-56. Arrived 11-10-23		1-24

■ **[1]** Registered to Ben Cox. **[2]** Identity confirmed. **[3]** Served with 436th's 79th TCS initially from Bottesford, then Membury – D-Day through to end of war. Plan is to operate it from Membury. **www.night-fright.com** **[4]** Cockpit, imported into the UK in 2006, to be used as a travelling exhibit for the *Night-Fright* project.

RED HILL on the A46 between Alcester and Stratford-upon-Avon

The fuselage of the former Long Marston Sea Prince is at a *private* location here.

	Registration	Code	Type	Other ID	Year	History	Date
❑	G-RACA	'571'	Percival Sea Prince T.1	WM735	52	ex Long Marston, Staverton, Kemble, WM735, 750, BTU, A&AEE. SOC 16-9-80, de-reg 28-11-95. Shark's mouth. Fuselage, first noted 2-20	10-23

STOCKTON east of the A426 north of Southam

Richard Adams: Has, or *had*, a Vampire T.11 cockpit for conversion to a simulator.

	Registration	Code	Type	Other ID	Year	History	Date
❑	WZ553	'40'	DH Vampire T.11	G-DHYY	53	ex Coventry, G-DHYY (de-reg 7-11-02), Hurn, Bruntingthorpe, Cranfield, Lichfield, Winthorpe, S' Wigston, B'thorpe, Loughborough, E Midlands, Speke, Woodford, Chester, St Athan, 4 FTS, 7 FTS, 202 AFS. Hawarden-built. SOC 2-12-68, Cockpit	3-10

STRATFORD-UPON-AVON

Peter Turner: Peter has many other Messenger and Gemini sections and other Miles material. The former Australian Gemini is expected to be handed on, to form the basis of a static restoration in Cheshire.

◆ *Prior appointment* **only** - *situated on private estate*

	Registration	Type	Other ID	Year	History	Date
❑	G-AKDK	Miles Gemini 1A		47	ex Coventry, Seaton Ross, 'Stratford', Denmark, G-AKDK	12-23
❑	G-ALAH	Miles Messenger 4A		45	ex Sabadell, Spain, Henlow, NAPS (1967), RH377 n/s. CoA 18-4-65. Arrived 22-9-14	12-23
❑	VH-GBB	Miles Gemini 1A	G-AKEN	47	ex Australia, VH-BTP, G-AKEN. Fuselage – see note above	12-23
❑	VP-KJL	Miles Messenger 4A	G-ALAR	48	ex Redhill, Woodley, Stoke-on-Trent, Coventry, G-ALAR, RH371, BAFO CW, AEAF CS. Fuselage and tail	12-23

WARWICK

A *private* airstrip in the locality.

	Registration	Type	Year	History	Date
❑	G-AAOR	DH Moth	29	ex EC-AAO. CoA 17-11-05, de-reg 1-3-19	7-19

WELLESBOURNE MOUNTFORD AERODROME south of the B4086, E of Stratford EBBW

Wellesbourne Wartime Museum: Operated by the **Wellesbourne Aviation Group**, charting the history of the airfield centred on the restored underground Battle Headquarters. ◆ **www22otu@gmail.com** | **www.facebook.com/22otu/**

	Registration	Code	Type	Year	History	Date
❑	RA-01378	'14'	Yakovlev Yak-52	83	ex Sov AF	12-23
❑	WV679	'O-J'	Percival Provost T.1	54	ex Dunkeswell, H' Blagdon, Halton 7615M (13-10-59), 2 FTS	12-23
❑	XJ575	'SAH-13'	DH Sea Vixen FAW.2	60	ex Long Marston, Helston, Culdrose SAH, A2611, 766, 890, 893, FAW.1, 766. Christchurch-built. SOC 24-3-71. Cockpit	12-23

❑ XK590	'V'	DH Vampire T.11	56	ex Witney, Brize Norton, CATCS, 4 FTS, 7 FTS. Hawarden-built. SOC 6-2-70		12-23

XM655 Maintenance and Preservation Society: The Vulcan hit the headlines on 16th September 2022 when a taxi run ended off the 'hard', into the grass and with its nose perilously close to the Stratford Road. This necessitated the carriageway's closure while the recovery operation was completed.

◆ *Occasional ground-running days* | **email** via website | **www.xm655.com**

❑ XM655		Avro Vulcan B.2 G-VULC	64	ex N655AV, G-VULC, Wadd Wing, 44, 101, 50, 12, 35, 9. Flew in 11-2-84, de-reg 25-3-02	[1]	1-24

■ **[1]** XM655 is owned by John Littler of Radarmoor.

WILTSHIRE

Includes the unitary authority of Swindon

AMESBURY on the A303 west of Andover

Gary Dean: Gary's exceptional P-51D cockpit procedure trainer is kept in the area. During 2023 the project was given an update, replacing the windshield assembly and the 'top decking'. It is a tribute to Gp Capt John Francis Xavier 'Sam' McKenna AFC, Empire Test Pilots' School commandant, killed while testing Mustang IV KH648 on 19th January 1945.

◆*Prior arrangement* **only** | **geeede@ntlworld.com**

❑ '44-11175'	NAA P-51D Mustang SIM	04	BAPC.512, *One More Time*. Unveiled 14-6-14	1-24

BOSCOMBE DOWN AIRFIELD south of the A303 at Amesbury EGDM

MoD Boscombe Down: Home of the **Aircraft Test and Evaluation Centre** and defence technology and security specialists **QinetiQ Group plc**. Within Hangar 104 is the **Apprentice Training Centre** (Apps).

Departures: Gazelle HT.3 XW906 (with the boom of AH.1 ZA804), last noted in 12-17, became G-CMFK in 4-22; **Jaguar** GR.1 XX956 moved to Spey Bay, Scotland, by 4-22; **Merlin**s migrating to Gosport, Hampshire: **HM.1**s ZH852 (15-11-22); ZH830; ZH838; ZH848; ZH849, ZH855; ZH863; **HC.3**s ZJ117 (9-6-22); ZJ135 joined the HC.4 conversion programme; **Navajo** fuselage ZF622 to Farnborough, Hampshire, by 7-23.

❑ 'MK356'*	'21-V'	V-S Spitfire IX FSM	03	BAPC.298, ex Cosford. First noted 9-19, displayed	[1]	11-23
❑ XL629		EE Lightning T.4	59	ex ETPS, A&AEE. Last flight 3-11-75. Displayed		1-24
❑ XS765		Beagle Basset CC.1 G-BSET	64	ex Cranfield, G-BSET (CoA 28-7-98, de-reg 25-3-04), ETPS, 26, 207, 32, MCS, SCS, NCS, HS. Fuselage, Apps		12-17
❑ XX172		HS Hawk T.1	77	ex Shawbury, Yeovilton, FRADU, 19, 4 FTS, 234, 4 FTS. Bird strike 15-12-06, SOC 7-8-17. Apps		12-17
❑ XX379	'Y'	Sud Gazelle AH.1	75	ex Shawbury, 6 Flt, 658, 3/4 Rgt, 8 Flt, 658, 656, 2 Flt. Westland-built. Arrived by 5-15, Apps		6-17
❑ ZD285		Westland Lynx AH.5X	85	ex A&AEE, RAE Farnborough. Apps	[2]	12-17
❑ ZD559		Westland Lynx AH.7	85	ex AH.5X, ETPS, RAE Bedford. Retired by 2-13. Apps		12-17
❑ 82-23762*		Boeing CH-47D Chinook	66	ex Benson, Odiham, US Army, Fort Rucker, CH-47A 66-0122. Arrived UK 1-07. Forward fuselage, first noted 7-23		7-23

■ **[1]** The *real* MK356 can be found at Coningsby, Lincs, while *another* 'MK356' is at Hawkinge, Kent. **[2]** Lynx AH.5Xs were interim airframes prior to the AH.7. ZD285 has a substantially modified nose section.

Joint Aircraft Recovery and Transport Squadron (JARTS): An RAF 'lodger' unit tasked with moving airframes by road and loads-in-transit can be found 'over-nighting' or staying for longer periods; only long-termers are given here. JARTS has an 'out-station' at Newquay, Cornwall - which see.

❑ G-BCWR*		BN-2A-20 Islander	75	ex St Athan, Bembridge, OY-RPZ, G-BCWR. De-reg 26-10-94. FBN-built. Fuselage	[1]	7-23
❑ XS180	'21'	Hunting Jet Provost T.4	63	ex '8238M', St Athan 8338M (6-8-73), Lyneham, St Athan, Halton, Kemble, CAW, 6 FTS		10-23
❑ XS646		HS Andover C.1	68	ex DERA etc, RAE, 84, 46. Forward fuselage		7-23
❑ XX165		HS Hawk T.1A	77	ex Wittering, Boscombe Down, Shawbury, 208, FRADU, 4 FTS, CFS, 74, CFS, 4 FTS, CFS. SOC 7-8-17. Fuselage		7-22
❑ XX173		HS Hawk T.1	77	ex Shawbury, FRADU, 6 FTS, 4 FTS. NEA 12-19. Arr 11-3-20		7-22
❑ XX240*	'840'	HS Hawk T.1	78	ex St Mawgan, Shawbury 736, FRADU, 19, 74, 6 FTS, 4 FTS. First noted 10-23		10-23

	Identity	Type		Year	History	Note	Date
❑	XX329*	HS Hawk T.1A		80	ex Valley RTP, 100, 74, 19, 92, T.1, 2 TWU. Bitteswell-built. NEA 25-11-21. First noted 6-22		7-23
❑	XX346*	HS Hawk T.1A		80	ex Valley RTP, 100, FRADU, 19, T.1, 2 TWU. Bitteswell-built. NEA 25-11-21. First noted 6-22		7-23
❑	'XZ615'	Westland Lynx AH.7	XZ209	79	ex St Athan, Fleetlands, Middle Wallop, 655, 656, 662, 659		10-23
❑	XZ646	Westland Lynx AH.7		80	ex St Athan, Fleetlands, Yeovilton, 847, 657, 656, 664, 656, 669, 654, 654. Crashed 21-2-05. Cabin	[2]	7-23
❑	ZA560 'EB-Q'	Panavia Tornado GR.4		81	ex Wittering, Marham, 617, GR.1, DERA, SAOEU. SOC 20-3-18. Fuselage. Arrived 15-7-21		7-23
❑	'ZA718'	Westland Lynx AH.7	XZ183	78	ex Wittering, St Athan, Middle Wallop, Fleetlands	[3]	10-23
❑	ZJ807	Eurofighter Typhoon T.3		04	ex Coningsby. Arrived 5-2-20. Fuselage		10-23
❑	TAD.019*	Sud Gazelle AH.1	XW912	74	ex Lyneham, Boscombe D JARTS, Arborfield, Fleetlands, 655, 3 CBAS, 656, 655, 3 CBAS. Westland-built. JARTS by 3-22		10-23
❑	162737	BAe/McDD AV-8B Harrier II		86	ex VMAT-203. Fuselage. First noted 4-17		3-22

■ [1] Islander written out of *W&R24* (p322) at St Athan as last noted 1-10. **[2]** Boom of XZ646 is on XZ649, see Weston-supper-Mare, Somerset. **[3]** The *real* ZA718, the famous Chinook, is to be found at Cosford, Shropshire. **[3]**

Solstice Business Park: Just off the A303, at the end of the westbound slip road to the services, within sight of the airfield, a Gazelle 'sculpture' which is almost lost within the sprawl of building development.

	Identity	Type	Year	History	Note	Date
❑	ZA804 'I'	Sud Gazelle HT.3		ex airfield, Shawbury, 2 FTS, CFS. Westland-built	[1]	8-23

■ **[1]** Much-altered, the Gazelle forms a 'sculpture' that is part helicopter, part dragonfly. It was officially unveiled 11-6-07. The original boom of ZA804 is fitted to XW906 – see above.

CHIPPENHAM

Maria Merry: and son Freddie converted an Agusta 109 into a 'Heli-Party Pad' complete with cocktail bar and a widescreen TV. It is *believed* extant. ◆ *Prior appointment* only

	Identity	Type	Year	History	Date
❑	G-GBCA	Agusta 109A	84	ex Weston-super-Mare, Denham, Helicopter Film Services. De-reg 3-9-85. Cab. Arrived by 7-18	10-19

CRICKLADE south of the A419 between Cirencester and Swindon

In September 2022 the predominantly Dove/Devon store at a yard in the locality was auctioned and cleared. The fuselage of Dove 8 G-ARJB was roaded to St Athan, Wales, on 13th December 2022. Two items under the hammer had eluded the pages of *W&R* since being written out of the 24th Edition under Little Rissington, Glos, (p67) as last noted in June 2011; former DH/HAS/BAe 'bus' G-ARBE and DR.400 G-BAGS. Dove *Bravo-Echo* made the trek to East Midlands, Leics, 13th December 2022; no 'forwarding address' for the Robin. Devon C.2/2 VP955 (G-DVON) reportedly failed to sell at the auction; it departed by the end of 2022 to 'Wigan', or ''Harrogate', or 'Preston' – take your pick...

LARKHILL north of the A303, northwest of Amesbury.

Royal Artillery Institution: As predicted in *W&R28*, Phoenix UAV ZJ469 departed in June 2022, for Old Sarum, Wilts.

LYNEHAM west of the A3102, southwest of Royal Wootton Bassett

REME Museum: Covering the Royal Electrical and Mechanical Engineers, its predecessors and the legacy of Lyneham.
◆ *Prince Philip Barracks, SN15 4XX* | **01249 894869** | **enquiries@rememuseum.org.uk** | **www.rememuseum.org.uk**

	Identity	Type		Year	History	Note	Date
❑	XV141	Westland Scout AH.1		68	ex Arborfield, Wroughton, 657, 659, 654, 661. Arrived 11-15. In the 'World Gallery'		12-23
❑	ZJ449	GEC-Marconi Phoenix UAV		c95	ex Arborfield. Acquired 7-10-08, arrived 11-15. Stored		12-19
❑	'XZ191'	Westland Lynx HC.28	TAD.016	77	ex Arborfield, M Wallop, Almondbank, Wroughton, Qatar Police QP-32. First noted 4-16. Displayed outside	[1]	12-23

■ **[1]** The *real* XZ191 is with the DCTT, below.

Defence College of Technical Training (DCTT): A one-off abbreviation is used in the listing below: MW = Middle Wallop.

Disposals: **Gazelle** AH.1 TAD.019 (XW912) returned to Boscombe Down, Wilts, by 3-22; TAD.021 (XW860) to Honington, Suffolk, 11-22; Lynx AH.7 XZ617 to Yeovilton, Somerset, by 2-23.

	Identity	Type	Year	History	Date
❑	XT623	Westland Scout AH.1	66	ex Arborfield, Wroughton, 655, 659, 655. First noted 4-16	7-17
❑	XX444*	Sud Gazelle AH.1	76	ex Wattisham, Fleetlands, 25 Flt, 662, 663, 656, 663, 656, 658, 656, 658, ARWS, ARWF. Westland-built. Arrived 23-3-23	3-23
❑	XZ170	Westland Lynx AH.9	77	ex Arborfield, Yeovil, A&AEE. Arrived 1-9-15	7-17

❑ XZ172 Westland Lynx AH.7 77 ex Arborfield, 653, 655, Yeovil, LCF/671, IPTU. F/n 7-17 7-17
❑ XZ180 Westland Lynx AH.7 78 ex MW. SOC 11-4-15. Arrived 9-11-15 7-17
❑ XZ191 'R' Westland Lynx AH.7 78 ex Fleetlands. SOC 4-9-13. Arrived 25-6-15 [1] 7-17
❑ XZ214 Westland Lynx AH.7 79 ex MW. SOC 11-4-15. Arrived 9-11-15 7-17
❑ XZ222 Westland Lynx AH.7 79 ex MW. SOC 9-5-15. Arrived 10-11-15 7-17
❑ XZ316 'B' Sud Gazelle AH.1 77 ex Arborfield, Cosford, Shawbury, 666, 670, ARWS, ARWF [2] 11-17
❑ XZ332 Sud Gazelle AH.1 77 ex Arborfield, MW, 670, ARWF, 656, 664. Arrived 26-8-15 [2] 7-17
❑ XZ333 Sud Gazelle AH.1 77 ex Arborfield, MW, 670, ARWF, F-Wxxx. SOC 18-4-19 [2] 9-20
❑ XZ345 'W' Sud Gazelle AH.1 78 ex B' Down (trials 9-20), Fleetlands, MW. SOC 18-4-19 [2] 9-20
❑ XZ642 Westland Lynx AH.7 80 ex MW. SOC 11-4-15. Arrived 10-11-15 7-17
❑ XZ653 Westland Lynx AH.7 80 ex Fleetlands. SOC 11-4-15. Arrived 17-6-15 7-17
❑ XZ666 Westland Lynx AH.7 81 ex Arborfield, 669, 655, 665, 655, LCF, 651. F/n 7-17 7-17
❑ XZ679 Westland Lynx AH.7 82 ex MW. SOC 11-4-15. Arrived 3-9-15 7-17
❑ XZ731 '311' Westland Lynx HMA.8SRU 80 ex St Athan, MW, Boscombe Down, 815, HAS.3, 702, HAS.2, 815. SOC 23-9-16. Arrived 24-7-19 3-21
❑ XZ732 '315' Westland Lynx HMA.8SRU 81 ex St Athan, MW, 815, 702, 815, HAS.3, 702, 815, HAS.2, 829, 702, 815 3-21
❑ ZA735 Sud Gazelle AH.1 80 ex Arborfield, 25 Flt. Arrived 26-8-15 [2] 7-17
❑ ZA769 'K' Sud Gazelle AH.1 80 ex Arborfield, MW, 670, ARWF. F/n 7-17 [2] 7-17
❑ ZD259 '474' W'land Lynx HMA.8SRU 83 ex St Athan, MW, 815, HAS.3, 702, 815 3-21
❑ ZD260 '313' W'land Lynx HMA.8SRU 83 ex St Athan, MW, 815, HAS.3, 815, 829, 815. SOC 23-9-16 3-21
❑ ZD261 '314' W'land Lynx HMA.8SRU 83 ex St Athan, MW, 815, 702, 815, HAS.3, 702, 829, 815 3-21
❑ ZD262 '316' W'land Lynx HMA.8SRU 83 ex St Athan, MW, 815, 702, 815, HAS.3, 702, 815 3-21
❑ ZD268 '366' W'land Lynx HMA.8SRU 83 ex St Athan, MW, 702, 815, HAS.3, 815 3-21
❑ ZE381 'X' Westland Lynx AH.7 84 ex Arborfield, Yeovil, 671, 25 Flt, 657, 655, 659, 655, 665. First noted 4-16 7-17
❑ ZJ191* McDD Apache AH.1 02 ex Middle Wallop. SOC 8-12-23 [2] 12-23
❑ ZJ223* McDD Apache AH.1 03 ex Middle Wallop. SOC 9-11-23 [2] 12-23
❑ TAD.001 Sud Gazelle CIM ~ ex Arborfield, MW. Cabin. First noted 4-16 [2] 4-16
❑ TAD.007 Westland Lynx CIM ~ ex Arborfield, MW. Fuselage number TO.42 4-16
❑ TAD.011 Westland Lynx CIM ~ ex Arborfield, MW. First noted 4-16 4-16
❑ TAD.012 Westland Lynx CIM ~ ex Arborfield, MW. First noted 4-16 4-16
❑ TAD.015 Sud Gazelle AH.1 ZB668 92 ex Arborfield, MW, Arborfield, Fleetlands, UNFICYP, Crashed 30-11-92. First noted 4-16 [2] 7-17
❑ TAD.023 Sud Gazelle AH.1 XX454 76 ex Arborfield, Waddington, MW, 663, 662, 656, 657, 659, 669, 664, 654, 669, 659 [2] 7-17

■ **[1]** XZ191 has a doppelganger on show at the museum, above. **[2]** All Westland-built.

MALMESBURY

Dyson Campus Institute of Engineering Technology: Harrier GR.7 ZD462 departed by road on 17th July 2022, ending up at North Weald, Essex. ◆ **Private** *location, prior arrangement* **only** | **www.dysoninstitute.ac.uk**

❑ XM173 'A' EE Lightning F.1A 60 ex Old Sodbury, Newton (Lancs), Bentley Priory, Binbrook 8414M (28-5-74), Binbrook TFF, Leuchars TFF, 226 OCU, 56. Arrived 11-2-13, 'flies' in the canteen, 56 Sqn colours 7-23

MARLBOROUGH on the A346 south of Swindon

A Dominie is *believed* to still be at a *private* location in the *general* area.

❑ N19XY 'J' HS Dominie T.1 XS731 66 ex Kemble, Cranwell, XS731, 55, 3 FTS, 6 FTS, 1 ANS. F/n 2-15 5-15

MELKSHAM on the A350 south of Chippenham

Adrian Brimson and **John Phillips** acquired Skeeter AOP.12 XL765 on 5th August 2000, moving it to this location on 22nd July 2001. Since then, the pair amassed a large stock of parts to aid its restoration. Impressed with the Wight Aviation Museum, they donated it and XL765 made the the trek to Sandown, Isle of Wight, on 16th October 2022.

No.**2385 (Melksham) Squadron Air Cadets**: Lancaster Road, Bowerhill.

❑ WP863 DHC Chipmunk T.10 G-ATJI 55 ex Boscombe Down, Hurn, Marlborough, Chippenham 8360M, Shawbury, G-ATJI (de-reg 3-1-68), RAFC, 664, RAFC. SOC 4-4-73. Hawarden-built. Cockpit 1-24

OAKSEY PARK AERODROME south of Cirencester, east of the A429 EGTW

As part of the 'tidy up' (see page 7) Airtourer G-ATCL has been deleted.

❑ G-ANJK	DH Tiger Moth	41	ex Yarcombe, T6066, 1 GU, 2 GS, 2 RFS, 25 RFS, L'pool UAS, 28 EFTS, 24 EFTS		N11-21
❑ NL985	DH Tiger Moth G-DHBZ	44	ex G-BWIK, Thruxton, Sywell, Cranfield, Leighton Buzzard, Bushey, Hendon, Finningley, Colerne, Cwmfelinfach 7015M (10-4-53), 9 AFTS, 2 GS, Lon UAS, Queen's UAS, 11 RFS, 5 RFS, Birm UAS, 16 EFTS, 14 EFTS. Morris-built. Damaged 23-5-71, SOC 2-6-71	[1]	5-21

■ **[1]** Once on charge with the RAF Museum, *India-Kilo* was badly damaged by fire at Hendon 23-5-71 and was replaced by T6296 from Fleet Air Arm stocks (on show at Cosford, Shropshire). 'DHBZ' is as close to 'DH82' as you can get in letters.

OLD SARUM AERODROME east of the A345 north of Salisbury EGLS

Boscombe Down Aviation Collection (BDAC): This superb collection celebrated a decade at Old Sarum on 1st July 2022. It charts trials and test aviation in general as well as the activities at nearby Boscombe Down and the incredible heritage of Old Sarum. Make sure you visit the World War One gallery – an exceptional display of material.

BDAC has always had a policy of extra access and the website proudly declares: "Sit in more aircraft cockpits than anywhere else in the UK" – no idle boast. A marvellous detail is an 'ops' room-like blackboard showing exhibit status, including what's new, what's being restored, and which cockpits are open. Visitors enter the display hall through a fuselage 'slice' of Hercules C.1 XV196, acquired in July 2017.

Meteor NF.11 WD686 ended its loan at Defford, Worcs; ownership was then transferred to Wattisham Station Heritage and it relocated directly to Wattisham, Suffolk. Phoenix UAV BAPC.356 was returned to Rochester, Kent, on 13th July 2022. Phoenix UAV ZJ469 arrived from Larkhill, Wilts, in June 2022 to supply parts for ZJ477. It was in turn passed on, moving to Bournemouth, Dorset, 25th October 2022.

A one-off abbreviation is used in the listing below, Boscombe Down = BD: the collection's former home.

◆ *Hangar 1 South, SP4 6DZ* | **01722 323636** | **email** via website | **www.boscombedownaviationcollection.co.uk**

❑ 'G-AMKL'*	Auster B.4 replica	19	BAPC.645, ex Newark. Arrived 14-10-22	[1]	1-24
❑ G-VIVM	BAC Jet Provost T.5 XS230	65	ex N Weald, G-BVWF, XS230 ETPS, T.5 prototype, 27 MU, BAC, T.4. Luton-built. Crashed 16-6-21, CoA 8-8-21. 'Fly Aviation UK' titles. Arrived 7-10-21	[2]	1-24
❑ '2783'	Royal A/c Factory BE.2c rep	07	BAPC.332, ex BD. BDAC-built. *Virgo Intacta*	[3]	1-24
❑ MS968	Taylorcraft Auster 5 G-ALYG	44	ex Henstridge, Charlton Mackrell, Heathrow, Irby, AOP.5 MS968, 661, 653. CoA 19-1-70, de-reg 15-10-14. Arrived 10-4-15	[4] [5]	1-24
❑ 'PD130'	Avro Lancaster I FSM	18	BAPC.482, forward fuselage. Arrived 10-19. Completion continuing	[6]	1-24
❑ WA577	Bristol Sycamore 3 G-ALST	r49	ex Sunderland, King's Heath, Shirley, St Athan 7718M (12-4-61), A&AEE, G-ALST (de-reg 17-10-50). Arrived 4-6-21		1-24
❑ WD321	DHC Chipmunk T.10 G-BDCC	51	ex BD, Husbands Bosworth, G-BDCC (crashed 29-8-99, de-reg 8-4-04) WD321, A&AEE, DH. Hawarden-built. Acquired 12-07		1-24
❑ WD790	Gloster Meteor NF.11	52	ex Usworth, Darlington, Leeming, 8743M (30-10-81), RAE Llanbedr, RRE, Ferranti, TRE. Arrived 3-11-18. Cockpit		1-24
❑ WG763	EE P.1A	55	ex Manchester, Henlow 7816M (7-8-63), RAE. Last flight 7-12-59. Arrived 31-1 *and* 1-2-22	[7]	1-24
❑ WH876	EE Canberra B.2(mod)	53	ex BD, Aberporth, BD, Chalgrove, Martin Baker, B.2(mod), A&AEE, U.10, B.2(mod), A&AEE, Pershore, 728, U.14, 73, 207, 11. Short-built. Acquired 22-5-01. Cockpit		1-24
❑ WJ865	EE Canberra T.4	54	ex BD, Bromsgrove, Stamford, Stock, Farnborough, ETPS, A&AEE. SOC 6-1-82. Acquired 7-07. Cockpit		1-24
❑ WK800	Gloster Meteor D.16	52	ex BD, Llanbedr, DS&TL, RAE, RAAF A77-876, U.21A, 23, 77 RAAF, F.8, RAF. Last flown 11-10-04. Acquired 1-09, arrived 23-7-12	[8]	1-24
❑ WN890	Hawker Hunter F.2	54	ex BD, Doncaster, Firbeck, Robertsbridge, Stamford, Hedge End, BD, A&AEE, AWA. AWA-built. SOC 21-1-63. Acquired 6-05. Cockpit	[9]	1-24

		Type		History	Notes	
❑ WT648		Hawker Hunter F.1	54	ex BD, Salisbury, Kexborough, Stock, St Athan, Weeton 7530M (22-11-57), DFLS. Acquired 4-02. Cockpit	[9]	1-24
❑ WT859		V-S 544	56	ex BD, Long Marston, Brooklands, Ruislip, Foulness, Culdrose, Fleetlands, Culdrose, Lee-on-Solent A2499, RAE, A&AEE. SOC 29-11-60. Acquired 7-02. Cockpit		1-24
❑ WV910		Hawker Sea Hawk FGA.4	55	ex BD, DERA, DRA, ETPS, 806. Damaged 2-5-58. Acquired 2000. ETPS colours. Cockpit		1-24
❑ WZ736		Avro 707A	53	ex Manchester, Waddington, Cosford, Finningley, Colerne, 7868M, RAE Bedford, A&AEE. Bracebridge Heath-built. Arrived 31-1 *and* 1-2-22	[7]	1-24
❑ WZ753		Slingsby Grasshopper TX.1	52	ex Southampton, Halton, London. Arr 7-4-19, dismantled		1-24
❑ XF113		V-S Swift F.7	56	ex BD, Salisbury, Bath, Frome, Farnborough, ETPS, A&AEE, Handling Sqn. SOC 31-10-61. Acquired 2000. Cockpit	[4]	1-24
❑ XF375	'6'	Hawker Hunter F.6A G-BUEZ	55	ex BD, Spanhoe, Duxford, G-BUEZ (de-reg 28-8-01), Cranwell 8736M, (10-1-82), ETPS, EE, RR. AWA-built. Acquired 4-07. ETPS colours. Outside		1-24
❑ XG290		Hawker Hunter F.6	56	ex BD, Salisbury, Hurn, Bruntingthorpe, Swanton Morley, Bentley Priory, Halton 8711M (20-10-81), Laarbruch SF, A&AEE. Acquired 6-11. Cockpit	[4]	1-24
❑ XJ476		DH Sea Vixen FAW.1	57	ex BD, Southampton, BD, A&AEE, HSD, ATU Woomera, DH, A&AEE, RRE. Christchurch-built. Acquired 6-06. Cockpit	[10]	1-24
❑ XK699		DH Comet C.2	57	ex Lyneham, Henlow 7971M (last flight 13-6-67), 216. Hatfield-built. *Sagittarius*. Arrived 12-11-13. Forward fuselage, outside		1-24
❑ 'XN149'	BMU	Slingsby T.21B	62	ex North Coates, East Kirkby, 9G-ABD, BGA.1085. *Spruce Goose*. Crashed 22-9-97, CoA 27-9-97. Arrived 30-11-14. Stored	[4] [11]	1-24
❑ XN726		EE Lightning F.2A	61	ex BD, Rayleigh, Foulness, Farnborough, 8545M, Gütersloh, 92, 19. Cockpit. SOC 1-4-77. Arrived 4-02	[12]	1-24
❑ XP899	'D'	Westland Scout AH.1	63	ex M Wallop, Arborfield, M Wallop, ARWF. Crashed 1-11-79. Arrived 14-9-15	[13]	1-24
❑ XR650	'28'	Hunting Jet Provost T.4	63	ex BD, DERA, Halton 8459M (19-12-75), SoRF, CAW, CATCS, 3 FTS, CAW, 7 FTS. Acquired 4-02. Outside		1-24
❑ XR898		Northrop Shelduck D.1	62	BAPC.365, ex 'XT005', Rochester, Purfleet, Rochester, Chatham, Amesbury (?). Arrived 5-3-18	[14]	1-24
❑ XS231		BAC Jet Provost T.5 G-ATAJ	65	ex BD, South Molton, Barnstaple, Ipswich, Bruntingthorpe, Hurn, Scampton, Shawbury, A&AEE, G-ATAJ (de-reg 10-3-65). Acquired 9-09. Cockpit	[4] [15]	1-24
❑ XS743		Beagle 206 Z2	64	ex QinetiQ, ETPS, A&AEE. Last flight 7-11-14. Arrived 9-3-22. *Eric Fitzpatrick* and *Bertie*	[16]	1-24
❑ XS790		HS Andover CC.2	64	ex BD, DERA, DRA, RAE, Queen's Flight. Acquired 11-98. Much-modified nose. Cockpit		1-24
❑ XT437	'423'	Westland Wasp HAS.1	65	ex BD, Lee-on-Solent A2721[2] (23-3-88), A2641[2], 829, *Diomede* Flt, 829. Acquired 2001. *Del Boy*		1-24
❑ XV148*		HS Nimrod proto	67	ex St Mawgan, Malmesbury, Guildford, Woodford, Bedford, Pershore, A&AEE. Cockpit, arrived 27-4-23	[17]	1-24
❑ XV784		HS Harrier GR.3	70	ex BD, DS&TL, Wittering 8909M (10-6-86), 233 OCU, 4, 1, 4. Damaged 2-4-86. Acquired 2002. Cockpit	[18]	1-24
❑ XW560		SEPECAT Jaguar S.06	69	ex BD, East Grinstead, Farnborough, Warton, A&AEE. Damaged 11-8-72. Acquired 4-04. Cockpit	[4] [19]	1-24
❑ XX145*		SEPECAT Jaguar T.2A	74	ex Cosford, Bruntingthorpe, Woodhouse, Cranwell, BD, ETPS, 226 OCU, JOCU. ETPS colours. Arrived 24-8-23		1-24
❑ XX154		HS Hawk T.1	74	ex BD, ETPS, Llanbedr, DRA, RAE, HSA. Last flight 19-12-18, arrived 21-8-19. ETPS colours	[20]	1-24
❑ XX343		HS Hawk T.1	81	ex BD, DERA, ETPS. Crashed 8-4-97. Acquired 2000. ETPS colours. Cockpit	[4]	1-24
❑ XX734		SEPECAT Jaguar GR.1	74	ex Charlwood, Abingdon, Coltishall 8816M (21-11-84), Farnborough, Shawbury, Warton, Indian AF JI014, G-27-328, 6, JOCU. Arrived 5-5-13	[18] [21]	1-24

❑ XX761		SEPECAT Jaguar GR.1A	75	ex BD, DERA, DRA, Warton, 226 OCU, 14. *Pudsey*. Damaged 6-6-78. Acquired 2002. Cockpit	[18]	1-24
❑ XX919		BAC 111-402	66	ex BD, DERA, RAE, D-AFWC, PI-C-1121. Acquired 2001. Cockpit		1-24
❑ XZ335		Sud Gazelle AH.1	77	ex Doncaster, Sunderland, Shawbury, 6 Flt. Westland-built. Pod. Arrived 7-19		1-24
❑ XZ457	'104'	HS Sea Harrier F/A.2	79	ex BD, Yeovilton, 899, 800, 801, 800, 899, 800, 899, 700A. Crashed 20-10-95. Acquired 5-03. *The Sharp End*	[22]	1-24
❑ ZA242		Short MATS-B Mk.1A UAV	82	ex 'ZA220', Nether Wallop, Chandler's Ford, Larkhill, Manorbier. Last flight 5-2-83. Arrived 20-7-16	[23]	1-24
❑ ZA319		Panavia Tornado GR.1T	79	ex Bicester 9315M (19-3-02), St Athan, 15, TTTE, Warton, A&AEE. Arrived 4-11-21		1-24
❑ ZD936	'AO'	Panavia Tornado F.2	85	ex BD, 'Manchester', Bedford, St Athan, 229 OCU. Acquired 7-04. 229 OCU colours. Cockpit		1-24
❑ ZJ477		GEC-Marconi Phoenix UAV	98	ex Larkhill. Arrived 15-9-20. Displayed in 'folded' form		1-24
❑ ZJ748*		Meteor Mirach 100/5	c05	ex QinetiQ, Aberporth. Arrived 31-1-22		1-24
❑ 3150		Target Tech Banshee 400	~	ex Swansea, Manorbier. Acquired 11-13, arrived 12-13		1-24
❑ A92-466		GAF Jindivik 103BL	c75	BAPC.485, ex BD, Cardiff Airport (restoration 4-10 to 10-11), BD, Welshpool, Llanbedr, 'A92-664', 'A92-999', DRA, RAE. Last flight (= shot down) 8-7-69. Acquired 11-06	[24]	1-24
❑ 42-93510*	'CM'	Douglas C-47A-25-DK Skytrain	43	ex Welford, -?-, Kew, Ottershaw, Kew, Cranfield, 6W-SAE, F-GEFY, Senegal AF, French AF, OK-WAR, USAAF 42-93510. Oklahoma City-built. Cockpit. Arrived 16-3-22. 435th TCG, 78th TCS colours	[25]	1-24

■ **[1]** Reproduction of the rear-loading ambulance one-off of 1951; based on an unidentified 'donor' airframe. **[2]** Built at Luton as a T.4, converted to T.5 aerodynamic prototype and first flown at Warton 28-2-67. **[3]** BE.2b was built by a BDAC team at Boscombe Down over a 4½ year period by Don Evans, David Acton, Peter Shorten and Gordon Elliott. Piloted by Lt 'Bill' Heaton, 2783 made the first operational sortie from Boscombe Down, 25-11-17, and is known to have also operated from Old Sarum. **[4]** Airframes co-owned by John Sharpe and BDAC. **[5]** 653 Sqn was based at Old Sarum; MS968 flown by Capt D H G 'Dickie' Thrush to France on 19-6-44 and flown almost exclusively by him all the way through to Germany by 4-45. **[6]** Lancaster portrays Mk.I Special (Grand Slam) PD130. When staffing allows, public have access – the panels etc are all 'live'. Owned by Malcolm Goosey. **[7]** WG763 and WZ736 on loan from RAF Museum. **[8]** WK800 is on loan from Trevor Stone. **[9]** WN890 and WT648 on loan from the Air Defence Collection / Tony Dyer - see below. **[10]** Sea Vixen on loan from Solent Sky - see Southampton, Hampshire. **[11]** T.21 was regularly flown by former Luftwaffe test-pilot Hanna Reitsch when she was CFI of Ghana's Accra Gliding Club in the 1960**s**. As BGA.1085 it was converted to - or intended to be converted - to a motor glider. Restored to represent a Sedbergh TX.1 flown from Old Sarum by 622 GS. **[12]** XN726 on loan from Hugh Trevor. **[13]** Scout on long term loan from MoD. **[14]** Shelduck owned Steve Hall from 13-6-19. **[15]** XS231 bult at Luton as a T.4, first flown 16-3-65 as T.5 engine development airframe then brought up to full T.5 aerodynamic status. **[16]** Strictly not a Basset CC.1; this was the second pre-production example for the RAF, and as such the 206Z2. Fitted with a variable-stability system at Cranfield 71-72. **[17]** Unfinished Comet 4, became first 'full' - ie Spey-powered - Nimrod prototype; first flown by John Cunningham at Hawarden 23-5-67. Cockpit restored and on loan from Martin Painter. **[18]** XV784, XX734, XX761 co-owned by Ron Fulton and BDAC. **[19]** UK prototype Jaguar, first flown by Jimmy Dell 12-10-69. **[20]** Prototype Hawk, first flown at Dunsfold 21-8-74 by Duncan Simpson, delivered courtesy of 27 Sqn Chinook HC.6A ZH892 exactly 45 years later! Owned Chris Hodson. **[21]** XX734 is fitted with the wing of XX731. **[22]** XZ457 is a Falklands veteran: operating from *Hermes* two separate pilots accounted for two A-4 Skyhawks on 21-5-82 and two Daggers on 24-5-82: the 'kill tallies' are painted on the nose. **[23]** MATS-B on loan from UAV guru Mike Draper - see Stockbridge, Hampshire. When it was built at Castlereagh it should have become ZA242 but it was painted in error as ZA220 and never altered. **[24]** Jindivik is a composite, including parts from A92-244, -390, -442, -466 and -490. It *was* believed to be largely A92-664 and it wore this identity from about 1983 to 2010. It has been restored as A92-466 which was discovered under layers of paint on the rear fuselage. A92-466 was shot down by a Navy Sea Slug missile on its 25th sortie, 8-7-69. **[25]** C-47 on loan from Dave Hawkins. An alternative 'back story': it could be 1944 and Oklahoma-built C-47A-30-DK 43-48020, which became RAF Dakota III KG737, serving with 525 Sqn and 1381 TCU until SOC 7-11-46. It then served KLM as PH-TDT, later F-OAFS, transferring to the Senegalese identity 6V-AAE. Over to you!

North Hangar light aircraft: Within BDAC's second display hangar a residual number of aerodrome residents had been located with the bulk moving out by road during 2022-2023: Stolp Starlet G-AZTV 3rd October 2023 to Hinton-in-the-Hedges; Renegade Spirit G-RENE 12th April 2022; Sky Arrow G-ROME 2nd August 2023; Skylark G-SGNT 13th November 2023 to Upper Catford; Auster 5 NJ633 (G-AKXP) 22nd May 2022 for 'Gloucestershire'. That leaves...

❑ G-ANNG	DH Tiger Moth	42	ex Farnborough, 15 EFTS, DE524. Morris-built. CoA 8-6-19	10-23

Air Defence Collection (ADC): Two of Wiltshire-based **Tony Dyer**'s cockpits (Hunters F.1 WT648 and F.2 WN890) are on loan to BDAC – see above – so this is an ideal 'port of convenience' under which to feature the remainder of his collection. Other projects include: a Sopwith Camel cockpit including many original fittings; *Aurora* (Tony likes naming his creations) a Spitfire I that he refers to as a "slice through cockpit"; a substantial chunk of the cockpit of Seafire F.46 LA546 *Bea* (acquired in

2006, see also Colchester, Essex); and many recovered parts - around 85% of the fuselage - from P-51D Mustang 44-13835 *Dam Yankee* (crashed 8th February 1945). The cockpit of Lynx HAS.3 ZD264 was passed on to a collector at Blandford Forum, Dorset. ◆ ***Not** open to the public, some airframes with BDAC - see above* | **rocketeer1940@aol.com**

❑ P3554	Hawker Hurricane I	40	ex Salisbury, Swanage, 607, 213, 56, 32. Shot down 5-10-40. *Jessamy*	[1]	1-24
❑ –	V-S Spitfire V	~	fuselage. *Valerie*	[2]	1-24
❑ KF532	NAA Harvard T.2B	44	ex Sywell, Winthorpe, Lossiemouth, 781, 799, 727, 799, 733, 758. SOC 9-4-54. Noorduyn-built. Cockpit. Arr 10-4-21		1-24

■ **[1]** Started in 1978 with the intention to create an airframe 85% composed of wartime Hurricane material. To date over *100* Hurricanes have 'provided' parts. Main cockpit items come from P3554 - Plt Off D Evans of 607 Sqn baled out from it over Swanage after combat with a Bf 109. **[2]** Follows the same lines as the Hurricane; extends from Frame 5 (the firewall) to Frame 13.

SALISBURY

Secret Spitfires Memorial: At Hudson's Field, Castle Road - the A345 south of the Old Sarum Iron Age Fort - to commemorate the local dispersed Spitfire assembly site. ◆ **www.secretspitfiresmemorial.org.uk**

❑ 'EN398'	'JE-J'	V-S Spitfire IX FSM	20	BAPC.580, ex Old Sarum. GB Replicas (Norwich)-built. Plinth-mounted 7-2-21	[1]	1-24

■ **[1]** There are other 'EN398s': Coningsby, Lincs; Taunton, Somerset; Pyle, Wales.

Also: Turbulent G-ASHT and Currie Wot G-BANV have been deleted.

SALISBURY PLAIN

Ultimately a location in this sprawling site will be the venue for the new **Royal Artillery Museum**, previously at Woolwich, Gtr Lon, and closed in June 2016. Previous exhibits Auster AOP.9 XR271, Shelduck XT583 and Phoenix ZJ356 are held at Wroughton, Wilts. Keep an eye on **https://royalartillerymuseum.com**

Within the vast Copehill Down exercise zone – known as the FIBUA, Fighting In Built-Up Areas – are two Lynx cabins.

❑ XZ171		Westland Lynx AH.1	77	ex 664, 671, RR, A&AEE	5-19
❑ XZ203	'F'	Westland Lynx AH.7	79	ex M Wallop, 671, LCF	5-19

SWINDON

Restoration of a Currie Wot continues in the *general* area.

❑ G-AYMP	Currie Wot	72	CoA 4-10-94	9-23

WARMINSTER

Last noted at the wargaming site in May 2010, Sparrowhawk II G-BOZU has been deleted.

WESTBURY on the A350 between Trowbridge and Warminster

Nigel Coward: Handed on both of his projects by mid-2023: Chipmunk T.10 WD387 (G-BDDD) destination unknown and Canberra T.4 WT486 to the Warton, Lancs, area.

WINTERBOURNE GUNNER east of the A338 northeast of Salisbury

Defence Chemical, Biological, Radiological and Nuclear [Event] **Centre** and the **Defence Science and Technology Laboratory**-run the Porton Down 'Danger Area'. The Dominie is used by the Health Authority Response Team. Lynx AH.9A ZG920 travelled to Wattisham, Suffolk, by July 2023.

❑ XS736	'S'	HS Dominie T.1	66	ex Ipswich, Cranwell, 55, 3 FTS, 6 FTS, RAFC, CAW	4-21

WROUGHTON on the A4361 south of Swindon

National Collections Centre (NCR) / **Science Museum Group**: The publicly accessible, vast artefacts and documents facility is on course for a grand opening in 2024: the first items began to arrive in June 2021. Managed by the Science Museum, ten former RAF hangars are held: four 'L' type, four 'D' type and a pair of 'Cs': three of which are not in use. All national museums will keep artefacts – large and small – at the site.

Unlike the NCR, it seems the Science Museum airliner collection and airframe store remains a closed book.

◆ *Prior arrangement* **only** | **www.sciencemuseum.org.uk**

❑ G-ACIT	DH Dragon	33	ex Southend, Beagle, ANT Blackpool, BEA, Scottish, Highland. Last flight 19-9-71, de-reg 26-4-02. Acquired 8-83	1-22

Reg		Type	Year	History	Note	Noted
❑ G-ALXT		DH Dragon Rapide	43	ex Strathallan, Staverton, 4R-AAI, CY-AAI, G-ALXT, Dominie NF865, 5 MU, 18 MU, MCS. Brush-built. Arrived 12-81. Railway Air Services colours, *Star of Scotia*		1-22
❑ G-APWY		Piaggio P.166	59	ex Southend, Marconi. CoA 14-3-81, last flown 1-6-83, de-reg 20-10-00		1-22
❑ G-APYD		DH Comet 4B	60	ex Dan-Air, Channel G-APYD, Olympic SX-DAL, BEA, G-APYD. Hatfield-built. CoA 3-8-79, last flown 1-11-79, de-reg 23-11-79		1-22
❑ G-ATTN		Piccard hot-air balloon	66	ex South Kensington, Hayes, South Ken'. De-reg 5-12-77. Acquired circa 1978		1-20
❑ G-AVZB		LET Z37 Cmelak	67	ex Southend, OK-WKQ. CoA 5-4-84, last flew 25-6-88, de-reg 21-12-88		1-22
❑ G-AWZM		HS Trident 3B-101	71	ex Heathrow, BA, BEA. CoA 13-12-85, last flew 28-2-86, de-reg 18-3-86		1-22
❑ G-BBGN		Cameron A-375 hot-air balloon	74	ex South Kensington, Hayes, South Ken'. *Daffodil II*. De-reg 22-8-89. Gondola, acquired 1989		2-18
❑ G-BGLB		Bede BD-5B Micro	c79	ex Booker. CoA 4-8-81, de-reg 21-11-91. Arrived 11-93		2-18
❑ G-BXXR		Lovegrove Four-Runner	98	de-reg 3-11-09		2-18
❑ G-IPSY		Rutan Vari-Eze	82	CoA 6-8-09, de-reg 16-7-09		2-18
❑ G-MMCB		Huntair Pathfinder II	r83	de-reg 23-11-88. Acquired 9-85		2-18
❑ G-RBOS		Colt AS-105 hot air airship	82	CoA 6-3-87, de-reg 3-4-97. Acquired 9-87		2-18
❑ BQT*		EoN 460 Srs 1	64	BGA.1156, ex Manchester, Seighford, Staffs GC, EGC / BGA.2666, BGA.1156. CoA 18-4-97. First noted 6-20		6-20
❑ –		Lilienthal Glider	c1894	BAPC.52. ex South Kensington, Hayes, South Kensington, Oxford, Berlin. Acquired 1920	[1]	1-22
❑ –		Newbury Manflier MPA	76	BAPC.162. Major elements, acquired 9-81		2-18
❑ –		Chargus Midas	78	BAPC.172. Acquired 1981		2-18
❑ –		Birdman Grasshopper hg-g	77	BAPC.173. Acquired 1980		2-18
❑ –		Bensen B-7 gyroglider	c74	BAPC.174. Acquired 1980		2-18
❑ –*		Volmer VJ-23 Swingwing	77	BAPC.175, ex Manchester, Old Warden. Last flight 8-5-81. Acquired 29-9-83, first noted 6-20	[2]	6-20
❑ –		Wood Ornithopter	c63	BAPC.182, ex Manchester, Hale. Incomplete, stored	[3]	12-18
❑ –		McBroom Cobra 88 h-g	76	BAPC.188. Acquired 10-85		2-18
❑ –*		Flexiform hang-glider	c82	BAPC.252, ex Manchester, Lancaster. Built Macclesfield. Acquired 1990, first noted 6-20		6-20
❑ –		Hartman Ornithopter	59	BAPC.276. Ex Cranfield. Acquired 1993		2-18
❑ –		Skyhook Safari	c79	ex Manchester. Acquired 1998, first noted 6-20	[4]	6-20
❑ EI-AYO		Douglas DC-3A-197	36	ex Shannon, N655GP, N65556, N225JB, N8695SE, N333H, N16071. Last flown 25-12-78		1-22
❑ N18E		Boeing 247	33	ex Wings and Wheels, Orlando, Sky Tours, N18E, N18, N13340 CAA, United/National A/T. Last flown 3-8-82		1-22
❑ N7777G		Lockheed L-749A-79 Constellation	47	ex G-CONI (de-reg 13-6-84), Dublin, Lanzair, KLM PH-LDT, PH-TET. Arrived 12-8-83		1-22
❑ OO-BFH		Piccard gas balloon	32	ex South Kensington, Hayes, South Kensington. Gondola, acquired circa 1937		2-18
❑ VP975	'M'	DH Devon C.2/2	49	ex RAE Farnborough, A&AEE, CCCF, 19 GCF, CPE. Last flew 2-86		1-22
❑ XP505		Folland Gnat T.1	62	ex South Kensington, RAE, MinTech, Dunsfold, CFS. Last flew 18-11-84		1-22
❑ XR271		Auster AOP.9	62	ex Woolwich, Larkhill, St Athan, M Wallop. NEA 8-11-68	[5]	10-16
❑ XT583		Northrop Shelduck D.1	65	ex Woolwich. 'Army' titles	[5]	10-16
❑ ZJ356		GEC-Marconi Phoenix UAV	c95	ex Woolwich. 'Army' titles	[5]	10-16
❑ ZJ452		GEC-Marconi Phoenix UAV	c95	'Army' titles		2-18
❑ 100509		Focke Achgelis Fa 330A-1 Bachstelze	44	ex South Kensington, Farnborough. Weser Flug-built. Acquired 2-46		2-18

■ **[1]** No.11 'Normalapparat' hang-glider built by Otto Lilienthal and brought to the UK in March 1895. **[2]** VJ-23 flown by David Cook across the Channel 9-5-78 - first powered hang-glider to do so. **[3]** Built by Benjamin Graham Wood of Bowdon, Gtr Man, a hopeful Kremer Prize chaser... **[4]** Skyhook flown by Len Gabriel London to Paris 27-8-79 and presented to the (Manchester) museum by Len. **[5]** Stored on behalf of the Royal Artillery Museum – see Salisbury Plain, Wilts

WORCESTERSHIRE

BEWDLEY on the A456, west of Kidderminster

Ross McNeill ◆ *Prior arrangement* **only** | **rossmcneill@btinternet.com**

❑ 'Z5663'		Hawker Hurricane II	~	fuselage, complex composite	1-24
❑ -		Avro Anson II	~	ex Canada, RCAF. Cockpit	1-24
❑ XH175	'AR'	EE Canberra PR.9	60	ex Stock, St Athan, 1 PRU, 39, 58. Short-built. Cockpit	1-24

BIRLINGHAM on the A4104, east of the B4080 to the west of Evesham

◆ **Private** *collection, prior appointment* **only**

❑ WF299		Hawker Sea Hawk FB.3	54	ex 'WN105', Helston, St Agnes, Topcliffe, Catterick 8164M, Lee-on-Solent, Culdrose SAH-8 A2662, A2509 (21-7-61), 802, 738, 736. AWA-built	8-23
❑ WH166		Gloster Meteor T.7	51	ex Digby 8052M (9-9-69), CFS, 5 CAACU, CAW, 4 FTS, 205 AFS, 210 AFS, 208 AFS	8-23
❑ WZ425		DH Vampire T.11	52	ex Cardiff-Wales, Woodford, Chester, St Athan, 5 FTS, RAFC, 229 OCU, CGS. Christchurch-built. SOC 24-11-67	6-22
❑ XF526	'78' *and* 'E'	Hawker Hunter F.6	56	ex St Athan, Halton 8679M (9-11-81), Laarbruch SF, 4 FTS, 229 OCU, 56, 43, 56, 63, 66	8-23
❑ 'XN623'		Hunting Jet Provost T.3 XN632	61	ex Eaglescott, Chivenor, St Athan 8352M (16-7-73), Kemble, Shawbury, 3 FTS	8-23

BROMSGROVE on the A448 northwest of Redditch

Jason Allen, Brian Barrett and Bob Dunn of the **Wolverhampton Aviation Group** keep their Hunter cockpit locally.

❑ XE597		Hawker Hunter FGA.9	56	ex Moreton-in-Marsh, Halton, Bentley Priory 8874M (4-10-85), Brawdy, 1 TWU, 2 TWU, TWU, 229 OCU, W Raynham SF, 1, 54, MoA, 208, 56, 63, 66. Cockpit, acquired 19-3-02. 1 Squadron colours	1-23

DEFFORD on the A4104 southwest of Pershore

RAF Defford Museum: Established and run by the **Defford Airfield Heritage Group** in association with the National Trust. Visitors pay Croome Park's admission charge; there is no additional charge to visit this fascinating museum.

The loan of Meteor WD686 from BDAC, delayed by Covid, was completed on 8th September 2023 when it was passed on to Wattisham, Suffolk, and covered accommodation.

◆ *Within Croome Park, WR8 9DW* | **email** via website | **http://deffordairfield heritagegroup.wordpress.com** – superbly detailed site | also **www.nationaltrust.org.uk/croome**

❑ WD956		EE Canberra B.2	51	ex Cosford, Aldridge, Pershore, RRE, RAE, Vickers. SOC 30-12-64. Cockpit [1]	1-24

■ **[1]** Served with Vickers, Wisley, testing the RED DEAN missile. Later joined RAE/RRE: the cockpit *may* have been grafted to WD931.

EVESHAM on the A46 northeast of Cheltenham

The Valley Evesham: The retail complex at the junction of the A44 and A46 has a Cherokee as an attraction/obstacle in the adventure golf course. ◆ **www.thevalleyshopping.co.uk**

❑ G-SMTH*		Piper Cherokee 140	70	ex Hurn, G-AYJS. De-reg 2-08-17. Arrived 15-2-22	1-24

Holdair: Martyn Holder *should* still have a *private* workshop in the area.

❑ XX665		SAL Bulldog T.1	74	ex Selby, Wellesbourne M', Halton, Newton 9289M, E Low, Abn, E Low UASs. Crashed 20-9-97. Cockpit. Arrived by 4-18	5-18

HONEYBOURNE north of the village, on a minor road between Bretforton and Mickleton

All Things Wild: 'Hands on' animals and other attractions. ◆ **www.allthingswild.co.uk**

❑ XP346		Westland Whirlwind HAR.10	62	ex Long Marston, Tattershall Thorpe, Shawbury, Lee-on-Solent, Akrotiri 8793M (2-9-83), 84, 22, 225. F/n 12-14	1-24

KIDDERMINSTER

Paintball Park Kidderminster: Blakedown. ◆ *Prior arrangement* **only** | **www.paintballpark.co.uk**

❑ XZ193	'4'	Westland Lynx AH.7	78	ex Weeton, Hixon, Fleetlands, 671, 656, 665,656, 653, ARWF. Cabin. Arrived 2-18	7-22

WORCESTER

Jungle Safari Adventure Golf: Within the Ravenmeadow Golf Centre. ◆ **www.adventuregolfworcester.com**

❑ G-AVWN	Piper Arrow 180	67	CoA 10-4-09, de-reg 13-3-09. First noted 7-19	12-23

EAST YORKSHIRE

Includes the unitary authority of Kingston upon Hull

BEVERLEY AERODROME or Linley Hill, on minor roads north of Beverley

Hull Aero Club: Cherokee G-BEYT had gone by April 2022 – no 'forwarding address'.

BREIGHTON AERODROME in between Bubwith and Breighton, east of Selby

Real Aeroplane Company (RAC): Aircraft operated by Tony 'Taff' Smith, Rob Fleming and friends including the airworthy Aeronca 100 G-AEVS, Dart Kitten G-AEXT, Magister T9738 (G-AKAT), Argus HB751 (G-BCBL) etc are based at this delightful former bomber airfield. Elements of Nigel Ponsford's collection are also kept here - see also under Selby, N Yorks.

Listed below are non-flyers, stored, or long-term restoration projects. Chilton DW.1 G-AESZ was back in permit by 2023. Abiding by the 'tidying up' outlined on page 7, the following have been deleted: DR.400 G-BAHL, Jodels G-BDDF and G-BDJD and Emeraude G-BJVS. Evans VP-1 G-BAAD departed by road on 10th November 2023 – after three decades of residence – for restoration in Norfolk. ◆ *RAC members* **only** *but rates* very *reasonable* | *Selby, YO8 6DS* | **www.realaero.com**

❑ G-ADXS		Mignet HM.14 'Flea'	35	ex Cambridge, East Tilbury, Andrewsfield, Southend, Staverton, Southend. CoA 1-12-36, de-reg 1-12-46. *The Fleeing Flea*	[1]	1-24
❑ G-AFSV		Chilton DW.1A	39	ex Warwick, 'Coventry'. CoA 12-7-72. Arrived 3-9-20		1-24
❑ G-AMAW		Luton Minor	48	ex Batley, Old Warden, Hitchin. CoA 6-8-88	[2]	1-24
❑ G-AXEI		Ward Gnome	67	ex East Kirkby, Tattershall. De-reg 30-5-84	[3] [4]	1-24
❑ G-AYDV		Coates Swalesong SA.2	74	CoA 8-8-07	[2]	1-24
❑ G-JUNG		Bücker Jungmann	52	ex Spanish AF E.3B-143. CASA-built. CoA 30-6-<u>09</u>. Arr 10-19		1-24
❑ G-MMUL		Ward Elf	r84	ex Newark area. De-reg 12-4-89	[3] [4]	1-24
❑ G-OMIC		Bücker Jungmeister	40	ex HB-MIC, USA, Swiss AF U-86. Last flown 1967. Arrived 21-9-20. Off-site		1-24
❑ G-TYAK		Yakovlev Yak-52	89	ex RA-01038. IAR Bacau-built. CoA 29-4-16		1-24
❑ 'F50'		Mignet HM.14 'Flea'	89	BAPC.329, ex Harrogate	[4]	1-24
❑ N102L		Bücker Jungmann	39	ex HB-UTT, Swiss AF A-77. Dornier-built. Off-site		1-24
❑ 491273	'51'	Aero L29 Delfin	~	ex Chester, YL-PAG, Soviet AF. Displayed		1-24

■ **[1]** 'Flea' built by Christopher Storey at Southend, it first flew 15-11-35 and gained Authorisation No.20. **[2]** G-AMAW was built by J A Coates and was also known as the Coates SA.1 Swalesong. Original design G-AYDV was also built by John. **[3]** On loan from Nigel Ponsford - see also Selby, N Yorks. **[4]** Gnome, Elf designed and built by Mick Ward, 'Flea' built by Mick.

Tony Brier: Has a *private* workshop in the area.

❑ 356	Kader Gomhouria Mk.6	~	ex Gainsborough, Egyptian AF	[1]	1-24

■ **[1]** Gomhouria is a licence-built Zlin Z.381. The Z.381 was itself a version of the Bücker Bü 181 Bestmann. Gomhourias were built by the Heliopolis Aircraft Works / Kader Industries.

BRIDLINGTON on the A165, south of Scarborough

Aircraft Preservation Foundation (APF): Run by <u>G</u>eremy Britton and Sarah Thorpe, there is a workshop in the *general* area. Three APF airframes are on loan at Exeter, Devon, assisting in tuition at the Future Skills Centre. Victor procedure trainer is at Woodford, Gtr Man. Present projects are Airbus A300B and Boeing 737-100 cockpit simulators, both of which will go out on loan when restoration is completed. ◆ *Prior arrangement* **only** | **info@aircraftpreservation.co.uk** | **www.aircraftpreservation.co.uk**

BROUGH south of the A63 west of Hull

BAE Systems Military Air Solutions: Volunteers have built two full-scale models/replicas which are kept within the factory site. Additionally, there is a scale replica Blackburn Kangaroo '1416' floatplane: while impressive it is not *W&R* material! Last noted in February 2015, the anonymous Typhoon cockpit/centre fuselage has been deleted.

❑	'G-AEBJ'*		Blackburn B.2 FSM	20	see above, first noted 1-23	[1]	12-22
❑	–*		Blackburn Monoplane	20	see above, first noted 1-23		12-22
❑	ZJ100*		HS Hawk Mk.102D	92	ex Finningley, Warton, Brough. Last flown 13-12-12	[2]	12-22
❑	–		HS Hawk T.53	83	ex Hurn, Indonesian AF LL-5313, G-9-498. BAE Systems c/s. Displayed, since 2005	[3]	1-24
❑	–	AJ-1	Lockheed F-35A EMU	c09	arrived 2009. 'Lifetime' fatigue testing airframe		11-17

■ **[1]** See Shuttleworth, Beds, for the *real* G-AEBJ. **[2]** Listed under Humberside, Lincs, in W&R28 (p132). Not so stored dismantled here in the structures hall, probably since 2016. **[3]** Composite, based upon T.53 LL-5313 but with a Srs 100 nose and other mods. **[4]** Referred to as SIFT - Single Seat Fatigue Test.

DRIFFIELD on the A614 north of Beverley

A Pup is at a *private* workshop to the north of the town.

❑	G-AXSD	Beagle Pup 100	69	ex Turweston, Bagby, Prestwick, G-35-139. CoA 10-5-08, de-reg 2-2-11. Arrived 3-1-18	1-22

FULL SUTTON AERODROME south of the A166, east of Stamford Bridge

Lake LA-250 G-LAKE is due for export to the USA as N250SP. Cessna 310 N315P and 421C N421CA have been deleted.

❑	G-BARV	Cessna 310Q	73	ex Elstree. CoA 18-8-09, de-reg 3-3-11. First noted 5-16	1-24
❑	G-COLH	Piper Cherokee 140	67	ex G-AVRT. De-reg 13-9-16. Fuselage	1-24

GILBERDYKE on the B1230 east of Goole

Joe and Lyndon Blackburne – The Provost Boys: The Canberra cockpit is being restored to represent a former Pershore B.6(mod) test bed. ◆ *Prior arrangement* **only | lyndon.blackburne@everquip.co.uk**

❑	WK124	'CR'	EE Canberra TT.18	54	ex Binbrook, South Clifton, Manston, Wyton 9093M, 100, 7, FRU, B.2, 213, 59, 103. Avro-built. Last flew 26-3-91. Cockpit. Arrived 26-10-17	[1]	1-24
❑	XD377		DH Vampire T.11	53	ex Doncaster, Firbeck, Barton, Thornaby, Elvington, Cosford, Birmingham, Shawbury 8203M (28-7-72), Hawarden, 66. Hawarden-built. Cockpit, stored		1-24
❑	XR662	'25'	Hunting Jet Provost T.4	63	ex Shrewsbury, Tettenhall, Baxterley, Wolverhampton, Bicester, Kemble, Finningley, Halton 8410M (6-6-74), SoRF, CAW, CATCS, RAFC, CAW, 6 FTS, CAW. F/n 10-17		1-24

■ **[1]** Centre section and starboard wing were with JARTS enclave at Newquay, Cornwall, in 2020.

KINGSTON UPON HULL

St Stephen's Shopping Centre: Ferensway, off the A1079. **www.ststephens-hull.com**

❑	'G-AAAH'	DH Moth FSM	17	BAPC.470. Ex railway station. *Jason*	[1]	12-23

■ **[1]** There is another replica at Sunderland, N&T, and – of course – the real thing at South Kensington, Gtr Lon.

Streetlife Museum of Transport: Five extensive galleries ranging between bicycles, cars, carriages, and railways.
◆ *High Street, Hull, HU1 1PS* | **01482 300300** | **www.hullmuseums.co.uk/streetlife-museum**

❑	'G-EBVO'	Blackburn Lincock FSM	99	BAPC.287, ex Brough	1-24

Also: The Miles types are at a *private* location in the *general* area.

❑	G-AGOY	Miles Messenger 3	43	ex West Chiltington, Hatch, Southill, Castletown, EI-AGE, HB-EIP, G-AGOY, U-0247. CoA 25-11-53	12-23
❑	G-AHAA	Miles Mercury 6	46	ex OY-ALW, D-EHAB, G-AHAA. First noted 1-19	12-23

LITTLE WEIGHTON west of the A164 and Cottingham

The former Pocklington Short 330 is *thought* to remain at a *private* location here.

❑	OY-MUB	Short 330-200	81	ex Pocklington, Alton, Hurn, G-BITX, G-14-3069. Fuselage	6-17

OTTRINGHAM on the A1033 east of Hedon

A long out-of-use Cessna 120 is stored at a *private* location in the *general* area.

❑ G-BRPG | Cessna 120 | 46 | ex N7203. CoA 29-8-94 | 8-20

PATRINGTON on the A1033 east of Hedon

A Vampire is kept at a *private* venue in the *general* area.

❑ XD542 'N' DH Vampire T.11 | 53 | ex Beverley, Montrose, Edzell, Cranwell, 'XD429', Colerne, Melksham 7604M (22-6-59), FWS, CGS. Hawarden-built | [1] | 6-21

■ **[1]** The booms of XD542 can possibly be found at Birkin, N Yorks.

PAULL on minor road south of Hedon

Former **Fort Paull Armouries and Visitors Centre**: *W&R28* (p265) repositioned XB259 at North Duffield, N Yorks, with the hopeful suffix 'Due'. Just like 'moving' a Typhoon from Duxford to Newark, this was an act of optimism. The mighty airlifter remained here, partially dismantled. In January 2024 the brave and determined lads at the Solway Aviation Museum, Carlisle, Cumbria, stepped up to launch a rescue with a fighting fund of £60,000 to be raised. Take a look at **www.solway-aviation-museum.co.uk** to see how you can help. Here's hoping by the next edition XB259 has a new home.

◆ *Prior arrangement* **only**

❑ XB259 | Blackburn Beverley C.1 G-AOAI | 55 | ex Beverley, Paull, Luton, RAE, G-AOAI (15-3-55 to 30-3-55). Last flown 30-3-74. See notes above | 1-24

POCKLINGTON AERODROME east of the A1079, west of the village

A Delfin is kept locally.

❑ '29' | Aero L29 Delfin | 893046 | ~ | ex '142', Market Drayton, Romanian AF | [1] | 3-19

■ **[1]** L29 is a composite, with outer wings and tailplane from another, or other, aircraft.

PRESTON on the B1239 north of Hedon

Wright's Garage: Staithes Road.

❑ WL627 | Vickers Varsity T.1 | 53 | ex Hull, Newton 8488M (3-3-76), 6 FTS, 2 ANS, 1 ANS, BCBS. Hurn-built. Cockpit | 9-21

SEWERBEY off the B1255 northeast of Bridlington

Sewerby Hall and Gardens: Amy Johnson opened the house in 1936 and to celebrate this there is a permanent exhibition dedicated to the locally born aviator. ◆ *Church Lane, Sewerby, YO15 1EA* | **www.sewerbyhall.co.uk**

SOUTH CAVE off the A1034, north of Brough

A *private* strip in the *general* area.

❑ G-AYZU*	Scheibe Falke	71	CoA 10-6-07, de-reg 24-11-22. Slingsby-built T.61A. F/n 12-21	12-21
❑ G-BAXE	Hughes 269A	64	ex N8931F. CoA 21-12,93, de-reg 17-10-19. Cab	8-21
❑ G-BLPI	Slingsby T.67B Firefly	84	de-reg 13-3-19. Cockpit	8-21
❑ G-SHPP	Hughes 269A	68	ex N80559. Cr 28-7-08, de-reg 9-12-08, CoA 3-6-09. Cab	8-21

STORWOOD on a minor road south of Elvington

A *private* store in the locality. ◆ *Prior arrangement* **only**

❑ G-VOCE*	Robinson R22 Beta	89	ex Doncaster, G-BSCL. De-reg 16-5-19	10-21
❑ XM565	Saro Skeeter AOP.12	59	ex Leeds, Ivybridge, M Wallop, Fleetlands, M Wallop, Southampton, M Wallop 7861M (17-9-64), 651	7-22
❑ XR627 'X'	Westland Scout AH.1	64	ex Townhill, Ipswich, Wattisham, Arborfield, Dishforth, M Wallop, Wroughton, Garrison Air Sqn, 3 CBAS	7-22
❑ XT788 '316'	Westland Wasp HAS.1 G-BMIR	67	ex Dunkeswell, Faygate, Tattershall Thorpe, Wroughton, 829. SOC 19-12-85. De-reg 22-12-95	7-22

NORTH YORKSHIRE

Includes the unitary authority of York

BAGBY AERODROME, or Thirsk, on the A19 southeast of Thirsk — EGNG

Cherokee Six G-SIMY was flying again by 2023. As part of the light aircraft 'tidy up' - details on page 7 - the following have been deleted: Warrior G-BSOK; Cessna 206 G-CCRC (bound for the USA); Tomahawk G-TMHK; Arrow N88NA.

	Reg	Code	Type	Year	Details	Note	Last noted
❑	G-ARLR		Beagle Terrier 2	48	ex Auster AOP.6, VW996, AAC, 663. CoA 9-9-01		12-23
❑	G-AZSW		Beagle Pup 100	69	ex PH-VRT, G-35-140. Cr 3-9-06, CoA 15-6-09, de-reg 15-2-11		12-23
❑	G-BGGM*		Piper Tomahawk 112	78	de-reg 28-4-21. Fuselage, first noted 3-22		12-23
❑	G-BXZA*		Piper Tomahawk 112	79	ex Eshott, Barton, N2480N. De-reg 26-10-16. First noted 3-22		12-23

BIRKIN east of the A162 and north of the A645, northeast of Knottingley

The paintball site has closed. As of late 2023, the Lynx and the Vampire remained. ◆ *Prior arrangement* **only**

	Reg	Code	Type	Year	Details	Note	Last noted
❑	–		Westland Lynx EMU	84	ex -?-, Weston-super-Mare, Yeovil. Zebra-striped	[1]	10-23
❑	XE874	'61'	DH Vampire T.11	54	ex Montrose, New Byth, Valley 8582M, Woodford, Chester, Shawbury,1 FTS, 4 FTS, 8 FTS, 4 FTS, 1 FTS, 4 FTS, 7 FTS. Christchurch-built. SOC 30-10-67	[2]	10-23

■ **[1]** Built at Yeovil in 1984 using Lynx and WG.30 parts. **[2]** XE874 was fitted with the booms of XD528. These lie nearby, semi-submerged in a small lake. XE874 has booms fitted which *may* come from XD542.

CROFT south of Darlington, Croft-on-Tees and the A167

Point Blank Paintball: On the former No.2 Communal Site of the wartime airfield.

◆ *Prior arrangement* **only | www.pointblankpaintball.co.uk**

	Reg	Code	Type	Year	Details	Note	Last noted
❑	G-ATSY		Wassmer Baladou IV	66	ex Rufforth, CoA 23-11-91, de-reg 6-3-15. Arr 26-3-15		3-23
❑	OY-XGP	'K6'	Scheibe SF.25B	70	ex D-KOSC. Displayed		3-23

DINSDALE on a minor road south of Middleton St George

Anthony Harker: Keeps a Lightning at a *private* location in the area.

	Reg	Code	Type	Year	Details	Note	Last noted
❑	XR718	'DA'	EE Lightning F.3	64	ex Walpole, Wattisham 8932M (9-2-87), ABDR, LTF, 11, LTF, 11, 5, LTF, 5, 11, LTF, 5, LTF, 5, 226 OCU, 29, 56		3-23

■ **[1]** There is a partial 'imposter' of XR718 at Bruntingthorpe, Leics.

ELVINGTON off the B1228 southeast of York

Yorkshire Air Museum and Allied Air Forces Memorial: As well as the aircraft, the watch tower and other World War Two buildings, the famed 'NAAFI' remains a 'must do' at this atmospheric site. A walk through the many wartime huts is a fascinating tour through the history of the region with memorials across the site. There are regular special events, including 'Night Shoots', 'Thunder Day' runs and pre-bookable tours of the Halifax re-creation.

YAM stepped up to offer the **Shackleton Preservation Group** a home for the taxiable AEW.2 WR963 and the cockpit of T.4 VP293 from Coventry, Warks. As *W&R* closed for press, the AEW.2 had yet to make the trek north; but it is listed here in anticipation. **shackleton963@outlook.com | www.facebook.com/avroshackleton**

◆ *Off the A64, YO41 4AU* | **01904 608595 | museum@yorkshireairmuseum.org | www.yorkshireairmuseum.org**

	Reg	Code	Type	Year	Details	Note	Last noted
❑	'G-AFFI'		Mignet HM.14 'Flea'	75	BAPC.76, ex Hemswell, Cleethorpes, Nostell, Rawdon. Yeadon Aeroplanes-built. Arrived 1989	[1]	1-24
❑	G-AVPN		HP Herald 213	64	ex Channel Express, I-TIVB, G-AVPN, D-BIBI, HB-AAK. CoA 14-12-99, de-reg 8-12-97. Flew in 20-10-97. Cockpit		1-24
❑	G-MJRA		Mainair Tri-Flyer	r82	ex Wetherby. (Demon 175 wing) De-reg 24-1-95. Arr 2001		7-21
❑	G-TFRB		Air Command 532	90	ex Hartlepool. CoA 6-8-98, de-reg 7-6-01. Arrived 11-01		1-24
❑	G-YURO		Shaw Europa 001	92	ex Wombleton. CoA 9-6-95, de-reg 22-4-98. Arrived 1997		1-24
❑	–		Wright Flyer replica	66	BAPC.28, ex Leeds, Eccleston, Cardington, Finningley. Arrived 11-99	[2]	1-24
❑	–		Cayley glider replica	72	BAPC.89, ex Manchester, Hendon, Lasham. Southdown Aero Services-built. Unveiled 12-8-99	[3]	1-24
❑	–		Blackburn 1911 replica	78	BAPC.130, ex Stoke, Helston, *Flambards*. Arrived 10-1-95		1-24
❑	'9970'		Royal Aircraft Factory BE.2c replica	62	BAPC.41, ex '6232', St Athan, Halton. 1 SoTT, Halton-built. Arrived 10-94		1-24

Local product, the Europa prototype, G-YURO, built at Kirkbymoorside, October 2022. *Brian Downs*

	Serial	Code	Type	Year	History	Notes	Date
❑	'9828'		Avro 504K replica	68	BAPC.42, ex 'H1968', St Athan. 1 SoTT, Halton-built. Arr 10-94		1-24
❑	'F943'	'S'	Royal Aircraft Factory SE.5a replica G-BKDT	r82	ex Selby, Elvington, Selby, G-BKDT. De-reg 11-7-91. Arrived 1987. Taxiable	[4]	1-24
❑	'N540'		Port Victoria Kitten rep	c80	ex Selby. Arrived 1996. Taxiable	[5]	1-24
❑	'P3873'	'YO-H'	Hawker Hurricane I FSM	99	BAPC.265. Arrived 10-00. 401 Sqn RCAF colours		1-24
❑	'R6690'	'PR-A'	V-S Spitfire I FSM	96	BAPC.254. TDL Replicas-built. Unveiled 9-96. 609 Sqn c/s		1-24
❑	FK338		Fairchild Argus II G-AJOZ	42	ex Woodhall Spa, Tattershall, Wigan, Mkt Drayton, Wigan, Southend, Sywell, G-AJOZ, FK338, Kemble, ATA 2 FP, 42-32142. Crashed 16-8-62, de-reg 27-2-67. Arrived 2000		1-24
❑	KN353		Douglas Dakota 4 G-AMYJ	44	ex 'KG427', Coventry, SU-AZF, G-AMYJ, XF747, G-AMYJ, KN353, 110, 96, 243, USAAF C-47B-25-DK 44-76384. CoA 4-4-97, de-reg 12-12-01. Arrived 10-12-01. Taxiable		1-24
❑	'LV907' *and* 'NP763'		HP Halifax recreation	44	BAPC.449, *Friday 13th*, 158 Sqn colours, Mk.III 'NP-F', to port, Mk.VI 'H7-N', 346 Sqn colours to starboard	[6]	1-24
❑	RA854		Slingsby Cadet TX.1	43	ex Wigan, Woodford, RAFGSA, 186 GS, 41 GS. Otley Motors-built. Arrived 6-4-00		1-24
❑	VP293*	'X'	Avro Shackleton T.4	51	ex Coventry, Duxford, Coltishall, Winthorpe, Coventry, Woodford, Coventry, E Kirkby, Strathallan, RAE, MOTU, A&AEE, MR.1, 206, 42, 224, 236 OCU. SOC 23-5-75, last flown 3-5-76. *Zebedee*. Cockpit, trailer-mounted. Arr 19-12-23	[7]	1-24
❑	VP967		DH Devon C.2/2 G-KOOL	48	ex Redhill, Goodwood, Redhill, East Surrey Tech G-KOOL (de-reg 13-1-12), 'G-DOVE', Biggin Hill, VP967, Kemble, Culdrose SF, 21, 207, SCCS, SCS, WCS, SCS, NCS, SCS, MCS, MCS, CCCF, 38 GCF, TTCCF, FCCS, 2 TAF CS, MCCS, RAFG CS, 2 TAF CS, Wahn SF, RCCF. SOC 1-4-82. Arrived 6-10-10. 207 Sqn colours, taxiable		1-24
❑	VV901		Avro Anson T.21	49	ex Bacup, Burtonwood, Cosford, Irton Holme, Leconfield, CFCCU, Dur UAS, 1 RFS. Arrived 8-6-93		1-24
❑	VW993		Beagle Terrier 2 G-ASCD	48	ex 'TJ704', Holme-on Spalding Moor, Nympsfield, Blackbushe, PH-SFT, G-ASCD (CoA 26-9-71, de-reg 5-10-89), Auster AOP.6 VW993, 651, 663. Arrived 1988		1-24
❑	WH846		EE Canberra T.4	54	ex Samlesbury, St Athan, Laarbruch SF, 231 OCU. SOC 29-1-82. Arrived 19-5-88		1-24
❑	WH903		EE Canberra B.2	54	ex 102, 617. Arrived 1992. Short-built, cockpit	[8]	1-24
❑	WH991		Westland Dragonfly HR.5	53	ex Storwood, Tattershall Thorpe, Tattershall, Wisbech, Taunton, Fleetlands, Culdrose SF, 705, 700, Eglinton SF, *Centaur* Flt, 705, *Illustrious* Flt. SOC 8-6-70. Arrived 10-94		1-24
❑	WK640	'C'	DHC Chipmunk T.10 G-BWUV	52	ex Halton, FSS, East Mids UAS, 7 AEF, RAFC, QUAS, St And UAS, 1 FTS, St And UAS, 1 RFS, 17 RFS. Hawarden-built. Cr 20-2-09, CoA 24-2-11. Cockpit. Arr 12-20. Stored	[9]	2-23

	Serial	Code	Type	Year	History	Note	Status
❑	'WK864'	'C'	Gloster Meteor F.8 WL168	54	ex Finningley, 'WH456', St Athan, Swinderby, Finningley, Heywood 7750M (10-5-62), APS Sylt, 604, 111. Arrived 12-4-96. 616 Sqn colours		1-24
❑	WR963*	'B-M'	Avro Shackleton AEW.2 G-SKTN	54	ex Coventry, N963WR, Waddington, Lossiemouth, 8 *Ermintrude*, 205, 28, 210, 224. *Gp Capt Dave Hencken*	[10]	**due**
❑	WS788	'Z'	Gloster Meteor NF(T).14	54	ex Leeming 'WS844', Patrington 7967M (5-9-67), 1 ANS, 2 ANS, NF.14, 152. AWA-built. Acquired 6-89, arrived 16-3-92		1-24
❑	XH278	'42'	DH Vampire T.11	55	ex Felton, Henlow 8595M, Upwood 7866M (9-11-64), 27 MU, RAFC. Hawarden-built. Arrived 10-2-02. RAFC c/s		1-24
❑	XH767	'L'	Gloster Javelin FAW.9	57	ex Leeming, Norwich, Monkton Farleigh, Worcester 7955M (10-7-67), Shawbury, 228 OCU, 11, 25, FAW.7. Arr 4-2-01		1-24
❑	XL231		HP Victor K.2	62	ex 55, 57, Witt Wing, Victor TF, Witt Wing, 139. Flew in 25-11-93. *Lusty Lindy.* Taxiable	[11]	1-24
❑	XL502		Fairey Gannet AEW.3 G-BMYP	61	ex Sandtoft, Carlisle, G-BMYP (CoA 29-9-89, de-reg 22-2-05), Leuchars 8610M (1-12-78), 849, Pershore, 849. Arr 11-3-05		1-24
❑	'XL571'	'V'	Hawker Hunter T.7 XL572	58	ex Brough, Hurn G-HNTR (de-reg 11-10-91), Cosford 8834M (23-8-84), XL572, 1 TWU, 2 TWU, TWU, 229 OCU. Arrived 12-1-95. 92 Sqn, 'Blue Diamonds' colours		1-24
❑	XM553		Saro Skeeter AOP.12 G-AWSV	59	ex Wattisham, Saxmundham, M Wallop, G-AWSV (de-reg 23-5-95), 15 MU, 5 Flt, 1 Wg. SOC 25-11-68. Arr 2009		1-24
❑	XN582	'95'	Hunting Jet Provost T.3A	61	ex Sleap, Bruntingthorpe, Teversham, Cambridge, Teversham, Cosford 8957M (11-3-88), 7 FTS, 1 FTS, 3 FTS, RAFC. *Spirit of Shropshire.* Arrived 9-12-21		1-24
❑	XN589	'46'	Hunting Jet Provost T.3A	61	Linton-on-Ouse 9143M, 1 FTS, T.3, RAFC. Last flight 18-3-92. Arrived 31-10-19. 1 FTS colours		1-24
❑	XN974		Blackburn Buccaneer S.2A	64	ex Warton, Holme on Spalding Moor, RAE Bedford, HoSM, A&AEE, Driffield, HoSM, A&AEE, RAE Bedford, A&AEE, HoSM. Flew in 19-8-91. Royal Navy colours, taxiable		1-24
❑	XP640	'M'	Hunting Jet Provost T.4	62	ex Halton 8501M (13-9-76), CATCS, 6 FTS, CAW, CFS, 3 FTS. Arrived 10-93		1-24
❑	XS903	'BA'	EE Lightning F.6	66	ex Binbrook, 11, 5-11 pool. Flew in 8-5-88. 11 Sqn colours	[1]	1-24
❑	XV168	'AF'	Blackburn Buccaneer S.2B	66	ex Brough, Lossiemouth, 12, 208, 12, 801. SOC 15-10-93. Arrived 18-8-13. 12 Sqn colours	[12]	1-24
❑	XV250		HS Nimrod MR.2	71	ex Kinloss, Kin Wing, Kin & St M Wing, MR.1, 42, Kinloss, 202, Kinloss. Flew in 13-4-10. Taxiable		1-24
❑	XV748	'3D'	HS Harrier GR.3	69	ex Cranfield, Bedford, 233 OCU, 1, GR.1, 233 OCU, 1. Arrived 21-10-00	[13]	1-24
❑	XX901		Blackburn Buccaneer S.2B	77	ex Kemble, St Athan, Lossiemouth, 208, 12, 237 OCU. 208. SOC 10-1-95. *Kathryn - The Flying Mermaid / Glen Elgin.* Arrived 26-5-96, handed over to YAM 12-10-22	[14]	1-24
❑	XZ233*		Westland Lynx HAS.3S	77	ex Selby, Ipswich, M Wallop, St Athan, 702, Fleetlands, Yeovilton, HAS.2, 815, Falklands, 700L. Arrived 25-3-22	[15]	1-24
❑	XZ383*	'AF'	SEPECAT Jaguar GR.1	77	ex Cosford 8901M (23-5-86), Coltishall, 14, 17. Arrived 5-8-23		1-24
❑	XZ631		Panavia Tornado GR.4	78	ex Warton, Panavia, A&AEE. Arrived 22-3-05. 2 Sqn colours		1-24
❑	ZA354		Panavia Tornado GR.1	82	ex Warton. Arrived 29-4-05		1-24
❑	–	'1'	Hunting Jet Provost T.3	c62	ex Linton-on-Ouse. Procedure trainer. Arrived 10-92		1-24
❑	–	'2'	Hunting Jet Provost T.3	c62	ex Linton-on-Ouse. Procedure trainer, 1 FTS badge	[16]	1-24
❑	–*		BAE Systems HERTI-1	c06	ex Stafford, BAE Systems, Afghan deployment 2007. Marshall Slingsby-built. First noted 10-23	[17]	1-24
❑	21417		Lockheed CT-133 Silver Star	54	ex Germany, 414 Sqn, CAF 133417, RCAF 21417. Arrived 25-6-93. Canadair-built		1-24
❑	45	'BR'	Dassault Mirage IVA	66	ex Paris, French AF. Last flight 11-9-91. Arrived 30-3-17	[18]	1-24
❑	538	'3-QH'	Dassault Mirage IIIE	68	ex 3 Esc, French AF. Arrived 1995		1-24
❑	'15919'	'1'	M'schmitt Bf 109G FSM	94	BAPC.240, ex Garforth. Arrived 5-94	[19]	1-24
❑	QA-10		Hawker Hunter FGA.78	68	ex 'N-2' Hurn, Qatar AF QA-10, G-9-286, Dutch AF N-268. Arrived 25-4-92		1-24
❑	'319764'	'329'	Waco CG-4A Hadrian	~	BAPC.157, ex '237123', Bacup, Ormskirk. *Bonjour Julie*		1-24

■ **[1]** Airframes on loan: the 'Flea' from Dave Allan; Lightning from Peter Chambers. **[2]** Built by RAF Finningley Vintage Aircraft Group; its first and only(?) 'hop' there 11-9-66. **[3]** Cayley test flown at Lasham 1972, also flown – and damaged – at Brompton Hall, Scarborough, Cayley's ancestral home. **[4]** Built by John Ketley and Bill Sneesby, Selby. Not flown... see John's other SE.5a G-ERFC at Shuttleworth, Beds **[5]** Kitten was built by Bill Sneesby; fitted with a Citroen 2CV. **[6]** Halifax re-creation is a complex composite: rear fuselage section from former 58 Squadron Mk.II HR792 which crashed Stornoway on 13-1-45; centre section and inner wings from Hastings C.1 TG536 from Catterick; unused outer wings from a Hastings C.1; myriad Halifax detail parts; Hercules engines courtesy of the French Air Force and ex-Noratlas, plus new-build cockpit and rear section. **[7]** VP293 is on loan from Norman Thelwell. **[8]** Original nose, airframe converted to T.11 in 1964 and T.19 in 1966 going as 8584M to fire pits at Marham 21-12-77. The 'back end' post-conversion served with 228 OCU, West Raynham TFF, 85, RAE, 85 and 100. **[9]** Airworthy OGMA-built Chipmunk G-CERD wears 'WK640'. **[10]** WR963 on loan from the Shackleton Preservation Group, contact details above. **[11]** Victor acquired on behalf of YAM by André Tempest and his late father, Gerry, it regularly taxies. **[12]** XV168 donated by BAE Systems and dedicated 18-8-13 to the company aircrew who gave their lives during the type's development. **[13]** XV748 - see also Coventry, W Mids, for at least one set of its wings. **[13]** Title transferred from the Buccaneer Aircrew Association to YAM, 12-10-22. **[15]** Lynx on loan from Jet Art Aviation, Selby, N Yorks. **[16]** 'JP' '2' is *very likely* XM373, ex Cranwell 7726M, crashed 29-6-61 with 2 FTS. **[17]** HERTI - High Endurance Rapid Technology Insertion UAV, based on a re-engineered J&S Aero Fregata motor glider. Work sub-contracted to Marshall Slingsby Advanced Composites of Kirbymoorside, so spot-on for YAM's regional collection. **[18]** Mirage IV first flown 6-5-66; last flight was also the final ever flight of a IVA; total time 6,309 hours. **[19]** Bf 109G *Black 1* was built by Danny Thornton of Garforth, W Yorks.

FELIXKIRK AERODROME between the A19 and A170 northeast of Thirsk

❑ G-AIPR	Auster J4 Archer	47	ex Popham. CoA 27-9-07		N2-19

INGLETON on the A65 southeast of Kirkby Lonsdale

Brian's Used Tractors: A well-known local landmark. **www.briansusedtractors.co.uk**

❑ G-MBWF	Flexiform Solo Striker	82	CoA 29-6-95, de-reg 6-11-00		7-21

LEEDS EAST AIRPORT or Church Fenton EGXG

Jet Art Aviation (JAA – see Selby, N Yorks) keeps its Tornado F.2A and 'SHAR' at the airport.

◆ **Not** *available for inspection without prior arrangement*

❑ N250DM	Bell UH-1H Iroquois	66	ex Sparkford, 66-16114		7-23
❑ N338CB	Bell UH-1H Iroquois	66	ex Sparkford, N312RB, 66-16118		7-23
❑ ZD902	Panavia Tornado F.2A	84	ex Boscombe Down, DERA, 229 OCU. Arr 11-12-15	[1] [2]	12-23
❑ ZH798 '002'	HS Sea Harrier F/A.2	96	ex Culdrose, Shawbury, Yeovilton, 801, 800, 899, 801, 800. 801 Sqn colours. Arrived 1-2-21. Taxiable	[1]	12-23

■ **[1]** Held by JAA. **[2]** One-off F.2A was heavily modified to TIARA status - Tornado Integrated Avionics Research Aircraft.

LEEMING AIRFIELD east of the A1, west of Bedale EGXE

RAF Leeming:

❑ XX253	HS Hawk T.1A	78	ex Scampton, 'Red Arrows'. Collision 23-3-10. F/n 9-22	[1]	1-24
❑ XX317* 'CO'	HS Hawk T.1A	80	ex 736, 100, 19, 74, 208, 4 FTS, 1 TWU. For display 6-22		1-24
❑ ZH552	Panavia Tornado F.3	92	ex Boscombe Down, QinetiQ, 56, F3 OCU. Last flight 5-7-12. Displayed since 2015	[2]	1-24

■ **[1]** Collided with XX233 (pilot ejected OK) over Kastelli, Crete; XX253 successful forced-landing and SOC. **[2]** Tornado carries a trio of unit badges on the fin: 11, 23 and 25 Squadrons, each one-time based at Leeming on the type. It also carries five cine-camera 'zaps' denoting its role as a camera-ship during MBDA Meteor missile trials out of Boscombe Down.

Hawker Hunter Aviation (HHA): Previously based at Scampton, HHA is a major contractor for the military and aerospace industry and while the operational machines are beyond the terms of reference for *W&R*, it would be a crime not to mention them: Hunter F.58 ZZ190 and T.72 XE688. Only airframes under major restoration or long-term store are formally listed: HHA maintains an airframe store at Scampton, Lincs. ◆ **Strictly** *prior appointment* **only** | **www.hunterteam.com**

❑ ZZ191*	Hawker Hunter F.58	59	ex Scampton, G-HHAD, G-BWFS, Swiss AF J-4058. Arrived 8-11-22		12-23
❑ ZZ194*	Hawker Hunter F.58	59	ex Scampton, G-HHAC, Duxford G-BWIU, Swiss AF J-4021. Arrived 12-22		12-23
❑ J-4110*	Hawker Hunter F.58A G-CJWL	72	ex Scampton, Norway, Swiss AF, G-9-328, A2561 (17-3-63), F.4 XF318, 229 OCU, 130. Squires Gate-built. Arr 14-12-22		12-23

LEEMING BAR junction of the A1 and A684, northeast of Bedale

Exelby Services: ***Note*** at **Coneygarth**, to the north of the A684 and the Leeming Bar Services. Acquired the former Scampton gate guard: it will be pylon-mounted in due course.

❑ XX306*	HS Hawk T.1A	80	ex Scampton. Shawbury, 'Red Arrows', 4 FTS. Bitteswell-built. Last flight 20-10-12, SOC 18-8-15. Arrived 10-7-23	[1]	1-24

■ **[1]** XX306 entered service with the 'Reds' 3-7-80. Total time 7,378 hours.

LEYBURN on the A684, south of Richmond

GPSV Auctions / Agility Defense and Government Services UK Ltd: (Yes, that's defense with an 's'.) Offers vast amounts of former military hardware via tender or auction. This location is a storage/holding venue but airframes tend to linger only fleetingly. See also Froghall, Staffs. ◆ **Strictly** *prior arrangement* **only | https://agilitystoke.com**

MALTON northeast of York

Eden Camp Modern History Museum: Each hut in this former prisoner of war camp has a different theme and the level of presentation is breath-taking. There is a Link trainer display, a plotting room, and items on 617 Squadron.

◆ *Off the A64 north of Malton, YO17 6RT* | **01653 697777 | admin@edencamp.co.uk | www.edencamp.co.uk**

❑ 'P2793' 'SD-M'	Hawker Hurricane FSM	93	BAPC.236, G B Mouldings-built. 501 Sqn colours	[1]	1-24
❑ 'V7357' 'SD-F'	Hawker Hurricane FSM	93	BAPC.399, ex 'P2793', 501 Sqn colours		1-24
❑ 'RK838' 'GE-W'	V-S Spitfire FSM	91	BAPC.230, ex 'AB550', 'AA908'. TDL-built. 349 Sqn colours		1-24
❑ –	Fieseler Fi 103 (V-1) FSM	93	BAPC.235, TDL Replicas-built		1-24

■ **[1]** After gale damage to the original 'P2793' *another* was commissioned for display. The first lies dismantled in a Queen Mary trailer.

NEWBY WISKE northwest of Thirsk, near South Otterington

FRED G-BBBW has been 'tidied up' and deleted.

❑ G-BGFK	Evans VP-1	r92	de-reg 7-4-99	12-22

NORTH DUFFIELD AERODROME on the A163 northeast of Selby

Condor Aviation: The placing of Beverley XB259 under this heading with the suffix 'Due' was an act of optimism – see under Fort Paul, E Yorks. By November 2022, the fuselage-cum-dwelling of HS.125 VP-CFI moved to Montrose, Scotland.

◆ *Prior arrangement* **only**. | **www.condoraviation.co.uk**

❑ OE-KDW	Prescott Pusher	~	pole-mounted as 'windsock' (!), first noted 10-16	1-24

PICTON on a minor road west of the A19, south of Yarm

Battlezone Paintball ◆ *Prior permission* **only | www.battlezonepaintball.co.uk**

❑ G-BFGS	MS Rallye 180GT	75	ex Spalding, F-BXYK. CoA 23-12-11, de-reg 24-1-12	9-21
❑ XN385	Westland Whirlwind HAS.7	60	ex Bolton, Chorley, B'thorpe, Hurn, Wroughton, Culdrose, Wroughton, HS, A&AEE, 771, 824, 825, 824. SOC 18-9-92	9-23

RUFFORTH AERODROME south of the A1237, west of York

McLean Aviation: On the 'West' site. ◆ *When conditions permit, a charity donation allows a glimpse inside.*

❑ G-BCHX	Scheibe SF-23A Sperling	59	ex Netherthorpe, D-EGIZ. Damaged 7-8-82, de-reg 22-3-02		4-23
❑ G-BUFN	Slingsby Venture T.2	77	ex ZA631. Wrecked 5-1-12, de-reg 12-1-12		4-23
❑ XK819	Slingsby Grasshopper TX.1	55	ex Selby, Breighton, Warmingham, Stoke-on-Trent, Cosford, Malvern, 2 MGSP, Kimbolton. Arrived by 4-14		6-22
❑ XP463	Slingsby Grasshopper TX.1	61	SOC 4-2-88	[1]	2-19

■ **[1]** See under Lasham, Hampshire, for *another* - or *this* - 'XP463'.

York Gliding Centre: On the 'West' site. ◆ *Prior arrangement* **only | www.yorkglidingcentre.co.uk**

❑ XZ551*	Slingsby Venture T.2	77	G-BUGT. De-reg 10-7-18. First noted 7-21	7-22
❑ XZ553	Slingsby Venture T.2	77	G-BUJX. CoA 4-9-14. Frame	7-22

SCALBY Sea Kings XZ589, ZE369 (which arrived 20-1-22) and ZE370 relocated to Scarborough, N Yorks, by March 2023.

SCARBOROUGH

Helicopter Glamping, Pinewood Park: Boasting "Spacious, warm, luxury, unique, awesome!", a trio of SAR yellow Sea Kings are arrayed in dispersal form. ◆ *Racecourse Road. Prior arrangement* **only | https://helicopterglamping.co.uk**

❑ XZ589*	'E'	Westland Sea King HAR.3	78	ex Scalby, Gosport, Fleetlands, 22, 202, SKTU, 22, 202, SKTU		1-24
❑ ZE369*	'S'	Westland Sea King HAR.3	85	ex Scalby, Charlwood, Horsham, Fleetlands, 22. Acquired 20-1-22		1-24
❑ ZE370*	'E'	Westland Sea King HAR.3	85	ex Scalby, Froghall, Gosport, 202, 22		1-24

Locally: At another, *private*, location, restoration of the Austers is believed to continue.

❑ G-AHCK		Auster J1N Alpha	46	ex Thwing, Spilsby, Croft, Skegness. De-reg 22-4-94	6-21
❑ G-AJRC		Auster J1 Autocrat	47	ex Thwing. CoA 14-7-02, de-reg 22-2-08	6-21

SELBY on the A19 south of York

Jet Art Aviation Ltd (JAA): With a passion for Harriers, Tornados and all other things fast jet, Chris and Melanie Wilson's family-run business specialises in the restoration, supply and transportation of static display or museum airframes. Tornado ZD902 and Sea Harrier ZH798 are kept at Leeds East, N Yorks (aka Church Fenton) – which see. *Cockpitless* Harrier GR.3 XW922 arrived from Manston, Kent, on 2nd December 2020: it does not get a formal entry below.

Departures: **Jaguar** T.2 cockpit XX140 to Sittingbourne, Kent, by 3-23; GR.1 XX747 exported to Mauritius 1-22. **Jindivik** 'A92-255' arrived at the Bloodhound Museum, Menzingen, Switzerland on 18-11-21. Thanks to Trevor Stone (of Meteor WK800 and 'Drone Corner' at Old Sarum, Wilts) some light relating to its composite nature. *At least* the centre section is from a very early UK Jindivik: *very likely* A92-105, lost into the sea on its first flight, 22-6-60. **Lynx** HAS.3 XZ233 departed for Elvington, N Yorks, on loan 25-3-22. **Sea Harrier** F/A.2 ZH811 to Chippenham, *Cambridgeshire*, by 6-22. Tornado F.2 ZD899 after extensive restoration also to Chippenham, Cambs, by mid-2023.

◆ ***Strictly private*** *location*, ***NO*** *public access* | **www.jetartaviation.co.uk**

❑ XM191		EE Lightning F.1A	61	ex North Scarle, EP&TU Cranwell 8590M, St Athan, Abingdon 7854M, Wattisham, 111. Crashed 9-6-64. Arrived 10-13. Shark's mouth. Cockpit		1-21
❑ XR751		EE Lightning F.3	65	ex Queensbury, Ipswich, Tremar, Binbrook, 11, LTF, 29, 226 OCU, EE. SOC 21-6-88. Arrived 7-11. Cockpit		1-16
❑ XS177	'N'	Hunting Jet Provost T.4	63	ex Westbury, Gilberdyke, Binbrook, Metheringham, Ipswich, Cosford, Valley 9044M (24-4-90), Shawbury, CATCS, 3 FTS, 2 FTS. First noted 8-21		8-21
❑ XV779		HS Harrier GR.3	70	ex Hitchin, Llantrisant, Welshpool, Stafford, Abingdon, Hamble, 3, Wittering SF, 3, 20, GR.1, 20, 4, 1. Cockpit	[1]	1-16
❑ XW175		HS Harrier T.2/4	69	ex Cosford, Boscombe Down, QinetiQ, RAE, HSA. Last flown 19-11-08. *John Farley OBE AFC*. Arr 17-7 -19	[2]	12-23
❑ XW870	'F'	Sud Gazelle HT.3	73	ex Manston 9299M, Shawbury, 2 FTS, CFS. Westland-built. Crashed 8-8-95. Arrived 2-12-20		2-23
❑ XX116		SEPECAT Jaguar GR.3A	73	ex Manston, St Athan, 16, 226 OCU, 6, Indian AF JI-008, G-27-316, GR.1, 226 OCU, JOCU. Arr 2-12-20. Black c/s		2-23
❑ XX121	'EQ'	SEPECAT Jaguar GR.1	73	ex Charlwood, Cosford, Shawbury, Warton, Shawbury, 6, 54, 226 OCU		2-23
❑ XX175		HS Hawk T.1	77	ex St Athan, Shawbury, Valley, Shawbury, 208, FRADU, 208, 19, CFS, 4 FTS. SOC 7-8-17. Arrived 14-10-20		12-23
❑ XX226		HS Hawk T.1	78	ex St Athan, Shawbury, Yeovilton, 100, 74, CFS, 74, 4 FTS. Accident 20-4-07, SOC 7-8-17. Arrived 14-10-20. 74 Sqn c/s		12-23
❑ XX257		HS Hawk T.1A	79	ex Charlwood, St Athan, Red Arrows. Cr 31-8-84. Arr 15-1-15		7-18
❑ XX290	'U'	HS Hawk T.1W	79	ex St Athan, Shawbury, 100, FRADU, 208, 100, 234, 4 FTS, 'Red Arrows', 4 FTS. SOC 7-8-17. Arrived 14-10-20		12-23
❑ XX341		HS Hawk T.1	81	ex Woodmancote, Boscombe Down, ETPS, A&AEE, ETPS. SOC 8-1-18. Arrived by 12-19	[3]	12-23
❑ XZ107	'FH'	SEPECAT Jaguar GR.3A	76	ex Ipswich, St Athan, 41, GR.1, 41, 6, 2		2-23
❑ XZ364	'FS'	SEPECAT Jaguar GR.3A	76	ex Tunbridge Wells, Ipswich, Shawbury, 41, 54, GR.1, Gulf Det, 54, 2. SOC 28-11-05. Cockpit		12-19
❑ XZ400	'FQ'	SEPECAT Jaguar GR.3A	78	ex Ipswich, St Athan, 41, GR.1, 54, Shawbury, 6, 54, Warton		2-23
❑ XZ455		HS Sea Harrier F/A.2	79	ex Queensbury, Ipswich, Yeovilton, FSAIU, 801, 899, 800, 899, 801, 899, 700A. Crashed 14-2-96, Arrived 7-11	[4]	1-16
❑ ZA359	'B-55'	Panavia Tornado GR.1	81	ex Warton, TTTE. Arrived 24-1-14		1-16
❑ ZB601		HS Harrier T.4	82	ex Yeovilton, Dunsfold, St Athan, ETS Yeovilton, 899, 233 OCU. SOC 5-6-00. Arrived 9-9-15. Forward fuselage		2-23

❑ ZD613	'122'	HS Sea Harrier F/A.2	85	ex Leeds, Shawbury, 800, 899, 801, 899, 801, 800, 899, 801, 899, 801, 899. SOC 8-9-03. Arrived 18-3-21		12-23
❑ ZE168		Panavia Tornado F.3	86	ex East Cowes, Leeming RTP, 43, 25, F3 OEU, 23, 5, 11, 111, 229 OCU. Cockpit. Arrived 9-16	[5]	3-18
❑ ZE965		Panavia Tornado F.3	89	ex Church F', Leeming, 111. Cockpit. Arr 17-7-17		3-18
❑ ZH804	'003'	HS Sea Harrier F/A.2	97	ex Culdrose, Shawbury, Yeovilton, 801, 899, 800, 899, 800. Arrived 29-1-21		12-23
❑ ZH807		HS Sea Harrier F/A.2	98	ex East Cowes, Newport, Basingstoke, St Athan, accident 1-5-02, 899. Cockpit		1-21
❑ –		V-S Swift CIM	~	ex Newark, Hemswell. Arrived by 6-13		1-16
❑ –		HS Harrier	~	ex Ipswich, Wittering, Warton. Fuselage	[6]	2-18
❑ –		HS Harrier GR.1 or 3	~	ex Ruthin. Cockpit, flying control rig		1-16
❑ –		SEPECAT Jaguar SIM	~	single-seater		12-23
❑ –		BAe/McDD Harrier GR.9	~	ex Welshpool, Hixon, Wittering. Procedure trainer		1-16
❑ 163205		BAe/McDD AV-8B Harrier II	88	ex Queensbury, St Athan, USMC, VMA-223. *Spanky*. Forward fuselage	[7]	1-16

■ **[1]** XV779 belly-landed at Wildenrath 16-12-74; pilot safely ejected. XV779 was rebuilt with a spare cockpit and is to be found at Wittering Cambs. Original nose was rebuilt and held as a spare. **[2]** VAAC – Vectored-Thrust Aircraft Advanced Control; T.2 airframe transformed under Cranfield Institute guidance 1983-1986 with rear cockpit fitted with a digital fly-by-wire control system and at same time brought up to near-T.4 status. Carried out the first ever deck landing using a unified control system, on HMS *Illustrious*, in 1986. John Farley flew XW175 in VAAC guise during 1999. **[3]** Converted at Cranfield to ASTRA - Advanced Stability Training and Research Aircraft. **[4]** XZ455 flew 58 Falklands combat sorties, scoring two air-to-air 'kills'. Then, in its *second* war, it crashed on return from a patrol over Bosnia; the pilot ejecting safely. **[5]** ZE168 scored two air-to-air 'kills' against QF-4 Phantom drones during ASRAAM trials out of Elgin AFB in April 2002. **[6]** Unflown airframe built around the time of the GR.1 Development Batch (XV276 to XV281, 1966-1967), Kestrel-like intake side fairings with 'punch-in' doors. Fitted with 'needle' nose during static/wind tunnel trials at Warton. **[7]** As flown by Capt S C Spang USMC.

Anne and **Nigel Ponsford** / **Ponsford Collection**: Located in the *general* area and at a *separate* site from Jet Art. See also Breighton, E Yorks. ◆ *Airframes held in deep storage or under restoration in the locality: visits are* **not** *possible*

❑ G-AEFG	Mignet HM.14 'Flea'	36	BAPC.75, ex Breighton, Leeds, Harrogate, Kirkby Overblow, Accrington. CoA 31-3-38	[1]	1-24
❑ G-APXZ	Payne Knight Twister	r60	ex Breighton, Tumby Woodside, Loughborough, Biggin Hill. De-reg 26-3-73. Frame		1-24
❑ ALX	Hawkridge Dagling	47	BGA.491, ex Leeds, Great Hucklow		1-24
❑ AQY	EoN Primary	48	BGA.588, ex Breighton, Hemel Hempstead. Stored		1-24
❑ BVM	Slingsby Dart 17R	66	BGA.1269, ex Breighton, Rufforth. CoA 25-7-90		1-24
❑ –	Hutter H.17a	36	ex Leeds, Accrington		1-24
❑ –	Dickson Primary	31	BAPC.340, ex Leeds, Harrogate		1-24
❑ –	Addyman STG	34	BAPC.14, ex Leeds, Harrogate, Wigan	[2]	1-24
❑ -	Addyman STG	34	BAPC.15, ex Wigan, Warmingham, Wigan, Harrogate.	[2]	1-24
❑ –	Addyman Ultralight	36	BAPC.16, ex Leeds, Harrogate, Wigan	[2]	1-24
❑ –	Killick Gyroplane	c63	BAPC.18, ex Leeds, Harrogate, Irlam		1-24
❑ –	Addyman Zephyr	33	BAPC.39, ex Leeds, Harrogate. Substantial parts	[2]	1-24

■ **[1]** 'Flea' built by John Nolan at Accrington, tested at Barton by 9-36, Authorisation to Fly No.51. **[2]** Addyman was the prolific E T W Addyman of Harrogate, who designed and built a series of gliders or in the case of the unfinished Ultralight, a powered aircraft based on the STG. STG = Standard Training Glider; the Zephyr was a more refined sailplane.

SHERBURN-IN-ELMET AERODROME on the B1222 east of the town, east of Leeds EGCJ

The clubhouse serves quite possibly the best aerodrome bacon butties *in the world*. If you're looking for the supreme outside of aviation, they're found at 'Two Flags' on the A47 just north of Barrowden in Rutland!

❑ G-OPTZ	Pitts S-2A Special	73	ex G-SKNT, G-PEAL, N81LF, N48KA. Aerotek-built. CoA 26-8-17	12-23

SKIPWITH on minor roads east of Riccall and the A19

Yorkshire Paintball Centre: Escrick Park Estate. ◆ *Prior arrangement* **only** | **www.ypc.co.uk**

❑ G-AXRL	Piper Cherokee 160	62	ex Sturton, North Cave, PH-CHE, D-EFRI. De-reg 12-8-94	12-20

SUTTON BANK AERODROME on the A170 west of Thirsk, engage low gear

Yorkshire Gliding Club ◆ *Prior arrangement* **only** | **www.ygc.co.uk**

❑ G-BFRY	Piper Pawnee 260	74	ex SE-GIB. CoA 10-7-15, de-reg 8-8-22	1-24

THORPE UNDERWOOD north of the A59 northwest of York

Queen Ethelburga's School: The Jungmeister is *thought* to fly on. ◆ *Prior arrangement* **only** | **www.qe.org**

❑ 'G-BUTX'		Bücker Jungmeister FSM	~	displayed in atrium	12-19

■ **[1]** 'The real G-BUTX is airworthy and is based in the south of England.

WOMERSLEY south of the M62, west of the A19

Blue Lagoon Diving and Leisure Centre: As well as the Hunter displayed on the surface, see also Appendix D : *Submerged.* ◆ *Prior arrangement* **only** | **www.facebook.com/divebluelagoon**

❑ WT799	'879'	Hawker Hunter T.8C	55	ex Exeter, N Weald, Ipswich, Shawbury, FRADU, FRU, 759, RAE, F.4, 4, 11. SOC 3-4-95. Displayed	12-23

YORK

Strensall Barracks: Strensall Road, northeast of the city centre. A Puma is used as an embarkation trainer.

❑ XW202		Sud Puma HC.1	71	ex Shawbury, Benson, 33, 230, 33, 27, 230, 1563 Flt, 33, 1563 Flt, 33, 1563 Flt, 33, 240 OCU, 230, A&AEE, 230, 240 OCU, 230, 240 OCU. Westland-built. Arrived 14-5-14	12-23

Also: Chevalier G-BICP has been 'tidied up' and deleted.

SOUTH YORKSHIRE

Includes the unitary authorities of Doncaster, Rotherham and Sheffield

BARNSLEY

FlyMe: A 'Virtual Airport' is located at the Shortwood Business Park with a wholly synthetic 737-800 'sim' and a former Jet2 737. Another element of the business is 'Sky-Pods', customising airliner fuselage sections as 'posh sheds'.
◆ *Prior arrangement* **only** | **www.flyme.co.uk**

❑ G-CELG		Boeing 737-377	88	ex St Athan, Jet2, S7-ABD, VH-CZN. De-reg 18-5-18. Forward fuselage	12-23

BAWTRY on the A638 south of Doncaster

Bawtry Paintball and Laser Fields ◆ *Prior arrangement* **only** | **www.bawtrypaintballfields.co.uk**

❑ XL840		Westland Whirlwind HAS.7	57	ex Long Marston, Norwich, Sibson, Blackpool, Fleetwood, Wroughton, 705, Brawdy SF, Culdrose SF, 705, 820. SOC 26-6-76	1-24
❑ XZ211		Westland Lynx AH.7	79	ex Croft, M Wallop. Boomless, first noted 2-15	1-24
❑ ZD255		Westland Lynx HAS.3GMS	83	ex Croft, Fleetlands, 815	1-24
❑ ZD263	'632'	Westland Lynx HAS.3S	83	ex Croft, Fleetlands, 702, 815, 702. Arrived 7-14	1-24

DONCASTER Leisure Park, Lakeside – former Doncaster aerodrome site

South Yorkshire Aircraft Museum (SYAM): The appeal of this dynamic, ever-so-friendly museum continues to soar – it now scores 22,000-plus in its annual visitor count. There was a time when the author would take a deep breath before tackling the 'Duxford' section... Now, it's 'Doncaster' that provides a mild dose of trepidation as the stock of midnight oil is assessed in order that I try to stay ahead of SYAM's vibrancy and the team's endeavours to keep this book out of date! This is meant as rich praise, the achievements here and the 'can do' co-operative ethos with the rest of the 'community' is a shining beacon to all of us. That respect has also recently been recognised by the RAF Museum passing on its Dragon Rapide and the MoD releasing a Hawk – both feathers in the cap of the SYAM crew!

Since March 2008 SYAM has been the custodian of the rear fuselage of Lancaster 10(AR) KB976. This was the unfortunate G-BCOH of the Strathallan Collection, mortally damaged in a hangar collapse at Woodford 12th August 1987. Exported to Florida in 1993, the bulk of KB976 lies in Fantasy of Flight's 'Pending' file. See under East Kirkby, Lincs, for the role KB976's rear is playing in putting NX611 into the air.

The K.8 and Dart glider cockpits owned and restored by James Stables clinched a Spirit of *CockpitFest* award at the 2022 event at Newark. Debuting there was another 'lockdown' creation from Bill Fern, the extreme nose (from the windscreen forward, complete with instrumentation) of a Meteor. Beyond the remit of the book, it deserves an honorary mention. Parts come from several Meteors, be they fighter, trainer, or night-fighter, hence Bill's designation: 'Meteor 4711'.

SYAM has given the Newark Air Museum's *CockpitFest* gathering stalwart support ever since it was established in 2000. For the 2022 event, the team adopted the label 'Civvie Street', but for the following year decided 'The Doncaster Mafia' was more fitting! To reward this burst of honesty (!) the Valetta cockpit bagged a *W&R* 'Spirit of *CockpitFest*' prize and Jaguar GR.1 XX736 was presented with the hallowed 'Grand Champion' award.

Many airframes that are in store or under restoration are *not* available for public inspection – see beyond the main list. Working with SYAM and co-based is the **Yorkshire Helicopter Preservation Group** - see separate entry. SYAM curator Naylan Moore bases his **Classic Aircraft Collection** here. Naylan has a Hurricane project under way but it is not at the stage of a formal listing. See also Moore's Restorations later. Ercoupe G-AVTT was disposed of to 'Nottinghamshire, in 2023. Cockpit of Canberra PR.7 WT534 departed in 2019 for Wisbech, Norfolk.

◆ *Off the A638 beyond 'The Dome' | Airborne Road, DN4 7FB* **but** *DN4 7NW for sat-nav junkies* | **01302 761616** | **contact@southyorkshireaircraftmuseum.org.uk** | **www.southyorkshireaircraftmuseum.org.uk**

	Identity		Type	Year	History	Notes	Last noted
❑	'K-158'		Austin Whippet replica	90	BAPC.207, ex Sunderland, Stoke-on-Trent. Arrived 1-00		1-24
❑	G-ACBH		Blackburn B.2	32	ex Redhill, 'Kent', Ingatestone, W Hanningfield, Wickham Bishops, Downham, Ramsden Heath, Brentwood 2895M, CoA 27-11-41, de-reg 14-7-42. Arrived 21-2-12. Fuselage	[1]	1-24
❑	G-AEJZ		Mignet HM.14 'Flea'	36	BAPC.120, ex Hemswell, Cleethorpes, Brough. CoA 28-5-37, de-reg 12-38. Arrived 2004	[2]	1-24
❑	G-AHED*		DH Dragon Rapide	46	ex Stafford, Cosford, Wyton, Cardington, Henlow, Dominie II RL962 n/s. Brush-built. CoA 17-4-68, de-reg 3-3-69. Arrived 14-12-22		1-24
❑	G-APMY		Piper Apache 160	58	ex Firbeck, Connah's Quay, Halfpenny Green, EI-AJT. CoA 1-11-81, de-reg 25-11-81. Acquired 4-96		1-24
❑	G-ARYZ		Beagle Airedale	62	ex Spanhoe. CoA 26-2-01. Arrived 12-4-15	[3]	1-24
❑	G-ATXH		HP Jetstream 200	67	ex Cranwell, Finningley, Prestwick, Filton. De-reg 22-4-71. Arrived 2005. Cockpit	[4]	1-24
❑	G-AVAA		Cessna F.150G	67	ex Firbeck, Shobdon, Hurn. Reims-built. CoA 5-7-96, de-reg 16-4-96. Arrived 26-11-97		1-24
❑	G-BCLW		American AA-1B Trainer	74	ex Finningley. Damaged 12-2-13, CoA 9-6-13. Arr 27-4-13		1-24
❑	G-BNNA		Stolp Starduster Too	73	ex N8SD. Cr 20-6-17, de-reg 11-7-17. Forward fuselage		1-24
❑	G-BTYX		Cessna 140	76	ex Spanhoe, Uckfield. Rochester, N76568. CoA 23-2-98, de-reg 10-4-01. Arrived 12-4-15. Cockpit	[5]	1-24
❑	G-BUUV		Lindstrand LBL.77A HAB	93	ex Lancing. CoA 16-5-97, de-reg 9-6-97. Arrived 2011	[6]	1-24
❑	G-DDCD		DH Dove 8	62	ex Cricklade, Little Rissington, Kemble, Staverton, Biggin Hill, G-OEWA, G-DDCD, G-ARUM. CoA 7-10-91, de-reg 24-5-05. Arrived 28-2-20	[7]	1-24
❑	G-DELB		Robinson R22	88	ex Firbeck, Sherburn, Retford, N26461. Cr 27-12-94, De-reg 20-4-95. Acquired 11-97		1-24
❑	G-MJKP		Hiway Skytrike	r82	CoA 31-12-86, de-reg 9-12-94. Arrived 2001		1-24
❑	G-MMDK		Mainair Tri-Flyer	83	CoA 30-5-99, de-reg 2-12-10. Arrived 2009		1-24
❑	G-MVNT		Whittaker MW-5-K	90	CoA 5-5-07, de-reg 27-5-11. Arrived 2009		1-24
❑	G-MYJX		Whittaker MW-8	93	de-reg 31-7-01. Arrived 2007	[8]	1-24
❑	G-OPFW		HS HS.748-2A/266	72	ex Haverigg, Emerald, G-BMFT, VR-BFT, G-BMFT, 5W-FAO, G-11-10. CoA 16-2-07, de-reg 15-6-09. Arrived 4-9-10. Parcelforce colours. Cockpit		1-24
❑	–		Cayley glider rep	03	BAPC.639, ex Brough. BAE Heritage Group-built. Arr 10-11-21		1-24
❑	–		Blériot XI replica	09	BAPC.307. Unveiled 2010. 'Delagrange'	[9]	1-24
❑	–		Bensen B-8	c65	BAPC.533. Built in Doncaster. Arrived 2009		1-24
❑	–	'W-F'	'MisFire'	~	cockpit, travelling exhibit. *MisFire*	[5] [10]	1-24
❑	BGA.1008	BJP	Slingsby Swallow	c61	ex Dunstable	[5]	1-24
❑	BGA.1268	'404' / BVL	Slingsby Dart 15	66	ex 'Lincs', Shipdham, Newark GC, Devon & Somerset GC, Acquired 9-17. Cockpit, travelling exhibit	[11]	1-24
❑	BGA.1567		Slingsby Swallow	c69	ex Wroot. Cockpit. Arrived 11-17	[12]	1-24
❑	GGA.522		Schleicher K.8b	~	BGA.3257 / FCQ, ex Spalding, RAFGGA.522 Laabruch, D-0322. Luftsportverain Bayer-built. Acquired 2002 Cockpit, travelling exhibit	[11] [13]	1-24
❑	EI-BBK	G-ARXB	Beagle Airedale	62	ex Spanhoe, Abbeyshrule, G-ARXB, EI-ATE, G-ARXB. CoA (Irish) 11-11-83. De-reg 22-11-23. Arrived 6-6-20. Cockpit	[5]	1-24

	Identity	Code	Type	Year	History	Notes	Date
❑	EI-JWM		Robinson R22	90	ex G-BSLB. Arrived 2004		1-24
❑	HB-NAV	'A'	Beagle Pup 150 G-AZCM	71	ex Dover, Henley-on-Thames, Woodley, Henlow, Redhill, HB-NAV (de-reg 12-2-85), G-AZCM (de-reg 4-5-72). Arrived 2009. Forward fuselage, trailer mounted	[5]	1-24
❑	HB-XMO		Enstrom 280C	80	ex Sudbury, Switzerland. Crashed 23-5-97. Arrived 29-10-15. Travelling exhibit	[11]	1-24
❑	N4565L		Douglas DC-3-201A	39	ex Framlingham, Ipswich, Dublin, LV-GYP, LV-PCV, N129H, N512, N51D, N80C, NC21744. De-reg 7-6-13. Arr 6-8-03		1-24
❑	N9399		DH Tiger Moth	39	ex Old Sarum SF, M Wallop SF, Baginton SF, 1 AACU, 1618 Flt, 287, 24 EFTS, 28 EFTS. SOC 28-3-50. Fuselage. Arr 2004	[5]	1-24
❑	FX322		NAA Harvard II	44	ex Worksop, Doncaster, Bruntingthorpe, Stoke, ?, French AF, FX322, n/s. Cockpit		1-24
❑	LB314		Taylorcraft Plus D OY-DSZ	42	ex Denmark, D-ELUS, G-AHHX, Auster I LB314, Llanbedr SF, 83 GCF, 43 OTU, 656, 652, 654. Arrived 12-2-18		1-24
❑	SN280		Hawker Tempest V	45	ex Napier. SOC 30-12-49. Acquired 2010. Cockpit/firewall and growing!	[14] [15]	1-24
❑	VP519		Avro Anson C.19/2 G-AVVR	47	ex W'hampton, 'Manchester', Dukinfield, Hadfield, Stockport, Peel Green, Cosford, Wigan, Irlam, Halfpenny Green, G-AVVR (de-reg 16-9-72), Shawbury, FCCS, 11 GCF, MCS, 31, Malta CF, TCDU. SOC 19-2-68. Arrived 2011. Cockpit		1-24
❑	WA662		Gloster Meteor T.7	50	ex Firbeck, Willington, Chalgrove, Llanbedr, Farnborough, FCCS, 3, Wildenrath SF, Gütersloh SF, 3. Acquired 1994		1-24
❑	WB733		DHC Chipmunk T.10 G-ATDE	50	ex Firbeck, Sevenoaks, Shawbury SF, G-ATDE (de-reg 19-1-68), Marham SF, 4 SoTT 'hack', Lyneham SF, Upavon SF, Hull UAS, 11 RFS. Hawarden-built. SOC 12-9-73. Acquired 1995		1-24
❑	WB969		Slingsby Sedbergh TX.1	50	BGA.2036, ex Wroot, RAFGSA.247, WB969, CGIS, 168 GS. Crashed 24-8-80, CoA 8-10-80. Arrived 10-01		1-24
❑	WD935		EE Canberra B.2	51	ex Birdlip, Bridgnorth, Ottershaw, Egham, St Athan 8440M (17-4-75), 360, 97, 151, CSE, EE, BCDU, RAAF A84-1. Arrived 2003. Cockpit		1-24
❑	WE987	DZX	Slingsby Prefect TX.1	50	BGA.2517, ex Newport Pagnell, ACCGS, CGS, 633 GS, 642 GS, 2 GS. CoA 17-7-89. Arrived 12-01		1-24
❑	WH779	'CK'	EE Canberra PR.7	54	ex Winthorpe, Castle Donington, Boscombe D', Farnborough, Marham, RAE, 100, 13, Wildenrath 8129M (10-3-71), Brüggen, 31, 80, 13, 542. Arr 11-1-15. Cockpit. 13 Sqn c/s	[16]	1-24
❑	WJ476		Vickers Valetta T.3	52	ex Cardington, Henlow, ATC unit (?), 5MU, 2 ANS, MEAF CS, Special CS, Fayid. Arrived 2001. Cockpit	[17]	1-24
❑	WJ565		EE Canberra T.17	53	ex Harrington, North Coates, Coventry, North Coates, Binbrook, Bruntingthorpe, Cosford 8871M, St Athan, 360, B.2, A&AEE. HP-built. Arrived 22-3-03. Cockpit		1-24
❑	WJ903		Vickers Varsity T.1	52	ex Firbeck, Dumfries, Glasgow Airport, 6 FTS, AE&AEOS, 1 ANS, 2 ANS, 3 ANS. SOC 5-2-75. Hurn-built. Acquired 14-3-97. Cockpit, 6 FTS colours by late 2020		1-24
❑	WJ975		EE Canberra T.19	53	ex Hemswell, Cleethorpes, Cambridge, 100, 7, 100, 85, West Raynham TFF, 228 OCU, B.2, 44, 35, 231 OCU. Avro-built. SOC 21-5-80. Arrived 2005. Cockpit	[5]	1-24
❑	WK626	'85'	DHC Chipmunk T.10	52	ex Firbeck, Salisbury, Welling, White Waltham 8123M (4-8-72), Bicester SF, Odiham SF, Ox UAS, S Cerney SF, 1 FTS, Bicester SF, Odiham SF, FTCCS, Lon, Cam UASs, Colerne SF, Leeds, Nott UASs, 16 FRS, 18 RFS. Hawarden-built. Acquired 1997. Fuselage	[5]	1-24
❑	WL131		Gloster Meteor F.8	53	ex Firbeck, Guernsey 7751M, APS Sylt, 601, 111. SOC 16-11-62. Acquired 9-95. Cockpit	[5]	1-24
❑	WT319*		EE Canberra B(I).6	55	ex Lavendon, Castle Carey, Filton, Samlesbury, 213, Laarbruch SF, 213. SOC 8-12-69. Cockpit. Arr mid-21	[18]	1-24
❑	WT525*	'855'	EE Canberra T.22	55	ex St Mawgan, 'Spitfire Corner', Wyton, South Woodham Ferrers, Stock, St Athan, FRADU, 17, 80. Short-built. SOC 10-5-92. Cockpit. Arrived 9-6-23		1-24

	Serial		Type	Year	History	Note	Date
❑	WT536		EE Canberra PR.7	55	ex Walcott, Southampton, Bruntingthorpe, Cosford 8063M (19-11-69), 80, 31, 13, 17. Short-built. Cockpit		1-24
❑	WT741	'791'	Hawker Hunter GA.11	55	ex Hemswell, Macclesfield, Bitteswell, HSA, 738, F.4, 118. SOC 13-7-71. Arrived 2005. Cockpit. 738 Sqn c/s	[14]	1-24
❑	'WV314'	'B'	Hawker Hunter F.51 E-424	56	ex Firbeck, East Kirkby, Tattershall, Cosford, Dunsfold, G-9-445 (20-2-76), Danish AF, Esk.724. Acq 1988. 92 Sqn c/s		1-24
❑	XE317		Bristol Sycamore HR.14 G-AMWO	54	ex Firbeck, Winthorpe, Portsmouth, CFS, 275, G-AMWO (de-reg 30-9-53). SOC 6-5-72. 275 Sqn c/s. Arrived 1997		1-24
❑	XE797		Slingsby Cadet TX.3	53	ex Topcliffe, Dishforth, Catterick, Dishforth, 645 GS, 2 GC, 641 GS, 27 GS. SOC 28-9-78. Cockpit. Arrived 30-10-16		1-24
❑	XE935		DH Vampire T.11	55	ex Firbeck, Sibson, Hitchin, Woodford, Chester, St Athan, 8 FTS. Hatfield-built. SOC 8-11-67. Acquired 1986		1-24
❑	XG297	'Y'	Hawker Hunter FGA.9	56	ex Firbeck, Newton-le-Willows, Bacup, Macclesfield, Bitteswell, HSA, 20, 28, 20, F.6, 4. SOC 12-2-76. Acquired 1995. 20 Sqn colours. Cockpit	[5]	1-24
❑	XH584		EE Canberra T.4	55	ex Firbeck, Sunderland, Marham, 231 OCU. SOC 12-7-66. Acquired 1993. Cockpit	[5]	1-24
❑	XL149		Blackburn Beverley C.1	57	ex Winthorpe, Finningley 7988M (7-11-67), 84, 30, 84, 242 OCU. Arrived 2005. Cockpit. 84 Sqn colours		1-24
❑	XL388		Avro Vulcan B.2	62	ex Walpole, Honington 8750M (2-4-82), 50, Wadd Wing, Scampton Wing, 9. Arrived 7-4-03. Cockpit. *Mayflower III*, 9 Squadron colours		1-24
❑	XM350		Hunting Jet Provost T.3A	58	ex Firbeck, Church Fenton 9036M (10-11-89), 7 FTS, 1 FTS, RAFC, A&AEE. Acquired 1995		1-24
❑	XM411		Hunting Jet Provost T.3	60	ex Firbeck, Otterburn, Halton 8434M (10-11-74), St Athan, Shawbury, Kemble, CFS. Acquired 1999. Cockpit		1-24
❑	'XM651'		Saro Skeeter AOP.12 XM561	59	ex Firbeck, East Kirkby, Tattershall, Moston, M Wallop, Arborfield 7980M (4-8-67), 15 MU, HQ 1 Wing, HQ 2 Wing, 651. Acquired 1993		1-24
❑	XN238*		Slingsby Cadet TX.3	59	ex Barnstaple, Doncaster, Firbeck, Robertsbridge, St Athan, 622 VGS, ACCGS, 1 GC, 626, 634, 614 and 662 GSs. SOC 20-10-83. Forward fuselage. Arrived by 6-23	[5]	1-24
❑	XN386	'435'	Westland Whirlwind HAR.9	60	ex Lancaster, Blackpool, Heysham, Wroughton A2713 (10-8-76), Fleetlands, *Endurance* Flt, HAS.7, 846, 814. Arrived 1999. Boomless		1-24
❑	XN511	'12'	Hunting Jet Provost T.3	60	ex Firbeck, Robertsbridge, 'XM426', Lutterworth, Blackpool, Liversedge, Kemble, CFS, 1 FTS, CFS. SOC 28-5-76. Acquired 1997. Cockpit	[18] [19]	1-24
❑	XP190		Saro P.531-2	61	ex Firbeck, Wroughton, Arborfield, M Wallop, BSE Filton, A&AEE. SOC 1-5-72. Acquired 27-8-92		1-24
❑	XP706		EE Lightning F.3	63	ex Hemswell, Strubby, Binbrook 8925M (9-2-87), LTF, 11, 5, LTF, 23, 111, 74. Arrived 19-11-02		1-24
❑	XP902		Westland Scout AH.1	63	ex Firbeck, Otterburn, Edinburgh, Dishforth, Netheravon, Wroughton, Garrison Air Sqn, 3 CBAS. Acquired 1999. Cockpit		1-24
❑	XS216		Hunting Jet Provost T.4	64	ex Goole, Finningley, 6 FTS, CAW. Damaged 7-5-73. Cockpit. Arrived 2003. Marked 'CRAN22/1'		1-24
❑	XS481		Westland Wessex HU.5	63	ex Firbeck, Dishforth, Wroughton, Yeovilton, Culdrose, Yeovilton, 771, 707. SOC 21-7-92. Acquired 6-98		1-24
❑	XS735	'R'	HS Dominie T.1	66	ex Walcott, Penwyllt, St Athan, CTTS, Sealand, Cranwell 9246M (28-10-96), 55, 6 FTS, RAFC, CAW. First noted 8-17		1-24
❑	XV139		Westland Scout AH.1	67	ex Wattisham, 'XV137', Yeovil, Arborfield, Wroughton, 657, Falklands, 656, 662, 653. Arrived 6-09		1-24
❑	XV280 '31121RN'		HS Harrier GR.1	67	ex Yeovilton, Culdrose, Yeovilton A2700[2] (1-11-90), Foulness, Boscombe Down, A&AEE, HSA. Cockpit, Sea Harrier style, trailer-mounted. First noted 6-16		1-24
❑	XV281		HS Harrier GR.1	67	BAPC.484, ex Welshpool, Cannock, Preston, Samlesbury, Dunsfold, Boscombe D', A&AEE, BSE. Forward fuselage.	[20]	1-24
❑	XV677	'269'	Westland Sea King HAS.6	70	ex Gosport A2619 [3] (7-6-99), Fleetlands, 814, 810, 819, 706, 814, 820. Arrived 25-7-06		1-24

	Reg	Code	Type	Yr	History	Note	Date
❑	XV752	'B'	HS Harrier GR.3	69	ex Bletchley, Cosford 9078M, 4, 3, 1, 233 OCU, GR.1, 1, 233 OCU. Arrived 5-12-11	[21]	1-24
❑	–		Blackburn Buccaneer S.2 EMU	69	ex Stamford, Croydon, Popham, Brough. Arrived 2005, acquired 10-20. Cockpit	[22]	1-24
❑	XW666		HS Nimrod R.1	73	ex Long Marston, Warton, Woodford, Kinloss, 51, A&AEE. Crashed 16-5-95. Arrived 2001. Cockpit		1-24
❑	XX238*		HS Hawk T.1	78	ex Shawbury, 208, 19, 74, 19, 6 FTS, CFS, 4 FTS. NEA 12-19. Arrived 3-10-23		1-24
❑	XX411	'X'	Sud Gazelle AH.1	75	ex Chichester, 3 CBAS. Shot down 21-5-82, San Carlos. Westland-built. Arrived 5-02		1-24
❑	XX495	'C'	HP Jetstream T.1	75	ex Bedford, Shawbury, Cranwell, 45, 3 FTS, 45, 6 FTS, METS. SAL-completed. Arrived 13-2-19		1-24
❑	XX669	'B'	SAL Bulldog T.1	75	ex Halton, Andover, Llantrisant, Bruntingthorpe, Cosford 8997M, 2 FTS, Birm UAS, Man UAS. Damaged 6-9-88. Arrived 2006. Birmingham UAS colours		1-24
❑	XX736		SEPECAT Jaguar GR.1	74	ex Chesterfield, Brough, Coltishall 9110M, Shawbury, Warton, Indian AF JI013, G-27-327, 6, 226 OCU. Arrived 2007. Cockpit. 54 Sqn colours. See notes above	[5]	1-24
❑	XX888		Blackburn Buccaneer S.2B	74	ex Barnstaple, Dundonald, Ottershaw, Shawbury, St Athan, 16, 15. SOC 10-10-91. 16 Sqn colours. Cockpit, arr 7-7-21		1-24
❑	XZ246	'434'	Westland Lynx HAS.3S(ICE)	78	ex Ipswich, 815, *Endurance* Flt, HAS.2, 815, 702. Arrived 8-16. HMS *Endurance* colours		1-24
❑	XZ431		Blackburn Buccaneer S.2B	77	ex Newark, Selby, Newport, Market Drayton, B'thorpe, Marham 9233M, 12, 208, 12, 208. Arrived by 6-16. Nose	[23]	1-24
❑	ZD938		Panavia Tornado F.2	85	ex Chester, Market Drayton, Shawbury, St Athan, 229 OCU. Arr 28-6-11. Forward fuselage. 229 OCU c/s	[24]	1-24
❑	0767 'A-4-116'		Aermacchi MB.339AA	81	ex Derby, Mickleover, Filton, Yeovilton, Stanley, Argentine Navy. First noted 11-13	[25]	1-24
❑	AE-406		Bell UH-1H Iroquois	72	ex Valley, M Wallop, Greenford, M Wallop, Fleetlands, Stanley, Arg Army AE-406, 72-21491. Boomless cabin, Griffin colours. Arrived 8-8-18		1-24
❑	N-302		Hawker Hunter T.53	58	ex Firbeck, Chelford, Macclesfield, Leavesden, Elstree, Hatfield, Danish AF Esk.724 ET-273, Netherlands AF N-302. Acquired 1996. Netherlands AF colours. Cockpit	[5]	1-24
❑	–		Waco CG-4 Hadrian rep	97	BAPC.443, ex Hatfield, *Saving Private Ryan*. Cockpit	[5]	1-24

■ **[1]** At some stage G-ACBH had elements of G-ADFO grafted on - both identities can be discerned on the airframe. (G-ADFO was written off 3-9-40.) **[2]** Built by Leslie Crosland in Hull, flew: Authorisation No.82. **[3]** *Yankee-Zulu* gifted by Carl Tyers/Windmill Aviation. Wings held in store. **[4]** Prototype Jetstream, first flown 18-8-67. **[5]** Airframes on loan from Bill Fern. **[6]** Balloon on loan from the Mobberley Balloon Collection. **[7]** Served the National Coal Board as G-ARUM from new – 11-61 – to 1-84 when it became G-DDCD. As such, *Uniform-Mike* was a 'regular' as Doncaster. **[8]** MW-8 prototype, built by the designer, Mike Whittaker. **[9]** Full-size replica Blériot XI built by Ken Fern to celebrate the 100th anniversary of the first aviation meeting in the UK - at Doncaster racecourse 15/18-10-09. It depicts Léon Delagrange's machine that established a world speed record of 49.9mph at the event. **[10]** A cockpit, firewall and cowling from unidentified homebuild type - see *W&R28*, p328 for more details. Codes stand for William (aka 'Bill') Fern. **[11]** Dart, K.8 and Enstrom owned by James Stables. **[12]** Swallow built by Roy Greenslade at nearby Wroot, c/n RG.103. **[13]** GGA - RAF Germany Gliding Association; Two Rivers Gliding Club, Laarbruch. **[14]** On loan from Naylan Moore's Classic Aircraft Collection. **[15]** SN280 served exclusively with Napier and was SOC 30-12-49. This may, or may not be, BAPC.536. **[16]** PR.7 WH779 on loan from Darren Headleand. **[17]** Identity now confirmed. **[18]** On loan from Sam Scrimshaw and Andy Carnill – Wingless Wonders. **[19]** 'XM426' denotes confusion/exchange with this airframe: both XN511 and XM426 were at 5 MU Kemble at the same and SOC on the same date 28-5-76. Both were reduced to cockpits and issued to ATC units - 2490 at Liversedge and 1151 at Wallsend, respectively. They *may* have swopped identities, or just 'paperwork'. For a goodly period XN511 was referred to as XM426 (*W&R* just as guilty): the history sequence as given is believed to be functional! **[20]** XV281 has the rear of a P.1127 test-rig. **[21]** XV752 on loan from 1053 Sqn ATC, Armthorpe, S Yorks. **[22]** **C**ockpit was acquired from Bill Fern in October 2020 by Carolyn Cordran (mum) and Marcus Cordran. Marcus refers to this venture as a 'rig' with the build/contract number B3-2-69 and that it was most likely within the batch XV870 to XV879 which was cancelled when HMS *Victorious* was decommissioned in March 1968. Two cockpits were built at Brough for use as Redifon simulators; one went to Lossiemouth, *perhaps* this was the other. It was used inside Brough's 'Shed B' - restricted entrance - for cockpit ergonomics trials. It was sold off from Brough in the late 1980s. Any leads on this cockpit's pedigree, or offers of help with kitting it out, via **buccaneerxn979@gmail.com** **[23]** XZ431 cockpit on loan from John Hoole. **[24]** Tornado owned by Simon Pulford - see Chester, Cheshire. **[25]** MB.339 was fitted with the forward fuselage of 0761 at Yeovilton, circa 1984; its cockpit section was never brought to the UK. Last used by Rolls-Royce as a mock-up for the US Navy/USAF JPATS programme, 1995.

Deep Store and **Workshop**: SYAM is happy to offer 'back lot' tours of the storage area – applications in advance **only** – see above for contact details. Auster AOP.9 XR238 represents no less than 30 years of tracking down its identity by *W&R* stalwart David Burke. Acquired by Bill Fern as a fuselage and battered wings, it has been used for spares reclamation and reduced to a cockpit – an SYAM speciality. This machine was one of a cache held by a collector in Rugby, Warks, and in *W&R16* was tied down as c/n AUS.176, XR239, with XR238 as a possibility. Last noted in May 2005 under Rugby' in *W&R26* (p287) it was written out; only to 'surface' care of Bill. Inspection of the fin in early May 2023 found a faint 'J' above the flash on each side. To quote David: "Then the penny dropped, it was not a 'J' but an Arabian dagger!" Photographic evidence of XR238 having been 'zapped' by 8 Squadron (badge, a sheathed Arabian dagger) while in service with the Odiham-based 38 Group Comms Flight and the build plate reading 175, clinched it! (Many a time *W&R* correspondents have pointed out the omission of the code 'J' for 8 Squadron Shackleton AEW.2s!) After stripping for spares, the original frame of AOP.9 XP282 was scrapped by October 2023. (See under Woodhall Spa, Lincs, for its 'second coming'.)

	Identity	Type	Year	History	Notes	Last noted
❑	G-AHHP	Auster J1N Alpha	46	ex Dunkeswell, G-SIME, G-AHHP. De-reg 22-2-99. Arrived by 9-18. *Saucy*	[1]	1-24
❑	G-AOKO	Percival Prentice 1	49	ex Coventry, Southend, VS621, CFS, 2 FTS, 22 FTS. CoA 23-10-72, de-reg 9-10-84. Arrived 9-5-00		1-24
❑	G-ARGI	Auster 6A Tugmaster	46	ex Newark-on-Trent, Chirk, Heathfield, AOP.6 VF530, 661. CoA 4-7-76, de-reg 23-8-77. Arrived 1-00. Frame	[2]	1-24
❑	G-BAML	Bell JetRanger	67	ex Walton Wood, N7844S. Crashed 30-5-03, de-reg 7-7-03. Arrived 2004		1-24
❑	G-BBNJ	Cessna F.150L	73	ex Spanhoe, Sherburn. Reims-built. De-reg 10-3-20	[3]	1-24
❑	G-BECE	AD Skyship 500	76	ex Cardington, Old Warden, Cardington, Kirkbymoorside. Gondola, damaged 9-3-79, de-reg 30-5-84. Arrived 1-08		1-24
❑	G-DDEA	Slingsby T.59D Kestrel	75	ex BGA.2046. De-reg 24-11-15. In trailer. Arrived 7-5-21		1-24
❑	G-FTAX	Cessna 421C	77	ex Stafford, Cambridge, N8363G, G-BFFM, N8363G. CoA 16-5-01, de-reg 8-7-03. Forward fuselage. F/n 7-21		1-24
❑	G-MJPO	Eurowing Goldwing	82	de-reg 9-4-02. Arrived 2003		1-24
❑	G-TPTR	Bell JetRanger II	79	ex Weston-super-Mare, Lyneham, G-LOCK, N2951N, N2951W, Agusta-built. Cr 1-3-89, de-reg 9-10-94. Arrived 28-4-17		1-24
❑	BGA.1863	Scheibe L-Spatz 55	~	ex Wroot, D-8225, D-6425. Arrived 11-17	[4]	1-24
❑	–	Stewart Ornithopter	c65	BAPC.61, ex Boston, N' Coates, Louth, Tumby Woodside, East Kirkby, Tattershall, Wigan, Irlam, South Reston. Built by Alan Stewart. *Bellbird II*. Arrived 9-5-16		1-24
❑	–	Hawker Typhoon	c42	ex Boscombe Down, Salisbury. Cockpit project	[5] [6]	1-24
❑	–	Hawker Typhoon	c42	ex Staverton. Cockpit	[5] [6]	1-24
❑	RA848*	Slingsby Cadet TX.1	43	ex Hooton Park, Wigan, Harrogate, Wigan, Handforth, Gt Hucklow. Otley Motors-built. Cockpit. Arrived 15-10-22		1-24
❑	WK393	DH Venom FB.1	53	ex Lavendon, Doncaster, CGS, FWS, Silloth, Firbeck, Dumfries, Silloth. Hawarden-built. SOC 28-2-58. Acquired 12-3-17. Cockpit	[5]	1-24
❑	WP255	DH Vampire NF.10	51	ex Haverigg, Firbeck, Ecclesfield, Bingley, Church Fenton, CNCS, 1 ANS, CNCS, 23. SOC 30-11-59. Acq 1991. Cockpit	[5]	1-24
❑	WX788	DH Venom NF.3	54	ex Elvington, Kenilworth, Long Marston, Cardiff, Bledlow Ridge, Connah's Quay, DH. Christchurch-built. SOC 25-11-57. Arrived 2-02		1-24
❑	WZ822	Slingsby Grasshopper TX.1	52	ex Firbeck, Robertsbridge, Halton, London. Acquired 5-97		1-24
❑	XA293*	Slingsby Cadet TX.1	52	ex Hooton Park, Stoke-on-Trent, Long Marston, Redditch. Forward fuselage. Arrived by 10-22		1-24
❑	XK421	Auster AOP.9	57	ex Woodhall Spa, S Molton, Eggesford, Doncaster, Firbeck, Thurcroft, Firbeck, Hedge End, Fownhope, Long Marston, Innsworth, Bristol, Caldicot, Bristol, 8365M (7-11-63), A&AEE, 1 Wing, M Wallop, LAS. Arrived 2017	[5] [7]	1-24
❑	XP905	Westland Scout AH.1	63	ex Ipswich, Arborfield, M Wallop, Wroughton, 656, 655, 652, 654, 652. First noted 7-21		1-24
❑	XR238*	Auster AOP.9	61	ex Rugby, Popham, -?-. 38 GCF, AAC Centre M Wallop. SOC 1-6-72. Cockpit by mid-2023 - see notes above.	[3]	1-24
❑	XT793	Westland Wasp HAS.1 G-BZPP	67	ex Old Sarum, Thruxton, Babcary, Lee-on-Solent, Thruxton, G-BZPP (de-reg 7-9-12), East Dereham, Bruntingthorpe, Fleetlands, HHU, 829, A&AEE, 829, HHU. Arr 16-7-19		1-24

	Reg	Code	Type	Other reg	Yr	History	Note	Date
❑	333		DH Vampire T.55		53	ex Barton, Chelford, Hadfield, Dukinfield, New Brighton, Chester, Iraqi AF. Christchurch-built. Arr 2-03. Cockpit	[3] [8]	1-24

■ **[1]** *Hotel-Papa* flew from Doncaster 1969-1973. **[2]** *Golf-India* was a tug with Doncaster and District Gliding Club 1961-1971. **[3]** Airframes on loan from Bill Fern. **[4]** *Likely* identity; may well have been flown locally. **[5]** Airframes on loan from Naylan Moore's Classic Aircraft Collection. **[6]** One of these may be BAPC.534 and the other BAPC.535, then again... **[7]** Parts from XP286 used in restoration. **[8]** Delivered to Iraq 1953. Airfreighted to Hawarden 1960 for trial installation of ejector seats, not returned.

Yorkshire Helicopter Preservation Group: Not suitable for a 'formal' listing is a Whirlwind hydraulic system training aid constructed from gearbox, rotor head and tail rotor components by Bristow Helicopters trainees at Redhill. This carries the fictitious registration 'G-YHPG' and attracts a lot of attention in the main aircraft hall! As well as the airframes, the group has a wealth of artefacts and documentation. ◆ *Most airframes on display within SYAM; workshop by appointment only*

	Reg	Code	Type	Other reg	Yr	History	Note	Date
❑	WN499	'Y'	Westland Dragonfly HR.5		53	ex Caernarfon, Higher Blagdon, Blackbushe, Culdrose SF, 705. SOC 1-6-44. Arrived 3-6-06. Dismantled	[1]	1-24
❑	XA862	'704'	Westland Whirlwind HAR.1	G-AMJT	53	ex Colerne, Weston-super-Mare, Coventry, Wroughton, Lee-on-Solent A2542 (20-5-66), Seafield Park, Haslar, L-o-S, Fleetlands, 781, 771, 700, 705, G-AMJT (de-reg 13-3-53). Arrived 13-7-05. Cockpit	[2]	1-24
❑	XA870	'911'	Westland Whirlwind HAR.1		54	ex Helston, Predannack, Lee-on-Solent A2543 (18-5-66), 705, 155, 848. Arrived 1-12-02. Sectioned		1-24
❑	XJ398		Westland Whirlwind HAR.10	G-BDBZ	57	ex Elvington, Oxford, Luton G-BDBZ (de-reg 28-3-85), XJ398, Culdrose, RAE, ETPS, DH Engines, A&AEE, HAR.5, HAR.3. Arrived 27-6-03. 202 Sqn colours	[3]	1-24
❑	XP345	'N'	Westland Whirlwind HAR.10		62	ex Elvington, Storwood, Tattershall Thorpe, Lee-on-Solent Cyprus 8792M (2-9-83), 84, 1563 Flt, 202, CFS. Arrived 6-7-02. 84 Sqn UN colours		1-24
❑	XT150		Bell Sioux AH.1		65	ex Netheravon, M Wallop 7883M, Wimbourne, Andover, Arborfield, Seletar, 42 Cdo. Crashed 6-2-68. Agusta-built. Arrived 7-8-08. Off-site	[4]	1-24
❑	XT242		Bell Sioux AH.1		66	ex Firbeck, Hooton Park, Warmingham, Long Marston, Wimborne, Middle Wallop, 'Blue Eagles'. Acquired 13-2-03. 'Blue Eagles' colours	[5]	1-24

■ **[1]** WN499 will be restored to represent HC.4 XB251 of 194 Sqn in Operation FIREDOG, in Malaya. **[2]** Remainder of XA862 - well battered - is/was in the fire training area at Colerne, Wilts. This was the first Yeovil-built S-55, first flown at 12-11-52 by Derrick Colvin. **[3]** XJ398 was the prototype HAR.10. Fitted with a GE T58 it first flew on 28-2-59. **[4]** XT150 is a composite, incorporating elements of the purely instructional 7884M. **[5]** Owned by YHPG's Alan Beattie and is a composite, with parts of XW179 included.

Moore's Restorations: Located off-site and run by SYAM stalwart, **Naylan Moore**, the workshop is listed here as a 'port of convenience'. As well as airframes, he specialises in classic Minis. Naylan is custodian of the expanding **4 Squadron Collection**. The cockpit of Harrier T.4 XW927 was exported to Hermeskeil, Germany, by October 2023.
◆ *Prior arrangement* **only** | **www.facebook.com/mooresrestorations**

	Reg	Code	Type	Other reg	Yr	History	Note	Date
❑	G-ASWF		Beagle Airedale		64	ex Newark-on-Trent, Leicester. CoA 27-4-83, de-reg 3-2-89		1-24
❑	N55XJ		Cassutt M11		03	ex Bungay area. Original fuselage		1-24
❑	WD293		DHC Chipmunk T.10		50	ex St Athan, Aberdare, Newport, Caerleon, Cwmbran, Filton 7645M (4-7-60), Queen's, St And, Glas, St And UASs, Chatham Flt, SoMR, 1 BFTS. Hawarden-built. Cockpit		1-24
❑	WG463*		DHC Chipmunk T.10	G-ATDX	51	ex Evesham, Breighton, Ipswich 8363M (22-8-73), S'ton, Nott, St A, Cam UASs, Colerne CF, Oxf, Abn UASs, CoAT G-ATDX, 24 GCF, Cott CF, 3 BFTS, 16 RFS. Hawarden-built. Cockpit	[1]	1-24
❑	XP888		Westland Scout AH.1		63	ex Ipswich, Arborfield, M Wallop, Wroughton, 651, 652, 14 Flt. Cabin		1-24
❑	XV806		HS Harrier GR.3		71	ex Workshop, S Molton, Boscombe D, Culdrose, A2607[3], A2602[2] (18-4-91), Cosford, 4, 3, 4, 20. Fuselage	[1]	1-24
❑	XX246*		HS Hawk T.1A		78	ex RAMCO Skegness, Valley RTP, Shawbury, 74, 208, T.1, 19, 2 TWU, 1 TWU. Arrived mid-2023	[1]	1-24
❑	XZ131		HS Harrier GR.3		76	ex Spark Bridge, Brierley Hill 9174M, St Athan, 233 OCU, 1417 Flt, 233 OCU, 4, 1, 4. Cockpit	[1]	1-24
❑	ZJ138*	'X'	EHI Merlin		02	ex 'Scotland', Farnborough, Boscombe Down, Gosport, Yeovil, 28. Crashed 23-6-10. Cockpit	[1]	1-24

❑ – HS Sea Harrier FRS.1 EMU ~ ex Halesworth [1] 1-24
❑ 162074 BAe/McDD AV-8B Harrier II 84 ex USMC. Cockpit [1] 1-24

■ **[1] 4 Squadron Collection** - more details on **www.the4squadroncollection.org**

DONCASTER town centre

Danum Gallery, Library and Museum: (The previous Museum and Art Gallery.)

◆ *Waterdale and Chequer Road, DN1 2AE* | **01302 734293** | **www.doncaster.gov.uk/museums**

❑ 'G-AEKR' Mignet HM.14 'Flea' 71 BAPC.121, ex Breighton, Firbeck, Nostell Priory, Crowle, Oakington. *This is the 'Flea' that Claybourne's Built.* Acquired 22-3-97. Stored, off-site [1] 4-23
❑ – Bensen B-7 c61 BAPC.275. Acquired 2001. Stored, off-site [2] 4-23

■ **[1]** Original G-AEKR, first flew at Doncaster 28-5-36, Authorisation No.87. It became part of the RAF Finningley 'Station Museum' in the 1960s but was burnt out in a hangar fire 5-9-70. Some metal parts incorporated in this 'replacement' built largely at Oakington. Completed project handed over at Finningley 18-9-71, **[2]** Bensen built by S J R Wood of Warmsworth.

DONCASTER SHEFFIELD (ROBIN HOOD) **AIRPORT** or Finningley, east of A638, north of Bawtry EGCN

Vulcan to the Sky Trust (VTST): The year 2021 ended with disappointment, a major fund-raising push, 'Operation Safeguard' failed to meet its target and the Trust announced "a period of reflection" was required regarding the future. This was put into sharp focus on 13th July 2022 when the management of Doncaster Sheffield Airport (DSA) declared: "aviation activity on the site may no longer be commercially viable". They weren't kidding, the last commercial flights were staged on 4th and 5th November 2022 and airport infrastructure was quickly wound down. Along with this came the obvious: VTST would not have its tenancy renewed beyond June 2023. VTST reported it was evaluating "two potential new homes" for XH558 and examining the chances of a one-shot ferry flight – the latter quickly died as an option. The local authority took a robust view that DSA should continue to function as an airport, technology park and other forms of employment. In January 2024 VTST issued a statement that included: "Negotiations on the future of [DSA] are continuing between the City of Doncaster and Peel L&P [Peel Land and Property Group, owners of DSA]... we are hopeful that a resolution will be reached that sees DSA re-open to the public and XH558 remain as a key attraction..."

Page 4 contains some further discussion of this situation. Meanwhile VTST held hopes that visitor days could be held in 2024 – keep an eye on the website. *W&R28* outlined plans to bring Canberra B(I).8 WT327 (N30UP) back from the USA: this airframe included the original nose of WK163 – see below. This scheme is believed to be on hold.

◆ **enquiries@vulcantothesky.org** | **www.vulcantothesky.org**

❑ WK163 EE Canberra B.2/6 G-CTTS 55 ex Baginton, G-BVWC, DRA Farnborough, RAE Bedford, RRE Pershore, Napier, ASM Bitteswell. Avro-built. CoA 29-6-08, handed over 19-5-16. 617 Sqn colours [1] 1-24
❑ XH558 Avro Vulcan B.2(MRR) G-VLCN 60 ex Lyneham, Bruntingthorpe, Waddington, VDF, Marham, Waddington, 50, Wadd Wing, A&AEE, Wadd Wing, 27, 230 OCU, 27, Wadd Wing, 230 OCU. *Spirit of Great Britain.* Arrived 29-3-11, last flight 20-10-15, de-reg 19-8-17 1-24

■ **[1]** Registered to VTST. When fitted with a Napier Double Scorpion booster rocket, WK163 clinched the world altitude record on 28-8-57, reaching 70,310ft. At Pershore, WK163 was substantially re-engineered with B.6 wings, engines and the cockpit of B.6 XH568.

Also: Boeing 727 EC-DDX had gone by the spring of 2023, believed axed; Citation N80364 is unaccounted for.

❑ G-GAVA BAe Jetstream 3102 87 ex SE-LDI, C-FHOE. De-reg 1-3-18. First noted 4-18 7-23

Locally: Tim Wood's Swift moved off site in May 2019 and is reported to have changed hands by 2022: it is listed here as a 'port of convenience'. Another owner keeps a Chipmunk cockpit in the *general* area.

❑ WK275 V-S Swift F.4 55 ex VTST site, Selby, Upper Hill Hatfield, Filton, C(A). SOC 25-5-59. Arrived 15-5-19: off-site 5-21
❑ WK638 DHC Chipmunk T.10 G-BWJZ 52 ex Swindon, Long Eaton, Eccleshall, Stamford, Manston, 9 AEF, RAFC, 9 AEF, York UAS, 1 FTS, 1 AEF, Ox UAS, 1 RFS. Hawarden-built. Crashed 22-8-99, CoA 17-1-02, de-reg 4-4-00. Arrived 2015. Cockpit 6-20

FISHLAKE on minor roads, west of Thorne

Jet Provost Preservation Group: Paul Flynn's 'JP' relocated here. ◆ *Prior arrangement* **only** | **www.facebook.com/xs186**

❑ XS186* '10' Hunting Jet Provost T.4 64 ex Metheringham, Ipswich, N Luffenham, Halton 8408M (7-10-74), St Athan, Kemble, Shawbury, CAW. F/n 9-22 2-23

NETHERTHORPE AERODROME north of the A619, west of Worksop EGNF

By August 2022 the cabin of F.172 G-NIUS had gravitated to Blackbushe, Hampshire.

	Reg	Type	Year	Notes	Date
❑	G-ARJT	Piper Apache 160G	62	ex N10F. CoA 18-8-07, de-reg 17-10-17	7-22
❑	G-BBKF	Cessna FRA.150L	74	ex Sibson. Reims-built. CoA 13-6-91, de-reg 15-2-07. Fuselage	6-22
❑	G-BEIA	Cessna FRA.150M	76	ex Sibson. Reims-built. CoA 27-10-03, de-reg 3-3-11. Fuselage	6-22

SHEFFIELD

Structural Dynamics Laboratory for Verification and Validation: Europa Avenue. Run by Sheffield University, this high-tech facility specialises in acoustic and vibration testing. ◆ *Prior arrangement* **only** | **www.lvv.ac.uk**

	Reg	Type	Year	Notes	Date
❑	XX184 'CQ'	HS Hawk T.1	77	ex Boscombe Down, Portsmouth, B' Down, Portsmouth, B' Down, 100, 208, 234, 4 FTS. SOC 7-8-17. F/n 11-19	12-23
❑	ZE376	Westland Lynx AH.9A	85	ex M Wallop. SOC 3-10-18. First noted 11-19	12-23

WEST YORKSHIRE

Includes the unitary authorities of Barnsley, Bradford, Calderdale, Kirklees, Leeds and Wakefield

BIRD'S EDGE Abiding by the tidying up outlined on page 7, Jodels G-BFXR and G-BKIR have been deleted.

DEWSBURY

Two helicopters are stored in a *private* location in the area. *Alpha-Romeo may* be destined for Scotland.

	Reg	Type	Year	Notes	Date
❑	G-BHAR	Bell Sioux AH.1	65	ex XT194. Westland-built. CoA 8-9-11	12-19
❑	G-USAI	Bell 47J-2A Ranger	63	ex D-HACK, 5B-CAF, Cyprus CR-1, N83701. Agusta-built	12-19

HUDDERSFIELD AERODROME or Crosland Moor, south of the A670 west of the city

The forward fuselage of Boeing 737-300 D-AGEE (identity confirmed) departed – destination unknown – during 2022. Active restoration Jodel D.117 G-AYKK has been deleted.

	Reg	Type	Year	Notes	Date
❑	G-BIIZ	Great Lakes 2T-1A	29	ex Squires Gate, N603K. Cr 8-8-98, CoA 4-2-99. Off-site	12-23

LEEDS-BRADFORD AIRPORT or Yeadon EGNM

Last noted in late 2018 in the rescue training area, Robinson R44 G-PROG is believed to have perished while the fuselage of Short 360 EI-BPD is reported to have been removed – no 'forwarding address'.

Written out of *W&R28* (p281) the cockpit of HR.200 'G-OTAA' is extant locally at a ***private*** location as a plaything, complete with 'Red Arrows' colours and markings. The same cannot be said for the cockpit of Cessna G-ATND which is believed to have been handed on to another owner: no further details.

	Reg	Type	Year	Notes	Date
❑	G-MFLC*	Robin HR.200-120B	97	ex 'G-OTAA', de-reg 16-9-14. Cockpit, 'Red arrows' colours	9-23

LEEDS HELIPORT or Coney Park

Heli Jet Aviation: As outlined on page 7, the following have been deleted: Robinsons G-CHPA, G-LOLZ and G-WIRL; JetRanger G-HMPT; Bell 222s N153H and N800HL and UH-1H N911DN.

◆ *Has a viewing area, but access to the hangars is* strictly *prior arrangement* **only** | **www.helijet.co.uk**

	Reg	Type	Year	Notes	Date
❑	G-MRSN	Robinson R22 Beta	91	de-reg 2-9-20	12-23
❑	G-RAMI	Bell JetRanger III	79	ex N1080N. CoA 5-9-16, crashed 6-6-15	12-23
❑	DU-103	Bell JetRanger	~	ex Dubai Air Wing. Arrived 23-11-15	12-23

SOWERBY BRIDGE on the A646 west of Halifax

Ryburn Valley High School: Enquiries in autumn 2023 revealed that Piper Cadet G-SACU is no more...

SCOTLAND

Scotland comprises 32 unitary authorities ranging from Orkney, Shetland to Dumfries and Galloway and Borders

ABERDEEN AIRPORT or Dyce

EGPD

As well as the 'pukka' training aids, there is a purpose-built rig for HUET - Helicopter Underwater Escape Training.

❑ G-BHIC		Cessna F.182Q	80	ex Kemble, Alton, Kidlington. Reims-built. Damaged 9-06, CoA 3-8-08, de-reg 4-5-07. Fuselage, rescue trainer		9-21
❑ -		Sud Dauphin II	~	BAPC.563, ex CHC Scotia. Composite	[1]	11-21
❑ XZ232	'Falck 4'	Westland Lynx HAS.3GMS	77	ex Ipswich, Fleetlands, 815, 702, HAS.2, 702, 700L. Red scheme	[2]	9-23
❑ XZ372	'FV'	SEPECAT Jaguar GR.3A	76	ex Ipswich, St Athan, 41, 6, GR.1, 6, 226 OCU, 20, 14. Last flown 5-7-05. Rescue trainer		9-23
❑ XZ647		Westland Lynx AH.7	80	ex Falck NUTEC, M Wallop. Red scheme. Rescue trainer		9-21
❑ ZA110	'563'	HP Jetstream T.2	81	ex Ipswich, Culdrose, 750, F-BTMI. SOC 29-10-10. SAL-built. Fuselage, rescue trainer		9-23
❑ ZG916*		Westland Lynx AH.9A	91	ex 'Ipswich', Middle Wallop. First noted 3-23		3-23

■ **[1]** Dauphin is with Survivex on the western perimeter industrial estate. It is fitted with a 'N2-model tail if that helps. Apparently, it deserves a heritage number. **[2]** Lynx HAS.3 is a fire-trainer on a mock-up oil rig heli-pad with Falck NUTEC on the eastern perimeter.

ABOYNE south of the A93 west of Banchory

Deeside Activity Park ◆ *Prior arrangement* **only** | **www.deesideactivitypark.com**

❑ G-OANN	Zenair CH-601 Zodiac	00	ex airstrip, crashed 23-4-06. Fuselage in 'crash' scene	[1]	9-23

■ **[1]** Zodiac G-OANN was rebuilt and is airworthy – this is the original fuselage.

ABOYNE AERODROME south of the A93 west of Banchory

A homebuilt amphibian is stored at a local, *private*, location.

❑ G-BAHP	Volmer Sportsman	73	CoA 18-10-93	N6-23

ACHARACLE on the southern tip of Loch Shiel, a long way west of Fort William

A Sea King is held at a *private* location in the *general* area.

❑ XV648	Westland Sea King HU.5SAR	69	ex Colsterworth, Fleetlands, 771, Gannet Flt, 819, DERA, 706, HAS.2, 706, Falklands, 825, 706, HAS.1, 706, 737, 826, 700S. First noted 10-16	1-21

AYR east of the A77 southwest of Kilmarnock

Ayrshire College: Bulldog XX612 (G-BZXC) moved to Glasgow Prestwick, Scotland, 30th November 2024.
◆ *Prior arrangement* **only** | **www.ayrshire.ac.uk**

❑ G-AZHK	Robin HR.100-210B	71	ex Dalcross, G-ILEG, G-AZHK. CoA 22-10-71, de-reg 30-9-21	9-21

BALADO AERODROME or Balado Bridge, on the A91 west of Milnathort

❑ XM412	'41' *and* '49'	Hunting Jet Provost T.3A	60	ex Ipswich, N Weald, Binbrook, Colsterworth, Halton 9011M (10-8-89), 1 FTS, 3 FTS, 2 FTS. Displayed	9-23

BANCHORY on the A93 west of Aberdeen

A pair of Airedales are cherished at a *private* location in the *general* area.

❑ G-ARXD	Beagle Airedale	62	ex Netherley. CoA 13-6-86	N7-22
❑ G-ASAI	Beagle Airedale	62	ex Dundee, Islay. CoA 20-5-77	N10-22

BLANTYRE on the A724 south east of Glasgow

A *private* owner has a Gnat in the *general* area.

❑ XM697	'S'	Folland Gnat T.1 G-NAAT	61	ex Carluke, Market Drayton, Exeter, Hurn, Dunsfold, Hurn, Woking, HSA, A&AEE, HSA. SOC 23-9-68, de-reg 10-4-95. 'Red Arrows' colours. First noted 4-16	9-21

BRIDGE OF WEIR on the A761 northwest of Paisley

Neil Geddes: Has a *private* store/workshop in the locality.

❑ G-AJAJ	Auster J1N Alpha	46	CoA 12-6-15		7-21
❑ G-CDUW	Aeronca C.3	35	ex F-AZKE, N64765, N14631		7-21
❑ WZ824	Slingsby Grasshopper TX.1	52	ex Dirleton, Strathaven, Ringmer, Dishforth, St Bees. SOC 9-3-88	[1]	7-21
❑ XK820	Slingsby Grasshopper TX.1	56	ex Strathallan, Aberdeen, Lancing, Locking. SOC 21-6-88	[2]	7-21

■ **[1]** See also under Carlisle, Cumbria. **[2]** XK820 has wings from WZ754 and WZ778.

BRIGHOUSE BAY on the B727 west of Kirkcudbright

Brighouse Bay Holiday Park: Note more precise location. | **www.brighousebayholidaypark.co.uk**

❑ WS792 'K' *and* 7965M	Gloster Meteor NF(T).14	54	ex Carlisle (Kingstown), Cosford 7965M (19-6-67), 5 MU, 1 ANS, 2 ANS, no service as NF.14. AWA-built. 85 Sqn colours	12-23

CARLUKE on the A73 southeast of Motherwell and Wishaw

Reynard Nursery: Within the nursery, the Convair is used by **Runway Studios Makeup Lounge** as a 'surgery'.
◆ *Visitors welcome during open hours, but best to check beforehand* | **www.reynardgardencentres.co.uk** | **www.facebook.com/runwaystudiosmakeup**

❑ G-CONV	Convair CV-440-54	57	ex Coventry, CS-TML, N357SA, N28KE, N4402. De-reg 20-12-06	12-23

CARRUTHERSTOWN on the A75 between Dumfries and Annan

Hetland Garden Centre: A Cessna, in the inevitable crash pose, is in the 'Dino Park' segment. ◆ **www.hetland.co.uk**

❑ N310WT	Cessna 310R	78	ex Perth, G-BGXK, N6070X. De-reg 17-10-01. First noted 4-21	7-21

CHAPELTON on the A276 northwest of Strathaven

A *private* store of light aircraft in the locality.

❑ G-AOEH	Aeronca 7AC Champion	46	ex Newtownards, OO-TWF, N79854. CoA 19-7-10	6-21
❑ G-AWUS	Cessna F.150J	68	Reims-built. Crashed 22-11-86, de-reg 4-7-94	6-21
❑ G-AYXV	Cessna FRA.150L	68	Reims-built. Crashed 5-9-79, de-reg 24-9-79	6-21
❑ G-AZHT	Victa Airtourer T3	69	ex Glasgow, Abbotsinch. AESL-built. Crashed 29-4-86, de-reg 7-12-22	6-21
❑ G-BGWV	Aeronca 7AC Champion	46	ex OO-GRI, OO-TWR. Crashed 8-6-86, de-reg 9-1-13	6-21
❑ N170AZ	Cessna 170A	48	ex Strathallan, HB-CAZ	6-21

CULLODEN southeast of Inverness

The Belfair is extant in the *general* area.

❑ G-APOD	Tipsy Belfair	58	ex Dundee, OO-TIF. CoA 23-8-88, de-reg 6-9-00	3-22

CUMBERNAULD AERODROME north of the A80, north of Cumbernauld EGPG

Dragon G-ACET was flying again by April 2023. Islander S7-AAU had been reduced to a mid-fuselage section by June 2022.

❑ XV268	DHC Beaver 1	G-BVER	66	ex G-BTDM, XV268, M Wallop. CoA 23-4-95, de-reg 20-12-16	5-22

CUPAR on the A91 west of St Andrews

Scottish Deer Centre: ◆ Bow of Fife, KY15 4NQ | **email** via website | **https://scottishdeerpark.co.uk**

❑ XW530	Blackburn Buccaneer S.2B	70	ex Elgin, Lossiemouth, 208, 12, 208, 216, 16, 15, 16. Arrived 11-12-21	6-23

Locally: A Victor cockpit is kept at a *private* venue in the area.

❑ XA917	HP Victor B.1	56	ex Crowland, Barnham, Marham, Wittering 7827M (13-12-63), A&AEE, HP. Damaged 2-3-61. Cockpit	[1]	7-21

■ **[1]** The first production Victor B.1, XA917 hit the headlines on a sortie out of Radlett 1-6-57 with John Allam at the helm; in a shallow dive at around 40,000ft, it clocked 675mph - Mach 1.02 - becoming the largest aircraft at the time to go supersonic.

Cupar's Scottish Deer Centre is home to Buccaneer S.2B XW530, June 2023. *David S Johnstone*

DINGWALL on the A862 northwest of Inverness

A farm in the *general* area has taken on the former Batman film props. ◆ *Prior arrangement* **only**

❑ G-EEST*	BAe Jetstream 3102	87	ex Evanton, *The Dark Knight Rises*, Inverness, Millom, Humberside, Eastern, Wick, SE-LGM, OY-SVY, C-FASJ, G-31-781. Damaged 17-9-03, de-reg 5-11-07. Fuselage, f/n 12-22		12-22
❑ –*	Embraer Bandeirante	~	ex Evanton, *The Dark Knight Rises*. Fuselage, f/n 12-22		12-22

DIRLETON on the A198 west of North Berwick

A *private* airstrip in the locality. Starduster G-JIII has been deleted.

❑ G-BBBO	SIPA 903	51	ex Eggington, F-BGBQ. CoA 9-9-09		6-21

DUMFRIES off the A701 northeast of Dumfries on the former airfield

Dumfries and Galloway Aviation Museum: The restored watch tower that forms the centrepiece of the museum contains a huge array of artefacts, including an impressive engine collection. Within the Airborne Forces Hall is a beautifully restored/constructed Horsa fuselage section, lacking cockpit it is not formally listed.

'JP' T.4 XP557 travelled to Kinloss, Scotland, 16th April 2023.

◆ *DG1 3PH* | **01387 251623** | **email** via website | **www.dumfriesaviationmuseum.com**

❑ G-AWZJ	HS Trident 3B-101	71	ex Prestwick, BA, BEA. CoA 12-9-85, de-reg 7-3-86. Arrived 1999. Forward fuselage	[1]	1-24
❑ G-AYFA	SAL Twin Pioneer 3	58	ex Hooton Park, Morecambe, Mold, Carlisle, Hooton Park, Warmingham, Sandbach, Shobdon, Prestwick, G-31-5, XM285, SRCU, 225, Odiham SF, 230. De-reg 16-5-91. Cockpit. Arrived 9-13	[2]	1-24
❑ G-AZIL	Scheibe Falke	71	CoA 13-10-14, de-reg 3-3-22. Slingsby-built T.61A. Arrived 10-2-19. Off-site		1-22
❑ G-RAYE	Piper Cherokee Six	66	ex Doncaster, Stamford, Tatenhill, G-ATTY, N11C. CoA 27-9-08, de-reg 2-6-08. Arrived by 4-14. Fuselage, off-site		3-20
❑ –	HS HS.748-2B	89	ex Perth, Woodford. Cockpit	[3]	1-24
❑ CHQ*	Slingsby Tandem Tutor XN247	59	BGA.1559, ex Hooton Park, Selby, Bury St Edmunds, Leeds, RAFGSA.316, XN247, 622 GS. CoA 1-7-82. Arrived 15-10-22		10-22
❑ P7540 'DU-W'	V-S Spitfire IIa recreation	40	ex Pickhill, Loch Doon, 312, 266, 609, 66. CBAF-built. Crashed 25-10-41. Salvaged 1988. Unveiled 16-7-17	[4]	1-24
❑ –	Avro Anson I	~	ex Canada, RCAF. Complete frame plus additional cockpit. 'Unveiled' 6-21		1-24
❑ –	HP Halifax rep	~	BAPC.322, ex Linton-on-Ouse. Cockpit. First noted 3-18		1-24
❑ –	GAL Hotspur II	~	BAPC.397, ex Duxford, Aldershot. Cockpit. First noted 6-17		1-24
❑ –	GAL Hamilcar	~	forward fuselage; entrance to Airborne Forces hall		8-22

Reg	Code	Type	Year	Details	Note	Date
❑ WA576		Bristol Sycamore 3 G-ALSS	51	ex East Fortune, Strathallan, Halton 7900M (5-1-66), RAE, A&AEE, G-ALSS de-reg 17-11-50. Arrived 7-6-87		1-24
❑ WJ880		EE Canberra T.4	55	ex Firbeck, N Weald, Halton 8491M (2-4-76), 7, 85, 100, 56, Laarbruch SF, RAE, 16, Laarbruch SF, Gütersloh SF, 104. Arrived 1995. Cockpit, travelling exhibit		1-24
❑ WL375		Gloster Meteor T.7(mod)	52	ex West Freugh, RAE. SOC 16-6-69, acquired 1977. RAE colours by 6-22	[5]	1-24
❑ WP860*	'6'	DHC Chipmunk T.10 G-BXDA	52	ex Eshott, Ballyboy, WP860 12, 13, 6 AEFs, Abn UAS, Leeds UAS, 9 AEF, Leeds, Abn, St And, Perth, St And UASs, CNCS, 5 FTS, CNCS, RAFC. Hawarden-built. CoA 21-11-14. Arrived 9-10-22 - off site. Travelling display airframe		4-23
❑ WT746		Hawker Hunter F.4	55	ex 'XF506', Saighton, Halton 7770M (28-11-62), St Athan, AFDS. Arrived 1999. *Clara*, 'Black Arrows' colours		1-24
❑ XL497	'041'	Fairey Gannet AEW.3	61	ex Prestwick, Lossiemouth, 849, A&AEE, 849. SOC 7-12-78. Arrived 13-4-05		1-24
❑ XT148*		Bell Sioux AH.1	65	ex Chester, Hooton Park, Sunderland, Weston-super-Mare, Halton, Panshanger, Wroughton, ARWF. Agusta-built. Cab, no 'bubble'. Arrived 2-4-23		1-24
❑ XT236*	'12'	Bell Sioux AH.1	66	ex Hooton Park, Chester, Doncaster, Sunderland, M Wallop, Sek Kong. Westland-built. Arrived 2-4-23		1-24
❑ XT280	'323'	Blackburn Buccaneer S.2B	65	ex Dundonald, Birtley, East Fortune, Lossie', 208, 12, 208, 12, 16, 809, A&AEE, 809. SOC 10-4-94. Arrived 2-03. Cockpit		1-24
❑ XT486		Westland Wessex HU.5	66	ex Altcar, Brize Norton 8919M (3-2-87), Wroughton, 848, 847, 772, 707, 781. Arrived 13-6-07		1-24
❑ XW363	'36'	BAC Jet Provost T.5A	71	ex Haverigg, Swinton, Warton, Samlesbury, Preston, Warton, RAFC, 6 FTS, 1 FTS. SOC 11-1-91. Arrived 2010, off-site		10-22
❑ XX483	'562'	HP Jetstream T.1	74	ex Welshpool, Weston-on-Trent, Shawbury, 750, CFS, 5 FTS. Arrived 2002. 750 Sqn c/s. Cockpit, travelling exhibit		1-24
❑ ZF584		EE Lightning F.53	68	ex Edinburgh, Turnhouse, Warton, Saudi AF 211, 307, 53-682, G-27-52. Last flown 22-1-86, arrived 22-5-06. 111 Sqn c/s		1-24
❑ FT-36		Lockheed T-33A-1-LO	55	ex Sculthorpe, Belgian AF, USAF 55-3047. Last flew 26-11-79, arrived 8-9-81. *Little Miss Laura*	[6]	1-24
❑ 318	'8-NY'	Dassault Mystère IVA	c57	ex Sculthorpe, French Air Force. Last flown 15-5-79. Arrived 1981. 'Tiger' stripes	[6]	1-24
❑ Fv35075	'40'	SAAB J35A Draken	c61	ex Duxford, Swedish AF F16. Arrived 19-8-05	[7]	1-24
❑ '241079'		Waco CG-4 Hadrian replica	03	BAPC.370, ex Cosford, Shawbury, Lubbock, Texas. Fuselage. Arrived 11-18	[8]	1-24
❑ '54-005'		NAA F-100D-11-NA Super Sabre	54	ex Sculthorpe, FAF, USAF 54-2163. Last flown 24-5-77, arrived 11-1-79. USAF colours, *Miss Shillelagh*	[6]	1-24
❑ 68-0060		GD F-111E Aardvark	68	ex 20 TFW. Escape pod. Crashed 5-11-75. Arrived 1990		1-24

■ **[1]** *Zulu-Juliet*'s is open to the public and includes an interior display and 30-seat lecture hall. **[2]** 'Twin Pin' on loan. **[3]** HS.748 cockpit is no longer thought to be off the line, but a dedicated customer mock-up. **[4]** Based at Ayr with 312 (Czechoslovak) Sqn, P7540 was flying ultra-low over Loch Doon, near Craigmalloch, 25-10-41, when a wing tip hit the water and it crashed. **[5]** Meteor fitted with an F.8 rear fuselage and 'tail feathers' – making it a so-called T.7½ - and an FR.9 or PR.10 nose cone. **[6]** Part of the National Museum of the USAF's Loan Program. **[7]** Draken was signed over to the museum from the IWM during 2012. **[8]** From the Assault Glider Trust.

Locally: The Austers are at a nearby, *private*, workshop. With **1153 (Dumfries) Squadron Air Cadets**: The status of the CoZy, which was destined to become a simulator, is uncertain. The Chipmunk cockpit is kept by a D&G member in the area.

Reg	Type	Year	Details	Note	Date
❑ G-ALNV*	Taylorcraft Auster 5	44	ex Newark-on-Trent, Nottingham, Leicester, AOP.V RT578, 341, 329. CoA 4-7-50, de-reg 1-5-59. Arrived 26-2-22		5-23
❑ G-AOCP*	Taylorcraft Auster 5	45	ex Newark-on-Trent, AOP.V TW462, 666. Damaged 4-70, de-reg 24-6-71. Arrived 26-6-22, spares for G-ALNV	[1]	10-22
❑ G-CESP	Puffer CoZy Mk.4	07	ex Perth. Unfinished project, de-reg 5-11-10		1-14
❑ WB670*	DHC Chipmunk T.10	50	ex Carlisle, Newcastle, Morpeth, East Fortune, Currie, Southend, London Colney, Welwyn Garden City, 8361M (22-8-73), Hatfield, MoS, 5 FTS, LAS, 12 RFS, 5 RFS. Hawarden-built. Cockpit, 1 AEF colours. Arrived by 6-22	[2]	6-22

■ **[1]** G-AOCP is a composite, including parts from G-AKOT - crashed 9-9-62, de-reg 16-10-62. **[2]** WB670 was used for life-extension trials at Hatfield and SOC as tested to destruction 31-12-71.

DUNDEE

Dundee Museum of Transport: Among the cycles, cars, vans and fire engines is a replica of a Dundee pioneer.

◆ *Unit 10 Market Mews, DD1 3LA* | **email** via website | **www.dmoft.co.uk**

❑ –*	Watson Biplane No.1 rep	21	BAPC.642. Built by Dundee Model A/c Club. F/n 6-22	[1]	1-24

■ **[1]** First biplane design - strictly an inverted sesquiplane - designed and built by Preston A Watson c1908/1909; reconfigured as a glider in 1910 and used by the Dundee Aero Club.

DUNDEE AIRPORT or Riverside

EGPN

❑ G-BXET	Piper Tomahawk 112	80	ex N25089. CoA 26-8-11, de-reg 23-6-11. Cockpit, rescue tnr		7-20

EAST FORTUNE north of the A1, west of East Linton

National Museum of Flight Scotland: Part of National Museums Scotland - see Edinburgh for the 'headquarters'. As well as the hangars: Hangar 2, military aviation, Hangar 3 - civil aviation, Hangar 4 Concorde and the 'Jet Age' exhibition, several other wartime buildings are open. Hangar 1 is devoted to conservation and is not *generally* available to the public.

◆ *Signed from the A1 near Haddington, EH39 5LF* | **0300 1236789** | **info@nms.ac.uk** | **www.nms.ac.uk/flight**

Hangars 2, 3, 4 and external exhibits:

❑ G-ACYK	Spartan Cruiser III	35	ex Hill of Stake, Largs. Crashed 14-1-38, de-reg 8-6-38. Arrived 1973. Fuselage		1-24
❑ G-AGBN	GAL Cygnet II	41	ex Strathallan, Biggin Hill, ES915, MCCS, 52 OTU, 51 OTU, 23, G-AGBN. CoA 28-11-80, de-reg 15-11-88. Arrived 11-8-81		1-24
❑ G-AHKY	Miles M.18-2	40	ex Perth, Strathallan, Blackbushe, HM545, U-0224, U-8. CoA 20-9-89, de-reg 19-3-92. Phillips & Powis-built. Arr 1991		1-24
❑ G-ANOV	DH Dove 6	54	ex CAFU, G-5-16. CoA 31-5-75, de-reg 6-7-81. Arr 10-78		1-24
❑ G-APFJ	Boeing 707-436	60	ex Cosford, British Airtours, BOAC. CoA 16-2-82, de-reg 30-5-84. Arrived 4-06. BOAC colours. Forward fuselage		1-24
❑ G-ARCX	Gloster Meteor NF.14	53	ex Ferranti, WM261. CoA 20-2-69, de-reg 25-10-73. AWA-built. Arrived 8-75	[1]	1-24
❑ G-ARPH	HS Trident 1C	64	ex Cosford, BA, BEA. CoA 8-9-82, de-reg 24-5-82. Arrived 2006. BA colours. Cockpit		1-24
❑ G-ASUG	Beech E.18S	56	ex Loganair, N575C, N555CB, N24R. CoA 23-7-75, de-reg 12-5-75. Arrived 1976		1-24
❑ G-ATOY	Piper Comanche 260B	66	ex Elstree, N8893P. Crashed 6-3-79; de-reg 14-5-79. Arrived 1979. *Myth Too*. Fuselage, in 'Fantastic Flight'	[2]	1-24
❑ G-AVMO	BAC 111-510ED	68	ex Cosford, Hurn, BA, BEA. *Lothian Region*. CoA 3-2-95, de-reg 12-7-93. Arrived 9-9-06. Outside		1-24
❑ G-AVPC	Druine Turbulent	73	CoA 28-9-99, de-reg 13-9-02. Arrived 4-03		1-24
❑ G-BBVF	SAL Twin Pioneer 2	59	ex Shobdon, XM961 / 7978M, SRCU, Odiham SF, 230, 21. Damaged 11-3-82, de-reg 8-8-83. Arrived 19-8-82		1-24
❑ G-BDIX	DH Comet 4C	62	ex Lasham, Dan-Air, XR399, 216. CoA 11-10-81, de-reg 13-6-83. Hawarden-built. Arrived 30-9-81. Outside		1-24
❑ G-BELF	BN Islander G-HEBZ	77	ex Cumbernauld, D-IBRA, G-BELF - CoA 12-3-01, de-reg 21-3-09. G-HEBZ de-reg 8-11-18. Arrived 7-7-05. Scottish Ambulance colours	[3]	1-24
❑ G-BOAA	BAC/Sud Concorde 102	75	ex London, BA, G-N94AA (1-79 to 7-80), G-BOAA. CoA 24-2-01, de-reg 4-5-04. Arrived 19-4-04	[4]	1-24
❑ G-JSSD	HP Jetstream 3100	69	ex Prestwick, N510F, N510E, N12227, G-AXJZ. CoA 9-10-90. De-reg 4-1-96. Arrived 2-96	[5]	1-24
❑ G-SJEN	Icarus C42 FB80	04	ex Strathaven. Last flown 5-10, de-reg 10-8-10. Arr 7-11		3-20
❑ G-UNIV	Montgomerie Two-Place	96	ex Glasgow, G-BWTP. CoA 18-1-05, de-reg 16-1-14	[6]	3-20
❑ W-2	Weir W.2	34	BAPC.85, ex Edinburgh, East Fortune, Glasgow, EF, Hayes, Knockholt, Hanworth, Cathcart. Acquired 1986	[7]	1-24
❑ –	Scotkites Cirrus III hang-glider	77	BAPC.197, ex Lothian Hang Glider Club, Edinburgh. Last flown and arrived 1987		3-20
❑ –	Firebird Sierra h-glider	c83	BAPC.313, ex Huntly. Arrived 2002		3-20
❑ –	Airwave Magic Kiss h-g	89	BAPC.312, ex Biggar. Arrived 2005		3-20
❑ 591	Schleicher Rhönlerche II	59	ex D-0359. Arrived 1987		10-21

❑	VH-SNB		DH Dragon I	42	ex Strathallan, VH-ASK, RAAF A34-13. Arrived 1981	[8]	1-24
❑	VH-UQB		DH Puss Moth	30	ex Strathallan, Bankstown, G-ABDW. Arrived 1981		1-24
❑	N14234		HP Jetstream 1	69	ex Hatfield, East Midlands, N14234, N102SC, N200SC, N1BE, G-BBBV, G-8-12. Arrived 5-94. Fuselage	[9]	1-24
❑	TE462		V-S Spitfire XVI	45	ex Ouston 7243M (14-12-54), 101 FRS, Finningley SF. CBAF-built. Arrived 19-2-71. Plinth-mounted		1-24
❑	VM360		Avro Anson C.19	47	ex Strathallan, Thruxton, Kemps, G-APHV (de-reg 21-1-82), TRE, A&AEE. SOC 18-11-57. Arrived 8-77		1-24
❑	VX185		EE Canberra B.5	52	ex Wroughton, South Kensington, EE. Arrived 10-97. *The Record-Breaking Canberra*. Cockpit	[10]	1-24
❑	WF259	'171'	Hawker Sea Hawk F.2	54	ex Lossiemouth A2483 (24-6-59), Lossiemouth SF, 736. AWA-built. Arrived 10-7-72. 804 Sqn colours		1-24
❑	WW145	'680'	DH Sea Venom FAW.22	55	ex Lossiemouth, 750, 891. Christchurch-built. SOC 13-2-70. Arrived 1972		1-24
❑	XA228		Slingsby Grasshopper TX.1	53	ex store, Glenalmond School. Arrived 6-00		1-24
❑	XM597		Avro Vulcan B.2	63	ex Waddington, 50, 35, 101, 9, 50, 35, Wadd W, 12. Arrived 12-4-84. Outside		1-24
❑	XN776	'C'	EE Lightning F.2A	62	ex Leuchars 8535M (1-4-77), 92, 19. Arrived 8-5-82		1-24
❑	XV277		HS Harrier GR.1	66	ex Ipswich, Yeovilton A2602[2], A2600[2] (28-11-88), Filton, HSA. Arrived 4-00		1-24
❑	XX308		HS Hawk T.1	80	ex Shawbury, 'Red Arrows', 4 FTS. Bitteswell-built. Last flown 18-4-13. SOC 5-12-17. Arrived 30-11-17	[11]	1-24
❑	XZ119	'FG'	SEPECAT Jaguar GR.1A	76	ex Cranwell, Coltishall, 41, Warden Det, 41, Gulf Det, ETPS, 41. Arrived 27-4-09. *Katrina Jane*		1-24
❑	ZE934	'TA'	Panavia Tornado F.3	89	ex St Athan, 56, 111, 11, 43, 11, 111, 5. Arrived 13-9-05		1-24
❑	9940		Bristol Bolingbroke IVT	42	ex Strathallan, RCAF 5 B&GS. SOC 21-8-46. Fairchild Canada-built. Arrived 8-8-81. RCAF yellow c/s		1-24
❑	3677	613677	Mikoyan-Gurevich MiG-15*bis Fagot*	53	ex Cáslav, Ostravian Air Regt, Czech AF. Letov-built S-103		1-24
❑	191659	'15'	Me 163B-1a Komet	44	ex Cambridge, Cranfield, Brize Norton, RAE, Husum, II/JG400. Arrived 1976		1-24

■ **[1]** *Charlie-Xray* factoids: Built as an NF.11, it was fitted with the NF.14 clear canopy and was the prototype for that variant, first-flying at Bitteswell 15-7-53 and despatched to Boscombe Down for trials 13 days later. With the Ferranti test fleet its colour scheme gave it the nickname *Mentadent*, after a toothpaste of the time! Retired in 1969 with just 346 hours 'on the clock'. **[2]** The unrestored Comanche fuselage, was flown solo around the world by Sheila Scott in 1966. **[3]** Although wearing G-BELF, this registration was cancelled 21-3-07 and on that day it was re-registered as G-HEBZ. **[4]** *Alpha-Alpha* factoids: Withdrawn from BA service 12-8-00, total hours 22,769, landings 8,064. It is on long-term loan from British Airways. **[5]** Handley Page-built as a Series 1, first flown at Radlett 21-7-69; converted to BAe Series 31 prototype and first flown at Prestwick 28-3-80. **[6]** Built in Glasgow, full designation Montgomerie-Parsons Two-Place (mod). Donated by Glasgow University's Department of Aerospace Engineering. Used for a variety of trials, with instrumentation in the second cockpit. **[7]** W-2 coincidently has the 'B Condition' ('B Class', or 'trade-plate') identity W-2, used by G & J Weir Ltd of Cathcart. Previously recorded as on loan from the Science Museum, this was the case until 1986 when it was donated to NMS by Viscount Weir. **[8]** Built by DH Australia at Bankstown, NSW, for the RAAF; *believed* no active service. **[9]** Airframe used as engineering mock-up for the BAE Jetstream Super 31. **[10]** Canberra B.5 VX185 has been quoted in previous editions as 7631M. This 'M' number was indeed allocated to VX185, in 1959. But this was *after* it had lost *this* cockpit, and it was converted to the prototype B(I).8 in 1954; it was broken up at Filton 30-4-64. *With* this cockpit, the crew of Beamont, Hillwood and Wilson made the first-ever out-and-back crossing of the North Atlantic in VX185 on 26-8-52 in an elapsed time of 10 hours 3½ mins, hence the lettering on the nose. **[11]** There is *another* 'XX308' - see Cranwell, Lincs.

Deep store and Hangar 1: Hangar 1 is the conservation workshop and not generally available to the public. The museum also has a storage site at Granton, Edinburgh – also ***not*** available for inspection. Criquet 'FI+S' (G-BIRW) moved to Duxford, Cambs, in late 2023. The anonymous 'JP' SIM moved to Montrose, Scotland, by April 2022.

❑	G-AMOG	Vickers Viscount 701	53	ex Cosford, Cardiff, BOAC, Cambrian, BEA G-AMNZ. CoA 14-6-77, de-reg 17-5-76. Arrived 17-8-06. BEA colours, *Robert Falcon Scott*		5-23
❑	G-AXEH	SAL Bulldog Srs 1	69	ex Prestwick, Shoreham. CoA 15-1-77, de-reg 19-6-78. Arrived 23-12-84. Beagle-built	[1]	1-22
❑	G-BCFN	Cameron O-65 HAB	74	CoA 15-5-97, de-reg 24-1-19		12-17
❑	G-BDFU	Dragonfly MPA	81	ex Blackpool, Warton, Prestwick. De-reg 15-12-83. Arr 1981		10-21
❑	G-BVWK	Air and Space 18A	65	ex Kinnettles, SE-HID, N6108S. De-reg 18-10-00. Arr 10-04		3-20
❑	G-MBJX	Hiway Super Scorpion	r82	ex Halton. De-reg 13-6-90. Arrived 1998		10-21

❑	G-MBPM		Eurowing Goldwing	80	CoA 21-8-98, de-reg 3-8-00. Arrived 4-99		10-21
❑	G-MMLI		Solar Tri-Flyer / Typhoon	r84	BAPC.244, ex Glasgow. De-reg 7-9-94. Arrived 1998		10-21
❑	BJV	'M8'	Slingsby T.21A	49	BGA.1014, ex Feshiebridge, SE-SHK. CoA 30-4-81. Arr 28-5-82		10-21
❑	–		Chargus 18/50 h-glider	75	BAPC.160, ex Tranent. Arrived 1975 - from new		12-17
❑	–		Birdman Moonraker h-g	77	BAPC.195, ex Edinburgh. Arrived 1987		12-17
❑	–		Southdown Sigma II h-g	c80	BAPC.196, ex Penicuik. Arrived 1987		12-17
❑	–		Electra Floater h-g	79	BAPC.245, ex Edinburgh. Arrived 1995		12-17
❑	–		Hiway Cloudbase h-g	79	BAPC.246, ex Edinburgh. Arrived 1995		12-17
❑	–		Albatros ASG.21 h-g	77	BAPC.247, ex Edinburgh. Arrived 1995		12-17
❑	–		Eurowing Catto CP-16	c81	BAPC.262, ex Gifford. With wings of G-MJEN. Arrived 1983		10-21
❑	–		Goldmarque Gyr	c82	BAPC.314, ex Huntly. Arrived 2002		12-17
❑	TS291	BCB	Slingsby Cadet TX.2	44	BGA.852, ex Portmoak, TS291. CoA 12-66. Arr 1980		10-21
❑	WV493	'29'	Percival Provost T.1 G-BDYG	53	ex Strathallan, G-BDYG (de-reg 4-11-91, CoA 28-11-80), Halton 7696M, 6 FTS. Arrived 11-8-81		5-23
❑	XL762		Saro Skeeter AOP.12	58	ex Wallop, Halton 8017M, 2 RTR, 9 Flt, 652, 22 Flt, 654, 651. SOC 27-5-68. Arrived 1-11-75		1-22
❑	XT288		Blackburn Buccaneer S.2B	66	ex Lossiemouth 9134M (10-4-91), A&AEE, 208, 12, FAA 800. Arrived 7-94		5-23
❑	XV241		HS Nimrod MR.2	70	ex Kinloss, Kinloss Wing, Kin/St M Wing, 42, MR.1, A&AEE, Kin Wing, 203, Kinloss. Arrived 10-2-11. Forward fuselage		5-23
❑	309	3309	Mikoyan-Gurevich MiG-15UTI *Midget*	53	ex Polish AF. WSK-built SBLim-2. Cockpit		1-22
❑	BF-10		Bristol Beaufighter TF.10	44	ex South Africa, Portuguese AF BF-10, RD220 n/s. Arrived 9-12-00		5-23
❑	–		Waco CG-4A Hadrian	44	BAPC.317, ex Aberlady. Arr 1980. Nose. *The Bunhouse*		12-17
❑	155848	'WT'	McD F-4S-MC Phantom II	68	ex Yeovilton, VMFA-232, USMC, F-4J US Navy. Arrived 13-5-99. VMFA-232 colours	[2]	5-23

■ **[1]** *Echo-Hotel* was the prototype Bulldog, first flying from Shoreham 19-5-69. See under Sandown, Isle of Wight' for another 'G-AXEH'. **[2]** The F-4 is on loan from the US DoD.

❖

Aviation Preservation Society of Scotland (APSS): The main workshop is at Congalton Gardens Farm, to the north of East Fortune, on the B1367 towards Kingston. (See also under Edinburgh, Scotland, for another workshop.) Full-scale, flyable, Sopwith 1½ Strutter 'F2211' (G-CMDN) moved to Kirknewton, Scotland, in readiness for flight test on 3rd April 2023. Wassmer-built Jodel D.120 G-BKCW (permit lapsed in February 2020) is also on the stocks and makes good progress.
◆ *Prior arrangement* **only** | **www.facebook.com/strutterapss/**

EAST LINTON just north of the A1, east of Haddington

The Tin Shed: This 'community focal point' *should* have a Tomahawk. **www.themart.co.uk**

❑	G-BMKG	Piper Tomahawk 112	82	ex Perth, ZS-LGC. CoA 17-1-13, de-reg 5-2-18	3-18

EDINBURGH

National Museum of Scotland: The National Museum of Flight at East Fortune (above) is a part of the group. The airframes are imaginatively displayed, including a 'formation' from Pilcher to Tomahawk – reminiscent of the heady days at East Fortune. ◆ *Chambers Street, Edinburgh, EH1 1JF* | **0300 1236789 | info@nms.ac.uk | www.nms.ac.uk**

❑	G-ACVA	Kay Gyroplane	35	ex East Fortune, Edinburgh, Glasgow, Strathallan, Perth, Glasgow, Perth. De-reg 5-5-59. Acquired 1998		1-24
❑	G-AOEL	DH Tiger Moth	40	ex East Fortune, Strathallan, Dunstable, Mk. II N9510, 7 FTS, 2 GU, 11 RFS, 1 RFS, 7 RFS, 7 EFTS. CoA 18-7-72, de-reg 21-1-82. Acquired 1980, first noted 7-16		1-24
❑	G-AXIG	SAL Bulldog 104	71	ex Dirleton, Compton Abbas, Blackbushe, SAL. Beagle-built. CoA 12-11-11, de-reg 21-4-11. Acquired 7-11	[1]	1-24
❑	G-BGXB	Piper Tomahawk 112	79	ex East Fortune, Alton, Cardiff, N9728N. CoA 16-8-04, de-reg 22-2-10. First noted 7-16		1-24
❑	–	Pilcher Hawk	1896	BAPC.49, ex East Fortune, Edinburgh. Accident 30-9-1899. On loan from 1909, acquired 24-3-1920	[2]	1-24

Edinburgh's impressive cascade, May 2023. From the rear: Pilcher Hawk, Slingsby Gull, Tiger Moth, Terrier 2, Tomahawk.
Terry Dann

❑ BED		Slingsby Gull I		38	BGA.902, ex East Fortune, Edinburgh, Newbattle, 'G-ALPHA'. Acquired 1968. First noted 7-16	[3]	1-24
❑ VF581	'G'	Beagle Terrier 2	G-ARSL	46	ex East Fortune, Eggesford, Auster AOP.6 VF581, 664. De-reg 4-8-14. First noted 7-16		1-24

■ **[1]** *India-Golf* completed at Prestwick by SAL as the second prototype and first flew 14-2-71. **[2]** Designed and built by Percy Pilcher with help from his sister Ella, the Hawk was first flown in 1896 and is the UK's oldest heavier-than-air flying machine. Pilcher crashed this machine while flying at Stanford Hall, Leics, on 30-9-1899 and died of his injuries two days later. (There is a Hawk replica at Stanford Hall - qv.) **[3]** Gull I is *possibly* the former VW912.

Aviation Preservation Society of Scotland: See under East Fortune, Scotland, for more details. Tiger Moth F-AZDH was not held by APSS at this site, remaining in private hands at a private location near Duns.

❑ –	Bensen gyroglider	~	BAPC.315, Acquired 2015	10-16

Edinburgh Academy: In Kinnear Road, close to the Botanic Gardens, is *believed* to still have its Grasshopper.

❑ WZ773	Slingsby Grasshopper TX.1	52	SOC 16-6-88	6-12

EDINBURGH AIRPORT or Turnhouse

EGPH

❑ 'L1067'	'XT-D'	V-S Spitfire FSM	89	BAPC.227, ex 'L1070', 'XT-A', 603 Sqn colours. *Blue Peter*. Plinth-mounted near entrance	[1]	1-24

■ **[1]** The 603 (City of Edinburgh) Squadron Association look after the Spitfire FSM.

ELGIN Contrary to *W&R28* (p289), Airtourer G-ATJC did not move to Perth; it was scrapped locally.

ERROL south of the A90, east of Perth

The trio is kept by a *private* collector locally: the Gannet outside, the other two internally.

❑ 'XE897'		DH Vampire T.11	XD403	54	ex Leuchars, Errol, Strathallan, Woodford, Chester, 4 FTS, 1, 7, 8, 5 and 4 FTSs. Christchurch-built. SOC 2-12-68		4-22
❑ XG882	'771'	Fairey Gannet T.5		57	ex Lossiemouth 8754M (21-7-82), 845, Culdrose SF. Arrived 30-5-91	[1]	4-22
❑ XN981		Blackburn Buccaneer S.2B		65	ex Lossiemouth, 12, 208, 12, 809, 12, 800, 801, 700B. SOC 11-4-94		4-22

■ **[1]** Gannet is a composite, including parts from AS.4 XA463 and T.5 XG889.

EVANTON on the B9176 southwest of Alness

Classically, *W&R28* (p289) wrote out the fuselages of Jetstream G-EEST and an unidentified Bandeirante as last noted in May 2017. They exist but not here: turn to Dingwall, Scotland.

FIFE AERODROME or Glenrothes, on the A92 north of Kircaldy

EGPJ

The Tiger is *believed* to be extant in the general area.

❑ G-AREH	DH Tiger Moth	41	ex Bridge of Weir, Lochwinnoch, Kilkerran, G-APYV, 6746M, DE241, 22 RFS, 22 EFTS. Morris-built. CoA 19-4-66. Off-site	N1-21

FORDOUN On the A90 between Brechin and Stonehaven

Neil Butler: (Previously listed under Laurencekirk.) Continues to work his magic on a series of projects. F.150K G-BHIY was flying again by 2022. ◆ *Prior appointment* **only**

❑ G-AWSS		Druine Condor		69	ex Montrose, Fordoun. Rollason-built. CoA 19-10-94	4-21
❑ G-BTDY		Piper Super Cub 150		61	ex N24570. CoA 23-7-94	4-21
❑ VS356		Percival Prentice T.1	G-AOLU	50	ex Montrose, Stonehaven, Perth, Strathallan, Biggin Hill, EI-ASP, G-AOLU, VS356, CFS, 2 FTS. Blackburn-built. CoA 8-5-76. Stored, first noted 8-17	4-21
❑ VS610	'K-L'	Percival Prentice T.1	G-AOKL	49	ex Montrose, Old Warden, Bassingbourn, VS610, 1 FTS, 22 FTS, RAFC, 22 FTS. CoA 20-9-96. Stored, f/n 8-17	4-21
❑ 454537	'J-04'	Piper J3C Cub	G-BFDL	45	ex HB-OIF, L-4J 45-4537. CoA 27-6-18	4-21

FORFAR Cessna 182K G-AVID is believed to have been scrapped; Kachina G-DJCR has been deleted.

GALSTON on the A71 east of Kilmarnock

Galston Adventure Centre: Part of the Scottish Assault Courses franchise, has a Dauphin carcass playing the role of a "real downed helicopter". ◆ **https://scottishassaultcourses.com/locations/ayrshire**

❑ G-CEYU*	Sud Dauphin	88	ex N97SV. De-reg 13-11-17. First noted 6-22	12-23

GLASGOW

Kelvingrove Art Gallery and Museum: There is a huge amount going on within this superb building, but from the *W&R* point of view, the main attraction is the Spitfire which 'flies' in the main hall.

◆ *Kelvin Park, Argyle Street, G3 8AG* | **0141 2761450** | **kelvinhall.lf@glasgowlife.org.uk** | **https://kelvinhall.org.uk**

❑ LA198 'RAI-G'	V-S Spitfire F.21	44	ex Kelvin Hall-Glasgow, East Fortune, Cardington, St Athan, Leuchars, Locking, Worcester, 7118M (19-2-54), 3 CAACU, 602, 1. 602 Sqn colours	1-24

Riverside Museum: Sub-titled 'Scotland's Museum of Transport and Travel' and in a whiz-bang new building with many more exhibits than the previous Museum of Transport, there is, however, little in the way of aeronautical content.

◆ *Pointhouse Place, G3 8RS* | **0141 2874350**| **info@glasgowlife.org.uk** | **www.glasgowmuseums.com**

❑ -	Pilcher Hawk replica	66	BAPC.48, stored	[1]	3-10
❑ -	Pilcher Bat II replica	07	BAPC.316, ex Prestwick. Unveiled 23-11-07	[2]	3-20

■ **[1]** Hawk built by 2175 Squadron ATC, Glasgow, and awaits restoration. **[2]** Bat built by the Pilcher Glider Reproduction Project team; volunteers from BAE Systems at Prestwick who took 10 years to complete it.

The Experience: Montrose Avenue, Hillington Park. The venue *appears* to have closed.

❑ VP-BRV	Boeing 737-528		ex Kemble, Yamal Airlines, F-GJNB. Forward fuselage. Arrived 14-10-15, Chequers colour scheme	1-23

Mission Aviation Fellowship (MAF): The charity's base in Challenge House, Canal Street, is home to a Cessna used as a travelling demonstrator. ◆ *Prior arrangement* **only** | **www.maf-uk.org**

❑ P2-MFA	Cessna 172	~	ex Perth, Papua New Guinea, MAF. Accident 2013	[1]	3-21

■ **[1]** Fitted with the wings of 150 G-BTIN.

GLASGOW PRESTWICK AIRPORT previous listed as good old Prestwick Airport EGPK

If you are like this scribe, the idea of Boeing 787 Dreamliners being scrapped - sorry, recycled - seems alien, well the time is nigh. *W&R28* (p297) recorded former Norwegian Boeing 787s that entered external storage over May-September 2019, "but are bound to be up and running before too long." Well, partially right... LN-LND arrived 18th September 2019 and departed as EI-LND 3rd November 2022. LN-LNG, here since 2nd July 2019, became EI-LNG and left 7th April 2022. These were youngsters having been born at Everett in 2014. Younger by a year, LN-LNH, which touched down 20th August 2019 was registered as M-ABSD in July 2023, ready to rejoin the fray.

Such a fate was not on the cards for LN-LNA and LN-BNB, apparently positive geriatrics with a 2013 birth date and destined to be the first of breed to be parted out. (LN-LNA arrived 27th May 2019, later re-registered VP-CVL; LN-LNB arrived 17th September 2019, later VP-CVM.) Dismantling took two months, a task completed in February 2023; parts recycling etc was handled by Irish-base EirTrade. The job was challenging because of the Dreamliner's carbon composite fuselages and wings, requiring very different disciplines in recycling/destruction. Sections of fuselage were sent to ECube at St Athan, Wales, and to Boeing for investigation of disposal techniques.

Fuji FA.200 G-BCNZ is *believed* to have been broken up. Rallye G-BCVC, Cessna 152 G-BFFE and Cessna 310 N1909G have been deleted.

❑ G-ARMD	DHC Chipmunk T.10	50	ex Kemble, Redditch area, WD297, 666, 1 BFTS. Hawarden-built. CoA 5-6-76, de-reg 26-6-15. In ISO container		10-21
❑ G-AWJF*	Tipsy Nipper T.66	68	ex Stewarton. Slingsby-built. De-reg 17-9-91. F/n 10-22		3-23
❑ G-BDEU	DHC Chipmunk T.10	52	ex WP808, Edin, Nott, Edin, Lpl, Nott UASs, Detling SF, Birm UAS, 15 RFS. Hawarden-built. CoA 27-1-13, de-reg 8-5-14. Cockpit		3-23
❑ G-CELR	Boeing 737-330	86	ex TF-ELR, D-ABXB. De-reg 8-9-17. Forward fuselage		3-19
❑ G-ORJX	HSA HS.146 RJX85 T1	01	ex Woodford, de-reg 12-12-02	[1]	6-11
❑ G-BSOU*	Piper Tomahawk 112	81	ex N23373. De-reg 5-9-19. Cockpit, first noted 12-22		3-23
❑ G-11-068	BAe ATP	93	fuselage. Rescue trainer		12-23
❑ OO-JLO*	Boeing 737-800	07	ex CN-RPG, G-FDZD, D-ATUB. Flew in 9-10-21. Presented to fire service 2-23		12-23

❑ XX612* '03' *and* 'A' SAL Bulldog T.1 G-BZXC 74 ex Ayr, Prestwick, Dunfermline, Dundee, Wales, S'ton UASs, RNEFTS, QUAS, CFS. CoA 15-1-09, de-reg 5-3-08. Arrived 30-11-23 11-23

■ **[1]** Prototype RJX (first flown 28-4-01), used as an engineering design aid by BAE Regional Aircraft (amends *W&R27*) in support of the 146/RJ fleet. It comprises fuselage, starboard wing, and tail. It arrived on site 8-6-11. It last flew 10-1-02 and clocked 321:59 hours.

Locally: The Wagtail Flying Group keeps its Tipsy in the area.

❑ G-AISC Tipsy B 48 ex Cumbernauld, Henstridge. CoA 23-5-79, de-reg 8-1-24 N9-18

GRANGEMOUTH on the M9 east of Falkirk

No.1333 (Grangemouth) Squadron Air Cadets' memorial to the site of the former RAF Grangemouth, on Bo'Ness Road

❑ 'X4859' 'PQ-N' V-S Spitfire FSM 08 BAPC.319. 58 OTU colours 3-23

HOUSTON on the B790 west of Glasgow Airport

Delta Force Paintball: Turningshaw Road. ◆ *Prior arrangement* **only** | **www.paintballgames.co.uk**

❑ XZ690 '640' Westland Lynx HMA.8 79 ex Upminster, Ipswich, Fleetlands, 815, HAS.3, 702, HAS.2, 829, 815. SOC 27-10-10. First noted 11-16 11-21

INCHINNAN on the A8, north of Glasgow Airport

Rolls-Royce Heritage Trust Scotland Branch: The branch has a collection of engines and artefacts at the Inchinnan Business Park. This includes material on the Hillington plant that built Merlins 1939 to 1947.

◆ *Prior appointment* only | **www.rolls-royce.com/about/heritage-trust**

INSCH AERODROME west of the B992 at Auchleven

❑ G-BALK Stampe SV-4C 46 ex Aboyne, 'Cheshire', Liverpool, Littleborough, F-BBAN, French mil No.387. Nord-built. De-reg 4-12-96. Fuselage 4-22

❑ T6830 DH Tiger Moth G-ANJI 43 ex 'A17-376' C-GIZA, N548DH, F-BHIQ, G-ANJI, T6830, 2 RFS, 21 EFTS. Morris-built. Arrived 3-9-18, off-site 9-21

❑ 479781 Piper L-4H Cub G-AISS 44 ex D-ECAV, SL-AAA, 44-79781. CoA 25-6-97 4-22

INVERNESS

Behind the Radar – Inverness: A former wartime radar filter room that ended up as the Highland Council's Emergency Planning centre until it was sold off in 2019. Known as 'The Bunker', it is 'guarded' by a Lynx.

❑ XZ218* Westland Lynx AH.7 79 ex Colsterworth (?), Rugby, Barby, Fleetlands, 655, 662, 653, 652, 662. 'US Army' titles. First noted 7-21 1-24

◆ *Prior arranged tours **only**. Mackintosh Place, IV2 3TX* | **www.behind-the-radar.co.uk**

■ **[1]** Written out of *W&R26* (p183) leaving Barby, Northants, early in 2016, bound for Cobham, Surrey. That destination was in error, it moved to a military vehicle specialist in Rugby, Warks, prior to arrival in Inverness.

INVERNESS AIRPORT or Dalcross EGPE

The Buccaneer and 'JP' are stored in a compound within the airport's business units.

❑ XK532 '632' Blackburn Buccaneer S.1 61 ex Lossiemouth 8867M, Manadon A2581 (22-2-68), Arbroath, Lossiemouth, 736. Arrived 23-9-92 [1] 9-23

❑ XW375 '52' BAC Jet Provost T.5A 71 ex St Athan, Cosford, 9149M (7-6-93), Halton, CFS, 6 FTS, RAFC. Arrived 25-2-21 9-23

❑ XW419 '125' BAC Jet Provost T.5A 71 ex B'thorpe, Hurn, Basingstoke, Booker, Wickenby, Cosford, Halton 9120M (16-9-91), 7 FTS, 1 FTS, RAFC. Off-site [1] 11-21

❑ XW433* BAC Jet Provost T.5A G-JPRO 72 ex Coventry, St Mawgan, Coventry, Humberside, Shawbury, 7 FTS, 3 FTS, 7 FTS, 3 FTS. CoA 8-1-20. F/n 9-23 [2] 9-23

■ **[1]** Previously with the former Highland Aviation Museum which closed its doors here in 2019. **[2]** Last recorded in *W&R26* (p287) as bound for Inverness.

Highland Aviation Training: Operates a gyrocopter school from the airport. Most of the 'museum' gyros previously at Rufforth, N Yorks, arrived in February 2021. ◆ *Prior appointment* only | **www.highlandaviation.com**

❑ G-ARTJ Bensen B-8M 62 ex Rufforth, Leven, Cupar, East Fortune, Cupar, Currie. De-reg 6-6-75 2-21

❑ G-BXCJ	Campbell Cricket	97	ex Rufforth. CoA 28-4-09		2-21
❑ G-CDBE	Bensen B-8M	05	ex Rufforth. CoA 7-9-04, de-reg 28-11-22		2-21
❑ G-IIXX*	Montgomerie-Parsons	93	ex Crosshill. Unflown. First noted 9-22		9-22
❑ 'PCL-132'	PFA Rotaglider 001	~	BAPC.440. Ex Rufforth	[1]	2-21
❑ –	'Gyroglider'	~	ex Rufforth. Unknown 'species'		2-21

■ **[1]** Built by Peter Lovegrove, *thought* original design.

Also: Abiding by the tidying up related on page 7, Cessna F.150H G-AWMT has been deleted.

❑ G-BNHG	Piper Tomahawk 112	80	ex N91435. De-reg 27-9-17. Towing training	8-21
❑ G-BTCI	Piper Vagabond	48	ex N4839H, NC4839H. CoA 9-8-05	8-21

KEITH on the A96 between Fochabers and Huntly

A *private* collector has the forward fuselage of a Nimrod at a location in the area.

❑ XV252	HS Nimrod MR.2	71	ex Kinloss, Kinloss Wing, MR.1, Kinloss, 51 (loan), 203, 42, St Mawgan. Forward fuselage	7-21

KILMARNOCK northeast of Ayr

No.**327 (Kilmarnock) Squadron Air Cadets**: The exact nature – and status – be it synthetic or F.4-based, is unresolved.

❑ –	Hawker Hunter	~	cockpit -see comments above	11-14

KINGSMUIR or Sorbie, on the B9131 southeast of St Andrews

A Super Cub project is under way at a *private* location in the locality.

❑ G-PGEE	Piper L-18C Super Cub	51	ex Fordoun, G-BIYJ, Italian AF MM 51-15303, I-EIST, Italian AF MM51-15303. CoA 6-6-17. First noted 12-20	12-20

KINLOSS north of the A96, west of Elgin

Morayvia Sci-Tech Experience Project: Brings together disciplines from aerospace and astronomy to technology and arts-related activities, serving the northeast of Scotland, the Highlands and beyond. Not all airframes are on site. Along the coast at Spey Bay is a workshop and some airframes are held in store off-site - see separate entry below.

There is also a Super Puma cockpit sim ('G-TIGA'), acquired from Bristow at Aberdeen, and an F-35 cockpit '04', the latter a film mock-up from *Terminator Dark Fate*, and not deserving a formal listing.

By April 2022, a Tornado cockpit had moved to East Midlands, Leics.

◆ *Abbeylands, North Road, IV36 3YA* | **01309 691916** | **admin@morayvia.org.uk** | **www.morayvia.org.uk**

❑ G-APWJ*	HP Herald 201	63	ex Duxford, Norwich, Air UK, BIA, BUIA. Last flight 7-7-85, de-reg 10-7-85. Air UK colours. Arrived 24-3-22		1-24
❑ G-ASVO	HP Herald 214	64	ex Inverness, Glenrothes, Perth, Shoreham, Hurn, Channel Express, PP-SDG, G-ASVO, G-8-3. Damaged 8-4-97, de-reg 25-9-01. Forward fuselage. Arrived 4-17		1-24
❑ G-BNCY*	Fokker Friendship 500F	77	ex Beauly, Pershore, Bournemouth, Guernsey, Air UK, VH-FCE, PH-EXH. *Lilly Langtree*. Damaged 7-12-97, de-reg 19-2-98. Cockpit, poor state. Arrived 14-7-22	[1]	1-24
❑ G-MJSV	MBA Tiger Cub 440	r83	ex local scrapyard, Kinloss. De-reg 9-11-89. Arrived 2016		1-24
❑ G-UIST	BAe Jetstream 3102	87	ex Westerton, *Batman - The Dark Knight Rises*, Iver Heath, Inverness, N190PC, N331QH, N840JS, G-31-750. CoA 4-6-10, de-reg 5-5-11. Cockpit. Arrived 16-3-19	[2]	1-24
❑ '14' red	Antonov An-2R *Colt* HA-MKE	74	ex 'Red 14', France, Air Foyle, UR-07714, CCCP-07714. WSK PZL-Mielec-built. Arrived 2-6-16		1-24
❑ 'L1019' 'LO-S'	V-S Spitfire I FSM	12	BAPC.308, ex Currie. Fuselage. Arr 12-12-21. 6-2 Sqn c/s	[3]	1-24
❑ WJ721	EE Canberra TT.18	53	ex Gairloch, Oban, Dundonald, Bacup, Samlesbury, 7, B.2, 50, 40. SOC 19-11-81. Cockpit. Arrived 3-6-15	[4]	1-24
❑ WM145	Gloster Meteor NF.11	52	ex Durham-TVA, Dinsdale, Gatenby, Great Ayton, Rotherham, Finningley, 5, 29, 151, 219. AWA-built. SOC 30-10-63. Cockpit. Arrived 18-12-18	[5]	1-24
❑ WN957	Hawker Hunter F.5	54	ex Stockport, Welshpool, Llanbedr, Stafford, North Weald, Chivenor, Leconfield, St Athan 7407M (21-2-57), RAE. AWA-built. Cockpit. Arrived 5-16. 1 Sqn colours		1-24

❑ WP495	'915'	Westland Dragonfly HR.3	53	ex 'G-AJOV', Cosford, Biggin Hill, Banstead, Warnham, Wimbledon, Blackbushe, Culdrose SF, 705, *Victorious* Flt, *Centaur* Flt, *Victorious* Flt, HR.1, Culdrose SF, Ford SF. SOC 1-6-64. Acquired 27-7-17	[6]	1-24
❑ WR971*	'Q'	Avro Shackleton MR.3/3	56	ex West Walton Highway, Narborough, Cosford 8119M (14-12-70), 120, Kinloss Wing, 201, 120, Kin' Wing, CA. Cockpit etc. Arrived 31-3-23	[7]	1-24
❑ WZ557		DH Vampire T.11	53	ex Durham-TVA, Dinsdale, Gatenby, Gt Ayton, Huntingdon, Acaster Malbis, Woodford, Chester, St Athan, 5 FTS, 16. Hawarden-built. SOC 13-11-67. Arr 18-12-18. 5 FTS c/s	[5]	1-24
❑ XD425	'44'	DH Vampire T.11	54	ex Seaton Burn, Millom, Dumfries, W Freugh, Stranraer, Woodford, Chester, St Athan, 8, 5, 7 FTSs, 202 AFS. Hawarden-built. SOC 30-11-67. Arrived 2015. Cockpit		1-24
❑ XD875		Vickers Valiant B.1	57	ex Inverness, Winthorpe, Bruntingthorpe, Marham, Firbeck, Coventry, Cosford, 7, 138, 207, 49, 207. SOC 9-11-62. Cockpit. Arrived 1-2-18	[5] [8]	1-24
❑ XG692*	'668' *and* '444'	DH Sea Venom FAW.22	57	ex Stockport, Baxterley, Hatton, Alcester, W' Mountford, Sydenham, Castlereagh, Sydenham, 750, 891. Hawarden-built. SOC 20-8-70. Arr 4-6-23. Cockpit, 750 / 891 Sqn c/s	[9]	1-24
❑ XH563		Avro Vulcan B.2MRR	60	ex Durham-TVA, Dinsdale, Bruntingthorpe, Banchory, Rotherham, Scampton 8744M (31-3-82), 27, 230 OCU, Wadd W, 230 OCU, 12, 83. Cockpit. Arrived 18-12-18	[5]	1-24
❑ XJ380		Bristol Sycamore HR.14	56	ex Old Sarum, Boscombe Down, Crowland, Montrose, New Byth, Drighlington, Finningley 8628M, Catterick, CFS, MoA, Handling Sqn, 275. SOC 22-3-68. Oldmixon-built. Arrived 19-5-21		1-24
❑ XJ723		Westland Whirlwind HAR.10	55	ex Newcastle upon Tyne, Montrose, Wroughton, 202, 228, HAR.4, 155. SOC 29-3-79. Acquired 25-7-17	[10]	1-24
❑ XM402*		Hunting Jet Provost T.3	59	ex West Walton Highway, Narborough, West Raynham, Halton, Newton 8055AM (21-11-69), Shawbury, 6 FTS, 2 FTS. Arrived 22-3-23		1-24
❑ XN351	'M'	Saro Skeeter AOP.12 G-BKSC	59	ex Norwich, Saxmundham, Lossiemouth, Inverness, Shobdon, Cardiff, H' Blagdon, Old Warden, Wroughton, 652, 651. CoA 8-11-84, de-reg 11-10-00. Arr 3-6-19		1-24
❑ XN607		Hunting Jet Provost T.3	61	ex Inverness, Great Ayton, Leeds, 3 FTS. SOC 28-5-76. Grey colours. Cockpit. Arrived 1-2-18	[5]	1-24
❑ XP557*		Hunting Jet Provost T.4	62	ex Dumfries, Hemswell, Firbeck, Bruntingthorpe, Halton 8494M (30-6-76), 6 FTS, RAFC. Arrived 16-4-23		1-24
❑ XR447		Northrop Shelduck D.1	61	ex Elgin. Crashed 16-6-61, wreckage. First noted 9-21	[11]	1-24
❑ XR528		Westland Wessex HC.2	64	ex Little Rissington, Lyneham, Gosport, Culdrose, Predannack, St Mawgan, 72, 60, 28, 240 OCU, 78. SOC 5-12-08. Arrived 17-8-17. Yellow, 22 Sqn SAR colours		1-24
❑ XS176		Hunting Jet Provost T.4	63	ex Inverness, Stamford, Luton, Solihull, Bruntingthorpe, Salford, Halton 8514M (24-3-77), CATCS, 3 FTS, 2 FTS. Arrived 11-11-12. Cockpit		1-24
❑ XS713	'C'	HS Dominie T.1	65	ex Shawbury, Cranwell, 55, 3 FTS, 6 FTS, 1 ANS, CAW, 1 ANS, CAW, 1 ANS. Arrived 18-11-20		1-24
❑ XT466	'528'	Westland Wessex HU.5	65	ex Kemble, Bentwaters, Lichfield, Gosport, A2617 [4], Weeton 8921M (3-2-87), Cosford, Wroughton, 847, 771, 848, 845. Acquired 13-12-17. 771 Sqn colours	[12]	1-24
❑ XV240		HS Nimrod MR.2	70	ex Kinloss, Kin Wing, St M, 42, Kin, MR.1, Kin, 42, Kin, 203, Kinloss. Acquired 12-11. Forward fuselage		1-24
❑ XV586*	'010'	McD Phantom FG.1	69	ex Yeovilton, Leuchars 9067M (19-8-91), 43, 892. Arrived 21-2-23. 892 Sqn colours		1-24
❑ XX743*	'EG'	SEPECAT Jaguar GR.1	74	ex Cosford, Halton 8949M (3-12-87), Shawbury, 6. Arrived 22-10-22. 6 *and* 238 Sqn colours		1-24
❑ XZ113	'A' *and* '30'	SEPECAT Jaguar GR.3A	76	ex Musselburgh, Bentwaters, St Athan, FJ&WOEU, SAOEU, 41, GR.1, Granby Det, 41, 2, 41. Arrived 11-5-17. 2 Sqn colours, *Samantha Jayne* to port; 41 Sqn c/s to stb		1-24

❑ XZ592	'H'	Westland Sea King HAR.3	78	ex Fleetlands, 202, SKTU, 22, SKTU, 78, 202, SKTU, 78, 1564 Flt, 202. Arrived 16-7-15		1-24
❑ ZH821		EHI Merlin HM.1	97	ex Shawbury, Yeovil. Arrived 26-6-19		1-24
❑ _*		Panavia Tornado GR.4 sim	~	ex Lossiemouth. Thales-built. F/n 7-21		1-24
❑ _*		Short Tucano T.1 sim	~	ex Church Fenton. Forward cockpit. F/n 7-21		1-24
❑ J-1172*		DH Vampire FB.6	52	ex Stafford, Cosford, Wyton, Cardington, Manchester, Cosford, 8487M, Colerne, Swiss AF. Swiss-built. Arrived 20-12-23		1-24

■ **[1]** F.27 written out of Pershore, Worcs, in *W&R27* (p291) as going to to a rock concert venue near Inverness 2016... used as a DJ 'platform' since... Poor state... **[2]** *Sierra-Tango* on loan from Paul Gibbs. **[3]** Spitfire donated by Robert Whitton; ongoing project, being completed in-house. **[4]** Canberra was on loan from Bruce Hudson, but 3-23 acquired by Morayvia. **[5]** On permanent loan from a N Yorks-based collector. **[6]** WP495 on long term loan from Surrey and Sussex APS. Names on the nose are of the Lord Lieutenant of Moray, Lt Col Grenville S Johnson, a huge supporter of the project, and his father Lt Col W D Johnston who served at Lossiemouth in the 1950s and was involved with Dragonflies. **[7]** Comprises: cockpit/nose section, a 'chunk' of centre fuselage and rear fuselage. A 'slice' of WR971 is also held at Flixton, Suffolk. **[8]** XD875 was the last of 107 - including prototype - Valiants, issued to the RAF on 27-8-57. **[9]** XG692 owned by Bob Pountney: '668' from its days with 750 Sqn at Lossiemouth, 1968; '444' from 891 Sqn on *Centaur* 1960. **[10]** On 27-12-65 winchman Sgt John Reeson of 22 Sqn in XJ723 was involved in a rescue from the collapsed North Sea oil rig *Sea Gem* and was awarded a GM. **[11]** Salvaged from a local scrapyard, XR447 crashed on its *first* UK sortie 16-6-61. **[12]** XT466 is owned by famed SAR winchman Bob Pountney.

Off-site: workshop and storage: ***Not*** available for public inspection. It is reported that Hunter F.1 WT569 will return to Kenfig Hill, Wales, after restoration.

❑ WT507*	'44'	EE Canberra PR.7	54	ex Mansfield, Halton 8548M (24-3-77), 8131M, St Athan, 31, 17, 58, A&AEE, 58, 527, 58. Cockpit. Arrived 20-2-23		1-24
❑ WT569*		Hawker Hunter F.1	55	ex Kenfig Hill, St Athan 7491M (21-11-57), A&AEE, Hawker. Arrived 11-11-22. See note above		1-24
❑ XL875		Westland Whirlwind HAR.9	58	ex Perth, Wroughton, Lee SAR Flt, Culdrose SAR Flt, 847, HAS.7, 848, 815. SOC 2-5-77. Arrived 21-5-21		1-24
❑ XM169		EE Lightning F.1A	60	ex Inverness, Great Ayton, Thirsk, Leuchars 8422M (13-6-74), Leuchars TFF, 23, Binbrook TFF, 111, A&AEE. Cockpit	[1]	1-24
❑ XS510	'626'	Westland Wessex HU.5	64	ex Crowborough, Gosport, A2676 [2], A2765 (24-3-88), Lee-on-Solent, 772, Lee SAR Flt, 707, 848. Arrived 2-19,		1-24
❑ XV725	'C'	Westland Wessex HC.2	68	ex Manston, Cosford, Gosport A2707 [2], Shawbury, 72, 18. Arrived 18-12-20		1-24
❑ XV867		Blackburn Buccaneer S.2B	68	ex Inverness, Great Ayton, Leeming, 208, 12, 208, 237 OCU, FAA, 809, 736, 803. Cr 10-9-93. Arr 1-2-18. Cockpit	[1]	1-24

■ **[1]** On permanent loan from a N Yorks-based collector.

Kinloss Barracks: The former RAF base displays Morayvia's Nimrod - see above.

❑ XV244	HS Nimrod MR.2	71	ex Kin Wing, 42, Kinloss, 203, 42, Kinloss. *Duke of Edinburgh*	1-24

KIRKNEWTON Between the A70 and A71 southwest of Edinburgh

Delta Force Paintball: By late 2022 Lynx HMA.8 XZ698 had made the move to Seaton Burn, N&T.

LEUCHARS AIRFIELD on the A919, northwest of St Andrews EGQL

Waterloo Barracks: Leuchars still roars, acting as a 'satellite' for Lossiemouth. Within the base **2345 (Leuchars) Squadron Air Cadets** has a presence with a Harrier and Tomahawk that attend local events.

❑ G-CWFB		Piper Tomahawk 112	78	ex G-OAAL, N4471E. CoA 8-2-07, de-reg 8-12-10. Cockpit, first noted 7-16		7-19
❑ XW265	'W'	HS Harrier T.4A	70	ex ??, St Athan, Cosford 9258M (3-10-96), Shawbury, 20, 233 OCU, A&AEE. Cockpit		7-16
❑ ZE967	'UT'	Panavia Tornado F.3	89	ex 56, 43, 111, 43, 25, 23, 25, 43, 11, 111. Displayed, unveiled 10-9-04	[1]	8-23

■ **[1]** Tornado wears 43 Sqn c/s to port, 111 on starboard and 56 on both sides of the tail.

LONGSIDE AERODROME Jungster G-BLDC and Sakota G-BYRE have been deleted.

LOSSIEMOUTH AIRFIELD south of the B4090, west of Lossiemouth EGQS

RAF Lossiemouth: The resident Typhoon units tend to allocate weapons loading trainers - WLTs - for short periods and then rotate them back into operational service: so, *W&R* will avoid them, unless they are seriously long term.

Former gate guardian Tornado GR.1B ZA475 moved to Spadeadam, Cumbria, in June 2023.

❑ LA255 'JX-U' V-S Spitfire F.21 45 ex Leuchars, Coningsby, Cottesmore, Wittering 6490M, W Raynham, Cardington, Tangmere, 1. Accident 13-11-47. Displayed within base on occasions; arrived 11-14 [1] 1-24
❑ XX119* 'AI' SEPECAT Jaguar GR.3A 73 ex Cosford, Coningsby, 6, GR.1, 54, 16, 226 OCU, 8898M, 226 OCU,A&AEE, 54, 226 OCU, JOCU. Last flown 29-3-06. 'Tiger' colours. 6 Sqn 'mascot'. Arrived 7-12-23 1-24
❑ ZA463 Panavia Tornado GR.4 83 ex Marham, 12, 15, 12, GR.1, 15. Unveiled 7-23 [2] 1-24

■ **[1]** LA255 is owned by the 1 (Fighter) Squadron Association. **[2]** ZA463 fitted with the fin of GR.4 ZA554 - SOC 4-2-19 and scrapped here 7-19. ZA463 carried out last ever RAF Tornado flight, call-sign 'MRM74' on 14-3-19, crewed by S/Ls Ian Dornan and Stephen Boardman. Unveiled to commemorate the three killed in a collision 3-7-12 over the Moray Firth between ZD473 and ZD812.

MAYBOLE Last noted in June 2017, Zodiac G-RWMW and Rallye OO-NAT have been deleted.

MOFFAT east of the A74(M) north of Lockerbie

Dr Hamish Macleod: The Spitfire is in a *private* garden. A donation to the RAF Benevolent Fund permits photography.

❑ 'PT462' 'SW-A' V-S Spitfire IX FSM ~ BAPC.318. 253 Sqn colours [1] 8-22

■ **[1]** The *real* PT462 is based at Duxford, Cambs.

MONTROSE on the A92 north of Arbroath

Montrose Air Station Heritage Centre: Montrose was Britain's first operational military air station: the original hangar block, known as 'Burke's Shed' dates from 1913. The restoration workshop is ***not*** open to the public.

Delete reference to Grasshopper WZ791: it remains a denizen of Hendon!

◆ *Broomfield Industrial Estate, Waldron Road, DD10 9BD* | **01674 678222** | **enquiries@rafmontrose.org.uk** | **www.rafmontrose.org.uk**

❑ G-MMLM MBA Tiger Cub 440 84 ex Dundee. De-reg 22-5-00. Arrived 2011. *Red Baron* 1-24
❑ '471' Royal A/c Factory BE.2a rep 15 BAPC.321, unveiled 12-8-16. 2 Sqn colours [1] 1-24
❑ 'B7320' 'P' Sopwith Camel replica c72 BAPC.59, ex 'B5577', E' Fortune, Cosford, St Athan, 'D3419', St Mawgan, 'F1921', St Athan, Colerne. Arrived 2006 [2] 1-24
❑ DG590 Miles Hawk Major G-ADMW 35 ex Stafford, Cosford, Wyton, Cardington, M Wallop, Henlow 8379M, Ternhill, G-ADMW, Swanton Morley SF, Wyton SF, G-ADMW. Phillips & Powis-built. CoA 4-6-83, de-reg 16-9-86. Arrived 15-2-17 [3] 1-24
❑ 'EP121' 'LO-D' V-S Spitfire V FSM 12 BAPC.320. GB Replicas-built. Arrived 17-7-13, unveiled 26-7-13. 602 Sqn colours, *Red Lichtie* 1-24
❑ TX226 Avro Anson C.19 46 ex Coventry, Duxford, Little Staughton, East Dereham, Colerne 7865M (22-1-65), Shawbury, FTCCF, OCTU Jurby, 187, Hemswell SF, Coningsby CF, CBE. Arrived 4-18 [4] 1-24
❑ WF825 'X' Gloster Meteor T.7 51 ex Redhill, Yatesbury, Malmesbury, Monkton Farleigh, Lyneham 8359M, Kemble, CAW, 33, 603. SOC 6-2-69. Arrived 3-12-09 1-24
❑ WT619 Hawker Hunter F.1 54 ex Stafford, Manchester, Henlow, St Athan, Weeton 7525M (22-11-57), 233 OCU, 222, 43. Sectioned. Arrived 28-10-19 1-24
❑ XA109 DH Sea Vampire T.22 53 ex Leuchars, Easr Fortune, Lossiemouth, Lossie' SF, 831, Culdrose SF, 781. Christchurch-built. SOC 17-3-67. Arr 3-8-11 1-24
❑ ZD744* '092' Panavia Tornado GR.4 84 ex Marham, GR.1, 14. SOC 1-3-19. Arrived 19-5-22 1-24
❑ –* Hunting Jet Provost CIM ~ ex East Fortune, Leuchars, Rosyth. Cockpit. Arrived by 4-22 1-24

■ **[1]** Based at Montrose from February 1914, 2 Sqn was the first RFC unit to deploy to France on the outbreak of war. After an epic series of 'hops' southwards, Lt Hubert Dunsterville Harvey-Kelly was the first British airman to touch down 'in anger' in France, landing BE.2a 471 at Amiens on 13-8-14. Construction of the replica took place 2014-2016. **[2]** Camel painted as one flown by Capt John Todd, who instructed at Montrose in 1918. **[3]** Tested by Charles Powis at Woodley on 31-7-35, G-ADMW is the oldest surviving Miles aircraft in Britain (although the Miles-designed Southern Martlet G-AAYX at the Shuttleworth Collection was built in 1930). **[4]** Acquired from Glenn James, owner of airworthy Anson T.21 WD413 (G-VROE).

Petrofac Training Services - Montrose Training Centre: Forties Road. WG.30 N1116WG was put up for sale in October 2022 and by April 2023 had moved locally - see below.

Basin Art Centre: Brechin Road. Took on the former Petrofac – above – WG.30 | **www.facebook.com/TheBasinArtCentre**

❑ N116WG* Westland WG.30-160 85 ex Petrofac, Weston-super-Mare, Yeovil, PanAm, G-BLLG, G-BLLG G-17-20. First noted 4-23 [1] 4-23

■ **[1]** Fitted with the boom of G-17-12, for those that have the urge to know, that would be from G-BKKY (013) or VT-EKJ (026).

Locally: The fuselage of a HS.125 is in store awaiting a plan to turn it into a glamping' pod-thing at a farm.

❑ VP-CFI* HSA HS.125-700B 79 ex North Duffield, Hurn, OD-BBF, OD-HHF, G-OURB, G-NCFR, G-BVJY, RA-02802, G-BVJY, C6-BET. Fuselage 11-22

NETHERLEY on the B979 north of Stonehaven

Alba Power: The turbine specialists have a 'guardian' at the Mill of Monquich. **www.albapower.co.uk**

❑ N-315 Hawker Hunter T.7 58 ex Long Marston, Hucclecote, Batley, Amsterdam, and NLS spares, XM121, n/s 9-23

NORTH ROE on the A970 north of Lerwick, 'Mainland' Shetland Islands

Duncan Feather: The Potez is extant locally. ◆ *Prior arrangement* **only**

❑ F-BMCY Potez 840 62 ex Sumburgh, N840HP, F-BJSU, F-WJSU. Damaged 29-3-81 8-23

PERTH

BlueSky Experiences: XX892 is reported to have migrated south to 'Lincolnshire' in May 2022. No 'forwarding address' – how do you hide just shy of 30,000lb of icon? ◆ **Strictly** *by prior arrangement* | **www.blueskyexperiences.com**

❑ XX892 Blackburn Buccaneer S.2B 75 ex Forres, Lossiemouth, 208, 237 OCU, 16. Cockpit 7-21

Perth College – University of the Highlands and Islands: Behan Campus, Crieff Road. Linked with AST at the airport (see below). ◆ *Prior arrangement* **only** | **www.perth.uhi.ac.uk**

❑ G-BATW Piper Cherokee 140 72 ex Scone, N742FL. CoA 24-10-14, de-reg 18-11-16 3-20

PERTH AIRPORT or Scone EGPT

Air Service Training - Perth College: See also Perth College, above. Jetstream G-NFLC travelled by road to St Athan, Wales, on 23rd June 2022. Departing at the same time and to the same destination was Cessna 310 G-AYGB. This was written out of *W&R28* (p295) as having moved on – destination unknown – by May 2021, but it had lingered.

◆ **Strictly** *prior arrangement* **only** | **www.airservicetraining.co.uk**

❑ G-BEWP Cessna F.150M 77 Reims-built. Crashed 4-10-83, de-reg 5-12-83 1-22
❑ G-BWYE Cessna 310R II 79 ex F-GBPE, N26369. CoA 10-9-09, de-reg 7-7-11 1-24
❑ SX-ROD* BAe Jetstream 41 95 ex Cranfield, Sky Express, G-CEYW, N560HK, G-4-07. Arrived 21-7-22 1-24
❑ – BAe ATP ~ ex Prestwick. Cockpit, simulator [1] 11-17
❑ ZE413 Agusta 109A 98 ex Ipswich, Lichfield, 8 Flt. Arrived 1-11-16 [2] 1-24
❑ MM81220 Agusta 109A ~ ex Italy, Guardia di Finanza. Arrived 21-5-21 1-24
❑ MM81335 Agusta 109A ~ ex Italy, Guardia di Finanza. Arrived 21-5-21 1-24

■ **[1]** The ATP cockpit *could* be from the prototype Jetstream 61 G-JLXI. **[2]** Contributor Jim Simpson found the serial on the 'Hereford Gun Club' Agusta, it's on the entrance door. As he noted: "It's not the ghost of its old serial, it really is white on white!"

Also: *W&R28* (p289) reported Airtourer G-ATJC as gravitating here. Not so, it remained at Elgin awaiting its fate.

❑ EI-APF Cessna F.150G 66 ex Anstruther, Kirknewton, Perth, Sligo. Reims-built. CoA 8-98. Fuselage, rescue trainer 10-22

PETERHEAD on the A90 south of Fraserburgh

Score Energy Ltd: The Lightning 'guards' the GLEN Test Facility, which handles industrial R-R Avons, among other types.

◆ *Private site, entrance* **strictly** *by prior arrangement* | **www.score-group.com**

❑ XR749 'DA' EE Lightning F.3 65 ex Tees-side, Chop Gate, Leuchars 8934M, 11, LTF, 11, LTF, Binbrook pool, 29, 226 OCU, 56. Damaged 17-2-87. LTF c/s 9-23

PRESTWICK AIRPORT The compiler has given in to modernity: this is now listed under Glasgow Prestwick Airport

SCALLOWAY on the A970, west of Lerwick, Shetland

Scalloway Museum: As well as displays on the famous 'Shetland Bus', the risky trawler run across the North Sea to re-supply Norwegian partisans during the German occupation 1940-1945, there is an unfinished Luton Minor on show.
◆ *Castle Street, ZE1 0TP* | **01595 880734** | **email** via website | **www.scallowaymuseum.org**

❑ G-AMUW		Luton Minor	52	ex Orkney. De-reg 13-4-73. Unfinished, uncovered airframe. Unveiled 5-15	[1]	1-24

■ **[1]** Project started by Bill Petrie at St Margaret's Hope on Orkney; later to Shetland-based Jim Smith.

SPEY BAY on the B9014 north of Fochabers

Spey Bay Salvage Ltd: A diverse operation combining metal recycling and a fleet of recovery and transport vehicles. The proprietor is an enthusiast and a great supporter of Morayvia (Kinloss, Scotland). This is the 'off-site' facility that stores and prepares exhibits for the museum: like the rest of the Spey Bay site, it is *not* readily open to the public.

As hinted at in *W&R28* the following airframes were 'processed' here by early 2022: Canberra B(I).6 WT308; Wessex HU.5 XT773; Phantom FGR.2 XV411; *noseless* Merlin HC.3 ZJ128. ◆ *Prior arrangement* **only**

❑ XX956*	'BE'	SEPECAT Jaguar GR.1	75	ex Boscombe Down, Gibraltar, Ipswich, Halton 8950M (3-12-87), Shawbury, 17, 31, 17, 14, 17. Arrived 4-22		4-22

STRANRAER

Stoneykirk Aviation Museum: Steve Austin and friends have turned their award-winning restorations and many artefacts into a museum. Extending the collection's prize 'cupboard', the Buccaneer was given a Spirit of *CockpitFest* award at the June 2022 event. ◆ *Mid Cairngarroch Croft, DG9 9EH. Open 'most Sundays' in summer – check beforehand – or by prior arrangement* | **info@2av8.co.uk** | **www.2av8.co.uk**

❑ WE191		EE Canberra T.4	54	ex Dumfries, Warton, Samlesbury, Bracebridge Heath, Kemble, Indian AF B.52 Q497, Samlesbury, Kemble, WE191, 231 OCU, 237 OCU, 231 OCU, 245. SOC 1-2-78. Cockpit	[1]	1-24
❑ WV903	'128'	Hawker Sea Hawk FGA.6	55	ex Hooton Park, Mold, Yeo'ton, Dunsfold, Lee-on-Solent, Culdrose A2632, Halton 8153M, Sydenham, 801, FGA.4, 802, 897, 811, 804. SOC 20-1-71. AW-built. Cockpit. Arr 6-15		1-24
❑ XA903		Avro Vulcan B.1	57	ex Wellesbourne Mountford, Sidcup, Cardiff, Farnborough. Last flight 22-7-79, SOC 19-7-79. Cockpit	[2]	1-24
❑ XE921	'VR'	DH Vampire T.11	55	ex St Mawgan, Newbridge, Yarmouth, Welshpool, Stoke, Barton, Firbeck, Retford, Firbeck, Keevil, Exeter, 3/4 CAACU, 1 FTS, CFS. Hatfield-built. SOC 16-12-71. Arrived 3-17. CFS colours. Cockpit		1-24
❑ XK533	'229'	Blackburn Buccaneer S.1	61	ex East Fortune, Arbroath, Lossiemouth, 809, 700Z, A&AEE, 700Z. Crashed 10-10-63. Cockpit. Arrived 30-10-21		1-24
❑ XN983*		Blackburn Buccaneer S.2B	65	ex West Walton Highway, Terrington St Clement, 12, 208, 15, 12, 809, A&AEE, RR. SOC 10-4-94. Cockpit, arr by 6-22		1-24
❑ XP558	'20'	Hunting Jet Provost T.4	62	ex Sheffield, Ipswich, Norwich, Honington 8627M, St Athan, Culdrose, A2628 (13-5-74), CAW, 3 CAACU, RAFC. Cockpit		1-24
❑ XP925	'752'	DH Sea Vixen FAW.2	63	ex Chorley, Haslemere, Farnborough, Tarrant Rushton, FRADU, FRU, 899. Hawarden-built. SOC 19-11-81. Cockpit		1-24

■ **[1]** WE191 was acquired by BAC 24-5-65 and converted to B.52 status for the Indian Air Force. Frustrated by the Indo-Pakistan war of 1965, it was stored at Kemble from 5-7-66 on behalf of BAC, before transferring *back* to the RAF on 15-10-70. It never returned to active service and was declared a non-effective airframe 30-6-72. **[2]** XA903 has a fabulous trials provenance: Blue Steel trials (57-61), Olympus 593 test-bed (64-71), RB.199 test-bed and Mauser cannon static tests (73-79).

STRATHALLAN AERODROME Last noted in June 2017 para-trainer Cessna U.206 G-BAGV has been deleted.

STRATHBLANE on the A381 north of Glasgow

A Sea King is kept in the *general* area. ◆ *Inspection* **not** *possible*

❑ XV705		Westland Sea King HAS.2	71	ex Woodmancote, Colsterworth, Gosport, 824, HAS.1, 814, 824, 737, 706, 771, Gosport A2618 (28-8-01), 771, Gannet Flt, 771. First noted 1-20		1-21

THORNHILL on the A873 northwest of Stirling

Mains Farm Wigwams: Among the choice of exotic places to sleep is a Sea King. The 'Twin Pin' awaits conversion.

◆ *Prior arrangement* **only** | **www.mainsfarmwigwams.com**

❑ G-APRS		SAL Twin Pioneer 3	59	ex Coventry, Staverton, G-BCWF, XT610, G-APRS, PI-C430. CoA 15-7-08, de-reg 6-12-17. *Primrose*. Arrived 13-7-18		1-24
❑ ZA127	'509'	Westland Sea King HAS.6	80	ex Colsterworth, Gosport A2846 (19-7-01), 706, HAS.5, 810, A&AEE, 820. Arrived 19-4-16		1-24

WINCHBURGH on the B9080 east of Edinburgh

A *private* house in the area has a pink HS.125 cockpit, believed used as a simulator and possibly from a Series 400.

❑ –		HSA HS.125	~	cockpit, see note above. First noted 5-16		4-21

WALES

Comprises 22 unitary authorities ranging from Anglesey and Flintshire to Pembrokeshire and Rhondda

AMMANFORD on the A483 north of Swansea

No.**2475 (Ammanford) Squadron Air Cadets**: Penybanc Road.

❑ WH739		EE Canberra B.2	53	ex St Athan, 100, 85, 45, 75 RNZAF, Upwood SF, 50, 101. SOC 27-7-76. Cockpit		2-23

CAERNARFON AERODROME or Llandwrog north of the A499, southwest of Caernarfon EGCK

Caernarfon Airport Airworld Museum: The museum tells the story of aviation in general and specifically in North Wales. The mountain rescue exhibit is a graphic story of wartime crashes, both Allied and Luftwaffe, and includes a large amount of salvaged wreck items. Among the many interesting exhibits is a 'Turtle' narrow-gauge railway shunting engine, salvaged from what was RAF Hell's Mouth (west of Abersoch on the Lleyn Peninsula).

Enquiries in August 2022 relating to the stored airframes revealed that Skycraft Scout G-MBBB (and very likely the anonymous, incomplete, example) and Weedhopper G-MJSN "were disposed of some years ago".

◆ *Caernarfon Airport, LL54 5TP* | **01286 832154** | **info.airworldmuseum.com** | **www.airworldmuseum.com**

❑ 'G-EGCK'		Mignet HM.14 'Flea'	c36	BAPC.286, ex St Athan, 'local area'. Arrived 12-02	[1]	1-24
❑ G-BSMX		Bensen B-8MR	90	de-reg 17-5-10. Unassembled kit, in store		1-24
❑ –		Blériot XI replica	11	BAPC.448, unveiled 2011	[2]	1-24
❑ –		Vickers Varsity T.1 EMU	c52	ex Higher Blagdon, Oakington. Arrived 1988	[3]	1-24
❑ 'N5137'		DH Tiger Moth G-BNDW	39	ex Shobdon, Fownhope, N6638, Fairford SF, 27 GCF, St Mawgan SF, Prestwick SF, 25 EFTS, 22 EFTS, 22 E&RFTS. De-reg 19-7-12. Arrived 26-11-97	[4]	1-24
❑ WM961	'J'	Hawker Sea Hawk FB.5	54	ex Higher Blagdon, Culdrose A2517, FRU, 802, FB.3, 811. SOC 17-1-62. Arrived 1988		1-24
❑ WT694		Hawker Hunter F.1	54	ex Newton, Debden 7510M (22-11-57), 229 OCU, DFLS, 54. Arrived 26-9-95. 245 Sqn colours		1-24
❑ WV781		Bristol Sycamore HR.12 G-ALTD	52	ex Finningley, Odiham, Digby 7839M (16-3-61), HDU, CFS, ASWDU, G-ALTD. Arrived 1986. Forward fuselage		1-24
❑ XA282		Slingsby Cadet TX.3	52	ex Syerston, 635 VGS, 617 GS, 1 GC, CGIS, 105 GS. SOC 19-8-86. Arrived 1986		1-24
❑ XH837		Gloster Javelin FAW.7	57	ex Northolt, Ruislip, 71 MU 8032M (21-2-62), 33. Arrived 9-4-86. Cockpit		1-24
❑ XJ726		Westland Whirlwind HAR.10	55	ex Sibson, Wroughton, 2 FTS, CFS, ME SAR Flt, 22. SOC 4-2-81. Arrived 1986		1-24
❑ XK623	'56'	DH Vampire T.11	56	ex Hurn 'G-VAMP', Moston, Woodford, Hawarden, St Athan, 5 FTS. Hawarden-built. SOC 6-12-68. Arrived 1986		1-24
❑ XW269	'TB'	HS Harrier T.4A	71	ex Selby, Queensbury, Boscombe Down, Wittering, SAOEU, 233 OCU, 3, 1, 233 OCU, 4. 4 Sqn c/s, T.2 era. Arr 2-10-12		1-24
❑ XX309*		HS Hawk T.1	80	ex Shawbury, St Athan 'hack', 208, 19, 6 FTS, 234, 4 FTS. Welsh dragon colours. Arrived 15-5-23		1-24

■ **[1]** Former University of Wales Air Sqn St Athan 'Flea' is *believed* to be largely new-build, but with Scott A2S engine. From circa 2006 it incorporated the metal elements - including the unique undercarriage - from the Idwal Jones-built example BAPC.201 acquired from nearby Talysarn – see Hooton Park, Cheshire. The 'registration' is derived from the aerodrome's ICAO Location Indicator. **[2]** Blériot *perhaps* built to a reduced scale. **[3]** Varsity cockpit - within the 'Astra' cinema area *underneath* the mountain rescue display - carries a Marshall of Cambridge mod plate and is *very* substantial. **[4]** Tiger comprises a fuselage and mocked-up port wings.

Others:

Reg		Type	Year	History	Date
❑ G-AWUK		Cessna F.150H	68	ex Shobdon, Stansted, Oaksey Park, Bristol, Biggin Hill. Reims-built. Cr 4-9-71, de-reg 13-4-73. Cockpit, rescue tnr	11-22
❑ XD165	'B'	Westland Whirlwind HAR.10	54	ex Doncaster, Storwood, Wattisham, Netheravon, Halton 8673M (2-2-81), SARTS, 202, 228, 22, 225, 155. Rescue tnr	8-23

CARDIFF

Cardiff University School of Engineering: Hawk T.1 XX263 made the trek to St Athan, Wales, on 22nd April 2022.

Dean Smith: Keeps his *W&R Spirit of CockpitFest* award-wining cockpit in the *general* area.

Reg	Type	Year	History	Date
❑ G-BOCB*	HSA HS.125-1B/522	66	ex St Athan, Porthcawl, Doncaster, Cardiff, Hatfield, G-OMCA, G-DJMJ, G-AWUF, 5N-ALY, G-AWUF, HZ-BIN. CoA 16-10-90, de-reg 22-2-95. *Winnie* (port), *Peter* (stb). Cockpit	12-22

CARDIFF AIRPORT or Rhoose

EGFF

Airport: In a compound on the southwest side, the fire crews have a synthetic trainer and a BAC 111.

Reg	Type	Year	History	Date
❑ G-AVMT	BAC 111-510ED	68	ex Hurn, European, BA, BEA. CoA 5-12-03, de-reg 17-12-04	10-23

International Centre for Aerospace Training: Part of Cardiff and Vale College. ◆ *Prior application* ***only*** | **www.cavc.ac.uk**

Reg		Type	Year	History	Date
❑ D-AGEG		Boeing 737-300	88	ex Kemble, Germania, UR-GAF, D-AGEG, G-EURP. Arrived 14-11-12. Forward fuselage	10-23
❑ XX487	'568'	HP Jetstream T.2	74	ex Culdrose, 750, T.1 n/s. SAL-completed. Arrived 18-6-11	10-23
❑ XX687	'F'	SAL Bulldog T.1	75	ex Shawbury, EM UAS, Liv UAS. Arrived 18-7-01	10-23

CAREW CHERITON on the A477 east of Pembroke

Carew Control Tower Group: Based at the unique watch tower at the former airfield, visitors are in for a treat at this superbly put-together and very friendly museum. The Anson is a long-term project.

◆ *On Showground edge, SA70 8SX* | **info@carewcheritoncontroltower.co.uk** | **www.carewcheritoncontroltower.co.uk**

Reg	Type	Year	History	Date
❑ VM325	Avro Anson C.19	47	ex Gloucestershire, Bentham, Staverton, Coventry, Halfpenny Green, WCS, NCS, WCS, TCCF, Upavon CF, 173, 4 FP. SOC 19-9-68. Arrived 23-8-05. Workshop	12-23

CHIRK on the A5 north of Oswestry

◆ **Private** *location; prior application* ***only***

Reg	Type	Year	History	Date
❑ G-AJBJ	DH Dragon Rapide	44	ex Coventry, Husbands Bosworth, Peel Green, Squires Gate, Dominie NF894, 18 MU, HQ TCCF. Brush-built. CoA 14-9-61, de-reg 16-12-91	6-22
❑ 'G-AJCL'	DH Dragon Rapide G-AIUL	45	ex Southend, British Westpoint G-AIUL, Dominie NR749, Kemble, 2 RS. Brush-built. CoA 29-9-67, de-reg 6-4-73	9-21
❑ G-AKOE	DH Dragon Rapide	42	ex Booker, X7484, PTS. CoA 25-2-82, de-reg 18-6-02. British Airways colours, *Sir Henry Morgan*	6-22
❑ G-ANFC	DH Tiger Moth	42	ex London Colney, Dunstable, DE363, 22 EFTS, 4 FIS. Morris Motors-built. CoA 9-10-03, de-reg 25-5-23	6-22
❑ G-AZMX	Piper Cherokee 140	68	ex Connah's Quay, Chester, Halfpenny Green, SE-FLL, LN-LMK. CoA 9-1-82, de-reg 9-1-84	10-22
❑ G-BAYL	Nord Norecrin	48	ex Ivychurch, Solihull, Bodmin, F-BEQV. De-reg 14-11-91	6-22
❑ G-BEDB	Nord Norecrin	48	ex Liverpool, Chirk, F-BEOB. CoA 11-6-80, de-reg 14-11-91	9-21

CONNAH'S QUAY on the A548 west of Chester

Coleg Cambria ◆ *Prior application* **only** | **www.cambria.ac.uk**

Reg	Type	Year	History	Date
❑ N66SW	Cessna 340	~	ex N5035Q. *Flyer* titles, dismantled, stored	11-23

❑ –		HSA HS.125-1000	~	BAPC.382, ex Hawarden. Unflown forward fuselage, stored	11-23
❑ XW291		BAC Jet Provost T.5 G-BWOF	69	ex N Weald, Hurn, SOC 18-3-96, Shawbury, 6 FTS, 3 FTS, RAFC, CFS, RAFC, CFS. CoA 6-5-16. First noted 7-18	11-22
❑ XW423	'14'	BAC Jet Provost T.5A G-BWUW	72	ex Little Snoring, RAF, Shawbury, 3 FTS, RAFC, 1 FTS, 3 FTS. CoA 14-2-02, de-reg 29-6-06	11-22

COWBRIDGE on the A48 west of Cardiff

Task Force Paintball ◆ *Prior application* **only** | **www.taskforcepaintball.co.uk**

❑ XG592	W'land Whirlwind HAS.7	57	ex Cardiff, Wroughton, 705, 846, 705, 700, HS. SOC 5-5-76	1-22

CWMBRAN on the A4051 north of Newport

Mark Gauntlett: The cockpits are *believed* extant. ◆ *Prior application* **only**

❑ XE985	DH Vampire T.11	55	ex Exeter, Bridgend, Cwmbran, Bridgend, London Colney, Woodford, Chester, St Athan, 5 FTS. Hawarden-built. SOC 17-11-67. Cockpit	7-11
❑ QA-12	Hawker Hunter FGA.78	56	ex Woking, Hurn, Qatar AF, G-9-284, Dutch AF N-222. Cockpit	7-11

FONMON

Fonmon Castle Park and Gardens: 'JP' T.5A XW320 returned to St Athan, Wales, by September 2022. By then the venue had gained the fuselage of a 737 to turn into a cafe. ◆ *CF62 3ZN* | **info@fonmoncastle.com** | **www.fonmoncastle.com**

❑ N470AC*	Boeing 737-300	90	ex St Athan, Bournemouth, HZ-AMG, N570LL, 9M-AAE, B-2653, N2332Q, G-OABD, 9V-TRC, OY-MME. Last flown 8-10-10. Fuselage, arrived 3-22	1-24

HAVERFORDWEST on the A4076 north of Milford Haven

Welsh Spitfire Museum: *Bridge Street* | **info@welshspitfire.org** | **www.facebook.com/people/Welsh-Spitfire-Museum/**

❑ JG668	V-S Spitfire VIII G-CFGA	44	ex Oxford, Australia, Oakey, RAAF A58-441 (SOC 22-5-46), JG668 no service	[1]	5-23

■ **[1]** Registered to TSIB Ltd.

HAVERFORDWEST AERODROME or Withybush, on the A40, north of Haverfordwest EGFE

❑ G-BLTT	Slingsby T.67B Firefly	85	CoA 5-8-00, de-reg 28-7-04. Rescue trainer	9-21

Forward fuselage of JG668, Welsh Spitfire Museum, May 2023. *Chris England*

HAWARDEN AIRFIELD or Broughton, on the B5129 west of Chester EGNR

North Wales Military Aviation Services: The restoration and operation of jet 'warbirds', especially 'JPs' and Strikemasters, is a speciality. Only those under long-term restoration and storage are listed. Chipmunk T.10 G-BCOO was flying again by 2021 and Strikemaster Mk.84 311 (G-MXPH) was airworthy by 2023. MiG-23ML '04' and MiG-27K '71' at the Newark, Notts, are on loan from NWMAS. ◆ *Prior arrangement* **only** | **www.nwmas.com**

❑	G-OEDB		Piper Tomahawk 112		78	ex G-BGGJ, N9694N. De-reg 25-5-19. Fuselage		10-21
❑	CCCP-07268		Antonov An-2R	YL-LEV	~	ex Latvia, USSR. Arrived by 12-93		5-23
❑	CCCP-17939		Antonov An-2R	YL-LFC	~	ex Latvia, USSR. Arrived by 12-93		5-23
❑	CCCP-19731		Antonov An-2R	YL-LEU	~	ex Hooton Park, Chester, Latvia, USSR. Arrived by 12-93		5-23
❑	CCCP-19733		Antonov An-2R	YL-LEZ	~	ex Latvia, USSR. Arrived by 12-93. 'Chocks Away'		1-24
❑	CCCP-20320		Mil Mi-2 *Hoplite*	YL-LHN	~	ex Latvia, Latvian AF 154, USSR. Arrived by 12-93		5-23
❑	CCCP-20619		Mil Mi-2 *Hoplite*	YL-LHO	~	ex Latvia, Latvian AF 153, USSR. Arrived by 12-93		5-23
❑	CCCP-40748		Antonov An-2R	YL-LFA	~	ex Latvia, USSR. Arrived by 12-93		5-23
❑	CCCP-40749		Antonov An-2R	YL-LFD	~	ex Latvia, USSR. Arrived by 12-93		5-23
❑	CCCP-40784		Antonov An-2R	YL-LEY	~	ex Latvia, USSR. Arrived by 12-93		5-23
❑	CCCP-40785		Antonov An-2R	YL-LFB	~	ex Latvia, USSR. Arrived by 12-93		5-23
❑	CCCP-54949		Antonov An-2R	YL-LEX	~	ex Latvia, USSR. Arrived by 12-93		5-23
❑	CCCP-56471		Antonov An-2R	YL-LEW	~	ex Latvia, USSR. Arrived by 12-93		5-23
❑	'37' yellow		Aviatika MAI 890	YL-MIG	~	ex Latvia, USSR. Arrived by 12-93		5-23
❑	'38' yellow		Aviatika MAI 890		~	ex Latvia, USSR. Arrived by 12-93		5-23
❑	WK620	'T'	DHC Chipmunk T.10		52	ex Enstone, Twyford, Tattershall Thorpe, M Wallop, BFWF, Hull, Mcr, Queen's and Bristol UASs, 22 RFS. Hawarden-built. Damaged 19-5-93		4-23
❑	XN459*		Hunting Jet Provost T.3	G-BWOT	61	ex North Weald, CFS, 1 FTS, A&AEE, 1 FTS. CoA 25-4-20. First noted 5-23. Stored		8-23
❑	XW299*	'MB' *and* '60'	BAC Jet Provost T.5A	G-CLJW	70	ex Selby, Boscombe Down, Selby, Cosford, Halton, 9146M (18-5-92), 1 FTS, RAFC, 1 FTS.	[1]	4-23
❑	XW409	'123'	BAC Jet Provost T.5A		71	ex St Athan 9047M (29-6-90), 7 FTS, 1 FTS. Stored, off-site		9-14
❑	323		BAC Strikemaster Mk.81	N21419	69	ex Singapore ADC, S Yemen AF 504, G-27-36, G-AXFX, G-27-36, S Yemen AF 504		9-14
❑	'18' red		Aero L29 Delfin			YL-PAF, ex Latvia, USSR. (591771). Dismantled		1-24
❑	'23' red		Mikoyan-Gurevich MiG-27M *Flogger*		81	ex Latvia, USSR. Arrived by 12-93. At 'Chocks Away'. (83712515040)		1-24
❑	'35' red		Sukhoi Su-17M3 *Fitter*		77	ex Latvia, USSR. (25102). Arrived by 12-93		1-24
❑	'54' red		Sukhoi Su-17M *Fitter*		74	ex Latvia, USSR. (69004). Arrived by 12-93		1-24

■ **[1]** Written out of *W&R27* at Selby (p300) as bound for Australia; registered to an Australian owner.

Also:

❑	G-BYJF	Thorp T.211	98	ex N2545C. Venture Light A/c-built. CoA 14-6-12		9-21
❑	G-EGEE	Cessna 310Q	69	ex G-AZVY, SE-FKV, N7540Q. CoA 22-3-08, de-reg 15-2-11		9-21
❑	P4-JET*	HSA HS.125-800B	93	ex EI-RJL, OH-SAQ, EI-RJL, N524XL, G-6-349. De-reg 16-5-19	[1]	8-23
❑	5N-JMA	HSA HS.125-800XP	93	ex N658XP. First noted 6-18		8-23

■ **[1]** P4-JET is currently a Falcon 50EX.

Aviation Park: The 'Chocks Away Diner', which is well worth a visit, is 'guarded by MiG-27 '23' and An-2 CCCP-19733 - see above. Also on the site is **Cokebusters**, nothing to do with fizzy drinks or more powerful stimulants, the company is a specialist in decoking Industrial processes and pipe inspection. ◆ *Aviation Park, CH4 0GZ* | **https://cokebusters.com**

❑	'AB196'	SA Spitfire Mk.26	G-CCGH	07	CoA 6-6-13. Displayed, first noted 8-20	[1]	1-24

■ **[1]** Australian scale kitplane by Supermarine Aircraft, registered to Cokebusters Ltd.

Tornado Heritage Centre: Offers pre-bookable 'Aircrew' experience days, including 'time' on a Tornado F.3 procedures trainer/simulator. ◆ *Aviation Park, CH4 0GZ* | **www.facebook.com/p/Tornado_Heritage_Centre**

❑	XP585*	'24'	Hunting Jet Provost T.4	62	ex Wrexham, Halton 8407M (7-10-74), St Athan, RAFC, 6 FTS, RAFC. Arrived 13-8-23	1-24
❑	ZE966	'VT'	Panavia Tornado F.3	89	ex Wroughton, Swinton, St Athan, 111, 56, 11, 25, 11, 43. 56 Sqn colours. Acquired 30-9-16, arrived 18-2-17	1-24

No.2247 Squadron's Vampire T.11 XE852, May 2022. *Ian Humphreys*

No.**2247 (Hawarden) Squadron Air Cadets**: In Manor Lane to the west of the airfield. Vampire XE852 is one of the oldest 'running' ATC airframes - clocking up 37 years with the unit.

❑ BGA.1733		SZD Pirat	c72	cockpit, first noted 5-21. Stored	[1]	4-22
❑ XE852	'58'	DH Vampire T.11	54	ex Woodford, Chester, Shawbury, 1 FTS, 4 FTS. Hatfield-built. SOC 30-10-67. Arrived 3-11-87		1-24

■ **[1]** Pirat was accepted as a complete airframe – date unknown – and cut down to a cockpit.

Locally: Chipmunk WK620 is stored on the airfield, see above.

KENFIG HILL north of the B4281 east of Pyle

No.**2117 (Kenfig Hill) Squadron Air Cadets**: A landmark in and around Main Street since it was delivered in March 1964 Hunter F.1 WT569 was craned off the site on 11th November 2022 and delivered to Kinloss, Scotland. It is reported that it will return after restoration.

LLANBEDR AIRFIELD west of Llanbedr and the A496 on the road to Shell Island

Snowdonia Aerospace Centre: ◆ *Prior arrangement* **only**

❑ ZJ503		GAF Jindivik 104AL	c98	ex RAAF A92-908. Trolley-mounted, displayed	[1]	7-23

■ **[1]** On loan from 2445 (Ardudwy) Squadron, Air Cadets.

LLANGEINOR on the A4064 north of Bridgend

IrvinGQ: The rescue equipment manufacturer has a Draken on display. **www.irvingq.com**

❑ 35515	'49'	SAAB J35F Draken	c68	ex F10, Swedish AF	8-22

NANTGARW on the A470 northwest of Cardiff

National Collections Centre: Large object store for the National Museum of Wales.

◆ *Prior appointment* **only** | **https://museum.wales**

❑ XM300	Westland Wessex HAS.1	59	ex Cardiff, Cardiff-Wales, RAE Farnborough, RAE Bedford, A&AEE, Westland. SOC 1-8-79. SAR colours	8-23

NEWBOROUGH Anglesey, on the B4421, at the southern tip of the island

Anglesey Transport Museum – Tacla Taid: Amid the cars, armoured vehicles, agricultural machinery and more, is a Hunter.

◆ *Tyddyn Pwrpas, Newborough, LL61 6TN* | **email** via website | **www.angleseytransportmuseum.co.uk**

❑ WV396	'91'	Hawker Hunter T.8C	55	ex Valley 9249M, Yeovilton, FRADU, 759, F.4, 229 OCU, 20. SOC 16-5-95. 4 FTS colours. Arrived by 6-17	8-23

NEWBRIDGE-ON-WYE on the A470 north of Builth Wells

Quackers Indoor Play Centre: At Newmead Farm, a 'JP' is in the grounds. | **www.quackersnow.com**

❑ XM358		Hunting Jet Provost T.3A	59	ex Twyford, North Scarle, Colsterworth, Halton 8987M (10-1-89), 1 FTS, 3 FTS, 1 FTS, CFS, RAFC, CFS, 7 FTS, 2 FTS	8-22

PEMBREY FOREST RANGES west of the A484 and Llanelli

❑ XR523	'M'	Westland Wessex HC.2	64	ex Torpoint, Fleetlands, Gosport, S'bury, F'lands, 72. Arr 4-16	6-21
❑ XV372		Sikorsky SH-3D Sea King	66	ex St Mawgan, Culdrose, Predannack, St Mawgan, Trowbridge, Yeovil, Aston Down, Lee-on-Solent, Pyestock, BSE, Westland. SOC 1-11-71, arrived by 4-16	6-21
❑ XX958	'BK'	SEPECAT Jaguar GR.1	75	ex Cosford 9022M, Shawbury, 17, 14. Arrived 2-7-19	6-21
❑ XX966	'JJ'	SEPECAT Jaguar GR.1A	75	ex Cosford, Halton 8904M (23-5-86), Shawbury, 6, 54, 20, A&AEE, 20, 17	6-21

PEMBROKE DOCK on the A477 northwest of Pembroke

Pembroke Dock Heritage Centre: Administered by the **Pembroke Dock Sunderland Trust**, the centre displays many recovered parts, including two Pegasus radials, from 210 Squadron Sunderland I T9044 which sank in a gale at Pembroke Dock on 21st November 1940. Recovery of other items is on-going. Displays chart the history of this famous flying-boat haven and the general history of the maritime complex.

◆ *Royal Dockyard, SA72 6YH* | **01646 684220** | **enquiries@pdht.org** | **https://pdht.org**

PORT TALBOT east of Swansea on the A4241

A *private* owner in the *general* area has taken delivery of a Vampire cockpit.

❑ XE982*		DH Vampire T.11	55	ex Tetbury, Newbridge, Weston, Dunkeswell, Hereford, St Athan 7564M (15-5-58), RAFC. Hawarden-built. Cockpit. First noted 3-22	3-22

PYLE on the A48 west of Bridgend, north of junction 37, M4

JBT AeroTech: Village Farm Industrial Estate, a Spitfire FSM is displayed. | **jbtaerotech.gse@jbtc.com**

❑ 'EN398'	'JE-J'	V-S Spitfire IX FSM	~	BAPC.552. Unveiled 6-12-13	[1]	3-19

■ **[1]** Other 'EN398s' can be found at: Coningsby, Lincs; Taunton, Somerset; Salisbury, Wilts.

RADYR south of the M4, west of Cardiff

Delta Force Paintball: Tyla-Morris Farm. *May* still have a Lynx. ◆ *Prior arrangement* **only** | **www.paintballgames.co.uk**

❑ ZD565	'404'	Westland Lynx HMA.8	80	ex Upminster, Ipswich, Fleetlands, 815, 702, HAS.3, 702. First noted 11-17	11-17

REDBERTH on the A477 east of Pembroke Dock

Apple Camping: As well as the JetStar, the site also offers 'Arabian Nights' in the fuselage 'barrel' of a former Etihad A319. Cockpitless, it is beyond the remit of the book, but it is most likely from A6-EID.

◆ *Prior arrangement* **only** | **www.applecamping.co.uk**

❑ N25AG		Lockheed JetStar II	76	ex Kemble, Alton, Kemble, 3C-QRK, P4-CBG, VP-CBH, EC-FQX, EC-232, N20GB, N333KN, N717X, N717, N5528L. Last flown 26-9-06. Fuselage, arrived mid-16	12-23

RUTHIN on the A494 southwest of Mold

Phantom Preservation Group: Mark A Jones *should* still have his cockpits in the locality. ◆ *Prior arrangement* **only**

❑ XV419		McD Phantom FGR.2	69	ex Terrington St Clement, Stock, Wattisham, 19, 228 OCU, 29, 56, 29, 228 OCU, 29, 111, 14, 111, 54, 228 OCU, 54. SOC 5-10-92. Cockpit	3-14
❑ ZE788	'HV'	Panavia Tornado F.3	88	ex Selby, Leeming, 111. Cockpit	2-19

ST ATHAN AIRFIELD on the B4265 west of Barry EGSY

South Wales Aviation Museum (SWAM): From the moment of entry the exhibition hangar through a section of former RAF VC10 fuselage the warm welcome, accessibility and informality assures visitors that this is a very special venue. As well as the eclectic airframes and cockpits, the number of ancillary exhibits, displays, dioramas and artefacts is rewarding and absorbing. Up on the second floor is the excellent café, which also offers great views of the aircraft hall.

SWAM was founded by two aviation professionals, supported by an increasing band of enthusiasts. Gary Spoors is mentioned several times in this book and is the leading light of GJD Services and GJD AeroTech, headquartered at St Athan. GJD provides specialist parting out, maintenance, transport and other engineering tasks – see also below. John Sparks runs the resident Horizon Aviation Services and affiliated concerns, with a penchant for the operation and restoration of 'classics' - see separate entry. SWAM occupies the famous Picketston Site - a 'peninsula' that extends northwards from the vast former RAF St Athan site.

Gary Spoors also has airframes on loan as follows: East Midlands, Leics, VC10 forward fuselage XV108, Jetstream XX494, Sea King ZD477; Filton, Glos: Sea Harrier ZD610; Gloucestershire, Glos: Vulcan cockpit XM569 (along with David Price); Woodford, Gtr Man, VC10 cockpit XV106.

Given that SWAM is part of a large airfield complex, there will be some to-ing and fro-ing of airframes; so please bear this in mind when visiting. Likewise, aircraft given below as 'on show' may well go into restoration or store; or vice versa.

Departures: Lynx HMA.8 XZ729 moved to Gosport, Hampshire, by 4-22.

◆ *Hangar 872, Picketston Business Park, CF62 4QR* | **01446 788476** | **info@swam.online** | **www.swam.online**

❑	G-APFG		Boeing 707-436	60	ex Pershore, Cove, Bruntingthorpe, Cardington, Stansted, British Airtours, BOAC. Last flight 3-11-80, CoA 24-5-81, de-reg 24-4-81. Flightdeck		1-24
❑	G-BCTT		Evans VP-1	77	CoA 25-3-05, de-reg 15-4-14. Arrived 22-4-21		1-24
❑	G-BMMF		Clutton FRED Srs II	90	ex Glamorgan, CoA 18-7-03. Acquired 2019		1-24
❑	G-BTUS		Whittaker MW-7	92	CoA 20-6-06. Arrived 10-6-21		1-24
❑	G-BVPM*		Evans VP-2	90	ex Locking. CoA 31-5-94. Arrived 4-22	[1]	1-24
❑	G-BYMT		Pegasus Quantum 15-912	99	ex Manchester, Strathaven. De-reg 10-8-10. Arr 30-10-21		1-24
❑	G-CHPT*		Aviastroitel ME7 Mechta	95	ex Wem, BGA.4102. CoA 28-8-15. Arrived 6-7-22		1-24
❑	G-CHUO*		Aviastroitel ME7 Mechta	96	ex Wem, BGA.4217. CoA 26-5-20. Arrived 16-2-22		1-24
❑	G-CLAX		Jurca Sirocco	68	ex Barry, G-AWKB. De-reg 19-7-19. Fuselage, in cafe	[2]	1-24
❑	G-ELLE		Cameron N90 HAB	98	envelope. CoA 15-6-07, de-reg 4-10-19. Arrived -20		8-20
❑	G-MMNN		Sherry Buzzard	84	ex Stoke. Unfinished, de-reg 28-7-17. Arrived 13-6-20	[3]	1-24
❑	–*		Hiway Spectrum	c80	BAPC.251, ex Wroughton, Manchester, Lytham. Arr 1-22		1-24
❑	B-HUI		Boeing 747-467	93	ex Bruntingthorpe, Cathay, VR-HUI. Last flight 31-10-16. *Nick Heard / Simon McGlynn*. Flightdeck, arrived 12-1-19		1-24
❑	F-BTGV	'1'	Aerospacelines Super Guppy 201	71	ex Bruntingthorpe, Airbus Skylink, Aeromaritime, N211AS. Last flight 1-7-96. Flightdeck, arrived 4-2-21	[4]	1-24
❑	VX113*	'36'	Beagle Terrier 1 G-ARNO	48	ex Southend, Auster AOP.6, AAC, 651, 662. Accident 7-6-22, CoA 9-3-23. Arrived 4-3-23		1-24
❑	WK128		EE Canberra B.2	54	ex Pershore, Llanbedr, FRL. Avro-built. Cockpit		1-24
❑	WP321		Percival Sea Prince T.1 G-BRFC	53	ex Horizon site, Hurn, N7SY, G-BRFC (CoA 28-5-87, de-reg 21-11-99), N Weald, Bourn, WP321, Kemble, 750, 744. SOC 16-9-80	[5]	1-24
❑	WR974	'K'	Avro Shackleton MR.3/3	57	ex Burtonwood, Charlwood, Cosford 8117M (9-12-70), Kinloss W, 203, 42, 203, SWDU, ASWDU. Arrived 7-20		1-24
❑	WZ869	'6'	DHC Chipmunk T.10	53	ex Leicester, Bruntingthorpe, South Molton, Handforth 8019M, 1 FTS, RAFC, Dishforth SF, Benson SF, Oxf UAS, Dur UAS, 64 GCF, Colerne SF. Crashed 20-5-68. Hawarden-built. Fuselage, less tail. RAFC colours		1-24
❑	XE956		DH Vampire T.11 G-OBLN	55	ex Rochester, Pen-Coed, Bridgend, St Albans, Hatfield, CATCS, 1 FTS, 8 FTS, 3 CAACU, APS, 67. Hatfield-built. SOC 2-2-71. De-reg 14-4-23. Arrived 9-7-18	[6]	1-24
❑	XF690*		Percival Provost T.1 G-MOOS	55	ex Old warden, Yeovilton, N Weald, Cranfield, Thatcham, Wymeswold, Leicester, Hendon 8041M (25-11-68), CATCS, CNCS, 64 GCF, QUAS. CoA 14-9-19. Arrived 21-12-23		1-24
❑	XH560*		Avro Vulcan K.2	60	ex Rayleigh area, Marham, Waddington, 50, Wadd W, 27, Akrotiri Wing, Cott W, Wadd W, Cott W, 230 OCU, 12, MoA, 230 OCU. SOC 5-1-84. Cockpit. Arrived 9-12-22		1-24

❑ XH670*		HP Victor B.2	59	ex Rayleigh, East Kirkby, Tattershall, Woodford, Radlett, MoA. SOC 31-10-75. Cockpit. Arrived 9-12-22		1-24
❑ XK895		DH Sea Devon C.20 G-SDEV	56	ex St Mawgan, G-SDEV (CoA 17-9-01, de-reg 4-1-19), Coventry, Kemble, Swansea, Bruntingthorpe, Cambridge, Culdrose SF, 781 Sqn. Arrived 8-7-18		1-24
❑ XL500		Fairey Gannet AEW.3 G-KAEW	61	ex Horizon site, Exeter, N Weald, Chatham, Culdrose, Fleetlands, Lee-on-Solent, Dowty-Rotol, Culdrose SAH A2701, A&AEE, 849. Last flown 28-2-85	[5]	1-24
❑ XL573		Hawker Hunter T.7 G-BVGH	58	ex Horizon site, Exeter, N Weald, Exeter, Shawbury, 237 OCU, Laarbruch SF, 237 OCU, 4 FTS, 229 OCU, FCS. Arrived St Athan 15-12-11. CoA 6-10-15		1-24
❑ XM833		Westland Wessex HAS.3	60	ex Usworth, Lasham, Wroughton, 737, 820, 814, HAS.1, 819, 700H. SOC 24-11-81. Arrived 14-5-19		1-24
❑ XP672	'03'	Hunting Jet Provost T.4 G-RAFI	62	ex Bruntingthorpe, Retford, Ipswich, N Weald, Hurn, Jurby, Halton 8458M (19-12-75), SoRF, CAW, CATCS, CAW, 2 FTS. CoA 11-3-00, de-reg 22-11-10. Arrived 9-4-18		1-24
❑ 'XR993'		Folland Gnat T.1 XP534 G-BVPP	63	ex Bruntingthorpe, N Weald, Cranfield, G-BVPP (CoA 14-1-05, de-reg 22-5-09), XP534, Halton 8620M, 4 FTS, CFS, 4 FTS, CFS, 4 FTS. Damaged 17-9-04, Arrived 6-4-19. 'Red Arrows' colours	[7]	1-24
❑ XV582	'M'	McD Phantom FG.1	69	ex Cosford, Leuchars, 9066M (6-9-90), 43, 228 OCU, 43, 111, 43. *Black Mike*. All-black colours. Arrived 21-11-18		1-24
❑ XW320	'71'	BAC Jet Provost T.5A	70	ex Fonmon, St Athan, Cosford, '9015M', 9016M (20-11-89), Halton, 1 FTS, Leeming SF, 3 FTS, RAFC. F/n 9-22		1-24
❑ XW420	'MU' *and* '83'	BAC Jet Provost T.5A	71	ex Horizon site, Woodvale, Cosford 9194M (7-6-93), 1 FTS, RAFC. Arrived at St Athan 8-9-17		1-24
❑ XW436*	'68'	BAC Jet Provost T.5A	72	ex Horizon site, Cosford, Halton 9148M (18-5-92), 1 FTS, CFS, 3 FTS, Leeming SF, 3 FTS, RAFC. Arrived (St Athan) 16-10-20; first noted 9-22		1-24
❑ XX727*	'ER'	SEPECAT Jaguar GR.1	74	ex Cosford, 8951M, Shawbury, 6, 54, 6, JOCU. Last flown 26-7-84. Arrived 26-5-23		1-24
❑ XX889*	'T'	Blackburn Buccaneer S.2B	75	ex Cosford, Bruntingthorpe, Kemble, Staverton, Bentham, Staverton, Enstone, St Athan, 12, 208, 12, 16. Arrived 23-2-23. 208 Sqn colours		1-24
❑ ZA195	'710'	HS Sea Harrier F/A.2	83	ex Tangmere, Farnborough, Booker, Yeovilton, St Athan, Warton, BAE, 899. Arrived 7-19		1-24
❑ ZA326		Panavia Tornado GR.1	83	ex Bruntingthorpe, Boscombe Down, DERA, RAE Bedford. Arrived 27-10-18. First ground run 7-2-20	[8]	1-24
❑ ZA612	'074'	Panavia Tornado GR.4	82	ex Winterbourne Gunner, Marham, GR.1. Last flown 21-1-19. Arrived 6-21		1-24
❑ –		HS Hawk SIM	~	ex Pershore, Farnborough. First noted 4-19		4-19
❑ –		Short Tucano	~	front cockpit procedure tnr, 'shark's mouth. First noted 5-21		7-23
❑ 55-4439	'WI'	Lockheed T-33A-1-LO	55	ex Sunderland, Sculthorpe, French AF, USAF 55-4439. Last flown 25-1-78. Arrived 1-20	[9]	1-24
❑ HA580*		Hawker Tempest II	45	ex Haverfordwest, Hemswell, Chichester, Blackbushe, Poona, Indian AF (1-6-48), RAF MW758 n/s. Arrived 26-2-23		1-24
❑ 272*		Westland Lynx SH-14D	79	ex Woodmancote, Gilze-Rijen, Netherlands Navy, G-17-23. Arrived 13-8-22		1-24
❑ 526	25887	Mikoyan-Gurevich MiG-29 *Fulcrum*	~	ex West Walton Highway, Fairford, Sov AF. Crashed 24-7-93. Cockpit, poor state		9-23

■ **[1]** On loan from The Helicopter Museum, Weston-super-Mare. It was built at 'WSM' by Peter Marigold and 'clocked' about 10 flying hours. Enclosed cockpit, 'clamshell' access doors. **[2]** The fuselage of unfinished project G-CLAX graces the cafe. It has been cut in half vertically and both sides have been mounted on the wall, nose to nose. It is best left to the reader to decide if this is still an airframe or 'installation art'! **[3]** Buzzard designed and built by Ernie Sherry. **[4]** *Golf-Victor* was the first 337SGT conversion, maiden flight 24-8-70. It is composed of Boeing C-97 Stratofreighter wings, cockpit, fin/rudder, and new-build fuselage. **[5]** Airframes from Mark Stott. **[6]** *Lima-November* registered to Jon Vivash. Total time 2,456 hours. **[7]** Gnat on loan from Red Gnat Ltd, North Weald. **[8]** ZA326 factoids: first flown 31-3-83 and last flown 13-12-05 by which time it was the last flying GR.1. Donated to the Panavia Tornado Preservation Group by Elliott Atkins – **https://ptpg.org**. **[9]** Part of the National Museum of the USAF's Loan Program.

Lynx 272 settling in to its new home, September 2022. *Ken Ellis*

GJD Services/AeroTech and SWAM restoration and storage: Airframes and cockpits are held away from the publicly accessible ramp and hangar at several sites. Some are in the museum's 'pending tray', others may well be used for spares or exchange. This area is viewable ***only*** by prior arrangement.

Departures: By 2022 the cockpit of HS.125 G-BOCB had moved to the Cardiff, Wales, area: Lynx HMA.8 ZF557, on loan, moved to Woodmancote, W Sussex, during 2020; Sea King HC.4 ZG822 left for Wainfleet, Lincs, 4-10-23. Navajo N477PM arrived from Staverton, Glos, 3-11-22, but moved on again - with no 'forwarding address' - 4-10-23.

❑ G-APSA	Douglas DC-6A	58	ex Baginton, 4W-ABQ, HZ-ADA, G-APSA, CF-MCK, CF-CZY. CoA 23-5-09, de-reg 17-5-21. British Eagle c/s. Arr by 9-21	11-23
❑ G-ARJB*	DH Dove 8	60	ex Cricklade, Little Rissington, Kemble, Cumbernauld, Carlisle, Rocester, East Midlands. CoA 10-12-73. *Exporter*. Fuselage. Arrived 13-12-22	11-23
❑ G-AVFM	HS Trident 2E	69	ex Pershore, Cove, Bristol, BA, BEA. CoA 2-6-84, de-reg 20-3-84. Arrived 16-4-19. Flightdeck	9-21
❑ G-AWMI*	AESL Airtourer 115	68	ex Cardiff-Wales. Glos-Air assembled. CoA 8-5-08, de-reg 7-12-10. Arrived 10-4-22; on loan	11-23
❑ G-AYGB*	Cessna 310Q	70	ex Perth, N7611Q. CoA 23-10-87, de-reg 23-6-94. Arrived 22-7-22	11-23
❑ G-AZHJ	SAL Twin Pioneer 3	59	ex off-site Coventry, Prestwick, Staverton, Prestwick, G-31-16, XP295, Odiham SF, 1310F, Odiham SF, 230. CoA 23-8-90, de-reg 23-7-97. Arrived 11-11-20	9-21
❑ G-BDXG	Boeing 747-236B	78	ex Bruntingthorpe, Hurn, European, Saudia, European, BA. CoA 30-6-06, de-reg 29-3-06. Flightdeck	9-21
❑ G-BDXH	Boeing 747-236B	79	ex Bruntingthorpe, Hurn, Filton, European, BA. Last flight 12-11-04, CoA 13-4-04, de-reg 7-3-06. Flightdeck	9-21
❑ G-CEAG	Boeing 737-229	75	ex Bruntingthorpe, European, SABENA OO-SDL. CoA 14-6-06, de-reg 23-1-09. Flightdeck	9-21
❑ G-CELH*	Boeing 737-330	86	ex Channel Express, Lasham, D-ADXD, TF-ABL, D-ABXD. Last flight 22-10-18, de-reg 11-12-18, arrived 18-7-20. Cockpit	9-23
❑ G-JIBO	BAe Jetstream 3102	86	ex OY-SVJ, G-BTYG, N415MX, G-31-711. CoA 29-4-16	2-23
❑ G-MKCA	Boeing 747-285	80	ex Bruntingthorpe, Kemble, MK Airlines, 9G-MKM. N207BA, Korean HL7454. Last flight 7-8-09, de-reg 30-9-15. Flightdeck	9-21
❑ G-NFLC*	HP Jetstream 1	69	ex Perth, Cranfield, G-AXUI, G-8-9. CoA 3-6-05, de-reg 3-8-04 Arrived 23-6-22	6-22
❑ G-SIXC	Douglas DC-6A/B	58	ex Baginton, 'DC-6 Diner', Air Atlantique, N93459, N90645, B-1006, XW-PFZ, B-1006. CoA 4-4-05, de-reg 2-8-11. Air Atlantique colours. Arrived 5-8-21	11-23
❑ A7-ABX	Airbus A300B4-622	90	ex Bruntingthorpe, Qatar, Korean HL7537, HL7293, F-WWAU. Last flight 19-11-13. Flightdeck	7-23

❑ B-HUE		Boeing 747-467	93	ex Bruntingthorpe, Cathay, VR-HUE. Last flight 5-1-15. Flightdeck, arrived 12-1-19		3-20
❑ CS-TTJ*		Airbus A319-111	99	ex TAP Air Portugal, D-AVYM. Hamburg-built. Flew in 29-9-21, scrapped 2-22. Forward fuselage		2-23
❑ N470AC		Boeing 737-300	90	ex Hurn, HZ-AMC, B-2653, N2332Q, G-OABD, 9V-TRC, OY-MME. Fuselage. Arrived 5-8-20		9-21
❑ N437TH*		BAe Jetstream T.3	85	ex Dunsfold, 'HB-VEM', Manston, Cranwell, ZE441, Culdrose, 750, *Heron* Flt, 750, *Heron* Flt, 750, G-31-667. Arrived 28-4-23		11-23
❑ N747KD		Boeing 747-236F	80	ex Bruntingthorpe, Kemble, Cathay B-HVY, VR-HVY, BA G-KILO. Last flight 29-4-08. Flightdeck		3-20
❑ N858WL		Boeing 737-406	90	ex Bruntingthorpe, KLM PH-BDW. Last flight 16-11-11. Arrived 12-1-19. Cockpit		6-21
❑ SX-OAD		Boeing 747-212B	79	ex Bruntingthorpe, 'G-ASDA', Olympic, 9V-SQI. *Olympic Flame*. Last flown 12-6-02. Flightdeck. Arr 4-2-21		2-21
❑ 'VH-FDT'		DHA Drover II G-APXX	51	ex Horizon, Booker, Lasham, Blackbushe, Southend, Squires Gate, G-APXX (de-reg 26-11-73), VH-EAS	[1]	9-21
❑ VP-BTU*		Airbus A319-114	99	ex Siberia Airlines, N303NB, D-AVWF. Hamburg-built Flew in 26-4-21, scrapped 10-22. Flight deck		9-23
❑ 2-SEVN*		Boeing 727-281	63	ex Lasham, N724YS, N240RC, HL7357, JA8355. Forward fuselage, arrived 27-10-22		9-23
❑ 5U-BAG*		Boeing 737-200	78	ex Lasham, Niger Government. Last flown 11-9-14. Cockpit, arrived 21-11-23		1-24
❑ WF784		Gloster Meteor T.7	51	ex Staverton, Quedgeley, Kemble 7895M (30-11-65), 5 CAACU, CAW, FTU, 130, 26. Arrived 2-9-21		1-22
❑ WJ945*		Vickers Varsity T.1 G-BEDV	53	ex St Mawgan, Duxford G-BEDV (CoA 15-10-87,de-reg 15-6-89), CFS, 5 FTS, AE&AEOS, CFS, 115, 116, 527. Hurn-built		**due**
❑ WJ992		EE Canberra T.4	53	ex Hurn, DRA Bedford, RAE, 76. Avro-built. Cockpit, arrived 9-2-21		5-21
❑ WK126*	'843'	EE Canberra TT.18	54	ex Staverton, Bentham, Staverton, Hucclecote, N2138J, St Athan, FRADU, B.2, 100, 9. SOC 26-10-90. Arr 17-8-22		9-23
❑ WL405		Gloster Meteor T.7	52	ex 'Liverpool', Hooton Park, Bruntingthorpe, Yatesbury, Chalgrove, Martin-Baker, Farnborough, BCCS, 1 GCF, 231 OCU, Wittering SF, JCU, Hemswell CF. SOC 1-4-69. Cockpit. Arrived 23-9-19	[2]	1-22
❑ XL472	'044'	Fairey Gannet AEW.3	59	ex Horizon site, Charlwood, Boscombe Down, 849 'B', HQ, 'A' Flts. SOC 6-12-78	[1]	9-23
❑ XL929		Percival Pembroke C.1 G-BNPU	56	ex Coventry, Shoreham, Sandown, Shawbury, 60, Kemble, 207, SCCS, TCCS, FCCS, BCCS. De-reg 11-8-88. Arr 11-11-20		9-23
❑ XN584	'E' *and* '88'	Hunting Jet Provost T.3A	61	ex Treforest, Bruntingthorpe, Halton 9014M (10-9-90), 1 FTS, CFS, RAFC, CFS, RAFC, TWU, RAFC. Arrived 4-8-21	[3]	11-23
❑ XP150	'18'	Westland Wessex HAS.3	62	ex Moreton-in-Marsh, Lee-on-S' A2764, A2719 (8-8-84), Wroughton, 772, 737, 814, HAS.1, 706. Arrived 22-5-19. Scrapped for spares 9-22; flightdeck		11-23
❑ XS507	'27'	Westland Wessex HU.5	64	ex Higher Purtington, Benson, Gosport, Lee-on-Solent A2674 [2], A2762 (21-3-88), 772, 845, 707, 848, 847, 772, 2 FTS, 772, 707, 846, 845, 707. Arrived 18-5-21		10-23
❑ XV104	'U'	Vickers VC10 C.1K	67	ex Bruntingthorpe, 101, 10. Arrived 26-1-19. Flightdeck	[4]	2-23
❑ XV109	'Z'	Vickers VC10 C.1K	68	ex Bruntingthorpe, 101, 10. Arrived 26-1-19. Cockpit	[4]	2-23
❑ XV254		HS Nimrod MR.2	71	ex Inverness, Kinloss, Kinloss Wing, A&AEE, Kin W, St Mawgan W, 42. Arrived 2-21. Forward fuselage		9-23
❑ XV499	'I'	McD Phantom FGR.2	69	ex Bruntingthorpe, Hixon, Leeming, 74, 19, 228 OCU, 29, 228 OCU, 29, 228 OCU, 23, 19, 92, 41, 228 OCU, 29, 228 OCU, 6, 228 OCU. SOC 5-10-92. Cockpit		3-20
❑ XX263*		HS Hawk T.1A	79	ex Cardiff, Shawbury, 19, Shawbury, T.1, 2 TWU, 1 TWU, . TWU. SOC 11-1-18. Arrived 22-4-22		2-23
❑ XX845*	'EV'	SEPECAT Jaguar T.4	75	ex Predannack, Cosford, St Athan, 6, T.2, 6, 226 OCU, 41, 226 OCU, 14, 17, 2, 20, 17. Last flown 1-6-05. Arr 7-7-22		11-23

Serial	Code	Type	Reg	Year	History	Note	Date
❑ XZ969*		HS Harrier GR.3		80	ex Predannack, Culdrose A2612, Manadon A2610 (24-4-91), St Athan, 4, 1, 3. Arrived 7-7-22		11-23
❑ ZA148*	'G'	Vickers VC10 K.3	N148ZA	67	ex St Mawgan, Brize Norton, 101 Sqn, Srs 1154, Filton, East African A/W 5Y-ADA. Last flight 28-8-13. Cockpit. Arrived 17-11-23		11-23
❑ ZD627	'WO'	Westland Sea King HC.4		84	ex B'thorpe, Gosport, 848, 846, 707. Cockpit. F/n 10-18		3-20
❑ ZE700*		HSA HS.146 CC.2	G-CMFY	84	ex Northolt, 32, QF, G-6-201, ZE700, G-5-07, G-5-02. Hatfield-built. Arrived 17-3-22	[5]	1-23
❑ M25-04		SAL Bulldog 102		72	ex Kemble, R Malaysian AF FM1224. Fuselage. F/n 7-19		9-21
❑ SL-01*		Westland Commando Mk.2C		76	ex Lee-on-Solent, Dunsfold, Sierra Leone, Qatar QA-23, G-17-26. Arrived 1-9-23		11-23

■ **[1]** Airframes from Mark Stott. **[2]** WL405 owned by Jason Holloway. **[3]** The wings of XN584 are fitted to XP627: see Sunderland, N&T. **[4]** The centre fuselage of XV106 is also on show: its cockpit is as Woodford, Gtr Man. **[5]** 50 days after ZE700 made its last ever flight it was registered to Lingfield-based Aircraft Maintenance Services; the paperwork needed to smooth engine and ancillaries sales from a *civilian*, instead of a military airframe.

Horizon Aviation Services: (See introductory notes to SWAM above.) Manages jet warbirds and other types, on behalf of a series of owners: these are not given a formal listing. Only long-term restoration projects or stored airframes are presented. **Mark Stott** has a collection of airframes several of which are with SAWM: Drover 'VH-FDT', Sea Prince T.1 WP321, Gannet AEW.3s XL472 and XL500.

Departures: Sea Price T.1 WF118 to Blackpool, Lancs, 6-6-23; 'JP' T.5A XW436 had moved to the SWAM ramp - above - by 9-22. Gnat T.1 G-FRCE (XS104) was in permit by 12-22 and has been deleted. Strikemaster Mk.80 G-FLYY, in RNZAF colours as 'NZ6300', was flying by 2020 and was re-registered as G-RNAF 1-23. ◆ *Prior arrangement* **only**

Serial	Code	Type	Reg	Year	History	Note	Date
❑ G-AKVF		Chrislea Super Ace		48	ex Dublin, Coventry, Dunsfold, AP-ADT, G-AKVF. CoA 31-5-13. Arrived 3-7-20		7-20
❑ G-AWTS*		Beech Musketeer Sport		69	ex OO-BGN. De-reg 8-7-21		11-23
❑ G-AYIG*		Piper Cherokee 140		70	De-reg 8-6-23		11-23
❑ G-FLSH		Yakovlev Yak-52		87	ex N Weald, RA-44550. IAR Bacau-built. CoA 29-10-10, de-reg 26-3-10. Arrived 20-11-18		9-23
❑ G-JMGP*		Aero L39ZO Albatros		78	ex RA-3537K, Sov AF (?). De-reg 30-9-19		11-23
❑ WV740*		Percival Pembroke C.1	G-BNPH	55	ex Hurn, 27 MU, 60, 21, WCS, MCCFS, MCS, Eastleigh (Kenya) SF, 78, Khormaksar SF, 84, Aden Prot. SF. CoA 31-3-20		11-23
❑ XL954		Percival Pembroke C.1	G-BXES	57	ex Weston, Coventry, N4234C, Tatenhill, W Waltham, 9042M, Northolt, 60, RAFG CS, 2 TAF CS. CoA 4-10-17, de-reg 4-3-21. Arrived 14-12-21		10-21
❑ XV753*		HS Harrier GR.3		69	ex St Mawgan, Predannack, Culdrose A2691[2] (24-4-96), Halton, Abingdon 9075M, St Athan, 233 OCU, 1, GR.1, 3, 233 OCU. Arrived 29-6-23		11-23
❑ XW289	'MU'	BAC Jet Provost T.5A	G-JPVA	71	ex N Weald, Cranfield, G-BVXT, Shawbury, 1 FTS, 3 FTS, RAFC, 1 FTS, RAFC, CFS. CoA 6-1-17, de-reg 4-11-16. Arr 11-16		12-22
❑ XX342		HS Hawk T.1	G-HAWC	81	ex Boscombe Down, ETPS. First noted 7-19	[1]	6-21
❑ XZ440*	'DD40'	HS Sea Harrier F/A.2		79	ex Culdrose, Yeovilton, 800, BAe, FRS.1, 801, 800, A&AEE. Arrived 14-11-23		11-23
❑ ZB603*	'DDT03'	HS Harrier T.8		83	ex Culdrose, St Athan, 899, 233 OCU. Arrived 5-1-24		1-24
❑ ZD579*	'DD79'	HS Sea Harrier F/A.2		85	ex Culdrose, Shawbury, Yeovilton, 800, 801, 800, 801, 899, FRS.1, 800, 801, 800, A&AEE, 801, 899, 800, 899. Arrived 28-11-23		1-24
❑ ZD990	'DDT90'	HS Harrier T.8	G-RNTB	87	ex Culdrose, St Athan, 899, T.8, 20, 3, T.4. Arrived 15-8-17	[2]	6-21
❑ ZE690*	'DD90'	HS Sea Harrier F/A.2		87	ex Culdrose, Yeovilton, 801, 899, 801, 800, 801, 800, 801, 899, FRS.1, 899. Arrived 7-11-23		11-23
❑ ZE692*	'DD92'	HS Sea Harrier F/A.2		87	ex Culdrose, Yeovilton, 899, 801, 899, 800, 801, 899, 801, 899, FRS.1, 801, 899. Arrived 21-11-23		11-23
❑ ZH797*	'DD97'	HS Sea Harrier F/A.2		95	ex Culdrose, Yeovilton, 801, 899. Arrived 27-10-23		11-23
❑ ZH802*	'DD02'	HS Sea Harrier F/A.2		96	ex Culdrose, Yeovilton, 899, 800, 899, 800, 801. Arrived 27-10-23		11-23
❑ ZH803	'DD03'	HS Sea Harrier F/A.2	G-RNFA	96	ex Culdrose, Shawbury, Yeovilton, 801, 800. Arrived 8-8-17	[2]	11-21

❑ ZH813* 'DD13'	HS Sea Harrier F/A.2		99	ex Culdrose, Shawbury, Yeovilton, 801, DERA. Arr 19-12-23	12-23
❑ A23-005*	Pilatus PC-9/A		87	ex RAAF. HDH-assembled. Arrived 2021	11-23
❑ A23-013*	Pilatus PC-9/A	G-SBST	87	ex RAAF. HDH-assembled. Arrived 2021	11-23
❑ A23-033*	Pilatus PC-9/A	N625PC	89	ex RAAF. HDH-built. Arrived 6-20	11-23
❑ A23-051*	Pilatus PC-9/A		89	ex RAAF. HDH-built. Arrived 2022	11-23

■ **[1]** Registered to L39 Aviation Ltd. **[2]** Registered to Fly Harrier Ltd.

MoD Saint Athan: (*W&R* will continue to call it St Athan!) Operating as an enclave within the Welsh Government-owned site is **4 School of Technical Training** - formed here on 1st September 1938.

❑ VN-A190	Boeing 737-4H6	94	ex Kemble, Jet Star Pacific, Malaysian 9M-MQJ. Arrived 6-13. Training airframe	6-20
❑ 'JP098'	Eurofighter Typhoon EMU	~	dumped out on the East Camp. First noted 7-11	6-19

Airliner parting out: Both **GJD Services** and **GJD AeroTech** – see narrative for the South Wales Aviation Museum, above - and **eCube Solutions** have extensive facilities and operations at St Athan, storing, decommissioning and recycling jetliners. This work is relatively rapid and beyond the scope of *W&R*: long-terms only a noted. Boeing 767 ZS-DJI succumbed to the axe by late 2020. With eCube, scrapping of Boeing 747 G-BYGC began on 16th August 2023 and by October it had been reduced to rubble.◆ **Strictly** *by prior arrangement* **only**

❑ ER-AXV*	Airbus A320-211	96	ex Air Moldova, VH-HYR. Toulouse-built. Arr 29-11-19	1-24

Cardiff University: A Jetstream has been acquired as a static test-bed for hydrogen/electric propulsion research under Project 'Dragonfly'. ◆ **Strictly** *prior arrangement* **only**

❑ G-NFLA*	BAe Jetstream 3102	84	ex Cranfield. G-BRGN, G-BLHC, G-31-637. CoA 21-8-21. Ferried in 15-4-23	11-23

Happy Jakes Touring Caravan Park: At Flemingston, just north of the SWAM site.
◆ *Prior arrangement* **only** | **www.happyjakes.wales**

❑ G-CONY	BAe Jetstream 3101	87	ex SWAM, N22746, N331QE, G-31-745. De-reg 27-2-17. Fuselage. First noted 6-20	10-23

SEALAND on the A494 north of Queensferry

Defence Electronics and Components Agency: The former RAF Sealand has a GR.4 as a 'guardian'.

❑ ZA607 'EB-X'	Panavia Tornado GR.4	82	ex Marham, 41/FJWOEU, GR.1, 9. Arrived 18-2-19, unveiled 22-2-19	11-23

SWANSEA

National Waterfront Museum: Part of the National Museum of Wales. ◆ *Oystermouth Road, SA1 3RD* | **0300 1112333** | **waterfront@museumwales.ac.uk** | **https://museum.wales/swansea/**

❑ –	Watkins CHW	1909	BAPC.47, ex Nantgarw, Cardiff, St Athan, Cardiff. *Robin Goch*	[1]	1-24

■ **[1]** Single-seat monoplane designed and built by C H Watkins at Maendy, Cardiff, 1907-1909. Fitted with a 40hp 3-cylinder also designed by Watkins. Claimed to have made its first hop in 1909, a cross-country in 1910 and flown extensively until 1916.

SWANSEA AIRPORT or Fairwood Common EGFH

Tempest II HA580 was briefly here – first noted June 2022 – before moving on to St Athan, Wales, on 23rd February 2023.

❑ 'G-STNR'	Aero L29 Delfin	RA-01611	~	ex St Athan, Germany, Sov AF. 'Tiger' colours Arrived 7-15, displayed	[1]	8-23

■ **[1]** The *real* G-STNR is a Yak-52 - see Henstridge, Somerset.

TALGARTH AERODROME east of the A479 south of the town

Black Mountains Gliding Club: ◆ *Prior arrangement* **only** | **www.blackmountainsgliding.co.uk**

❑ G-BLDG	Piper Pawnee 235	68	ex Rufforth, SE-FLB, LN-VYM. CoA 4-9-15. Arrived 30-10-19	N2-21

TREFOREST on the A473 southeast of Pontypridd

University of South Wales: The Jetstream is *believed* to be still ensconced in the purpose-built Aerospace Centre at the Faculty of Advanced Technology. ◆ *Prior arrangement* **only** | **www.southwales.ac.uk**

❑ G-JXTC	BAe Jetstream 31	86	ex Eindhoven, PH-KJG, G-JXTC, G-LOGT, G-BSFH, PH-KJG, G-31-690. De-reg 7-10-11	4-12

VALLEY AIRFIELD south of the A5, southeast of Holyhead EGOV

RAF Valley: The resident Babcock-run Aircraft Maintenance and Repair Organisation (AMRO) is handling the now dwindling Hawk reduce to produce (RTP) programme, although it is doubted airframes will endure here long. As predicted in *W&R28* (p308) Hawk T.1A XX157 which had been rejected for rework for the 'Reds' joined the RTP programme by August 2022. The hulks of several airframes (eg XX157 and XX332) were dispatched to Skegness-based disposal specialist RAMCO in late 2022. A wholly 'synthetic' Hawk training aid is on the dump.

❑ XX156		HS Hawk T.1	75	ex CFS, 19, DTEO/DRA, A&AEE, RAE, HS, A&AEE. SOC 10-7-17. Displayed from 29-8-18	[1]	1-24
❑ XX161*		HS Hawk T.1	76	ex Culdrose, 19, 234, 'Red Arrows', 4 FTS, CFS, 4 FTS, CFS. Arrived 26-10-22. Instructional		1-24

■ **[1]** Second prototype Hawk, first flown at Dunsfold 19-5-75.

WELSHPOOL on the A483 west of Shrewsbury

Military Aircraft Cockpit Collection: Run by Sue and Roy Jerman. ◆ **Private** *collection, prior arrangement* **only**

❑ WH775		EE Canberra PR.7	54	ex Bruntingthorpe, Cosford 8868M/8128M (11-3-71), 100, 13, 31, 17, 31, 13, 82, makers. Cockpit		12-19
❑ WK102		EE Canberra T.17	54	ex Bruntingthorpe, Cosford 8780M, 360, B.2, 45, RNZAF, 207. SOC 18-2-83. Avro-built. Cockpit		12-19
❑ XJ758		Westland Whirlwind HAR.10	56	ex Oswestry, Shrewsbury, Shawbury, Ternhill 8464M (10-2-76), Wroughton, CFS, 230, CFS, HAR.2, 217, 1360F, 22. Cockpit	[1]	12-19
❑ XM652		Avro Vulcan B.2	64	ex Burntwood, Sheffield, Waddington, 50, Wadd Wing, Cott Wing. SOC 20-2-84. Cockpit		12-19
❑ XM692		Folland Gnat T.1	60	ex S Molton, East Tilbury, Boscombe D', Robertsbridge, Salisbury, Southampton, Fareham, Foulness, A&AEE. SOC 28-3-69. Forward cockpit		3-13
❑ XS923	'BE'	EE Lightning F.6	66	ex Bruntingthorpe, Cranfield, Binbrook, 11, LTF, 5-11 pool. SOC 24-6-88. Cockpit		12-19
❑ XT277		Blackburn Buccaneer S.2B	65	ex Bruntingthorpe, Cosford 8853M (21-5-85), Shawbury, 237 OCU, 12, 800, 809, 801. Cockpit		12-19
❑ XZ356	'FU'	SEPECAT Jaguar GR.3A	76	ex Ipswich, St Athan, 41, SAOEU, 54, GR.1, Shawbury, 6, Gulf Det, 41, 14, 17, 41		12-19
❑ XZ993*	'M'	HS Harrier GR.3	81	ex Upwood, Selby, Welshpool, St Athan 9240M (25-7-94), Laarbruch,St Athan, 4, 1, 1453 Flt, 3. Cockpit. Arrived 28-4-17		12-19

■ **[1]** Whirlwind cockpit is on loan from Dave Higgins - see also Norwich, Norfolk.

Also: Based locally is a Robinson R22 used as a travelling fund-raiser for the Wales Air Ambulance.

❑ G-GDAY		Robinson R22 Beta	87	ex Squires Gate. Crashed 24-4-99, de-reg 28-9-19. Red scheme, trailer-mounted		4-23

WREXHAM 'JP' T.4 XP585 moved to Hawarden, Wales, on 13th August 2023.

YSTRAD MYNACH on the A469 south of Pontllanfraith

Coleg y Cymoedd: The Jetstream is *believed* to still serve. ◆ *Prior arrangement* **only** | **www.cymoedd.ac.uk**

❑ –	G-ATXJ	HP Jetstream 41 EMU	67	ex Rhoose, Luton, G-ATXJ, HP. CoA 8-2-71, de-reg 11-4-72. Fuselage. 'Ystrad Mynach Airways' titles		3-10

■ **[1]** Jetstream factoids: Based on G-ATXJ, the third prototype; first flying 28-12-67. Became the Srs 200/300 prototype: maiden flight 16-12-69. Last flight 5-3-70, total time 636 hours. Was an exhibit with the former Wales Aircraft Museum.

CHANNEL ISLANDS

The Islands are self-governing British Crown Dependencies - part of the British Isles, but not part of the United Kingdom

ALDERNEY AIRPORT

EGJA

❑ G-ASHV	Piper Aztec 250B	63	ex Guernsey, N5281Y. CoA 22-7-85, de-reg 20-6-88. Rescue trainer	11-19
❑ G-BDTN	BN Trislander	76	ex Guernsey, Aurigny, S7-AAN, VQ-SAN, G-BDTN. CoA 10-6-98, de-reg 5-1-11. Rescue trainer	11-19

GUERNSEY

Mark Hollingsworth: Is restoring the front 21ft of a Herald.

❑ G-BAZJ	HP Herald 209	74	ex airport, Air UK, 4X-AHR, G-8-1. CoA 24-11-84, de-reg 4-1-85. Forward fuselage	1-20

Oatlands Visitor Centre: At St Sampsons, within Oatey and Joey's Playbarn is the dramatically posed Trislander. Grub's good at the café too! | **www.oatlands.gg**

❑ G-JOEY	BN Trislander	75	ex airport, Aurigny, G-BDGG, C-GSAA, G-BDGG. FBN-built. Last service 28-6-14. De-reg 19-10-16. Arrived 10-4-18	9-23

Others: Some references are long-in-the-tooth but *believed* current. Each is held at a different *private* venue.

❑ G-ATEP	EAA Biplane	67	CoA 18-6-73, de-reg 14-7-86	5-03
❑ G-ATHN	Nord Noralpha	48	ex F-BFUZ, Fr mil No.84. CoA 27-6-75, de-reg 16-12-91	1-20
❑ G-FTSE	BN Trislander	77	ex airport, Aurigny, G-BEPI. Fairey BN-built. Crashed 17-1-11, de-reg 14-8-14. Forward fuselage, trailer-mounted	9-23
❑ 5N-AHN	Bell JetRanger	68	ex Bristow, G-AWFV. Forward fuselage - sim	5-11

GUERNSEY AIRPORT

EGJB

❑ G-BDTO	BN Trislander	76	ex Aurigny, G-RBSI, G-OTSB, G-BDTO, 8P-ASC, G-BDTO, C-GYOX, G-BDTO. De-reg 10-2-17. Rescue trainer	9-23
❑ N97121	Embraer Bandeirante	~	ex City-Link, PT-SDK. Rescue trainer	1-20
❑ XM409	Hunting Jet Provost T.3	60	ex Firbeck, Moreton-in-Marsh, Halton 8082M (13-5-70), Shawbury, 2 FTS. Cockpit	4-23

JERSEY AIRPORT

EGJJ

The Heron is a project with the **Jersey Airlines Duchess of Brittany Heritage Group**. The 'JP' *should* still serve the fire crews.

❑ G-AORG	DH Sea Heron C.1	56	ex Coventry, XR441, *Heron* Flt, 781, G-AORG, G-5-16. Jersey Airlines c/s, *Duchess of Brittany*. CoA 24-7-19	9-21
❑ XP573	Hunting Jet Provost T.4	62	ex Halton 8336M (21-3-73), '8236M', Kemble, Shawbury, R-R, 1 FTS, CFS. Rescue trainer	9-18

Guernsey-based Trislander G-FTSI visiting Jersey, September 2023. *Dave Murray*

NORTHERN IRELAND

ANTRIM on the M22 northwest of Belfast

At a *private* location in the *general* area David and Matthew McCullough have the cockpit of a tri-gear Europa mounted on a gimbal – Link Trainer fashion.

❑ G-TAGR		Shaw Europa XS	04	crashed 19-4-14, de-reg 27-11-15. Cockpit, NASA colours	12-21

ARMAGH, or Woodview, on the A3 / A28 northwest of Newry

Airframes held at a *private* location in the *general* area. Jodel D.112 G-ARDO has been deleted.

❑ G-APXR		Piper Tri-Pacer 160	60	CoA 31-3-11	9-22
❑ G-AREV*		Piper Tri-Pacer 160	58	ex N9628D. De-reg 11-1-19. First noted 9-22	9-22
❑ G-MCCY*		Yakovlev Yak-52	90	ex LY-AQF. ICA Bacau-built. CoA 20-11-08. First noted 9-22	11-23

AUGHNACLOY at the A5/A28 junction, north of Monaghan

AWOL Outdoor Adventure: ◆ *Prior arrangement* **only | www.awolpaintball.ie**

❑ EI-BDK		MS Rallye Club 100ST		ex Abbeyshrule, F-BXMZ. De-reg 25-11-08	8-14

BALLYMAGORRY on the N14 northwest of Strabane

A long out-of-use microlight lingers in the area.

❑ G-MTCZ		Solar Wings Tri-Pacer 250	r87	de-reg 3-8-94	1-20

BALLYMONEY on the A26 southeast of Coleraine

A yard in the area *might* still hold a Sierra.

❑ G-BBSC		Beech Sierra 200	73	ex Aldergrove. Damaged 4-12-97, de-reg 27-7-01. Fuselage	7-19

BANNFOOT northwest of Craigavon

Clearing up *W&R28* (p310), Rallye G-BDWA "went south", but the FRED is still present at a *private* location.

❑ G-PFAL		Clutton FRED II	81	CoA 27-7-88, de-reg 12-10-10	9-22

BELFAST

Crumlin Road Gaol: Known as 'The Crum', the website boasts it was the scene of umpteen executions, less gory attractions include a Wessex. ◆ *Crumlin Road, BT14 6ST* | **info@crumlinroadgaol.com** | **www.crumlinroadgaol.com**

❑ XR529	'E'	Westland Wessex HC.2	64	ex Aldergrove 9268M, 72, SARTU, 2 FTS, 18, 78, 72. Arrived 15-1-19	4-22

BELFAST AIRPORT or Aldergrove

EGAA

❑ G-AVFE		HS Trident 2E	67	ex BA, BEA. CoA 6-5-85, de-reg 20-3-85. Rescue trainer, forward fuselage by 11-19	11-23
❑ PH-PTD		Piper Navajo 350	78	ex Quick Airways, N27583. Fuselage, rescue trainer	11-19
❑ XT456	'XZ'	Westland Wessex HU.5	65	ex 8941M (11-11-87), Wroughton, Yeovilton, Wroughton, 845, 847, 846, 845, 707. Rescue trainer	11-23

Joint Helicopter Command Flying Station Aldergrove. Cockpits XE643 and XR700 moved to Long Kesh, N Ireland.

❑ XX443	'Y'	Sud Gazelle AH.1	76	ex Gosport, M Wallop, 658, 662, 663, 3 Regt, 669, 659. Westland-built. Crashed 28-9-97. Displayed, first noted 3-17	11-23

Also: Close to the airport, a *private* collector *should* have a Vampire cockpit.

❑ XD525		DH Vampire T.11	54	ex Belfast, Holywood, Belfast, Aldergrove 7882M (8-4-65), 1 FTS, 4 FTS, 5 FTS, 7 FTS. Christchurch-built. Cockpit	2-14

BELLARENA AERODROME north of Limavady

In June 2023 Kirby Kite BGA.327 returned to its owner in Bedfordshire.

❑ G-ARAP	Champion 7EC Traveler	60	ex Londonderry, Eglinton. Cr 22-9-81, de-reg 30-5-84	7-21
❑ ALA*	Short Nimbus I	47	BGA.470, ex Holywood, Bishop's Stortford, Duxford. CoA 8-75. First noted 6-23	6-23
❑ XA225	Slingsby Grasshopper TX.1	53	ex Lasham, Odiham, Keevil, Upavon, Keevil, Petersfield	9-23

BROUGHSHANE, on the A42, northeast of Ballymena

❑ G-MZGB	Cyclone AX2000	97	ex Blackhill. CoA 19-5-08, de-reg 6-11-15	12-21

CAUSEWAY AERODROME near Aghadowey, south of Coleraine

❑ G-BASO	Lake LA-4-180	67	ex Londonderry, N2025L. CoA 19-6-06	1-23
❑ G-BOLL	Lake LA-4-180	64	ex EI-ANR, N1133L. CoA 29-8-18	1-23
❑ G-BVRY	Cyclone AX3/582	95	crashed 9-7-98. CoA 2-3-99, de-reg 21-11-02	1-23
❑ N216HK	CGS Hawk Arrow	r92	G-MWYP, de-reg 9-2-93	1-23
❑ N217HK	CGS Hawk Arrow	r92	G-MWYR, de-reg 9-2-93	1-23

DUNGANNON on the A29 between Cookstown and Armagh

The 337 'pod' was written out of *W&R28* (p311) as last noted in July 2013. It lives on; it has had a respray to red and white and gained helicopter-ish rotors.

❑ G-AVJG	Cessna 337B	67	ex N2415S. CoA 31-5-92, de-reg 30-7-96. See notes above	11-22

ENNISKILLEN Rallye EI-BBI was auctioned on 3rd March 2022 and moved on – no 'forwarding address'.

ENNISKILLEN AERODROME or St Angelo EGAB

Reference the 'rules of engagement' given on page 7, R44 G-SWAT has been deleted.

❑ EI-AVC	Cessna F.337F	~	ex Dungannon, Castlerock, Abbeyshrule, N4757. Reims-built. De-reg 26-6-03. Rescue trainer	2-20

FINTONA on the B46 / B122 south of Omagh

❑ G-BMYF	Bensen B-8M	86	de-reg 6-4-09	10-18

FIVEMILETOWN on the A4 east of Enniskillen

Blessingbourne Carriage and Costume Museum: Within the Blessingbourne Estate.

◆ *Prior appointment* **only** | *Tyrone, BT75 0QS* | **info@blessingbourne.com** | **www.blessingbourne.com**

❑ XT208	Bell Sioux AH.1	66	ex Sek Kong, 656. Ditched 16-3-72, cabin	[1]	5-23
❑ XW795	Westland Scout AH.1	72	ex M Wallop, Almondbank, Wroughton, 659, 655, 669		5-23

■ **[1]** A door opened in flight while low over Tolo Harbour, Hong Kong. Distracted while closing the door, the chopper struck the water.

GILFORD on the A51 north of Newry

Two airframes are stored at a *private* house in the *general* area.

❑ G-BKAF	Clutton FRED Srs II	83	CoA 30-5-97, de-reg 8-9-22	6-21
❑ EI-AUT	Forney F.1A Aircoupe	60	ex Bannfoot, Cork, G-ARXS, D-EBSA, N3037G. De-reg 27-5-11	6-21

GLENGORMLEY on the A6 north of Belfast

Scrapyard Golf: The website declares: "Probably the worlds [sic] craziest indoor golf adventure..." Two substantial airframes, and the wings from Rallyes EI-BBJ (see Dunshaughlin, Ireland) and EI-BMB, are among the bizarre obstacles. Fear not, there are also regular selfie points. ◆ **www.scrapyardgolf.co.uk**

❑ EI-BSO*	Piper Cherokee 140	~	ex Craddenstown, C-GOBL, N8241W. Fuselage	7-22
❑ G-MZEV*	Mainair Rapier	97	ex Newtownards. De-reg 25-11-21	7-22

HOLYWOOD on the A2 east of Belfast

Ulster Transport Museum: Part of National Museums NI, the transport element is co-located with the **Ulster Folk Museum**, on either side of the A2 Belfast to Bangor road. Time really should be taken to visit *both*. The Transport Museum is on the banks of Belfast Lough and a series of halls take the visitor through railways, buses, trams, cars, horse-drawn vehicles, shipping models, a special *Titanic* exhibition and then the small, but pleasing, aviation section.

Sealand G-AKLW and McCandless G-ATXX had been moved to the storage site – see below – by September 2023.

◆ *Cultra Manor, Holywood, BT18 0EU* | **028 90428428** | **email** via website | **www.nmni.com/uftm**

	Reg	Type	Year	Details	Note	Noted
❑	G-BKMW	Short Sherpa	82	ex Belfast City, CoA 14-9-90, de-reg 14-11-96. Cockpit		1-24
❑	G-BREL	Cameron O-77 HAB	78	de-reg 12-10-98. Basket. First noted 11-18		1-24
❑	XG905	Short SC.1	57	ex Sydenham, Thurleigh, BLEU, RAE. Acquired 20-5-74	[1]	1-24
❑	–	Ferguson Mono replica	73	IAHC.6, ex Dublin. Acquired 4-5-76		1-24

■ **[1]** XG905 made the type's first full transition from vertical to horizontal flight at Thurleigh 6-4-60. It crashed fatally following an autostabilsation failure at Sydenham 2-10-63. It was rebuilt and flying again in 1966.

Deep storage sites: ***not*** available for inspection. Last noted in December 2018, Short Nimbus BGA.470 had moved to Bellarena, N Ireland, by June 2023.

	Reg	Type	Year	Details	Note	Noted
❑	G-AJOC	Miles Messenger 2A	47	ex East Fortune, Strathallan, Dunottar, U-9. CoA 18-5-72, de-reg 5-1-82	[1]	9-23
❑	G-AKEL	Miles Gemini 1A	47	ex Kilbrittain Castle. CoA 29-4-72, de-reg 30-5-84. Cockpit, wings, tailplane	[2]	9-23
❑	G-AKLW	Short Sealand 1	51	ex USA, Jeddah, Saudi AF, SU-AHY, G-AKLW. Acquired 8-86		9-23
❑	G-ALCS	Miles Gemini 3	47	ex 'Limerick', Kilbrittain Castle. CoA 30-11-72, de-reg 30-5-84. Cockpit and wing stubs.		12-18
❑	G-AOUR	DH Tiger Moth	43	ex Belfast, NL898, 15 EFTS. Morris -built. Crashed 6-6-65, de-reg 8-7-65		9-23
❑	G-ARTZ (1)	McCandless M2	66	ex Killough	[3]	9-23
❑	G-ATXX	McCandless M4	68	ex Killough. De-reg 9-9-70. Acquired 1987		9-23
❑	–	Ferguson Mono replica	75	IAHC.9, ex Belfast Airport, Holywood. Off-site		9-23
❑	VH-UUP	Short Scion I	34	ex East Fortune, Strathallan, G-ACUX, VH-UUP, G-ACUX		9-23

■ **[1]** Built at the Miles plant at Newtownards, N Ireland. **[2]** As well as G-AKEL, the rear fuselage and tail 'feathers' of G-AKGE - see under Dromod, Ireland - are held. **[3]** Registration G-ARTZ has been used twice, both times on Rex McCandless' products. The second candidate was last recorded at St Merryn, Cornwall.

KILKEEL on the A2 east of Newry and Warrenpoint

	Reg	Type	Year	Details	Note	Noted
❑	G-BYTA	Kolb Twinstar Mk.3	00	crashed 16-11-07, CoA 14-2-08, de-reg 21-3-11		12-21

LETTERKENNY on the N56, west of Londonderry

A collection of microlights is *believed* extant in the area at a *private* address.

	Reg	Type	Year	Details	Note	Noted
❑	G-MBWL	Huntair Pathfinder 1	r84	de-reg 6-1-93		1-16
❑	G-MJBT	Eipper Quicksilver	~	de-reg 24-1-95		3-17
❑	G-MVXW	Rans Coyote	90	ex Frosses. CoA 14-9-06, de-reg 6-2-07	[1]	12-16
❑	G-MZFI	Lorimer Iolaire	97	de-reg 25-3-09		3-17

■ **[1]** The Coyote was de-registered as sold in Ireland.

Others: A local scrapyard has/had a Rallye.

	Reg	Type	Year	Details	Note	Noted
❑	EI-AWU	MS Rallye Club	67	ex Rosnakill, G-AVIM. De-reg 27-6-08		2-19

LISBELLAW Whittaker G-BUOA has been deleted.

LONDONDERRY / DERRY

Greater Shantallow Community Arts at Studio2: On the Skegoe Industrial Estate, *may* keep an AA-5 as a travelling exhibit.

◆ *Prior arrangement* **only**

	Reg	Type	Year	Details	Note	Noted
❑	EI-BNR	American AA-5A	r83	ex Abbeyshrule, N9992Q, CS-AHM. Crashed 21-2-88		6-19

Oakfire Adventures: ◆ *Prior arrangement* **only** | **www.oakfireadventures.com**

	Reg	Type	Year	Details	Note	Noted
❑	G-BFWK	Piper Warrior 161	78	ex Belfast, N9589N. CoA 8-12-99, de-reg 26-5-98		1-24

LONDONDERRY AIRPORT or Eglinton, on the A2 east of Londonderry EGAE

	Reg	Type	Year	Details	Note	Noted
❑	G-BWWX	Yakovlev Yak-50	85	ex LY-AOI, Sov AF. CoA 11-6-09, de-reg 4-2-15		9-23
❑	EI-DIF	Piper Navajo 350	77	ex G-OAMT, G-BXKS, N350RC, EC-EBN, N27230		12-19

Jaguar GR.1 XZ389 arriving at Long Kesh, 19th November 2023. *Ian Thompson*

LONG KESH west of Lisburn, close to J7 of the M1

Ulster Aviation Society Heritage Collection (UAS). With the sub-title 'Where History has Wings', the collection continues to grow and mature and truly deserves *national* status. The team conducts a vigorous outreach policy and is engaged in an extensive restoration programme. The ejection seat test-bed's arrival is very relevant: Martin-Baker's trials centre is at Langford Ledge, near Crumlin. Major refurbishment of the hangars, and the expected arrival of *three more complete aircraft* in early 2024, has meant that some airframes have been placed in external store as a temporary arrangement until 2026/2027 when those involved will return indoors.

Hawk T.1A XX286 arrived from Shawbury on 30th July 2022. Lovely machine but with great respect, not a 'Red'. The offer of the former 'Red Arrows' XX260 was too good to refuse and XX286 was offered for auction via the Froghall, Staffs-based Agility website in May 2023. Local transport contractor Beers Heavy Recovery stepped in and acquired it, donating it *back* to UAS. In another refreshing UAS initiative, XX286 will be used for a 'work experience' programme.

One-off abbreviation for this section: LL = Langford Lodge, the collection's previous home.

Air and Space 18A EI-CNG was due to be returned to its owner at the end of its loan agreement in early 2024.

◆ *Maze Long Kesh, Halftown Road, BT27 5RF.* **Only** *available on pre-arranged basis* – **bookvisit@ulsteraviationSociety.org** | **hello@ulsteraviationsociety.org** | **www.ulsteraviationsociety.org**

❑	G-AVCS	Beagle Terrier 1	52	ex Lisburn, Auster AOP.6 WJ363, Odiham SF, AAC, 1900 Flt. Crashed 18-10-81, de-reg 3-4-89. Arrived 8-7-17		1-24
❑	G-BDBS	Short 330	75	ex LL, Belfast City, Short, G-14-3001. CoA 2-9-92, de-reg 1-7-93. Acquired 7-4-93		1-24
❑	G-BEHX	Evans VP-2	81	ex Coalisland. CoA 22-1-90, de-reg 16-12-02. *Ulster Flyer.* Arrived 5-6-16		1-24
❑	G-BNZR	Clutton FRED II	91	ex Belfast. CoA 25-5-99, de-reg 11-8-10. Acquired 31-5-10		1-24
❑	G-BTUC	Embraer Tucano	83	ex LL, Belfast City, Short, G-14-007, PP-ZTC. CoA 20-8-91, de-reg 20-12-96. Acquired 16-1-01		1-24
❑	G-CDUX	Piper Cherokee Six	73	ex Newtownards, EC-DUX. De-reg 29-1-15, crashed 6-6-14. Fuselage. Arrived 21-11-17		1-24
❑	G-CJEN	Ferguson Mono rep	16	built at Long Kesh. Flown 5-16, de-reg 1-6-16. Handed over 28-9-16	[1]	1-24
❑	G-MBJV	Rotec Rally 2B	r82	ex Armagh. De-reg 13-6-90. Arrived 12-10-13	[2]	1-24
❑	G-MJWS	Eurowing Goldwing	r83	ex LL, Newtownards. De-reg 23-6-97. Acquired 29-7-00	[3]	1-24
❑	G-MZHM	Team Hi-Max 1700	97	CoA 26-10-06. Acquired 13-9-07	[4]	1-24
❑	G-RENT	Robinson R22	88	ex LL, Newtownards, N2635M. Damaged 30-9-92, de-reg 11-12-03. Acquired 28-2-03	[5]	1-24
❑	G-TANK	Cameron N-90 HAB	95	CoA 28-5-14, de-reg 25-5-16. *DFDS Hoyer*	[6]	1-24
❑	G-14-1	Short SB.4 Sherpa	53	ex Flixton, Rochester, Duxford, Staverton, Bristol, G-36-1, Cranfield, G-14-1. Fuselage, replica wings. Arrived 16-7-08, acquired 10-12		1-24

Reg		Type	Yr	History	Note	Date
❑ EVN		Monnett Monerai	r85	ex Bellarena, BGA.2988. CoA 6-11-88. Arrived 15-3-17	[7]	1-24
❑ –		Mignet HM.14 'Flea'	35	ex Moneymore. Fuselage, arrived 1-18. Stored	[8]	1-24
❑ –		Chargus Cyclone	79	BAPC.263, ex LL, Ballyclare. Last flight 4-4-88. Acquired 11-94		1-24
❑ –		Eipper Quicksilver	80	arrived 18-2-12. Ross's (mineral water) logos	[9]	1-24
❑ –		Rogallo hang glider	77	BAPC.266, ex LL Last flown 1978, acquired 2-00		1-24
❑ 'NI-UAS'		Aerosport Scamp	~	arrived 31-8-13	[10]	1-24
❑ –		Hapi Cygnet SF-2A	~	unassembled, in kit form. Arrived 31-8-13	[11]	1-24
❑ –*	TA-05	Learjet 75	c94	ex Sydenham. Bombardier-built test fuselage. Arrived 26-3-22	[12]	1-24
❑ –		Short Tucano EMU	c86	ex Sydenham. Acquired 1-12. Stored		1-24
❑ EI-BUO		Aero Composites Sea Hawker	87	ex LL, Newtownards. Ditched Strangford Lough 9-91. Acquired 1998. Stored	[13]	1-24
❑ N80BA		Pitts S-1A	~	ex Killinchy, Newtownards. Cr 7-11-99. Arr by 9-13. Stored		1-24
❑ 'P7823'	'FT-M'	V-S Spitfire FSM	13	BAPC.369, ex 'P7895', Seaton Burn, Linton-on-Ouse. GB Replicas-built. Arrived 21-12-13. 504 Sqn colours, *Belfast Telegraph – Down*		1-24
❑ HB612		Fairchild Argus II G-AJSN	43	ex Dromore, Cork, HB612, ATA, 43-14885. Dam 10-6-67, de-reg 12-3-73. Arrived 3-3-12		1-24
❑ JV482	'S-C'	Grumman Wildcat V	44	ex LL, Newtownards, Castlereagh, Lough Beg, 882. Crashed 24-12-44. Acquired 30-4-84		1-24
❑ VP957		DH Devon C.2/2	48	ex Lisburn, Bishop's Court 8822M, Belfast, Northolt, 207, 21, C.1, WCS, SCS, NCS, SCS, WCS, SCS, Andover SF, 38 GCF, AAFCE, 2 TAF CS, BAFO CS. Last flown 4-7-84. Cockpit. Arrived 2-14		1-24
❑ WA634*		Gloster Meteor T.7(mod)	49	ex Cosford, St Athan, Martin-Baker. Arrived 9-12-22		1-24
❑ WF122	'575'	Percival Sea Prince T.1	51	ex Doncaster, Bruntingthorpe, Helston, Culdrose A2673 (5-2-79), 750, Sydenham SF, Arbroath SF, Lossiemouth SF, 700Z Flt, Lossiemouth SF, FOFT, 750, Eglinton SF, 744. Arrived 13-10-17. Sydenham SF colours		1-24
❑ WF911	'CO'	EE Canberra B.2	52	ex Alveley, Gloucester, Hooton Park, Charnock Richard, Bacup, Preston, Samlesbury, G-27-161, 231 OCU. SOC 21-5-69. Arrived 19-10-13. Cockpit, stored		1-24
❑ WN108	'033'	Hawker Sea Hawk FB.3	54	ex LL, Sydenham, Hurn, FRU, 806, 895, 897, 800. SOC 26-9-63, acquired 17-10-89		1-24
❑ WZ549	'F'	DH Vampire T.11	53	ex LL, Sydenham, Coningsby, Tattershall, Coningsby 8118M (last flight 19-12-70), CATCS, 1 FTS, 8 FTS, FTU, C(A). Christchurch-built. Acquired 10-91		1-24
❑ XA460	'768'	Fairey Gannet AS.4	56	ex Doncaster, Connah's Quay, Brawdy, Gannet Supp Unit, 849, AS.4, 831, ECM.6, 849, AS.4. SOC 10-2-71, Last flight 22-1-71. Arrived 29-12-11		1-24
❑ XE643*		Hawker Hunter FGA.9	56	ex Aldergrove, Abingdon 8586M, 208, F.6, 56, 63, 66, 92. Crashed 9-12-61. Cockpit, stored		1-24
❑ XH131		EE Canberra PR.9	59	ex Kemble, Marham, 39, 1 PRU, 39, 13, 39, MoA. Short-built. Last flight 31-7-06, acquired 13-12-10		1-24
❑ XJ918* *and* 8190M		Bristol Sycamore HR.14	56	ex Cosford (museum) and 2 SoTT 8190M (15-12-71), 32, MCS, Kemble, Wroughton, 110, Seletar, A&AEE, 275. Oldmixon-built. Arrived 9-12-22		1-24
❑ XM414	'101'	Hunting Jet Provost T.3A	60	ex LL, Dundonald, Binbrook, Colsterworth, Halton 8996M (10-4-89), 7 FTS, RAFC, 1 FTS, RAFC, 2 FTS. Acquired 23-12-04		1-24
❑ XN239*	'G'	Slingsby Cadet TX.3	59	ex Duxford, Henlow 8889M (3-3-86), ACCGS, 644 GS, CGS, 644 GS. Arrived by 9-22: under restoration, off-site		1-24
❑ XR517	'N'	Westland Wessex HC.2	64	ex LL, Shoreham, Ipswich, Fleetlands, 60, 72, 18. Acquired 3-12-05		1-24
❑ XR700*		Hunting Jet Provost T.4	63	ex Aldergrove, Abingdon 8589M, Shawbury, CATCS, 3 FTS, 1 FTS. SOC 1-10-71. Cockpit, stored		1-24
❑ XT864	'007'	McD Phantom FG.1	68	ex Leuchars 8998M, 111, 892, 767, 700P. Arrived 15-6-15. Unveiled 28-4-18, in 892 Sqn colours		1-24
❑ XV136	'X'	Westland Scout AH.1	68	ex Netheravon, Almondbank, Wroughton. Arrived 2-3-14		1-24

Reg		Type	Yr	History	Note	Date
❑ XV361		Blackburn Buccaneer S.2B	68	ex LL, Lossiemouth, 208, 15, 208, 12, 15, 809, 800. Last flight 18-4-94		1-24
❑ XW222		Sud Puma HC.1	72	ex Benson, 230, 33, 230, 33, 230, 27, 1563 Flt, 18, 230. Last flown 12-12. Westland-built. Arrived 29-7-14		1-24
❑ XX260*		HS Hawk T.1A	79	ex Shawbury, 'Red Arrows'. Bird strike 7-8-11. NEA 12-19. Arrived 15-5-23		1-24
❑ XX286*		HS Hawk T.1A	79	ex Shawbury, 208, 234, 19, TWU. NEA 12-19. Arrived 30-7-22. 208 Sqn colours. See note above	[14]	1-24
❑ 'XX613'	'A'	SAL Bulldog T.1 XX637	74	ex 'XX530', Glasgow, Kinloss, Cranwell, St Athan 9197M (7-6-93), York UAS, North UAS, 2 FTS. Arrived 1-12-19	[15]	1-24
❑ XZ389*	'BL'	SEPECAT Jaguar GR.1	77	ex Cosford, Halton 8946M (13-11-87), Shawbury, 17, 31, 20. Arrived 19-11-23		1-24
❑ ZF167		Short Tucano T.1	89	ex Sydenham, Shawbury, 1 FTS, 7 FTS. Arrived by 9-14		1-24
❑ ZG771		Panavia Tornado GR.4	91	ex Boscombe Down, Marham, 9, 31, 12, 15, Warton, 15, 617, 14, 617, 12, 9, 13, 15, GR.1, 9, 13, 9, 2, 9, 13, 9, 31, 9, 14, 31, 17, 31, 17, 31. Last flown 28-2-19, arr 29-9-21	[16]	1-24
❑ –*		Panavia Tornado F.3	~	trailer-mounted cockpit. Arrived 25-3-22		1-24
❑ –*		Short-Bristol Vindicator UAV	~	remotely-piloted target drone. First noted 3-23		1-24
❑ 202		Sud Alouette III	72	ex Baldonnel, IAC. Ditched 20-10-95. Acquired 27-5-09	[17]	1-24
❑ 203		Cessna FR.172H Rocket	72	ex Baldonnel, IAC. Reims-built. Last flew 4-10-19. Arr 6-11-21		1-24
❑ 218		Fouga CM.170-1 Magister	~	ex Baldonnel, Shannon, Baldonnel, IAC, Austrian AF 4D-YU. Last flew 30-4-98. Arrived 6-11-21		1-24
❑ –		Fieseler Fi 103 (V-1) FSM	c09	BAPC.403, acquired 1-10	[18]	1-24

■ **[1]** Ferguson replica built for BBC Belfast for a documentary screened in 9-16. Based on Harry Ferguson's second design of 1911. Construction led by boat-builder Alastair Duffin at Long Kesh 2-16. Piloted by William McMinn, it was flown at Bellarena in 5-16. Civil registration very brief, allocated 9-5-16, de-registered 1-6-16! **[2]** Rotec donated by Stuart Wilson. **[3]** Eurowing Goldwing donated by Jeff Salter. **[4]** Hi-Max built and donated by Maurice McKeown. **[5]** Robinson is on loan from Harold Hassard. **[6]** Cameron donated by Robin Mercer. **[7]** Monerai donated by Loudon Blair. **[8]** 'Flea' was built by the late Robert Wilbert Harris in the town in 1937. It is *believed* to have flown, at least once. It was used as a 'floatplane' in the 1936 coronation pageant at Moneymore. Reports that the wings and a propeller survive are being tracked down. **[9]** Quicksilver was built by Ernie Patterson. In August 1980 he flew it from the sands of Dundrum Bay, Newcastle, NI, to commemorate Harry Ferguson's flight of three miles on 8-8-1910. **[10]** Scamp partly built by Don Chisholm and finished by UAS volunteers. [11] Cygnet kit acquired by Don Chisholm; not assembled. **[12]** Donated by Spirit AeroSystems. Belfast production of composite Learjet 75 fuselages ended in 2021. TA = test article, completed 59,200 'flights' - three design lifetimes... **[13]** Jon Horswell notes that this machine was initially registered (in 3-93) as a Glass S005E, the Sea Hawker having originated as the QuikKit Glass Goose = hence the nearly spelt-out S005E. **[14]** After initial acquisition by UAS, re-offered at auction and donated by Beers Heavy Recovery 5-23. **[15]** XX637 repainted as 'XX613' 'A' which served QUAS 1974-1992 in memory of QUAS CO S/L Robert John Burge, killed in XX613 16-10-92; dedicated 15-10-22. **[16]** Digging into ZG771's history, UAS volunteers pleasantly discovered that the specially-marked aircraft was the last Tornado to visit Northern Ireland, 13-2-19, with a classic low-level 'beat up' at Aldergrove. **[17]** Alouette taken on charge by the IAC 22-3-72, ditched on 20-10-95 and struck off charge 31-10-95, with 7,100 hours on the clock. **[18]** V-1 was built by member James Herron.

MOY on the A29 southeast of Dungannon

Moy Antiques: The Square. ◆ **https://moyantiques.com**

Reg		Type	Yr	History	Note	Date
❑ XW281	'T'	Westland Scout AH.1 G-BYNZ	69	ex Dungannon, Gortin, Plymouth Thruxton, G-BYNZ (crashed 24-9-00, de-reg 5-2-01). Arrived 27-7-21	[1]	9-23

■ **[1]** Scout is/was fitted with the boom of XP883 - the rest of the latter is at Wymeswold, Leics.

NEWTOWNARDS AERODROME south of the town, between the A20 and A21 EGAD

Reg	Type	Yr	History	Date
❑ G-ARSX	Piper Tri-Pacer 160	56	ex Rathfriland, N2907Z. CoA 19-5-02, de-reg 12-2-02. Frame	1-20
❑ G-BANF	Luton Minor	77	ex Moneymore. CoA 5-6-92	1-20

PORTADOWN on the A3 southwest of Belfast

Gerald Hamill and Sons: The prototype Short 330 *may* linger at the yard. ◆ *Prior arrangement* **only**

Reg	Type	Yr	History	Note	Date
❑ G-BSBH	Short 330	74	ex Sydenham, G-14-3000. De-reg 8-12-88	[1]	8-23

■ **[1]** *Bravo-Hotel* was the prototype, first flown 22-8-74.

Also: Written out of *W&R24* (p327) at Castlerock, N Ireland, the fuselage of a Super Skymaster has appeared locally.

Reg	Type	Yr	History	Date
❑ G-RORO*	Cessna 337B		ex Castlerock, G-AVIX, N5454S. Crashed 25-6-99, de-reg 9-12-02. Fuselage	11-22

RANDALSTOWN at the end of the M22 west of Antrim

Escarmouche Action Park: A *thinking* paintball site - escarmouche is French for skirmish!
◆ *Prior arrangement* **only** | **www.escarmouche.com**

Reg		Type	Yr	Details		Noted
❑ G-KNAP		Piper Warrior II	81	ex Aldergrove, G-BIUX, N9507N. Cr 13-7-99, de-reg 12-1-10.		5-15

SAINTFIELD on the A7 southwest of Belfast

A Wessex is kept at a *private* location in the *general* area.

Reg		Type	Yr	Details		Noted
❑ XS865		Westland Wessex HAS.1	65	ex Ballykinler, Lee-on-Solent, A2694, Wroughton, 771, 820. SOC 10-10-80. Camouflaged. First noted 6-13		9-23

STRABANE on the A5 south of Londonderry

Within the area, in *separate* locations, are two airframes.

Reg		Type	Yr	Details		Noted
❑ G-BDRL		Stits Playboy	62	ex Londonderry, N730GF. CoA 17-6-98, de-reg 11-5-01		1-20
❑ G-BSZI		Cessna 152	84	ex N95139. De-reg 20-6-13		1-20

UPPER BALLINDERRY on the A26 north of Moria

A collector at a *private* location in the area *should* still have two airframes.

Reg		Type	Yr	Details		Noted
❑ EI-BAG		Cessna 172A	60	ex Langford Lodge, Upper Ballinderry, Portadown, Enniskillen, Abbeyshrule, G-ARAV, N9771T. CoA 26-6-79		2-14
❑ WD386	'O'	DHC Chipmunk T.10	51	ex Dumfries, Firbeck, Cranfield, Tenby, St Athan, 1 FTS, Oxf UAS, 22 RFS, 2 BFTS. SOC 29-7-70. Hawarden-built	[1]	2-14

■ **[1]** WD386 has the rear fuselage of WD377 - see under Balcombe, W Sussex.

IRELAND

ABBEYSHRULE AERODROME northwest of Mullingar, south of the N4 EIAB

Although very dated, the Tiger Moth is *believed* extant locally.

Reg		Type	Yr	Details		Noted
❑ EI-AOP		DH Tiger Moth	40	ex Dublin, G-AIBN, T7967, 18 EFTS, 1667 CU, 1 GCF, 16 PFTS. Morris Motors-built. Crashed 5-5-74, off-site		9-20
❑ F-GAIF		Wassmer Piranha	~	de-reg 6-07		9-20
❑ ZK-EVC		Piper Tomahawk	~	first noted 9-18		1-20

ARDAGH on the R521 south of Foynes

A *private* airstrip and glider store includes a long retired Rallye.

Reg		Type	Yr	Details		Noted
❑ EI-BNG		MS Rallye Commodore	~	ex Abbeyshrule, D-EDZO, F-BRGY. De-reg 5-8-87		6-21

ASHBOURNE between the N2 and the N3 northwest of Dublin, Meath

Leo Murray's *private* and eclectic collection, the **Meath Aero Museum**. The plan to move Dove VP-YKF to Shannon did not come to fruition. ◆ *Prior arrangement* **only**

Reg		Type	Yr	Details		Noted
❑ 'EI-ABH'		Mignet HM.14 'Flea'	99	fuselage and rudder		1-24
❑ EI-AWR		Malmo MFI-9 Junior	~	ex Bray, LN-HAG, SE-EBW		1-24
❑ VP-YKF		DH Dove 6	50	ex '176', Omagh, New Ross, Waterford, Cork, Dublin 3D-AAI, VQ-ZJC, G-AMDD. Accident, Cork, 8-82		1-24
❑ VM659		Slingsby Tutor	47	ex Galway, Gort, Castlebridge, Cork, IGA,6, IAC.6, VM659. SOC 23-5-57. Arrived 20-3-01	[1]	1-24

■ **[1]** Identity confirmed.

The Ark Puddenhill: Activity centre, *may* still have its 337. ◆ *Prior arrangement* **only** | **https://the arkpuddenhill.ie**

Reg		Type	Yr	Details		Noted
❑ EI-BHM		Cessna F.337E	77	ex Dublin, Farranfore, OO-PDC, OO-PDG. Reims-built. CoA 9-7-82		11-14
❑ E-402		Hawker Hunter F.51	56	ex Farnborough, Hurn, Kemble, Hurn, Macclesfield, Dunsfold, G-9-433 (8-8-76), Danish AF Esk.724		10-23

BALDONNEL AIRFIELD or Casement, west of Dublin

EIME

Irish Air Corps Museum and Heritage Centre: ◆ *Prior arrangement* ***only*** | *Baldonnel, Dublin 22, Ireland*

	Identity	Type	Reg	Year	Details	Note	Noted
❑	C-7	Avro Cadet ✈		34	ex New Zealand ZK-AVR, Southampton, Abbeyshrule, Terenure, EI-AGO, EI-AFO, IAC C-7		9-23
❑	'98'	Cessna 172B	G-ARLU	61	ex Southend, G-ARLU, N8002X. Dam 30-10-77, de-reg 6-8-80		10-18
❑	141	Avro XIX Srs 2		46	ex Dublin, Baldonnel		9-23
❑	164	DHC Chipmunk T.20		52	Hawarden-built		9-23
❑	172	DHC Chipmunk T.20		52	ex Castle Archdale, Baldonnel. Hawarden-built. Fuselage		9-23
❑	183	Percival Provost T.51		55	ex Dublin, Baldonnel	[1]	9-23
❑	191	DH Vampire T.55		61	ex Gormanston, Dublin, Baldonnel. Hawarden-built		9-23
❑	199	DHC Chipmunk T.20	G-APTF	51	ex Gormanston, G-APTF, T.10 WG320, TTCCF, Wyton SF, 18 RFS. Hatfield-built. Fuselage		9-23
❑	206	Cessna FR.172H Rocket		72	Reims-built		9-23
❑	215	Fouga CM.170-1 Magister		~	ex Dublin, Baldonnel, Katanga AF not delivered, Austrian AF 4D-YJ. First noted 1-19		9-23
❑	219	Fouga CM.170-1 Magister		~	-		9-23
❑	231	SIAI-M SF-260WE Warrior		77	-		9-23
❑	WZ762	Slingsby Grasshopper TX.1		~	EI-135, ex Gowran Grange, Cosford, Rugby	[2]	9-23
❑	– c/no 1012	Sud Alouette III		~	non-flying training rig.	[3]	3-19
❑	–	Wright Flyer replica		03	built on site		9-18

■ **[1]** Provost 183's wings are fitted to fellow 184 at Dromod, Ireland – which see. The ones it is fitted with now have no attribution. **[2]** Grasshopper WZ762 is fitted with the wings of WZ756. **[3]** Alouette has the constructor's number 1153 painted on it.

Irish Air Corps Headquarters: FR.172H 208 was registered as EI-HFE in November 2022 – see Ballyboy, Ireland.

	Identity	Type	Year	Details	Note	Noted
❑	195	Sud Alouette III	63	ex F-WJDH. '30 Years' markings. Training aid		9-23
❑	205	Cessna FR.172H Rocket	72	Reims-built. Last flew 4-10-19		9-23
❑	221 '3-KE'	Fouga CM.170-2 Magister	~	ex French Air Force No.79. Fuselage, stored		9-23
❑	EI-BXO	Fouga CM.170-2 Magister	c62	ex Dungannon, Saggart, Swords, Shannon, N18FM, Finnish AF FM-28. Valmet-built. Arrived by 4-14, fuselage	[1]	9-23
❑	EI-RJZ	HSA HS.146-RJ85	98	ex CityJet, N512XJ, G-6-326. Woodford-built. Flew in 17-4-20. Instructional		4-20
❑	G-ASNG	DH Dove 6	57	ex Waterford, Cork, (EI-BJW), Coventry, HB-LFF, G-ASNG, HB-LFF, G-ASNG, PH-IOM. Fuselage	[1]	7-23

■ **[1]** CM.170 and the Dove both used as 'travellers' for emergency exercises – eg 'deployed' to Dublin Airport in 9-23.

BALLINAMORE on the R199/R202 northeast of Carrick-on-Shannon

At a ***private*** workshop in the *general* area, a Bell Ranger is being restored.

	Identity	Type	Year	Details	Note	Noted
❑	G-BFPP	Bell 47J-2 Ranger	63	ex Lee-on-Solent, F-BJAN, TR-LKD, F-OCBU. Crashed 11-7-97, CoA 11-11-99. First noted 8-21	[1]	8-21

■ **[1]** Tail boom of AB 47J-3B-1 EC-AXZ also present.

BALLYBOY AERODROME east of the N52 southwest of Tullamore

Irish Historic Flight Foundation: The fleet currently stands at: Boeing N2S-5 EI-HFD; Chipmunk T.20s 168 (EI-HFA), 169 (EI-HFB) and '170' (EI-HFC), Tiger Moth EI-AHI; Piper L-4 44-80762 (EI-BBV); and the 'custodianship' of Dragon EI-ABI – see under Dublin, Ireland. The organisation is working towards a full-blown visitor centre at Ballyboy but for now the 'outreach' is attendance at air events. ◆ *Prior arrangement* **only** | **www.irishhistoricflight.com**

	Identity	Type	Reg	Year	Details	Noted
❑	208*	Cessna FR.172H	EI-HFE	72	ex IAC, Baldonnel. Reims-built. Last flew 4-10 19	9-23

Also:

	Identity	Type	Year	Details	Noted
❑	EI-CUB	Piper J3C-65 Cub	46	ex G-BPPV, N88392. Off-site	9-23
❑	EI-ETC	Aeronca 15-AC Sedan	49	N915TC. ex G-CETC, HB-ETC	8-20
❑	G-MTKE	Thruster TSM Mk.1	87	CoA 27-8-03, de-reg 20-3-09	8-20
❑	G-MVMM	Aerial Arts Chaser	88	CoA 30-7-04, de-reg 29-1-19	8-20

BANDON off the N71 southwest of Cork

ICP NewTech: The company builds remotely operated vehicles (ROVs) and has an ATR 42 in use for training 'drivers'.

◆ ***Strictly*** *by prior arrangement* **only** | **www.icpnewtech.com**

❑ EC-LMX	ATR 42-320	88	ex Shannon, EI-SLI, 5Y-BVD, EI-SLI, CS-TLR, PT-MTO, XA-TPZ, XA-MAR, F-WWEL. Fuselage. Arrived 23-5-15	6-21

CARLOW on the N9 southwest of Dublin

South East Technological University: (Note name change.) Kilkenny Road ◆ *Prior arrangement* **only** | **www.setu.ie**

❑ EI-AMI	Piper Colt 108	61	ex Wexford, G-ARSU, EI-AMI, G-ARSU	9-19
❑ EI-AUE	MS Rallye Club	69	ex Kilkenny, G-AXHU	11-18
❑ EI-BGJ	Cessna F.152 II	r79	ex Kilrush. Reims-built	6-23
❑ EI-CUP	Cessna 335	80	ex Sligo, N2706X	11-18
❑ –	Monnett Sonerai II-LW	~	fuselage frame, c/n SAAC.23. Arrived during 2013	11-18
❑ G-HUGS	Robinson R22	90	ex Enniskillen. CoA 23-3-11, de-reg 21-2-11	6-23
❑ 220	Fouga CM.170-1 Magister	~	ex Baldonnel, IAC	6-23

CELBRIDGE south of the M4, west of Dublin

A pair of dismantled Duchesses are stored at a *private* location in the locality.

❑ G-WACI	Beech Duchess	79	ex Weston, N6703Y. CoA 22-11-12, de-reg 5-9-17	10-21
❑ G-WACJ	Beech Duchess	80	ex Weston, N6700Y. Damaged 10-7-11. CoA 22-7-11, de-reg 15-2-18	10-21

CLOUGHAN on the N52 northeast of Mullingar

A Whirlwind *may* still be stored at a *private* location in the area.

❑ XP354	W'land Whirlwind HAR.10	62	ex Cricklade, Colsterworth, Halton 8721M (4-11-81), 22, 202	10-23

CLONBULLOGUE AERODROME on the R401 south of Kinnegad EICL

❑ EI-BNK	Cessna U206F	71	ex G-HILL, PH-ADN, D-EEXY, N9506G. De-reg 31-10-12	10-21

CORK

Munster Airsoft: The site is *believed* to have closed: no details for Rallye EI-BBO and Cessna 182 EI-BPJ.

Locally: A VP-2 is stored at a *private* location in the *general* area.

❑ EI-BVT	Evans VP-2	c76	ex G-BEIE (de-reg 2-8-91). *Birdy*	3-21

CORK AIRPORT EICK

Irish Aviation Historians: *May* still keep a Spitfire cockpit FSM at the airport.

❑ - 'FY-Y'	V-S Spitfire FSM	~	cockpit	6-19

CRADDENSTOWN AERODROME north of the R156, between Mullingar and Trim

❑ EI-BUA*	Cessna 172M	~	ex Weston, N5458H. Fuselage	2-22
❑ EI-BKN	MS Rallye 100ST	~	ex Clonbullogue, Weston, F-GBCK. De-reg 5-11-10. Fuselage	10-23
❑ EI-BVK	Piper Tomahawk 112	~	ex Newcastle (Wicklow), OO-FLG, OO-HLG, N9705N. Fuselage	2-22
❑ EI-CCK*	Cessna 152 II	~	ex Weston, N24251. De-reg 5-11-12. Fuselage	2-22
❑ EI-CCL*	Cessna 152 II	~	ex Weston, N24791. Crashed 4-5-93. Cockpit	2-22
❑ EI-CDV*	Cessna 150G	~	ex Weston, N2777S. Fuselage	2-22
❑ EI-GSE*	Cessna F.172M	~	ex Weston, D-EDXO. Reims-built. De-reg 27-1-14. Fuselage	2-22
❑ G-BHIA*	Cessna F.152 II	80	ex Weston. De-reg 23-7-92. Reims-built. Fuselage	2-22
❑ G-BPBI*	Cessna 152	79	ex Weston. De-reg 11-2-91. Fuselage	2-22
❑ EI-DXN	Zenair CH-601	~	ex Newcastle (Wicklow). De-reg 20-1-20	9-21

CROOKSTOWN on the N9, south of Newbridge

Crookstown Craft Village: *May* still have a Cessna 401 on display.

❑ N9146N	Cessna 401B RAM	70	ex Weston	11-18

DROGHEDA on R132 north of Dublin

A gyrocopter is *thought* still to be stored in the locality.

❑ G-BRVR	Barnett J4B-2	89	ex Frosses. De-reg 21-4-09		5-19

DROMOD on the N4, north of Longford

South East Aviation Enthusiasts Group (SEAEG): Thanks to the **Cavan and Leitrim Railway** SEAEG has a great base within this extensive and friendly railway and transport centre. When staffing permits, some cockpits are open for access. See also Dublin, Ireland, for more of Phil Bedford's collection.

◆ *On the L1600 out of Dromod | SEAEG: Philip Bedford,* **pbedford707321@gmail.com** | ***Cavan and Leitrim**: Station Road, Dromod,* | **dromodrailway@gmail.com** | **www.cavanandleitrimrailway.com**

❑ EI-BDM	Piper Aztec 250D	69	ex New Ross, Waterford, Kildimo, G-AXIV, N6826Y	[1]	1-24
❑ EI-BNJ*	Evans VP-2	c83	ex Bartlemy. Arrived 29-1-23		1-24
❑ EI-BRW*	Ultra-Lite Deltabird	85	ex Bartlemy. Crashed 1986. Arrived 29-10-22	[2]	1-24
❑ EI-CAJ*	O'Leary Biplane	89	ex Bartlemy. De-reg 6-7-94. Arrived 29-10-22		1-24
❑ EI-CVW	Bensen B-8V	98	arrived 14-8-21	[3]	1-24
❑ EI-ETE	MS Rallye Club	71	ex Newcastle (Wicklow), G-BXZT, OO-EDG, D-EBDG, F-BSVL. Arrived 23-6-17.		1-24
❑ EI-100	SZD Mucha	58	ex OY-XAN. CoA 1-7-97		1-24
❑ EI-139	Slingsby Cadet TX.3	53 EI-GMH	ex New Ross, Gowran Grange, BGA.3485, Falgunzeon, Motor Cadet III G-BOKG, TX.3 XE789, 553 GS, 662 GS, 663 GS, 661 GS, 31 GS. CoA 2-8-97	[1] [4]	1-24
❑ –	Mignet HM.14 'Flea'	35	IAHC.1, ex New Ross, Waterford, Dublin, Coonagh. *St Patrick*. Off-site	[5]	1-24
❑ G-AKGE	Miles Gemini 3C	47	ex New Ross, Waterford, Kilbritain, EI-ALM, G-AKGE. CoA 7-6-74, de-reg 30-5-84. Cockpit	[1] [6]	1-24
❑ G-ANIS	Taylorcraft Auster 5	44	ex Longford, AOP.V TJ375, 1952 Flt. CoA 19-9-76, de-reg 8-10-81		1-24
❑ G-AOIE	Douglas DC-7C	56	ex 'EI-AWA', New Ross, Waterford, Shannon, PH-SAX, G-AOIE, Autair, Caledonian, BOAC. *County of Perth*. De-reg 1-5-81. Forward fuselage	[1]	1-24
❑ G-OGGS	Thunder Colt Ax-8 HAB	89	CoA 10-2-95, de-reg 12-12-01		1-24
❑ CBK	DFS Grunau Baby III	c48	BGA.1410, ex New Ross, Naas, Breighton, Stoke-on-Trent, Firbeck, RAFGSA.378, D-4676. CoA 2-4-83	[1]	1-24
❑ CBZ	Slingsby Tutor	c44	BGA.1424, ex New Ross, Naas, Gowran Grange, Jurby, RAFGSA.214, RA877. CoA 4-4-78. Stored in a bus	[1] [7]	1-24
❑ VP-BDF	Boeing 707-321	61	ex New Ross, Waterford, Dublin, N435MA, G-14-372, G-AYAG, N759PA. *Spirit of 73*. Cockpit	[1]	1-24
❑ NC285RS	NAA Navion	46	ex New Ross, Naas, Abbeyshrule, N91488. Crashed 11-6-79. *My Way*. Cockpit, rear fuselage, tail	[1]	1-24
❑ 173	DHC Chipmunk T.20	52	ex New Ross, Waterford, Gormanston, IAC	[8] [9]	1-24
❑ 184	Percival Provost T.51	55	ex New Ross, Waterford, Baldonnel, IAC	[8] [10]	1-24
❑ 187	DH Vampire T.55	56	ex New Ross, Waterford, Baldonnel, IAC. Cockpit	[8] [9]	1-24
❑ 192	DH Vampire T.55	61	ex New Ross, Waterford, Baldonnel, IAC	[8] [9]	1-24
❑ RA881	Slingsby Cadet TX.1	c44	ex New Ross, Breighton, Halfpenny Green, RAFGSA 163. Cockpit, stored	[1] [7]	1-24

■ **[1]** Airframes on loan from Philip Bedford. **[2]** Type as officially registered, believed to be a Bimax Osprey. Gained fame by flying under the Blackwater Viaduct, near Fermoy 21-9-86. **[3]** Bensen built, and owned by, Fergus Kavanagh. **[4]** EI-139 has been brought back to Cadet TX.3 status. It is hoped to fly it again as EI-GMH. **[5]** 'Flea' on loan from the Aviation Society of Ireland Preservation Group. A 1935 Douglas flat twin has been acquired for it. **[6]** See also Holywood, Northern Ireland, for more on G-AKGE. **[7]** Phil Bedford is restoring T.8 Tutor CBZ to its original 1944 condition as a long-span Cadet TX.2. CBZ was converted into an enclosed cockpit motor glider and will use the cockpit of RA881 in the rebuild. Phil owns CBZ along with Damian Smyth. **[8]** Airframes on Department of Defence loan. **[9]** Chipmunk and Vampires Hawarden-built. **[10]** Provost 184 has the wings of 183 (see Baldonnel, Ireland).

DUBLIN

National Museum of Ireland: Within the impressive Collins Barracks. ◆ *Benburb Street* | **www.museum.ie**

❑ 34	Miles Magister	39	ex Baldonnel, Dublin, Baldonnel, RAF N5392 n/s. Phillips & Powis-built	[1]	1-24

❑ 198	DH Vampire T.11	55	ex Baldonnel, XE977, 8 FTS. Hawarden-built	[2]	1-24

■ **[1]** Magister 34 was delivered from new 22-2-39 and became an instructional airframe 11-3-52. **[2]** Vampire 198 was never operated by IAC, having been acquired ex-RAF as a training aid 30-8-63.

Philip Bedford: Keeps his Auster and Proctor at a *private* site in the locality. See also Dromod, Ireland.

❑ EI-ACY	Auster J1 Autocrat	46	ex Dromore, G-AIBK. Crashed 6-4-67	1-24
❑ G-AHWO	Percival Proctor V	46	ex Whitehall, Dublin, (EI-ALY). Cr 5-5-59, de-reg 17-11-60	1-24

Merchants Arch Bar and Restaurant: Wellington Quay. A Sonerai 'soars' over the diners. **www.merchantsarch.ie**

❑ –	Monnet Sonerai II	78	c/n SAAC.6. Unflown, installed 3-16	1-24

Wayfinder Centre: Glasnevin. Opening in April 2024, this institution provides training for people with disabilities to use transport of all kinds. The A319 forward fuselage has had the underfloor baggage bays etc 'sliced' away and is fully equipped internally with seating etc. ◆ *Prior arrangement* **only** | **www.ncbi.ie/wayfindingcentre**

❑ F-GRHL*	Airbus A319-100	00	ex Knock, Air France, D-AVWT. Last flight 29-11-22. Hamburg-built. Forward fuselage	1-24

Others: A Viscount cockpit is preserved and a Pup is being worked on at *separate*, *private* locations in the general area.

❑ EI-AOH	Vickers Viscount 808	67	ex Dublin Airport, Aer Lingus, PH-VII. Scrapped 12-72. *St Fiacre*. Cockpit	1-24
❑ G-AXMW*	Beagle Pup 100	69	ex Audley End, G-35-101. De-reg 19-2-21. Arrived 7-23	8-23

DUBLIN AIRPORT or Collinstown

EIDW

Dragon EI-ABI is stored at the airport. It is part of the Irish Historic Flight Foundation – see Ballyboy, Ireland. Boeing 737 EI-CJD was broken up 16th August 2022.

❑ EI-ABI	DH Dragon	36	ex EI-AFK, G-AECZ, AV982, EE, 7 AACU, 110 Wing, G-AECZ. *Iolar.* Stored by 9-19	[1]	12-23

■ **[1]** EI-ABI represents the first Aer Lingus aircraft, 1936. Factoid: The original EI-ABI was previously G-ACPY and returned to the UK in 1938. It was shot down by a Ju 88 off the Scilly Isles on 3rd June 1941.

Technological University Dublin – Aviation Technology Centre: Within the Dublin Airport Business Park. The cockpit of Bonanza N7205R had been scrapped by mid-2022. ◆ *Prior arrangement* **only** | **www.tudublin.ie**

❑ EI-AWH	Cessna 210J Centurion	69	ex Rathcoole, G-AZCC, 5N-AIE, N616FN, N1734C. De-reg 13-4-99. Arrived 14-1-19		10-22
❑ EI-CGU	Robinson R22	81	ex Dublin, G-BSNH, N9065D. De-reg 16-4-97. DIT titles		10-22
❑ G-NJIB*	HS 146-300	90	ex Simtech, B-1776, G-BSXZ, G-6-174. CoA 11-4-04, de-reg 27-1-07. CityJet colours, Cockpit	[1]	10-22
❑ N829AA	Learjet 25B	72	ex N25TK, N741F, N741E, N262JE		10-22

■ **[1]** 146 written out of *W&R28* (p320) as "no longer used" at airport-based Simtech Flight Crew Training: last physical sighting 8-11.

DUBLIN WESTON AIRPORT near Leixlip

EIWT

Goose N4575C was ferried to Coventry, Warks, 14th December 2023. By February 2022 there had been a migration of fuselages from the dump to Craddenstown, Ireland: 172 EI-BUA, 152 EI-CCK; 150 EI-CDV; F.172 EI-GSE; F.152 G-BHIA; 152 G-BPBI; and cockpit of 152 EI-CCL not previously listed here.

❑ EI-AUH	Cessna F.172H	~	ex Kilkenny. Reims-built. Cr 10-5-72, de-reg 28-8-86	7-23
❑ EI-BSF	HS HS.748-1/105	62	ex Baldonnel, Dublin, Ryanair, EC-DTP, G-BEKD, LV-HHF, LV-PUM. *Spirit of Tipperary.* CoA 21-5-87, de-reg 26-7-94. Fuselage, rescue trainer. Arrived 10-14	12-23
❑ EI-CFN	Cessna 150G	~	ex N5446K. De-reg 13-11-07. Rescue trainer, f/n 10-21	10-21
❑ EI-CGG	Forney Aircoupe 415C	~	ex N2522H. CoA 10-00. de-reg 6-11-12. Rescue trainer	12-23
❑ G-JBDB*	Bell JetRanger II	70	ex G-OOPS, G-BNRD, Oman AF 602. Agusta-built De-reg 23-4-19. Simulator with National Flight Centre	12-23
❑ G-SEAI	Cessna U.206G	77	ex N756FQ. CoA 12-6-08, de-reg 20-5-21. Floatplane	10-21

DUNSHAUGHLIN on the N3 northwest of Dublin

A cache of French types is held at a *private* storage site in the locality. The wings of Rallye EI-BBJ had appeared at Glengormley, N Ireland, by July 2022.

❑ EI-ATS	MS Rallye Club	~	de-reg 14-6-11	1-20
❑ EI-BBJ	MS Rallye Club	~	ex Clonbullogue, Weston, F-BUVX. De-reg 5-11-10. See above	1-20
❑ EI-BMJ	MS Rallye Club	~	ex Coonagh, F-BXTG. De-reg 6-10-09	1-20
❑ EI-BNU	MS Rallye Club	~	ex Weston, F-BPQV	1-20
❑ EI-BUG	SOCATA ST-10 Diplomate	71	ex Weston, G-STIO, OH-SAB. CoA 8-98	1-20
❑ G-HOLY	SOCATA ST-10 Diplomate	70	ex F-BSCZ. CoA 26-9-05, de-reg 22-10-15	1-20

Others: Also in the locality are three other aircraft, at *separate* locations.

❑ EI-AKM	Piper J-3C-65 Cub	~	ex N88194. CoA 30-6-60	12-21
❑ EI-AUS	Auster J5F Aiglet Trainer	52	ex Powerscourt, G-AMRL. CoA 2-12-75, de-reg 18-11-12	2-16
❑ EI-FFT	Forney F.1A Aircoupe	61	ex G-AROO, N25B	1-20

EDGEWORTHSTOWN on the N4 between Longford and Mullingar

Midland Karting and Paintballing ◆ *Prior arrangement* **only** | **www.actionsports.ie**

❑ EI-ATK	Piper Cherokee 140	67	ex G-AVUP. De-reg 22-2-11. Fuselage	11-23
❑ EI-BKE	MS Rallye	~	ex F-BKUN, F-WKUN. De-reg 16-9-86. In woods	11-23
❑ EI-CFV	MS Rallye Club	71	ex Abbeyshrule, G-OLFS, G-AYYZ. Alongside racetrack	11-23
❑ EI-CHN	MS Rallye	67	ex Abbeyshrule, G-AVIO. Fuselage, in woods	11-23

Rallye EI-CFV awaiting a thorough splatting, November 2023. *Ian Thompson*

ENNISCRONE or Inishcrone, on the R297 north of Ballina

Quirky Nights Glamping Village: Development of this ambitious site, which includes railway carriages, buses and specialised 'pods', continues. The 767 has yet to be converted into a 'dwelling'. ◆ *Prior arrangement* **only**

❑ EI-CZD	Boeing 767-216ER	86	ex Shannon, Transaero, N762TA, CC-CJU, N4529T. Arrived 5-16	5-23

FOYNES on the N69 west of Limerick

Foynes Flying-Boat and Maritime Museum: This exceptional venue is within the former transatlantic flying-boat terminal and control tower. The fantastic Boeing 314 'Clipper' 'walk-in' exhibit must be sampled to be believed. In September 2023 a €5m expansion and upgrade to existing facilities was opened, including a cinema. There is also special exhibition devoted to Maureen O'Hara – Irish film star married to flying-boat maestro Charles Blair. Discover the origins of Irish coffee and sample it in the well recommended O'Regan's Restaurant.

◆ *Foynes, Limerick, Ireland* | **00 353 69 65416** | **info@flyingboatmuseum.com**| **www.flyingboatmuseum.com**

❑ -	Boeing 314 'Clipper'	06	BAPC.594. 'Walk-in' recreation. PanAm c/s, *Yankee Clipper*	1-24

FROSSES on the R262 between Killybegs and Donegal

A Tiger Cub is stored at a *private* site in the locality.

❑ G-MMJS	MBA Tiger Cub	c87	ex Drogheda, Newry. De-reg 7-9-94	1-22

KILKENNY on the N76 / N10, north of Waterford

National Reptile Zoo: The entrance hall is graced by a microlight, in a suitably reptilian colour scheme.
◆ *Hebron Business Park* | **info@nationalreptilezoo.ie** | **www.nationalreptilezoo.ie**

❑ G-MZNY	Thruster T600 450N	98	de-reg 17-3-21. First noted 7-21	7-21

KILRUSH junction of the N67 and N68, southeast of Kilkee

Evans VP-2 EI-BDL was donated to a school for instruction and moved out on 18th December 2023 – destination unknown.

KNOCK IRELAND WEST AIRPORT on the N17, southwest of Charlestown EIKN

❑ YU-AON	Boeing 737-3Q4	87	ex Air Serbia, JAT, N181LF, S7-RGL, PT-TEF. Last flight 28-3-14. Rescue trainer, less tailplane	8-22

LIMERICK on the N24 southwest of Shannon

A Silvaire is kept in the *general* area. The cockpit of a former Shannon 727 *may* still be at the United Metals yard.

❑ G-AFZK	Luscombe 8A Silvaire	39	ex N25118. CoA 15-6-09	N9-20
❑ EC-CFA	Boeing 727-256	73	ex Shannon, N907RF, Iberia. *Jeres Xeres Sherry*. Cockpit. Arrived mid-2018	6-19

LIMETREE AERODROME north of Portlaoise

❑ G-MNGB	Mainair Gemini Flash	84	CoA 19-4-98, de-reg 4-5-01	11-18

LISTOWEL on the N69 northeast of Tralee

A museum to commemorate Irish-American service in the US military is in the process of being set up. A UH-1H arrived at Cork docks in November 2023 and will be prepared for display by International Aerospace Coatings at Shannon prior to arriving on site. The 'Huey' will be marked as UH-1H 67-17428 *Dolphin 428*, as flown by Tralee-born 2nd Lt John I O'Sullivan of the 174th Av Co, 14th Av Battalion, who was awarded a DSC for action at Quang Ngai, Vietnam, 1st April 1970.

❑ N704TF*	Bell UH-1H Iroquois	71	ex Fort Worth, US Army 71-20201. De-reg 5-11-10. Arrived Ireland 11-23. See notes above	11-23

MAYNOOTH AERODROME or Dolly's Grove, north of the M4 and the town, south of the R156

The three airframes are dramatically mounted alongside the hangars.

❑ ES-YLK		Aero L29 Delfin	~	ex Cork	9-23
❑ LY-AFO		Antonov An-2 *Colt*	~	ex Cork	2-22
❑ XZ995	'3G'	HS Harrier GR.3 G-CBGK	86	ex Lowestoft, Shoreham, Ipswich, St Mawgan 9220M, Chivenor, 1417 Flt, 4, 3, 233 OCU, 3. De-reg 14-3-05	9-23

Also: An Auster is *believed* stored in the area.

❑ EI-AMY	Auster J1N Alpha	50	ex Powerscourt, Kells, G-AJUW. De-reg 18-10-12. Fuselage	12-15

MILTOWNPASS AERODROME on the N6 west of Dublin EIMP

❑ EI-DUV	Beech Baron B55	73	ex N3045W. Fuselage	8-20

NEWBRIDGE north of the M7, southwest of Dublin

A Venom cockpit is kept in the *general* area.

❑ 'WR360'	'K'	DH Venom FB.50 G-DHSS	56	ex Portarlington, Hurn, Swiss AF J-1626. CoA 22-4-03, de-reg 5-3-13. Swiss-built. Cockpit.	1-20

NEWCASTLE AERODROME on the R671 north of Wicklow EINC

❑ G-BTSN	Cessna 150G	67	ex N3806J. CoA 16-12-14, de-reg 4-6-18. Fuselage, rescue tnr	5-19
❑ N19F*	Cessna 337A	65	ex N6289F. Roberston mods. First noted 4-22	9-23

PORTLAOISE at the N7 / N8 junction southwest of Dublin

Portlaoise Plane Restoration Project: Plans for a permanent display have yet to come to fruition. ◆ *Visits* **not** *yet possible.*

	Reg	Type	Year	Details	Note	Date
❑	–	Aldritt Monoplane	1909	IAHC.2, ex Donabate, Wannock, Portlaoise. Acquired 27-11-18; unveiled 21-8-21	[1]	8-21

■ **[1]** Designed and built by motor engineers Frank and Louis Aldritt at Portlaoise, it carried out a limited number of flights from 11-09.

RATHCOOLE AERODROME south of the N72 and Dromagh EIRT

Although dated, both airframes are *thought* to be current.

	Reg	Type	Year	Details	Note	Date
❑	EI-AFN	BA Swallow 2	38	ex G-AFGV. Off-site		5-16
❑	G-AXVV	Piper J3C-65 Cub	44	ex F-BBQB, L-4H 43-29572. CoA 16-6-73, de-reg 12-4-99		9-23

ROSCREA at the N7 northeast of Limerick

A Jodel is held at a *private* location in the *general* area.

	Reg	Type	Year	Details	Note	Date
❑	G-BMLB	Jodel D.140A Paris-Nice	65	ex F-BNCI. CoA 20-10-09, de-reg 16-5-11. Wassmer-built	[1]	8-20

■ **[1]** De-registered as sold in Ireland.

ROUNDWOOD on the R765 west of Newtown Mount Kennedy

Special Ops East – North Wicklow: Last noted in November 2017, the anonymous, camouflaged, Rallye fuselage has been deleted. 'Campaigners' now have a crude helicopter mock-up to fantasize over. ◆ **www.specialops.ie**

SHANNON AIRPORT on the N19 between Limerick and Ennis EINN

Atlantic Airadventures: **Shannon Aviation Museum** and **Shannon Flight Simulation Centre**, on the airport industrial area. During August 2022 a permanent exhibition was opened by Brigadier General Rory O'Connor on the heritage of the Irish Air Corps during its centenary year. The transfer of Dove VP-YKF did not transpire: it remained at Ashbourne, Ireland.

◆ *Aviation Education Centre, Link Road* | **00 353 061363687** | **info@shannonaviationmuseum.com** | **https://shannonaviationmuseum.com**

	Reg	Type	Year	Details	Note	Date
❑	EI-CIA	MS Rallye	68	ex Toomyvara, G-MONA, G-AWJK. De-reg 3-2-11		12-23
❑	EI-CIN	Cessna 150K	70	ex Shannon Training Centre, Weston, G-OCIN, EI-CIN, G-BSXG, N6228G. Stored		12-23
❑	EI-COZ	Piper Cherokee 140C	70	ex Abbeyshrule G-AYMZ, N11C. De-reg 16-5-13		12-23
❑	EI-SLM	ATR 42-310	94	ex Aer Lingus, Air Contractors, N643AS, F-WWLC. Accident 17-7-11. Forward fuselage		1-22
❑	G-AVMZ	BAC 111-510ED	69	ex Alton, Hurn, European, BA, BEA. CoA 17-2-02, de-reg 10-6-03. Forward fuselage		12-23
❑	G-BAHI	Cessna F.150H	68	ex Little Staughton, PH-EHA. Reims-built. CoA 14-12-07. De-reg 4-7-19. Fuselage		1-22
❑	G-BHYN*	Evans VP-2	c89	ex Ballina. De-reg 1-4-97, arrived 25-9-22		12-23
❑	G-BTVV	Cessna F.337G	73	ex Weston, PH-RPD, N1876M. Reims-built. CoA 12-1-03, de-reg 19-2-14		12-23
❑	G-CDPF	HSA HS.146-300	89	ex Lasham, Southend, Air Wisconsin N614AW, G-5-132. Hatfield-built. Cockpit - simulator. De-reg 23-6-07		12-23
❑	–	Monnett Monerai	~	fuselage. Built by Larry Kelly, SAAC.38	[1]	12-23
❑	–	Bede BD-5B Micro	~	ex Glasgow. PFA 014-10048. Long-span wings		12-23
❑	–	Dragon 150	~	arrived 10-21	[2]	1-22
❑	C-GAPW	Boeing 737-275	74	ex Canadian, N127AW, C-GAPW. Simulator	[3]	1-22
❑	D-3229	Scheibe Bergfalk 55/II	~	suspended in main building		1-22
❑	5N-ABJ	Boeing 707-3F9C	71	ex Limerick, Shannon, Nigeria Airways. Cockpit. Arr 2-9-15	[4]	1-22
❑	210	Cessna FR.172H Rocket	72	ex IAC, Baldonnel. Reims-built. Last 'up' 4-10-19. F/n 8-20		12-23
❑	216	Fouga CM.170-1 Magister	~	ex Baldonnel, Cork, Baldonnel, Austrian AF 4D-YK. Arrived 10-12-21		12-23
❑	-	V-S Spitfire FSM	c98	ex Lytham St Annes. Cockpit, built by Richard Jones		12-23
❑	VS562	Avro Anson T.21	48	ex Market Drayton, Coventry, Crowland, Llanbedr, Portsmouth, Llanbedr 8012M (9-4-65), A&AEE. Forward fuselage		12-23
❑	'VV612'	DH Venom FB.50 G-VENI	55	ex Dublin area, Portarlington, Hurn, 'WE402', Swiss AF J-1523. Swiss-built. CoA 25-7-01, de-reg 5-3-13. F/n 12-21		9-23
❑	'WR421'	DH Venom FB.50 G-DHTT	56	ex Dublin area, Portarlington, Hurn, G-BMOC, Swiss AF J-1611. Swiss-built. CoA 17-7-99, de-reg 5-3-13. F/n 12-21		9-23

❑ 'WR410'		DH Venom FB.50 G-DHUU	54	ex Portarlington, Hurn, G-BMOD, Swiss AF J-1539. Swiss-built. CoA 24-5-02, de-reg 5-3-13. 6 Sqn c/s		12-23
❑ XM144		EE Lightning F.1	60	ex Spark Bridge, Pershore, Booker, Eaglescott, Burntwood, Leuchars 8417M (28-5-74), Leuchars TFF, 23, Leuchars TFF, 226 OCU, 74. Arr 12-13. Cockpit. 74 Sqn c/s.		12-23
❑ XX826	'JH'	SEPECAT Jaguar GR.1	75	ex Market Drayton, Welshpool, Ipswich, Cosford 9021M (10-1-90), Shawbury, 2, 20, 14. Cockpit		12-23
❑ XX897		Blackburn Buccaneer S.2B	76	ex Hurn, DRA Bedford, RAE, RRE. Tornado nose cone	[5]	12-23
❑ XZ654		Westland Lynx AH.7	80	ex Ipswich, M Wallop. First noted 6-15	[6]	9-23

■ **[1]** Monerai on loan from Larry Kelly. **[2]** Dragon donated by Olly Conway. **[3]** *Papa-Whisky* factoids: 71,151 hours, 74,613 landings and is now a fixed-base trainer for a 737-800 series. **[4]** The 707 cockpit is a returnee to Shannon, it flew in there in 1989 and was scrapped in 1998. It was latterly at the University of Limerick. **[5]** XX897 converted by Marshall of Cambridge in 1980 with Tornado F.2 style nose as part of the Foxhunter radar development programme. **[6]** Boom on XZ219 / 'XZ654' at Bramley, Hampshire.

Shannon Training Centre: ◆ *Prior arrangement* **only**.

❑ G-ORHE	Cessna Citation 1	74	ex Enniskillen, N619EA, G-OBEL, G-BOGA, N932HA, N93WD, N5220J. CoA 24-7-08, de-reg 19-8-11. Arr 22-10-18	10-18

SLIGO on the N16 west of Enniskillen

Gerry O'Hara: The airframes are *thought* to be still stored at a *private* location in the area.

❑ EI-BOV	Rand KR-2	r84	*Kitty Hawk*	3-16
❑ –	Sligo Concept	~	IAHC.7, single seat low wing monoplane, unflown	3-16
❑ –	O'Hara Gyroplane	~	IAHC.8, on Bensen lines, unflown	3-16

SLIGO AIRPORT or Strandhill, west of the town EISG

Bulldog T.1 XX631 (G-BZXS) had moved to Enniskillen, N Ireland, by September 2022 in readiness for certification.

❑ G-ECAT	Fokker Friendship 500	86	ex G-JEAI, VH-EWY, PH-EXL. Damaged 2-11-02. CoA 16-12-02, de-reg 12-8-03. Rescue trainer	4-17

TOOREEN on the N83, north of Ballyhauris

Flanagan Motors: Within the showroom is a Cessna fuselage. This 150 was written out of *W&R22* at Newry (p331), having been last noted there in March 2008.

❑ EI-BHW*	Cessna F.150F	66	ex Newry, G-ATMK. De-reg 2-5-88	3-22

TRIM Tri-Pacer EI-UFO has been deleted.

TUAMGRANEY on the R463/ R352 north of Killaloe, on the western shores of Lough Derg

Wastelands Salvage: An amazing recycling/upcycling/industrial-and-architectural salvage site, always worth a browse, still holds the exotic T-37 'Tweet'. ◆ **https//wastelandssalvage.com**

❑ 0931	Cessna T-37C	70	ex N3127M, N5432M, 0931 Brazilian Air Force. De-reg 15-7-10. Fuselage, first noted 2-18	9-23

Opposite: Red tailed Jaguar line-up at Cosford, June 2023. Left to right: T.2 ZB615, ACT GR.1(mod) XX765, T.2A XX145. *David Willis*

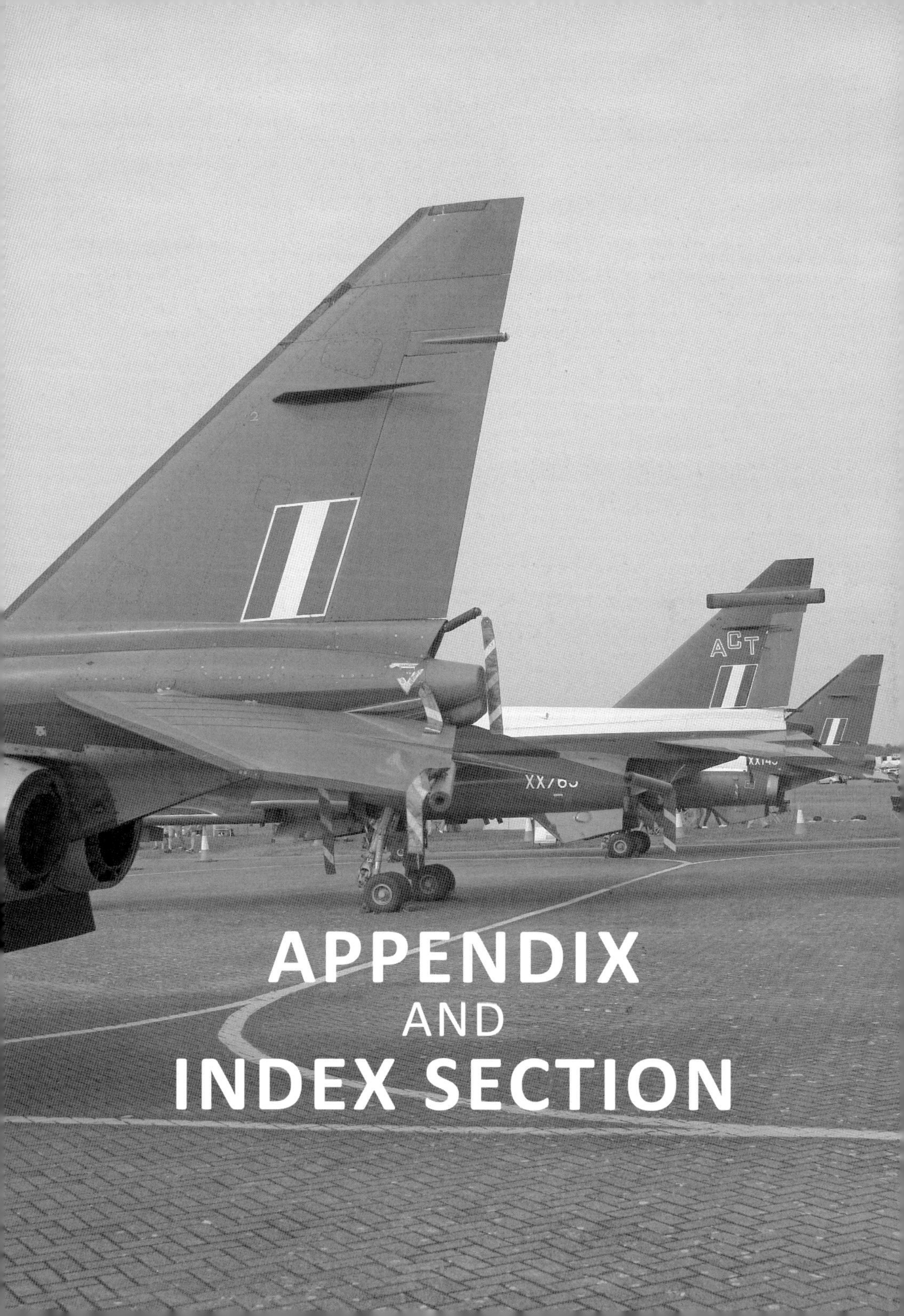

APPENDIX
AND
INDEX SECTION

Appendix A : 1974 AND ALL THAT...

With thanks to Sellar and Yeatman, who were writing about 1066 onwards, for the inspiration for this section's title. Discussion about how to mark the author's half-century determined that it would be a GOOD THING to provide a taste of 1974 for both those that remember the time and those who think it ancient history. *W&R4*'s cover (opposite) featured low-tech Letraset titles, and the book was illustrated with a grand total of 24 images in glorious black and white.

The following pages contain photos used in *W&R4* and others from the era. Some of these came from the trusty Ellis Kodak Instamatic camera which of course used 'wet' film. (Younger readers can Google these...) We've used the same layout and caption style as the colour sections in this edition but opted for place and county names then generally still in use. *W&R5* adopted the 'new' counties of the 1972 Local Government Act that came into force on 1st April 1974 – there are still some readers who cannot forgive the author for abandoning Middlesex. Extra context and notes regarding the subject's present status, or its fate, have been added.

BUCKINGHAMSHIRE

Provost T.1 7697M (WV495), May 1972
1 School of Technical Training, Halton
Exported to USA 1993 for use as spares
Roy Bonser

CAMBRIDGESHIRE

P-51D Mustang '472258' (RCAF 9246)
Imperial War Museum, Duxford, June 1974
Current, as '411631', American Air Museum, Duxford
IWM

ESSEX

Beverley C.1 XB261
Historic Aircraft Museum, Southend – arriving 6th October 1971
Scrapped on site May 1989, flightdeck current at Newark Air Museum
KEC

ESSEX

Douglas DC-7C PH-DSL
Civil Aviation Authority Fire School, Stansted, July 1975
Scrapped on site July 1981
Daniel Ford

GLOUCESTERSHIRE

Meteor F.8 WH364
Kemble, March 1972
Current Jet Age Museum, Staverton, Glos
Roy Bonser

GLOUCESTERSHIRE

Scimitar F.1 XD324
Dowty-Rotol compound, Staverton, April 1972
To Foulness, Essex, ranges 1975; perished by 1981
Ken Ellis

LANCASHIRE

Firefly AS.5s/AS.6s
Unimetal yard, Failsworth, 1972
Site cleared 1981-1982, *perhaps* those at Newton Abbot, Devon
Ken Ellis

LANCASHIRE

Viscount 701 G-ALWF
Viscount Preservation Trust, Speke, 1972
Current Duxford Aviation Society, Duxford
VPT

MIDDLESEX

C-10A Jetstream hulks
R J Coley yard, Hounslow, July 1972
Yard cleared by 1974
Ken Ellis

SUFFOLK

Meteor T.7 VZ634
Wattisham crash rescue,
June 1973
Current Newark Air
Museum
Ken Ellis

SCOTLAND

Avro XIX G-AHKX
Strathallan Aircraft
Collection, Strathallan,
August 1974
Airworthy Shuttleworth,
Beds, as 'TX176'
Scott Meredith

Appendix B : RAF OVERSEAS

British military aircraft in the *W&R* categories to be found on *Crown* territory or property, now reduced to only one venue.

CYPRUS

RAF Akrotiri: As the base has expanded, what was the main entrance – bedecked by the Lightning and Whirlwind – is now an 'inner' gate. Noted for the first time in October 2023 and well worth a mention, No.**1 (Overseas) Squadron Air Cadets** has its headquarters within the base and a Cessna 150/152 cockpit for instruction and as a travelling exhibit.

❑	–*		Cessna 150 / 152	~	*We Fly*, cockpit – see notes above	10-23
❑	XD184		W'land Whirlwind HAR.10	54	ex 8787M (2-9-83), 84 'A' Flt, 1563F, 228, 155. Displayed since 9-84, at 'inner' gate. 84 Sqn colours	10-23
❑	XR504		Westland Wessex HC.2	63	ex 9327M, 84, 22, SARTS, 18, 1 FTU. Displayed by 9-08, outside 84 Sqn HQ. 84 Sqn colours	10-23
❑	XS929	'L'	EE Lightning F.6	67	ex 8970M (20-5-88), Binbrook, 11, LTF, 11, 56, 11. Last flight 20-5-88. Displayed since 23-4-89, at 'inner' gate. 56 Sqn colours	10-23
❑	XV470	'BD'	McD Phantom FGR.2	69	ex 9156M, 56, 228 OCU, 11, 43, 228 OCU, 56, 228 OCU, 18, 228 OCU, 29, 228 OCU, 92, 228 OCU, 92, 56, 228 OCU, 31, 17, 14. Arrived 7-92. Stored	10-21

Left: 1 (Overseas) Squadron ATC Cessna cockpit. *John Phillips*

Left: 84 Squadron's mascot, Wessex HC.2 XR504. *John Phillips*

Bottom: Lightning F.6 XS929. All Akrotiri, October 2023. *John Phillips*

Appendix C : EXPORTS

All known exports are of course listed in the text, but not highlighted as such. This table highlights 'heritage' and former military exports: excluding general aviation types. Column 4 gives the location under which it was to be found within *W&R* and Column 5 the destination.

G-BKXP		Auster AOP.6	Winsford, Cheshire	Belgium 23-9-22
KK116	G-AMPY	Dakota 4 ✈	Coventry, Warks	USA 17-5-22
VX461		Vampire FB.5	Cosford, Shropshire	Australia 11-22
WG655	G-INVN	Sea Fury T.20S	Duxford, Cambs	USA 12-23
XW927		Harrier T.4	Doncaster, S Yorks	Germany, by 10-23
XX747		Jaguar GR.1	Selby, N Yorks	Mauritius, 1-22
XZ920		Sea King HU.5 ✈	Gosport, Hampshire	Ukraine (via Portland), 11-22
ZA134		Sea King HU.5 ✈	Portland, Dorset	Ukraine UR-H034 13-5-23
ZA296		Sea King HC.4	Solent, Hants	Slovakia, late -22
ZF163 plus 22		Tucano T.1	Shawbury, Shropshire	USA, 2020 – see p188
ZG791		Tornado GR.4	Marham, Norfolk	Australia 1-22
'A92-255'		Jindivik 102BL	Selby, N Yorks	Switzerland 18-11-21
84001		C-103H Hercules	Cambridge, Cambs	Sweden 7-22
84003		C-103H Hercules	Cambridge, Cambs	Sweden 7-22
'626/18'	N6268	Travel Air D-2000	Turweston, Bucks	USA 2023
584219		Fw 190F-8/U1	Hendon, Gtr Lon	Germany 23-10-23
997		Ohka 11	Cosford, Shropshire	USA 2022
1211	G-MIGG	MiG-17 *Fresco*	North Weald, Essex	Poland 10-23
'413573'	N6526D	P-51D Mustang	Cosford, Shropshire	Australia 11-22

Appendix D : SUBMERGED

Unless readers are wet suit-equipped, airframes at dive sites are inaccessible. For completeness, this section gives brief details of 'aquatic' aircraft: 'Last noted' – more accurately 'last dived' dates are given in brackets. Thanks to Anthony Mills for much of this material.

BLETCHLEY south of the A5, near Milton Keynes. **Blue Lagoon Diving Centre**: Cessna 150E G-ASVF was sunk here in 1984 (6-15). **www.mksac.co.uk**

CAPERNWRAY on the A6 north of Carnforth. **Capernwray Diving Centre**: Cessna F.150L G-BFWL (4-10); HS.748-2A G-BVOV (sunk 29-3-10); Dragonfly HR.3 WP503 (4-10); Wessex HU.5 XS491 (4-10). **www.dive-site.co.uk**

CLIFFE at the end of the B2000, north of Rochester. **Buckland Lake Reserve – Polaris Scuba**: Aztec 250E N54211 (submerged circa 5-12, it was last noted dumped on the lakeside 8-13) and the fuselage of Falcon 20 9M-BCR (8-13.) Site *thought* no longer active.

CROMHALL east of Thornbury. **Cromhall Quarry Diving Centre**: Wessex HU.5 XS488 (with the rear end of XR497) from Layer Marney, Essex, had arrived by late 2020, Also reported was Commander N5834N. **www.cromhallquarry.com**

ECCLESTON on the B5250 south of Leyland. **Delph Scuba Diving Centre:** The forward fuselage of a Short 330 G-SSWR and Jet Provost T.4 XP688, both noted 6-16. **www.thedelph.com**

GODSTONE junction of A22/A25 east of Redhill. **Divers Cove**: Cherokee 140 G-ZANG (8-16). Cherokee 180C cockpit G-ATXM (ex Southend) was noted as here from 8-16: however, see under Teesside Airport, D&C. **www.diverscove.co.uk**

HARLECH *The Maid of Harlech*, **Lockheed P-38F Lightning 41-7677**, became the first legally designated marine crash site during 2019. This 14th FG machine force-landed just off the coast on 27th September 1942, the pilot was rescued.

LOUGH FOYLE Northern Ireland. Sometimes visible off shore - eg 11-22 - is the hulk of **Corsair II JT693** 'R' of 1843 Squadron, which crashed on 9th October 1944. Good viewpoint at Engine Corner, Shore Road, north of Ballykelly.

MONEYMORE north of Cookstown, Northern Ireland. The fuselage of Cessna F.172P EI-ING is submerged in a scuba lake at The Jungle. **www.thejungleni.com**

NORTH CAVE west of Hull. **Eight Acre Lake**: The unidentified Puma has been tracked down. HC.1 XW234, written off in Northern Ireland 21-1-02. **www.scubadream.co.uk**

PLYMPTON east of Plymouth. **New England Quarry**: Thanks to Jon Horswell, the fate of a Whirlwind last mentioned in *W&R*11 (p84) can be tied up. Moved from Shawbury to Tattershall Thorpe, Lincs, in 6-87, HAR.10 XP395 was used in a BBC programme, in which it was marked 'XJ729', then disposed of. It was submerged at this site by 9-88. No references on a dive club operating currently.

PORTSMOUTH Defence Diving School: Since 1997 Wessex HU.5 XT760 has been in a lake off Horsea Island. It is/was fitted with the rear fuselage of XT604 – see East Midlands Airport, Leics.

STONEY STANTON on the B581 east of Hinckley**. Stoney Cove – The National Diving Centre**: Wessex HU.5 XT768 (4-17), the forward fuselage of Viscount 814 G-AWXI (4-17) and Partenavia P.68 G-LOUP (4-17). There is only one Wessex here, the other, HU.5 XT770, is reported to have come here from Shawell, Leics, in 2008. **www.stoneycove.com**

TAMWORTH Dosthill Diving Centre: The fuselage of Jetstream 31 G-WMCC (7-17) was delivered from Sandwell, W Mids, on 12-4-15 for submerging in the lake. **www.dosthillquarry.com**

TIDENHAM, on the A48 northeast of Chepstow. The *former* National Diving and Activity Centre: HS.146-100 G-JEAU (sunk 17-12-07); an Aztec; Sea Devon C.20 XK896 fuselage (G-RNAS - 2-08); Wessex HAS.3 XS122 (12-13) and Wessex HC.2 XT607 (1-12). Announced in 9-23, the whole site is being redeveloped by ocean technology and exploration company DEEP as a research facility.

UPPER VOBSTER on minor road west of Frome. **Vobster Quay**: Sea King HC.4 ZA299 (submerged 23-1-18) and HS.748-2A G-AVXJ (5-17) is split into three sections. **www.vobster.com**

WHITTLESEY on the A605 east of Peterborough. **Dive In**: Short 360 G-ROOM (7-17) and Jet Provost T.3 XM467 (7-17). **www.divein.co.uk**

WOMERSLEY south of the M62, west of the A19. **Blue Lagoon Diving and Leisure Centre**: As well as Hunter T.8C WT799 on show on the surface (see main section) in the depths is MS Rallye G-BLIY (sunk 2012) and Hunter F.6A XJ639, (sunk 7-06). **www.facebook.com/divebluelagoon**

WRAYSBURY south of Colnbrook. **Wraysbury Dive Centre**: The forward fuselage of Boeing 737 G-CELA arrived from Cotswold (Kemble) 5-19 and submerged 26-8-20 (5-22). **www.wraysbury.ws**

Corsair II JT693 of 1843 Squadron, based at Eglinton, force landed in the shallows of Lough Foyle on 9th October 1944; the pilot was uninjured. Its hulk has been observed on occasions ever since: in this instance November 2022. *Ian Thompson*

Appendix E : *COCKPITFEST*

Staged at the Newark Air Museum, *CockpitFest* is a unique occasion in the aviation 'year'. Awards are as follows: 'Grand Champion' (GC) as judged by the attending public; 'Cockpiteers' Cockpit' (CC) voted for by the attending 'cockpiteers'; and *Wrecks & Relics* 'Spirit of *CockpitFest*' (*W&R*) awarded by the author of this 'ere book! Occasionally, a 'Spirit' prize is also given by the museum. Presentations are also made for instrument clusters, control columns, flying clothing etc, but these are not applicable here.

Information is given as follows: Column 1 gives type and identity plus award (if applicable); Column 2 location at that time. Readers seeking more information should look at: **www.newarkairmuseum.org**

CockpitFest XXII Newark, 25th-26th June 2022

Type and identity	Award	Location
Buccaneer S.1 XK533	*W&R*	Stranraer, Scotland
Buccaneer S.2 EMU		Doncaster, S Yorks
Buccaneer S.2 XX888		Doncaster, S Yorks
Buccaneer S.2B XX899	GC	resident
Canberra PR.9		resident
Dove 6 G-ANAP		March, Cambs
Harrier GR.3 XV810		Walcott, Lincs
Jet Provost T.4 XS181		Spark Bridge, Cumbria
Jet Provost T.5 G-BYED		Metheringham, Lincs
Lightning F.6 XR757	CC	resident
Lightning F.6 XS922		Spark Bridge, Cumbria
Lightning F.6 XS932		Walcott, Lincs
'Missfire'		Doncaster, S Yorks
P-51D Mustang SIM		Amesbury, Wilts
Phantom FGR.2 XV490		resident
Provost T.1 'XF545'		Leicester, Leics
Schleicher K.8b GGA.522	*W&R*	Doncaster, S Yorks
Sea King HAS.6 ZG875		Crewe, Cheshire
Shackleton T.4 VP293		Coventry, Warks
Slingsby Dart '404'	*W&R*	Doncaster, S Yorks
Tempest V SN280		Doncaster, S Yorks

Notes: Additionally, Chris Bennett's *all* of superb Scout AH.1 XV130 (G-BWJW) attended from its Maidstone, Kent, base: regularly running up its Nimbus.

CockpitFest XXIII Newark, 24th-25th June 2023

Type and identity	Award	Location
Buccaneer S.1 XK533	*W&R*	Stranraer, Scotland
Buccaneer S.2 EMU		Doncaster, S Yorks
Buccaneer S.2B XX899	GC	resident
Cadet TX.3 XN797		Doncaster, S Yorks
Cadet TX.3 XN238		Doncaster, S Yorks
Canberra PR.9 EMU		resident
Chipmunk T.10 WG362		Grimsby, Lincs
Dove 6 G-ANAP	*W&R*	March, Cambs
Harrier GR.3 XV810		Walcott, Lincs
Jaguar GR.1 XX736	GC	Doncaster, S Yorks
Jaguar GR.1 SIM		Worksop, Notts
Jet Provost T.3 XN511		Doncaster, S Yorks
Jet Provost T.5 G-BYED		Metheringham, Lincs
Lightning F.6 XR757	CC	resident
Lightning F.6 XS922		Spark Bridge, Cumbria
Phantom FGR.2 XV490		resident
Provost T.1 'XF545'	CC	Leicester, Leics
Scout AH.1 XT640		South Clifton, Notts
Slingsby Swallow BJP		Doncaster, S Yorks
Spitfire I P9451		Hooton Park, Cheshire
Tempest V SN280		Doncaster, S Yorks
Valetta T.3 WJ476	*W&R*	Doncaster, S Yorks

Notes: Chris Bennett's Scout AH.1 XV130 (G-BWJW) was again in attendance.

Kent-based Chris Bennett brought his immaculate and *whole* Scout AH.1 XV130 to both the 2022 and 2023 events. *Ken Ellis*

Appendix F : FURTHER READING / GAZING

Magazines

Air North, North East Branch of Air-Britain, monthly | **ajmurray1967@blueyonder.co.uk** | **www.airnorth.org**
Aviation News and Review, LAAS International, monthly | **laasint@btinternet.com** | **www.laasdata.com**
FlyPast, monthly magazine from Key Publishing | **subs@keypublishing.com** | **www.key.aero/flypast**
Humberside Air Review, Humberside Aviation Society, monthly 'e-zine', also an annual *Residents Review* | **pwildf117@yahoo.com**
Irish Air Letter, published by Paul Cunniffe, Karl E Hayes and Eamon C Power, monthly (also available as an 'e-zine') | **ial.magazine@upcmail.ie**
Military Aviation Review, Military Aircraft Photographs, monthly and 'e-zine' plus sister journal *@MAR* | **redbrae99@gmail.com** | **www.militaryaviationreview.com**
Scottish Air News, Central Scotland Aviation Group, monthly (also available as an 'e-zine') Also publishes the annual *Scottish Register* | **scansubs@gmail.com** | **www.scottishairnews.co.uk**
Ulster Air Mail, published by the Ulster Aviation Society, monthly | **membership@ulsteraviationsociety.org** | **www.ulsteraviationsociety.org**

Books

The following have been on and off the shelves with great speed and are regarded as trusted friends:
British Civil Aircraft Register 1919-1999, Michael Austin, Air-Britain, 1999
Category Five, RAF Aircraft Losses 1954 to 2009, Colin Cummings, Nimbus Publishing, 2010, plus ***Final Landings*** (2001) and ***Last Take-off*** (2000) in this exceptional series
Fleet Air Arm Fixed-Wing Aircraft since 1946, Ray Sturtivant with Mick Burrow and Lee Howard, Air-Britain, 2004 – a masterpiece!
Fleet Air Arm Helicopters since 1943, Lee Howard, Mick Burrow and Eric Myall, Air-Britain, 2010 – likewise!
Flying Units of the RAF, Alan Lake, Airlife, 1999
Great Aviation Collections of Britain, Ken Ellis, Crécy Publishing, Manchester, 2013
Local Aviation Collections of Britain, Ken Ellis, Crécy Publishing, Manchester, 2017
Royal Air Force Aircraft XA100 to XZ999, Jim Halley, Air-Britain, 2001 – and others in the series
Royal Air Force Flying Training & Support Units since 1912, Ray Sturtivant, John Hamlin, James J Halley, Air-Britain, 2007
Royal Air Force Squadrons, Wg Cdr C G Jefford, Airlife, 1988
Royal Navy Instructional Airframes, Ray Sturtivant and Rod Burden, British Av Research Group/Air-Britain, 1997
Squadrons and Units of the Fleet Air Arm, Theo Ballance, Lee Howard and Ray Sturtivant, Air-Britain, 2016

Websites

Many web sites are mentioned within the main narrative, but the following have been of great use and proven worth:

www.caa.co.uk – the excellent GINFO database run by the Civil Aviation Authority
www.demobbed.org.uk – great database on former British military aircraft from the stalwarts of the Wolverhampton Aviation Group. Not content with this, the group also runs the UK Serials Resource centre – **www.ukserials.com**
www.flyinginireland.com – comprehensive site devoted to Irish aviation

Appendix G : ABBREVIATIONS

Without the use of abbreviations for the 'potted' histories of the aircraft listed in *W&R*, the book would be twice the size. To save repetition, abbreviations that are clearly combinations of others are not listed in full, eg MEAFCS, breaks into MEAF and CS, ie Middle East Air Force Communications Squadron.

AA	Air Attaché
A&AEE	Aeroplane and Armament Experimental Establishment. From the late 1980s became the Aircraft and Armament Evaluation Est.
AAC	Army Air Corps
AACU	Anti-Aircraft Co-operation Unit
AAFCE	Allied Air Forces Central Europe
AAIU	Air Accident Investigation Unit
ABDR	Aircraft Battle Damage Repair
ABG	Air Base Group (USAF)
ACC	Allied Control Commission
acq	Acquired by organisation listed, not necessarily at the venue given
ACSEA	Allied Command, South East Asia- *see Note 1*
ACU	Andover Conversion Unit
ADS	Air Director School
AE&AEOS	Air Engineers and Air Electronic Operators School
AEF	Air Experience Flight
AES	Air Engineers School
AES	Air Engineering School
AETW	Air Engineering Training Wing
AFDS	Air Fighting Development Squadron,
AFDU	Air Fighting Development Unit
AFEE	Airborne Forces Experimental Establishment
AFN	Air Forces North
AFNE	Air Forces Near East
AFS	Advanced Flying School
AFTS	Advanced Flying Training School
AFU	Advanced Flying Unit
AFWF	Advanced Fixed Wing Flight
AIU	Accident Investigation Unit
ALAT	Aviation Legere de l'Armee de Terre
ALE	Aviation Legacy Enthusiast
AMARC	Aerospace Maintenance& Regeneration Center, Arizona, USA
AMIF	Aircraft Maintenance Instruction Flight
AMS	Air Movements School - see DMS / DMTS
ANG	Air National Guard
ANS	Air Navigation School
AONS	Air Observer and Navigator School
AOTS	Aircrew Officers Training School
APS	Aircraft Preservation Society
APS	Armament Practice Station
AR&TF	Aircraft Recovery and Transportation Flight, St Athan – tri-service 'mover' of fixed-wing airframes. (See MASU)
arr	Arrived at venue, by road or air
ARW	Air Refueling Wing (USAF)
ARWF	Advanced Rotary Wing Flight,
AS	Aggressor Squadron
AS&RU	Aircraft Salvage and Repair Unit
ASF	Aircraft Servicing Flight
ASS	Air Signals School
AST	Air Service Training
ASWDU	Air-Sea Warfare Development Unit
ATA	Air Transport Auxiliary
ATAIU	Allied Technical Air Intelligence Unit
ATC	Air Training Corps (Air Cadets)
ATDU	Air Torpedo Development Unit
ATF	Airframe Technology Flight
Att	Air Attache
AuxAF	Auxiliary Air Force
aw/cn	AWaiting CollectioN - *see Note 2*
AWFCS	All Weather Fighter Combat School
AWOCU	All Weather Operational Conversion Unit
AWRE	Atomic Weapons Research Establishment,
BA	British Airways
BAAT	British Airways Airtours
BAC	British Aircraft Corporation
BAe	British Aerospace
BAE	BAE Systems - the 'B' 'A' and'E' apparently standing for nothing!
BAF	British Air Ferries
BAFO	British Air Forces of Occupation
BAH	British Airways Helicopters
BAM	Booker Aircraft Museum
BANS	Basic Air Navigation School
BAOR	British Army of the Rhine
BAPC	British Aviation Preservation Council
BATUS	British Army Training Unit, Suffield (Can)
BBMF	Battle of Britain Memorial Flight
BBML	British Balloon Museum and Library
BC	Bomber Command.
BCBS	Bomber Command Bombing School
BDRF	Battle Damage Repair Flight
BDTF	Bomber Defence Training Flight
BDU	Bomber Development Unit
BEA	British European Airways
BEAS	British Executive Air Services
BFTS	Basic Flying Training School
BFWF	Basic Fixed Wing Flight
B&GS	Bombing & Gunnery School (RCAF)
BG	Bomb(ardment) Group (US)
BLEU	Blind Landing Experimental Unit
BMA	British Midland Airways now bmi
BOAC	British Overseas Airways Corporation
BPPU	Bristol Plane Preservation Unit
BRNC	Britannia Royal Naval College
BSE	Bristol Siddeley Engines
B&TTF	Bombing & Target Towing Flight
BTF	Beaver Training Flight
BTU	Bombing Trials Unit
BUA	British United Airlines
BW	Bomb(ardment) Wing (US)
C(A)	Controller (Aircraft) see also CS(A) - *see Note 3*
CAA	Civil Aviation Authority
CAACU	Civilian Anti-Aircraft Co-operation Unit
CACF	Coastal Artillery Co-operation Flight
CACU	Coastal Artillery Co-operation Unit
CAF	Canadian Armed Forces
CAFU	Civil Aviation Flying Unit
Cam Flt	Camouflage Flight
CATCS	Central Air Traffic Control School
CAW	College of Air Warfare
CBAF	Castle Bromwich Aircraft Factory
CBE	Central Bombing Establishment
CC	Coastal Command.
CCAS	Civilian Craft Apprentices School,
CCF	Combined Cadet Force
CF	Communications Flight as suffix with other unit, or for an airfield

CFCCU	Civilian Fighter Control and Co-op Unit
CFE	Central Fighter Establishment - see CFE-EAF.
CFE-EAF	Central Fighter Establishment - Enemy Aircraft Flt
CFS	Central Flying School
C&TTS	Communications and Target Towing Sqn
CGS	Central Gliding School
CGS	Central Gunnery School
CIFAS	Centre d'Instruction des Forces Aeriennes Strategiques
CIT	Cranfield Institute of Technology
CNCS	Central Navigation and Control School
CoA	Certificate (or Permit) of Airworthiness.
Cott	Cottesmore, in relation to V-Bomber wings
CPF	Coastal Patrol Flight
cr	crashed, or other form of accident
CR	Crash Rescue, training airframe.
CRD	Controller, Research and Development
C&RS	Control and Reporting School
CS	Communications Squadron, as a suffix with other units, or for an airfield.
CS(A)	Controller, Supplies (Air), see also CA - *Note 3*
CSDE	Central Servicing Development Establisment
CSE	Central Signals Establishment
CSF	Canberra Servicing Flight
CTE	Central Training Establishment
CTTS	Civilian Technical Training School
C&TTS	Communications & Target Towing Squadron
CU	Communications Unit, as suffix
CU	Conversion Unit, as suffix
DARA	Defence Aviation Repair Agency, Fleetlands, St Athan, Sealand
DB	Development Batch – early Lightnings
dbr	damaged beyond repair, to distinguish an aircraft that was written off but did not crash
deH	de Havilland
de-reg	de-registered (from a civilian identity)
DEMS	Defence Explosives Ordnance Disposal, Munitions and Search School
DERA	Defence Evaluation and Research Agency — replaced DRA and DTEO.
Det	Detachment, flight or other unit detached from main base
DFLS	Day Fighter Leader School
dism	dismantled
DLO	Defence Logistics Organisation
DMA	Doesn't Mean Anything
DMS /DMTS	Defence Movements School, later Defence Movements Training Squadron
DPA	Defence Procurement Agency replaced MoD(PE)
DRA	Defence Research Agency – see DERA
DSA	Disposal Ss Agency
DSDA	Defence Storage and Distribution Agency
DTEO	Defence Test and Evaluation Organisation – see DERA
DU	Development Unit, as suffix
EAAS	East Anglian Aviation Society
EASAMS	European avionics consortium
ECTT	Escadre de Chasse Tous Temps
EE	English Electric
EFTS	Elementary Flying Training School
EOD	Explosive Ordnance Disposal
EP&TU	Exhibition, Production and Transport Unit
E&RFTS	Elementary & Reserve Flying Trng School
ERS	Empire Radio School
Esc	Escadre, French squadron
ETPS	Empire Test Pilots School
ETS	Engineering Training School
ETU	Experimental Trials Unit
EWAD	Electronic Warfare and Avionics Detachment
EWE&TU	Electronic Warfare Experimental & Training Unit
F / Flt	Flight, suffix to number
FAA	Fleet Air Arm
FAA	Fuerza Aerea Argentina
FAAHAF	Fleet Air Arm Historic Aircraft Flight
FAAM	Fleet Air Arm Museum
FAF	French Air Force.
FAH	Fuerza Aerea Hondurena
FC	Fighter Command.
FCS	Fighter Control School
FCTU	Fighter Command Trials Unit
FEAF	Far East Air Forces - *see Note 1*
FECS	Far East Communications Flight
FF	Ferry Flight
FF&SS	Fire Fighting and Safety School
FGF	Flying Grading Flight
FLS	Fighter Leader School
f/n	first noted
FOAC	Flag Officer, Aircraft Carriers
FOCAS	Friends of Cardington Airship Station
FOFT	Flag Officer, Flying Training
FONA	Flag Officer, Naval Aviation
FONAC	Flag Officer, Naval Air Command
FP	Ferry Pool
FPP	Ferry Pilots Pool
FRADU	Fleet Requirements and Direction Unit
FRL	Flight Refuelling Ltd
FRS	Flying Refresher School
FRU	Fleet Requirements Unit
FS	Fighter Squadron (US)
FSM	Full Scale Model
FSS	Ferry Support Squadron
FSS	Flying Selection Squadron
FTC	Flying Training Command
FTS	Flying Training School
FTU	Ferry Training Unit
FU	Ferry Unit
FW	Fighter Wing (USAF)
FWS	Fighter Weapons School
GIA	Ground Instructional Airframe
GS	Glider School
GSU	Group Support Unit
GTS	Glider Training School
GU	Glider Unit
GWDS	Guided Weapons Development Squadron
HAB	Hot air balloon
HAM	Historic Aircraft Museum, Southend
HC	Home Command
HCEU	Home Command Examining Unit
HCF	Hornet Conversion Flight
HDU	Helicopter Development Unit
HGSU	Heavy Glider Servicing Unit
HHU	Helicopter Holding Unit
HMTS	Harrier Maintenance Training School
HQ	Headquarters
HS	Handling Squadron
HSA	Hawker Siddeley Aviation
HTF	Helicopter Training Flight
IAAC / IAC	Irish Army Air Corps / Irish Air Corps
IAF	Indian Air Force
IAM	Institute of Aviation Medicine

IA-PVO	(Russian) Air Defence Fighter Force
IFTU	Intensive Flying Trials Unit
IGN	Institut Geographique National
IHM	International Helicopter Museum
ITF or 'S	Instrument Training Flight / Squadron
IWM	Imperial War Museum
JASS	Joint Anti-Submarine School
JADTEU	Joint Air Delivery Test and Evaluation Unit - replaced JATEU
JATE	Joint Air Transport Establishment - see JATEU
JATEU	Joint Air Transport Evaluation Unit – see JADTEU
JCU	Javelin Conversion Unit
JEHU	Joint Experimental Helicopter Unit
JMU	Joint Maritime Unit
JOCU	Jaguar Operational Conversion Unit
JTU	Joint Trials Unit
JWE	Joint Warfare Establishment
LAS	Light Aircraft School
LC	Logistics Command
LCS & 'U	Lightning Conversion Squadron / Unit
l/n	last noted
LRWE	Long Range Weapons Research Est
LTF	Lightning Training Flight
LTW	Lyneham Tactical Wing (Hercules)
MAM	Midland Air Museum
MASL	Military Aircraft Spares Ltd
MASU	Mobile Aircraft Support Unit – DARA Fleetlands, tri-service 'mover' of helicopters See AR&TF
MBA	Museum of Berkshire Aviation
MC	Maintenance Command
MCS	Metropolitan Communications Squadron
MEAF	Middle East Air Force- *see Note 1*
MECS	Middle East Communications Squadron
METS	Multi-Engine Training School
MGSP	Mobile Glider Servicing Party
MinTech	Ministry of Technology, see also MoA, MoS - *see Note 3*
MoA	Ministry of Aviation, see also MinTech, MoS - *see Note 3*
MoD(PE)	Ministry of Defence (Procurement Executive) – see DPA
MoS	Ministry of Supply, see MinTech, MoA - *see Note 3*
MoTaT	Museum of Transport & Technology, NZ
MOTU	Maritime Operational Training Unit
MPA	Man-powered aircraft
MU	Maintenance Unit - *See Note 4*
NAAS	Navigator and Airman Aircrew School
NACDS	Naval Air Command Driving School
NASA	National Aeronautical and Space Admin
NASU	Naval Aircraft Servicing Unit
NBC	Nuclear, Bacteriological and Chemical
NCS	Northern Communications Squadron
nea	Non effective airframe - *See Note 2*
NECS	North Eastern Communications Squadron
NFLS	Night Fighter Leaders School
NGTE	National Gas Turbine Establishment
NIBF	Northern Ireland Beaver Flight
n/s	No service - UK military only
NSF	Northern Sector Flight
ntu	Not taken up, registration applied for, but not worn, or paperwork not concluded
(O)AFU	(Observers) Advanced Flying Unit
OCTU	Officer Cadet Training Unit
OCU	Operational Conversion Unit
OEU	Operational Evaluation Unit
OFU	Overseas Ferry Unit
OTU	Operational Training Unit
(P)AFU	(Pilot) Advanced Flying Unit
PCSS	Protectorate Comms and Support Squadron
PEE	Proof & Experimental Establishment
PFA	Popular Flying Association
PFS	Primary Flying School
PFTS	Primary Flying Training School
PP	Pilots' Pool
PPS	Personal Plane Services
PRDU	Photo Reconnaissance Development Unit
PRU	Photographic Reconnaissance Unit
PTC	Personnel and Training Command
PTF	Phantom Training Flight
PTS	Primary Training School
PVO	(Russian) Air Defence Force
QF	Queen's Flight
RAAF	Royal Australian Air Force
RAE	Royal Aircraft / Aerospace Establishment
RAeS	Royal Aeronautical Society
RAF	Royal Air Force
RAFA	Royal Air Force Association
RAFC	Royal Air Force College
RAFEF	Royal Air Force Exhibition Flight
RAFFC	Royal Air Force Flying College
RAFG	Royal Air Force Germany
RAFGSA	Royal Air Force Gliding & Soaring Assoc
RAFHSF	Royal Air Force High Speed Flight
RAFM	Royal Air Force Museum
RAN	Royal Australian Navy
RC	Reserve Command
RCAF	Royal Canadian Air Force
RCN	Royal Canadian Navy
RCS	Rotary Conversion Squadron
Regt	Regiment
RFS	Reserve Flying School
RHK	Royal Hong Kong
RMAF	Royal Malaysian Air Force
RNAY	Royal Naval Aircraft Yard
RNEC	Royal Naval Engineering College
RNEFTS	Royal Navy Elementary Flying Training School
RNGSA	Royal Navy Gliding and Soaring Association
RNHF	Royal Navy Historic Flight
RNoAF	Royal Norwegian Air Force
RNZAF	Royal New Zealand Air Force
ROC	Royal Observer Corps
RPRE	Rocket Propulsion Research Establishment
RRAF	Royal Rhodesian Air Force
RRE	Royal Radar Establishment
RRF	Radar Reconnaissance Flight
RRHT	Rolls-Royce Heritage Trust
RS	Radio School
RSRE	Radar and Signals Research Establishment
RSS & 'U	Repair & Servicing Section / Unit
RTR	Royal Tank Regiment
RWE	Radio Warfare Establishment
SAAF	South African Air Force
SAC	School of Army Co-operation
SAF	School of Aerial Fighting
SAH	School of Aircraft Handling
SAOEU	Strike Attack Operational Evaluation Unit
SAR	Search and Rescue
SAREW	Search and Rescue Engineering Wing
SARTS	Search and Rescue Training Squadron
SARTU	Search and Rescue Training Unit
SC	Signals Command
Scamp	Scampton, to distinguish a V-Bomber wing
SCBS	Strike Command Bombing School

SCS Southern Communications Squadron
SEAE School of Electrical and Aeronautical Engineering
SF Station Flight, usually with an airfield name
SFDO School of Flight Deck Operations
SFTS Service Flying Training School
ShF Ship's Flight
SHQ Station HQ
SKTU Sea King Training Unit
SLAW School of Land/Air Warfare
SMR School of Maritime Reconnaissance
SOC Struck off charge - *See Note 2*
SoRF School of Refresher Flying
SoTT School of Technical Training - *See Note 5*
SRCU Short Range Conversion Unit
SRW Strategic Reconnaissance Wing
SS Signals Squadron
SS Support Squadron
SU Support Unit
SVAS Shuttleworth Veteran Aeroplane Society
TAC The Aeroplane Collection
TAF Tactical Air Force
TAW Tactical Airlift Wing
TC Transport Command
TCS Troop Carrier Squadron (USAAF)
TCW Troop Carrier Wing (USAAF)
TEE Trials and Experimental Establishment
TES Tri-Partitie Evaluation Squadron
TEU Tactical Exercise Unit
TF Training Flight
TFF Target Facilities Flight
TFS Traget Facilities Squadron
TFS Tactical Fighter Squadron
TFTAS Tactical Fighter Training Aggressor Squadron
TFU Telecommunications Flying Unit
TFW Tactical Fighter Wing
TGDA Training Group Defence Agency
Thum Flt Temperature and HUMidity Flight
TLA Three-letter abbreviation
TMS Tornado Maintenance School
TMTS Trade Management Training School
TOC Taken on charge - *See Note 2*
TOEU Tornado Operational Evaluation Unit
TRE Telecommunications Research Establishment
TS Training Squadron
TTC Technical Training Command
TTF Tanker Training Flight
TTTE Tri-National Tornado Training Establishment
TTTE Thomas The Tank Engine
TTU Torpedo Training Unit
TWDU Tactical Weapons Development Unit
TWU Tactical Weapons Unit
UAS University Air Squadron - *See Note 6*
UNFICYP United Nations Forces In Cyprus
USAAC United States Army Air Corps
USAAF United States Army Air Force
USAF United States Air Force
USMC United States Marine Corps
USN United States Navy
VAFA Vintage Aircraft Flying Association
VAT Vintage Aircraft Team
VGS Volunteer Gliding School – and, from 2005: Volunteer Gliding *Squadron*
VVS KA (Russian) Soviet Army Air Force
VVS VMF (Russian) Soviet Naval Air Force
Wadd Waddington, denoting a V-Bomber wing
WCS Western Communications Squadron
wfu Withdrawn from use
Witt Wittering, denoting a V-bomber wing.
WLT Weapons Loading Trainer
WSF Western Sector Flight

Notes on UK military airframes

1 **RAF 'Holding Units'**: For administrative purposes, the history cards of some RAF aircraft become fairly vague when transferred to either Middle East or Far East theatres of operations. Accordingly, the following abbreviations denote the 'operator' for the segment of an aircraft's life in that theatre, even though it may have been used by several front-line units: ACSEA, FEAF, MEAF.

2 **History Card 'milestones'**: There are several RAF aircraft history card 'milestones' referred to in the main text. Essentially an aircraft starts off as AWaiting Collection (Aw/cn) - a signal from the manufacturer that the aircraft is ready for issue to service; it is then taken on charge (toc) and becomes a part of the RAF; after service life, it may eventually to be declared a non-effective airframe (nea) and down-graded to instructional or fire-training use; the final act is for it to be struck off charge (SOC), either being written-off in an accident, scrapped, sold to another user etc etc.

3 **Government 'owning' bodies**: Technical 'owner' of UK military machines is the C(A) or CS(A) and at times these are noted within the aircraft history cards instead of a unit, although it may well be a pointer to the aircraft being operated at that time of its life by a test or trials unit. In similar manner, MinTech, MoA or MoS can appear, frequently meaning operation by the RAE, or DRA.

4 **Maintenance Unit** (MU): Frequently mentioned in the text are: 2 - Sealand, 5 - Kemble, 6 - Brize Norton, 7 - Quedgeley, 8 - Little Rissington, 9 - Cosford, 10 - Hullavington, 12 - Kirkbride, 13 - Henlow, 14 - Carlisle, 15 - Wroughton, 16 - Stafford, 18 - Dumfries, 19 - St Athan, 20- Aston Down, 22 - Silloth, 23 - Aldergrove, 24 - Tern Hill, 25 - Hartlebury, 27 - Shawbury, 29 - High Ercall, 32 - St Athan, 33 - Lyneham, 34 - Montford Bridge, 36 - Sealand, 37 - Burtonwood, 38 - Llandow, 39 - Colerne, 44 - Edzell, 45 - Kinloss, 46 - Lossiemouth, 47 - Sealand, 48 - Hawarden, 51 - Lichfield, 52 - Cardiff, 54 - Cambridge, 57 - Wig Bay, 60 - Leconfield, 71 - Bicester. Note that several locations had more than one MU, eg Sealand, St Athan.

5 **School of Technical Training** (SoTT): The following are mentioned in the main text: 1 - Halton, 2 - Cosford, 3 - Manston, later Blackpool, 4 - St Athan, 5 - Locking, 6 - Hednesford, 7 - Innsworth, 8 - Weeton, 9 - Newton, 10 - Kirkham, 11 - Credenhill, 12 - Melksham, 14 - Henlow, 21 - Burtonwood.

6 **University Air Squadron** (UAS): Prefixed with a university name: Abn - Aberdeen, Dundee and St Andrews, Bir - Birmingham, Bri - Bristol, Cam - Cambridge, Dur - Durham, Edn - Edinburgh, Elo - East Lowlands, Ems - East Midlands, G&S - Glasgow & Strathclyde, Lee - Leeds, Liv - Liverpool, Lon - London, Man - Manchester and Salford, Nor - Northumbrian, Not - Nottingham, Oxf - Oxford, QUB – Queen's University Belfast, Sotn - Southampton, Wal - Ws, Yor - Yorkshire.

Index I : BY TYPE

For the purposes of this index, no distinction is made for replicas, full-scale models etc.

Index II : LOCATIONS

This index also includes a decode of alternative names to help you find John Lennon!

Wanna know the rest? Hey, buy the rights!
OMC 'How Bizarre', PolyGram NZ, 1995

Montrose Air Station Heritage centre's Tornado GR.4 ZD744, December 2022. *Jim Simpson*

On Guard

The history of Britain's military 'gate guardian' aircraft

In the post-war hey-days of the RAF, almost every military aviation base in the UK was graced by a 'gate guardian' - a retired military aircraft symbolically guarding the entrance to the airfield. Many of these aircraft were historically significant and would be highly prized today, but were often under-appreciated at the time.

There were also a vast number of airframes used for instruction and display by Air Training Corps (ATC) squadrons up and down the country.

The story of these aircraft has always fascinated aviation enthusiasts and yet over the decades, there have been almost no books on the subject and no comprehensive guide to all this fascinating aspect of Britain's military aviation heritage.

Now, from the desk of Ken Ellis, compiler of 'Wrecks & Relics' for five decades, comes the complete story of the UK's Gate Guardians, told in full for the first time. Laid out in 'Wrecks & Relics' style, aircraft are listed by location, with cross-referencing that enables readers to follow the most mobile 'guardians' as they moved from base to base; together with disposals and fates. Full 'biographies' of significant examples are covered. Also in 'On Guard' are the aircraft that 'guarded' the RAF's overseas outposts and the Spitfires and Hurricanes that were rescued for the epic 1969 film 'Battle of Britain'.

In 1988 it was realised that keeping historic aircraft on external display was wrong and negotiations with a warbird restorer allowed several Spitfires to go back into the air, in exchange of full-size replicas taking their place on gates. This amazing transformation is revealed as are the rare types were saved for museums – for example greatly boosting the RAF Museum collection in its formative years. The RAF Museum also used a number of former 'guardians' as collateral in worldwide bartering to achieve types missing from the collection. In addition, the rare machines that 'got away are highlighted.

An at-a-glance survey details those airframes and replicas still 'on duty' at British military bases and a further section charts the hundreds of aircraft used for instruction and display by Air Cadet squadrons.

Copiously illustrated, including 'then and now' images, and fully indexed, this is the definitive history of a fascinating aspect of Britain's aviation heritage.

Provisional publication date: **Spring 2025**

Also by **KEN ELLIS**

Testing to the Limits Volume 1
British Test Pilots Since 1910
Addicott to Huxley
ISBN: 9780859791847
£24.95

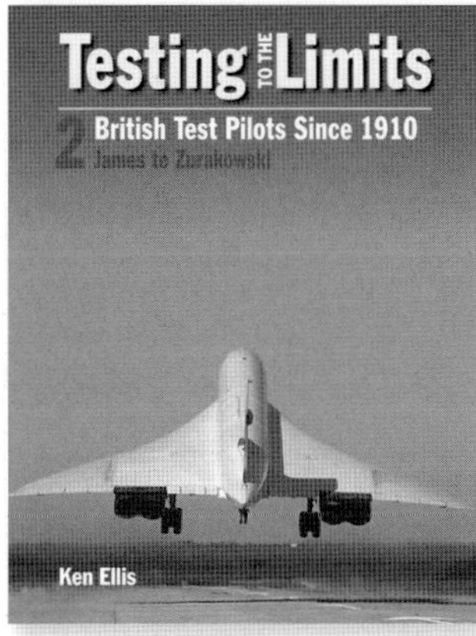

Testing to the Limits Volume 2
British Test Pilots Since 1910
James to Zurakowski
ISBN: 9780859791854
£24.95

Crécy
www.crecy.co.uk

Also by **KEN ELLIS**

WRECKS & RELICS

Is your Wrecks & Relics collection complete?

Available from Crécy Publishing:

Wrecks & Relics Ed 20
(2006)
ISBN 978185780235 £15.99

Wrecks & Relics Ed 21
(2008)
ISBN 9780859791342 £17.95

Wrecks & Relics Ed 22
(2010)
ISBN 9780859791502 £18.95

Wrecks & Relics Ed 23
(2012)
ISBN 9780859791724 £18.95

Wrecks & Relics Ed 24
(2014)
ISBN 9780859791779 £18.95

Wrecks & Relics Ed 25
(2016)
ISBN 9781910809037 £18.95

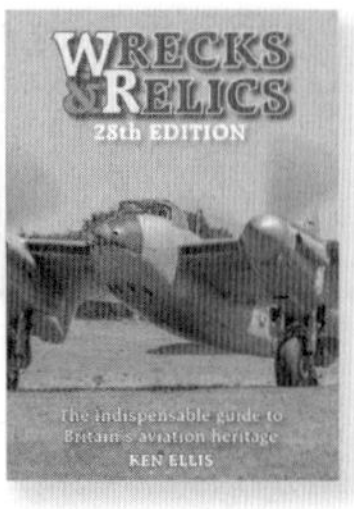

Wrecks & Relics Ed 28
(2022)
ISBN 9781800351387 £19.95

Crécy
www.crecy.co.uk